The

THOUGHT OF THE EVANGELICAL LEADERS

The

THOUGHT OF THE EVANGELICAL LEADERS

Notes of the Discussions of
The Eclectic Society, London
During the years 1798–1814

EDITED BY
JOHN H. PRATT

THE BANNER OF TRUTH TRUST

THE BANNER OF TRUTH TRUST
3 Murrayfield Road, Edinburgh EH12 6EL
PO Box 621, Carlisle, Pennsylvania 17013, USA

*

First published by James Nisbet 1856
Reprinted by the Banner of Truth Trust 1978
ISBN 0 85151 270 4

Printed in Great Britain by Robert MacLehose and Company Limited
Printers to the University of Glasgow

PREFACE.

THESE Notes of Discussions on religious topics, at Meetings of the Eclectic Society of London, have been prepared from Memoranda made at the time by the late Rev. Josiah Pratt, B.D., during the period that he was a Member of that body.

Some of the papers in this Volume have already appeared in print in India, and have been so much sought after for their original character, intrinsic value, and general interest, that the Editor has availed himself of the opportunity afforded by a visit to this country to lay the whole collection before the public.

The character of the subjects discussed may be gathered from the Table of Contents which follows. The Editor feels, however, that it is well to throw in a caution in calling attention to this Table,—by observing, on the one hand, that the subjects were not always discussed to the full extent marked out by the theses ; and, on the other, that the records now published are but Notes of what chiefly struck an individual Member.

J. H. P.

LONDON, *July* 21, 1856.

CONTENTS.

NOTES OF DISCUSSIONS

AT THE MEETINGS OF

THE ECLECTIC SOCIETY.

THE ECLECTIC SOCIETY was instituted early in the year 1783 by a few of the London Clergy, for mutual religious intercourse and improvement, and for the investigation of religious truth.

The first meeting was held at the Castle-and-Falcon Inn, Aldersgate Street, January 16, 1783, and consisted of the Rev. John Newton, the Rev. Henry Foster, the Rev. Richard Cecil, and Eli Bates, Esq. Its members were subsequently increased to twelve or fourteen, besides as many country members or occasional visitors. The meetings were afterwards held once a fortnight, at the Vestry-room of St John's Chapel, Bedford Row; and the Society comprehended, according to the original design, two or three Laymen and Dissenting Ministers.

At the date at which our Notes commence, January 8, 1798, the Society consisted of the following members:—The Rev. John Newton, the Rev. H. Foster, the Rev. G. Pattrick, the Rev. Thos. Scott, the Rev. R. Cecil, the Rev. W. J. Abdy, the Rev. J. Venn, the Rev. Basil Woodd, the Rev. W. Goode, the Rev. John Davies, and the Rev. Josiah Pratt; besides the Rev. John Clayton, and the Rev. J. Goode, Dissenting Ministers, and John Bacon, Esq., senior, Layman. Among the country members were the Rev. Charles Simeon, and Charles Grant, Esq. These are now all numbered with the dead; but in respect to all of them it may be said that their works do follow them, and in respect to many, that their memorial still abides amongst us. The Rev. John Newton, by his published Letters and his Olney Hymns; the Rev.

Thomas Scott, by his invaluable practical Commentary on the Holy Bible; the Rev. Richard Cecil, by his "Remains," and the Rev. Josiah Pratt, as Secretary of the Church Missionary Society—will long live in the memories and hearts of multitudes.

Although it much enhances the interest of these records that several of the members of a community so small should have risen, in various ways, to eminence, it must be borne in mind that there was a considerable disparity in their relative standing, when these Notes were taken; all of them had not arrived at that ripeness of knowledge and maturity of wisdom for which in subsequent years they were deservedly esteemed. At the date of the first of the records which we now publish, Mr Newton had attained the good old age of 73; while Mr Scott was only 51, and had yet 21 years to be added to his life; Mr Cecil was 50, and lived to 62; and Mr Pratt was at this time only 29, and survived to the age of 76.

The following notices by a friend recently deceased, who was personally known to the various parties, will serve as a clue to the characters of such of the members as have not been so generally known to the public. It is not transgressing the bounds of decorum thus freely to write, as they have belonged to an age long gone by.

The Rev. H. Foster was a plain and deeply pious man; without any peculiar decoration of taste, style, or eloquence in his general preaching; his ministrations were much valued, chiefly on account of their heart-searching and experimental character. On certain subjects, so great was his solemnity of manner, especially when discoursing upon death and eternity, that the late Mr Wilberforce used to say that he was on those occasions the most eloquent man he knew.

The Rev. G. Pattrick, a humble, pious, retiring man, but much esteemed by his people.

The Rev. W. J. Abdy was a mild, affectionate man, of a devout spirit rather than of a powerful mind. He was Curate, and afterwards Rector, of St John's, Horsely-down. When he first went to that parish, he suffered treatment in opposition to his efforts for the spiritual benefit of his flock amounting almost to persecution. He was advised by his best friends to act with more spirit; but his mild disposition interfered with his following this advice, and he gradually made way by patient continuance in well-doing.

The Rev. John Venn was the author of the published Sermons, and was Rector of Clapham; the son of the eminent Rev. Henry Venn, whose Memoir has been published, and the father of the present Honorary Secretary of the Church Missionary Society.

The Rev. Basil Woodd, a devout and excellent man; he called

himself a Baxterian. He was minister of Bentinck Chapel, Paddington, belonging to the Established Church.

The Rev. W. Goode was at first Curate of the Rev. W. Romaine, and afterwards Rector of St Ann's, Blackfriars, London; he was father of the present Rev. W. Goode, author of *Divine Rule of Faith and Practice,* and other works.

The Rev. John Clayton, and Rev. J. Goode (brother of the above), were both excellent Independent ministers, men of piety and judgment. "More like Watts and Doddridge," says our informant, "than like Dissenters of the present day." Mr Clayton died a few years ago, at the age of 89.

John Bacon, Esq., senior, was the elder of the two celebrated sculptors, father and son. He was a man of imagination; a quick discerner of the points of men's characters. Genius was more conspicuous in his own than solidity of judgment.

JANUARY 8, 1798.

WHAT IS THE NATURE, EVIL, AND REMEDY OF SCHISM ?—Proposed by the Rev. J. Venn.

The Rev. J. Venn—

The NATURE of Schism.—It is a separation from the Church in discipline, ceremonies, &c., in opposition to doctrine.

When it is on account of doctrine, it is Apostasy or Heresy. Heresy is a sin against God. Schism is a sin, not primary, but secondary, because God has not ordained a system. It is our duty to separate on account of doctrine, if false.

The New Testament has not ordained anything express concerning the time of worship—or ministers, as to a family—or the precise form of Church Government. What rule, then, is there for Rites and Ceremonies ? I answer, "The Church hath power to decree rites or ceremonies." Who is to do it ? Power must be somewhere. Where but in the Church ?

EVILS.—These are great. Schism breaks the unity of the Church. The consequences are serious. 1. Want of affection. 2. It weakens the strength of the Church : "*Jerusalem is built as a city that is at unity with itself.*" 3. Rule, order, government, discipline, are relaxed. A great part of the strength of the Church is spent in opposing Schism, whilst the common enemy preserves a united phalanx. 4. Party spirit is produced. A schismatic spirit is a narrow, jealous, selfish spirit.

A schismatic spirit arises from giving importance to unimportant matters. A man who sets out on bad principles, shews it in all he does. When the best times of the Church come, a Baptist, Independent, Presbyterian, or Episcopalian Minister will be the first to say, "Brethren ! of what small consequence are our particular notions." A schismatic spirit is a spreading spirit, a gangrene, schism on schism : it gives opportunity to the evils of the day. When it has its perfect work, it is like liberty degraded into licentiousness. Schism tends to diminish humility in our hearers. It produces bigotry and uncharitableness, and is evil in its influence on the world at large, which laughs, and retorts, " We will believe you, when your creed is settled."

REMEDY.—Not persecution ; the reverse. The Civil Magistrate or Church has no right on matters of opinion. On the part of the Church, simplicity, moderation. On the part of the people, let them learn submission. 1. Submit in some measure to the majority. 2. Consider of how little importance ceremonies in themselves are.

The Rev. J. Goode—

Those Churches which are framed by the policy of man arrogate too much to themselves :—*they* have "got the thing ! " Schism is a division, a rupture, a rent. It is generally taken for separation, on account of externals. Yet there is Schism without separation. Comparing it to the body, we are taught that it is an unnatural want of affection. See the account of the Church of Corinth.

Mr Venn remarked, that the Church of Corinth is not in point. We mean by Schism, separation. There was *disorder* rather in that Church. Separation was not then known.

The Rev. H. Foster—

The Schism of this country shews the awful depravity of human nature. Men in power have occasioned it ; but the men who made it, should have borne more.

The Church has power to decree rites and ceremonies. Every Church assumes it.

The Rev. R. Cecil—

If we take the matter as Jones does, " This particular Church," &c., we stand on untenable ground. Venn has taken a wider and safer stand.

I have marked Schism. I think the wicked state we are in is the reason why we never talk in public of so great an evil. It is a lust of the flesh, a shocking sin breaking out in the heart of man : and yet we never touch it in the pulpit ! I have seen it. I have felt it. I have seen again and again a separating self-sufficient spirit—one of the lusts of the flesh—a restless spirit. He cannot be contented in the ranks. *He* go to Church and sit in the pew with the ear and the heart of a child ! Perhaps he is a tallow-chandler. What does he do ? He says to the butcher—" I think we are not right," &c. The devil will help the man to reasons. This is not the spirit of a godly man like W. This is not the spirit of a conscientious Dissenter. He is a man brought up in the Church. He knows his minister to be a godly man ; but he is disposed to set up his own post and pillar and tabernacle. And one fungus grows out of another. A tailor starts up. This tailor is a talking man. He takes it into his head that his minister is in a gross error, because his minister does not hold eternal justification. " No, he does not hold imputed sanctification ; whereas, if you look into Gill, you will find it there." What is to be done ? " Take a garret—take any place—let us but have the pure Gospel." While this is all sheer evil—the acrimony of the heart.

Such a man rose in my parish. He got into my kitchen. My maid was to become a member of his new and pure Church. But, happily for the exposure of hypocrisy, there was what is called a consecration of colours in the neighbourhood. Thither the tailor went, and thence was he brought home in a cart, alas! drunk. This is not a solitary specimen. It is in the very heart of man; because man is a self-sufficient creature. Wherever good is doing in the world, the devil will set up Schism. There is, indeed, some good arising from it. Every house must have a sewer.

REMEDY.—Godliness, humility, patience, peaceableness, righteousness. Nothing short of these is a sufficient remedy. There is great difficulty in treating this disorder so as to be most likely to obtain success. I should be sorry to be misunderstood. I find little is to be done by attacking the thing directly. We must attack the root of the evil; and the root is the want of a quiet mind—thankfulness to God. Manna is rained plentifully about the tents, but men want it seasoned. Some want music, and some detest it; but carnality of mind is at the bottom. The schisms I have witnessed have been chiefly propagated by a relaxation of godliness, under the idea of furnishing the people with the pure Gospel. The man has baited for the flesh. He pretends to make the road easier. The cross, self-denial, &c., have been kept in the shade. Ignorance is determined not to enter by the gate, and then gets Vain Hope to ferry him over the river.

The Rev. B. Woodd—

If uniformity were established, the same spirit would still creep in. It exists everywhere now. The spirit of strong attachment to us, ministers, personally, is this spirit. Schism is not separation from a corrupt Church, as the Greek from the Roman, the Waldenses from the Roman, Protestants from the Roman. Schism is separation on account of modal peculiarities, innovations, &c.; there were Dissenters prior to the Act of Uniformity.

REMEDY.—Establish very catholic terms of communion, as the Trinity, the divinity of Christ, the agency of the Spirit, the atonement, necessity of faith and obedience. Allow, in inferior things. Modern Churches tend more to produce than prevent Schism. The Act of Uniformity has the spirit of Satan.

Look at the state of the Universities, and the difficulty of good men getting orders. Hence, people must starve or go away. Godly men must be silent. A godly minister in contemplation of his own death must advise his people to go.

Christian unity consists not in the subjection of many Churches to one, or in uniformity of worship. Look into history. The proper unity of the Church is in harmony and love.

The Rev. T. Scott—

The crime of Schism is only implicitly spoken of in Scripture. It grows out of the passions of men mixing together. *Whence come wars,*

&c. Thence comes Schism. No man has a right, however, to bind my conscience. Let us consider ourselves as so many battalions in an army—one listed in one battalion and another in another. In the present state of the Church, we should go on separately, but lovingly. To mould all into one mass would be to form another sect.

The Rev. J. Clayton—

The essence of Schism is an unpeaceable spirit. Heresy is a corruption of the doctrine of the Church; Schism an attack on peace. Persons differing in ceremonies, may be yet enemies to Schism. Unity of spirit and Uniformity are different. The Apostle settles this—*He who regardeth the day, regardeth it unto the Lord; and he that regardeth not the day, to the Lord he doth not regard it,* &c.—Rom. xiv. 6.

The next subject, it will be observed, was discussed not long after the time when the admirable modern system of Sunday schools was first devised—in which members of the congregation to which the children belong devote a portion of their time on the Lord's-day to instructing the young of the flock. This excellent practice had not yet spread itself over the kingdom—a circumstance which should be borne in mind in reading the following observations, as it invests them with an additional degree of interest.

JANUARY 22, 1798.

WHAT MAY BE DONE TOWARDS THE INTERESTS OF THE CHILDREN OF A CONGREGATION ?—Proposed by the Rev. R. Cecil.

The Rev. R. Cecil—

There are many children in our congregations. Parents cannot come ; but they will send their children. I collected mine on benches ; but they tattled and were troublesome. I was obliged to remove my benches, and to put them under the care of a man and woman. But these were not able to manage them. Every one will sing his own tune.

Besides, the number is very large ; and I feel my difficulty and responsibility. For here seems to be a large harvest. It is difficult to speak to children before a congregation, especially where the people are made of lacework.

I generally have recourse to terrible images. I explain salvation by a house on fire ; for I remember, when I was a child, and learned from bad companions to curse and lead a wicked life, I thought I would keep on, if I could but escape hell.

The Rev. J. Newton—

What is agreeable to children is agreeable to children of six feet high. Particularly the Apostle's method among children, *I determined to know nothing amongst you save Jesus Christ and him crucified.* Talk to children about God abstractedly, and it is all in vain. But they can think on

One who is now in heaven, though once a child.   Go through the life of Christ, and all the historical parts of Scripture.

The Rev. J. Pratt—

The case of children is of greater importance in the present day, than in any former.   It is a subject of vast difficulty.   The Moravians sit down with the elder people, and think it easy.

ATTENTION is to be kept up.   The MEMORY to be impressed.   The JUDGMENT to be descended to.   The AFFECTIONS are to be won.   VOLATILITY is to be fixed.

How is this to be done?   Any how.   Even eccentricities may be useful here.   Children cannot judge of what is in correct taste, and what not.   The question is, how to produce most effect?   If we talk so as to meet the parents, we shall produce a far less effect.

It is not simplicity alone at which we must aim ; but we must clothe what we say with such circumstances as affect children.   A wise man will stand by and approve as to children, though he is little benefited himself.   His very presence, however, cramps the minister in the discharge of this duty.

Don't ask children to *define*.

Have *patience*.   " How do you do the thing?" said one to Miss More.   " I tell them the same thing over and over and over again."

In reply to Scott, I should ask questions, but not questions that imply knowledge.

G. has said that little can be done on Sunday.   I think otherwise. Give subjects for children to prove, &c., from Scripture : this is an excellent exercise.   It sets to work—and that is a great step gained.

The Rev. J. Venn—

I once thought it absurd to teach children the Catechism, which they did not comprehend.   So I determined to address their understandings.   I got them round me, talked to them in a familiar way, and all went on well.   But I compared them with a stupid maidservant, who had been educated in the old way : and found to my surprise that *she* was *the best!*   So I altered my opinion.

Consider a child's mind.   Lay up the means of knowledge, rather than expect it.   Combine both methods.

1*st*. ENGAGE THE ATTENTION.   Children like " Pilgrim's Progress," though they do not understand it.   Images and stories are useful to engage attention.   Teach but little.   Fletcher of Madeley preached on robin red-breast and flowers.

2*d*. STORE THE MIND WELL.   There is no fear of burdening their young memories.   I have known children get 70 chapters by heart. Perhaps the best way is thus to store the memory.   Children are machines.   Employ them properly.   I would teach (1.) The Church Catechism.   (2.) The Catechism broken into short questions.   Then (3.) I would break the Sermon into short questions.   And (4.) make them get Scripture by heart.

I would teach by intervals.   None should be present but children, because if others are there, the Minister will be aiming at them.

The Rev. R. Cecil concluded by saying : Let a man find out his talent, and then employ it. I differ with Woodd as to age. Children are early capable of receiving impressions. I imprinted on my daughter, at an early age, the idea of Faith, by getting her to throw some favourite beads behind the fire from confiding in me, and then rewarded her with more.

The exceedingly happy manner in which Mr Cecil thus succeeded in giving his daughter a lively impression of the meaning of Faith, is so admirably described in the volume of his " Remains," gathered and published by the Rev. Josiah Pratt, that we shall not apologise for introducing it here :—

Children are very early capable of impression. I imprinted on my daughter the idea of Faith, at a very early age. She was playing one day with a few beads, which seemed to delight her wonderfully. Her whole soul was absorbed in her beads. I said—" My dear, you have some pretty beads there. " " Yes, papa !" " And you seem to be vastly pleased with them." " Yes, papa !" " Well, now, throw 'em behind the fire." The tears started into her eyes. She looked earnestly at me, as though she ought to have a reason for such a cruel sacrifice. " Well, my dear, do as you please : but you know I never told you to do anything which I did not think would be good for you." She looked at me a few moments longer, and then (summoning up all her fortitude, her breast heaving with the effort) she dashed them into the fire. " Well," said I, " there let them lie : you shall hear more about them another time ; but say no more about them now." Some days after, I bought her a box full of larger beads and toys of the same kind. When I returned home, I opened the treasure and set it before her : she burst into tears with ecstasy. " Those, my child," said I, " are yours ; because you believed me, when I told you it would be better for you to throw those two or three paltry beads behind the fire. Now that has brought you this treasure. But now, my dear, remember, as long as you live, what FAITH is. I did all this to teach you the meaning of Faith. You threw your beads away when I bid you, because you had faith in me that I never advised you but for your good. Put the same confidence in God. Believe everything that he says in his word. Whether you understand it or not, have faith in him that he means your good."

<hr>

FEBRUARY 5, 1798.

IN WHAT SENSE ARE WE WITHOUT THE LAW TO GOD, BUT UNDER THE LAW TO CHRIST ?—Proposed by the Rev. J. Goode.

Rev. J. Goode—

The Apostle had not scratched out the word *accommodate*. He had a mind free from bigotry ; enlarged with comprehensive views of the Gospel. He kept the grand end in view. Guyse supposes by " Jews " that he means so. My question is—How may a believer be said to be not without law to God, and yet under the law to Christ ? See 1 Cor. ix. 20–22. This is an important question. I hope to be furnished with arguments against the false maxim—" The law not a rule of life." The law stands upon the immutable distinction of moral good and evil, and so for substance must be preserved under every dispensation. Christ fulfilled the law ; explained it ; enforced it ; illustrated it by example ; recommended it by redeeming love.

Rev. Thomas Scott—

The Apostle speaks chiefly of the ceremonial law ; a cancelled deed ; a bond given for payment, now paid. Many believers did not see this. The Apostle sets an example of giving up where truth is not concerned. He is as firm as a rock where truth is concerned ; as pliable as a willow, when not. He seems in all his epistles deeply aware of the tendency of human nature to corrupt everything. Therefore he comes in with a parenthesis, *Being not without law to God, but under the law to Christ.* Let us never think men can be left at random. He changes from the ceremonial to the moral law. In reading Paul's epistles, we must always attend to his different uses of the word " law." [Here Mr Scott proceeded at length upon the subject of the moral law being the rule of a man's conduct.] The due regard of the moral law leads to the regard of the evangelical system. If a man loves God truly, it will lead him to receive every sentiment God reveals. Here is one proof of Christ's divinity—that there is not a disposition enjoined towards God in Scripture, which is not enjoined towards Christ in the New Testament.

Rev. Josiah Pratt—

Take the train of the Apostle's argument *to the Jews* (v. 20), *i. e.,* Judaising Christians, who coupled the law with faith in Christ. See Gal. iv. 21 : *I became as a Jew, i. e.,* as though I were a Jew in religion, or in sect ; like a Jew in some actions and exterior observances, in ceremonies, in some things which were not repugnant to faith in Christ : see example, Acts xxi. 23, &c. *To them that are under the law, i. e.,* the ceremonial law, meaning the unbelieving Jews ; *as under the law, i. e.,* a proselyte, for the proselytes subjected themselves to the law : see example, Acts xvi. 3. *To them that are without law, i. e.,* the Gentiles, ἀνόμοις, not in its frequent sense of " lawless," but as under no obligation to the observance of either the ceremonial or judicial law given to the Jews ; *as without law, i. e.,* behaving himself as though he had been a Gentile, by forbearing the observance of the Levitical law ; and as far as he might with propriety, taking them up on their own ground. See example in his speech at Athens (Acts xvii.), requiring no other postulata than reason might seem to admit ; demonstrating to them, that, upon their own principles, they stood convicted of ignorance of God, and therefore ought to listen to one who said he had the means of enlightening them ; not hereby involving the surrender of any truths, though he kept them behind. But in doing this, he was guided by this rule—*being not without law to God, but under the law to Christ, i. e.,* to guard against the misunderstanding or abuse of calling himself ἄνομος, he would have them recollect that in this delicate management he had a sure and steady bound which he did not trespass; and it was this—Though he brought not before the Gentiles the Levitical institutions which were done away in Christ, and though he required as few principles and as general as possible, yet he did not sacrifice any part of God's law which was in present and general force and obligation; but held himself bound by that, while he was more especially subjected to Christ's law, and used the liberty given him by that law of overstepping the narrow fences and restrictions of the Levitical institutions. See Poli, *Synopsis et Ann.*, *in loco*. The Apostle means neither the moral nor the ceremonial law, but, "*q. d.*, μη ανομος θεω, I am subjected to God in being ἐννομος Χριστῳ, submitted to Christ."

In reply to Goode, I should rather consider from this question the Apostle's SYSTEM OF CONDUCT, than the EXCELLENCE AND NECESSITY of the moral law. The Apostle seems not to allude to the moral law particularly, but to describe his own system of proceeding towards others.

Rev. J. Clayton—

To the Jews I became as a Jew; i. e., reasoning with them from the Old Testament. *To them that are under the law, as under the law; i. e.*, accommodating himself, as in circumcising Timothy. *To them that are without law, as without law; i. e.*, addressed them from the internal evidence of the Gospel. His whole system of accommodation was to bring them to God. *Under the law to God; i. e.*, though I sacrifice some punctilios, I govern myself by God's holy law. *Under the law to Christ; i. e.*, sweetened to me by Christ's mediatorship.

Rev. J. Newton—

The Apostle speaks of some startling questions about the law from those who *understand not what they say, nor whereof they affirm.* The law is the result of that relation subsisting between God and us as intelligent creatures. It is the law of our nature, that we must love and serve Him with all our hearts. It was a kind of instinct when man was upright. It was then as natural to him, as to a bird to fly. A believer in Christ is free from the condemning power of the law. The Apostle gives us an example of his accommodating spirit. See also Rom. xiv. Let not him who worships under a steeple condemn him who worships under a chimney. True Christians are willing to live as saints, and to die as sinners.

Rev. B. Woodd—

This passage is an illustration of the accommodating spirit of the Gospel. He introduces the law of Christ as being under an additional obligation by Christ's redemption. I cannot say that I particularly fall in with Pratt's idea of his having a reference to the law of liberty under Christ. The law of God is the criterion and character of all truth. There are very few Antinomians in the world, properly so called; but rather an excess of zeal for the grace of the Gospel, as

Pharisaism is rather an excess of zeal for the law of God. Some of these regard the moral law only as a part of the Mosaic economy. As such, Baxter says it is abolished.

The means to be adopted to remedy Antinomianism are not direct opposition, which irritates, but conciliation of all parties. Let us shew that our differences are often unmeaning distinctions, and that we are quarrelling with brethren about words and phrases. This law applies in all cases and circumstances of intelligent beings—God (see Hooker, 1st book)—angels—Jesus Christ—believers as creatures, redeemed, delineated on their hearts by the Holy Spirit.

Rev. Thomas Scott—

Was Paul wrong when he directly attacked the false principles of Judaising teachers?

Rev. B. Woodd—

I think not. I only think the way wrong in us.

Rev. W. Goode—

The text is a general rule, to be applied to general cases. I look up to God through Christ. I receive the law now only through Christ. I do not receive it as from an awful God, but through Christ, as one who knows my circumstances, as one who takes away my guilt, as one who gives me motives and power.

I believe with Woodd, that many Antinomians differ from us only in terms. Some of them have as sincere a regard to holiness as any. " What are you guided by?" They will answer, " The Apostle's precepts." By which we comprehend the whole system. They love the precepts they find in the Epistles, but love not the same in Exodus.

Rev. John Venn—

I agree with Pratt in the general view of the Apostle's reasoning, but should differ, perhaps, with him in his consideration of the different persons to whom he addressed them. *Jews*—unbelieving Jews. *Under the law*—I would not say Judaising Christians, but Christians of tender conscience, with reverence to the old fabric. *Without law*— Gentiles. Huntingdon would not have qualified this expression.

It shews that the Apostle had something in his mind, and feared he might be misunderstood as leading to lawlessness. His words *to them that are without law, as without law,* might lead to the inference that, had you seen him in heathen places, he would be as a heathen. He therefore adds, *not without law to God, i. e.,* the Moral Law,—*to Christ, i. e.,* a qualification of being *not without law to God.* Go back to what Christ did with reference to the law in his conduct. He did not tell his disciples that he came to abrogate. *Think not that I am come to destroy the law, but to fulfil.* Christ thus confirmed the authority of the law. Where, then, is the difference? He took away some institutions, and thus left us at liberty. The prejudices of the Gentiles were strong against Levitical ceremonies; and then he would win them to the Gospel, which is free from the obligation of these ceremonies.

A peculiar historical interest attaches itself to the next topic, as it has reference to the state and exigencies of the times when it was discussed.

During the course of the last six years, affairs had worn a very gloomy and threatening aspect in England. French revolutionary principles seemed to be spreading wide their mischievous influence. Unremitted pains were taken, not only to agitate and mislead, but to corrupt and poison the minds of the populace by every artifice that malice could suggest; and such had been the success of these efforts, and of the inflammatory publications by which they were carried on, that the perverted feelings and imaginations of men appeared to be propelling them fast into the same abyss into which the French had already fallen.

At such a crisis, the importance of devising some means of counteracting the growing evil naturally presented itself to the minds of the members of the Eclectic, and the following topic was discussed on—

FEBRUARY 19, 1798.

WHAT CAN BE DONE AT THE PRESENT MOMENT TO COUNTERACT THE DESIGNS OF INFIDELS AGAINST CHRISTIANITY?—Proposed by Mr Bacon.

Mr Bacon—

It belongs to us to consider; and to consider in order to act. I have had many designs, but thought at last that I could do nothing, and that I must act merely as a private man. But I have been stimulated by conversation and reading. Robison's book roused me.* The old story with me, and I thought it indolence. I remembered Shipley, the suggester of the Society for Promoting Arts; and thought *I* might be the means of suggesting. I had an idea all parties could be united; but I now almost give that up. But all should be either under one controlling Committee, or we should form different Societies in different bodies.

The Rev. Thomas Scott—

Non omnia possumus omnes. Give me a doctrine to define, and I can do it. But I have thought about this scheme again and again, and can make nothing of it. If the plan were adopted, I would give an opinion. 'I had thought, if the object were to defend Christianity, then politics should not be introduced.

The Rev. John Newton—

An honest woman said to me, " I don't know how it is, but your clever men are seldom good, and your good men are seldom clever."

---

* This was Professor Robison of Edinburgh, the author of the four volumes on Mechanical Philosophy. He published in 1798 a work to which allusion is made above, and which attracted, in an uncommon degree, the attention of the public. Its title was, " Proofs of a Conspiracy against all the Religions and Governments of Europe, carried on in the Secret Meetings of Freemasons, Illuminati, Reading Societies," &c. —See Chalmers's *Biog. Dict.*

The Rev. J. Pratt—

Nothing effectual can be done without a large fund. The Ministry and Opposition are obliged to spend large sums in throwing their pamphlets into circulation. If *party-spirit* will not stimulate, I'm afraid *religion* will not.

PRIVACY must be the first character of any Society to answer our end. Strike, but conceal the hand.

THE CONTROL OF LITERATURE must be the second grand principle. Literature is at present the great engine acting upon society.

If a Society be not practicable, yet the times call on Individuals to square their exertions to particular objects.

The Rev. W. Goode—

To know whether the plan is practicable, it must be tried. The beginning must be small. Let us look to God for His blessing. But, humanly speaking, even with the same exertions, we shall not have the same success as Infidels ; for they have the natural heart of man with them. They act in secrecy—are cordially united—and have enlisted literature on their side.

The Rev. J. Venn—

Too much must not be aimed at. I would consider this Society as a presiding spirit. Let it use the Barlett's Buildings' Society. The chief uses of our proposed Society would be :—

1. To AFFORD A MEDIUM OF CIRCULATION.

A man in a country parish knows only what he hears at his parish feast. But united to a Society, he is no longer a loose grain of sand —he becomes an acting principle. Barruel would not reach many men in the country two or three years to come.* Remember the fable of the bundle of sticks. A number of able and wise men, forming a soul for the rest of the body, will put that in motion which was before a *caput mortuum*.

2. Another use will be the COMMUNICATION OF KNOWLEDGE. Just as the spider in her web—touch any part, and she feels.

3. Moreover, it will CALL OUT ZEAL. When a man is called out to speak and act, he feels spirit. Energies are created by Societies. What are men in a desert island ?—sunk into nothing. Revolutions produce vigour—powers are called forth in the same manner.

Our Society should creep before it goes. I never knew of a Society professing great things that did not fail, and *vice versâ: e.g.*, the Royal Society and the Eclectic ! ! The Sierra Leone Company has failed from attempting too much. The Colony of Georgia did not succeed, because it was taken up by Parliament on a large scale. It cost more than all the other Colonies. This is a law of nature, which must be followed if we would succeed. We should tell people in the country what evil principles are urged in various ways. I agree with Pratt on the necessity of secrecy.

* L'Abbé Augustin Barruel wrote, as Professor Robison did, soon after the French Revolution, an able work exposing the arts and wickedness of the French and German conspiracy against Christianity and all settled governments.

My idea of such a Society is, therefore, a medium of circulation, and for the communication of knowledge in the most ready way.

It appears from our Note-Book that a good deal of desultory conversation arose at this meeting. But the discussion was not without its effect. The members of the Eclectic exerted themselves in various ways to carry out their object; they used their influence with their friends in the country, and were not backward on their own part to do everything they could to meet the crisis.

Already had the powerful pen of Hannah More been most successfully employed in this important service, and her incomparable little tract, *Village Politics*, by *Will Chip*, had, with astonishing rapidity, reached every corner of the kingdom: many hundred thousands were circulated in London alone: many thousands were sent by Government to Scotland and Ireland; and men of the soundest judgment went so far as to affirm, that it had most essentially contributed, under Providence, to prevent a revolution.

Others were now pressing into the same service; and pamphlets and tracts multiplied on all hands. To this desire to meet the infidelity and recklessness of the times, it is that we are indebted for the volume of *Essays*, in the works of the Rev. Thomas Scott, *on the most important subjects in religion*, which were at first published in penny-numbers, once a fortnight, and reached many editions, besides those printed in America. The author states, in his preface, that his original design was, by a series of Essays, each comprised in a single number, to guard the minds of young people especially against the infidelity and scepticism of modern times; as well as to give a distinct view of the grand peculiarities and excellent tendency of genuine Christianity. He purposed not to be strictly methodical, argumentative, or systematic; but to treat a variety of subjects in a familiar, easy, and engaging manner.

He seems, however, to have distrusted his ability for the task he had undertaken, and in some degree to have underrated his own performances. For he says the attempt soon convinced him that he had not the requisite talents for Essays of this description; and that he felt obliged to leave it to persons of a more versatile and happy genius to furnish that species of publication, which seemed specially suited to the circumstances of the times, and best adapted to the taste of modern readers.

As, however, the Essays first published met with great encouragement, and had considerable circulation, he proceeded on the plan to which he found himself most competent, and at length completed a work which has been of eminent service—the origin of which we may thus distinctly trace to discussions in the Eclectic Society.

But these deliberations led also to another method of calling attention to the signs and dangers of the times.   The clerical members of the Eclectic, joined by various friends in the country, commenced a series of Lectures in their several Churches and Chapels upon this important subject.   They lasted for nearly three years. The Rev. Thomas Scott commenced the course.   His opening sermon was afterwards published in the form of a pamphlet, at the request of the Eclectic Society, and widely circulated.   In the body of the tract, reference is made to the circumstances which led to this method of arousing the public mind; and we find distinct allusion to this very meeting of the Eclectic on February 19, 1798, of which we have given a few scattered notices above.   We shall, therefore, conclude this article by appending the interesting account which Mr Scott gives of the state of feeling of good men, and the part the Eclectic Society took in these perilous times :—

" The more serious persons," he writes, "value our civil and religious privileges, the greater in this view will be their apprehensions on attentively considering the signs of the times, and the deeper their conviction that the Lord might justly give us up into the hands of our enraged enemies.   On whatever side we turn our eyes, we must witness such atrocious crimes as tend to dismay our hearts more than all the menaces of our haughty assailants ; and we can find nothing suited to relieve our terrors, except we advert to the remnant of real Christians scattered through the land.   In subordination to the Lord's infinite mercies, our hope of preservation rests on this company and on their supplications and exertions ; and this consideration leads us anxiously to inquire, What can be done to stir up this whole remnant to attend, as with one soul, regardless of party distinctions, to the alarming signs and important duties of the times, and what individual or collective efforts may be made to increase the number of those who are indeed " the chariots and horsemen" of the nation ?

Some ministers in the metropolis, having frequently conferred together on this subject, at length deliberately entered into a consultation on the best means of accomplishing these desirable ends, in their several situations, and by their combined endeavours.   It was very obvious that prayer for the Church and Nation was peculiarly seasonable and obligatory ; and we unanimously determined that, by the help of God, we would earnestly recommend the same to our several congregations, exhorting them to join their supplications for the land to those of their brethren, on every day, but especially to make this topic a prominent part of their devotions on the evening of the Lord's-day, both in their families and in private.

These considerations, however, did not rest here, but produced a general conviction that the present emergency called us and our people

to other duties likewise, and that it would be very useful for us particularly to examine the subject.   This appeared the more seasonable,
when we reflected that numbers, aware of the evil of political discussions from the pulpit, and of rendering religious ordinances subservient
to the gratification of men's passions and prejudices, are ready to conclude that we have nothing to do with the state of public affairs, or,
in other words, that *in this respect* we have actually no duties at all !
while others seem to take it for granted, that no one who differs from
them in political sentiment can possibly be influenced by religious
principles.

It was therefore agreed among a few friends, that a Sermon should
be preached weekly, on the usual lecture-day and hour, in our several
churches and chapels by rotation, on the Signs and Duties of the Times,
by some other of the company than the stated pastor ; and that other
ministers of the Established Church should be invited to join us, by
giving their pulpits and employing their labours in the same cause.

This was begun about a year ago, and is still continued with considerable encouragement ; and as we greatly desire to unite our brethren throughout the land in similar measures, we have at length
determined to publish an account of our designs, both in order to excite attention, to prevent misapprehension, to obviate prejudice, and to
stimulate others to imitate us, as far as our conduct is judged to accord
with the principles of sacred Scripture.

We would therefore propose our sentiments on the following subjects to the candid attention of pious Christians, however distinguished,
in every part of Great Britain :—

I. The duty of intercession for the Nation and for the Church in
seasons of danger and distress.

II. The nature and special objects of those prayers which may be
supposed to be availing on such occasions.

III. The prevalency of acceptable prayer, according to the Scriptures.

IV. And lastly, The other duties which are incumbent on us, along
with our prayers, in the present emergency.*

This series of Lectures came to a close in the year 1802, Mr
Scott being invited to preach the last, as he had the opening sermon.   This admirable discourse, upon Ps. cxvi. 2—*Because he hath
inclined his ear unto me, therefore will I call upon him as long as
I live*—was a thanksgiving sermon for the merciful interposition
of the Almighty in behalf of our country.   It was published at
the unanimous request of the Society, by whom the course was
maintained.

The past fifteen months had brought on a wonderful change in
the aspect of public affairs.   The prospect at the beginning of
that period was then very gloomy.   Our allies had left us (perhaps unavoidably) to sustain alone the apparently unequal contest—the powers of the north combined to deprive us of our naval

* Rev. Thomas Scott's Works, vol. v. p. 494.

superiority—even our rulers were evidently not without apprehensions that an invasion would be attempted—a scarcity, approximating to famine, pressed upon our people at home—it became doubtful whether supplies from abroad could be procured to sustain the people till harvest, and what that harvest would be, who could tell? Urged by such distresses, what might not have been feared from the suffering multitudes! what advantages might not the disaffected at home, as well as our foreign enemies, have obtained! No doubt the more our country was pressed and alarmed, the greater earnestness in prayer was excited. "Man's extremity is God's opportunity." These clouds were now all dispersed. A plentiful harvest had supplied the people's wants. Our successes and negotiations had quelled the northern storm—peace was made with France. "*My* tongue," said the preacher, "cannot do justice to the change which, in little more than a year, has taken place. I can only stand astonished, and call on you, my brethren, saying, *Oh magnify the Lord with me, and let us exalt his name together!*"

———

THE next subject from our Eclectic Notes is one which chiefly concerns the Ministers of religion, although it was proposed and opened by a Lay Member of the Society. It is a topic which must carry interest with it to every person who has the success of the preaching of the Gospel at heart.

After the observations of the members, we shall, by way of illustration, add, at some length, what information we have been able to collect regarding the various gifts which they themselves possessed as preachers.

MARCH 5, 1798.

WHAT CONSTITUTES WHAT IS TERMED EFFECT IN PREACHING ?—Proposed by Mr Bacon.

Mr Bacon—

1. We need not expect much pulpit effect, if all is made to rest on what is done in the pulpit.

To produce effect, the Minister's character must be established. Honesty gives substance. A man may go once to an exhibition, but he cannot live with pictures ; he has to live with men. Even the behaviour of his wife and children may affect his ministry—their dress and manner of deportment.

The nature of his previous prayer is of consequence to the effect which is to follow.

2. The text selected must be plain, or capable of being made so. When a man shews us what we could not easily see ourselves, he makes a lodgment in our minds.

3. The Minister must interest, and make an impression, in order to

B

produce an effect. He must awaken men ; and, as it were, open the pores that they may inhale the sentimental effluvia. Animation in the preacher aids the importance of truth.

Medicine must be prepared according to the Dispensatory of the College.

He who made man's heart knows how to address it ; the Minister must therefore look up to Him for his assistance. Christ should be the subject of a sermon in the sense in which he is the subject of the Scriptures.

The Rev. Thomas Scott—

Poeta nascitur non fit. Many would have Whitfield's spirit if they could catch it. If we cannot get a sword, let us go with a sling and a stone. Let the Minister do what he can, and go with simplicity. If he has none of the imagination with which some are gifted, still God will bless him. The greatest hindrance to effect is the want of the apostolic spirit.

We should go forth as if to work miracles—miracles of grace in the conversion of sinners. Men aim not at a *right* effect. They may produce great effect while preaching ; but all is soon forgotten for want of the right effect being produced. Massillon sent Louis away dissatisfied with himself.* This was a right effect. But many go away satisfied with themselves—and then no effect, or a bad one, has been produced.

The Rev. Josiah Pratt—

1. Effect depends *ceteris paribus* upon the STATE OF RELIGION IN THE MIND OF THE PREACHER.

Quintilian has a chapter (lib. xii. ch. 1) to prove that an orator must be a good man. The mind *feels* truth only as it is liberated from vice. *Nihil tam occupatum, tam multiforme, tot ac tam variis affectibus concisum atque laceratum, quam mala mens.*

---

* This is the eminent French preacher, John Baptist Massillon, born in 1663. The first efforts of his eloquence were made at Vienne : his funeral oration on Henri de Villars, Archbishop of that city, was so universally admired, that it led to his being called to Paris. His powers were immediately felt and acknowledged, when he made his appearance at court ; and when he preached his first sermon at Versailles, he received this compliment from Louis XIV., to which allusion is made by Mr Scott in his remarks above—"My father," said that monarch, "when I hear other preachers, I go away much pleased with them ; but whenever I hear YOU, I go away much DISPLEASED with—MYSELF."

On one occasion, the effect of a discourse preached by him " on the small number of the elect" was so extraordinary, that it produced a general though involuntary murmur of applause in the congregation. The preacher himself was confused by it ; but the effect was only increased, and the pathetic was carried to the greatest height that can be supposed possible. His mode of delivery contributed not a little to his success. " We seem to behold him still in imagination," said they who had been fortunate enough to hear his discourses, " with that simple air, that modest carriage, those eyes so humbly directed downwards, that unstudied gesture, that touching tone of voice, that look of a man fully impressed with truths which he enforced, conveying the most brilliant instruction to the mind, and the most pathetic movements to the heart." The famous actor Baron, after hearing him, told him to continue as he had begun. " You," said he, " have a manner of your own, leave the rules to others." At another time, he said to an actor who was with him : " My friend, this is the true orator ; we are mere players."—See Chalmers's *Biog. Dict.*

Effect depends much on the propagation of sympathy.*

2. There are some COMMON CAUSES OF EFFECT in which all must agree.

(1.) The people must be interested.   (2.) The preacher must be intelligible.   (3.) The preacher must be armed with Truth.   God's great ordinance—CHRIST JESUS—he blesses, and that in an especial manner. (4.) Truth must be exhibited with Simplicity and Fidelity.   The preacher must, in a certain sense, be above his hearers.   His soul must be wholly imbued with the dignity of his office.   (5.) Truth must be accommodated to his hearers.

3. There are some CIRCÙMSTANTIAL CAUSES OF EFFECT peculiar to men or stations.

No common and universal standard can be laid down.   There is danger in our judging for others.   If a preacher has the common principles, few men can judge for him further.

As to MAN :—

Every man has one way in which he can be most effective.   His cast of mind, his education, his associations, his prejudices, his habits, his friends, all combine to form him *sui generis*—solitary.   His duty is to find out his talent—by *any* means.   His duty is to correct his exuberances, but to push his talent.   If a man be an honest inquirer into these things, he is himself the best judge of the way in which he will be most efficient.

So as to STATIONS :—

There are many circumstances peculiar to each man's calling, which must go far to decide the wisest and most likely way of his producing effect by his ministry.

The Rev. J. Clayton—

There are different kinds of effect : there is—

A NATURAL EFFECT, which operates on our natural feelings :

A MORAL EFFECT, which changes men's manners : but the great thing is—

A SPIRITUAL EFFECT, which brings God and the Soul together.

That effect may be produced upon an auditory—they should be impressed with the feeling, that " this man is in his place ; " that his doctrine is the doctrine of the Bible—and eminently Jesus Christ.   He should apply it in detail—should ferret them.   His manner, his spirit, his love to Christ, his compassion for souls, his faithfulness, should all

---

* The following remark, taken from Whately's Elements of Rhetoric, where the author is speaking of the effect of sympathy between a speaker and his audience, will illustrate this statement :—

" It is to be observed, that we are disposed to sympathise with any emotion which we believe to exist in the mind of any one present, and hence if we are at the same time otherwise disposed to feel that emotion, such disposition is in consequence heightened. In the next place, we not only ourselves feel this tendency, but we are sensible that others do the same ; and thus we not only sympathise with the other emotions of the rest, but also with their sympathy towards us.   Any emotion, accordingly, which we feel, is still further heightened by the knowledge that there are others present who not only feel the same, but feel it the more strongly in consequence of their sympathy with ourselves.   Lastly, we are sensible that those around us sympathise not only with ourselves, but with each other also ; and as we enter into this heightened feeling of theirs likewise, the stimulus to our own minds is thereby still further increased."

be prominent, if he desires to produce the right effect. Out of the pulpit, he must maintain a character in keeping with all this. He should, moreover, pay marked attention to occasions of Providence. Providential occurrences and indications are teeming around us. Providences are pioneers to grace.

The Rev. J. Newton—

Effect, I believe, has been produced in my preaching by a solemn determination to bring forth JESUS CHRIST as the GREAT SUBJECT in all my discourses.

I try, moreover, to leave this impression on the people—that *I wish them well*.

The length and breadth of a preacher may be thus represented. His *length* is his measure in the pulpit; his *breadth*, his conduct and character out of it. A man may be very long, but a mere talker. He may be short, but well set.

I agree with the last speaker but one, that no general rule can be laid down for all.

There are two grand arguments which we must constantly put forth:
(1.) *I beseech you by the mercies of God.* (2.) I warn you by *the terrors of the Lord.*

There are two sorts of popularity which ministers attain to—one from the exertion of talents; the other by reaching the heart.

The Rev. B. Woodd—

1. WHAT IS EFFECT ?—Not the applause of our congregation. Not merely transitory impressions. Not collecting large assemblies. It is REAL CONVERSION, and all that follows.

2. HOW IS THIS EFFECT PRODUCED ?

I answer, solely by the Spirit of God; but to this end He uses means. The matter is gross upon which we have to act; and we are in more danger of *producing no effect* upon such matter, than of *wounding.*

(1.) We must endeavour to gain attention; and must therefore never be too long either in our paragraphs or in the whole sermon.

(2.) We must use plainness. *If the trumpet give an uncertain sound, who shall prepare himself for the battle ?*

(3.) Affection must be shewn in our manner. Affection steals insensibly on the heart. It conciliates attention when the subject will not.

(4.) We must manifest all solemnity. All ribaldry is destructive of effect.

(5.) Mixed addresses to the understanding will and affections are good.

(6.) Our subject should be of a mixed character—Doctrinal, Expository, and Practical.

(7.) Popular subjects—subjects the importance of which.is easily apprehended—should be often dwelt upon; such as Death, Judgment, the Love of God in Christ, &c.

(8.) On the mode of exhibiting our subject, the following hints might be considered:—State the heads. Explain terms. Quote a few apposite texts. Bring forward some familiar illustrations and suitable anecdotes—Scriptural anecdotes. Make due pauses. Adopt the questioning form. Make personal addresses. Speak in the second person. Nobody knows where " he " lives. If extempore, then have not too great a burden of notes. Study the subject sufficiently. Solemnise the mind previously by prayer.

(9.) The character must be good, the spirit congenial and sympathetic.

(10.) JESUS CHRIST must be ALL IN ALL in our preaching. His name frequently though properly introduced. There is a charm in this. The frequent repetition of it in successive verses in the Epistles is very observable. St Paul is guilty of continual digressions to this subject. Every doctrine and every duty should be brought forward with reference to Jesus Christ.

The Rev. W. Goode—

I like Clayton's divisions—NATURAL—MORAL—SPIRITUAL EFFECT.

Most rules produce the two former. It is the Spirit who uses means to produce spiritual effect. *Preaching Christ* is the great means. But WE must BE SEEN to believe the truth ourselves.

The Rev. J. Venn—

I have taken the question as effect indicative of the Spirit's influence.

1. To produce an IMPRESSION should be our aim. Massillon was famous for working up the people. Kirwan, the Irish preacher,* had

---

* Walter Blake Kirwan was an Irish preacher, remarkable for the command he obtained over the congregations he addressed. He was brought up and ordained in the Romish Church, but afterwards came over to the Protestant Episcopal communion. For some time after his conformity, he preached every Sunday in St Peter's Church, Dublin ; and so great was the effect, that the collections for the poor on every occasion rose four or five fold above their usual amount. Before the expiration of his first year, he was wholly reserved for the task of preaching charity sermons ; and on November 5, 1788, the governors of the general daily schools of several parishes entered into a resolution, " that from the effects which the discourses of the Rev. Walter Blake Kirwan, from the pulpit, have had, his officiating in this metropolis was considered a peculiar national advantage, and that vestries should be called to consider the most effectual method to secure to the city an instrument, under Providence, of so much public benefit." In the same year he was preferred by the Archbishop of Dublin to the Prebend of Howth, and in the next year to the parish of St Nicholas Without, the joint income of which amounted to about L.400 a-year. He resigned the prebend, however, on being presented, in 1800, by the Marquis Cornwallis, then Lord-Lieutenant, to the deanery of Killala, worth about L.400 a-year.

Wonders are told of his popularity. Whenever he preached, such multitudes assembled that it was necessary to defend the entrance of the church by guards and palisadoes. He was presented with addresses and pieces of plate from every parish, and the freedom of various corporations ; his portrait was painted and engraved by the most eminent artists, and the collections at his sermons far exceeded any that ever were known. Even in times of public calamity and distress, his irresistible powers of persuasion repeatedly produced contributions exceeding a thousand or twelve hundred pounds at a sermon ; and his hearers, not content with emptying their purses into the plate, sometimes threw in jewels or watches, as earnests of further benefactions. He died exhausted, as we are told, by the fatigues of his mission, October 27, 1805, leaving a widow with two sons and two daughters, to whom his Majesty granted a pension of L.300 a-year for the life of the widow, with reversion to the daughters. In 1814, a volume of his sermons was printed for the benefit of his sons, who were not included in the above provision. From this it would be difficult to discover the causes of his extreme popularity. There are in them many animated and brilliant passages addressed to the feelings and passions ; and these, we presume, were assisted by a manner suited to his audience, of which we can form no opinion. His talents, however, as directed to one point—that of recommending charity—were unquestionably successful beyond all precedent, and his private character well corresponded to his public sentiments. He was a man of acute feeling, amiable, humane, and beneficent.—See Chalmers's *Biog. Dict. ;* from which this account is taken.

such powers of description, that it is related that on one occasion when he was describing the unhappy disunion which sometimes is found in families, a countess in his congregation involuntarily exclaimed—"I am sure it is not I only that am to blame."

2. We should consider the MINDS TO BE IMPRESSED. Let us have Archimedes for mathematical truth. But people in general are affected by what belongs to man ; and this excludes abstruse truth. In all instances of effect being produced, there is some great truth brought down to the level of every man's capacity. Effect, in short, springs from setting truth before men so as to interest the passions.

Man is a selfish creature. How slow is he to be affected with the miseries described as existing in India ! He is more affected as the objects are nearer. That an effect may be produced, there must be no prejudice in the hearers.

With respect to the Preacher :—

It is an affair of taste. There is nothing in which people are so delicate or fastidious. The tone is material. This calls to my mind Garrick speaking Shakspeare.

[Garrick had naturally a very artificial and pragmatical manner of speaking ; nobody liked his manner or his articulation. But when repeating Shakspeare, he seemed to lose himself and to be transformed into his admired author. The metamorphose was wonderful.]

Monotony hinders effect. Extempore preaching is therefore likely to produce effect. Gesture should be neither outrageous nor stiff. The Preacher must not be conceited. The mind must be previously wrought up in the people. Whitfield gradually worked up his audience, and then struck the nail. Fox says the same thing over and over again, till he feels it felt :—the master-stroke of oratory. Pitt wants this effect. The distinctive marks ·in the eloquence of Fox and Pitt are chiefly seen in this, that Fox pushes till the effect is felt ; but Pitt strongly states the thing, and then leaves it, whether felt or not.

The Rev. R. Cecil—

There is a material difference between going to work on this subject as an ARTIST, and as an APOSTLE.

We shall now endeavour in some measure to illustrate this subject by the examples of the chief members of the Eclectic at this time in their characters as preachers, and shall append to these Notes such information as we have been able to gather on this subject.

Of the various speakers upon this occasion, there is no doubt that Mr Cecil stood pre-eminent as a preacher capable of commanding the attention of a congregation and producing upon them a corresponding effect. But the others were not without their excellencies, though differently estimated as preachers according to their various gifts and abilities. In this one thing, however, they all agreed—in setting forth JESUS CHRIST, in all the parts of the glorious Gospel, as the grand topic of ·their ministry. It will be interesting to notice in what various ways they were gifted, while they united in this one grand essential.

Mr Cecil had the power of exciting and preserving attention above most men. All his effort in the pulpit was directed, first to engage attention, and then repay it. Till this was gained, he felt that nothing could be effected. The following characteristic anecdote is related of him upon an occasion when his original mind suggested, in a case of emergent necessity, the adoption of a somewhat unusual method of arousing his hearers. " I was once preaching," he says, " a Charity Sermon where the congregation was very large, and chiefly of the lower order. I found it impossible, by my usual method of preaching, to gain their attention. It was in the afternoon, and my hearers seemed to meet nothing in my preaching which was capable of rousing them out of the stupefaction of a full dinner. Some lounged, and some turned their backs on me. ' I MUST HAVE ATTENTION,' I said to myself. ' I WILL be heard.' The case was desperate ; and, in despair, I sought a desperate remedy. I exclaimed aloud, ' Last Monday morning, a man was hanged at Tyburn!' Instantly the face of things was changed ! All was silence and expectation ! I caught their ear, and retained it through the sermon."

He was remarkable for his power of illustration. His topics were chiefly taken from Scripture, and from life; and his manner of illustrating his subjects by Scripture examples is said to have been of the most finished kind. His talent in discriminating the striking features, and connecting them with his matter, was so peculiar, that the histories of Abraham, of Jacob, of David, and of St Paul, seemed in his hands to be ever new, and to be exhaustless treasures of illustration.

His most striking sermons were, generally, those which he preached from very short texts, such as—*My soul hangeth on thee—All my fresh springs are in thee—O Lord, teach me thy way—As thy day is, so shall thy strength be.* In these sermons, the whole subject had probably struck him at once ; and what comes in this way is generally found to be more natural and forcible, than what the mind is obliged to excogitate by its own laborious efforts.

It is instructive to know what method so remarkable a man adopted in his preparation for the pulpit. He thus describes it himself :—

" I generally look into the portions of Scripture appointed by the Church to be read in the services of the day. I watch, too, for any new light which may be thrown on passages in the course of reading, conversation, or prayer. I seize the occasions furnished by my own experience — my state of mind—my family occurrences. Subjects taken up in this manner are always likely to meet the cases and wants of some persons in the congregation. Sometimes, however, I have no text prepared ; and I have found this to arise generally from sloth : I go to work : this is the secret ; make it a business—something will arise where least expected. . . . . It is a favourite method with me to reduce the text to some point of doctrine. On that topic I enlarge, and then apply it. I like to ask myself—' What are you doing ? What is your aim ?'

" To be *effective*," he adds, " we must draw more from nature, and less from the writings of men. We must study the Book of Providence, the Book of Nature, the heart of man, and the Book of God ; we must read the history of the world—we must deal with matters of fact before our eyes."

Impression appears to have been a leading feature of his ministry. The result upon his hearers was—to use the words of one who admired and accurately studied his character—" Determination grounded on conviction and admiration, rather than on emotion." * His dispensation, indeed, as we gather from his Memoir, was to meet a particular class of hearers, and this at a particular juncture in the history of the Church ; and he was wonderfully qualified by nature, education, and grace, to fill up his vocation. He was fitted, beyond most men, to assert the reality, dignity, and glory of religion—as contrasted with the vanity, meanness, and glare of the world. This subject he treated like a master. Men of the world felt that they were in the presence of their superior—of one who unmasked their real misery to themselves, and pursued them through all the false refuges of vain and carnal minds.

His successor, the present Bishop of Calcutta, thus describes his preaching in one of the funeral sermons he delivered upon the occasion of the death of his departed friend :—

" His *style of preaching* partook largely of his characteristic excellencies. His first object was, to awaken and command attention, in doing which he had an astonishing address. He next proposed his subject with strength and clearness. If any difficulties were connected with it, he stated them prominently, in the manner of Paley, and resolved them. His acute and penetrating mind then seized on the main topics of his argument. These he placed in an interesting point of view, and delineated, or rather touched them off, with a few masterly and powerful strokes. A lucid perspicuity shone throughout. His ideas, like the rays of the sun, carried their own light with them. Images and illustrations were at his command, and rendered his discourses not only instructive, but absolutely fascinating. They were living pictures. All was admirably grouped, and every principal figure stood off from the canvas. To confine himself to dry argumentative discussion was impossible—he was not, he could not be didactic. The

* See *A View of the Character of the Rev. R. Cecil*, by the Rev. Josiah Pratt, B.D., prefixed to his *Remains*, from which many of the above remarks are gathered.

genius of the man broke through on every occasion, and gilded and adorned the topics he handled. No ideas were presented naked and meagre, like the barren, leafless tree of winter ; all were clothed with luxuriance, and verdure, and fruitfulness. When his subjects were of the grander kind, and his powers were on their full stretch, there was a comprehension of mind, a native dignity, a sublimity of conception, a richness and fertility of imagery, which captivated and astonished his audience. No one can form an adequate notion of his powers as a public speaker from his printed sermons. Like every true orator, the soul of his discourses lay, in a large degree, in that pathos, that touch of nature, that surprising originality, that sublimity and grandeur of expression, which must considerably evaporate with the affections which produced them. I have, on the whole, no fear of affirming before this audience, who best know his excellencies, that he was not merely one of the most eminent preachers of his day, but one of a totally different order from others—a completely original preacher ; one who, while he was interesting to all, could be conceived of fully only by those who had some spark of genius kindred with his own."

But amidst all his great gifts and commanding powers, his grand and absorbing topic was never lost sight of. " Christ is God's great ordinance," he said : " nothing ever has been done, or will be done to purpose, but so far as he is held forth with simplicity. All the lines must centre in him. I feel this in my own experience, and therefore I govern my ministry by it." And this he felt to his dying day. A short time before his decease, he requested one of his family to write down for him in a book the following sentence :—" NONE BUT CHRIST, NONE BUT CHRIST, said Lambert, dying at a stake : the same, in dying circumstances, with his whole heart, saith Richard Cecil." The name was signed by himself, with his left hand, in a manner hardly legible through infirmity.

From this eminent minister, unquestionably one of the first preachers—perhaps the very first preacher—of his time, we turn to his companions in the Eclectic Society.

The prominent characteristic of Mr Newton's preaching was, TRUTH spoken in SIMPLICITY AND AFFECTION, and is strikingly portrayed in the text which he chose in opening his ministry at St Mary Woolnoth's, in the city of London, in 1779—*Speaking the truth in love.*

Mr Cecil was his biographer, and gives the following illustration of his friend's excellent sense and good management in adapting his ministry to his people :—

" Soon after he came to St Mary's, he remarked, in the course of conversation—' Some have observed, that I preach shorter sermons on a Sunday morning, and with more caution : but this I do upon principle. I suppose I may have two or three of my bankers present, and some others of my parish, who have hitherto been strangers to my views of truth. I endeavour to imitate the Apostle. *I became,* says he, *all things to all men:* but observe the END—it was in order to *gain some.* The fowler must go cautiously to meet shy birds, but he will not leave his powder and shot behind him. *I have fed you with milk,* says the Apostle: but there are some that are not only for forcing strong meat, but *bones* too, down the throat of the child. We must have patience with a single step in the case of an infant; and there are *one-step* books and sermons, which are good in their place. Christ taught his disciples, *as they were able to bear it;* and it was upon the same principle that the Apostle accommodated himself to prejudice. Now,' continued he, 'what I wish to remark on these considerations is, that this apostolical principle, steadily pursued, will render a minister *apparently* inconsistent: superficial hearers will think him a trimmer. On the other hand, a minister, destitute of the apostolical principle and intention, and directing his whole force to preserve the appearance of consistency, may thus *seem* to preserve it: but let me tell you, here is only the *form* of faithfulness, without the *spirit.*'"

With no very remarkable natural gifts like those which embellished Mr Cecil's ministry, he was nevertheless greatly blessed: and we may number among those to whom his ministry was eminently useful—the Rev. Dr Claudius Buchanan, to whose exertions in subsequent years India is so much indebted. And indeed a greater than he, the Rev. Thos. Scott, has recorded the practical benefit which he derived at an earlier period from Mr Newton's discourses at Olney. Mr Scott thus describes the effect they had upon him, at a time when his mind was gradually emerging from the darkness in which it had been enveloped even up to a period subsequent to his taking holy orders, and when— to use his own words—"the pride of reasoning and the conceit of superior discernment, though somewhat broken, had yet considerable influence." In this state of mind, he, nevertheless, "condescended," he says, "occasionally to attend Mr Newton's preaching," and adds:—

" I soon perceived the benefit; for, from time to time, the secrets of my heart were discovered to me, far beyond what I had hitherto noticed; and I seldom returned from hearing a sermon, without having attained to a further acquaintance with my deficiencies, weaknesses, corruptions, and wants; or without being supplied with fresh matter for prayer, and directed to greater watchfulness."

This was EFFECT of the right kind. Such testimonies as these cannot fail to afford encouragement to those ministers, who, while they are conscious of having no great commanding powers nor eminent gifts, are, nevertheless, *in simplicity and godly sincerity,* endeavouring to *speak the truth in love. We have this treasure in earthen vessels, that the excellency of the power may be of God, and not of us.* And though some, like Mr Cecil, may be endowed with remarkable gifts, intended no doubt to fit them for the particular spheres of duty to which they are called, yet ALL who set forth the Cross of Christ as the grand remedy for a ruined world, will, in one way or other, have seals given to their ministry, which will be their *joy and crown of rejoicing in the presence of Jesus Christ at his coming.*

Very much the same general description may be given of the preaching of the Rev. W. Goode, another member of the Eclectic, except that it was not characterised by the same flow of affection which distinguished Mr Newton's.

" As he was not a man of impassioned feelings, the impression of his sermons was gradual and permanent, rather than powerful and rapid.   They were addressed to the understanding, and enriched with that continued reference to the Holy Scriptures, which his long and humble study of the Bible, and his intimate acquaintance with the orginal languages, furnished."

Yet *he* also produced his effect, and had his reward in seeing many called through his means to the saving knowledge of the truth; for we are further informed, that

" His ministry was greatly blessed to the conversion of sinners, as well as to the consolation and instruction of true Christians.   He was cautious in committing himself to those who professed to be the con- verts of his ministry.   But when he thought he could rely on their integrity and steadiness, he intrusted himself to them with much affection."

And to what is this success to be ascribed?   The same in- formant, Bishop Wilson, in a funeral sermon to the memory of the departed in 1816, shall instruct us :—

" His great topic was JESUS CHRIST, in his person, offices, work, resurrection, and glory ; the covenant of grace, with its promises and duties ; the necessity of an entire regeneration of the heart by the Holy Spirit, of repentance for sin, and of living faith in the righteous- ness of Christ ; and the indispensable importance of the effects of faith and love in the subjugation of the tempers, the obedience of the life, and a holy conformity of the members of the Christian church with their Head."

Of another member—the Rev. Basil Woodd—the same discri- minating judge again shall speak.   Adverting to his character as a preacher, he says—

" Here he took a most important and honourable station.   If he did not attain the highest walk of popularity in the ordinary sense of the term, he was popular in the best and only scriptural sense—in the esteem and love of an attentive and numerous audience.   A mild, persuasive, affectionate statement of the Gospel, pervaded his dis- courses.   His subjects were well chosen, his divisions of them clear. He was of the old school—he preached JESUS CHRIST, and him cruci- fied."

The preaching of the Rev. John Venn, another valued member of the Eclectic Society, who died in 1813, at the early age of 54, is described as having been eminently distinguished for two excellencies which are not often found united in the same minister— FIDELITY in the interpretation and exposition of Scripture; and ORIGINALITY in "the rich, copious, and varied streams of piety, truth, and eloquence, which flowed from his lips." His discourses were marked often by "a noble and sublime train of thought;" they breathed such "spirituality and heavenly-mindedness" as to "make him occasionally speak of heaven, almost as if he had been there." "In these and many other qualities" he was "readily admitted, by all who knew him, to have been unequalled and unrivalled."* It is said of him upon his tomb, that "as a preacher he was affectionate and persuasive, intellectual and discriminating, serious, solemn, and devout: anxious to impress on others those evangelical truths which he himself so deeply felt."

The Rev. Thomas Scott affords another instance, similar to the three whose names we have brought before our readers, previously to Mr Venn's, though in a different manner, of great ministerial usefulness in the pulpit, although his preaching was attended by a mode of delivery and other defects which presented an effectual barrier to his becoming what is denominated a popular preacher. "An asthmatical affection," we are told, "added to a strong provincial accent, an inattention to style and manner, and prolixity, rendered his discourses less attractive than those of many very inferior men."

But Mr Scott was a man of very superior understanding and of a masculine grasp of mind. "Such were the richness and originality of his matter, such his acquaintance with Scripture, and with the human heart, and such the skill which he evinced as a Christian moralist, that by hearers of attentive and reflecting minds he was listened to, not only with respect, but with delight." †

We have ourselves heard the author of the above remarks observe, that when Mr Cecil used occasionally to ask Mr Scott to preach in his pulpit, while others, less capable of appreciating the rich profusion of thought and original illustration which flowed from his well-stored mind, were wearied and dissatisfied, Mr Cecil would involuntarily give vent in a whisper to bursts of admiration of the profundity of his knowledge of Holy Scripture, and of the human heart, and of his surprising power of applying this knowledge to all the varied concerns of men in all their relations in life.

For sixteen years, the late Mr Wilberforce was in the habit of

* Funeral Sermon by Rev. Hugh Pearson.
† Funeral Sermon by the present Bishop of Calcutta.

attending Mr Scott's ministry at the chapel of the Lock Hospital. His testimony to its effect upon his own mind, notwithstanding the sundry unfavourable peculiarities of manner, is particularly valuable, and will be read with interest :—

" It was in the winter of 1785–6 that the late Mr Newton informed me that the Rev. Mr Scott, a clergyman of a very superior understanding and of eminent piety, more peculiarly remarkable for his thorough acquaintance with the Holy Scriptures, was about to settle in London, having been appointed to the chaplaincy of the Lock Hospital.

" This was a period of my life when it was peculiarly important to me habitually to attend the ministrations of a sound and faithful pastor, and I willingly assented to Mr Newton's earnest recommendations of Mr Scott. I soon found that he fully equalled the strongest expectations that I had formed of him ; and from that time for many years I attended him regularly, for the most part accompanied by my dear friends—both, alas ! now gone to a better world—the Hon. Edward James Eliot,* and Mr Henry Thornton. We used to hear him at the Lock in the morning ; Mr Thornton and I often gladly following him for the afternoon service into the city, where he had the lectureship of Bread Street Church. All objections arising from an unfavourable manner were at once overruled by the strong sense, the extensive acquaintance with Scripture, the accurate knowledge of the human heart, and the vehement and powerful appeals to the conscience, with which all his sermons abounded in a greater degree than those of any other minister I ever attended. Indeed, the substantial solidity of his discourses made those of ordinary clergymen, though good and able men, appear comparatively somewhat superficial and defective in matter."

Of the other members of the Eclectic at the period to which the Notes refer, the only one of whom we can gather any information is the Rev. Josiah Pratt—at this time in his 30th year. During the six-and-forty years which were added to his life, he grew to great ripeness in the ministry.

The following prominent features in his pulpit ministrations are gathered from the Appendix to his Memoir. They are selected and illustrated by a writer (one of his stated hearers) in a very interesting manner, by quotations from his sermons :—

I. Constant, copious, unvarying, enlarged statements of the fulness of Christ—" His unsearchable riches." It was reckoned " a grace given" to declare these. The theme was felt to be, and made to be felt, " inexhaustible."

II. The glory and work of the Spirit was also another topic of frequent full discourse.

III. There was an apparent deference to the minds of the hearers, as persons able to receive and judge of the doctrine set forth. It was

---

* This gentleman had married the sister of Mr Pitt.

more like communication than dictation—in the manner of St Paul making his address to Christians ; and to them not as ignorant and indifferent listeners.   This secured attention and affection.

IV. The discourses were indeed full of truth, and always contained some weighty, succinct statements, which could be well remembered, and became as marks where the rest of the seed was sown.

V. A constant injunction and reference to "*closet*" duties.

VI. There was much uniformity in the discourses ; all solid truth, well wrought out.   If the hearer felt a difference, he was sensible it was in himself, not in his minister.

VII. Much might be added on the calm, dignified mode of delivery, and the good taste exhibited in the expressions.

VIII. There was an interesting mode of exhibiting Scripture characters.   Abraham, Jacob, Joseph, David, Peter, Jonah,—all seem to have been set forth by him with a touch that was his own, and thus rendered familiar and dear, as if they were our brethren—our well-known friends.

IX. There was an interesting application of divine truth to the various relations of life, and to providential events ; and there were cheering views of the future days of the Church of Christ.   Each opening year had its address to heads of families, to children, to females, to friends, to married, to unmarried, to servants.

A deep impression had evidently been left upon the writer's mind, and an effect produced of the best and most solid description.   Let the following quotation speak of this:—

" Can the Christian minister," he asks, " be esteemed too highly, if he be regarded as the appointed servant of the Great Shepherd, and if he be faithful and loving in the discharge of that trust ? Is it wrong for a spiritually-minded Christian to rejoice that he finds the regular ministrations of his pastor to keep pace with his own need ; and that in proportion as he himself grows in experience of the corruption of his own nature—of the grace and sufficiency of the Lord Jesus—of the glory and beauty of that adorable Redeemer—of the necessity for larger, stronger efforts to perfect holiness in the fear of God—he also perceives, by sweet communication of *public* instruction, apart from the least private or personal communion, that his minister also speaks in fuller, warmer, intenser terms, of the same truths ?   Can there fail to be found between such spirits a chain of union, the links of which and the strength of which will perhaps never be recognised, till in heaven, or in future blessedness, it is made manifest, without disguise, and with perfect ability to call it the " work of God ?"

After these marked allusions to the effective character of these ministrations to which death had put a stop, the writer assigns his reasons for committing his recollections to the public :—

" Such a connexion did once exist between a very humble individual and a pastor of well-known worth.   In vain has the affectionate heart looked out for a suitable or an adequate testimony to that excellence ;

other points in that character may have been more fully appreciated—this could only receive its testimony from experience. The few words that follow are intended as an expression of the deepest gratitude to God as the giver of this good, and as a memorial of grateful love towards a departed pastor."

And here we close our sketches; the Moral of which, we think, is this—

1. That no Ministry can be EFFECTIVE in the right sense, unless JESUS CHRIST, the Son of the FATHER, who gave Himself for us, our adorable Redeemer, Intercessor, Saviour, Lord and King, be set forth prominently, boldly, unreservedly, as the Sum and Substance, the Centre and Scope, the Beginning and the End of all our Preaching. It is CHRIST alone, through faith in his blood, that can give the sinner hope, or the believer peace. He is our only Refuge, and our only Hope of Glory. And therefore any Ministry which does not point habitually, and distinctly, and unhesitatingly, to HIM, His Sacrifice, Atonement, Intercession, and Coming again, is radically defective, and practically sets up other methods of salvation than that which GOD has ordained, and therefore CANNOT be blessed with that EFFECT which is alone valuable, and will alone stand the test of eternity—we mean, THE CONVERSION OF SINNERS, THE EDIFICATION OF SAINTS, AND THE SALVATION OF BOTH.

2. The other part of our Moral is this. Having this essential qualification—the determination to preach CHRIST and CHRIST ALONE to the exclusion of every thing that may derogate from the glory of His grace—every Minister may look with confidence for the blessing of God to rest upon his labours, however unworthy he may feel himself to be, and however unadorned by other gifts. Let every Minister, then, to use the words of one of the speakers of the Eclectic, "find out his talent by any means;" let him " correct his exuberances, but push his talent:" and in this way each will be using those gifts, great or small, which God has bestowed upon him, and by which he has fitted him for the post in which He places him—and thus the greatest good and the best EFFECT must be the happy consequence.

MARCH 19, 1798.

WHAT IS AN EXTERNAL CALL TO THE MINISTRY, AND HOW FAR IS IT INDISPENSABLE ?—Proposed by the Rev. Basil Woodd.

The Rev. B. Woodd—

First, passages of Scripture which are all clear and express, and intimate that an External Call is indispensable.

1 Tim. iv. 14—*Neglect not the gift that is in thee, which was given thee by prophecy, with the laying on of the hands of the presbytery.*

2 Tim. ii. 2—*And the things that thou hast heard of me among many witnesses, the same commit thou to faithful men, who shall be able to teach others also.*

Rom. x. 15—*How shall they preach except they be sent?*

1 Pet. v. 2—*Feed the flock of God which is among you, taking the oversight thereof, not by constraint, but willingly; not for filthy lucre, but of a ready mind.*

Col. iv. 17—*Say to Archippus, Take heed to the ministry which thou hast received in the Lord, that thou fulfil it.*

Acts xiv. 23—*When they had ordained them elders in every church, and had prayed with fasting, they commended them to the Lord, on whom they believed.*

Acts xiii. 2, 3—*As they ministered to the Lord, and fasted, the Holy Ghost said, Separate me Barnabas and Saul for the work whereunto I have called them. And when they had fasted and prayed, and laid their hands on them, they sent them away.*

1 Tim. v. 21, 22—*I charge thee before God and the Lord Jesus Christ, and the elect angels, that thou observe these things, without preferring one before another, doing nothing by partiality. Lay hands suddenly on no man, neither be partaker of other men's sins. Keep thyself pure.*

Titus i. 5—*For this cause left I thee in Crete, that thou shouldest set in order the things that are wanting, and ordain elders in every city, as I had appointed thee.*

Acts xx. 28—*Take heed therefore unto yourselves, and to all the flock, over the which the Holy Ghost hath made you overseers, to feed the church of God, which he hath purchased with his own blood.*

Secondly, passages which appear to lean to the other side, but which speak by application only, and are dubious.

Num. xi. 27–29—*And there ran a young man, and told Moses, and said, Eldad and Medad do prophesy in the camp. And Joshua, the son of Nun, the servant of Moses, one of his young men, answered and said, My lord Moses, forbid them. And Moses said, Enviest thou for my sake? would God that all the Lord's people were prophets, and that the Lord would put his Spirit upon them!*

Luke ix. 49, 50—*And John answered and said, Master, we saw one casting out devils in thy name; and we forbade him, because he followeth not with us. And Jesus said unto him, Forbid him not: for he that is not against us is for us.*

Acts viii. 4—*Therefore they that were scattered abroad went every where preaching the word.* See also Acts xi. 19, 20.

Acts xviii. 24–26—*And a certain Jew named Apollos, born at Alexandria, an eloquent man, and mighty in the scriptures, came to Ephesus, . . . and he began to speak boldly in the synagogue.*

1 Cor. xiv. 31—*For ye may all prophesy one by one, that all may learn, and all may be comforted.*

Turretin, in his Inst. Theolog., sect. xviii. quest. 23, gives many instances of unordained men performing ministerial functions.

Some take a middle course, supposing every private Christian at liberty to preach the Gospel, though others are expressly set apart for the public ministry of the Word and sacraments.

The Rev. J. Venn—

You may add to the affirmative passages, Heb. v. 4, *And no man taketh this honour unto himself, but he that is called of God, as was Aaron.* The Apostle here lays down a general principle and illustration, in Aaron and in Christ.

With regard to the passages on the other side of the question, I should except against all cases of *supernatural* interference. In the case of Apollos—he knew the baptism of John, and was sent by John : perhaps Aquila, or Priscilla, or both, who instructed him, were evangelists. Men were supernaturally appointed in the primitive church. The gift of tongues was a proof of special commission.

Now inquire whether, after excepting these supernatural cases, men should take upon themselves the Ministry. This is a question of expediency and order. God is a. God of order. Those men are most unfit, who are most intrusive.

Are there any indispensable requisites ? Are abilities requisite ? A man is not to judge of his own. Is learning necessary ? There should be some measure of education. It becomes, to say the least, a matter of prudence, that the Church should estimate these circumstances.

General particular considerations are to be taken into the account. A man perhaps hears others in pride ; and thinks himself called and qualified. It is necessary that there should be proper judges of this.

The call of the Spirit and of the Church ought to coincide. The Spirit's call consists in a great measure in the Church's call. I cannot think that the Spirit sanctions a man who has no call from some church of Christ, either dissenting or established. I call not ten or twelve men in a village a church. I would distinguish between a man devoting himself to the ministry and administering the sacraments—and his conferring with his neighbours, and exhorting them. If such a man has assembled a people, he should obtain a designation from some church. There must be in every case—

1. THE CALL OF THE SPIRIT. This consists in His giving a man grace, and a desire, accompanied by great humility and diffidence.

2. Then, besides this call, there must be SOME EXTERNAL FITTING. If a man had no voice, and would speak only in a whisper—if he were sickly and out of bed only once in ten days—or even of an infirm constitution, I should say he has no call. Impediments of this kind are often found to co-exist with fancies and desires after the ministry.

3. There should be a LEGAL DESIGNATION OF THE CHURCH.

The Rev. R. Cecil—

Venn has spoken as a wise and moderate man. If we go to extremes on either side, we run into absurdities.

Take the extreme on the side of the Church. I mean, trace it up to the Apostles. In following the line of succession backwards—here is a drunkard ! But I know some good people so tenacious of this point, that they could never come out of a dead Church into a sound Meeting-House. This spirit is productive of the greatest evil. *The temple of the Lord are* WE ! *The temple of the Lord are* WE ! This is a

charm for the Church of Rome.   No salvation, say they, but there !
Pascal speaks thus most strongly.   This spirit has bound rotten casks
with iron hoops.   The same *spirit* has been in the Church of England :
men comforted themselves with this.   Dissenters have it too.   Whitfield
answered Erskine * well.   " Come among us, for we are the Lord's
people."   " For that reason," said he, " I won't, for I am sent to the
Devil's people."

We need not wonder if we see God putting contempt upon this.
Men have scouted the spirit of His religion.   He will pour contempt
on their pride.   They shall have a lantern and no candle.   A dispensation of life and salvation in some barn ; while darkness, ignorance,
and prejudice reign within the Gothic walls.   This, it is conceived, is
something like provoking them to jealousy.   This begins often in
simplicity, but it proceeds to corruption.   Methodism itself becomes
high-churchism.

Take the New Testament as your guide.   You see nothing precisely
prescribed.   You see both these parties condemned.   Though God is
pleased to work by men, this is not a sufficient call.   There should be
some church authority.   Men are generally more influenced and
called to preach the gospel, who are not brought up for it, than those
who are.   Yet, though not originally designed, they are brought in
with excellent qualifications.   Some of these have not had access to a
Bishop ; or, if they have had, were not successful : yet they are
authorised ministers of Christ.   Extraordinary cases admit of extraordinary circumstances ; but generally some Christian Church should
call.   The Gospel is at this day under a great scandal from men going
out without this call.   " As a Tailor, a Cobbler, a Carpenter, I am
nothing—let me be something."—Such men come under demagogues.
They come under purse-proud men, are kicked about, and the ministry
sinks.

High-churchism is one extreme ; Methodism another extreme.   I
would take a middle course.

The Rev. T. Scott—

The Scripture lays down no full, express, and positive command on
the subject.   Certainly it is now a matter of prudence and expediency.
In all ordinary cases, no man should come forth till sanctioned by a
due call.   Some say, " Things are right ; " and others, " Things are
wrong."   I would say—" Do all the good you can in the short time
you have to live."

April 2, 1798.

In what sense are we to understand the Temptation of our
Lord ?—Proposed by the Rev. J. Venn.

The Rev. J. Venn—

Objections to a literal interpretation.

1. It seems to be ascribing too much to Satan to suppose that he

* An eminent Presbyterian Minister of Scotland.

had such power as to take our Lord from place to place : perhaps we have no proof of the personal appearance of Satan. That part, however, where he shewed our Saviour *the kingdoms of the world* seems to require a visible interposition. Some suppose Christ had the powers of vision supernaturally enlarged.

2. The Temptation is described to be in the wilderness. Now a literal interpretation would make part of it *out* of the wilderness. Scripture, moreover, represents it as taking place in *one* day. Christ was baptised at Bethabara (John i. 28). Bethabara was near to a large wilderness. Probably this was the wilderness in which the temptation occurred. This was nearly sixty miles from Jerusalem. After his baptism, Christ seems to have returned from some place (John i. 29–31). In returning, he saw John the Baptist at Bethabara. John points him out to his disciples. It seems probable, therefore, that he had ascended to this Eastern desert since his baptism, and was now returning. The geography seems not to countenance Christ's leaving the desert till forty days were expired.

3. Scripture represents Christ as being *tempted in all points like as we are.* Now Satan does not tempt us personally. If he were to come in personal appearance, it would put us on our guard. We must suppose, therefore, that he worked on Christ's human passions.

Calvin hesitates as to the manner, and says that in some parts the supposition of its being in vision answers best.

On the other hand :—

1. We must not depart unnecessarily from the literal sense.

2. If it were in vision, it would have been unnecessary to take Christ into a high mountain.

THE USE of Christ's Temptation.

1. It teaches us the end and object of Temptation being sent to a Minister.

Luther says three things are necessary to form a Minister :—

    (1.) Meditation. (2.) Temptation. (3.) Prayer.

2. From Christ's Temptation we may derive Consolation.

    (1.) Christ knows our Temptations. (2.) Christ will succour us.

    (3.) Christ has overcome, and broken Satan's power.

The Rev. R. Cecil—

The Bishop of London [Bp. Porteus] lately preached on this subject, and said—If the Evangelist wished to describe a fact, how could he have done it otherwise ? *

Maundrell describes a desert and mount suitably situated—whence the Tetrarchy of India may be seen.

I say—Why reject the power of Satan in representing to Christ *the kingdoms of the world?*

The Rev. Thomas Scott—

It is a universal rule, that we do not depart from literal interpreta-

---

* See the IVth of Bishop Porteus's Lectures on St Matthew. It is evidently this to which Mr Cecil alludes, and which he heard delivered. It contains many valuable remarks on the subject of our Lord's Temptation.

tion unnecessarily.   And, if we depart in one case, not to extend it to others unnecessarily.

If Satan shewed Christ the *kingdoms of the world*, he could not shew their glory.   Therefore some part must have been in vision.

1. Satan is possessed of powers superior to those we possess.   What, therefore, is supernatural to us, may not be so to him.

The Scriptures would not give us such charges against false miracles, if Satan had no supernatural powers.   So in Deuteronomy, where workers of miracles are to be stoned.   Satan has no power, but as God permits ; but he has vast power by his permission.

2. Satan's appearing to Christ does not prove that we are not tempted as Christ was ; at least, our not being tempted by Satan in visible appearance does not exclude another kind of temptation.

3. There is something suitable and grand in the idea, that as Satan baffled man in the garden, Christ, the second Adam, should baffle him in a wilderness.

4. How Christ went to Jerusalem we have no reason to inquire. Scripture speaks of His being in Jerusalem literally : His viewing the kingdoms literally ; but the glory, in vision.

Where Scripture can be taken up literally, never abandon that interpretation.

Where not, then and then only recur to another mode.

The Rev. Josiah Pratt—

I. Some contend that it was NOT A REAL TEMPTATION, but a VISION, because :—

1. It is unlikely that Christ should submit to be thus carried about. I answer :—

(1.) To be *forcibly* conveyed from place to place, would have been so : this was *voluntary*.

(2.) Nor would *that* have been so dishonourable, as the deception of His organs in vision.

(3.) We need not wonder, if Christ suffered himself to be carried about by Satan, since He endured to be crucified by his accomplices.

2. It is said, that all the Temptation was in the Desert.   See Luke iv. 14.   *Jesus returned.*   As he was led into the wilderness to be tempted, he could not be on a pinnacle, nor on a mountain.

I answer :—

(1.) In this way it may be equally affirmed or denied from St Luke's account, that all the Temptation was in the desert.

(2.) Though he says, *Jesus returned*, it does not follow that Christ had not been before translated to a pinnacle, or a mountain.   Though he was led into the wilderness, it does not follow that *all* the Temptation was there.

3. It is probable, some say, that Christ was tempted in the same manner as we are, viz., by suggestions.

I answer :—

(1.) Satan generally presents to us *external* objects, and through them insinuates suggestions.   Thus Christ must submit to the same.

(2.) Christ was perfectly sinless, and therefore could not be exposed in the way *we* are to Satan's internal suggestions.

4. Others affirm, that the Temptation on the mount was really *impossible*, and must therefore be referred to vision. This is certainly the strongest argument against the *reality of the Temptation.*

Yet I would observe :—

(1.) That some, as Origen, suppose that *the kingdoms of the world* were exhibited *allegorically*, and not *literally.* That they are not to be understood of the external kingdoms of the world, but of the kingdom which Satan exercises in the world; or of the kingdom, that is, the men, in whom he reigns by vices. But this savours of Origen. Why carry Christ to a mountain to shew him that Satan ruled in the world?

(2.) Some understand it of *appearances!* either externally offered to Christ's eyes, or internally to His imagination or intellect. But it is not credible that Christ's eyes should be deluded; or that Satan should have access to his imagination or intellect. But again, why lead Christ to a mountain to present these appearances?

(3.) Some understand this temptation, not as presented to the *eyes*, but to the *ears* of Christ.—They take it to refer not to *visible objects*, but to a discourse by Satan concerning the kingdoms of the world and their glory. But this is repugnant to the words of the Evangelist, and renders the translation to a mountain unnecessary. And why is *a* HIGH *mountain* mentioned?

(4.) But others—and with the greatest probability on their side—understand the words as in SYNECDOCHE, *i. e.*, that Satan shewed Christ part of the kingdoms of the world; and that which was most worthy of notice in these kingdoms; or that Satan shewed him different districts or provinces; and pointed out the glory, opulence, and splendour of each in particular.

Many ancient interpreters agree with this—supposing that Satan did not shew Christ the very kingdoms and cities and people; but rather the parts of the earth where they lay. So Moses saw all the land of Israel: Deut. xxxiv. He who shews *part* of a thing, and its *principal* part too, may in some sense be said to shew the *whole.*

5. *In a moment of time*—agrees, many think, rather with a vision than a real appearance.

I answer:—

(1.) The regions of the world might be exhibited to CHRIST, and beheld by Him in a Moment of Time.

(2.) It need not mean a mathematical point of time; but a brief space.

Thus the Syriac renders it. Ambrose remarks well, that it was not so much the swiftness of the view, as the fragility of the things viewed, which it is here designed to exhibit.

6. The manner of Satan's access to Christ cannot be known—his voice, his shape, &c.

But I answer, that neither is it *necessary* for us to ascertain his *form*, or his manner of approach. No doubt he came in a mild and insinuating manner. Salmerus fancifully says—In the first Temptation he came as a holy Hermit; in the second as an Angel; in the third as a King!

7. It is said, that Christ was carried to the pinnacle and the mountain in vision, just as the Prophet Ezekiel was apparently translated into the land of which he prophesied (Ez. xl.) And as John *seemed* to himself to be now in heaven, while he was really in Patmos.

But I answer, that these examples differ from the example of Christ. That the prophets were carried in vision, is either explicitly or implicitly declared in Scripture; there is no such notice here.

Some will inquire:—*How* was Christ carried by Satan?

It was not with *violence;* but *voluntarily.* This is gathered from—

(1.) The nature of the subject. It would be unsuitable to Christ's dignity and majesty to be borne here and there through the air by Satan.

(2.) The expressions of the evangelist. He uses words which denote leading rather than carrying: and thus the Syriac. It is probable that Christ voluntarily followed Satan up the steps of the Temple.

But here is an objection. Several days must have passed if Christ followed Satan on foot. I reply:—

(1.) The desert might be near to Jerusalem.

(2.) The motion of Christ might be rapid.

(3.) There is no absurdity in supposing the time to have been several days.

But though this voluntary following of Christ is probable, yet the opposite sentiment implies no contradiction: nor has it any difficulties which may not be removed, provided the carrying of Christ be considered voluntary, and not by violence.

This is to be ascribed not to Christ's weakness, but to Christ's patience and submission. Christ did many things for *moral instruction:* These are to be imitated. Christ did many things for *display of power :* These are not to be imitated.

II. That the TEMPTATION WAS REAL is evidenced by :—

1. The Text of the Evangelist.

(1.) *Led up* denotes local motion.

(2.) *Leaveth him*—indicates this also.

(3.) *Taketh—Placeth—Sheweth*—denote history. Whatever expressions *could* be employed to designate a true history are here used; nor does any word occur denoting a vision.

(4.) How could Satan require in vision an act of worship from Christ?

(5.) Angels *approaching* Christ, and Satan's *leaving* Him, denote historical fact.

(6.) In vision, how could bread be presented to Christ, or how could place be found for Temptation on that account, and for the quotation of Scripture?

2. Reason also points out that the Temptation was Real.

(1.) We are not lightly to depart from the literal interpretation. I have already said, that if it detract from the dignity of Christ to be thus tempted, his passion and crucifixion do so more. Therefore the Marionites believed, that these also occurred in vision.

(2.) There are many visionary actions mentioned in Scripture; but these are in the prophets and not in the historical parts. They are also sufficiently marked by the expressions.

(3.) The Temptation of Christ is destroyed in fact, if it is supposed to have been in vision. The subject of temptation must be in possession of his faculties. His judgment concerning temptation in vision is worthy of neither praise nor blame.

(4.) Christ's victory over Satan would be nugatory. This is a very strong argument.

(5.) As Christ's fast, so his temptation and his journey are all external, all in the same style and thread of narration.

(6.) If it had been in vision, there could be no danger in temptation to cast himself down.

(7.) The apostle refers to Christ's trials and temptations as real. Heb. ii. 18, and iv. 15. Vision would dim the consolation of the faithful.

(8.) It would be dishonourable to Christ that Satan should be able to deceive Him by internal delusions, and the impression of appearances, and that Christ should think himself carried about, when he was not. For either these delusions were perceived to be such, or not. If perceived, there was no room for temptation. If not, the mind of Christ was in an error, when He thought himself carried to a pinnacle and to a mountain, while He was yet in the desert.

(9.) The external suggestions offered to Christ by the Tempter answer to the temptations of our first parents. To Christ and to sinless Adam, there was no access to the Tempter but by external means. Vide F. Spanheimii, *Dub. Evang. disc. LV. LIX.*

The Rev. J. Newton—

I was never troubled with these doubts. I have always taken the thing *literally.*

Middleton* and others like him make the first temptation all vision. Some jeer at the history of Jonah. Christ seems to have selected this very history of Jonah, to silence our inquiries.

There is a correspondence between our Lord's temptations and those of His people,

1. To Despondency. 2. To Presumption. 3. To Ambition.

The Rev. Basil Woodd—

It was necessary for the efficiency of Christ's mediatorial office that he should, in suffering, be conformed to the first Adam—therefore in temptation. This was an initiatory trial.

I think Satan appeared in his proper person as the God of this world.

These temptations appear to have been addressed, not to sinful feelings, of which indeed CHRIST could have none, but to lawful desires.

The USES are these.

1. We learn remarkably, the right means of vanquishing Satan:— by the Word of God.

* Dr Conyers Middleton.

2. We see the necessity of avoiding temptation: and how dangerous are the approaches of Satan.

3. We learn humility—temptation is God's means.

4. Here is consolation for the tempted.   Christ can sympathise.

Mr Scott here interposed in consequence of something which had fallen from Mr Woodd:—Woodd thinks there is a difficulty in Christ's being at all the subject of temptation.

In proportion to the purity of the soul, the danger decreases; but the anguish increases.

In proportion to the impurity of the soul, the anguish decreases; but the danger and pollution increase.

Take the example of a woman tempted to murder her child.   Her danger is less in proportion to her love; but her anguish exquisite in the same degree.

The Rev. W. Goode—

Satan might take occasion in tempting our Lord from what *was* seen to enlarge on what was *not* seen; this would not be properly a vision.

These three temptations bear an analogy to the temptations of Adam in paradise.

1. To UNBELIEF : *Yea hath God said!—Make these stones bread.*

2. To PRESUMPTION : *Ye shall not surely die!—Cast thyself down.*

3. To AMBITION : *Ye shall be as gods!—These shall be thine.*

The Rev. J. Davies—

Though Satan's power may not be really miraculous, yet it may appear miraculous to us, from our ignorance.   This principle will in my mind account for all the difficulties in the subject.

APRIL 10, 1798.

WHAT IS THE OBLIGATION OF THE CHRISTIAN SABBATH ?—Proposed by the Rev. B. Woodd.

Mr Woodd—

The Sabbath was instituted for a moral and physical benefit.   As the Sabbath was appointed for the commemoration of creation, it appears clear that it was not abrogated with the ceremonial law.   It had a prior authority to the ceremonial law.   On the coming of Christ, an alteration was made in the day.   " Though great to speak the world from nought, yet greater to redeem."   As to the strictness of its observance, I wish to have a line pointed out whereby we may steer clear on the one hand of judaizing, and on the other of too much license.

The Rev. W. Goode—

There is no positive command in the New Testament on the subject. This must be sought in the Fourth Commandment.   Writers generally state, that the moral obligation of that command is the observance of a seventh part of our time. This is transferable to the Christian Sabbath. The transfer to a different day arises from the different dispensation of grace.

The Rev. J. Goode—

The obligation of the Sabbath rests on these points :—
1. It is put down among Moral Precepts.
2. It was instituted before the Law.
3. It was not considered as merely ceremonial by Christ.

The Rev. H. Foster—

I have had many embarrassing questions put to me at times by various persons. I have generally advised giving up any business not compatible with the obligation of the Sabbath. I did this, more from compliance with general custom, than from thorough conviction.

The Sabbath was designed for all men to whom the Gospel came— to slaves and men in all circumstances.

My private opinion has been, that a man *might* go, if in an inferior relative situation, after attending worship, to his usual employment. But I confess that there is danger in this way of talking, because men will plead for themselves.

But I have an idea that there is a liberty which men may take with a good conscience, which would be called by some a violation of the Sabbath.

The Rev. J. Davies—

It is said that there is no account of the Sabbath among the Patriarchs. And it has thence been urged, that the Sabbath is a part of the Jewish economy only.

But that it *was* observed by the Patriarchs appears from hints given incidentally ; as Noah's sending the dove after seven days ; Jacob's fulfilling Leah's week.

Moses, however, is very concise as an historian.

As to the manner of observance, I should say that whatever appears not to hinder personal religion, or the devotion of others, or public worship, seems allowable.

The Rev. Professor Farish, a visitor from Cambridge—

As to the Change of Day :—

If Christianity was to be addressed to all ranks, it required that points of this sort should be settled by custom, rather than by an unbending command.

There is great difficulty in this subject ; but the same attends the abrogation of several Mosaic commands.

Consider the commandments as (1.) Moral, (2.) Political, (3.) Ceremonial.

The Political were abrogated because there was no longer an occasion for keeping the Church distinct in its political character.

The Ceremonial commands were fulfilled in Christ and the Gospel dispensation.

The Moral commands were some of universal obligation, others somewhat circumstantial. The observance of the Sabbath partakes of both kinds. It is in part of Moral obligation, and in part of Political, to keep the Jews distinct, and so far the command is altered.

It seems manifest that Christ meant to relax the strictness of the Sabbath. A part, therefore, of the command is abrogated, as other political institutions were. Christianity is mild and accommodating.

Yet it is manifest that the religious and physical benefits are of great importance and necessity.

The Sabbath is therefore of perpetual obligation, though not in its strictness.

The Rev. R. Cecil—

It belongs to our very relation to God to set apart a portion of our time for rest from our ordinary occupations, and for the special service of God. It might have puzzled our conscience if it had been left to itself to determine what part of time should be wholly devoted to this.

Whether it be said to be in remembrance of His work of creation, or for any other reason, the thing remains the same.

Farish has taken up the ground I should have taken on the Sabbath, as Christian. Christianity is not a hedge round a peculiar people. A slave might enter into the spirit of Christianity, though obliged to work as a slave. He might be *in the Spirit on the Lord's day*, though in the mines of Patmos.

I allow with Foster, that I have had difficulties.

I tell barbers, and such as have to pursue their ordinary callings on the Sabbath—" If you have the spirit of Christianity, and are in an employment contrary to Christianity, you will work out, and God will open you a door."

If his heart be right he would not bounce out the first day, but he would be looking and praying, and God would open him a door.

Christ came not to abolish the Sabbath, as he did the rest of the Law, but to explain and enforce it.

It was not positively enjoined because the religion of Christ was to be practicable and to go into all nations. It goes stripped of its precise and various circumstances.

I was in the Spirit on the Lord's day, seems the soul of the Christian Sabbath.

A man may take occasion to plead the Lord's promise to get the rubbish of the week rubbed off.

Now, in this view, a thousand frivolous questions would be cut off. For instance—" What *can* I do?" Why, what godly men do. Bend not. Be *in the Spirit*. God will help."

In short, we are going to spend a Sabbath in eternity. The Christian man gets as much of the Sabbath spirit as he can in preparation for that.

In proportion to a man's godliness in any age, he will be found an observer of the Sabbath.

J. Bacon, Esq.—

Before the Law, the Sabbath was observed with reference to Creation; under the Law, to the deliverance from Egypt; after the Law, to the Resurrection of Christ. And this, because the peculiar genius and glory of the dispensation was to be first in our thoughts in drawing near to God.

The Rev. T. Scott—

I take up with Cecil the spirit of the Sabbath. This binds the conscience of the *believer*. I want to get a bond on the conscience of *all men*.

God peculiarly *blessed* and *sanctified* the day. It stands in the body of the moral law.

As a professing Christian nation we stand much on the ground of the Jewish nation. The Fourth Command seems addressed especially to Heads of Families.

The apostolic example establishes the observance of the Christian Sabbath.

The expression LORD'S DAY declares both the obligation and spirit of the duty.

The French, in abolishing the Sabbath, shew their *malice* and *wisdom*. Christianity will go if they succeed in this.

Fas est et ab hoste doceri. Let us learn to value the Sabbath from their enmity.

Where Christianity has flourished, the Sabbath is strictly observed; and *vice versâ.*

With regard to its observance :—

Preparations for the Sabbath are necessary.

I almost wish our Sabbath, as well as the Jewish, began in the evening.

We should put our children and household in posture for the day.

Rise early. A man should be the Priest of his family.

If a man have little *time* to care for his family on other days, and little *heart* to do it on the Lord's Day, he has little title to the name of Christian.

He who hallows the Sabbath, bears a public and impressive protest for religion.

The πρωτον ψευδος of the Methodists of this day is, that because external things are not religion, therefore religion has nothing to do with external things.

Therefore this is a most important ground for us in this day of Atheism.

Man should say—" I have been in a storm all the week; now I bring forth my instruments to make my observations."

Who feels not the renewal of spiritual strength in the holy observance of this day !

I would not make little things a question.

How can a man love heaven, the eternal Sabbath, if his soul is not deeply engaged in the Sabbath on earth ?

The Rev. Josiah Pratt—

I. The OBLIGATION of the CHRISTIAN SABBATH.

1. The proportion of time should be *one-seventh*. The seventh day was appointed to Adam in innocence (Gen. ii. 3.) It seems to have been observed by the patriarchs. When commanded to Israel (Exod. xvi. 23, &c.), it was referred to as a thing known. Though Moses is silent on the Patriarchal Sabbath, nothing is to be inferred from this against it. Indeed from this period must have flowed the universal ancient division of time by weeks. His account is short. He says nothing of the worship, nor of the sacrifices from Seth to the Deluge; yet both were doubtless observed.

2. The Jewish Sabbath was a sign between God and His people.

In Exod. xxii., God puts the Jews in mind of His rest in Creation, to give greater weight to the command.

In Deut. v. 15, God omits the reference to the rest in Creation, and refers to the deliverance from Egypt. This reason was peculiar, and was endeared to the Jews. It was the ground on which the Sabbath became to them a sign.

In Exod. xxxi. 13, God declares the Sabbath to be a sign. To the Jews then it became a Sacrament, by which God testified that he was in covenant with them; and they, by keeping it, declared they were in covenant with Him.

In Ezek. xx. 10–26, He calls the other nine laws *judgments and statutes*, which if they did they should live in them; but never the Sabbath a judgment or statute, but a *sign* of God's acceptance of them.

Thus God took that which was obligatory before upon Adam and the Patriarchs to make it a Sign of a Covenant, as He did the Rainbow which had previously existed.

3. The Jewish Sabbath is to be viewed as a sign abrogated, while the obligation of one-seventh of time remains.

Good men, seeing the Sabbath among moral precepts, have thought its institution entirely moral, and therefore of universal and perpetual obligation.

But this is an improper inference. It shewed, indeed, that God expected its religious observance. If the Jewish Sabbath were the very Seventh Day from Creation, this would add still greater reverence to it.

Thus it stood till Christ came. Then the Jewish Sabbath ceased as a *sign*, because the thing signified by it was now no more—the typical dispensation being fulfilled and falling.

Therefore Paul (Col. ii. 16, 17) places the Sabbath with clean and unclean meats, &c.—on the same ground of obligation.

If the Jewish Covenant itself were only a "shadow," then a single ordinance, which was the sign of that Covenant, was a shadow too.

Therefore Christ in His sermon on the Mount, when He mentions several principal laws of the decalogue, as the vi., vii., viii., and shews how they were to be understood in future, says nothing of the Sabbath, any more than of the Passover, &c., &c.

Yet while he lived, he reverenced the ritual law as of divine origin, though about to perish.

Excepting Christ's attendance at the Synagogue on the Sabbath-day, he treated that day with more marked disrespect than he shewed to any other Mosaic command. He cured chronical diseases, commanded to carry beds, suffered his disciples to pluck the corn. This was to shew them that he was the *body* of which the Sabbath was but the shadow. On these principles, his conduct is explicable.

The *durable* part of the Sabbath—that of universal and permanent obligation—he reverenced in attending the Synagogue.

The *perishing* part—that which was of positive institution, appropriate to the Israelites—the sign of God's covenant with them, viz., the rigid Sabbath rest—this he neglected, especially when coming in comparison with greater good.

The Jewish Sabbath fell, therefore, with the Jewish economy. The obligation to that economy was made void on the Cross, but the observance lasted till the destruction of the Second Temple. The efficacy of the services was gone ; but the Jewish converts, even though instructed in the nature and extent of Christian liberty, continued to observe them all the time.

4. The Christian Sabbath is substituted by divine authority in the place of the Jewish, so far as the Jewish was not a positive institution and a peculiar sign of God's covenant with that people.

Under Christ is a new covenant and a new church.

The old day of worship is altered, that therein, as in other cases, the alteration of the covenant might appear.

The day observed under the new covenant is the first instead of the seventh. On that day Christ rose, and the work was completed on God's part. On that day also, the Holy Ghost descended, and man was enabled to do his part.

After this, nothing more is to be done.

As the Jews were commanded to hallow the Sabbath, because God rested in creation, and they crossed the Red Sea ; so Christians observe the first day, because the work of redemption was on that day completed.

An objection brought forward is, that the institution of the seventh day was express and solemn ; while the institution of the first day is not warranted by anything like *a command* in express words throughout the New Testament.

Some have replied, that the observance of the patriarchal Sabbath is revived in the first day, as it was observed on that day before the giving of the law, and the Jewish Sabbath was confined to the seventh day. But this is a groundless distinction.

The proper answer is, the resurrection of Christ, and the mission of the Spirit on the first day, at the distance of fifty days, was not without design.

Christ's first appearance to his disciples was on the first day (John xx. 19) ; His second appearance to them was on the same (John xx. 26).

In St Paul's time, the faithful met together in very distant parts of the Christian Church to worship.

Before St John died, the First Day was called the LORD's DAY.

Now, whatever was generally observed by the Apostles, must certainly have been by direction of the Holy Ghost. *He shall guide you into all truth,* must refer to worship as well as doctrine.

Times of worship under the law were so marked, that they could not possibly be overlooked in the first planting of the Christian Church: and, therefore, when the Apostles made so great an alteration, it certainly could not be without direction.

Whatsoever ye shall bind on earth, shall be bound in heaven, &c. (Matt. xviii. 18). Lightfoot clearly shews, that the Jews understood, by *binding* and *loosing,* when treating of ritual subjects, a doctrine that anything was unlawful or lawful to be done.

The disciples understood Christ's language. He speaks, both in Matt. xvi. 19, and xviii. 18, in the neuter gender, of binding and loosing *things,* not persons.

Christians are bound, without doubt, to obey the Apostles' injunctions. Every Apostolic practice, therefore, which is not temporary, is obligatory on us. When, therefore, we find them observing the Lord's Day as a day of worship, breaking bread, collecting for the saints, &c. &c., we may certainly conclude that this day was *appointed* for a day of worship by the Apostles.

Thus by a *sufficient commission* the day was changed.

The Apostles then loosed the Jewish Sabbath, so long as the Second Temple stood, to win Jews.

Since that economy is dissolved to us, that Sabbath is " *bound.*"

The Decalogue is a federal body of laws to the Jews. How far they oblige us, our Lord shews upon the Mount, and the Apostles in various places.

Whatever becomes of the Fourth Commandment, we are not at any loss upon the subject of the other nine, which are clearly, and in their full extent, set home on us.

II. OBSERVANCE of the Christian Sabbath.

There is very little on this point in the New Testament.

The conduct of the churches founded by the Apostles is to guide us.

They constantly attended on the preaching of the Word of God, they broke bread, and collected for the poor.

The Jews to this day keep the Sabbath as a sign of a covenant between God and them.

We observe the Lord's day because the Apostles, who had the power of *binding and loosing,* set apart that day for the weekly remembrance of Christ's Resurrection and the effusion of the Spirit.

Christians, then, are guilty of great sin who transact worldly business, travel unnecessarily, absent themselves from public worship idly.

Since the Apostles are silent on other points, the manner of spending the rest of the day is to be left to the decisions of every church and the conscience of every Christian, who should surely seize this opportunity of growing meet for heaven, and spending there the eternal Sabbath.—See Wotton's *Miscellaneous Discourses,* Vol. I., Disc. iv.

On the 30th of the same month, no particular subject was entered upon, but a general conversation took place regarding *The propriety of making Intercession for the Nation.*

MAY 14, 1798.

WHAT ARE THE OBJECTIONS BROUGHT AGAINST THE LITERAL SENSE OF THE MOSAIC HISTORY OF CREATION, AND WHAT ARE THE PROPER ANSWERS TO THEM?—Proposed by the Rev. Josiah Pratt.

Mr Pratt—

I. THE HISTORICAL SENSE IS IMPORTANT.

It ascertains the Nature and Manner of Man's fall and recovery. Any other sense would give us uncertain ideas of either. Any other sense would unsettle the mind in interpreting other scriptures. The Historical sense lays the first link of a grand chain of Prophecy.

II. THE HISTORICAL SENSE IS MORE PROBABLE THAN THE ALLEGORICAL.

It is conformable to the simplicity of the historical writings of Moses. It is incredible that Moses should introduce his history with a fiction calculated to puzzle. No historian ever began his history with an incredible fable without apprising his readers of it.

The allegorical sense is not consistent throughout. In fables, every actor aptly represents some natural object. Apply this rule to the account of the fall, and it will bring us to a stand.

III. THE OBJECTIONS AGAINST THE HISTORICAL SENSE ARE NOT INSUPERABLE.

1st Objection.—Man came perfect out of God's hands. He wanted not an admonisher at his elbow. A law was implanted in his very nature directing him to his chief good. It is not credible that man should be left destitute of powers proper to preserve that perfection of nature in which he was created. Yet, in this narration, there is no trace of any natural law, nor of religion which reason could teach. Reason and nature appear to have had no rule in the paradisal state: all things were ordered therein miraculously and supernaturally— *therefore* this cannot be, they say, a history of real transactions.

That man was *created* with such a law and religion is taken for granted. That such a law and religion are natural to man is also taken for granted.

The objection is a strong argument against the existence of natural law or religion. Suppose Adam a learner through his senses, then this history is all consistent. Things are ordered just as we might expect them to be. Man's perfection did not consist in a moral law, which would remove freedom of action. His natural powers, his senses, all acted necessarily and constantly; so his appetites. No other power was natural to his soul than that of taking in ideas through the senses. The soul cannot do this of itself, nor the senses for it. Therefore God taught Adam.

Every thing *was* miraculous in Paradise, or Adam would have learnt no law nor religion. The Hutchinsonians enter at large into the character of Eden, as a school. We may admit the principle, without following all their deductions.

2d Objection.—The discourse of a serpent tempting and beguiling Adam and Eve is inconsistent, it is said, with history. It is impossible, if taken literally; the introduction of the devil under the form of a serpent embarrasses the case still more : the text ascribes the success of the serpent to the natural subtlety of the animal ; and it is contrary to our notions of God's goodness to imagine that he would expose our unarmed and uninstructed parents to the insidious wiles of a tempter so greatly their superior in craft and power, without interposing in so unequal a conflict.

Some reply—

1. As to serpent—

Moses relates facts without comment or explanation. He makes the serpent the seducer, and says nothing of the latent cause.

Thus the Jews think it was really the serpent, and that the serpent had originally reason and speech. Abarbinel thinks the serpent spoke by *actions*—by eating, &c.

Others think it was not a serpent, but the devil under that name. But if so, why is he called the most subtle beast of the field ? The punishment inflicted on the serpent, leaves no doubt that the serpent's body was employed.

The common opinion is, that the devil used the serpent's body, as the most fit instrument of his fraud. And the allusions in other passages of Scripture confirm this. Thus Rev. xii. 9 ; xx. 2. *That old serpent, the devil. He (the devil) was a murderer from the beginning.* Also Wisd. ii. 24. " By the envy of the devil, death came into the world."

Milton supposes the serpent to pretend that he had acquired the power of speech by eating the fruit ; and to argue, that if it was capable of producing such a change in *him*, how much more might be expected by Eve. Compare 2 Cor. xi. 3. *As the serpent beguiled Eve through his subtlety.*

The serpent was chosen by the devil because it was mild, gentle, and perhaps specially familiar with Adam and Eve. Probably it was a beautiful creature, and Eve thought it a superior being. Mede thinks Eve took the serpent for a wise, though fallen, angel. Bishop Burnet and Archbishop Tenison think she took it for an angel sent to revoke their decree.

Bate * replies, that it is not necessary from the text to believe that a *real* serpent was concerned. The serpent is mentioned, in order to convey ideas which its nature was better capable of conveying than any other creature.

The serpent was *subtle*, or rather, naked, *i. e.* unarmed, sly and treacherous. It *seems* harmless, but is in *reality* poisonous. It *glides* along the ground, and so appears to have no means of attacking ; but it really bites and wounds the heel.

2. As to the alleged inconsistency with the Divine attributes—

Adam and Eve were not unarmed nor uninstructed, as has been

---

* Junius Bate was an English divine of the Hutchinsonian school, of the founder of which he was an intimate friend to the day of the death of that remarkable man. One of Bate's various publications was " An Essay towards Explaining the Third Chapter of Genesis." Another was entitled, " The Use and Intent of Prophecy, and the History of the Fall Cleared." This latter was occasioned by Dr Conyers Middleton's examination of Bishop Sherlock's " Discourses on Prophecy," published in 1725.

insinuated. They were informed of their duty. The prohibition was positive ; no power nor force was used. It was a fair trial and probation of obedience.

3d Objection.—The curse denounced against the deceiver must be restricted to a mere serpent, and must have been pronounced exclusively of all other agents, or could not possibly be just.

Some reply, that God might hereby not intend indignation against the serpent ; but design to make him a monument of man's fall and God's displeasure against sin. This was not unjust, as inflicted upon the instrument of an enormous crime, and when in itself no actual misfortune to the serpent.

Bate replies, that this sentence is also descriptive of spiritual things in words applicable to both visible and invisible objects. The chief sense of the words, is to describe to us the devil—his employment—his delight—his manner of proceeding—his food and his punishment. If the nature of the common serpent were not such as it is, the sentence on the original serpent would be unintelligible to us. And if the devil answered not to the sly and treacherous character of the common serpent, the sentence would be unjust.

See Ancient Universal History, 8vo edit. 1747, vol. i., 122–132. Doddridge's Lectures, prop. cxix., sec. 2, 3. Theol. Tracts, vol. vi., particularly Middleton against Sherlock, and Bate against Middleton.

The Rev. J. Newton—

There are three or four passages in the Old Testament which unbelievers are continually nibbling at. One is about Balaam's ass speaking, and another Jonah's whale. Now Christ confirms one, and St Peter the other. God seems to have permitted this to exercise our faith.

God, if I may so say, could not make an independent creature. He only has immutability—and this is not to be communicated to a creature.

The Rev. B. Woodd—

There is no end if we adopt the allegorical interpretation. The Swedenborgians allegorise every part of Genesis.

The Rev. John Venn—

If you would describe a FACT, it would not be possible to do it in more simple terms than those of Moses. When anything is written allegorically, the style rises with a sort of inflation. As to its being miraculous, everything was miraculous. The whole is not to be judged of by our usual ideas of what passes in life. A full answer to the second objection is, that it was a miraculous age. It seems likely that some change took place in the serpent. The sentence in part applying to the devil, and in part to the serpent, rests on the general ground of imputation. This always exercised the objections of infidels. But it runs through Scripture ; *e. g.*, the curse on Ham's posterity. We are not perfectly competent to explain God's method of acting. We find in Scripture a double sense given to prophecy.

c

The Rev. R. Cecil—

Such a question as this should be previously considered—this I have not done. But I remember a result from a former examination ; it was this—*Hitherto shalt thou come, and no further.* It is something like the man with his hand under his cloak—" What have you under your cloak ? " " I carry it there that you may not know."

A man, in opening such a book as the Bible, has no chance of finding out anything without humility. God speaks with majesty. He asks not, " What think you of my creation ? " The sober man would say—" I expect everything to be wonderful in such an account."

There is much at the bottom of these objections which unbelievers bring forward. They strike at the root of the great doctrines of Sin and Regeneration. It has been objected, that there is the face of futility on this account. How can we conceive such a perfect Being to introduce imperfection into his own work ? God meant to bring glory to himself from the whole scheme. There is great impertinence and pride in the men who toss about this account. But the poison of some scorpions is said to be the antidote to their bite. So these men are an antidote to themselves.

Who can draw the line between the allegorical and historical ? Cain's history is a true history—and it all goes on in a continuous thread of connexion with the history of the Fall. If you take away the literal sense, it is reduced to *every* man's sense.

To answer these objections is much too grave a business. A sober man has something else to do than to give an answer to all the objections that ingenious men can bring forward. " Here are our documents," we say. No arguments can be brought against them resting on such a foundation ! But a fool may ask more questions than a wise man can answer.

Mr Bacon—

Though I may have made many mistakes in taking things too literally, I find, after all, that I have got from the whole the same important truths.

The Rev. Thomas Scott—

It is unphilosophical to suppose a Revelation in all things levelled to our capacity. The devil used the organs of the serpent as afterwards he used the organs of the demoniacs. No man knows how God taught Adam. But are not sin and misery in the world ? Who can give a better account of their introduction ? Where are we to stop, if we begin to allegorise ? Some have allegorised even the Crucifixion and the Resurrection.

———

May 28, 1798.

WHAT IS MEANT BY THE WEDDING GARMENT IN THE PARABLE OF THE MARRIAGE OF THE KING'S SON ?—Proposed by the Rev. J. Pratt.

The Rev. Thomas Scott—

The marriage of the king's son is prepared. The proposal made. Each, on several grounds, has his particular objection.

In this, our Lord points out the particular objections of the Pharisees to Christ's office and kingdom. None are taken from the road ready dressed. He here alludes to the wardrobes of great men.

The criminal is supposed to object to the garment of the king's ward. This man represents a specious, hypocritical professor. He is not a man that openly rejects; but he goes to his farm and other occupations. He is one who has *a name to live, but is dead.*

In Scripture, the simile of robes is taken also in another sense. God speaks in Gal. iii. of the sinner's so *putting on Christ,* as though God saw nothing but Christ.

Putting on Christ is the great thing meant by the wedding garment, but we must keep imputed and imparted righteousness distinct. Things go together which are not to be confounded.

Consider, too, the knowledge of the disciples, and the nature of the parable. Christ could not be understood when spoken of as afterwards. Christ points out men who would, however, receive him, after they might discover him. He also points out those who would *reject him* under every form.

He speaks not of either point exclusively in this parable—imparted or imputed righteousness. Especially in a parable we should not separate things. If I want to preach on either, I should take a text suited to the subject, and preach on it—not from a *general* subject. Some have supposed sincerity meant, but sincerity is good or bad, as it is used. We must profess Christ crucified, and be sincere in *that.* Without sincerity, it is of no value.

The Rev. J. Newton—

The man thought he had a right to attend.

Probably, as some say, the wardrobe was provided, and yet he went without getting such garment as was proper.

The Rev. B. Woodd—

Dr Hammond *in loco* cites the authorities concerning the custom of wardrobes.

The wedding garment seems to imply whatever God has said to be necessary for salvation. He requires the righteousness of justification, and the righteousness of sanctification; yet I like what Scott says, of *putting on the Lord Jesus Christ,* and then explaining it of each.

The Rev. W. Goode—

I have usually referred it to Christ as our righteousness and sanctification. We have nothing to do with what the Jews or apostles understood by it, but what our Lord meant by it. Christ knew it was to be recorded, and might be understood afterwards by the Church.

The robe appears to be a title—a ticket for admission.

We find sanctification, in another part of the parable, in the disposition of the people who would seek to gain admittance.

The Rev. J. Goode—

Stennett says, that it is just to establish a doctrine on the great outline of a parable; but dangerous to establish a doctrine on any particular part of a parable.

The Rev. W. J. Abdy—

The great design of the parable is to shew the Jews that they were in danger of exclusion from the kingdom of God, while others will be there whom they did not expect.

Perhaps Christ did not mean anything to be understood explicitly by the wedding garment.

I consider this man as a sly and specious hypocrite.

The Rev. J. Davies—

Where justification is, there is sanctification; so it is not of much consequence which way we take it.

St Paul, before his conversion, appears to have been such a man as here described. He speaks afterwards of rejoicing to put on the righteousness of Christ.

The Rev. H. Foster—

We have got into the way of applying every text to Christ's imputed righteousness.

But the materials of the feast seem to constitute or include election, and every blessing of the gospel.

Invitation is given to Jews and Gentiles. This man would come in without conforming to the rules of the feast.

The guests had nothing particular to do with him. He seems to have been a wicked, disorderly man.

When the king came in, then it was that he was detected.

If I preach in conformity to the general opinion, I would talk of imputed righteousness. But I think imputed righteousness is not here.

The Rev. R. Cecil—

I find nothing hit my idea so much as that particular Scripture— *Put ye on the Lord Jesus Christ.*

Ah! one says, that means putting on Christ as our righteousness. But put him on as wisdom, sanctification, and redemption also.

The man is different from the guests; but the guests could not see the difference. The king, however, could see it; and the question makes him speechless. He is found out to be Antinomian, not in Christ; not belonging to Christ.

If we narrow this ground, and make it mean any particular doctrine, we seem to put on our particular spectacles.

Two persons, a lady and a curate, looked through a telescope at the moon. The curate, smelling a cathedral, thought the horns looked like the two spires of a cathedral; while the lady thought them like the ends of Cupid's bow!

Making the wedding garment signify exclusively either justification or sanctification, is dividing Christ.

What will exclude me? No particular deficiency; but that I am separated from him.

J. Bacon, Esq.—

Christ seems to mean in general, by the parable, what is necessary for entering his kingdom.

He puts them on inquiry, whether they had what was required ; besides, coming into his kingdom is not sufficient. It confuses the matter to press it into particulars.

The man got into the church of God , but had not got the spirit and character of God's people.

We must drop the idea of its being an external thing. It seems to point out the character of the *friend of God.*

The Rev. Thomas Scott—

Foster is right and we are wrong, as far as that feast includes blessings ; and the wedding garment means regeneration, faith, and life, or the grand distinguishing principle.

I differ from Foster, in thinking him not a licentious, but doubtful character.

The Rev. J. Goode—

It does not appear that the rest did not see the man's unfitness.

The Rev. J. Clayton—

I like not that, because we should then be obliged to admit notorious sinners to communion. This is one of the grounds of dissent.

JUNE 11, 1798.

HOW FAR IS IT EXPEDIENT THAT A MINISTER SHOULD CONFINE HIS PREACHING WITHIN HIS OWN EXPERIENCE ?—Proposed by Rev. R. Cecil.

Mr Cecil—

As a man, the minister should honestly seek to preach according to his own knowledge and conception of the truth.

If he be a time-server, he will seek to preach what is fashionable. Yet another in sincerity inquires what he ought to preach. He hears others do what he approves, and he thinks he ought to aim at this.

Though we are all like travellers, travelling the same road, we are nevertheless influenced in different ways—some are chiefly affected by law-work ; others are drawn mildly. The Jailer and Lydia might have given different views of conversion and its evidences. The Jailer might reflect on Lydia, that she had not made enough of despair ; while Lydia might reflect on the Jailer that he had not made enough of the drawing influences of divine love.

The logical man insists on principles : the imaginative man on impressions.

No man will preach with much emphasis what he has not hold of himself. If a man utters what he does not feel, it is felt not to be *authentic.*

Mr Bacon—

If the minister confines his preaching to his own experience, he

may narrow the subject.   Perhaps experience is apt to warp opinions,
how much more if the preacher give himself up to this as a principle.

The Rev. Josiah Pratt—

God's great object is Jesus Christ.   The preaching of Jesus Christ is
the great engine for moving men.

Men should bring their experience to the subject.   The constitution
of men's minds is doubtless extremely varied.   God's wisdom is shewn
in this.   The effect is, that we exhibit Jesus Christ in various lights.
Paul, Peter, John are all different ; but JESUS is the subject.

Constitutional tendencies *may* lead a man *from* Jesus Christ, even
though he approves of the Gospel.   If he finds this, he should correct
himself.   He should pray for *more grace*.

Jesus Christ will warm every man's heart, if he stands near enough.

The Rev. J. Clayton—

We should define what we mean by *experience* in this question.   I
would not confine it to *impression*, but extend it to what I am *convinced of*.

No man is to make himself the standard.   This is the grand error
of Popery.   The Scriptures are the great rule.

A man must preach beyond his own experience, if his preaching is
to be conformed to the Bible ; or he cannot suit the various cases of his
hearers.

Indeed if he is not to do so, *stated* pastors are not to be preferred to
occasional.

The Rev. R. Cecil—

In the question I have proposed, I mean not *personal* experience of
God's dealings ; but a man's *view of truth*.

One man has a wide view of the *rationale* of truth.   Should another
imitate that without feeling it ?

The Rev. B. Woodd—

A minister must preach beyond his own experience, but there will
be a sensible difference between what flows from his own feelings and
knowledge, and what is borrowed.

We should converse much with Scripture—especially the Psalms—
and study the lives of good men.

Deep experience is only a deeper measure of what a man has already
possessed.

In the first stage of experience, a Minister is qualified, though not so
much as he afterwards becomes.   He may deliver sentiments which
others *feel* beyond the preacher.

The Rev. R. Cecil—

The question should have been worded " views of truth " instead of
" experience."

The Rev. G. Pattrick—

A man will blunder who enters on subjects which he does not
understand.   A sermon on the New Birth was once put into my hand,

and I preached it; some people came to converse upon the view I took, but I could not talk with them.

We are to adopt anything which Scripture lays down—as redemption, spiritual influence, sanctification—whether we feel these truths as we should or no.

The Rev. W. J. Abdy—

Impressing truth on others will make a minister feel it more himself.

My *forte* is to preach to ungodly persons. I give only general directions to the godly. On attempting to preach experimentally in imitation of others, I found I could do nothing, and was obliged to go back to my own system.

The Rev. J. Venn—

A minister is to exhibit the Gospel. This is his primary business.

But how is he to enter into an explanation of doctrines? Let him look up to the mind of the Church. This is in some cases necessary.

He must take care that what he says is Christ's.

There is danger in calling man "Master"—in imitating others; and therefore in going beyond experience.

I was reading Walker's *Christian*, and said to myself, "Must I give this to my people?" But my conscience responded, "Is not Walker, then, the standard?"

If a man feels the influence of doctrines on himself, he will preach them to others. If he finds his doctrines in Scripture, he is safe; he need not make his own experience or that of others his only standard. We should raise the standard higher than any that can be attained.

The Rev. H. Foster—

It is plain a man must not make experience the standard of doctrine. Look at the Bible.

When Peter was proud, he was left to fall. *When thou art recovered, strengthen thy brethren*—seems to prove that God trains men, that they may lead others. In that way, the minister will lead others best.

Is a man to use his *own* way of stating truth? Or is he to take one *he sees* to be better?

He must follow his feelings. To take another's way is to try to take another's talents instead of his own. Look at Mr Whitfield, Romaine, &c., &c. Man will do that emphatically which he feels. His feelings will lead him to *that*. His judgment directs him to a *larger* view.

The Rev. R. Cecil—

A man is to use his *own* talent. "That is yours," says the great Master; "*occupy till I come.*" We need not seek to sit in our *corner*—we are likely enough to be there!

While every man has a certain *talent*, yet every man *breaks down* somewhere. A man should consider how far his particular talent leads him to neglect other points which God charges on him.

A man who looks exceedingly at one thing cannot see another. This is a common thing in observation.

A Minister must often take his credentials out of his pocket and inquire, " Have I delivered all this ? "

A sanguine man's *talent* in one respect, is his *snare* in another.

JUNE 25, 1798.

IS THERE A MORAL SENSE, AND WHAT IS IT ?—Proposed by Rev. J. Venn.

The Rev. J. Venn—

Paley concludes there is not : and this is the general opinion. But a great argument *for* it is the idea of *responsibility* which is natural to us. The Apostle seems to argue upon this presumption.

I would make some distinctions upon the *nature* of Moral Sense.

Most ideas go on this, that man knows what is right or wrong. I would say, there is some faculty in man whereby he is *affected* with certain emotions when he thinks he has done right or wrong.

These two things are distinct—a knowledge of right and wrong, and an uneasiness or approbation consequent on them.

It is generally held, that there is no sin committed unless a man knows it to be sin. I should think, on the contrary, that most sins are committed without immediate consciousness.

Habit hardens the heart, and dims the eye. The heathen are accounted sinful—first, for not knowing God from the visible creation ; and, secondly, for not acting up to what they did know.

The Rev. J. Pratt—

I carry the idea further than Venn. Man has a *capacity* to determine on right or wrong. But he must undergo *instruction* before he can exercise it.

Mr Bacon—

I do not consider it necessary that innate ideas should exist in order to form responsibility. The judgment is crooked, but the passions are more so. Men often judge better for others than for themselves.

Our Lord's golden rule enters into the *rationale* of the Moral Sense. How should *you* like this ? I should like my neighbour's hatchet, &c. The man who condemns this feeling does not perhaps do so *formally*, but with a *consciousness*.

Wherever two or three persons come together, the *selfish* principle is so operative, as to bring occasions for this judging of the mind.

The Rev. H. Foster—

Reduce it to a *capacity*, and then men do not differ from brutes, but in the greater *degree* of this capacity. Brutes learn by *experience* to feel terror at a stronger brute, because of being goaded.

The Rev. J. Venn—

There is a distinction between terror felt from experience of punishment, and a sense of right and wrong.

But yet, continued Mr Foster, I think man does not go further than the brute in this respect.

The Rev. Mr Gambier, a visitor for the evening—

The attainment of moral is like that of scientific knowledge. There are no doubt axioms in morals, as in mathematics.

There are three ways of acquiring moral knowledge :—(1.) By investigating for ourselves. (2.) By divine revelation. (3.) By picking it up from others.

The Rev. J. Clayton—

Every living creature has a capacity for education according to its rank. Every creature has a natural instinct thus improvable.

Man has a soul elevated above the brutes; and therefore has a capacity of being educated to a higher degree.

No part of the world is without remnants of Revelation. These have lost their distinctness indeed, but still they suggest ideas.

Our conscience—what is it? Knowing with;—with whom? GOD.

Man differs only therefore from beasts in his capacity, in having a higher capacity.

It is similar in the spiritual world. Regeneration is a communicated principle. Present truth to a regenerate mind; it assimilates.

The Rev. Basil Woodd—

If there were a moral sense, it would be uniform and universal. History contradicts this. We read of children being exposed in woods, and afterwards shewing but poor signs of having a moral sense.

The Rev. W. Goode—

Man is born with no moral sense, but moral capacities. A child is a bundle of capacities.

The Rev. R. Cecil—

A strong proof against original Moral Sense is the fact, how little there is in men who have all possible advantages.

I know not whether there may not be a certain *low* degree of moral education attainable by *uninstructed* men, which would make them revolt at the case of Caius quoted by Paley.* This might be a selfish principle.

---

* The following is the case supposed by Paley :—

"The father of *Caius Toranius* had been proscribed by the Triumvirate. *Caius Toranius*, coming over to the interests of that party, discovered to the officers, who were in pursuit of his father's life, the place where he concealed himself, and gave them withal a description, by which they might distinguish his person, when they found him. The old man, more anxious for the safety and fortunes of his son, than about the little that might remain of his own life, began immediately to inquire of the officers who seized him, whether his son was well, whether he had done his duty to the satisfaction of his generals. 'That son (replied one of the officers) so dear to thy affections, betrayed thee to us; by his information thou art apprehended, and diest.' The officer with this struck a poniard to his heart, and the unhappy parent fell, not so much affected by his fate, as by the means to which he owed it."

Now the question is, whether, if this story were related to the wild boy caught some years ago in the woods of Hanover, or to a savage without experience, and without instruction, cut off in his infancy from all intercourse with his species, and, consequently, under no possible influence of example, authority, education, sympathy, or habit; whether, I say, such a one would feel, upon the relation, any degree of *that sentiment of disapprobation of Toranius's conduct* which we feel, or not?

They who maintain the existence of a moral sense; of innate maxims; of a natural

Cases of exposed children are not fair criteria, because the custom of the people among whom they come may *overwhelm* any indication of moral sense.

But if this low degree of moral sense exist, yet it is vastly below the knowledge of God. The apostles declare we know nothing of God but by *faith :* which goes on revelation, else on fancy.

It is very clear, then, that there is no moral sense to any *purpose.*

I rather think the thing has been decided by men with too much haste. A *very low state* I conceive possible.

The Rev. J. Venn—

I have conceived the subject much as Mr Cecil does.

Man was perfect in his original state. He retains all his faculties now. But all his faculties are in ruins—among these, his *conscience.* It nevertheless exists and acts, though in a weak and low degree. Perhaps it is the meanest of all his original faculties.

JULY 9, 1798.

To what Extent does Scripture authorise Typical Explanations ? —Proposed by the Rev. B. Woodd.

Mr Woodd—

Allegorical interpretation attenuates the force of Scripture, when pushed far. I rather hesitate at it.

Yet it is certain that many parts of the Old Testament are typical.

Where Scripture authorises, all is clear ; where not, it is dangerous to do so.

I ask, whether we are to consider the applications in the New Testament as authorising a general typical interpretation, or as confining the typical interpretation to those instances ?

If we confine it, we take away some *collateral* evidence to Scripture.

An advantage in typical interpretation is, that it enables a Minister oftener to bring forward the great subjects of the gospel, and to give greater variety to his subject.

A disadvantage is, that it gives weapons to designing men—opens the door to Swedenborgians, and such like.

What criterion, then, can be laid down, to keep us within the limits of sober interpretation, and yet avail ourselves of the real advantages of allegory ?

The Rev. J. Goode—

We may allegorise when—

(1.) There is a resemblance between the events of the old and new dispensations.

(2.) There is reason to think it is designed by the Holy Spirit.

(3.) When we take care not to stretch the clue till it breaks.

conscience ; that the love of virtue and hatred of vice are instinctive; or the perception of right and wrong intuitive (all which are only different ways of expressing the same opinion), affirm that he would.

They who deny the existence of a moral sense, &c., affirm that he would not.

And upon this, issue is joined.

Some follow, as Leighton says, allegory so far, after the monkish way, as to run it out of breath.

Attend to the distinguishing properties of each thing.

Pushing allegory too far, tends to play into the hands of infidels, and to carnalise spiritual things.

The Rev. J. Davies—

Goode's rules are excellent. But I have doubted whether Scripture authorises typical interpretations at all.

It has been said, that the Psalms said to be typical ought to be confined to one interpretation. If they refer to Jesus Christ, confine them to that sense.

The Rev. H. Foster—

I doubt not but that the whole is a typical institution. The difficulty is to assign the limits.

It is abused so, that men are sickened. But we are not to give up things because abused.

Strive to gain truth, and leave events, as to abuse, to God.

Many things are not to be defended but upon a typical interpretation.

Passages quoted in the New Testament seem to warrant us to apply *similar* passages.

It will require sobriety and caution.

Another thing—give the history clearly, and ground the allegorical sense upon this.

We see writers in the Old Testament often begin upon their family or nation; then taken by the Holy Spirit, and carried out to things of redemption.

These things, *fulfilled* in his family or nation, are evidence to them that what was designed would be fulfilled.

As to *accommodation*—

I could not well get on without it, yet I think it is a mark of want of matter.

Yet the extreme on the typical side is least dangerous. The man is most likely to get hold of the Gospel.

This is my general idea. The New Testament applications have given us a rule and *warrant* to apply similar passages.

I like the general caste of Horne's " Commentary on the Psalms."

The Rev. R. Cecil—

I am jealous of truth and its sanctions.

It is a different thing when talking of a typical dispensation, and one unrolled. Allegories go into the New Testament.

When talking of a typical dispensation, I admire a master like St Paul. But *modesty* is necessary here. Remember, *this is the house of God, the gate of heaven.* How dreadful, if I lead thousands with nonsense ; if I lose opportunities of bringing solid truths home ; if I waste their precious time !

I want to cut off occasion of objecting. I want to pin down men's consciences.

We must shew people we have no twist. Some are continually seeking reasons for letting themselves off. Simple poor people will do with a twist. But there is always some seeking occasion. Let us shew them here is a holy, resistless offer.

Allegory is important to shew that there is one and the same doctrine from beginning to end. Christianity was preached to *us* as to *them*.

This is one way of getting the yoke off the neck. Men make the Bible "*my* Bible." They want to get the shafts off their shoulders. They don't like to amble in the shafts.

The *meaning* of the Bible is the *Bible*: and no man can alter that, whatever his notions may be.

If you would preach on imputed righteousness, why preach from *the skies pouring down righteousness*, and then anathematise men for not believing the doctrine, when hundreds of places are so clear?

Most of the ribaldry on this subject is from the want of a holy awe upon the mind.

This may arise from an evil fashion: so far, the case is somewhat extenuated.

It is a very different thing, however, to allegorise the old dispensation and the new, the new being plainly *substances*.

I remember, when a careless young man, having pinches in my conscience from some; others let me off.

"Oh! this is weak and allegorical—foolish preaching;" and I was let off for the time, till I met with some plain, simple, solid person, who took the obvious meaning.

I shall, therefore, carry to my grave perhaps a deep conviction of the danger of entering far into typical or allegorical interpretation.

J. Bacon, Esq.—

Substantiate well every truth. Lay it on the solid foundation of the Gospel. Take not away the substance and bring forth its shadow, yet deal as much in imagery and allegory as can be done soberly. God seems thus to have dealt with man.

The Rev. R. Cecil—

The use of metaphors and images is important and useful under *all* dispensations.

But to bring out a subject and make it representative of spiritual things, when it is not of itself obvious, is dangerous.

The Rev. Thomas Scott—

Most parts of the old dispensation are representative of Christ and the gospel, as baptism, &c., of thing signified.

What is called the spiritual meaning is the mind of the Spirit in Scripture. If we speak of a type, then the spiritual meaning is the anti-type.

Other meanings are fanciful.

When men find a meaning which no one else has ever found, we may fairly conclude that this is not the mind of the Spirit.

This habit of finding fanciful meanings arises from (1.) absence of sobriety, and (2.) eagerness of popular applause.

Remember we preach mostly to those *within*. If we could hear what those without say, we should weep often.

It is good soberly to bring in accommodation to relieve the monotony of preaching. In this case, we should explain, first, the clear sense, and then lead the mind on to the accommodation.

Illustration is useful, if God give the talent. Confound not, however, illustration and proof.

The Rev. J. Newton—

There are plain texts which speak of all doctrines. Therefore I take plain texts, and use typical ones as illustration. I hesitate where the New Testament authorises not.

The Rev. Josiah Pratt—

From some applications of the Old Testament in the New, we may perhaps infer that in the apostolic times a general typical system was well understood and allowed.

What *is* found seems to be part of a wider system, and is always assumed as known and allowed.

The New Testament applications seem to be the only *certain* ground.

However, the ancient history and economy were a preparation for the Gospel.

Histories, events, and persons, were in the providence of God made to bear a reference to the Gospel.

We know that persons and things among the Jews sustained a double character—literal and prophetic.

They were so treated as to relate to *either* singly, or *both* united.

For example, what is said of Solomon, or of Jerusalem, is true either of them, or of what in the sacred allegory of the Jews they denoted.

It is safest to insist on none but New Testament applications. Use all others by way of accommodation, as *leading our thoughts* to such and such a truth.

Reject all idle and wanton applications.

Nothing is to be adopted to the prejudice of the literal sense.

Follow the thread of the New Testament interpretations.

Tread in the clear and undoubted steps of the prophet (Eph. ii. 20.) Let Christ be the main subject of our applications. (See Louth's Præl. xi.; Doddridge's Lect., vol. ii. p. 17, sect. 132, cor. 1, 2 ; Franckii Prog. iii. v.)

From Christ's mentioning the serpent lifted up in the wilderness, we may infer that the cities of refuge may be applied to spiritual things.

The use of typical explanations lies in this—that abstract truth produces little impression ; and typical interpretations aid the feelings and the memory.

JULY 23, 1798.

WHAT ARE THE REAL CAUSES OF ENMITY AGAINST THE GOSPEL ?—Proposed by the Rev. J. Venn.

Mr Venn—

The Gospel being a Revelation from God, proposes itself to the approbation of every intelligent being.

If it meet with opposition and enmity, these must therefore arise either from the blindness of the understanding, or the perverseness of the will.

The disposition in every man is to make himself the standard. Every man, therefore, in a degree, makes his own preconceived opinions the standard whereby he judges the Gospel. This accounts for many stumbling at its doctrines.

But, in general, the perverseness of the will leads men to hate the self-denial of the Gospel. If we did not press the Gospel home, men would not spurn it.

In different ages, there have been different grounds of enmity against the Gospel. The chief ground of enmity in the Jews, was the shock given to their prejudices. The ground of enmity in the present day, is a prejudice less against the doctrines than against the demands of the Gospel. Men will allow you to hold the doctrines as *your whim*, if you press them not home on their consciences. As soon as the minister urges self-denial as required by the Gospel, then it is that men rise up against the Gospel.

The Rev. J. Davies—

Man naturally hates God, and all who are like Him, and all that is calculated to make man like Him. A radical cause of this is pride. Men cannot bear to be brought down to the universal level.

The Gospel may be viewed, too, as a medicine. If medicine be even in itself *pleasant*, yet it is disagreeable *quasi* medicine. But the Gospel is an unpleasant medicine ; therefore men by nature hate it. Men, too, think they *need not* such a medicine.

Enmity to the Gospel may arise also from prejudice against the persons who preach it, or the manner in which it is ministered.

The Rev. Thomas Scott—

The causes of enmity against the Gospel are distinct from *occasional* prejudices.

Persons prejudiced against the manner, for instance, are under occasional prejudices, which do not arise from the *root of enmity.*

Man will not submit to God's justice. He refuses to believe himself damned justly—even the moral and virtuous feel this. The spirit and curse of the Law, therefore, are the causes of deep enmity. The offence of the Gospel is its being brought home to the heart, as requiring its sacrifice of everything to God. Few are affected with enmity by the mysteries of the Gospel.

In a workhouse or a palace, enmity rises up against the simple exhibition of Jesus as the Saviour. The virtuous matron won't come down and place herself on the level in point of merit of one who has led an irregular life. The scholar won't come to sit at Christ's feet with poor men. The rich man won't come to use his goods as a *steward*.

The offence of the Cross takes its stand in the lust of the heart.

The Cross *may* be so preached as *not* to give offence. But this will not be the Gospel.

The Rev. J. Clayton—

The cause of enmity against the Gospel lies in human nature, not in persons. An intelligent man's depravity operates against the mysteries of the Gospel.

The Pharisees' enmity appears against the Gospel as exhibiting salvation by grace. The moral class have enmity against the conviction of being sinners. The sensual man's enmity is against the holiness of God.

Different persons may feel different views operating on them; but the cause is the same.

The Rev. Josiah Pratt—

I. The perverseness of the will may shew its enmity to the Gospel by—

(1.) Indifference. Gallio did not like to be disturbed. *He cared for none of those things.*

(2.) Aversion to the object the Gospel has in view—to stamp the image of God again on the soul: the sacrifice of connexions is required; the heart cleaves to the world.

(3.) Pride against the means. The man would do the thing himself. Pride will not accept a gift. The Pharisee would be holy, but not by Christ. He will not submit to *believe:* but would *see.*

This perverseness of the will may make *pretences;* and these pretences are taken from the preacher, his manner, &c., &c.

II. The blindness of the understanding is another cause of enmity. But if detached from perverseness of the will, it may be a temporary cause of resisting, but *only* a temporary one; for it will open itself for instruction.

God has made the way *wide, open, clear,* to the *regulated will.*

In the parable of the king's son, the *causes* of enmity are to be traced to the *will.*

The Rev. Basil Woodd—

This spirit of enmity being universal against the Gospel, is a grand argument for the truth of the Gospel.

Pride, independence, sensuality are the causes of enmity.

Enmity shews itself in—

(1.) The pains men take to find a flaw in the evidence.

(2.) The pains they take to find a flaw in the characters of professors.

(3.) The glee with which any perversion of the Gospel is taken up. Men call their neighbours to feast at the slaying of the Two Witnesses.

The Rev. T. Dykes, of Hull, a visitor this evening—

The grand cause of enmity against the Gospel is, that it makes its subjects different in character from all around. Heathens would have allowed Christians to call Jesus Christ, God, but could not bear their presumption in rejecting *their* gods.

The Rev. W. J. Abdy—

The Gospel obliges us to preach with apparent want of charity.

The Rev. R. Cecil—

The *occasions* of enmity have not been sufficiently enlarged upon this evening.

We must not fail to recur to the causes; but we shall stop very short, if we do not ascend to the occasions.

Any man would put me to pain to bleed me; but if he tore up my wound with a *horse-nail!*

1. That which is *hard* to be received at best, may be rendered morally impossible by occasions.

2. Another *occasion* of enmity may be this. A man may be ignorant in everything but the way of salvation, but especially learned in *that*. Men see him a fool *off* his ground, and so think him a fool *on* his ground. It is a gross error to rail against human learning.

3. The Gospel was at first a *fight*: now it is a *trade*. What *trade* are you? The Gospel. People see this. This is a great occasion of enmity. Men of learning and character have clenched the nail. They have brought out the mischief and exhibited it to the world. There are some master-men among these. Warburton was like a bear among bees. Let any man look into his book of grace. He may sit down and wonder why God has suffered such a bear to have such stuff to pull about. Warburton was a constable—a rude constable indeed. Count Zinzendorff's obscenities would afford another illustration. The devil won't want journeymen to bring out these matters.

4. Fanatical times are another occasion of enmity to the Gospel. For example, Cromwell's days. Butler was raised up by the devil to make the best of this great subject for ridicule. As long as such men as Butler are in the world, it will furnish great occasion of enmity to the Gospel.

5. Buffoonery in the pulpit is another occasion.

6. An unholy, insolent professor is a cause of enmity. He scorns: and insults mankind. It is enough to make them scorn the truth he holds. Some men are allowed by the world to call it to account—" A holy and just man."

7. A religious quiz is an occasion of enmity to the Gospel. Ask him a question, he'll stare in your face and look very spiritual. I remember a person at Lewes who accosted another thus — " Farmer, what do you know of Jesus Christ?" There was a quantity of spiritual pride in this. A grievous want, too, of breeding and good sense. The world, therefore, forms this idea—Religion makes a man a fool or mad: therefore I won't be such a creature.

These are stumbling-blocks. *Woe unto the world because of offences;*

for it must needs be that offences come: but woe to that man by whom the offence cometh.

Every man who has zeal for the propagation of the Gospel should keep his eye upon these *occasions*, since the thing, *per se*, meets with such enmity in the heart.

AUGUST 6, 1798.

WHAT IS EMULATION, AND WHAT ARE THE EVILS ARISING FROM IT ?—Proposed by Rev. T. Scott.

Mr Scott—

EMULATION is the Desire of Distinction. In this view it is the offspring of Pride.

Wherein is it distinguishable from a proper desire of excelling? The desire of excelling is a positive thing. An angel desires to excel—to exert all his faculties for God. A good man would endeavour to do everything in the best manner.

This is distinct from Emulation in the following respects :—

1st. In a holy being, the desire to excel would operate as forcibly in retirement, as on a stage.

2d. The desire of excelling will carry a man forward against reproach : while Emulation shrinks from reproach. See St Paul's character.

3d. It will lead a man to prefer what is substantially right, to what is apparently so.

4th. It will sincerely rejoice to see others excel : and grieve to see others come short of their duty and aim.

Emulation is Envy in its better-day clothes. A leading principle of the heathen world was the spirit of evil Emulation.

A boy, if taught to emulate his fellows in Horace and Homer, will apply the same principle to boxing, &c. Tell him to aim at *Excellence* —not so ! he will *distinguish* himself. Bring him to the university. He will strive to become a mathematician, a classic for fame's sake. If he aimed at Excellence, he would choose divinity also for his study.

There are two evil effects in Emulation.

1. " What can I excel in ? " a man inquires. " If fiddling will get me a name, I'll fiddle, though a minister."

2. " What will *please?* " is another question men put to themselves. " I'll aim at *that.*"

This Emulation is of an universally mischievous tendency. It leads men to prefer applause to public good.

The Rev. Josiah Pratt—

1. ITS NATURE.

EMULATION and ENVY are distinct in their nature.

Envy is pain felt and malignity conceived at the sight of excellence or happiness. Emulation is a generous ardour kindled by the example of others, to imitate, rival, and, if we can, excel them.

Envy is compounded of Sorrow and Hatred. Emulation chiefly of

Admiration. Envy involves in it a hatred of the person whose attainments or conduct we Envy ; while Emulation involves in it esteem of him.

Envy refuses to great actions the praise due to them. Emulation admires them and strives to imitate them.

Envy is mean and seeks to lessen a rival. Emulation is generous and only thinks of surpassing him.

In Scripture, φθόνος is always Envy : as in Gal. v. 21. Ζῆλος is both Envy and Emulation ; when it means Envy, as Gal. v. 20, it differs little from φθόνος. See Rom. xiii. 13 ; 1 Cor. iii. 3 ; 2 Cor. xii. 20 ; James iii. 14, 16. When it means Emulation, it is compounded with παρα, as Rom. x. 19 ; xi. 11, 14.

For an illustration of Envy, see Mark ix. 33 ; of Emulation, see 2 Cor. ix.

Emulation desires good for its own sake, not as possessed by another, which Envy often does.

2. The USES of Emulation.

It acts as a motive in resisting sloth, &c. We are ready enough to interpret difficulties as impossibilities. Examples deprive us of this refuge. What *has* been done by others, *may* be by us. And we feel ashamed to be in the rear. *Extremos pudeat rediisse.*

3. The DANGERS.

Emulation borders on Envy and Vanity—on Envy if we succeed not, on Vanity if we succeed.

The Rev. John Davies—

Emulation is a desire to excel. Whether it be good or bad depends on—1. The object in which we desire to excel. 2. The end at which we aim in desiring to excel. *Let us provoke one another to love and to good works.*

The Rev. J. Venn—

Emulation in an evil sense operates most easily between persons near each other.

Thus a painter feels Envy if you propose to him as an example for imitation the works of a rival ; but not so if the example of Titian, &c. St Paul stirred up the Corinthians by the Macedonians, who were at a distance. It would not have been without danger had they been near.

Care, therefore, is to be used in selecting what examples we set before youth. If *near*, then will envy be excited.

Emulation operates in *discouraging* more than by *encouraging*. Men become but superficial scholars, from desiring to excel others without labouring. If Emulation, in bad sense, were not used at schools, there would be more real learning in the world. The means recommended and enforced by God are always ultimately most successful.

The Rev. R. Cecil—

Emulation is the fire of the heart, which a good spirit pokes, and an evil spirit pokes. In the heathen world the devil was poking the poets, poking the philosophers. Emulation, as the Apostle uses it, is like the king's messenger, who urges forward his horses : he is upon the king's business.

Emulation in a bad sense is that which you see between two Bow coachmen, who whip and spur for no earthly purpose but to beat each other.   Emulation in a bad sense is pride in action.

As man is a sluggish creature, he wants exciting causes.   Both good and bad men agree in fact.   *Rem facias*—say both.   *Quocumque modo* —says the bad man.   Man is an active creature, from concupiscence.   A holy man is like the rower who *must* go to a certain point.   He may be helped by the current ; but if against the current, he tugs the harder.

There is mechanism in man.   You must touch certain springs.   We must not deal with man as an abstract being, but seize every avenue. We must provoke to generous shame.   *I took wages of other Churches.* Such a people *were ready a year ago.*   All this is fair and right and necessary.

August 20, 1798.

WHAT TENDS TO ENLIVEN OR DEPRESS DEVOTION IN A CONGREGATION ? —Proposed by Rev. R. Cecil.

Mr Cecil—

Let us begin with man.   Who and what is man ?   It is a mistake both in Churchmen and Dissenters to look on man as a creature of intelligence solely.   It is thought that if we get hold of the brain, then all will follow the head.   But wiser men have considered him as a creature of feeling also.   Let us, however, get hold of him as we can.

But what use is there in exciting attention, if there be nothing to be attended to ?   It is therefore of first importance to put a meaning into all that is done—no matter how different men's faculties and means are.

But a proper medium should be observed ; for there may be no meaning in either extreme.   A dead preacher conveys no meaning ; so one all life, may be a rambler and have no meaning.

Too little attention is paid in reference to Man.   I would consult him in all points.   I would give him cushions, if he would then sit easier.   I would make him warm and comfortable ; and would not be so foolish as to tell him to be warm in God's service, while he actually shivers.   I would let no doors creak, no windows rattle, nor *night's foul bird* scream, &c.

The music should not be in Opera style, nor disgusting to a correct taste; wherever fantastical interludes are brought in, a corrupt prin- ciple is at work.   The Moravians, though they have too much of ding- dong, yet have a harmony and the simplicity of Christianity in the very aspect of their worship.

Say nothing and yet everything—that is a rare gift.   Here the effect most depends on the minister.   If he be dead, in one way or other he will bring the people down to a dead state.

Avoid, above all things, monotony.   If the mind is vagrant, mono- tony cannot recall it.   Monotony not only in *tone*, but in *subject*.

On the other hand, a man may be vehement, but find no attention excited, if the minister be dead. He may roar like a town-bull; but no, the congregation is dead. There is nothing to lead the mind into a train of useful thought.

Men of sense and literature treat things abstractedly. But simplicity, with good sense, is of infinite importance.

Order, also, is important in a congregation for maintaining a devotional spirit. If noise is suffered—persons coming in when they will —it begets lax and loose and indifferent habits of devotion.

Man is a sympathetic creature. What he feels others neglect, he will neglect himself. If a man reads the prayers, as though the business was not yet begun, people soon feel this.

We should take occasion frequently to impress on the people the importance of the place and work. It is not enough to take this for granted. In fact, take nothing for granted. Man needs to be reminded of everything. He soon forgets everything.

Avoid long extempore prayer, either at the beginning or end of your sermon. It gives the impression that the congregation had been doing nothing before.

Wherever there is an *attempt* at music, and the attempt is *apparent* —here is the first step towards carnality. " Now we are going to do it." To DO IT !! We should rather seek to fall into the proper exercise of devotion in a natural manner ; and not to begin by an attempt at doing it. Doing it with a *knack* leads to carnality. " Now we do it better than any where else."

Do it *well*, but not with affectation. Keep religion from being *abstract* or *curious*. If you have a curious remark, keep it for some other place.

Man gets away from the bustle and business of the week. He comes to the house of God trembling perhaps ; and wishes, if possible, to have his heart raised upward. If the minister comes in with curious etymologies and disquisitions, it chills and damps ! We should be men of business in the congregation ; and seek to excite as well as instruct, and to make it an interesting affair in all its parts.

Some would sooner have the Methodists to rouse men, even rather than an Owen himself with his 1st, 2d, 3d, &c.

Then we should seek to bind up the broken-hearted, to comfort the feeble-minded, and make all interesting. We should make a spirit of accommodation to the wants and necessities of our people visible.

Write over the door—*Whoever will, let him come and take of the water of life freely.*

All hands should conspire with the minister. And his influence should be as if he said, " You shan't oppose what I would establish."

The Rev. J. Venn—

Real life shews itself differently in different people. Thus even *silence* shews spiritual life. A Minister may encourage the noisy and external expressions of life, till it all degenerates into nothing but mischief.

Mr Cecil observed here, that he did not take the question as referring to the work of the Spirit of God, but to exciting or depressing the interest of the congregation.

The Rev. Thomas Scott—

Much is called life, which is most certainly affectation.

An interchange in the parts of worship, as in our litany, is calculated to keep up devotion. But employing a man dead to God to read prayers has a bad effect. There is no sympathy with him in worship. He is hasty perhaps, or indifferent, and it all produces a bad effect. If ministers did indeed pray and not read the prayers, an impression would be made. The fault is one of the heart more than the mind. We should learn to read well, when we are young ministers. But when reading, the minister should never *think* of reading well ; but should put his *heart* into it.

I would try to think it as much an honour to *lead the devotion* of a congregation as to *preach.* Teach your congregation, that WORSHIP is the great end of assembling.

The Rev. Josiah Pratt—

A distinction may be made between what men may be brought to by habit, and what is the best habit to which men may be brought.

There may be danger of a minister forming his congregation to his *own* taste.

But we should take up the thing in its widest form. What is most likely to depress or impress man ?

We should combine addresses to the *Passions* and the *Intellect.* Man is a mixed creature. *So* mixed, that our best prospect is in leaning to the passions more than the intellect. In Yorkshire, men may bear a preponderance in favour of intellect : in town, of the passions.

The *permanent* life of devotion is to be preferred to a *temporary* excitement.

With some a liturgy depresses, it requires exertion ; but in the end it is far best in effect.

The excitation of curiosity, and feeding the taste—in these there is a dangerous tendency to give *entertainment* rather than awaken devotion.

Some also think the liturgy too long, and that it might be divided.

A hireling reader will produce an evil effect. I well remember being much struck with the manner in which Mr Simeon read the liturgy on one occasion in the church my father attended. But all could not imitate him, nor should they. The sympathy of the minister with the people is a great matter. If he be a holy man, near to God, he propagates the feeling of his own heart.

The music should be spirited, simple : we should avoid new or double tunes.

The end of the sermon should be pointed : the application short, and the hymn adapted to the subject.

The Rev. B. Woodd—

The people audibly joining in the responses exalts devotion.

The reader's feelings will have a great effect.

Get the sentences you read in the mind, rather than keep the eye fixed on them.

The music should be varied—soft, spirited, grave, &c. Responsive singing is good.

A short extempore prayer at the beginning or end of the sermon enlivens.

Variety of subject in preaching and also of illustration should be aimed at.

Illustrations by Scripture History; well chosen anecdotes; improvement of providences in a neighbourhood, &c.

Variety in tones and pauses; occasional ejaculations; apostrophes; but *aim* at making truth the grand object, not merely the mode of its delivery.

SEPTEMBER 3, 1798.

WHAT IS THE MEANING OF ROM. VII. 8—" BUT SIN, TAKING OCCASION BY THE COMMANDMENT, WROUGHT IN ME ALL MANNER OF CONCUPISCENCE—FOR BY THE LAW IS THE KNOWLEDGE OF SIN?"—Proposed by the Rev. B. Woodd.

Mr Woodd—

I wish to get a clear idea of the *irritating power* of the law.

Sin is depravity in general, the *law in the members*.

But we are rebels in proportion as we are restrained.

The law came with power to the Apostle, though free from sin, especially from *heart* sins.

The Rev. Thomas Scott—

I would scout the expression, "the irritating power of the law."

Sin *taking occasion*.   The fault is not in the law, but in our nature.

Acrimonious humours are not the fault of the blister: where they exist, anything will do for a blister.

Man thinks himself *free* from what has not yet broken out into *act*.

The philosopher spurns perhaps at the character of the covetous, little thinking what he would do himself under temptation.

The very idea of something forbidden, and out of reach, is temptation enough.   The imagination sets to work: the natural heart or Satan works on it.   The imagination makes a forbidden thing appear desirable.   The man then murmurs against the command—"Why not take that?"   But the law forbids!   He kicks, then, at the law.

When a man is awaked, he feels, "What a wretch I am to covet what God prohibits!"

This is a grand means of destroying self-confidence.

Corollary.   We shall preach the Gospel with more effect, if we preach the law fully.

Keeping back the law is the reason of so many untouched professors.

The grand remedy of self-righteousness is to preach the spirituality of the law.

The Rev. H. Foster—

An honest Christian can understand the seventh chapter of the Romans. If any one says he does not understand it, I say it strikes at the root of his experience.

It is the process through which every Christian goes. He hates the sin, but it's *there*—it *is* there.

The irritating power of the law seems to be its setting the imagination to work, which finds more in an object than is there.

I feel the whole process in the character from day to day, and year to year. As I feel my corruption, I think all has been deception.

I know there is a Saviour, and am determined to begin again. I go to the Saviour, and get to the same place : this is well. If *this* won't do, I've nothing else.

I do not acquiesce in this process as necessary. It is a cause of humility. I beg of God to renew this work.

The Rev. R. Cecil—

I feel this continually : there is no question about it.

I am glad to detect the thing. But call such a one rascal. Don't antinomianise the rascal into a saint.

A man should be denominated after his better part.

At times, a Christian is under an influence which does not belong to him. At the time, he's another man. The man himself perceives it not at first. But he becomes giddy, mad, outrageous.

See Owen on *Indwelling Sin.* Doctrine will not resist temptation. A man under passion will rush through hell-fire, and trample on the blood of Christ. Nay more, he will rush because he knows there is a way of pardon.

———

The members who spoke upon the next occasion came together with various degrees of experience on the subject which engaged their attention. Mr Bacon was 58 and the Rev. T. Scott 52 years old; and at this time, both had children who were of age. The Rev. W. J. Abdy was 43, the Rev. B. Woodd 39, and the Rev. J. Venn 38; and all three had children, the eldest about 12 or 13 years of age. The Rev. J. Pratt was in his 30th year, and had then no children, his first-born and only child having died an infant. Of the other members whose observations are recorded, we have no information.

September 17, 1798.

WHAT ARE THE FIRST AND MOST PROMINENT DISCOVERIES OF DEPRAVITY IN CHILDREN, AND THE BEST METHODS OF COUNTERACTING THEM ?—Proposed by the Rev. T. Scott.

Mr Scott—

Self-will is a prominent feature in children. The present disorders of Europe may be assigned to the want of the old plan of discipline. We should teach children that they must obey a *master*. We shall never learn better wisdom than God has taught us in the Bible. Easy correction is the best way of counteracting self-will. Never give a child what he cries for : it's like paying a child for crying. I loved my mother better than my father, when a child ; yet he indulged me, but she did not.

It is a fashion to teach children things as *amusement*. But it is of great importance to get a child into habits of application and self-denial. This is of more importance than anything they acquire.

I began with my children when they were in arms : this gave less trouble.

Religious people fail herein more than others. A Christian parent finds anger rise, begins to fear, and therefore gives way.

When reason ripens, then reason with them.

The Rev. Josiah Pratt—

The chief vices of children are Greediness and Self-will. These are the parents of thieving, revenge, cruelty, &c.

There are two extremes—severity and laxity—which must be guarded against in the management of children. [These he illustrated by examples of persons known to his brethren.] Of the two extremes, severity is the least injurious in its effects. Laxity gives more trouble in the issue.

It is a nice thing, however, to preserve both *Love* and *Authority*. My own father, I always felt and others have observed, was a happy example of the combination of these.

Convince a child that you *intend* his good. Let him see no passion in you. ' Guard against repressing the natural workings of his mind, lest you make the child affected or hypocritical.

The Rev. J. Clayton—

There are early discernible in children both Envy and Jealousy. For instance, how soon we see in children, that a thing taken away by another child becomes valuable, though it was not esteemed so before.

We cannot renew the heart, but we can prevent evil habits. Much may be done to smooth the ruggedness of nature by education. Few children are well educated : they retain some peculiarity or manner for want of attention.

To chastise in wrath tends to strengthen the evil you desire to correct. Chastisement is an ordinance of God. Now we none of us think of going to God's ordinances in wrath : why, then, to this? I once brought guilt on my conscience by chastising a child in anger. I changed my manner, and profited by it, and have had no occasion for correction since. I have had great comfort in my children.

Care should be taken that what parents do should not be undone by servants. Servants speaking evil of the master or mistress of the house must have a mischievous effect. It is the duty of mothers to be as Sarah was—*much in the tent.*

Promiscuous visiting, allowing your children to mix in the company of neglected children, counteracts the efforts of parents. One such visit will desolate the cultivated garden. "What a mean room is this!"—said a little girl I knew, after returning home from a gay party of children to which she was unaccustomed.

The Rev. B. Woodd—

Parental authority will be despised, if it be not grounded on affection. Affection, also, will be despised, if it be not supported by authority.

The passion of Fear may be used to give weight to the passion of Love.

If indulgence has slain its thousands, severity has slain its ten thousands.

The prevalent evils I have observed in children are—Self-will and Selfishness; Petty Tyranny; Falsehood; Indolence; Gluttony.

The Rev. G. Pattrick—

I contended once a whole night with a child when seven months old. And it has left a permanent effect to this day.

The Rev. W. J. Abdy—

I have proceeded on too lenient a plan with my children: and I condemn myself. I have been in the habit, for instance, of commiserating illness in them too much; this tends to spoil them. Being of tender spirits myself, my children have seen this. But being thus of a sympathising and tender spirit in myself, I should have preserved a sort of reserve.

My child can put on a look that makes me smile even when I am displeased, and I am obliged to say—"Though I smile, yet I'm angry."

For great effects of depravity, I always stand firm.

Much allowance must be made for the weakness of children's understanding.

The Rev. J. Goode—

Passion may be seen even at the breast: Obstinacy too. My child kept me once for two or three hours before its obstinacy would give way; but I conquered, and have had no trouble since.

Lying, Pride if born of rich parents, are soon seen in children.

A man must be both Priest and King in his family, and Prophet too!

The Rev. J. Venn—

The affection of its parent must be the prevailing idea with the child. ˙Severity itself then proceeds from affection. The insubordination of the present day arises from the mismanagement of children.

Rousseau gave the tone; and many followed and repented too late.*

---

* This must refer to Rousseau's work on Education, an author infamous for the talent of rendering everything apparently problematical.

"In this work," says Chalmers, in his 'Biographical Dictionary,' "with many remarks that may be useful, there are others so mischievous and impious, that whenever it produces an effect, it must be of the worst kind. It was not, however, his dogmas on education only, which excited the public hostility to this work, so much as his insolent declamation against all which the world had agreed to hold sacred, mixed with an

A clergyman of Colchester followed it : his two sons died of intemperance before eighteen years of age.

God intrusted children to parents, that their wisdom, strength, and authority may supply the lack of them in children.   But parents often unwillingly forward the vices of their children.

Much evil arises, as has been observed, from servants.   My children's tempers became altered from a change of their nurse-maid.

Guard against children *ridiculing* other children.   They will turn out pests if this be not discouraged.

We should consider children not so much as objects of pleasure, as subjects of improvement intrusted to us.   This view will give the character and tone to all that a parent does.

We should learn a child's besetting sin—such as malignity, pride, sensuality, &c. &c.

We cannot lay down *one* measure and rule for all children.

We should get a clear view of children's disposition and character : and implant in them conscientiousness.   They should be taught to view with horror any infringement on conscientiousness.   They have an early capacity of feeling this.

We should use, also, all methods of counteracting depravity.

A combination of Authority, Affection, and Instruction should be aimed at.

Give your children an impression of the *importance* of religion.

A chapter in my father's "Duty of Man" on teaching children is important.   Keep up *consistency.*

Above all, a nursery-maid is the Devil's instructor for *vanity,* &c. &c. &c.

The Rev. Mr Stillingfleet, a visitor for the evening—

A sort of reserve is proper in our management of children.   It is a dangerous thing for them to see the follies of their parents : for they ought to look up to their parents with reverence.   They should have the idea of their parent being a *good man,* and one with *authority.*

The opposition of one parent to the other is often an obstacle.

I was under a severe parent : but should have been worse, if under an indulgent one.   I think of the two extremes, the severe produces the least evil as to its effect on children..   Indulgence leads children to despise their parents : for they know they merit correction, and ought to receive it, although their faults are passed by.

Mr Bacon—

We may teach children more sideways, than directly.   We should conduct everything in ourselves with reference to our children.

affected admiration of the morals of the gospel, and the character of its Founder ; and it is remarkable that, in this last *condescension,* he so much displeased his former colleagues, Voltaire, D'Alembert, &c., that they joined the public voice, although from different and concealed motives.   In truth, they thought, like others, that there was too much of an insane inconsistency about Rousseau, and that no party could rank him among its supporters.   In the meantime, as soon as published, the French parliament condemned this book, and entered into a criminal prosecution against the author, which forced him to a precipitate retreat."

Much depends upon the tone in which the parent brings things forward.

My experience leans rather to authority than indulgence.

OCTOBER 1, 1798.

WHAT LESSONS MAY WE LEARN FROM THE DISPENSATIONS OF PROVIDENCE ?—Proposed by Rev. B. Woodd.

Mr Woodd—

We learn humility. Man is thus taught to *feel* his weakness. He sees God confound his schemes, and is taught to abandon his own will.

The Rev. J. Davies—

We must be cautious in forming conclusions on the dispensations of Providence.

Success in a *favourite* scheme is often a snare. Men are then tempted to think that God is with them. So ill-success may in like manner be misinterpreted. We often judge too hastily from events : *e. g.*, the barbarians concerning St Paul in Melita. We should therefore be cautious of forming *general* conclusions from *particular* events.

By the Divine dispensations, we learn—(1.) God's sovereignty ; and (2.) Man's ignorance, weakness, &c.

The Rev. H. Foster—

From the Divine dispensations may be learnt, that God is determined to point out his own glorious character, and to demonstrate this to all intelligent beings. We have but partial views of this while in this state. The only right view is in the Word of God.

We may be satisfied in giving up ourselves into his hands. We understand but little now ; but we see enough to be quiet. The time will come when he will astonish us with a display of his goodness. God's scheme is a *long* scheme. But we are impatient. A mechanic at work does not so. " Wait ! wait !"—that should be our frequent motto.

If appearances are such as to excite gratitude—be thankful ; if they confound you—wait. Study the histories of Joseph and Job.

In our schemes, let us *intend* to promote God's glory as honestly as we can. A man sometimes feels—I *will* have that object.

Let us look back on past feelings. It may be that I shall find that I have suffered before from what I now desire. I was then brought to God's footstool thereby. Such is the use of God's dispensations. Let us dread anything that may give conscience an occasion of lashing us.

The Rev. J. Goode—

The Psalmist, in the 107th Psalm, teaches us who they are that will be taught the lovingkindness of the Lord (v. 43), even they who mark his providential dealings. A man of wisdom will hear the name of the Lord, will learn his character, power, &c.

Providence is not to be our rule. The history of Jonah might teach us this.

When two lawful things are before us, Providence often decides for the humble learner.

Providence fulfils the Scriptures, and so confirms Scripture. We are constrained to say, *Verily there is a reward,—Verily, there is a God who judgeth the earth.*

An attentive observation of Providence tends to establish us in the good ways of God. So the Psalmist in the 73d Psalm.

A wise observer of Providence is rich in experience. *O my God, my soul is cast down within me, therefore will* I REMEMBER *thee from the land of Jordan.*

Mr Bacon—

In judging of the dealings of Providence towards myself, I have no confidence till I have brought my mind to a state of willingness to give up what God requires me.

The greatest part of God's plan is within the veil. We are like a man looking into a spacious apartment through the key-hole ; he sees in only one direction.

God can as easily raise up a man as an author can put his name down on paper.

There are preparatory providences, of which we can make nothing at the time. The calico-printer can make nothing of his pattern till the dye comes.

Contrast is a great thing in our being. *Dark* parts give the *brilliancy* and *effect.*

The great intention of the present system is to *exercise* us.

We are too curious in speculation. Dispensations are to bring us near to God. We should be like a child, ready to take our Father's hand.

A child understands not the *principle* of his education. This is an operation to be thought upon by and by.

The Rev. T. Scott—

This is a wide subject. Providence is a fulfilling of Scripture—not only of prophecy, but of everything in the heart, and our families, and the world in which we move, according to what God has said in Scripture.

The providential government of the world is God's history of his ways and of his creatures. The plan is laid not only for man now, but for eternal ages. In prophecy, a grand geographical outline of God's ways is given. Cities and towns and minute objects are not laid down, but the great outline only. Wait, and you will see nothing that is not there.

All creatures serve him, willingly or unwillingly.

He has work of various kinds to do in the world ; and he uses a Pharaoh, a Sennacherib, and an Alexander.

Some episodes in the grand drama may be already in part finished.

And fewer instances may now be given us whereby to judge of the grand concern.   The most important of all advice is—WAIT!

His dispensations to our country shew us, that he designs not to *please* but to *use* us.   His dispensations to Christians shew us, that he puts less estimation on outward things than we do.

An observant Christian will see in God's dispensations a witness of the truth of God's promises.   He always steps in just at the crisis.   I could illustrate this in many ways in my own experience.   I never prayed for money but I got it.   *Verily there is a God who heareth prayer.*

One object is to subdue the propensities of our nature ; to bring out what is in our heart.   For instance, in the case I have mentioned, difficulties in money matters shewed me the tendency of the heart to covetousness.   But it also taught me to sympathise with others.

Temptations follow not only tempers but providences.

The Rev. J. Newton—

If we be sincere in intention, we cannot make a mistake of any great importance.   If a fever or a fall prevent a journey, we must not call it a *disappointment*, but a *leading*.

God deals not by angels, but by providences.

When we *mean* well, but are not following God's will, he will hedge up our way.   If we be in God's way, mountains sink into plains.

Some things which we call providences, are trials of our faith and singleness of eye for God's glory.   Thus when a large and valuable living is offered to a minister already usefully employed in an active sphere, it may be, not a providential leading, but a trial of his constancy.   Moses was not useful to the Israelites till he renounced all the honours of the Egyptian court.

Great events often spring from small causes.   There is no proportion between causes and their issue.   The sleepless night of Ahasuerus was the preservation of the Jews.

God sometimes changes his hand.   An angel is sent to tell Joseph to go into Egypt.   Why was not this means used to call him at first to Bethlehem ?   All the world is to be disturbed to bring this about.

The right hand of God is his *leading* hand ; and the left, that of *permission*.

I would bring this subject down to all the common incidents of life.   A knock at a door, or a turning a corner, may be events which lead to important consequences.   There is no such thing as accident.

OCTOBER 15, 1798.

WHAT ARE WE TO UNDERSTAND BY DOCTRINAL, EXPERIMENTAL, AND PRACTICAL PREACHING ?—Proposed by the Rev. J. Clayton.

Mr Clayton—

A preacher of Doctrine is one who gives the preference to doctrine over experience or practice.   His followers become dealers in notions, are fastidious and disputatious.

A preacher of Experience is not one who preaches in consequence of extensive observation, but who dwells much on vicissitudes and frames of mind. His flock is in danger of disregarding doctrine and practice : and of resting too much in frames.

A preacher of Practice dwells much on the practical part of religion as it respects man, rather than God. If his preaching is with energy, it will have a certain effect. His followers are in danger of becoming Pharisaical, of being pleased with themselves, and being severe against immoralities, and that in a bitter spirit : they will perhaps make light of Jesus Christ and the gospel of the grace of God.

The faithful preacher may bear harder on one string than another : but he has respect to all.

Bradbury says, religion is Doctrinal in the Bible ; Experimental in the heart ; and Practical in the life.

All this must enter into preaching, though a minister may have more to do with one than another.

The Rev. J. Davies—

The Doctrinal preacher is one who defends the outworks of Christianity ; the Experimental preacher confines himself to temptations, trials, &c. ; while the Practical is a mere moral preacher. The Experimental is preferable, if one is to be preferred.

Doctrinal preaching will only carry light to the understanding, and *may* promote hypocrisy and spiritual pride. Practical may lead men to rest on moral duties. Experimental has this evil, that it is addressed to one particular sort of people only, and is little calculated to convince the unconverted.

Faults of ministers lie in this, that though not *exclusively* inclined to one mode, yet they are so too *prevalently*.

The Rev. Mr Storry, a visitor—

Milner taught me to pray the Spirit to direct doctrine to experimental and practical ends. And this he said in reference to two errors :—(1.) Making too *much* of feelings ;—(2.) Making too *little* of them. He himself was a mighty man for the *energy* of things. He combined an exhibition of the Fall and of Justification, with a delineation of the spiritual application of this to the heart and in the life.

The Rev. W. J. Abdy—

The end of God is to restore the image of God in man. This is to be effected only by means of Truth. The foundation is laid in the great essential Doctrines of the Gospel—such as respect the work and offices of Jesus Christ. The foundation of these is in the nature of God and man. With this, Experience will be necessarily connected.

Doctrine is meant not merely to make us wise ; but to direct man to union with Jesus. Till he apprehends this, he will meet with doubts, &c.

Peculiar circumstances may require a minister to cleave to one mode for a time rather than another.

The Rev. H. Foster—

Owen says, there is a Jewish saying, "Every doctrine has its meat in its mouth." There is no doctrine of the Gospel but is fitted, if rightly stated, to have its weighty effect on the soul. If stated within the limits of Scripture, it is suited to fill the imagination, to answer the reason, to satisfy the conscience, to win the will.

I would state the Doctrine, and as I go along, point out its use to the heart. If a minister states the Doctrine and applies it to practice, he will benefit many. If he states the Doctrine and only applies it to the mind within, he may have many hearers bad-tempered, &c., in spite of his doctrine. We should lead them to the practical business of life, —into their shops, &c.

We are often defective in not stating Doctrine. People are lamentably ignorant even after hearing for twenty years.

There is a sort of preaching that is neither Doctrinal, nor Experimental, nor Practical. A preacher of *wonderful* things is such a one.

A considerable part of a minister's wisdom lies in portioning out things as God has done it.

The Rev. J. Goode—

In the members of our flock, there would be Sight, Feeling, and Obedience ; and to produce these, all three—Doctrinal, Experimental, and Practical Preaching—must be combined in their proper proportion.

Mr Bacon—

These three things play beautifully upon each other. Doctrine gives the momentum. Experience embodies, shews, exhibits the Doctrine. Practice tries, attests, &c.

Butler says, if Doctrines influence not, they render the mind harder.

Doctrine addresses the head ; Experience the heart ; and Practice the life.

Man is a creature of Intelligence, and therefore Doctrine is necessary ; of Sympathy, and therefore Experience draws him ; and this leads to Practice.

The Rev. J. Newton—

Doctrine is the trunk, Experience the branches, Practice the fruit.

These things I will that thou affirm constantly, that they which have believed in God might be careful to maintain good works.

The Doctrine of the Cross teaches the Evil of Sin—the worth of the soul, &c. &c.

Man must *taste* and experience before he can *exhibit :* and there must be something to be *seen* as well as *tasted.*

Tillotson on " Speak evil of no man," says, that people will object that there is nothing of Christ in his sermon. His answer is, there is nothing of Christ in the text. So he says little more than Seneca would have said.*

* The passage here alluded to is as follows. It occurs towards the close of a long practical discourse by Archbishop Tillotson on *To speak evil of no man :*—
" All that now remains is to reflect upon what hath been said, and to urge you and myself to do accordingly. For all is nothing, if we do not practise what we so plainly see

The Rev. T. Scott—

There is a *false* Doctrinal, Experimental, and also Practical preaching.
1st. Are the Doctrines scripturally stated, explained, and enforced?
Half only of the truth is a lie. The man who preaches justification
without shewing what a living and what a dead faith is, does not preach
the truth.

2d. A sort of prescription seems to have sprung up in the present
day for Experience. Things are said to be true, because they are according to experience. But *false* Experience may be preached. There
may be enthusiasm in visions, impressions, &c. This is not truth
making its way.

3d. There may be mere moral Practice, and not evangelical Practice.
There is a defect when any one—Doctrinal, Experimental, or Practical—preponderates ; unless occasions call not for it.

I would allow for different talents ; yet no minister should willingly
go on declaring part only of his message.

There is in Ministers sometimes a sort of spiritual self-indulgence.
A man, therefore, fond of the rod should take cordials : and a man fond
of cordials, should take the rod occasionally.

Too much lies on Ministers in this day. There were Catechists in
the ancient Church.

Doctrines must be repeatedly brought before the minds of the people.
If not, people will never understand what you are about. If we unite
not all three together, we may have a root, a stem, and a bunch of
grapes *tied* together at the top, but not *growing*.

Experience is truth under the Spirit's operation producing its effects
on the passions of the heart.

Practice goes into the detail of duties.

OCTOBER 29, 1798.

WHAT IS THE MORALITY AND USE OF DREAMS ?—Proposed by the Rev.
J Goode.

Mr Goode—

> " My waking dreams are best conceal'd ;
> For little good, much ill they yield."

Boston says, the Law extends to the imagination, and to dreams
which are bred there. He asks, What is to be thought of men's
dreams which break God's law? He replies, no doubt they are sinful,

---

to be our duty. Many are so taken up with the deep points and mysteries of religion,
that they never think of the common duties and offices of human life. But faith and a
good life are so far from clashing with one another, that the Christian religion hath made
them inseparable. True faith is necessary in order to a good life, and a good life is the
genuine product of a right belief ; and therefore the one never ought to be pressed to the
prejudice of the other.

" I foresee what will be said, because I have heard it so often said in the like case—that
there is not one word of Jesus Christ in all this. No more is there in the text. And
yet I hope that Jesus Christ is truly preached, whenever his will and laws, and the duties
enjoined by the Christian religion, are inculcated upon us."

and requiring pardon. These motions follow on what have been our waking cares. See his *Body of Divinity*.

Baxter says, that dreams are sinful as connected with *causes*. The antecedent causes are any sinful act which distempers the body, or any sin which inclines the fancy and mind to evil dreams, or the omission of what was necessary to prevent them. The causes which afterwards make them objectively sinful, are the ill uses which men make of them ; as when they take their dreams to be Divine Revelations, or trust to them, or are affrighted by them as ominous, or as prophetical ; and make them the ground of their actions, and seduce themselves by the phantasms of their own brains.

He gives the following directions regarding dreams :—
1. Avoid fulness of food. 2. Avoid sinful habits of mind. 3. Let not the thoughts run on evil during the day. 4. Commend yourselves to God by prayer before you take your rest. 5. Let your last thoughts be holy and quieting. 6. On tracing any evil in your dreams, make it an occasion of renewing your repentance. 7. Lay no undue stress on dreams.*

The Rev. G. Pattrick—

Think not to learn truth from dreams. Yet if what is brought to mind is consonant to God's word, despise it not.

The morality of dreams is to be ascertained from the habits of the waking man. The sin and pollution of unholy dreams are chargeable on the conscience. God may direct the dreams of a fine mind to its benefit.

The Rev. W. J. Abdy—

Melancholy people should be cautious not to make themselves more accountable for dreams than they ought.

Often the events of a night are the subject of humiliation in the morning : sometimes, though I went to sleep with comfort, I have yet waked in a disordered state. The great Enemy gets access to the soul.

The Rev. J. Davies—

My experience of dreams is *contrary* to my waking thoughts.

The Rev. H. Foster—

I am a Baxterian so far as I have heard of Richard Baxter's sentiments.

---

* We make the following quotation from Baxter's excellent remarks upon this subject : —" Direct. 5. *Let your last thoughts still before your sleep be holy, and yet quieting and consolatory thoughts.* The dreams are apt to follow our *last thoughts*. If you betake yourselves to sleep with worldliness or vanity in your minds, you cannot expect to be wiser or better when you are asleep than when you are awake. But if you shut up your day's thoughts with God, and sleep find them upon any holy subject, it is like to use them as it finds them. Yet if it be distrustful, unbelieving, fearful thoughts which you condole with, your dreams may savour of the same distemper. Frightful and often sinful dreams do often follow sinful doubts and fears. But if you sweeten your *last thoughts* with the *love of Christ*, and the remembrance of your former mercies, or the foresight of eternal joys, or can confidently cast yourselves upon some promise, it will tend to the quietness of your sleep, and to the savouriness of your dreams. And if you should die before morning will it not be most desirable that your last thoughts be holy ? "—See R. Baxter's *Directions Against Sinful Dreams*. Works, folio, vol. i. p. 323.

D

There are some intimations under the old Law concerning dreams.

A distinction there certainly is between waking sin and sleeping sin. Shame attaches to the soul in the morning after sinful dreams. I bring it to the blood of atonement.

I have felt that dreams are the result of indulgence of sin. I ought to have been knocked down. "What are you about now?" I've said. When I have found it a dream, I have been happy. Have you done such things against the character of the Gospel!

My happiness that it was a dream has been greater on such an occasion than any word of consolation could make it.

The Rev. R. Cecil—

Andrew Baxter refers dreams to separate spirits.* This is ingenious, but his theory left no conviction on my mind. Though dreams follow after a multitude of business, and therefore have a cause, yet they are sometimes supernatural. If important events follow a dream, then we may regard it as one of the links in the chain of Providence. I think that dreams are not philosophically or fairly to be referred to accident. To mention one. When I lost my health at Lewis, I went to B. for six months. I engaged one of the soldiers to take care of my horse. One night I waked at twelve o'clock, and said to my servant, "I have had a strange dream. I have seen my horse cut to pieces in so lively a manner that certain I am there is something in it." The reply was, "Sir, your horse is in the stable." "Well, I'll go and see." No horse was there. I went afterwards, and found him covered with sea-sand. He had been taken out by a smuggler who knew I was ill, and the horse had found its way back!—How can this be referred to accident?

I believe dreams are one of God's witnesses in the world. *He hath not left Himself without witness.* Not a witness like His *word*, indeed; but still a witness to His being and providence. They are in some sense a witness among the heathen to keep alive a sense of the immaterial principle. A sort of half-way house to the other world: a porch to the spiritual world.

It is unquestionable that God often encourages a man by dreams. I began to preach in a small place under great discouragements. I dreamt at that time that I saw a large magnificent church rise out of

---

* Andrew Baxter was an ingenious metaphysician and natural philosopher, born in 1686-7, at Old Aberdeen, in Scotland; and no relation of Richard Baxter, the eminent non-conformist divine who was born in 1615, in Shropshire. Andrew Baxter published a work entitled, *An Inquiry into the Nature of the Human Soul, wherein its Immateriality is evinced from the Principles of Reason and Philosophy.* In the second volume of this work is inserted a very copious Essay on the Phenomenon of Dreaming, and what he has advanced on this subject excited much attention at the time of its first publication. He endeavoured to prove, that the scenes presented to the soul in sleep, in which there is so much variety, action, and life, nay oftentimes speech and reason, cannot be the effect of mechanism, or any cause working mechanically. And further, that the φαντάσμα, or what is properly called the vision, is not the work of the soul itself. His conclusion was, that "our dreams are prompted by separate immaterial beings:" that there are living beings existing separate from matter; that they act in that state; and that they act upon the matter of our bodies, and prompt our sleeping visions. Some observations upon this subject, and several objections to Mr Baxter's hypothesis, may be found in Mr David Fordyce's "Dialogues concerning Education," vol. ii. p. 223-257.—See Chalmers's *Biographical Dictionary.*

the ground. I took courage. I was confident of success. And I was not disappointed.

I am persuaded also that dreams are *monitory*. I remember before my conversion, and when a wicked profligate, that I dreamt I was in hell! It gave my conscience a shake. I could not for some time sin with ease.*

Much more do dreams appear to me as intended to suffer man to act out his part, while he is saved from the consequences at the time, that he may learn the folly of his own heart, and God's restraining providence. " Come, you shall go and act the villain, *and see* what misery it ends in."

Dreaming is like thinking or acting. Dreams run in his own channel. We are creatures of habit. The habit will prevail. It's a man's scourge. Man will act his part in dreaming, as in waking. If he be a good man, Satan will worry him. This is one of his modes of temptation. If he can present a seducing image, he will. Yet we must not lean too much towards the superstitious side. Mr Wesley's people do this. Dreams can afford no implicit ground of comfort and guidance.

There is no doubt that a man's peculiar occupation has much to do with dreams. I think I could dream any given night on any given subject. Such and such dreams, I find, generally follow such and such conduct. I've a class of dreams which follow a particular habit. I'm in a burying-ground—or I see a body half consumed—or I see the hedge of the churchyard cut into the form of a dragon, &c. I've

---

* Mr Cecil, as may be seen in his Memoir, was one of those remarkable characters, of which every age of the Church has furnished its examples, in which the early instructions and persevering prayers of a pious mother have been ultimately rewarded by the marvellous rescue of a son from the toils of scepticism and profligacy, and his entire conversion to God. The following extract from his Memoir will interest our readers :—

" While Mr C. was proceeding in such a course of evil, it pleased God by his Spirit to rouse his mind to reflections, which gave a turn to his future life.

" Lying one night in bed, he was contemplating the case of his mother. ' I see,' said he, within himself, ' two unquestionable facts. First, my mother is greatly afflicted in circumstances, body, and mind ; and yet I see that she cheerfully bears up under all, by the support she derives from constantly retiring to her closet and her Bible. Secondly, that she has a secret spring of comfort of which I know nothing ; while I, who give an unbounded loose to my appetites, and seek pleasure by every means, seldom or never find it. If, however, there is any such secret in religion, why may not I attain it as well as my mother ? I will immediately seek it of God.' He instantly rose in his bed and began to pray. But he was soon damped in his attempt, by recollecting that much of his mother's comfort seemed to arise from her faith in Christ. ' Now,' thought he, ' this Christ have I ridiculed : He stands much in my way, and can form no part of my prayers.' In utter confusion of mind, therefore, he lay down again. Next day, however, he continued to pray to the Supreme Being : he began to consult books, and to attend preachers : his difficulties were gradually removed, and his objections answered ; and his course of life began to amend. He now listened to the pious admonitions of his mother, which he had before affected to receive with pride and scorn ; yet they had fixed themselves in his heart, like a barbed arrow : and, though the effects were at the time concealed from her observation, yet tears would fall from his eyes as he passed along the streets from the impression she had left on his mind. Now, he would discourse with her and hear her without outrage ; which led her to hope, that a gracious principle was forming in his heart, and more especially as he then attended the preaching of the Word. Thus he made some progress ; but felt no small difficulty in separating from his favourite connexions. Light, however, broke into his mind, till he gradually discovered that Jesus Christ, so far from ' standing ' in his way, was *the* only *Way, the Truth, and the Life,* to all *that come unto God by Him.*"

dreamt these dreams a hundred times; but have always said in the morning—" You drank porter for supper."

The Rev. J. Venn—

Laudanum will uniformly give dreams—this is another illustration of what you say.

But some people torment themselves more about dreams than about waking sins. [Allusions are here made by way, we suppose, of illustration to " Sir John Shore," and " Doddridge," and " Vansittart," and " My mother seeing the body of Christ," which we cannot decipher.]

Consider dreams as in the class of all other occurrences. God or Satan may use them. But forsake not the written Word for them.

The Rev. T. Scott—

I have been plagued with dreams about a torn prayer-book: the congregation waiting a long time for me. This dream I should not have had, if I had not been a preacher. The greyhound pursues the hare in his dream.

The devil will never be wanting if he can get access. Dreams often prepare the mind for sin. The devil will not put the man on gross dreams, but will lead him to an unlawful use of lawful things.

But the *new man* sometimes dreams. I have preached on a text which I got in a dream.

1. Let not dreams interfere with Scripture.

2. Make them no rule of duty.

The Rev. Josiah Pratt—

The morality of dreams depends on this. Do any circumstances in my constitution determine them ? *All* persons dream. There are rare instances of not dreaming; and they are but equivocal. Yet all are not equally liable to dream. The same person dreams more or less at different times. Therefore circumstances give rise to dreaming.

Man's imagination is freakish and wanton in dreaming : yet its freaks bear some relation to the character and habits while waking. The lover, the miser, the merchant, all have their dreams.

The Rev. J. Clayton—

Dreams are not to be despised. There is much in Scripture about them. God avails Himself of every avenue. His Word and providence work on each other. Though dreams bring no new Revelation, yet they may *enforce* Revelation.

The persons who dream are to be taken into consideration. Some persons' dreams are always sober. I have repeatedly heard a minister preach sermons in my dreams. My professional dreams are superior to all my waking feelings.

The Rev. J. Newton—

If there were only one person who had ever dreamed, none would believe him—so wonderful is it ! If a man dreams only once, he would think that night the most surprising in his life.

Dreams depend much on the state of the nerves. The imagination is like a harpsicord—open when asleep.

Dreams are monitory. Such are Henry IV.'s dream in Sully's Memoirs ; and Lord Lyttelton's dream.

On the next occasion, the 12th November 1798, the member, whose Note-book we are so fortunate as to possess, was absent.

On the 26th November, a subject was proposed connected with the times. The joyful tidings of the Victory of the Nile had just filled every heart with gladness through the whole extent of our beloved country : and the 29th November 1798 was appointed as a day of general thanksgiving for the success obtained on that occasion over the French fleet, and for " other recent interpositions of God's good providence in our behalf."

It is well known, that soon after the commencement of the bloody contests which had wasted Europe, and destroyed many millions of her inhabitants, Great Britain was specially marked out as the victim of that power whom God was employing as his scourge among the nations. British prosperity was envied ; our wealth, commerce, and naval prowess were coveted ; and bitter resentment for supposed injuries was avowed. Yet, while the nations of Europe, with but few exceptions, witnessed and experienced, in a most tremendous manner, the horrors and miseries of war, England, during a course of years, had peace in her borders.

"Doubtless our excessive affluence," said the Rev. Thomas Scott, in preaching upon the occasion, in language which might have been used in the present day with astonishing and unexpected exactness, " the fuel and incentive of as excessive pride and luxury, has been diminished ; and many hardships have been felt by numbers, who are entitled to our sympathy and assistance. But our cities have not been reduced to ruinous heaps by dreadful sieges ; we have not seen our streets flowing with human blood, or strewed with mangled bodies ; nor have we heard the piercing groans of the wounded and dying, nor the more durable lamentations of their distressed survivors. We are most of us happily unable to form a conception of the terrors and miseries incident to the seat of war ; or of the scenes which are witnessed when an insulting victorious army prescribes scarcely any bounds to rapine, cruelty, and brutal lust. Nor have desolated fields, and the smoking ruins of towns and villages, pained our eyes, when we have had occasion to journey through the country."

The Eclectic Meeting fell three days before this commemoration. The subject which had been selected for this meeting is the more interesting, because some persons of scrupulous minds, who justly feel that war in every aspect is to be looked upon with feelings of horror, demur as to the propriety of offering up thanksgivings to the Almighty for events, however successful in a military and political point of view, which have been the occasion of hurling thousands, perhaps, of immortal souls into an awful eternity, ill-prepared to meet their GOD. In this light, doubtless, thanksgivings would not only be ill-advised, but would betray a spirit of malignant exultation and cruelty which no one would dream of imputing. But larger minds view the matter in a more comprehensive light, as we shall see.

NOVEMBER 26, 1798.

WHAT IS THE BEST WAY OF IMPROVING THE NEXT THANKSGIVING DAY? —Proposed by the Rev. J. Venn.

Mr Venn—

1. What are the particular mercies for which we are to thank God?

How far should we go into the detail? Our opinions and passions often interfere in deciding on these questions. Some think that a mercy, which others regard as a curse.

2. What kind of direction should we, as ministers, endeavour to give to the National Joy?

3. What is principally to be avoided in our Sermons on the occasion?

On these topics I should like to know the mind of my brethren.

The Rev. H. Foster—

View God's interposition in behalf of CHRISTIANITY. God interposed both in Nelson's victory, and in the spirit given to Nelson.*

Yet our present state calls for Humiliation.

The Rev. R. Cecil—

Feelings of sorrow filled my mind after the Fast-day [March 6,

---

* This doubtless has reference to the distinct acknowledgment of the Divine interposition with which Nelson's despatches opened. The Rev. Thomas Scott, in his sermon on the occasion, has the following passage:—

" I cannot on this occasion conceal the satisfaction I felt in comparing the letter of our British admiral with the despatches from the French general in Egypt, which arrived about the same time. 'It hath pleased Almighty God to give a great victory to his Majesty's fleet,' says the victorious Nelson, whose courage and conduct have excited universal admiration ; thus rationally ascribing the glory to the Lord of hosts himself. On the other hand, the French commander states, that *(in waging war against superstition)* he and his soldiers unite in the celebration of *Mohammedan festivals:* he throws the blame of the defeat of the French fleet on the *destinies;* yet, speaking of *Fortune* as a real person, he makes her *his deity,* and says, she favoured him as long as she was necessary ! So long as God is thus openly acknowledged by us, and despised or defied by our enemies, we may hope that ' He will withdraw his hand, and work for his name's sake, that it should not be polluted in the sight of the heathen.'"

Also Mr Wilberforce, in writing to his friend, Mr Hey of Leeds, thus alludes to the same feature in Nelson's despatch :—

" I am scribbling amidst interruption, and must conclude ; yet not without one word of humble acknowledgment of the goodness of God in our late naval successes. I think Lord Nelson's letter has produced a disposition to speak more of Providence. May it have the effect of helping to awaken to recollection a people loaded with blessings ! "

1796 ?] that any had particularised at all. We must take higher ground, as men of God. *Let the potsherd strive with the potsherds of the earth* in the detail. Isa. xlv. 9.

I like not DETAILS at all. On general principles, we meet ALL. You remember the man who gave three *reasons* for not going to the play ; the last woefully undid the effect the other two produced—" I had no money !" Such is the advantage of detail !

In these public questions, there are the following objections in our way :—I KNOW NOT the details. I know not particular facts and consequences. We *ought not* to be politicians. He who can talk well on his own subject, feels how incompetent others are to do so who have not the same information. It is, moreover, safer : for you may set people to dispute with you.

There is enough for me of General Features. Can any man dispute the wickedness of this country under its peculiar privileges ? Can we dispute the leaning to the net and the drag, to the horse and the chariot ? Hab. i. 16 ; Ps. xxxiii. 17.

We may well be shocked at the language sometimes vauntingly used in reference to our foes—" We will sweep them from the earth !"

In His dealings with us, we hear the strong voice of God, as to Ephraim of old, How *shall I give thee up? &c.* He seems to say—"This kingdom shall not be given up." "It shan't smoke with vengeance just now."

Mind you talk not out of people's depth. Rousseau's remark is apt to mislead. "Strong minds require a strong way of speaking ; but the vulgar know not the grammar of the language."

People of *all classes* can see when the minister is *not* a man of the world : when his intention, aim, and sentiments are *higher :* when his object is to bring them to a victory over sin. Not that he can't feel with his countrymen, and join in the common joy ; but still the great victory at heart is the victory of the Cross. He would not damp the people's joy ; but he would make it a step to something better. A minister is in character in this—a gentleman allowed.

Shall we talk of *prayer,* and not of the *answer ?* People of God are too often like the ostrich, who lays her eggs and watches them not.

But let us avoid party spirit, invective, or vain confidence on account of Victory. Speak of the French as the rod in God's hand, but let us not indulge in terms of bitterness.

Let us beware of leaving men without settling the GREAT AFFAIR. Every public occasion is a sort of lever to manage men with. We say the same thing again and again in our ordinary preaching, till no hold is obtained. "Now he is going to preach about the Law," people say ; "now about the Gospel :" and so the routine goes round. But sometimes a door is *forced* open—and that by a remarkable event. An assault is made upon Ear-gate.

Mr Bacon—

God has of late been making a peculiar address, by his Providential Dealings with us as a Nation, to the Stupid, the Self-confident, the Covetous, those poisoned with Infidelity, the Sensual, the Conceited, the Despisers of Authority, those who are Proud of Distinction, the Discontented, the Delicate also, and the Desponding.

The Rev. Thomas Scott—

Ministers should take hold of the occasion.   Sailors use, as they can, every wind.

It is dangerous to enter into detail—

> . . . . *Incedis per ignes*
> *Suppositos cineri doloso.*

Beddoes was thought a bad physician because he was a bad politician. So let us avoid endangering our credit as Ministers, by abstaining from committing ourselves to details in matters which don't concern us.

The grand improvement of the Thanksgiving Day should be the encouragement of the people in respect of prayer.

Preach to people of their *own* duties.   We may set before ourselves Gilpin, telling the Court its duty, as an example of boldness and faithfulness worthy of imitation.*

The Rev. Charles Simeon, a visitor on this occasion—

Detail should be entered into so far as is necessary to point out GOD specially and particularly.   HEREBY *ye shall know that the living God is among you,* said Joshua.   Josh. iii. 10, 11.

Let a minister take heed to his own spirit in this matter, and he will guide his people aright.

The Rev. J. Clayton—

Generalise not away the mercies by dwelling too little on details. If you do so, you'll leave nothing for your people to look at.

The Rev. J. Davies—

We might improve these occasions more to *individuals.*

We should not enter into details as *politicians,* but as *ministers.*

————

The next meeting was held Dec. 10th, for which the following interesting subject had been proposed by the Rev. H. Foster :— WHAT EVIDENCE HAVE WE FROM FACT OF THE INTERCOURSE OF THE INVISIBLE WORLD WITH OUR SYSTEM ?   But no discussion appears to have taken place.   The cause of this we think we can trace in the sudden and unexpected illness of one of the Society's members,

---

* Bernard Gilpin, an eminent English divine, and, for his excellent character and usefulness, called the " Apostle of the North."   He was born in 1517, and was descended from a good family in Westmoreland.   Chalmers, in his *Biographical Dictionary,* writes as follows :—

" He was appointed to preach before the king, who was at Greenwich, which appears then to have been a custom before being presented to any benefice.   On this occasion, with the true spirit of a reformer, he inveighed against the luxurious and corrupt manners of the times among all ranks, and although the king was not then present, delivered what he intended as an address to his majesty, not doubting, as he said, but that it would be carried to him.   This courage recommended him to the notice of many persons of the first rank ; particularly to Sir Francis Russel, and Sir Robert Dudley, afterwards Earls of Bedford and Leicester, who from that time professed a great regard for him ; and, when in power, were always ready to patronise him."

only the day before the meeting. The following is an extract from the memoir of the Rev. Richard Cecil :—

Mr Cecil had for many years suffered greatly from a complaint, supposed to be a sciatica. On being seized by a more violent and acute attack, a consultation of the faculty was held on his disorder on Friday, December 7, 1790 ; the result of which was, that he was prohibited from preaching any more while the existing symptoms continued.   A scirrhus in the cæcum was apprehended, and his condition was thought dangerous. The following Sunday [the day before the Eclectic meeting] a most affecting seen took place at St John's. He had been announced on the preceding Sunday to preach a sermon in the morning of this day (Dec. 9) for the children of the Sunday school attending the chapel, and another in the evening to their parents. Notwithstanding his prohibition by his medical friends, he determined to make an attempt to address the people once more. Many circumstances conspired to render the scene affecting. A friend remarked, that a side-view which he caught of his face, before he uttered a word, chilled him to the heart—sunk, worn, and dejected ! *The strong was,* indeed, *become as tow,* and *the mighty fallen !* His text added to the solemnity of the scene :—*He which testifieth these things saith, Surely I come quickly. Amen! Even so, come, Lord Jesus !*

He told his congregation that he was preaching contrary to the advice of his physicians, and that he should not be able to meet them in the evening. He had not preached more than five minutes, before it was visible that he was in extreme pain, and his feeble tone of voice proved that he was worn down. He could not continue his discourse more than twenty minutes, and then dismissed the congregation—not with the usual benediction, but in the last words of the Bible immediately following his text. The presentiment of many that this sermon would close his ministry, gathered strength from his having chosen the concluding subject of the Scriptures, and ending his discourse with the benediction following. After this period, it pleased God, whose *ways are not our ways, nor his thoughts our thoughts,* to add twelve years to his life.

The following notes, taken down during the first days of his serious illness, seem to carry us again into the midst of the Eclectic itself—adjourned, however, from St John's vestry into the sick chamber. We introduce them as a pleasing though incidental indication of the brotherly love which subsisted among the members of the Society, and of the happy influence it must have had upon their meetings :—

Dec. 10.—To the Rev. Mr Newton, who was dropping him a seasonable word of consolation, he replied, " It is consistent neither with reason nor religion, to oppose sufferings to the love of God ; for *whom the Lord loveth, he chasteneth, and scourgeth every son whom he receiveth.*" In the evening of the same day, to another friend (the Rev. Mr Venn) he said, " I am not afraid to die ; but I am afraid of being worn out by pain. Nature shrinks at this prospect."

Wednesday, 12th.—To the Rev. Mr Pratt he said, "My illness gives me stronger hold of two points—1st, God must be brought near, to be lived on and fled to ; 2d, Comfort, to be sensible to my heart, must spring from God's making himself sensible to me.   There must be an incarnation.   I must, by faith, lay hold of my God—as he became man !"

The first question in the new year, and discussed January 7, 1799, was so important, that we regret that we have no record of the remarks made upon it.   The question was—Is RELIGION ON THE ADVANCE OR DECLINE IN THIS COUNTRY ? and was proposed by the Rev. H. Foster.

The next was proposed by John Bacon, Esq., R.A., the eminent sculptor ; and his opening remarks are the more interesting— considering the subject he selected—as coming from a layman.

JANUARY 21, 1799.

WHAT CIRCUMSTANCES HAVE DETERMINED THE POPULARITY AND UNPOPULARITY OF DIFFERENT PREACHERS, AND WHAT INSTRUCTION MAY BE DERIVED FROM THE CONSIDERATION OF THE SUBJECT ?

Mr Bacon—

Popularity is a means of usefulness.   Yet a minister is not always useful in proportion to his popularity.

The popularity of some depends on the easy and free gospel they preach.

Yet in all who attain to popularity there must be cleverness in some degree.   But the popular is often inferior in weight and influence to some who do not attain to that distinction ; yet these men are imitable in the particular point which renders them popular.   This is generally on the surface ; though it may be *connected* with a deep thing.   In that case, the popularity may be more permanent.   A diamond is of little value till polished.   One picture in the exhibition strikes us more strongly the first time of looking at it.   After many days, another produces the strongest effect.

Mr Bacon then enumerated some of the chief preachers of the day, both in and out of the Church, and noticed what were, in his opinion, their chief characteristics.

Whitfield was remarkable for feeling, susceptibility, force.

Romaine for realising faith ; he had one subject, indeed, but this was the panacea : there was some variety.

Berridge gained in some degree from the place in which he preached ; he was always in populous places : simplicity was his one object.

Rowland Hill is irregular, extravagant, bawling, &c., yet something extraordinary : upright, devoted ; comes out—fire, brilliance, genius ; talks rather than preaches ; strong comparisons, but they interest ; stories.

Jay has great natural powers : memory.

Brewer possessed moderate talents, but pathos ; was fervent, affectionate, savoury ; no peculiar tone to obstruct, and rather aided his manner. Encouragement to diligence was one of his frequent topics. Perhaps, compared with the drawling manner of some other Dissenters, he may be classed as above the average.

Medley :—had some party in his spirit : glib : jocular.

Huntington :—had promptitude : was easy : pleasant : fanciful : like a harlequin.

Cadogan :—had no variety, tone, or dash ; but perception of subject : determination : sawing through : energy : reality : he took by force ; the one object he kept in view.

Gunn :—without extraordinary talents, but gives direction and application to the truth : no tone or twang: addresses this and the other : *evidently* a good man : his preaching is not treating the *subject*, so much as dealing in address : deals in general truths.

Venn of Huddersfield :—some tone, but remarkably fiery : current : realising : heavenly : rapturous: holy: quickening.

Wesley :—good sense : promptitude : clear: treats all circumstances as belonging to a system : not that in his ministry which would independently have been popular.

Robinson of Cambridge :—had ease: comprehension : no turns, or twists, but new views of things, &c.

Fordyce :—an orator, but it looked not like the real thing: gilded —but it wore off!

Dodd : Harrison : Hodgson, &c. :—pleasing: inviting.

The Rev. Thomas Scott—

Non omnia possumus omnes. A quack doctor defined ague as a thing he could cure and others not. So might many popular preachers say.

Declaring the whole counsel of God renders a man unpopular. A faithful man may be popular, but only by circumstances. Some of these popular men had only a partial popularity.

There are three reasons of a man's unpopularity.

1. He is himself Culpable :—

When he is grown dry, languid, uninteresting ; there is something wrong in the heart. When he gets angry, disputatious, hard, and scolding. When there is a want of usefulness, of a spirit of prayer, of wrestling with God. When pride and ambition creep into the heart. When a minister's tone and manner might be corrected, but he won't listen.

2. It is his Cross.

He may have an awkward figure. Wilberforce says scarcely any thin man commands attention in the House of Commons. He may have a bad voice, an uncouth manner. Though he has natural talents, yet perhaps not genius, brilliancy, fire, &c. An ass cannot imitate a lap-dog, but must be content to carry panniers. Circumstances may be such as not to allow a man fair play.

3. It is his Honour.

When he offends by delivering his whole message. If he uses the fan, he lessens the heap. The minister should dread one of his flock saying to him, in the last day, " You told me such things were sufficient, and now I find you deceived me." "I lived in covetousness, but you followed me not home therein."

I have always fanned some away by relative duties.

The Grecian harp pleases simple ears, but not a complicated harmony.

The Rev. J. Newton—

Painters and Poets borrow from all subjects.

The model of a minister is *qualem nequeo monstrare et sentio tantum.*

The things which make ministers popular are of very various kind :— (1.) A deep experimental acquaintance with religion. (2.) An earnest love for souls. (3.) A great fund of general knowledge. (4.) A lively fancy. (5.) A pleasing elocution. (6.) A handsome figure, &c. But the gifts of the Spirit he distributes as it pleases him.

But a popular preacher needs not all the above qualifications. Whitfield led a bad fashion. He taught to laugh, and then to cry. Others laughed, but could not do the rest.

The popularity of many arises from the extreme ignorance and absurdity of their hearers.

"Have I said anything foolish ?" was Phocion's remark when applauded.

There can be no popularity without simplicity.

But what is desirable popularity ? *The Lord hath given me the tongue of the learned.* This is obtained in the school of the Cross. Taste, and fellow-feeling, and sympathy, with the cases of his congregation, are here acquired. *Haud ignara ac non incauta futuri.*

But what is Popularity compared with Fidelity ?

––––––

The next subject, that for the evening of the 4th February 1799, was proposed by the Rev. Josiah Pratt.—How FAR MIGHT A PERIODICAL PUBLICATION BE RENDERED SUBSERVIENT TO THE INTERESTS OF RELIGION ?

We regret that we have no remarks recorded in our Note-book, as the observations of the proposer proved to be the germ of a work which has since been very extensively useful to the Church, and especially so in the various eventful epochs through which the Church has passed — we allude to the CHRISTIAN OBSERVER. The only record of remarks we have been able to procure was made by the 'Chairman for the evening, the Rev. J. Venn. It is to the following effect :—

"The objects proposed by Mr Pratt were—'To correct the false sentiments of the religious world, and to explain the principles of the Church ;' in addition to which ' Religious Communications,' there were to be articles Miscellaneous ; Literary ; Reviews ; a Review of Reviews ; and historical events of the month, with a particular reference to Providence."

In 1844, the Editor of the *Christian Observer,* in noticing the recent decease of Mr Pratt, observes in reference to this discussion, held nearly half a century before :—

"Mr Pratt was, we believe, the projector of the *Christian Observer*, of which he was the original Editor, though he retained that office only a few months. The work began to be published in January 1802; but as long before as February 4, 1799, we find Mr Pratt proposing for consideration, in the Clerical Society above referred to, the question —'How far may a periodical publication be made subservient to the interests of religion?' We have only a brief note of his remarks, with which we are favoured by the Rev. H. Venn—a worthy scion of a venerated stock—from the memorandum-book of his father, who was present; but even this note exhibits an outline of the plan of the *Christian Observer*, as afterwards developed in the prospectus.

"Such a work was much wanted; and the projectors say in the prospectus, that it was to be conducted by members of the Church of England, and to advocate its principles; combining information upon general subjects, with religious instruction, and to furnish an interesting view of religion, literature, and politics, free from the contamination of false principles, grounding everything upon Holy Writ, and with an endeavour to uphold its doctrines and precepts. Mr Pratt, as we said, was its first Editor; but, with the concurrence of the Committee which superintended it, he resigned that office to Mr Macaulay before the first volume was completed."

A letter from the late Mr Z. Macaulay to the Editor of 1830 has been since published, in which some further light is thrown upon this subject. It is dated 16th March 1830 :—

"MY DEAR SIR,—For the original Prospectus of the *Christian Observer*, a paper of hints was furnished by Mr Hey of Leeds. It was drawn up by Josiah Pratt [nephew of Mr Hey by marriage], in conjunction with Mr Pearson of Golden Square, and myself. Mr Pratt was the first Editor; but he gave it up before three months had elapsed, and then the work fell *entirely* on myself. The Editorship was *shared* for a couple of months on one occasion by ———; and for about the same time by Robert Grant. *With these brief aids, I carried it on myself till your engagement.*

"The nominal Committee were Pratt, Pearson, H. Thornton, Wilberforce, Charles Grant (the father), John Venn, and myself. But after the first year, there was little or rather no interference, except in the way of criticism and suggestion after papers appeared.—Yours ever truly, Z. MACAULAY."

We have thought it worth while thus to trace the origin of a work which was for years written in by such persons as Hannah More, Lord Teignmouth, Dean Milner, Wilberforce, Charles Grant, and the present Bishop of Calcutta, and still maintains its standing.

———

At the meeting of 18th Feb. 1799, a general conversation only took place. It was on the important subject of A MISSION CON- NECTED WITH THE EVANGELICAL PART OF THE CHURCH OF ENGLAND. We proceed, therefore, to the next.

MARCH 4, 1799.

HOW FAR IS FASTING A CHRISTIAN DUTY?—Proposed by the Rev. J. Newton.

Mr Newton—

Christ came to fulfil the Law, not to frustrate it. If Fasting were of moral obligation, it would not have been spoken of as circumstantial by our Lord. Perhaps St Paul speaks of Fasting rather in accommoda- tion to the state of the Church.

The strongest point in favour of Fasting, as a matter of obligation, is what our Lord says. *This kind goeth not forth but by prayer and fasting.*

I have earlier in life kept four private fasts, which I generally kept abroad in the fields or woods ; three of which are—(1.) My own birth- day. (2.) My wife's birthday. (3.) 21st of March, the day I was saved from sinking in the deep.

The Rev. J. Venn—

Duties are of two kinds :—1. Positive. 2. Those of imperfect obligation.

1. Jewish ordinances in many cases were positive. *This* is to be done, and in *such* a way. Eat no leavened bread on the day of the Passover ; &c., &c.

2. It is not to be supposed that duties of imperfect obligation are as binding on us as those of positive obligation. That obligation is less accurately defined.

The spirit of the Jewish Dispensation abounded in duties of positive obligation. The spirit of the Christian abounds in duties of imperfect obligation.

The question, then, is—How far this duty binds? Positive duties are generally prohibitory in their character. "Thou shalt have none other Gods but me:" "Thou shalt do no murder :" &c.

Fasting is to be regarded in its Effect and Utility.

Consider it, first, as it relates to the PERSON.

Fasting is a means to an end. Constitution is to be considered. If more *hurt* than *advantage* would follow, it is no duty. The cases in which Fasting is mentioned were generally solemn. (1.) Setting apart to the ministry. (2.) Great national troubles, &c. &c.

Consider it, secondly, as it regards the CHURCH.

A duty of imperfect obligation may become of positive obligation. Yet here the capability is to be considered. But if incapable himself, yet it may be right that a minister should keep up the appearance ; and not let persons pass his windows and see him feast while others fast. He might make *some* difference. He should, moreover, explain to his servants the motives for his practice and conduct. He should act herein as St Paul about meat offered to idols.   In such cases, one complies with the imperfect obligation as much as possible.   Not to comply would be of disservice to religion.

There have been great blessings accompanying Fasting.   Take, for example, Cornelius and our Lord himself.   John's Disciples fasted in preparation for the Gospel Dispensation.   This was a part of John's Dispensation.

Christ said the day *should come* when his disciples would fast.   He might here look forward to occasions of public distress, &c.

The Rev. H. Foster—

Mr Venn has stated the thing fairly.   There is no difference between the Old and New dispensations with regard to fasting.   It always was an occasional thing.   The case of Daniel in *altering* his food may suggest some useful hints.   It shews that a godly man may take food, but afflict himself in the kind.

The Rev. T. Scott—

Fasting is not once prescribed under the Law.   The only expression like it is—*Afflict thy soul.*   Therefore it is not of perpetual obligation.

Yet it is of moral obligation whatever the obligation be.   It is a circumstantial, occasional thing.   It is an acknowledgment that we have forfeited our right to all the creatures of God.   Therefore it is a proper attendant on all occasions of Humiliation.

By analogy, it will teach the *inclination* to submit to the *judgment.* It will enthrone conscience and judgment in all points.

Fasting is of great use and expediency when we have any special blessing to seek from God.   It is spoken of in this view with great honour in Scripture.   In observing it, a devout man says, " I'll have my mind as much separated as possible."   " I'll be alone with God this day."

We seldom set apart a day in such a spirit without getting good. At the time it may be felt heavy perhaps, but good in the result.

MARCH 18, 1799.

WHAT METHODS CAN WE USE MOST EFFECTUALLY TO PROMOTE THE KNOWLEDGE OF THE GOSPEL AMONG THE HEATHEN ?—Proposed by the Rev. J. Venn.

Mr Venn—

1. All success in Missionary undertakings must be expected from the Spirit of God.   GOD is to be sought on all occasions.

In proportion as the thing is important, the foundation must be laid in prayer.

God's providence must be *followed*, not *anticipated.*   We must wait for His motion.   If He diffuse a Missionary spirit on any to offer themselves for the work, this will be His leading.

Let us imitate herein the primitive times.   The nearer we approach to the principles and manners of the ancient Church, the better.

2. Success will depend, under God, on *the persons sent on the Mission.*

He that goes forth should be taught of Heaven : should have Heaven in his heart : should tread the world under his foot.

Can you *make* such men ?   No !   God must have made them.

3. It is better that a Mission should proceed from *small beginnings !* and advance according to circumstances, rather than that we should enter upon a large scale at first.

Nature follows this rule.   Colonies creep from small beginnings. Christianity was thus first propagated.

Every Mission must support itself.   A large undertaking will be its own ruin—*mole ruit sua.*

These three principles Mr Venn illustrated in—(1.) The Primitive spread of the Gospel ; and (2.) By the Missions of the Moravians.

Our notes of this very important meeting are so scanty, that we are glad to avail ourselves of a memorandum which was made in short-hand at the time, by the Rev. W. Goode, one of the members, and has been happily preserved to the present day.*

" On the 18th of March, a question was formally proposed by the Rev. John Venn, in these terms :—' What methods can we use more effectually to promote the knowledge of the Gospel among the Heathen ?' Fourteen members were present   Mr Venn opened the discussion, by insisting upon the duty of doing something for the conversion of the Heathen.   He stated reasons which, in his judgment, prevented the Clergy from joining the (London) Missionary Society ; and the necessity that those who associated themselves in this work should have such a community of sentiments as to enable them heartily to work together.

" He laid down three chief principles which ought to be kept in view :—

" ' 1. Whatever success is expected, must be expected entirely through the influence of the Spirit of God.   His agency must enlarge the hearts of Christians.   His providential guidance must lead the way and open the door.   God's providence must be *followed,* not *anticipated.*

" ' 2. All success will depend upon the kind of men employed.   They must be men of the Apostolic spirit, such as Brainerd—men not careful about the things of this world.

" ' It is far better to commence a Mission on a small scale, and let it grow according to circumstances, than to make great attempts at first.

" Upon these principles, Mr Venn ' would not propose to raise funds in the first instance : ' this would be beginning at the wrong end.   In order duly to acknowledge the hand of God in this work, let the following Resolutions be adopted by the Society :—

" ' 1. That it shall be regarded as the duty of every Member of this Society, in his individual and social capacity, to admonish his people to promote the knowledge of the Gospel among the Heathen.

* See the Appendix to a Sermon preached in the Parish Church of St Mary, Islington, on occasion of the death of the Rev. Josiah Pratt, B.D.   By Rev. Henry Venn, B.D., Honorary Secretary of the Church Missionary Society.

" ' 2. That it be a constant petition in the prayer used at this Meeting —and that it be recommended in our daily devotions—that God would implant in our minds a deep concern for the nations lying in heathen darkness, and make us instrumental in conveying the knowledge of the Gospel to some of them.

" ' 3. That each member do seriously direct his meditation, study, and inquiry to the best method of beginning and carrying on a Mission —the discovery of a proper place in which to begin the Mission—the proper qualifications of the persons to become Agents of the Mission.

" ' 4. That each Member strive to influence others in this cause, by visiting or speaking to three at least of his Christian friends, endeavouring to excite the same spirit in them, directing their thoughts to the same object, and to look out for men endued with the true Missionary spirit.

" ' If it should please God, as we may well hope it will, to direct us to the proper sphere of labour, and to the selection of two or three persons of the true spirit, then, as a next step—

" ' 5. That this Society should take into consideration what are the proper methods to be pursued for employing those Missionaries among the Heathen.

" ' One important point to be considered respects the general character of the Mission. I think it ought to be founded upon the *Church principle*, not the *high-Church* principle.

" ' Regarding the great difficulty of finding Ministers, I would rather send out Laymen than none at all ; and allow Laymen to perform many functions usually confined to Ministers at home. This practice is justified by the conduct of the Society for Promoting Christian Knowledge. If it be objected that this is contrary to the strict rules of the Establishment, I reply, that I would do a great deal to keep up the Establishment, but not sacrifice the good of souls. Laymen may go out as Catechists ; not to administer the sacrament ; to baptise only in cases of necessity ; but to instruct the people and to gather a Church. Afterward we must find a minister ; if not, get the Catechist ordained.' "

The foregoing account is taken from the short-hand notes of the Rev. W. Goode. Mr Venn did not himself preserve any record of his own remarks on this occasion. The notes of what was said by the other speakers are, comparatively speaking, very scanty.

Mr Venn appears to have had the chief share in maturing the incipient design ; and after the formation of the Society, he was requested to draw up an Account or Prospectus of the Society, which was the foundation of all its future proceedings, and which will be found, on comparison, to embody many of the principles which were on this occasion so fully developed.

Several of the subsequent speakers objected to the adoption of Resolutions by the Eclectic Society, as not according with its character.

" Mr Charles Grant urged the founding of a Missionary Seminary.

" The Rev. Josiah Pratt advocated the adoption of the Resolutions, as 'breathing a quiet, humble, dependent spirit.' 'Let us regard ourselves as forming the Society. Let us consider to whom it would be desirable to communicate our plans. Let us not proceed to choose a Committee till we have a larger Meeting. Let some little Address be drawn up, stating our designs, and how we wish to act in following the leading of Providence. It should be known that there is such a design. Fix upon persons to write to. It must be kept in evangelical hands.'

" The Rev. Charles Simeon, with characteristic distinctness of purpose and promptitude of zeal, proposed three questions—

" 'What can we do? When shall we do it? How shall we do it? —'What can we do? We cannot join the (London) Missionary Society; yet I bless God that they have stood forth. We must now stand forth—we require something more than Resolutions—something ostensible — something held up to the public. Many draw back because we do not stand forward.—When shall we do it? Directly: not a moment to be lost. We have been dreaming these four years, while all England, all Europe, has been awake.—How shall we do it? It is hopeless to wait for Missionaries. Send out Catechists. Plan two years ago. Mr Wilberforce.'

" The Rev. T. Scott stated the objections which he felt to the plan of the (London) Missionary Society, but hoped that good would be done. 'We must not expect too perfect Missionaries.'

" The Rev. W. Goode urged the duty of making the attempt: the difficulties suggested only proved that there was not a Missionary spirit abroad; 'form a plan; publish it; send it to those friends who are likely to assist; and thus see what can be done.'

The result of this Meeting was a general consent that a Society should be forthwith formed, by inviting a few of those upon whose concurrence in their own views they could rely; and that a Prospectus of their proceedings should be afterward prepared; and that then their plans should be laid before the Heads of the Church.

———

A fortnight later, 1st April 1799, at the usual meeting, the subject, so much upon the minds of the brethren, was renewed; and a general conversation took place upon THE ESTABLISHMENT OF A MISSION. The time was now drawing near for the accomplishment of their wishes.

———

On the 12th April 1799, a meeting of friends to the cause was held at the Castle-and-Falcon Inn, Aldersgate Street, and the CHURCH MISSIONARY SOCIETY was instituted. Mr Venn was in the chair; sixteen Clergymen—of whom nine were members of the Eclectic—with nine Laymen, composed the meeting.

We cannot close our remarks on this subject without giving some extracts from an address which was delivered in London, on the 31st October 1848, during the Jubilee-year, by the late Rev. William Jowett, M.A., formerly Literary Representative of the Church Missionary Society in the Mediterranean, and subsequently for a time Clerical Secretary of the Society, upon the occasion of Ten Missionaries being dismissed to their several stations.

The occasion, Mr Jowett remarks, seemed a suitable one for looking back to the earliest friends of the Society, observing their characters, tempers, and measures; and reflecting how far they are a model to us at this time. Out of a multitude worthy to be remembered, he selected four: namely, the first two preachers before the Society; and two others: these, from their peculiar exertions and position, he considers to have been the principal founders and builders-up of the Society. Their names are Scott, Simeon, Venn, and Pratt. The following is his notice of them :—

Principal Founders and Builders-up of the Society.

The first of these, the Rev. Thomas Scott, was a Clergyman without private fortune, and deriving a bare subsistence from the revenues of the Church. He was a man of frugal habits, hardy, homely, humble. From taste, and still more from principle, he had a dislike for what are called the good things of this world; and by both precept and example, he bequeathed to his surviving friends an inveterate dread of the love of money. His, however, was not the stale, pretended poverty of monastic life; to which some have hinted that the Church of England must return, in order to meet the spiritual exigencies of our overgrown population. On the contrary, it was a laborious, honest, domesticated poverty. He worked on, struggling with adverse circumstances, dependent on God for daily bread, yet maintaining a cheerful independence of spirit, and always laying by somewhat for works of charity. Such a man was well adapted to stamp our earliest labours with the true Missionary character; forming them on an apostolic model, and leading them to the imitation of our great Master, who, *though He was rich, yet for our sakes became poor, that we through His poverty might be rich.*

He was not brought up at a University, and had none of the elegant refinements of literature; but being endued with a strong and capacious understanding, and possessing unwearied perseverance, he made himself a thoroughly learned man, especially in theology, of which his masterly work, the Commentary on the whole Bible, gives ample evidence; a work without the parade of learning, but rich with immense stores of thought and knowledge. It is the practice of our Society to place within reach of every one of our ordained Missionaries a copy of this valuable work. It is not to be calculated how many hundreds of our Clergy, and thousands of the Laity, partake of a daily portion of this Commentary.   Thus we may view this good man, as poor yet making many rich.   In a spiritual sense, we are plentifully fed with the crumbs that fall from this poor man's table.

Of the second preacher before this Society, the Rev. CHARLES SIMEON, it is not so easy to fix the character, it was compounded of extremes so wide apart.   Before his conversion, which took place early in life, he was passionately gay : in all his after-years, though cheerful in the highest degree, yet was he intensely serious and devout, living to God, and living near to God, labouring for souls, studious of his Bible, and wholly given to his ministerial duties.   He had about him much of what seemed rashness, and often really was such ; yet principle and habit formed him a remarkably prudent man, as his most intimate friends had long known, and his Memoirs, recently published, have proved, to the surprise of many who judged him only by the peculiarities of his exterior.   He was a single man, labouring more than fifty years in one and the same sphere, and that a sphere of peculiar delicacy—the University of Cambridge.   But his integrity and simplicity of purpose carried him over all difficulties.   He was a whole man to everything he undertook.   If he had a text before him, he expounded it as though he had no other work to do but give out the full meaning of that one text.   If he had the character of a person to study, he examined it to the best of his judgment, impartially, without respect of persons : and the same in any other matter of business. There were two traits in him peculiarly worthy to be noticed by a Missionary.   Though possessed of great bodily strength, and though abundant in labours, yet was he scrupulously careful of health.   The other point is, that he was a rigid economist, exact in his accounts to a penny ; which was the more remarkable as he always enjoyed a competency, and during many of his later years was in affluent circumstances : but he considered himself the steward, not the possessor, of this world's goods.

In the presence of his son and representative,* I should hesitate to speak of the third-mentioned individual, the Rev. JOHN VENN, who was the projector and principal founder of this Society ; but I am spared the difficulty, as his character has been already portrayed, and that by no common hand, in the following terms :—" He was endowed by Providence with a sound and powerful understanding ; and he added to an ample fund of classical knowledge, a familiar acquaintance with all the more useful parts of philosophy and science.   His taste was simple.   His disposition was humble and benevolent.   His manners were mild and conciliating.   As a Divine, he was comprehensive and elevated in his views, and peculiarly conversant with theological subjects ; but he derived his chief knowledge from the Scriptures themselves, which he diligently studied and faithfully interpreted.   As a Preacher, he was affectionate and persuasive, intellectual and discriminating, serious, solemn, and devout ; anxious to impress on others those evangelical truths which he himself so deeply felt.   By his family, among whom he was singularly beloved, his remembrance will

* The Rev. H. Venn, B.D., Hon. Secy., C. M. S.

be cherished with peculiar tenderness. Having been sustained, during a long and trying illness, by a steadfast faith in that Saviour whom in all his preaching he laboured to exalt, he died July 1, 1813, aged fifty-four years, leaving to his surviving family and flock an encouraging example of the blessedness of those who embrace with their whole hearts the religion of Jesus Christ."

To this it may be added, that the Society, at its first formation, was greatly indebted to the calm and wise spirit manifested by Mr Venn, in their negotiations with the ecclesiastical authorities of the day. At a moment when others, of a sanguine temperament, might have been tempted to precipitate measures, he, while pursuing, yet was patient. The well-known motto from Ennius—*Cunctando restituit rem*—indicating one of the highest qualities of a public character, may justly be applied to this friend and founder of the Society. In Scripture an expression occurs, of a far more exalted order, describing the origin of this moral firmness : *He that believeth shall not make haste.*

Of the fourth-mentioned, the Rev. Josiah Pratt, it may perhaps be difficult for me, as a brother-in-law, not to speak with some degree of partiality. But as he has not long been removed from among us, here are many able to confirm or to correct my testimony. He was a man all energy—grave, firm, undaunted energy ; with a mind comprehensive, sagacious, sound, and practical ; a mind always busy, going forth in its excursions throughout the land, and through the compass of the whole earth, ever devising good : yet, with no turn for novelties. Of the many weeds that so often spring up in the religious world, none took root in him. There were no partialities, no bye-paths, no corners in his mind : all was plain, open, and direct ; tending to usefulness on the large scale. With these original qualities of the understanding was combined a power of labour truly astonishing. Work was his element : there was no *vis inertiæ* about him ; and his exertions were all so arranged in method, and pressed on with perseverance, that it seemed natural for us to expect success in whatever he undertook. He knew well how to carry forward the theories of good and able men into practical results. Others might deliberate : he could deliberate and act too. The benefits which he conferred upon this Society, or rather, it should be said, through this Society upon the world at large, were immense. He was capable of moving or arresting the mind of large assemblies ; and in our Committee he was well qualified to sway his fellow-labourers, from combining a just confidence in his own judgment with such a genuine modesty, as led him to respect the opinions and even the prejudices of other minds. And this was the more remarkable, as he was by nature vehement ; but this temperament was softened down from his attaining, through grace, to an eminent degree of self-knowledge and self-command. When I entered on the office of Secretary, sixteen years ago, the only rule he gave me was, " Never shew temper :" counsel which was fetched, I doubt not, 'from the depths of his own experience. Then in the qualities of his heart he was truly large, fervent, and affectionate, as all his friends could testify. He had a remarkably keen discernment, almost in-

stinctive, of the infirmities of human nature ; and a most tender compassion for its sinful weaknesses.   "I never knew a man," Bishop
Gobat once said to me, "like him, able to ask of Missionary Candidates
such plain questions without offending."   He was peculiarly reverential,
and full of adoring thoughts toward his God ; which gave an impressive
character to all his duties, and to all his intercourse with the public
and with Missionaries.   He was a faithful, experimental preacher, rich
in doctrine, and close in practical application ; eminently devout in
prayer, both in the family and with his friends.   Thus from his closet,
his study, his pulpit, and the Committee-room, he helped with others
to move the world : and, God prospering them, they did move it in
good earnest.   In his prayers, he was ever wont to make mention of
the three Persons of the blessed Trinity.   He honoured the person and
work of the Holy Spirit ; and the Holy Spirit put honour upon him,
by blessing his labours abundantly.   Though not, like Mr Venn, the
prime mover in forming this Society, yet in rearing, advancing, and
establishing it, he had the chief hand.   Moreover, being the youngest,
he was spared longer than the other three to promote this blessed
work.   After the formation of the Society, Mr Scott lived twenty-two
years, Mr Simeon thirty six, and Mr Venn but fourteen, while Mr Pratt
survived forty-five,—very near seven times seven years.   It was he
who laid down this fundamental principle for the Society—"It must
be kept in evangelical hands :" and in unison with this, he often, in
his venerable age, expressed his alarm lest a new generation should
attempt to build the Church with men devoid of spirituality.

These were all of them honourable men in their generations—and
there were others like-minded with them—to whom we owe everything, under God, in the formation of this Society.   They were indeed
men of like passions and infirmities with ourselves ; and they were in
natural character many of them widely different, and even opposite :
yet that One Spirit who called them to this holy enterprise, made them
one.   When, therefore, we contemplate their characters as a whole,
and view them as persons who have finished their course with joy, we
are bound to thank God for the grace which was bestowed on them :
and we may well add our earnest prayers, that a double portion of
their spirit may rest upon us.

A double portion of their spirit we need : for how greatly altered
are our circumstances !   The condition of the political world is changed.
At that time, our fathers were startled by the outburst of the first
French Revolution : as I have heard them relate, all faces then
gathered blackness : how much more in this day, when throughout the
Continent the foundations of society are shaken and upturned !   The
condition, also, of the Church is changed ; but how greatly for the
better !   Then she had begun to bestir herself from a long lethargy :
she is now risen, and, as we hope, is putting on her beautiful garments.

As these four persons were members of the Eclectic—three of
them being regular attendants, and Mr Simeon being a country
member, who attended occasionally, and was indeed one of the
first to propose the subject of Missions to the brethren, which he

did as early as February 8, 1796—we have thought it not inappropriate to incorporate with our Notes this interesting sketch of their characters.

———

APRIL 15, 1799.

WHAT IS THE OBLIGATION AND THE MOST EFFECTUAL METHOD OF ADMINISTERING BROTHERLY REPROOF ? — Proposed by the Rev. B. Woodd.

Mr Woodd—

The subject of reproof should be some *palpable* evil.

No reproof is unseasonable when there is any prospect of good.

Let us look well to our own character and to our motive before we reprove.

It is quite possible for a man to reprove sin in the spirit of sin.*

We should set about it in the spirit of prayer—in which spirit we should continue.

Be tender, candid, prudent, and impartial. *Considering thyself, lest thou also be tempted* (Gal. vi. 1). *We ourselves also were sometimes foolish, disobedient, deceived, &c.* (Tit. iii. 3).

Be grave and serious. Christ, in his mode of reproving Peter, sets an example of benignity.

The Rev. J. Goode—

Disarm a man by your kindness. Take the fittest season. Abigail's conduct gives an interesting illustration of this.

Go from thy knees to reprove thy friend.

The Rev. J. Davies—

We should measure our reproof by the thing to be reproved. Consider, also, the temperament and constitution of the person to be reproved.

Guard your own spirit from pride and censoriousness.

Put yourself in the place of the person reproved.

The Rev. J. Venn—

Some have a happy manner of reproving. [He illustrated this by the example of Bayle reproving a nobleman for swearing ; and by his father, the Rev. H. Venn, reproving some officers in a coach].

Nothing reconciles the supercilious but *humility* and *affection*.

The Rev. Mr Gilbert, a visitor for the evening—

It is easier to deal with brethren than with men of the world. You

———

* Here some reference appears to have been made to Diogenes and Plato. Perhaps the speaker had in mind the following, from Lord Bacon's Apophthegms :—
" 107. Plato entertained some of his friends at dinner, and had in the chamber a bed, or couch, neatly and costly furnished. Diogenes came in and got upon the bed, and trampled it, saying, ' I trample upon the pride of Plato.' Plato mildly answered, ' But with greater pride.' "

know not how much a man will grant you.   It is a great step gained to find the Bible acknowledged.

Mr Bacon—

Point out the beauties of his character when you reprove a man. This conciliates.   Shew how the thing you wish to correct will affect his character or interest.

Suggest some way to escape the temptation into which he is likely to fall.

Silence is the most unexceptionable means of reproof on some occasions.   Reserve and gravity, when approbation is expected.

Confess any weakness under which you labour.

It is better for a *third* person to reprove a fault committed against *yourself.*

You may reprove in public a forward man by courting a modest man.

The Rev. Thomas Scott—

Do not that for *all,* which is due to *some.*

There is a *general* obligation of reproof, and a *special* obligation.

Where the obligation is special, it is constantly to be attended to. Where it is general, wait for opportunities; but be not distressed if they occur not.

Cowardice, love of credit, and fear of trouble—are at the root of reluctance to reprove.

A pious man, though through infirmity he may be angry with you for reproving him, yet will be *afterwards* grateful.

How reproof is *received*—is a touchstone of a man's character.

Don't enslave your conscience.   There is no necessity for you always to speak when you are with the world.   Wait for the opportunity ; and if it come, take it.

Reproof, if more practised, would prevent divisions among Christians.

A physician administers nauseous medicines in the way most likely to make them palatable.

Commend what you see to be right, and your reproof will not seem to arise from temper.

The Rev. J. Newton—

In reproving, our danger is to say what should not be said, and to leave unsaid what should have been spoken.

Reproof in *secret,* in *season,* and in *love*—this is the right thing.

In company, though we talk not *to* a person, we may talk *at* him. This he illustrated by a case of Wesley's reproving an officer by a glass of water.

The Rev. J. Clayton—

Though the subject should be, as Brother Woodd said, *palpable,* yet some *little* things are symptomatic of great things.

Stop the evil in its beginning, and therefore reprove.

Time and place are to be considered. Seize the cooler moment.
Reproof purchases no licence for a man to talk of himself.

APRIL 29, 1799.

THE SIN AND DANGER OF EMBRACING FALSE DOCTRINE.—Proposed
by Rev. J. Goode

Mr Goode—

" Never shall we be well informed of the truth, till we are conformed
to the truth," says a good writer.

I would know of the brethren—(1.) How to distinguish Truth
from Error; (2.) Wherein consists the Sin of False Doctrine; and
(3.) The danger of embracing Error and its pernicious effects.

The Rev. J. Venn—

Goode asks a question important indeed, but deserving a separate
discussion. The characters of error do not belong to this question.

The Sin and Danger of Error may be considered with reference—

(1.) To GOD. All error is hateful to Him.

(2.) To its Effects. No false doctrine can be unattended with bad
effects.

The most fashionable and dangerous opinion is, that opinions are of
no consequence, if the life be right. But no truths are so merely
speculative, as to have no effect at all. Connected with others, every
truth has its effect. Opinions now dormant may be quickly called
out. Error though innocuous now, may therefore have its evil consequences hereafter. There is no speculative opinion, therefore, which
may not be of *importance*.

There is a difference between Opinions and Principles.

All determinations are to be traced to the Judgment or the Passions.

The idea that evil might be innocuous arose from men's observing,
that people holding various opinions nevertheless often do the *same
works*.

But all *works* are of value, only as the *motives* which lead to them
are *pure*.

Even when men varying in opinion do agree in acts, what they do
is the consequence of agreement (so far as they go) in the principles
of truth.

There is a marked connexion between Democracy and Error in
Religion.

This he illustrated by the example of Muir and Palmer, two democratic leaders in the north.

Men who *hold the truth in unrighteousness* pervert the various doctrines of the Gospel to their own views and wishes.

The Rev. Thomas Scott—

The Innocence of Error is a most pernicious notion. It implies
that all are bigots who contend for doctrines. It brings in Jesus
Christ and his disciples as bigots.

I. Scripture charges Error on *the state of the heart*—not on want of evidence. For example, the Scribes and Pharisees. To them our Lord says, *How can ye believe, which receive honour one of another, and seek not the honour that cometh from God only?* (John v. 44.)

There is no one truth of God's Word, which is not opposite to some lust of the heart.

The tree of knowledge was the most dangerous in the Garden.

The evil, then, is, that men will be the Teacher and not the Scholar : hence Arianism, Socinianism, &c.

Men will not submit to the *purity* of the Gospel : hence Antinomianism, &c.

When any man deliberately adopts anything contrary to Scripture, it will be found at the day of judgment to have arisen from the state of his heart.

II. As to the danger of Error, it reciprocates.

Lust and Pride prepare for Error, and Error strengthens Lust and Pride.

Why was every dunghill-deity preferred to the God of Israel? Why were Mars and Bacchus and Venus ever tolerated as the objects of worship?

Let a man tell me his deity, and I'll tell him his character.

The Rev. J. Pratt—

If Error be actually invincible, then it is not sinful. But God only can ascertain its sinfulness, or the degree of it.

The Sin of Error consists in the *state* and *habit* of the soul which lead to its being embraced.

The Danger of Error is, lest God should *leave* the man who holds it. The greatest struggle is at the first. If indulged, it gradually becomes less. Dr Priestly was quoted in illustration. At last, men come to "*believe a lie.*" Then they *receive the recompense of their error which was meet.*

A sensual man is in less danger than a speculative man, from Error, because he is more easily convinced of his folly.

The Rev. J. Clayton—

How can men become more capable of bearing the image of Satan, than by imbibing Error?

Man is sinful in the means he resorts to. No man imbibes Error but he has neglected the ordinary means of guarding against it.

He leaves prayer and God's Word, to read men's works.

The Danger of Error is, the annihilation of all that is useful to society. For all Error will ultimately affect Practice.

The Rev. J. Newton—

I would preach on the favourite maxim of the misguided poet—

> " For modes of faith let senseless zealots fight,
>   His can't be wrong whose life is in the right."

But then I would turn it on the adversary. No life is right, which is not based on right principles.

We must get the man first, and engage his heart to the LORD. His acts are of no worth, if they proceed not from union with Him. He may be useful to society, but is of no acceptance with GOD.

Error is fatal, if it be about—(1.) The Person of Christ: (2.) The Atonement of Christ: (3.) The Influence of the Holy Spirit: (4.) Sanctification: (5.) The Future State.

The Rev. B. Woodd—

If the heart be right, Truth is wholly received the instant it is presented. There are instances of hearts prepared by the Holy Spirit before Truth is brought before it, when they have embraced it instantly.

I believe that a heart that is right would receive all the five points Brother Newton has enumerated. The characteristic of Satan is not Error, but Malice.

All good Arminians are real Calvinists. Things have been distorted before their minds. But bring the Spirit of Truth before them, and they acknowledge it.

The Rev. W. Goode—

The Sin of Error is in man's not acknowledging the authority of GOD.

None are infirm in head till infirm in heart.

The Danger of Error is in strengthening the evil which led to it. Its leading to false morality, &c.

Manners may be gentle and amiable, but Error is a poison which works secretly.

The spirit of the world marked in erroneous men.

The Rev. H. Jowett, a visitor from the country—

I learn a practical lesson from this conversation :— *Cleanse thou me from my secret faults. Keep thy servant from presumptuous sins, let them not have dominion over me.*

The Rev. H. Foster—

The tests of Truth are these :—(1.) Whatever tends to exalt the Saviour: or (2.) to degrade the sinner : or (3.) to promote holiness— that is Truth.

Error is the opposite to these :—(1.) Whatever tends to exalt the sinner : (2.) to degrade the Saviour : or (3.) to hinder holiness.

MAY 13, 1799.

WHAT RULES SHOULD GOVERN A CHRISTIAN IN DESIGNATING A SON TO THE MINISTRY ?—Proposed by the Rev. R. Cecil.

Mr Cecil—

It is not a question here, whether a man should at anyrate designate his son to the ministry. A father may make his son a *Clergyman*, though he cannot make him a *Minister*. To think he could, would be as absurd as to say he'll make his son a painter or a musician—without eyes or ears.

My question rather is, what should *authorise* a man to *advise* his son to proceed in the line of the ministry.

It is, moreover, no question with me, whether a man should give his son a learned education or not.

The Rev. Thomas Scott—

For a father to wish to make his son a conspicuous man, is all out of place for a Christian. Yet it is to be feared that many Christians act on this principle.

I enter my protest against the practice of putting children in the way of learning accomplishments, and *out* of the way of learning what is of higher importance.

I tell my sons not to think of the Ministry, except with a determination to take up the hardships which must attend it.

1. None should be designated to the Ministry without a *competency of talent:*—with a mind capable of understanding the subject he speaks on ; and of speaking on the subject he understands.

2. There must be a *preference of the work of the Ministry* above all other occupations:—and this after counting the cost, lest they be *like the children of Ephraim, who being harnessed, and carrying bows, turned themselves back in the day of battle.*

Take *encouragement* from impressions made on your child's mind ; but make them not rules of action.

The Rev. Mr ——, a visitor for the evening—

I will speak as I have felt, and acted.

My son was a grave boy ; had a love of the Bible ; a love of good men ; and a love of good authors. Yet he went off ! God may mean to shew me what I can't do. He may *yet* become a minister. This boy so promising seemed to be *my* work. I was therefore now brought down. What we should do without such signs, I know not.

The Rev. John Newton—

I pity the slaves—galley slaves ; but when I consider the case of a Minister toiling without spirituality, I pity him *more.*

I am no friend to *impressions.* Some children I've known set apart from a mere *impression* of their parents, that God designs them for the Ministry.

If a parent finds that a child is often near the heart in *prayer,* this is encouraging.

You can send no son to College or an Academy without risk. He goes to College as to an ordeal. If he *stand* there, it is an evidence of his having hold of the truth.

The Rev. J. Clayton—

I felt no desire on the birth of my children that they should enter the Ministry ; for I knew its difficulties and dangers. My sons were not designated, but put in train.

It is wisely ordered in Providence that persons should generally be attached to their professions.

I would lay down the following rules on the question before us :—

1. The motives of parents should be scriptural. Their motives are often secular.

2. Ascertain the reality of your son's religion. If he has none, he will be a burden to himself and others, if he enter the Ministry : he will find no pleasure.

3. Discover whether he has natural capacity for the duties of the Ministry.

The Rev. Josiah Pratt—

It is so important a matter, that it must be by God's own leading. I would keep it out of sight from a boy. I would not tell him.

A useful Minister is of God's making, not ours.

Our duty is to remove all obstacles, and use all due means.

I would follow the youth with prayer : would lay books in his way : introduce him to companions ; but the first proposition should come from him.

Probably I speak herein under the influence of my own education, and the conduct of my nearest friends.*

But yet I decidedly think, that any step further than this, would seem like taking the matter too much out of God's hand.

Being brought up in business is no real objection to a person entering the Christian Ministry. It begets habits of industry, application, method, and order.

The Rev. B. Woodd—

If the Ministry be represented in too awful a light, an undue objection against it may be fixed in the mind of a youth. I went to college more to please my mother than from any other cause.

---

* This will be better understood after reading the following extracts from Mr Pratt's Memoir, published in 1848 :—" His father introduced him into his own business as a manufacturer ; in which, from his natural habits of industry and accuracy, he might be expected to excel, and family tradition reports that the expectation was fully realised. But at a very early period he had imbibed a strong taste for books, and his mind became filled with an ardent desire for the acquisition of general knowledge. For several years, however, he kept this very much to himself, procuring and laying in books secretly, and indulging his literary propensity only in leisure hours, and in the retirement of his chamber. He imagined that his parents might think it unnecessary for him to spend so much time and money in pursuits which would not turn to account in that line of life for which he was intended."—(P. 4). Then, after his mind was more seriously awakened to a concern for his soul :—" He speedily became anxious to be a Minister of Christ ; a desire which was probably much promoted by the sympathies, if not the suggestions, of some of his companions, who had for some time judged that his mind was under preparation for further duties. His chief fear as to the accomplishment of such a wish arose from what he considered to be his father's inclination and future plans. . . Under these apprehensions, he made it a subject of earnest prayer to God, that if it were consistent with His holy will that he should enter ' the sacred Ministry of His Church,' he would incline the heart of his father to favour the proposal. He then, in a respectful way, and not without fear and trembling, disclosed his mind to his beloved parent. But so far was he from discouraging him, that he entered at once most kindly into his views, and rejoiced in thus giving up a son to the more immediate service of God. . . . The time which had been occupied [in business] was by no means thrown away. He was then acquiring those habits, and that practical turn of mind, which so eminently qualified him for many duties to which he was afterwards called."—(Pp. 6, 7.)

As to the exact question in hand, I should say that there should be—

(1.) A preparatory designation, and (2.) A practical designation.

For the first, natural talents are necessary ; for the second, moral training and spiritual training.

My preparation should consist in concentrating the youth's studies in Biblical learning.

Oxford men, I think, are better preachers than Cambridge men. Cambridge men are always niggling at points, instead of taking comprehensive views. Cambridge men, instead of applying what they say to mankind, are abstract, account for things, and try to square matters.

The Rev. W. Goode—

Some brethren have alluded to Samuel's early dedication to the temple service ; but designation to the Christian Ministry is a very different matter.

The Rev. J. Davies —

The chief question is, Is there an *aptitude* for the Ministry ?

The Rev. John Venn—

Cambridge men have an advantage, as it seems, in the discussion of this question, for Cambridge men would not have *digressed,* as some have done this evening.

Consider in what state things are in the Establishment. None are admitted who are not regularly prepared. And this, if properly done, requires time.

This, therefore, is a reason for a parent's coming to some determination. Another reason is, that the child should have a *direction* given to his mind, in order to be duly prepared.

Whoever dedicates his child to GOD, does a good thing.

Some difficulty arises from confounding the duty of the parent with that of the child. It becomes at the proper age the *child's* choice, not the *parent's.*

Circumstances may sometimes greatly facilitate the preliminary preparation. I am a clergyman, and the son of one, according to tradition, for thirteen generations.

MAY 27, 1799.

WHAT ARE THE CRITERIA OF DIVINE TRUTH, AND HOW MAY IT BE DISTINGUISHED FROM PLAUSIBLE ERROR ?—Proposed by Rev. Thomas Scott.

Mr Scott—

Hervey and others have said, that Divine Truth—

(1.) Humbles the sinner : (2.) Exalts the Saviour : (3.) Promotes holiness.

But this is not definitive enough. A goldsmith may say that gold is malleable ; this is true, but not sufficient.

I would lay this down :—

1. All Divine Truth magnifies the Holy Law of God, both in its precept and penalty;

2. Displays the harmony of the Divine Perfections and of the Divine Government;

3. Exalts Christ;

4. Is suited to destroy all self-confidence in the most self-virtuous and wise, and to give comfort to the broken-hearted.

For it connects the deepest humiliation and the greatest *encouragement.* There is some defect, perhaps, generally in our way of stating Divine Truth ; for it seldom *humbles,* without *depressing :* it seldom *cheers* without *injuring.* But this is not the legitimate effect of Scripture Truth.

5. Divine Truth makes *no compromise.*

There is no balancing of parties. Some of the old divines who began to deviate from the simple truth, considered " flesh" and " spirit" as meaning ".body" and " soul ;" so that as the body was mortified, pride grew. Whatever indulges the flesh is an error.

The Rev. Josiah Pratt—

There are—

1. FALSE or INADEQUATE Criteria.

This or that agrees with our *view* or *party.* One makes all parts of Scripture perfectly free from difficulties. Another selects all that is comfortable or enlightening.

2. TRUE and SUFFICIENT Criteria.

These (1.) Humble the sinner ; (2.) Exalt Jehovah-in-covenant.

We may apply these principles to—

(1.) Man's guilt. (2.) Man's inability. (3.) The way of obtaining an interest in the divine favour. (4.) The person of Christ and the Trinity. (5.) The obligation of holiness on believers. (6.) The future state.

If the heart be right, by applying these two criteria, a man will find the right way in these matters.

This is striking in the divine dispensations, that truth is clear to the *lowly* and the *seeker;* but is hidden to the *proud* and the *idle.*

We must look for the characteristics and criteria of truth in Scripture. Doddridge gives no characteristic marks of Revelation, but what he gets from Revelation itself.

We must judge of the criteria of truth more from *tendencies* than *effects.*

The Rev. J. Newton—

The criteria of truth are *experimental.* As a man waking at early dawn, opens his curtains, and sees the light : he sees the light because he has eyes. So if the Spirit has been at work in our hearts, we acquiesce fully with all the views in Scripture regarding ourselves and Jesus.

The Rev. B. Woodd—

These criteria—what humbles the sinner and exalts the Saviour, and promotes holiness—do not appear to me sufficient. They are capable of serving error as well as truth. [This was illustrated in a manner which our brief notes do not present in a very intelligible form ; and therefore we do not attempt to give the illustration.]

I would reject all criteria, except such as are supported by plain scriptural language.

The Rev. W. Goode remarked, that the three criteria which had been brought forward, are not to be taken *independently* of each other, as Mr Woodd appears to have done in shewing their insufficiency. They are not to be separated from each other ; but to be taken in combination.

The Rev. J. Venn—

Calling men "master," is a source of error. I would say, all are wrong in something or other.

He is right who agrees most with the *best* men, in *all* ages.

If we follow man as our guide, truth is one thing in the third century and another in the fourteenth. And no wonder that *men* should not always agree in their views, when even Apostles did not always fully agree in matters in which they were not guided by inspiration. This shews how little confidence is to be placed in any man's opinion.

The Rev. J. Clayton—

Truth supposes a standard. Truth is conformity to this standard.

Some of the things which have been said this evening may make truth vague and indefinite. But truth is not so.

Scripture seems to bring forward two leading things—(1.) What God will commit to us. (2.) What he expects from us.

Nothing is to be had but through Jesus Christ. The union of his offices of Prophet, Priest, and King, forms criteria of truth. Men are willing to hear of *God*, not of *Christ*. This opposition to the truth *as it is in Jesus* furnishes a basis for criteria. Plausible errors on this subject are to be distinguished by the *state of mind* with which they are taken up.

Plausible error is not generally taken up by us when we are in a humble and broken state of heart.

The end in view also must be considered : have we our party or God in view ?

Also, has the acquisition of what we esteem the truth been obtained by importunate prayer for the Spirit's teaching ?

Again, are we willing to make all sacrifices for it ?

JUNE 10, 1799.

HOW FAR IS GRAVITY BINDING UPON THE MINISTERIAL CHARACTER ?— Proposed by the Rev. R. Cecil.

Mr Cecil—

I have felt in myself the necessity of this question. Gravity is doubtless binding on us.

The Apostle connects it with SINCERITY. *Likewise must the Deacons be grave, not double tongued.* Yet it must be natural ; not affected.

In my unconverted state, I remember being in company when a minister came with such gravity, that it seemed that all was to be given in an oracular style. This disgusted me. It looked like affectation. I felt as though religion was the cause. Some there are with whom it is always Good Friday in their countenance. This is not sanctified gravity.

Others are always disposed to levity. I don't mean men of original fancy ; nor do I mean that men may not think in their own way. Newton said to me the other day, in a humorous manner—" What would you think of seeing a dray-horse leap over St Paul's ! And yet," he added, " this would be no more than a flea does in proportion to its dimension when it leaps." Now, this was not levity. This was his genius.

I mean, that a minister should consider that his character is not to be like other men in every respect. There should be a special stamp on his character.

Though it may not be difficult to himself, yet it is difficult for others, to make a transition from levity to gravity. Therefore he should not indulge in levity in their presence. Besides, prejudice is sometimes quickened by knowing that a man is given to levity. I could not bear for a long time to look into any work of my uncle, Dr G. : some family traditions of his levity had prejudiced me. But when I picked up some of his works, I saw it was innocent and natural.

This maxim may be laid down—even the solemn affectation of gravity is, in the pulpit, better than levity. On the other hand, better have levity in private, than a repelling and solemn severity. How far gravity is binding on a man in public is no question. Everything that looks like levity there, is incompatible with the place.

That was a good thing that Mr Venn said to —— one day : " Brother, don't you think *sincerity* binding on us ? " " Yes, certainly. Why do you ask ? " " It's associated with gravity." A thing, I fancy, every one of us felt. If God brings us into a trying situation, in which we feel it's an awful thing to suffer or die, gravity is natural ; all else is offensive.

I remember being at Windsor with a man of levity. We had spent the day. He was asked to pray. He replied, " Why, really I feel my spirit unfitted. I am wholly unframed. Ask such an one." It struck us. This tends insensibly to call in question whether the man is sincere.

Nevertheless, if a man takes up a right principle, but uses it wrongly, he makes a fool of himself. Gravity must be *natural* and *simple*. There must be *urbanity* and *tenderness* in it. A man must not formalise on everything. He who formalises on everything is a fool ; and a grave fool is perhaps worse than a light fool. I set out with indulging too much in levity, even in the pulpit. It was above two years before I could get the victory over it—though I strove under sharp piercings of conscience.

The Rev. T. Scott—

It is truly said, " Man is the only laughing animal." It is a

E

question whether God or Sin made him such. Christ sighed and wept, but never laughed.

What is gravity ? It is not severity nor moroseness. It is nothing inconsistent with cheerfulness or sociableness. If habitual, it is likely to set every one at a distance. Human nature is like a pendulum. It passes from one extreme to the other, without resting in the right place.

Levity in the pulpit is an evil indeed, against which I would ever set my face. I would always speak there, as a man about to die. We should aim at this.

In private, aim at a middle way. We should not let our families say, " He's *austere.*" Nor yet, " His religion is confined to the pulpit." There should be a holy savour in our conduct.

When we are conversing expressly on religion, gravity in its strictest sense should prevail.

When on *business,* we should be grave. But we are not always at business. We should unbend the bow.

If with openly ungodly people, gravity is generally binding.

The Rev. J. Newton—

Scott said, that Christ never laughed. This is true, probably. But levity is expressive of cheerfulness, not of joy. The perfectly happy man is not light. Jesus smiled, perhaps. But if he never smiled, it is no wonder ; for he was especially *a man of sorrows and acquainted with grief.* His example, therefore, is no proof of there being sin in levity.

Some allowance must be made for constitutional turn, in public as well as in private. Such sometimes is overruled for good. [This he seems to have exemplified by a reference to a friend, a Mr Burgess.]

If we *felt* as our understanding directs, we should always be miserable. A man may be always serious in Bartholomew's Hospital and Bedlam. And what is the world, but an Hospital and a Bedlam ? Half the world is *wounded* and half *mad.*

There is no time for a sinner, a pardoned sinner, living among miserable sinners, to spend in jocoseness. There is nothing in the New Testament, from beginning to end, recommending levity.

Levity is found among the followers of Mr Whitfield. Yet he soon changed levity into tears. *He* had a peculiar gift. But his followers and imitators fail here : they have found it easier to make men laugh than cry.

The Rev. B. Woodd—

We should be particularly careful not to introduce jesting in reference to Scripture—in any way.

The Rev. J. Pratt—

Men of a *caricaturing* turn are in danger of levity in the pulpit, even in describing the most solemn scenes. [This he exemplified in a preacher describing the Fall, and God's voice in the garden.] God in his goodness may prevent the evil effects of this levity, but it is highly dangerous, and therefore to be strictly guarded against.

Gravity is of peculiar obligation when levity is likely to be *misunderstood* or *can't be explained.* Therefore in the pulpit it is decidedly reprehensible. Also in the company of adversaries or strangers whom we have no prospect of seeing again.

It is a great error in men to give the rein to their constitutional propensities. Every man's duty is to consider where he *tends* to fail. He should settle it with himself that his constitution has some propensities to be corrected.

A disposition to levity needs habitual watchfulness.

Laughter, however, is a *duty* to some men. [He seems here to have made some reference to his own natural caste of character, and his habit of mind, as illustrative of this remark.]

The Rev. J. Venn—

This question depends on the distinctions between cheerfulness and levity. Cheerfulness sets pleasing objects before us; levity, ludicrous. The object of cheerfulness is to make happy; of levity, to excite laughter. Cheerfulness proceeds from benevolence; levity often from the contrary. Cheerfulness looks at the bright side; levity at the absurd. Cheerfulness regards times and seasons; levity has no regard to time. [This he illustrated by Mr Whitfield.]

Cheerfulness benefits the man and all around him; it makes him contented and happy. Levity does no good; it dissipates.

Cheerfulness arises from sincerity, and is mixed with it. Levity is often found with a hypocrite; it is a character too often assumed by him.

Cheerfulness is consistent with gravity and seriousness; a man may rise from prayer cheerful. Levity unfits for prayer—as Mr Cecil has shewn.

Cheerfulness leaves no guilt, no bad savour. Levity leaves a sting.

Let, then, a minister be as CHEERFUL as possible, but never indulge in LEVITY.

A fine example of this was to be seen in my own father.

Berridge's vein of levity was his failing and his plague, amidst all his excellencies. And he used to say, that when he prayed most, he was most grave.

In reference to this last remark of Mr Venn's, Mr Scott said, that Mr Whitfield, when first from his closet in the morning, was always grave.

JUNE 24, 1799.

WHAT IS THE BEST PREPARATION FOR THE PULPIT?—Proposed by the Rev. J. Pratt.

Mr Pratt—

I proposed this question two years ago; but it took then too general a turn.

I ask now, " What particular preparation is made for *each sermon?*" There can be no objection to the general preparation being gone

into again. The subject is always of the utmost importance to us.
But I wish to get information on the specific point of actual preparation.

Most of us have made up our principles, and formed our habits.

All may pick up useful hints, though too old to change.

But *I* am seeking a method; and so perhaps are others.

The Rev. J. Newton—

I am too old to learn a new method, though it be better than
mine. To bring others to my method, would be like making shoes
for all men at one last.

Luther had two maxims—" Meditation, Temptation, and Prayer
make a minister." And " *Bene orasse est bene studuisse.*"

The best preparation is, not to be too anxious about it. Anxious
care hinders liveliness and efficacy. It leads to too little dependence
on the Spirit.

Be not didactic. Aim at the conscience. Soldiers aim at the
faces.

Consider, I may be preaching my last sermon. This leads so to
setting forth Christ, as *the Way, the Truth, and the Life.*

The grand thing in preaching, is to produce effect.

Make Christ the prominent figure.

The four books I recommended in *Omicron* are abundant.

Pay less attention to dear self—" How I come off." *

The Rev. J. Goode—

We should begin sermons on our knees.

I follow no regular plan: and seldom begin early, as I undo at the
end what I did at the beginning.

I am best when I fix on Wednesday or Thursday: yet I seldom
begin till Friday or Saturday.

I speak on Tuesday without preparation: but cannot do so on the
Sabbath.

The Rev. W. J. Abdy—

If confessing would do good, I'd confess. It would give you a history of weakness.

I am interested in the question. I have seldom heard my brethren,
without feeling this question:—" Where did he get this sermon?"
This arose from (1.) Pride, and (2.) Humility.

I lament (1.) the want of a good foundation, (2.) natural defects,
(3.) trials.

I never copy: perhaps I take a page or two. I seldom write on a
text that struck me at the time: it is too hard, too sublime.

At a distance of one or two years those difficulties that first occurred
vanish when the text presents itself a second time. I have then
found those texts pleasant.

* The following story will illustrate this :—On Mr Newton descending the pulpit
stairs on a particular occasion, at St Mary Woolnoth's Church, after preaching an impressive sermon, a person who had felt its force leaned over and said, " A most excellent discourse, sir." " The devil told me that, sir, before you !" was Mr Newton's
reply, conscious of the temptation to self-approval.

I gave gone through the Ten Commandments, the Lord's Prayer, the Epistles to the Churches, the Creed.

I generally have spent three days in six in close study. My Sunday morning Sermon costs me now eighteen hours.

Generally on Sunday morning I preach a new Sermon. When not a new one, I have spent six hours in alteration.

On Thursday evening I generally preach on an Epistle in continuation.

After all is written, I put in a little extempore.

There are two extremes. Mine is one. Yet I owe something to my pulpit.

In Gospel preaching, there is often a puerility and trifling. If a great work is to be done in the land, God would raise up very different instruments from us.

We should commend ourselves to every man's conscience. We should shew men that good sense and knowledge are consistent with the Gospel.

The Rev. J. Davies—

Ministers are peculiarly exposed to temptation on this point. They are under temptation—

(1.) To make too much of preaching, and to shew self-dependence.

(2.) To make too little of preaching, and to be guilty of presumption.

How should we distinguish between Satanic and Divine influence in this? I have felt in my own case that I have not been able to distinguish.

On Saturday night I have felt a deadness on a prepared subject.

On Sunday, after being ready on one I have been forcibly struck with another, and have acted hereon; and yet I am hardly satisfied whether I am right.

I am irregular in the choice of a text, and in the time employed on a sermon.

I endeavour to point my sermons to the conscience.

I am obliged to make three new sermons a week. They vary in nature and quantity of notes. Sometimes these are few. But I always write much, and take an abridgment into the pulpit. I read all I take.

The length is forty or fifty minutes.

Resources. I look at none *first*.

The Rev. G. Pattrick—

People are kind in choosing texts: they send letters. I have seldom adopted them, if the letters are anonymous. They are frequently controversial. Such persons seem to want arguments, or to lie in wait.

I have hoped, by taking a subject from the Epistle or Gospel, to avoid offence.

The Rev. H. Foster—

1. I went through the *Lives* for 15 or 16 years; but one might be 200 years on the life of Christ.

Once, at Spitalfields, I took up *Words*—*e. g.*, Faith, &c.   This is a pleasant exercise.

My way of finding texts, when I have no such subjects before me, is various.   When in trouble, or reading an author, or on any other occasion, I set down such texts as occur.   I have found them afterwards, but wondered why I had selected them.

I then tried putting down the *manner* in which such texts struck me.

2. I approve in my judgment of a paraphrase on texts, and then applying them.   But I humour them.   I would have the application as we go along, and not all at the end.

3. The time varies : an hour or more.

4. At one time, I had six sermons a week.   When in a course, I am obliged to get on.

People forget sermons ; I find no difficulty in preaching the same sermon again.

5. I write one great sheet : I never write more, and leave it at home.

Sometimes I get out from Notes into the deep.

6. I am too long : sometimes an hour.   I wish about fifty minutes or forty-five.

7. I like to get hints ; but could never take up anybody's plan. Man's mind has its own form.

I totally disapprove of what Mr N. seemed to countenance—a young man not giving himself up to study.

The Rev. R. Cecil—

I heard N. with pain.   If he studied, he would preach the best sermons of the day.   Self is idle, as well as proud.   It is an injurious thing for a young Minister to propose to himself to be a great preacher : to seek texts to figure on.   This is a temptation.   Let not man be branded with this, because he is determined not to serve the Lord with what costs him nothing.   Timothy is to give himself to reading and meditation.

I set out in life exactly on Mr N.'s plan.   I had bad counsellors. Only going up and letting off a sermon, I really imagined it was trusting in the Lord and doing the thing cleverly.   I talked with a wise and godly man.   He said, "There is nothing like appealing to matters of fact."   We sat down and talked over names.   We found them disreputable.   This first set my mind right.   I saw a man might sometimes succeed ; but if he succeeded in his general interpretation of the Scriptures, if he does this creditably and as *a workman that needeth not to be ashamed*, depend upon it he's a laborious man.

1. I generally look into the portions of Scripture for the day.

In reading, talking, and praying, texts appear in new lights.

One's experience, family matters, state of mind, furnish texts.   One thus chosen, always meets some one in the congregation.

Sometimes I can get no text.   I have found it to arise from sloth, and go to work.   This is the secret.   Make it a basis.   The thing will arise where least expected.

2. My favourite method is to resolve the text into some one point. I talk on the topic and then apply it. I like to ask myself : " What are you about ? "

I do not forestall my thoughts by turning to commentaries. (1.) I talk the subject over to myself. (2.) Write all. And (3.) Arrange.

3. I like to begin early. If driven late, accidents arise. One reckons without the host. The last days may be occupied. It is an advantage while walking to have a subject to think about. Your production will probably be a raw thing if you are driven into a corner.

4. Much depends on one's state of health. I used to make three a week. I do not make less than two. I preached four times for many years.

5. Aim at three-quarters of an hour. Half-an-hour is long enough for a week-day sermon. A man should not allow himself an hour : he may do it occasionally, but not *allow* himself. And I think this because I never hear an hour without wishing it less. This is a grand impediment to be removed from carnal people—the length of the sermon. A large discretion applies to ministers but not to the people. You have a certain quantity of attention to work upon. Make the best use of it while it lasts. The iron will cool, and then nothing or worse is done. If a minister will leave unsaid all his former see-saws, he can easily get within forty minutes.

6. The man does not succeed best who goes to authors. After having settled the plan, I go to Dr Such-an-one to see if I mistake not. I then find it necessary to reject a great many good things which the Doctor says.

I derive more from nature and less from books. The book of Providence ; the Heart-Bible ; the History of the World ; passing occurrences—these are sources to draw from.

The Rev. Thomas Scott—

1. I ask myself what subject I have omitted. I get texts at the Asylum. I sometimes ask for them.

2. As well as I can, I never get two alike. One may be too didactic, yet there is another extreme. People should be made to understand discussion more. I endeavour to commend myself, by means of *truth*, to every man's conscience. I wish to have more of the impressive ; but I do as well as I can.

3. *Give thyself wholly to them.* We should read the Bible through and through, and dwell on every verse as if we had to preach on it. Get whole truth into the head. I seldom get a text till Saturday, and digest it in the morning.

4. I write nothing now ; formerly, I wrote all. I know of no medium.

5. I could say much *pro* and *con* as to the length of a sermon. There is a deal in fashion. I incline to an hour. If the people are tired, I blame myself. The grand thing is to consider those without, to accommodate them.

6. I agree with Mr Newton.

Nearly forty years after this discussion, Mr Pratt drew up for a young man who had just taken Holy Orders, the following Paper on this subject :—

RULES FOR SERMONS.

I. CHOICE OF A SUBJECT.

Always look through the Psalms, Epistle, Gospel, and Lesson of the day. If any passage in these suits particular circumstances, or strikes your mind, take that for your subject.

If any text or subject impress your mind in a lively manner, put that down, and note also the thoughts which are associated with it in your mind. Keep these papers by you to be looked over for subjects when you are not otherwise provided.

Occasionally preach short courses of sermons on connected passages of Scripture, such as the Lord's Prayer, the 17th chapter of St John, the 53d of Isaiah, 72d and 51st Psalms, one of the shorter epistles, and detached but connected portions of the larger epistles.

Short courses may also be preached with advantage on Doctrinal or Practical topics—as, on Regeneration, Faith, Repentance, Affiance in Christ's Justification, Sanctification, Love of God, Love of Man, Relative Duties.

II. MANNER OF HANDLING THE SUBJECT.

The primary meaning and application of the passage must first be diligently ascertained. Make no use of any passage but such as arises by fair inference and just application to present circumstances. Accommodation of passages is the parent of idle fancies.

Having ascertained the primary meaning and application of the text, and settled the manner in which it must be made to bear on your congregation, then consider in what way it may best be treated, —whether or not it falls into just and natural DIVISIONS, which should rarely exceed three ; whether the whole may not be best gathered into PROPOSITIONS on which you would discourse ; or whether OBSER-VATIONS on the passage would not best bring out its pith and marrow : these may sometimes be extended with advantage to four or five. But this, though a pleasant and profitable way of treating subjects, is apt to lead the mind from that *oneness* of object which the preacher should have in view—*i. e.*, he must labour to impress his hearers with *one* subject. However he may handle his text, he should make all his divisions, propositions, and observations bear upon the great leading topic ; and send his hearers away with the impression of that one topic on their minds.

There is one general rule of great importance to be observed on all occasions, whatever be the method of handling the subject as to divisions, propositions, or observations. This is, mingle *statement* and *appeal* together. Beware of the deadening effect of perpetual statement ; beware of the reaction which follows perpetual appeal. Plain, forcible, and wise statements of truth, presented with life to the hearer, and himself questioned, and entreated, and exhorted, and admonished, and comforted, as the case may be, upon that statement ; and that in a brief tone, but rigorous and affectionate manner—this is the perfection of both composition and delivery.

But besides these frequent addresses and applications to the hearer as a sermon proceeds, as you draw to a close, having first briefly but sufficiently recapitulated the subject, make a short application to different classes of hearers, or sum up the whole in one or more lessons or inferences ; but always keeping it in view to send your hearers away with one great subject on their minds.

III. TECHNICALITIES.

Write out, in brief, all the marginal references in the passage. Choose out the most important to be quoted in your sermon to the number of six or eight, as the case may be, as illustrations and explanations of your subject ; and disperse the rest without formal quotation, so as to enrich your composition with scripture ideas and language.

When your subject is chosen, and your manner of treating it determined on, and the marginal references placed before you, distribute those references to their proper places, and then work out the subject according to the views and feelings of your own mind. Having done this, turn over your commentaries, and by them correct any error into which you may have fallen, and from them extract such statements or appeals as may enrich your sermon.

Aim at the composition of one sermon weekly, and no more Having chosen your subject early, let it dwell in your mind as the week passes : enrich it by what passes before your eyes. Let any other sermons come as they may ; let one, and one only, have your whole mind for the week.

IV. UNCTION.

This respects both the *composing* and *delivery* of the sermon. You must labour to get into the spirit of your sermon by fervent prayer. Compose your sermon as a dying man dealing with dying men ; as an ambassador of Christ seeking to win souls to obedience ; as a gentle nurse cherishing her children ; and as a father exhorting, comforting, and charging them. See 1 Thes. ii. 1–12. Thus will vigour be united with affection, and fervour with wisdom. Of all such preaching it may be said in a sound sense, *It is not ye that speak, but the Spirit of your Father which speaketh in you.* An unction from the Holy One will attend such a ministry.

July 8, 1799.

WHAT ARE THE CAUSES AND SIGNS OF DECLENSION IN RELIGION ?— Proposed by the Rev. J. Newton.

Mr Newton—

Christians are often not aware how soon they may decline in their religious affections. The Israelites, when singing on the sea-shore, would little have credited one who told them that soon they would be murmuring.

"Declension begins," says one, "at the *closet door.*"

Satan waits his opportunity. He will not come when impressions are fresh. The heart will cool, if the means of grace are not habitually used.

The declining professor grows formal in prayer and reading the Scriptures.

It belongs to a young experience to lay stress on frames of mind. For their frames may soon go. Not having a solid judgment, they grow weary, if they have to wait.

It is often with us as with the Galatians : we are *soon removed from Him that called us.*

1. Laxness in the use of the means. 2. Itching ears in hearing the truth. 3. Listening to seducers. These are signs of decline.

The Rev. J. Venn—

Cause and Effect act reciprocally on each other.

The following are the chief causes of declension, as it appears to me :—

1. Great laxity.

It is a nice point in such a place as London to draw the line of consistency. The same difficulty attaches to almost every pursuit. For example, Music, Science, &c. This arises from our corrupt nature, and our love to things not spiritual. This draws the mind continually back from God. Worldly cares, troubles, sorrows, &c. &c., come in ; and there is nothing to meet them. Everything earthly has of itself a tendency to draw us away from God. Grace in our hearts, striving with nature, is like a candle exposed to a storm.

2. The fickleness of our nature is another cause of declension. A man has tried the thing, and is tired. He hankers after something else, and is again dissatisfied.

3. The sensuality of our nature is a third. Natural appetites indispose us for God and his service.

4. Creature-love ; love riveted upon earthly objects of affection.

5. Prosperity. The fool in the parable illustrates this. It is an institution of divine wisdom, that there are few who possess an independent fortune.

6. Adversity is another cause. Accumulated cares drive men to despair.

7. Habits of mind, such as indolence, listlessness, &c.

8. Error is a grand cause—the entrance of vital error into our creed. A chief mark of its entrance is the callousness and insensibility which come over the spiritual affections. The Word is no longer sweet and new to us. Providences are no longer observed with gratitude. The advice of friends is not valued or followed as before.

The Rev. J. Davies—

There are general causes : such as the Natural Corruption of the heart ; the access which Satan has to it, &c.

And particular causes; as—1. The discussion of politics.   2. Too much visiting.   3. Neglect of ordinances.   4. Hearing too much. 5. Sins of professors acting as a stumbling-block.

The Rev. H. Foster—

1. A man's nostrums.   A man is vigorous on his own points, lax on other subjects.   2. Divisions and Heresies.   3. Habitual connexion with loose professors.   4. The exercise of the talents we may possess. This is often hazardous to the exercise of grace.   Few men are not *injured*, yea, many are *ruined*, by the exercise of talent.   Therefore God often gives a thorn with the talent, to preserve us.   Every talent is liable to this abuse, and may lead in its exercise to a decline in grace —even in preaching, and the exercise of charity.   5. Attendance on divine ordinances, too, may lead to this, if it lead to an undue reliance on public means, to the neglect of private duties.   6. An undue regard to self—*e. g.*, Jonah.   7. Some flagrant sin allowed and not crucified.

The Rev. R. Cecil—

Decline is a consumption.   Some consumptions do not *kill* a man. He goes into the country and is cured.   We must therefore distinguish between—

1. Declensions in religion which bring a man to spiritual death; and, 2. Others which are temporary, and of which he recovers.

1. Total Declension or Apostasy.

The cause is, he was never regenerated.   *They went out from us, but were not of us; . . . they went out that they might be made manifest that they were not all of us.*   The root is not in such a man.   He is a stony-ground hearer.   Temptation and persecution are two main causes of his going out.   There is a good deal in novelty.   Like Pliable, he hears some one talk of the *good things* of the kingdom.   Such a man's declension is a natural consequence of his character.   Something crosses him.   There is not so much satisfaction as he thought.   But this man *must* die; his decline is a deadly one.

2. But the question respects also those who *have* root in themselves; and yet there is a miserable declension, which needs a thunder-storm to set matters straight.

Men may go a great way and yet not be altogether right with God. All know this.   Men may go far without being suspected.   They can keep up an outside appearance.   Everything seems to others to go on well.   But if he be at bottom a true man, he begins to suspect himself.   He finds it a great labour to keep up this outside appearance; especially if he be a minister.   His spiritually-minded hearers will find him out.   There is something in his way of talking over old matters —there is too much appearance of " saying the thing"—he is cold and dull.   Yet the poor often do not see it.   They say, " He's sound." And perhaps he's apparently sounder than ever.   There is a great tendency to soundness of view in such a state.

Where a man really has grace, this may be part of a dispensation to him.   He has been careless : and he is suffered to decline, that he may feel it and repent, and learn his weak points.

If he has some great besetting sin, it may please God to expose him, and to make him hang his head as long as he lives ; especially if he be a high-spirited man, like David or Hezekiah. But this is God's pulling down, in order to build up.

The CAUSES OF DECLENSION in religion are as follow :—

The world always has much to do in declension in religion. If the man is naturally vain, he will be in danger of sacrificing everything to a name.

A prevailing appetite, if always fed, will stupify at last. Religion is an abstract and elevated thing. *The way of life is above to the wise, that he may depart from hell beneath.*

Keeping on good terms with those who respect us is a grievous snare. The devil knows where to mock a man. Men talk of " taste." The devil has more taste than any man.

Speculation knows not where to rest : hence the " evil heart of unbelief " is soon carried away.

Vain-confidence thinks himself in no danger. He knows the truth, can dispute, &c. Here lies his danger. " What," says Alexander, " shall we fear ? " Why *this*—that we have no fear.

No man indulges himself in anything which his conscience tells him ought not to be done, but at length it eats out his spirit.

The SYMPTOMS OF DECLINE are many.

When a man begins to work off from God and a spiritual mind, he gets fond of gentlemanly company who can entertain him, and know how to respect his character. This " gentlemanly spirit " is a suspicious thing, for it's connected with pride, and with delicacy, and a love of ease ; in short, it's a worldly spirit. It is the reverse of condescending to mean things : the reverse of the spirit of Jesus.

When a man can fix on the sore places of a religious character, and instead of Paul's " weeping " (Phil. iii. 18), speak tauntingly—" Such a man is fond of praying ! but he is fond of money." This too, is a bad sign. This is a galloping consumption.

A strong sectarian spirit is a sign of declension. Honest men are for the vitals. Here is a racket about baptism ; there about something else. If the mind were right, it would see that this is not the *grand* question. Paul's view would be quite contrary to this. See his advice regarding eating herbs.

Aversion to reproof is another sign. The man can't bear to have the thing pointed out, even in the pulpit. Calls it Arminianism, legality, if it scrapes him. *Hast thou found me, O mine enemy ?*

Stupidity under chastisement is another mark. When we are not disposed to ask—*Wherefore dost thou contend with me ?* but are *kicking against the pricks.* Stricken, but not sensible of the Father's hand that smites us.

A high-minded, boasting, unhumbled man, capable of taking down everybody but himself, is in awful danger.

Constant occupation, in worldly concerns especially, is a great snare. The worst is, where a man of business *will* be rich, and keeps two or three shops. They tell me they don't feel it affect their religion.

I don't believe them.   Decline has taken hold of such a man before he begins such a pursuit.   A godly and spiritual man will find the bustle he is in, in his ordinary business, a sufficient snare.

The Rev. T. Scott—

The great cause of declension is, that the heart is not *really converted;* the " two or three shops," the determination to be rich, and such like marks, are an evidence of this.   *If any man love the world, the love of the Father is not in him.*

Some CAUSES OF DECLENSION in real Christians are the following :— (1.) Want of jealousy against temptation.   (2.) Resting in attainments.   (3.) Ministers not entering into the detail of sins.   (4.) Late visitings.   It is the *little foxes which spoil the vines*—*e. g.*, in these visitings, " sacred music," how may it be abused to gratifying the taste merely, without edifying the soul !   (5.) Preaching low experience ; saying what is, rather than what *should be.*   Not judging of the heart sufficiently by the conduct—*e. g.*, Johnson's speaking of Milton's not praying.*   (6.) A false charity.   Making the best of Christians, because they hold our doctrine.   (7.) Selfishness in religion.   (8.) Self-flattery.   (9.) Attachment to particular ministers.   (10.) Infection of lukewarmness.   (11.) Loose principles beget loose practices.   (12.) Quackery —bending the strength against one disorder, while others are all the while eating into the vitals of religion.

The SIGNS OF DECLENSION in religion are—

(1.) Excusing this or that worldly conformity.   *The highway of the upright is to depart from evil.*

(2.) Disproportionate zeal for forms or doctrines.   Zeal satisfies, without asking *what* zeal it is.

(3.) Confidence that all is well, when others doubt of us, and with good reason.   The Laodicean Church.

JULY 22, 1799.

THE PRACTICAL MEANING OF THE APOSTOLIC INJUNCTION, 2 Thess. iii. 6, " THAT YE WITHDRAW YOURSELVES FROM EVERY BROTHER THAT WALKETH DISORDERLY."—Proposed by the Rev. Thomas Scott.

Mr Scott—

" Walking disorderly" is too much the characteristic of the day. False charity is introduced in the place of the holy character of the Scriptures.   Walking disorderly is one of these two things :—Either a man refuses to acknowledge a fault, and he thus perpetuates the act : Or, there is something habitual in his spirit or conduct unchristian— habitual covetousness, habitual ill-temper, &c.

---

* " In the distribution of his hours, there was no hour of prayer, either solitary or with his household ; omitting public prayers, he omitted all. . . .   Prayer certainly was not thought superfluous by him, who represents our first parents as praying acceptably in a state of innocence, and efficaciously after their fall   That he lived without prayer, can hardly be affirmed ; his studies and his meditations were an habitual prayer. The neglect of it in his family was probably a fault for which he condemned himself, and which he intended to correct, but that death, as too often happens, intercepted his reformation."—*Johnson's Life of Milton.*

Such are *to be withdrawn from.* Not that they should incur excommunication, but you would wish to shew a disapproval. The idea is, *sending to Coventry.* Shew him that your silence and distance is a reproof.

The Apostle considered this as true charity.

Many, especially in London, get their bills indorsed by friends, and so pass. The recovery of the man should be one grand part of our aim.

The Rev. J. Pratt—

The Apostle's injunction seems to be directed against some known offenders. It is pronounced with apostolic authority. We can pass no such definitive judgment.

Yet we gather our duty by analogy. If it affect ourselves, we should beware of feeling resentment.

There are some of whom the Christian feels an instinctive disapproval. Many want to rank themselves with Christians who have no title to do so. It is of great importance to mark to the world whom you would hold with, and whom not.

The Rev. J. Clayton—

Discipline would be abused if exercised beyond Scripture authority. Remember the parable of the tares.

Some deny the visible order of the Church, under a pretence of its invisible unity.

" Disorderly" walkers are—(1.) Those who lead a disorderly life ; (2.) Persons of idle-talk ; (3.) Who neglect family government ; (4.) The captious ; (5.) Those who slight reproof.

" *Withdraw from* " such, *i. e.*—(1.) Exhibit a contrary character; (2.) Shew prudent reserve ; (3.) Fall in with these proceedings of the Church according to Christ's injunctions.

Grace in the heart is the principle of orderly walking.

Discipline of God's and man's invention are very different things.

The Rev. B. Woodd—

Scott and Clayton extend disorderly walking too much. If we are to withdraw from all of ill-tempers, covetous, who want family religion, we shall be withdrawing from almost all.

I hope to live in heaven with many with whom I would not wish to walk in the world. If we withdraw from all such, we should become insulated.

I should rather explain this passage by that other, *If any man that is called a brother be a fornicator,* &c. (1 Cor. v. 11.)

The Rev. J. Davies—

This is not so much aimed against flagitious Christians, nor against *every instance* of disorderly walking, nor even against the *habit* of such, as against what the world looks at.

It may not be a gross sin, but yet such as it requires us to bear testimony against to the world.

" *Withdraw,*" *i. e.*, separate from intimacy.

The Rev. J. Venn—

It is not charitable to be censorious; but we must bear in mind the degree of respectability that consorting with a man gives him.

Why are men so notorious? From the want of this separation. Influence is an engine not sufficiently considered. This is a direction of the Apostle in the use of this engine.

I honour Johnson for leaving Millar's shop when he heard that Hume was there.

This keeps up the land-marks.

Walking disorderly refers to venial offences in the world, not flagitious.

Let the degree of withdrawing be proportioned to the injury the man may be supposed to do to the truth.

He may not be the man of my heart; yet respect should be shewn where it is due.

We may go to extremes. The Pharisees got out of *sinners'* way.

Great mischief is done by an indiscreet application of the injunction. Ministers should hold up, and not relax, the standard.

A man may be right in doctrinal standards, but wrong in practice and conduct.

The Rev. H. Foster—

Davies' view of the passage is just—an idle, disorderly, tattling, preaching-and-praying man.

I am often more at a loss to do what I know is right, than to *know* what it is right to do.

One is exposed to extremes from constitution.

The Rev. R. Cecil—

The difficulty lies in the practice. The Christian is God's witness in a degenerate world. *If the salt have lost its savour, wherewith shall it be salted ?*

If nobody join, yet bear *your* testimony.

This disorderly walking is quite distinct from occasional infirmity.

I see such an one mournfully, not arrogantly, not pharisaically ; but with pity.

We are to apply the injunction not to *the fornicators of this world ;* we must *go over to them ;* but if there be any who is *called a brother.*

I have been afraid of a pharisaic sort of withdrawing ; it may have an appearance of pride, or crudity, censoriousness, lifting the nose too high.

It is injurious to lie under this apprehension, even in *his* view. It fortifies him against you.

This I am confident of, that when I have been cold and lax, I have been more disposed to shake hands with a disorderly brother. There is a charge against us on this ground.

There was a man at Lewes, my parish once, who would be affected by my preaching, and would shed tears. But he would go to the neighbouring church, wait at the door, dog the minister there, and tell him he didn't preach the Gospel. Should not I withdraw from such an one ?

It is a low bargain between hearers and preachers:—" Do you like me ? Then come and hear me."

We should attend more to state of things in society than in the Church.

On the 5th August 1799, the next occasion, the subject which was to have been discussed was postponed.   The following entry is made in the Note-book in our possession :—

Postponed the appointed question, and conversed upon the capture of the " Duff."

The event here alluded to was one of painful interest, connected as it was with the work of Missions, which at this time was engaging the thoughts and prayers of so many.

The " Duff " was a vessel of about 300 tons burden, which the Directors of the London Missionary Society purchased and fitted out, in 1794, to convey their first missionaries to the first scene of their missionary efforts—the South Sea Islands.   A lively and deeply interesting account of the first voyage, with all the preparations for it, will be found in Mr Ellis' History of the London Missionary Society, published a few years ago.   Thirty missionaries—a noble company—embarked on their high and holy errand, and after a prosperous voyage reached Tahiti.   They met with a favourable reception from the leading natives of that and of other islands ; and commenced their missionary operations with that promise of the divine blessing which has since been so abundantly manifested in this field.

The " Duff " returned by China, and reached England in 1798, having been about four years performing the whole voyage. Tidings of the safe arrival of the vessel, and of the success of the undertaking, reached London during the annual meeting in May 1798.   A large assembly of the friends of the Society was gathered together at the moment the letter was handed to one of the directors communicating the gratifying intelligence ; and the welcome news produced sensations of gratitude and joy quite beyond description.   Such was the prosperous commencement of the London Missionary Society.   But cloud and sunshine are intermixed in all our best undertakings.   This was the case with this institution in its early operations.

The directors of the Society took speedy measures to prepare the vessel for a second voyage ; and the " Duff " sailed again, in December of the same year, with twenty-nine more missionaries, nine of them married, embarking upon the same errand, and going forth with the blessing and prayers of thousands whom they left behind.   But GOD's *ways are not our ways, nor his thoughts our thoughts.* It pleased him to defeat this second attempt—no doubt for the trial of the faith and patience, both of those who had hazarded their lives in this Christian enterprise, and of those who looked forward with longing expectation for the salvation of the heathen tribes by their means. The vessel fell into the hands of a French privateer off the coast of South America. The missionaries and their families were subjected to great privations and many sufferings—besides the greatest of all, the entire overthrow of their high purpose. The vessel was sold as a prize, and the missionaries left to shift for themselves. Through the overruling providence of God, they reached their native shores in safety in October 1799, by the help of a Portuguese vessel—Portugal being at that time in alliance with England.

Tidings must have reached England of their unhappy lot some weeks before their own arrival, as the Eclectic meeting at which it formed the topic of conversation, as we have seen above, was held on the 5th August.

It appears that the Committee Meetings of the Church Missionary Society—so recently formed (as we noted at p. 98) by members of the Eclectic—were at this time held in the evenings of the days when the Eclectic Meetings took place. The following notice of the capture of the "Duff," taken from No. V. of the Church Missionary Society's Jubilee Tracts, published during the jubilee year, will shew that the sympathy of the Eclectic brethren did not evaporate in mere talk and words, but communicated itself to the Church Missionary evening Meeting which several of them attended, and shewed itself in a more substantial and practical form : and we are the more happy to introduce the extract here, as it illustrates the spirit of charity and kindly feeling which the Church Missionary Society has always shewn towards all other kindred societies, which are engaged in the same work.

After alluding to what took place at the Church Missionary Society's Committee Meeting of the 5th August 1799, the writer of the Tract in question says—

At this Meeting a measure was adopted, which, though not an official act, exhibits the spirit by which the founders of the Society were actuated. The account of the capture of the ship "Duff," the property of the London Missionary Society, having been just received, eleven members present entered into an immediate subscription, to an amount exceeding £50, as a testimony of regard and condolence towards that Society ; and, relying upon the concurrence of the absent Members of the Committee in the same feelings, they sent the sum of one hundred guineas the same evening to the Treasurer of the London Missionary Society.

The Directors of the London Missionary Society passed a Resolution on this occasion, expressive of their warmest gratitude, and conveying to the Committee of the Church Missionary Society the following generous assurance :—

"That, as we consider them to be engaged in the same glorious cause with ourselves, the success of their exertions will afford us the same pleasure, and excite within us equal thankfulness, with our own."

A notice of this also occurs in a volume of Mr Scott's Letters and Papers, p. 155, as follows. Writing to a friend about the Church Missionary Society, now in its earliest infancy, he says—

"You may depend upon it that our new Society is not needlessly losing time. We cast anchor for a while, to avoid running on rocks ; but we mean soon to go on, and we would wish not to make more haste than good speed. We mean to begin on a small scale, and afterwards to enlarge it if we can, and we have no fear of *not* getting money, if the Lord will but *form us Missionaries*. One thing we have done—as soon as we heard that the "Duff" was taken, we, as individuals of the Committee, sent the Missionary Society a hundred guineas, as a token of regard and condolence, which has tended greatly to conciliate them, and to convince them that we are coadjutors and not rivals."

At the following meeting also, August 19, 1799, the subject for the evening again gave way to one of a melancholy nature—the death of one of the members of their body. The notice of the evening runs as follows :—

Postponed the appointed question again, to be discussed the next evening ; and conversed upon the death of Brother Bacon, which took place on Wednesday, the 7th instant, rather suddenly.

Mr Bacon was the senior of the two celebrated sculptors, father and son, of the present and last century. His memoir was written by his friend and admirer—the Rev. R. Cecil, and is to be found in Mr Cecil's Works. He was taken ill on Sunday, the 4th August, and died on the 7th, in his 59th year. During this short illness, he expressed his firm reliance on that Sure Foundation on which he had long and consistently built :—

"Thus departed a man," says his biographer, after giving proofs of his friend's great genius, "who, though one of the most distinguished artists of his day, had a mind capable of esteeming this rank but a small attainment. He grasped at the higher honours and unfading rewards which he now enjoys. Amidst the infirmities and temptations to which our common nature is subject, and under which an enlightened eye and a sincere heart led him often bitterly to complain, he was decided in the grand point, and determinately pursued it. He desired to bear his testimony to it after his death ; and therefore ordered, by his will, a plain tablet, with the following inscription (after the name and date), to be placed near his grave :—

" WHAT I WAS AS AN ARTIST
SEEMED TO ME OF SOME IMPORTANCE WHILE I LIVED :
BUT
WHAT I REALLY WAS AS A BELIEVER IN CHRIST JESUS,
IS THE ONLY THING OF IMPORTANCE TO ME NOW."

Mr Bacon had for some time been the only lay-Member of the Eclectic.

SEPTEMBER 2, 1799.

AS DIFFERENT SPEAKERS ARE INTRODUCED IN SCRIPTURE, BY WHAT RULES CAN WE DISTINGUISH THE SURE TESTIMONY OF GOD FROM THE OPINION OF THE SPEAKERS ?—Proposed by the Rev. Josiah Pratt.

Mr Pratt—

A distinction must be preserved between what scripture itself says and what is only said in scripture.

The sacred volume is a collection of compositions of different kinds, and written at distinct times. Its composition is such, that though the authors were excited and assisted in writing, yet there are many others, besides the authors, introduced as speaking. Besides the historical books, there are passages in most of the others, which come under this description. Moreover, there are many passages, which, though they are not historical or narrative of things done, yet they are records of many sayings or expressions not belonging to the authors of the scripture, but reported as of others, or wherein the writer personates others.

1. Many of the persons were wicked characters. For example, Balaam.

2. Some of them are good men perhaps, but under an improper bias or an error of judgment at the time : as Job.

3. Some good characters there are, apparently under no bias or errors, who yet speak with *no authority*; as, for example, Hannah.

The sayings of such persons the Holy Ghost does not adopt, but merely registers. Nor does scripture affirm that what these say is true ; but only that it is true that they said it.

A historian, who records errors and crimes and blasphemies, must be *inspired* to record them, though they come not from inspiration.

Such things *must* be found there, if we consider the *end and use* of scripture.

Wicked men are necessary to exhibit God's character, and illustrate His providence. Many things are to be avoided, as well as many practised. It is necessary, therefore, to shew us, in the characters and failings of others, the rocks and shelves as well as the pole star. We could not be armed against the Tempter's methods, if we were altogether ignorant of them ; nor could we anywhere learn them so well as in *His* book, who can alone discover the wiles and depths of Satan, and track him through all his windings and labyrinths.

Here the *antidote* is exhibited with the *poison*. The defeats of victories of others may teach us, at *their* cost and without *our* hazard, the true art of their warfare in which we are all concerned.

As God fed his servant Elijah, sometimes by an angel, sometimes by a woman, and sometimes by ravens ; so He makes all persons in the Bible, whether good, bad, or indifferent, to supply His servants with that instruction which is the aliment good for their souls. See Boyle on the *Style of Scripture.*

The Rev. G. Pattrick—

I have felt the difficulty brought forward in this question. But I have found my chief relief to be in comparing any doubtful sentiments with passages of unquestionably inspired authors.

As to the third kind mentioned by Mr Pratt, I should think, that what they say would not have been introduced into scripture, unless it were of authority.

The Rev. R. Cecil—

1. Consider the characters speaking.

We are in no danger of being misled, by what a speaker in the scripture says, into an error about his character. Thus we are in no mistake about the character of Balaam, though he spoke excellent things.

Nor are we in danger of error from their sentiments. For consider the case of Job's friends, who, though they mistook Job's character, erred not in sentiment. They failed in the application of the sentiment. Job's friends were made to *confess* their failure : they caught their own thumb in the screw !

Now taking the *whole*, there is light enough to walk by.

2. Consider, too, the character not only of the speaker, but of those spoken to.

For instance, in the case of St James, Luther should have considered the *scope* of the Apostle and to whom he wrote, before he had doubts of the genuineness of his epistle.

Throughout scripture, the analogy of faith is to be kept in view. Accident and circumstances much affect things. Sometimes they are spoken under the influence of feeling, sometimes under temptation : as for example, when the prophet says, *Thou hast deceived me and I was deceived.* Are we likely to be misled by what *Jonah* said ? We must consider the circumstances of his case.

Again, the speaker may be in an *uninformed* state : as the disciples before the descent of the Holy Spirit.

I have no difficulty about the third class. I always consider what is found in scripture should be reverenced, for the very reason that it is there, unless there be some strong and sufficient reason against it.

Thus, with regard to an ascription of praise like Hannah's : we are told that *all scripture is given by inspiration of God;* and there is no intimation that it was a mere effusion ! This is a question which a captious man might make a puzzle of, while there would be no difficulty to an honest man. It reminds me of Soame Jenyns's remark about the cloak at Troas. Some men *contrive* to cavil.

The Rev. Thomas Scott—

1. *No scripture is of private interpretation.* We are not to try what we can make of scripture, but what God the Spirit means in the passage we may be reading. The instructions we are to derive from it is a distinct question.

2. The clear passages are to explain the obscure, and not the obscure the clear. Such as God's character and laws, and the gospel and the ground of it.

I have never thought of the third sort of speaker. I think with Cecil, that where no reason appears for its not being scripture, it ought to be accounted as such.

Nothing hurts so much as bringing proofs from *irrelevant* passages, somewhat after the spirit of Hervey. Nor would I bring one passage, if a stronger is to be found. I would not, for instance, bring Hannah's, *He keepeth the feet of his saints,* to prove perseverance, when I can bring such a proof as this in our Lord's own words, *They shall never perish, neither shall any man pluck them out of my hand.*

No doubt, God spake by Balaam. The gift of *prophecy* and the gift of *grace* are distinct.

There are certain grand principles in which Job and his friends all agreed. Now this may be set down as of authority, from that circumstance, if there be no other proof.

I go further than Cecil against Job's friends. They failed not only in application, but in some points in principles. For instance, they seem to have thought prosperity too closely connected with godliness.

The decision of the Almighty in the last chapter has helped me to interpret the book, as to the view I should have of the different speakers.

Job was wrong in his view of himself, and yet his doctrine was more true throughout, than that of his friends. They erred in principle. Elihu also was wrong in some points. I think that the idea of his being Christ is unfounded.

In the Psalms, where anything appears wrong, the Psalmist is led to correct himself, and shew that he was under an infirmity. The Psalms and other parts of Scripture present a standard of *genuine experience*, as well as of *genuine devotion.*

What Paul says of his own inspiration only proves a difference between a counsel and a command. But even if we suppose the Apostle to make a distinction between his *inspired* and his *uninspired* injunctions, this would confirm very strongly the authority of his inspired injunctions.

On the next evening, September 16, 1799, the subject was, WHAT IS THE NATURE AND EFFECT OF THE FEAR OF GOD? On this we have no remarks.

WHAT ARE THE CHARACTERISTICS OF A SPIRITUAL MIND, AND WHAT ARE THE MEANS OF GROWTH THEREIN ?—Proposed by the Rev. J. Pratt.

Mr Pratt—

I. What is spiritual-mindedness? What are its characteristics?

Spiritual-mindedness and a mind for spiritualising are distinct things.' Spiritual-mindedness is an affair of the heart : spiritualising, of the imagination. A man may spiritualise much, and yet not be spiritual : and, on the other hand, a man may be truly spiritual, and yet not much given to spiritualise.

A spiritually-minded man is one who walks closely with God. The characteristics of a spiritual mind are those feelings and habits which flow naturally from living near to Him.

But grace will take something of the colour of the vessel which contains it. And therefore the same degrees of grace are extremely different in their actings ; for example, in a phlegmatic and a sanguine disposition, a cold man and an impassioned man.

Spiritual-mindedness in the one shews itself in godly integrity, right aims, readiness to entertain religious subjects. He shews steadiness in the use of means. He may not read much, may not be lively, because he is not so by nature nor in common life. You must expect it in principle, rather than in ardour, in such a person.

Spiritual-mindedness in the other shews itself in his superadding something to the first, while it exposes the man to the charge of want of steadiness. It superadds, however, affection, quickly kindled, easily kindled. It brings principles into more apparent and obvious, and perhaps effective, action.

The word is sometimes used in the New Testament in contradistinction to ritual observances, carnal good things, &c. But it is also used there precisely in our sense ; *e. g.*, in 1 Cor. 2d and 3d chapters. Rom. viii. 6, *To be spiritually minded is life and peace.* Isa. xxxviii. 16, *O Lord, by these things men live, and in all these things is the life of my spirit.* So speaks Hezekiah.

The characteristics of spiritual-mindedness are to be found, in their degree, in all true Christians.·

1. It is seen in faith.

What is not of faith is sin, in this sense also. This is against Quakers. Don't turn *the cross* into a *spiritual mind ;* but let a spiritual mind flow from a believing view of the cross of Christ.

2. It supposes an edge on the conscience.

Such as have a spiritual mind *have their senses exercised to* discern *both good and evil.* Prejudice, selfishness, carnal bias, do not so exert their deadening effect on such a mind. There is no putting *bitter for sweet and sweet for bitter.* There is an instinctive uprightness and integrity in its actings. It detects the beginnings of sin at an immense distance.

3. It is also marked by an easy conscience.

There is a constant presence of principle. *The righteous is a sure foundation.* You may always know *where* and *how* to find him. *Herein do I exercise myself always to have a conscience void of offence*—and the conscience is at ease.

4. It is seen in the affections being habitually diverted from evil.

It is seen in the believer's jealously guarding the avenues which lead to any besetting sin, *e. g.*, any books, or pictures, or tales which may excite what is evil in us.

5. It is also manifested by the affections being habitually directed to good.

When objects and events turn the mind to devout and holy reflections, *e. g.*, when the sight of suffering excites in us grateful affections towards God for his mercy to *us*.

II. The means of growth in spiritual-mindedness.

These are much like those in the natural body.

1. EXERCISE is necessary. *Herein do I exercise myself.—By reason of use,* those of full age *have their senses exercised.—Exercise thyself unto godliness.*

2. FOOD is also requisite. *The sincere milk of the word, that ye may grow thereby. Strong meat belongeth to them that are of full age.*

The Rev. J. Clayton—

The spring of spiritual-mindedness is the new life—union with Christ.

I. Its characteristics are seen in its actings : in contest with sin in all its forms : in delight and refreshment in spiritual worship.

It discovers itself in our choice of society. It refines and corrects the relative affections.

II. Means of growth in spiritual-mindedness.

1. Retirement from sensible objects to meditation on the unseen. The life of sense is fed by the presence of sensible objects.

2. Attention to the most spiritual duties, *e. g.*, prayer, meditation, self-examination. When in secret, we are away from the sympathy of our companions ; warmth now kindles from the altar itself. There is a difference between borrowing fire from others and receiving it direct from Jesus Christ.

3. Attention to order and economising of our time in secular affairs.

4. Avoiding the society of carnal professors. We should collect good materials, to be treasured up in our thoughts, for meditation. The mind is easily carnalised. *Religious* politics, as well as *secular* politics, are often deeply injurious to spiritual-mindedness.

The Rev. J. Davies—

There is a distinction between a spiritual mind and a spiritual frame. A spiritual mind is that which a man receives under the various influences of the Holy Spirit—enlightening, comforting, sanctifying him.

It is not a characteristic of a spiritual mind that a man can talk much about religion.

I. The characteristics are these :—

1. An abiding sense of the presence of God on the mind. Psalm cxxxix.

We may be in this frame in the midst of worldly occupation. *Being in the fear of the Lord, all the day long.*

2. The affections drawn out after God—longing for His return when absent : delighting in Him when present : *Whom have I in heaven but thee, and there is none upon earth that I desire beside thee.—Many say, Who will shew us any good? Lord, lift up the light of thy countenance upon us!*

3. Delight in thinking much of Christ, and exulting in Him. *He, the Spirit, shall take of the things of Christ, and shew them unto you.*

4. Deep humility. This we see in Isaiah ; so in St John : *I fell at his feet as dead.* So also Abraham, in his conference with God.

5. Love in exercise. See this in the Apostle John.

6. Fondness for the company of those who are in a spiritual frame. *Come hither, and hearken, ye that fear God, and I will tell you what he hath done for my soul.—They that feared the Lord spake often one to another.*

II. Means of growth.

1. Setting apart a daily portion of time for private religious reflection. Isaac went out to meditate in the fields. Some of the Psalms appear to be the result of such particular seasons set apart for contemplation, *e. g.*, Ps. viii. ; Ps. xix.

2. Frequent converse with the godly. *Iron sharpeneth iron, so a man sharpeneth the countenance of his friend.*

3. Family religion ; especially if the events of the day are observed.

4. Preserve a due frame of body, keep it healthy and vigorous. Watch over its safety.

The Rev. H. Foster—

We all, with open face beholding as in a glass the glory of the Lord, are changed into the same image from glory to glory, even as by the Spirit of the Lord.

The spiritual man is an image of God. He is formed by contemplating God in the gospel of His grace.

The mind that was in Christ, was a spiritual mind. Christ being perfectly spiritually-minded, had—

1. An entire subjugation to the will of God.

2. Was deeply sensible to the misery of man ; and—

3. Though conversant with sinners, yet was he kept untainted by sin. Spiritual minds will come more and more to see God's glory.

The desire of going to heaven is equivocal in its motive. But when a man refers salvation and all he has and hopes for to the glory of God, he has much of Christ's mind.

I would recommend Owen's work, *On Spiritual-mindedness.*

The Rev. R. Cecil—

I. What is spiritual-mindedness ?

Owen says, Bring a man of a carnal mind into a large miscellaneous company, and he will have much to do. Take him into a company of Christians, he will shew but little interest. Go with him into a smaller company engaged in religious exercises, he will feel still less. Leave him in a closet and force him to think upon God and eternity, it is intolerable to him.

A spiritual man is born into a *new world*—he has a new *taste*. He *savours the things of the Spirit*. He is like the needle—when once magnetised, it will continually tend to the pole, in a way no other needle will.

This is a subject on which we can do little with the world : they have no taste for it.

It is what some think fanaticism. Even Horsley, though he will go with Christians into *principles,* thinks their *longing* for higher affections fanaticism.

The following are characteristics :—

Self-loathing is a characteristic of a spiritual mind.

The spiritual man is able to walk and talk with God. He has his transactions with his God. If he feel dead and heartless, this is a matter he can refer to his God. He seeks from Him a wisdom for the day, for the hour, for the affair in hand.

The spiritual mind deals much in referring its affairs to God. " Let the Lord manage this—His is a different way from mine. Let it be !" *Surely, I have behaved and quieted myself as a child that is weaned of his mother : my soul is even as a weaned child.*

The spiritual mind is like the sensitive plant. " I shall smart if I touch this or that." There is a holy shrinking from what is hurtful.

There is something in the spiritual mind which even surprises itself : there is the beaming in of a holy joy and satisfaction.

When bereaved of earthly comforts, it can find rest in Christ and in His promises ; and the man can say, " Well, it's enough ! Let Him take the rest."

I have tried much to direct young people, when shaken by the conversation of people of the world, to observe the marks of a spiritual mind. If you can't answer their arguments, mark their spirit. Mark what a contrary spirit you are called to.

A spiritual mind is a mortified mind. The Church of Rome talks of mortification, but it goes not deep enough. Simon Stylites on his pillar is very high in his pretensions, if he can get people to pray to him and ask him to pray for them. But the spiritual mind must have wings to carry it upwards, and must, therefore, mortify whatever would retard its flight.

A spiritual mind is an ingenuous mind. There is in us all a sort of hypocrisy. We are not quite stripped of our outward guise. One man covers himself with a rag of one sort, and another with one of another. People who think they don't do this, do it, and don't know they do it. The truly spiritual mind is ingenuous in proportion as it is spiritual. The axe is laid to the root of a vain-glorious spirit.

Yet the spiritual mind is a *sublime* mind. It has a vast, extensive view. It has seen Christ ; and therefore cannot admire the stones of the Temple. As Fenelon says, Christ had seen His Father's house, and therefore could not be taken with the glory of the earthly structure.

II. As to the means of maintaining spiritual-mindedness.

Touch not pitch, if you would not be defiled.

Men go on long, saying, *Is it not a little one?* Beware of this. There is much in mortifying the body. There are slow, silent marches which the flesh will steal on us :—the spirit and temper are too apt to rise up ; the tongue to get loose ; imagination, if we give her liberty, will ride on our back.

Vain company, though not wicked, will mar our spirit—carnal professors especially lower the tone. I caught a sort of contagion once from such men. When I had much schooling in my illness, I detected a thief, *a little thief.* I looked back on days spent in my study, when I waded through history and poets and journals, &c. &c. Oh, but I was in my study ! that seemed enough. Another man's trifling is notorious to all observers ; but what are *you* doing ? It has nothing to do with the spirit : nor, perhaps, has it any reference to the good of my people. I speak not of a chastened use of literature ; but against its abuse.

Beware of temptation. The mind, dwelling on sinful objects, is darkened for days. Shun idleness. *Exercise thyself unto godliness.* Plan for God. Keep the company of the godly : the very sight of a good man, though he says nothing, will cheer the soul. Confess Jesus Christ. Study his honour and glory. Be much in prayer : let the ejaculations of your heart rise to heaven. All this will help you to maintain a spiritual mind !

The Rev. J. Newton—

We can't reason ourselves into this spiritual-mindedness ; nor be persuaded into it by another.

The ground of a spiritual mind lies in the three resemblances of Light, Sight, and the New Birth.

We must have a *taste* for divine things. They are not to be understood but by tasting. No *description* of a fine apple will give any idea of its taste.

There must be the sympathy of the heart. How are we affected by a child returning from a foreign country ! The spiritual mind so looks for Christ, the unseen though not unknown Saviour.

Much of the spirit of prayer—this is a chief means of growth. A courtier acquires an air, in his intercourse at court, not to be got elsewhere. If we would be *like* our King, we must *live* with Him.

The Rev. Thomas Scott—

Brother Pratt seemed to think a sanguine more effective than a phlegmatic mind. But though a steady and solid man makes less noise, he is often more effective. The difference between the two constitutions is like the difference between brushwood and logwood.

Owen describes the spiritual mind by its quantity rather than by its quality. He has said what is likely to distress : we must therefore receive it with caution. Scripture represents it to be like gold. If there be but *one grain*, still its the thing. Owen must have a *certain quantity*.

God made man's nature—animal, rational, spiritual. Man has kept the animal and rational, but has lost the spiritual, till God re-implants it.

The spiritual mind does not spring from the view of spiritual objects ; a spiritual nature must first be given, before we can see spiritual objects. The capacity of perceiving the beauty and excellence of spiritual objects wherever they exist—this implies a spiritual mind. Spiritual objects exist principally in the scriptural character of God. They shine in the person of Jesus Christ, who is *chief among ten thousand, and altogether lovely*. He who loves not the loveliness of the divine character of Jesus Christ, has none of the right kind of love. Spiritual objects shine in the word of God, the law and the gospel. They are seen in their measure in God's people.

A truly spiritually-minded man loves spiritual-mindedness in another party more than a less spiritually-minded man in his own.

Spiritual conflict, in such a world as this, is a strong characteristic of a spiritual mind.

A spiritual mind keeps itself, *out of regard to God,* from besetting sins.

A spiritual mind uses lawful goods cautiously. *I will eat no flesh while the world standeth, lest I make my brother to offend.*

A spiritual mind will conform to society ; but will grow into a holy indifference about " what he eats, or what he drinks, or what he puts on."

We are behind Christians of the last century in spiritual-mindedness.

Brother Clayton once told us of an inquisitive Jew, who said, " I go to your church; there I hear morals. I go to your meeting; there I hear of Jesus Christ. But I have read over and over your New Testament ; there I read much of the SPIRIT ! "

October 14, 1799.

WHAT IS IT TO PREACH CHRIST, AND HOW FAR SHOULD CIRCUMSTANCES REGULATE THE METHOD OF DOING IT ?—Proposed by the Rev. Josiah Pratt.

Mr Pratt—

I. WHAT IS IT TO PREACH CHRIST ?

FIRST : It is to make Christ the SUBJECT of our preaching.

And this, in general, includes the whole sum of Gospel truths respecting man's salvation by Christ. " *We preach* CHRIST JESUS *the* LORD," says the Apostle.

But, in particular, the preaching of Christ, as the subject of our ministry, comprehends our setting Him forth—

1. In HIS SUBSTITUTION.

We must preach the law in its condemning power: and shew that *all* men are *concluded under sin;* are under arrest ; and in an utterly hopeless condition by nature. We must make them despair of discharging the debt of penalty, as well as of duty.

Then we must represent CHRIST to them as a SURETY, as a SUBSTITUTE, and His ability and willingness to discharge their debt *for* them ; that He *atones* for their crimes ; and that He works out *another righteousness* for them.

This is a most essential branch of His mediatorial excellence. It is a fundamental article of true Christianity. It is the ground of all our hopes. What He *did* and *suffered*, He did and suffered in *our stead*. 1 Pet. iii. 18 ; 2 Cor. v. 21.

2. In HIS SUFFICIENCY He must be set forth.

Here it is, through Him, that we are to procure the *agency of the Spirit*.

We must set forth His fulness and infinite divinity ; His grace—free and unbounded ; His power—almighty ; His willingness—without reserve.

In Him are found—all that righteousness which the law requires ; all that grace which the gospel promises ; all that a guilty, helpless, perishing sinner can want. And all is *freely offered*.

3. In HIS COMPLETENESS AND COMPREHENSIVENESS we must exhibit Him.

CHRIST should be made the centre of all the subjects we enter upon. Let us handle no subject as mere philosophers : but point at Jesus in all the *credenda* and *agenda*, and from Him draw all reasons, encouragement, stimulus, motives.

Is it the nature and perfections of God we are treating of ? These are displayed most eminently *in the face of* JESUS CHRIST. Is it the law in its strictness and spirit ? Remember that CHRIST *is the end of the law for righteousness to every one that believeth*. Are the uses of the law our topic ? *The law is our schoolmaster to bring us to* CHRIST. Are we dilating on the gospel promises and blessings ? These must be considered as purchased by the blood, and distributed by the grace, of CHRIST.

Are we preaching of *faith ?* Consider Christ as the author and finisher, and direct object of faith. Are we calling people to repentance ? 'Tis CHRIST, *exalted to the right hand of the Father*, who must *give repentance*, as well as *remission of sins;* and Christ crucified, and viewed by faith, must be the first spring of repentance. Are we enforcing gospel obedience ? This should be considered as a general fruit of faith in CHRIST and of union to Him, springing from constraining love to Him ; performed by strength and grace derived from Him, and accepted only through Him.

CHRIST must be considered as " ALL IN ALL," *the Alpha and Omega, the Author and Finisher*. The fountain from which all is derived ; the centre in whom all terminates. His righteousness ALL in justification. His spirit and grace ALL in sanctification. And enjoyment of Him ALL in glorification.

SECONDLY : To preach Christ, is to make CHRIST the END of our preaching, as well as the subject.

We preach not ourselves but Christ Jesus the Lord, and ourselves your servants, for Jesus' sake. We must aim at the glory of Christ : and make the advancement of His interest our ultimate end.

We should detect, expose, disclaim, sacrifice the grand idol—SELF. We may speak much about Jesus Christ, yet not preach Christ : yea, men may preach Christ, too, as the subject of their preaching, and yet not for Christ's glory, but their own. We should make His honour and interest the centre of all our labours and industry. We should fix our eye on it as our mark, and endeavour to steer towards it. Our business is to commend Christ, not ourselves : to win souls to Him, not to ourselves.

Let us set at a holy distance all respects and regards which interfere in any sort with this high end.

II. THE METHOD OF PREACHING CHRIST—how to be regulated.

The obligation to preach Christ fully is universal and unqualified. Our inquiry only concerns the manner of doing it acceptably.

It is easy to do it in the simple direct way. Yet circumstances may call a minister to search out a better way.

1. Circumstances concerning the preacher himself.

His mind may be of a peculiar form : his experience of a peculiar cast.

Every man is *sui generis*, both in mind and experience. Every man, therefore, has *his own way :* and is natural and graceful *only in that way.* But it is a great error to think there is no *danger* peculiar to him. Every man has his peculiar dangers, as well as his peculiar forte. A wise man will remember this, and guard.

2. Circumstances as concerning his hearers.

They may require to be brought round, to be treated wisely.

Now, there is great difficulty in all this. It is not easy not to follow one's own spirit or contrivances. Yet none should judge his brethren. But each should feel a godly jealousy of himself. He should beware of human respects and regards. For while lawfully and wisely attending to them, it is easy to slide into an unholy frame. It is better to lean to the plain evangelical side, than attempt to tamper. If we bring men round, it may be perhaps *not to the true gospel.*

The Rev. J. Clayton—

A minister should not try to unmake himself. Yet he should try to make the Bible his standard. There is always a danger, lest we should have an edition of truth of our own.

I should like to hear what the brethren say about preaching Christ personally and closely. There is a danger of being thought too pointed and personal. But it is a question whether the Epistles are not pointed at particular persons : and therefore, whether we should not use our preaching in the same close manner, and how far this is to be considered as necessary to usefulness. If you know of individual deficiencies in any particular person, is it or is it not bearing hard to mention them ?

The Rev. J. Newton—

It is necessary to preach the glory of Christ's proper deity. How rich He was before He became poor. This shews the exceeding sinfulness of sin.

The way to make known God's glory and greatness, is only in JESUS CHRIST.

The Moravians in North America began with CHRIST.

It has been a rule with me for years never to preach a sermon without such a view of Jesus Christ that a man shall understand the gospel from that sermon. I *have* preached *true* sermons, but not *wholly* true. My aim now is to bring forth Jesus, as *Alpha and Omega*.

The Apostles seem to make digressions, as we should call them, to *bring in* Jesus Christ.

Our preaching of Christ should be with personal application. We should not needlessly offend ; but be faithful. Christ will go before us, to tread our enemies under our feet, that we may follow Him to gather up the spoils.

The Rev. B. Woodd—

The preacher should *discuss* his subject. If he is on a duty he should discuss it, and then shew its connexion with Christ.

Christ's love should be the motive ; His Spirit the power ; His glory the end.

We are not to take the Fifth Commandment and preach justification from it. There are many passages of Scripture History, the observations flowing from which would be chiefly of a *moral* nature ; yet they should trace up to Christ as Lord of Providence, &c.

As to the influence of circumstances, I have no idea of any accommodation of the matter, though there may be as to *manner*. Expressions which may give offence are to be avoided.

Yet we must be careful to preach a clear and decisive gospel. We *may* so preach as to be received ; yet to no profit. There is more danger in giving *no* offence, than the contrary. The great features of the gospel can't be too pointed.

If the application be not particular, it is no application at all.

The Rev. J. Goode—

To preach Christ is to exhibit Him, more especially in the CROSS.— *Bostwick.*

The smallest wheel in a watch, if it be wrong, will stop the motion. So by misplacing one point in a sermon, we may remove the truth and efficacy of the whole.— *Walker.*

Christ, as the substance, centre, foundation, should be the *drift* of all preaching.

Preach Christ at all times with affection ; but also with *fidelity*. It is possible so to polish the arrow as to take off the barb. Paul was learned ; yet at Corinth he determined to know nothing but Jesus Christ and Him crucified.

The great aim of the gospel is to open the heart to Jesus Christ.

There would be no opposition from the powers of darkness, if there were no danger of the heart being opened to Christ.

God's great instrument to open the heart is the preaching of Christ. Nothing is so effectual, it reaches the conscience and the heart, when nothing else will.

The Rev. W. J. Abdy—

We blame sinners, and they are justly blameable; yet we look at them with *compassion*, and propose the great remedy.

In *what manner* shall I represent this remedy which I have, so as to lead them to use it and value it.

Circumstances must regulate. In time, circumstances may change. The great difficulty is to make the necessity of regeneration understood and received.

The large number of false professors is an obstacle.

I feel more difficulty myself in enlarging on Christian *duties* than on Christian *doctrines*. Yet the Epistle to the Ephesians is a fine pattern for us to follow. There is so much said of the Glory of God, the Love of Christ, and the Example of Christ.

The Rev. J. Venn—

What is it to preach Christ?

The answer will vary according to the cause for the question being put. If I am opposing Heathens, or Jews, or others in particular, then a limited sense must be put upon the question. If, for instance, it be in opposition to a *legal* preaching, the errors must be detected; and there will be no preaching Christ, without a clear and prominent setting forth of the ground of justification by Christ.

If the question were put by a pastor of a flock, and in a general way, I should answer, no part of the Gospel is to be left out, if you would preach Christ.

Hear the·Apostle : WHOM WE PREACH, *warning every man, and teaching every man in all wisdom, that we may present every man perfect, in Christ Jesus.*

He who leans to a particular and narrow preaching of Christ, will have his people become Antinomians, or legalists, or followers of some unsound views.

Circumstances should entirely regulate the preaching of Christ.

Consider the state of the people, and on that part in which they need instruction lay the stress. James preached Christ, when he refuted the idea of a barren faith without works being real faith; when he shewed the error of undue regard to riches.

The Epistles pointed at particular circumstances.

The Rev. J. Davies—

There is a *general* way of preaching Christ, with particular application, and there is a *smooth* way of preaching Christ, so as to *lull* men. But it is essential to hold Him forth in His whole character, as Prophet and King, as well as Priest : we should preach the Law and Gospel always *conjointly*.

Circumstances must often require *a choice of subjects*, and also that each sermon should have some one feature prominent.

The Rev. R. Cecil—

A common counterfeit of the truth is this—A man takes the Fifth Commandment, and goes off to the Gospel. A discerning person probably perceives that it is so far from the simplicity and truth of the Gospel, that he is offended. But good people, nevertheless, get good from it. Yet it gives a bad taste, and also forms a bad standard by which men are to be tried.

False professors plague us. But if I preach a *whole* Christ, I will find them out. Some seem to think that in the choice of a *wise* way, there lurks a trimming disposition. There is a secret in doing a thing which none but an honest man finds out. A knave is not wise enough. We must not judge for one another, it has been well said. It is sufficient for us to know what *we* can do. The Apostles did the thing in *different* ways. Nay, they *could not* do it in each other's way. Each was in his proper work.

There are two extremes which all should watch against, for we are all liable to fail. One is, falling into a driving way of preaching.

Another is, resorting to a kind of rational contrivance. An ingenious man thinks he can so preach Christ that people will not say, "This is not Tabernacle preaching." But the fear is, he has not delivered his message. People don't know what he means. He devises a carnal contrivance to avoid a cross, and he does no good.

The truth *must* be preached—better coarsely than not at all.

This is a maxim. If the Gospel is a medicine, and a specific which must be got down as it is, then any attempt to disguise the *matter* of which it consists must defeat the end. The Jesuits in China did this, and utterly failed.

Accommodation of manner must consist in *humility*—coming down to the capacity of men.

If you have to do with learned men, you may use your learning; but not otherwise.

Here is caution. If you so preach, mind not little cavillers.

On the other hand, be exceedingly cautious when men of God are the butt and scorn of the world, not to think that you can escape.

It is a foolish project to avoid giving offence. But avoid giving unnecessary offence. Offence is necessary if the *truth* give it; but unnecessary if a man's own spirit is the cause. If a man of a naturally tyrannical spirit lose himself and give offence, it may be said in truth—"The devil is roused!" Why, the devil roared through him.

St Paul is a great example, not only in other points, but in this in particular. How he laboured to make this and that thing reasonably plain, and another thing palatable.

In imitating examples, there are two rules to be observed:—

1. Do not stretch beyond your measure to reach unto another.

2. Do not, however, despise in another the measure you cannot reach yourself.

A sound head, and a simple heart, and a spirit dependent on Christ, are sufficient to conduct us in every variety of circumstance.

The Rev. T. Scott—

There is great danger of our preaching Christ *partially*.

Some, from the short account given us of the Apostle's preaching in the Acts, collect a particular way of preaching Christ. But compare the account of St Paul's preaching to the Thessalonians given there, with his Epistles to them.

There is an enthusiastic way of preaching Christ. Impressions, fancies, dreams, &c. But here you will always find that something sets aside Christ.

The dark ages had a superstitious way of preaching Christ. It's Christ in a corner—on a picture. One Christ to the senses, another Christ to the imagination.

An ardent man should guard against an imprudent way ; and a cold man against prudence.

The Gospel is a medicine-chest, rather than a medicine.

The Rev. H. Foster—

Does the Scripture preach Christ ? Yes, indeed, He is the sun illuminating all. Bring forth, then, what you will, CHRIST throws all the light on it which it has.

———

On the next occasion, October 28, 1799, the subject was, WHAT ARE THE PROPER SUBJECTS AND MODE OF CHRISTIAN BAPTISM?— This was proposed by the Rev. T. Scott.

On the 11th November 1799, at the next meeting, the following was discussed, having been proposed by the Rev. J. Davies. WHAT MANNER AND MEASURE SHOULD BE OBSERVED IN TREATING THE DOCTRINE OF ELECTION?—We regret that we have no notes on either of these important topics.

———

NOVEMBER 25, 1799.

ON WHAT GROUNDS HAS A MAN WARRANT TO CONCLUDE THAT HE IS IN A STATE OF ACCEPTANCE WITH GOD ?—Proposed by the Rev. H. Foster.

The Rev. H. Foster—

It is a matter of experience.

When I set out, I tried to *be* what God would be pleased with. I used the name of Christ, because I found it in the Scriptures ; but I used him not for any effectual purpose.

My first change was, that I supposed God would accept the *will* for the *deed*, since I saw I could not be what I desired to be. But sometimes I willed to sin, so I found that I could not rest here. " You said you willed to be holy, but now you will to sin "—I said to myself. Thus I went on. And in examining my motives closely, even to this

F

day, I find so little that is altogether pure, that I am driven to distrust the work.

I used Jesus Christ—I hope savingly ; but I found so much mixture, that I was driven to take salvation as plainly proposed in Scripture. I prayed for spirituality and humility. But why ? To get influence with the children of God. " You pray for spirituality and devotedness," I said, " in order to gain aceptance." The root is rotten, while it is apparently specious. I can't tell whether, after all, there is anything more than self at bottom. It is from this, being perplexed, that I have felt a sort of necessity—good, bad, or indifferent—that come I must to CHRIST, *simply* for salvation, simply to stand on the record.

The Rev. R. Cecil—

Try to set out with knowing nothing. I make out, perhaps, that God made the trees, and all around me. I attain to a certain conclusion ; but I am dissatisfied with my reasoning. I come, then, to *simple belief*—as to heaven and hell ! I can account for all Brother Foster says, from constitutional tendency. A sanguine man runs too fast. It is important for ministers to think of this.

I can go all the way with Foster, in feeling that nothing can be done but in proposing Christ to the soul as the only hope ; this is the *one* way. The utter bankruptcy of nature we *must* acknowledge. Man knows not himself if he thinks he can pay *anything* in the pound. If he *have* any degree of comeliness, 'tis the comeliness that is put upon him. Man cannot make up his mind comfortably, if he be not borne up on the two pillars of faith and repentance. There *must* be a moral change. But then it is necessary, in order to a well-grounded hope, that we renounce all this in point of dependence.

The mystical way is a way of danger. By " water and blood," " not by water only." Though I think that not even Crisp * himself has spoken too strongly of the " Rock," yet it should never be spoken of but in connexion with the fruits. This is an adjunct in order to safety.

A dying bed will give a man a spirit of inquiry of a new sort. Now, though we shall not then dare to *lean* on anything in ourselves, yet we may call in experience as a ground of comforting evidence. Thus Christian, when sinking in the river, was told by Faithful to look back on all the way the Lord had led him. Man feels his defects ; but these are no objection to his case being genuine. There are black marks in characters ; but these are not they. Why is Shakspeare the chief poet ? Because of an absence of defect ? No ! but because of the presence of excellencies. So in the Christian. A little bear may be licked into form by its mother. Judas even was, perhaps, a size higher in plausible character and bearing than such a warm man as

---

* Crisp was a Puritan writer of considerable eminence, born in London in 1600, and educated at Eton. He graduated at Cambridge, and afterwards at Oxford. He took a prominent part in a controversy on the freeness of the grace of God in Christ Jesus. After his death, three 4to volumes of sermons were published under the title, " Christ Alone Exalted." The author appears to have been unguarded in some of his expressions ; and it is doubtless to this that Mr Cecil alludes in his remarks at the Eclectic.

Peter   Now, with reference to Foster and myself—why, he would shame me in life, yet he knows not he is so much better.

A hypocrite is often much better than an honest man in appearance. Some constitutions there are which throw everything on the outside. I will not plead for these, but I will not be cast down by them. Renounce everything, as a plea for getting in at the wicket gate. Shew your roll at the gate, as an evidence, not as a title.   If a man live in such a way that he is doubtful whether anything is going on between him and God, he *ought* to doubt. We must take the Gospel as a scheme of *sovereign* mercy, or we should be as wretched as Johnson in his allusion to the measuring our good works—" Man is to weigh the quantity." *Weigh the quantity !*

The Rev. Josiah Pratt—

The warrant spoken of in the question, is entirely *the promise.*

All we have to do is with the *evidence.*   I have to ascertain whether I am the character to whom the promise is made.   For all promises are made to certain characters.

This is the question—" Am I the character to whom acceptance is promised ? "

I should answer—" Yes ; if a disposition is given me *to embrace the promise in all its conditions.*"

What is implied in such a disposition ?

(1.) Faith, (2.) Desire, (3.) Compliance.

Nobody can deny that the promise is made to a certain character. And if I really have not that character, I have no right to the comfort.

But if I am that character, I *ought* to be happy, whether I am so or not.

Here is the difficulty.   The really godly man's *appreciation* of his state is often different from the *truth* of his state.   And since he is governed by his appreciation, he must unjustly conclude against himself.

What is he to do ?   Consider what he is, now ; and what he was, once.   He can *look unto the rock whence* he is *hewn, and to the hole of the pit whence* he is *digged.*   He must say—*This hath God wrought !*

But the Christian is often called to acts of implicit faith in the divine veracity.   " This *may* be *presumption* "—he is inclined to exclaim. Never ; if his soul loathes itself !   Nay, in a self-renouncing frame, to throw himself on God, is the highest act of faith.   Presumption this would be, when conscience speaks and testifies that neglect has been indulged, and that yet he turns away.

God has graciously connected peace with sincerity and a close walk with him.

If guilt is on the conscience, confess it all to God.   There is no shorter way to favour.

The Scriptures are more liberal than we are in dealing out consolations.

The Rev. J. Goode—

I know Brother Foster ; and I believe him to be true.   But another man might talk so.   Let me see their evidences.   The ground is, the " blood " of Christ, but the evidence is the " water."

The Rev. J. Clayton—

What is it to be ACCEPTED ?   Not only to be *accepted* in the righteousness of Christ; but to be made *acceptable* to the holiness of God.
(Owen.)

Am I then standing on the right ground, and yielding fruit to God?
The existence of grace and the manifestation of its evidences are *inseparable*.

If there be not an exercise of grace in *some* way, we should not be
easy about ourselves.   We may not be joyful always ; no grace is seen
in mourning and desiring.   Not ground of *dependance* but *satisfactory
evidence*.

The Rev. J. Newton—

The young Christian is like a man walking on the ice.   He carries
a sense of his weight about him.   But put him on Westminster Bridge,
and if he were as heavy as a waggon, he would not fear.

If I had been born with one leg, I should go limping to the grave,
for conversation would not cure it.   Nor will my diseased nature ever
be so wholly cured in this life, as to prevent me limping.

The inward work in my soul will tell me, like a dial, what o'clock
it is if the sun shines, but not if the sun be absent.

The Rev. B. Woodd—

Negative evidence is honesty, &c.   Positive evidence is love to God,
&c.   There is often an adverting to evidence though the believer is not
conscious of it.   If he feels no love to God, this speaks for itself.

The Rev. W. Goode—

The warrant for coming to Christ is distinct from the evidence that
we do really come.

They who speak against evidences, immediately set up some of their
own.   This was quite the case with Romaine, who, while laying so much
stress on faith and love, made indeed the proof of the existence of these
his evidences.

It is improper, in setting up evidences, to insist on *certain degrees* of
it, instead of the *reality* of it.

———

On the 9th December 1799, the subject was—WHAT IS THE
VISIBLE CHURCH OF CHRIST ?—The Rev. B. Woodd proposed this;
but we have no notes upon it.

———

DECEMBER 23, 1799.

WHAT WAS THE APOSTOLICAL METHOD OF PREACHING, AND HOW IS
THERE ANY DEVIATION FROM IT IN THE PRESENT RACE OF EVANGELICAL
PREACHERS ?—Proposed by the Rev. Josiah Pratt.

Mr Pratt—

It may be objected, that this question is irrelevant to *us*.   But this is not the case ; for though it is true that the Apostles were peculiarly situated, it is to be expected that their general manner and character are proper for our imitation.

FIRST. What was the Apostles' method ?

1. Their SUBJECT.

There are three striking features in the subject of their preaching.

1. The FOUNDATION.

They gave a full, clear, strong representation of it : e. g., in the Epistles to the Romans, and the Galatians. St Paul betrays a godly jealousy, lest he should warp from it. He is breaking out continually to glance at it, and to speak of it. There are few verses without an express assertion of it, or a strong glance at it.

2. The SUPERSTRUCTURE.

They treat Christians as subjects of a kingdom. They state the laws and regulations of this kingdom. They constantly enlighten the conscience to become the man's monitor. Not only do they say in general, " Faith works by love ;" but they call on Christians to ramify the working of love. They tell men the manner of love's acting in them in all their relations in life. They insist on this—enlarge on this —urge it—and press it.

3. The CONNEXION of these together.

There is great *wisdom* in the Apostolic method of presenting these in one view. They melt the heart by the great truths, and immediately apply the seal. They heat the iron, and, while hot, fashion it. Almost every Epistle ends with warm exhortations to duties ; and if they exhort to duty, they catch up instantly the motive—*Work out your own salvation with fear and trembling, for it is God that worketh in you, both to will and to do of his good pleasure.*

II. The MANNER.

1. Each Apostle is *sui generis*. Paul was ardent ; Peter, sanguine ; James, pithy ; John, affectionate.

2. All are simple. There is no affectation—no *recherché*—all is obvious.

3. They are grave. They are at an infinite distance from the *toujours gai*. There is no fun—no drollery.

4. They are weighty. There is no trifling—they are full of their subject.

5. They are scriptural. It seems with them a point gained, to bring in a scripture testimony.

6. They are circumstantial. For example, Paul at Athens—before Felix—before Agrippa.

SECONDLY. What is our Present Deviation from the Apostolic Method ?

What are the most striking defects of the Christian profession in these days ? These are in a measure to be traced to the preaching of the day. The heart is wicked indeed, and the best preaching cannot cure it ; but defective preaching will give a tone the wrong way. There were various and sore evils complained of by the Apostles in their day. But this sprung from the *heart*, and not from the Apostles' method of preaching.

Our present defects seem to be—

1. A want of a clear hold on principles.

Why? The preacher himself perhaps was led to God by distrusting the creature and by no strong feeling of the malady of sin. It is taken too much for granted that people have a hold of the foundation, and *are in the habit* of connecting everything we say with it. Foundation sermons are advantageous : they should be full and strong in doctrinal statements, in imitation of the Apostle in the Ephesians.

2. An unsanctified resting in notions.

(1.) An approximation to the world—the spirit of which is to doubt, and ask, " What is truth ?" Such persons will *answer* you well ; but what is their spirit, their soul ? They add " house to house"—shop to shop—pleasure to pleasure.

(2.) A privilege of party, to the neglect of religious duties.

We go to *St John's ;* or to this *meeting ;* or to that *chapel,* &c. We *dress* in a certain way—we *think* in a certain way. But the husband and wife bicker—the master is furious and the servant saucy. It's a horrible disfiguring of Christianity.

Whence is all this?

1. The preacher *neglects* the superstructure ; or, 2. He touches on it slightly, as if afraid to offend; or, 3. He does not connect the foundation with the superstructure. The heart gets cold in long practical discussions. These are subjects for books, not for sermons.

The Rev. T. Scott—

The evils Pratt speaks of existed in the primitive Church—but as exceptions from the rule. *Now* they exist as the *tone,* and other persons are the exception to the rule.

The greatest difference between us and the Apostles is the want of the Apostolic spirit. If a man behaves with courage and determination in a good cause, he is called a Christian hero ! But we want the Apostolic spirit.

The pastors of the primitive Churches were far inferior to the Apostles ; but we are far inferior to them. The difference between the Apostles and their successors, shews that though God gives *some evangelists, and some pastors and teachers, for the perfecting of the saints,* yet He would let no human writings *approximate* to the Apostolic. If the primitive writings had approximated nearer, we should have been more entangled with them than we are.

We learn what the Apostles' preaching was from—(1.) the Acts, (2.) the Epistles. I've known excellent men take their standard from the Acts. But what is said in the Acts is said to men *not acquainted with the Gospels.*

The Apostles' method is to be found in the Epistles.

The Apostolic method of preaching to those WITHOUT was argumentative. For example,—St Peter's address on the day of Pentecost : all the addresses in the Acts of the Apostles : *He reasoned with them out of the Scriptures.* This was the Apostolic method. They opened the understanding, and through it addressed the conscience, and pressed home the truth on the affections. Things were not taken for granted, but proved and developed.

The Apostles preached with authority :—*Thus saith the Lord.* We may be inferior to our hearers everywhere, *but* in the pulpit. We too much forget that we are ministers.

The Apostles preached with gravity. They stamped doctrinal things practically, and practical things as flowing from doctrine. Where doctrine and practice are preached separately, each hangs as a lump of grapes on a dead vine.

The Apostles' preaching to those WITHIN was very particular.

We are too general in speaking of *doctrines* and *duties.*

Addressing the understanding will make *rational* Christians—addressing the passions will make *enthusiasts.* But the Apostles made the understanding the medium of access to the passions.

The strong attack was on the *conscience :—Commending ourselves to every man's conscience—We are made manifest in your consciences.*

Though we may be *comforted* by the approval of our hearers, yet we should have more care to *guard against deception.*

The Rev. J. Davies—

The great distinction is being *thoroughly in earnest.*

The Rev. J. Newton—

Whoever of us can say—*Ye are witnesses, and God also, how holily and justly and unblameably we behaved ourselves among you that believe*—may command and rule his people's souls.

Paul was a REED in NON-ESSENTIALS—an IRON PILLAR in ESSENTIALS.

A minister has almost hit the marks if, when his sermon is over, some call him an Antinomian, and some an Arminian.

There are not only ministers who bring "milk" and "strong meat" —but some who bring mere *bones.*

The Rev. B. Woodd—

The Moravians discarded the argumentative for plain statements.

The Rev. J. Venn—

One difference between us and the Apostles is this—*we* must make sermons to the same people : *they* addressed different people.

Most ministers, if their living were taken from them, would have another tone if sent abroad.

Wesley, if six weeks in one place, would preach myself and the people dead.

Now this is founded on human nature, and a man's own feeling.

Another difference is this.

The *Apostles* knew every man in their congregation : they were their own churches. We are appointed over a people of whom we, perhaps, know little.

These circumstances would lead the Apostles to more earnest preaching.

The cases are more exactly parallel between the Apostles and Mis-

sionaries, than between the Apostles and us.   The Apostles preached
so particularly, as to extend to almost everything they did.

They lived with their people—as, *e. g.* Brainerd.   The Apostles
were like tutors, watching over Christians.   *Our office is to preach.*

The Rev. H. Foster—

The great thing is to have such impressions from Scripture and the
Spirit of God, as to see into eternity.   Where God intends to do most,
He will work this.

There is much in what Pratt says of having to preach our sermons.

While people pay tithes and pew-rent, all is well, they think; they
smile if we are on doctrine, and frown if on duties.

If they find you mean little, they will modify your saying by your
practice.   If God designs us great things, I expect He will raise us
up men in this way.

The spirit is the main thing.   Fletcher was an illustration of this—
if I judge by his sentiments, I should say he had no grace; but if I
hear of the effects, I'm silent.

If I had more talents I should enter more into minutiæ.   Yet,
when I have heard this done, though I have felt it may be clever, it
gets cold.

The Rev. R. Cecil—

There is a naturalness about the Apostles.   They are neither the
Logician nor the Rambler.

There is a modesty in the Apostles.   There was something in the
Apostles which addressed the *good sense* of men.

The Apostles never affect to go beyond their education; but on their
subjects they are well informed.

Though they speak with authority, yet there is a condescension
about them.

A great attack on the conscience of men is *felt*, when it is associated
with a holy character in the preacher.

JANUARY 19, 1800.

WHAT IS THE NATURE OF THE INSPIRATION OF THE SCRIPTURES?—
Proposed by the Rev. J. Venn.

Mr Venn—

Inspiration is the communication of knowledge to a man, which is
not gained otherwise than by divine interposition.   Inspiration was
more frequent in the early ages than afterwards.   It appears to have
been a regular communication between God and man.   This communication went to a variety of particular instances—even to so trivial a
circumstance as Saul seeking the asses.   It was sometimes by voices
—*e. g.*, the calling of Samuel; or by sight, as in the Urim and
Thummim.

Consider Inspiration in two respects—

I. As PLENARY.

When the words were suggested, and the persons inspired knew not

what they said meant.   There are many passages of this kind in the
prophecies.   The change of style sometimes shews this.   We see an
unexpected burst from prose to poetry.

II. As SUPERINTENDENT.

When the writer is relating a plain fact of history, the penman
uses here his own style.   Most of the historical writings come under
this description.

What degree of superintendence was there over the Apostles ?—This
is a question worthy of consideration.   In the works of God, there is a
remarkable sparing of divine interpretation.   Superintendence *varied*
in its character according to circumstances.

How far did the Holy Spirit superintend each man's style and
phraseology ?—this is another question for thought.

The Rev. H. Foster—

I believe the writers were influenced not only as to *matter*, but as to
words.

The original Scriptures are, I believe, the words of the Holy Ghost
himself.   This is perfectly consistent with the preservation of the
capacities and characters of the men themselves.   He played on them
as instruments.   *Not in the* words *which man's wisdom teacheth, but which
the* Holy Ghost teacheth.

Soame Jennings' idea of Scripture being a History of Revelations, is
injurious to its divine authority.

A distinction of kinds of inspiration *may* be good and useful, but I
believe in the plenary inspiration of the whole Scriptures.

The Rev. R. Cecil—

Everybody agrees that *all* Scripture was under an inspiration of
superintendence.   But there is some danger in considering *all* Scripture as *equally* inspired.

God undertakes to furnish man with truth ; but he does not undertake to work miracles where no miracle is necessary.

> " Rapt into future times, the bard begun,
> A virgin shall conceive, a virgin bear a son ! "

But the bard cannot begin till the Spirit has " touched" his " hallowed lips with fire."

But in writing a transaction, there needs no more than a care over
the writer, to prevent his uttering anything which is not truth.

The Rev. Josiah Pratt—

It is said by some, that St John writes ungrammatically.   If so,
then the Holy Ghost writes by him ungrammatically.   But *if so*, it is
as God does in other things.   He would teach us to despise little
things.   Scripture is a trial of men's minds.

The Rev. Thomas Scott—

Where is there a book, except the Scriptures, with which you can
sit down and write on Virtues and Vices without fear of being
deceived ?

It is an astonishing truth, and an irrefragable evidence of divine inspiration, that shepherds and kings and men of such various characters should write a book agreeing in all its parts.   Burke's oratory carried him away into sophistry.   Isaiah's, never.

Superintendence was necessary, chiefly in preventing men's talents from running into extravagance and error.

The Apostle writes about his cloak left at Troas, and such like minute matters, and *this* was under superintendence, for he might have run out into circumstances of this kind in a manner which would be frivolous without this superintendence.   But as it is now, all does good.   Compare Wesley's and Whitfield's Journals with St Paul's Epistles in these respects.

The rule of faith and practice is not, after all, altered, if everything is given up against which a *reasonable* objection as to its inspiration might be brought.

The Rev. J. Newton—

Exceptions confirm the rule.   When St Paul says he speaks by *permission*, he implies strongly that on all other occasions it is by *direction*.

The Rev. J. Davies—

There are three views :—1. That the ideas and words are inspired. 2. The ideas, and not the words.   3. The ideas, and the words so far as to prevent the writer's delivering anything inconsistent with truth.   The latter seems the middle and true view.   The others are clogged with difficulties.

FEBRUARY 3, 1800.

WHAT IS IT FOR A MINISTER TO "MAGNIFY HIS OFFICE?"   Rom. xi. 13.—Proposed by the Rev. J. Goode.

Mr Goode—

A contempt of the ministerial office will grow into a contempt of religion.   We should neither claim excessive respect for it, nor allow the office to be looked upon as trivial.   Our vindication of it should be cautious.   A minister is not allowed the liberty, in this respect, of other men.   A vindication which would be allowed in others, would be regarded as arrogance in ministers.

Paul was not in love with the dignity and power of his office, but with the ministrations and effect of his office.   He would please others only when it was right to please them, and wrong not to please them. It should appear that we love our office for the *Lord's* sake and the *work's* sake.

Let us preserve in mind when in the pulpit—Jesus weeping over bloody Jerusalem—Abraham importunately pleading for filthy Sodom —Moses interceding for idolatrous and rebellious Israel—Jonah calling loudly on wicked Nineveh—John Baptist, rough in word, but strong in appeals to the conscience—Paul reasoning till an adulterer trembled. We shall magnify our office if we properly imitate the spirit of these.

The Rev. G. Pattrick—

We should take care and seek grace to magnify our *office*, and not the *man*. Our office is most effectually magnified when its objects are obtained.

These objects are—1. The glory of God. 2. The salvation of souls.

The opposite errors we have to shun are—1. Having an unbounded complacency in our office; and, 2. A cynical, morose, formal deportment.

Fletcher was a man who, in his deportment and fervour, magnified his office.*

The Rev. H. Foster—

A minister magnifies his office by saying little in defence of it. If a minister is zealous, and in earnest, and faithful, then all know it.

The Rev. R. Cecil—

What did the man do, who said he magnified his office? We must consider the character, spirit, and history of that man, to know how we may magnify ours. His life and death were one magnifying of his office. Mark the end! To win one soul! to execute the will of God!

As man swells, the office goes down; but as the office swells in his view, the man goes down. No studying before the glass; studying periods, contriving images, &c. &c., will do it.

Man is a miserable creature in himself. There must be a constant hostility against himself, and no self-magnifying.

I am for a *middle*-way in vindicating characters. Avoid *hasty* vindications. But if a man is charged with being a *dishonest* character, then if a fair *opportunity* offer, let him vindicate himself. It does not appear that Elisha sent after Naaman to vindicate himself about Gehazi. To me, a dignity appears herein. I should not have had *patience* for this.

This is a way in which we may magnify our office :—*What things were gain to me, those I counted loss for Christ.* This we may apply to our various characters and tastes, whatever they are. Cadogan set us an example of this.† So also in Scripture characters, Ezra and Nehemiah. *I am doing a great work, I cannot come down.* (Neh. vi. 3.)

* The Rev. Mr Fletcher of Madeley.

† The Hon. and Rev. W. B. Cadogan, the second son of Lord Cadogan. Mr Cecil wrote his Memoirs—they are published in the four volumes of Cecil's Works. He was Rector of St Luke's, Chelsea. The following passage in his Memoirs will explain the allusion made by Mr Cecil to his character :—

" When Mrs Cadogan imposed this task upon me, she opened his 'scrutoire, in order to examine if he had left anything that it might be proper to add to what had been already printed; and I confess I was surprised at the quantity of paper covered with his university studies. These occupied much room, besides that which contained a great number of written sermons, and what are called skeletons of sermons, as he, latterly, did not *read* his discourses.

" When I say I was surprised at this, it was not so much from observing how greatly his character had differed from that of many, who go to universities merely as a necessary introduction into a particular profession, and pay little regard to the other advantages which such seminaries afford; but because, after a long intimacy with him, I had remarked his indisposition to converse on those branches of science which I now found he had so laboriously cultivated. I had imputed the indisposition rather to his having never deeply pursued such subjects, than to what I afterwards found to be the real motive—namely, a habitual delight in, and eager pursuit after, sublimer objects; for latterly he counted all things *but* as *dross for the excellency of the knowledge of Christ Jesus his Lord.*"

We must make sacrifices, when called to it, if we would magnify our office.

A man will not *sell his office*, if he desire to magnify it.   Micaiah is an example of this, and even Balaam.

Let us leave God to vindicate His own truth, and not be too anxious to vindicate ourselves.

In speaking of self, even where it may be necessary or advisable, much turns on *character* and *occasion*.

The Rev. Josiah Pratt—

I. There is an INTERNAL magnifying of our office, when we appeal to God—God, the only Judge, who knows our different temperaments.

The filling up of our office must not be measured by our visible success.

Victory over man's self will be shewn in the future world.   God's glory in the Gospel is not fully seen here.   A man in *obscurity* may greatly magnify his office.

When does he internally magnify his office ?

When everything is brought into subjection to Christ.   When his peculiar and besetting idol is brought down to the ground.   When his peculiar talent is pushed to the utmost : when, having found it out, he is content with it, and has no envy towards others, no striving to excel them from ambition.

II. There is an EXTERNAL method of magnifying our office.

If the first exist, this will follow—

1. Let the man retreat behind the scene, and not push himself forward ; let him throw selfish ends away, and he is sure to magnify his office before men.

2. Carry a holy frame, a divine unction, into all your duties.   This must magnify your office in the eyes of reasonable men.   There will be in this a strong appeal to men's consciences, which they cannot resist.   See Fuller's view of this.   The *world* allows it.

3. Reprove gainsayers.

This, when done wisely, will magnify our office.   But he that can do this *well*, must be a man of known character, a man to whom *credit is given*.   It is only *consistent* characters that can do this.   Mere *authority* will not do.   *Thou that teachest another, teachest thou not thyself?*

The Rev. Thomas Scott—

Many excellent things have been said of—(1.) A minister's conduct, and (2.) The exercise of his ministry.

But this appears not to have been in St Paul's mind.   He meant not, I magnify *myself* in exercising my office.

In such a day as this, it is important to make the office *respected, however poor our discharge of it*.   A general contempt of the clergy partly arises from the clerical character.   In vindicating ourselves general charges may be neglected ; but specific refuted.   We should insist on the *importance of the word;* the *effects* on society when discharged aright ; the effects on *individuals*.

St Paul's meaning was this :—

"I would have you feel the OFFICE of immense *importance, difficulty,* and *effect*—whether *I* execute it well or not."

We don't, in this day, speak with the authority St Paul did, but still we should uphold the greatness of the office of a minister of Christ. We should avoid proud assumption.

A minister is like a *wall,* when he stands up for *God* and in God's name ; but like a *willow,* when for *self.*

The Rev. J. Newton—

In one respect, I can say that I have magnified my office. For I never saw any office so desirable !

When the heart is engaged in the work, this is my feeling—

If men threaten—" *shall such a man as I flee ?* "

If the world allures—" *I am doing a great work, I cannot come down.*"

An *ambassador* magnifies his office, when he keeps close to his instructions. He may stand sometimes upon his *p*'s and *q*'s, but not for himself, but for the honour of the *court* he represents.

On the next occasion of the members of the Eclectic Society meeting, the member whose notes we copy was not present. And on the following meeting his notes were so scanty, that we pass them over, and proceed to the next.

MARCH 17, 1800.

ON WHAT GROUNDS SHOULD A CHRISTIAN DISCOUNTENANCE THEATRICAL AMUSEMENTS ?—Proposed by the Rev. J. Clayton.

Mr Clayton—

God's name is taken in vain in the best theatres.

This proceeds from the corrupt heart, and it addresses the corrupt heart.

Mr Newton says, that theatres are as much means of men's destruction, as the means of grace are of salvation.

The best cure would be a higher tone of Christianity. Collier, Law, and Witherspoon have written well on the subject.*

* Jeremy Collier was an eminent non-juring Bishop, born in 1650. His life was an eventful one, and he published many works. "But the work of Collier which produced the greatest effect, and secured to him the most lasting celebrity, was his Short View of the Immorality and Profaneness of the English Stage, together with the Sense of Antiquity upon this Argument, published in 1698, in 8vo. In this work, with truth and justice on his side, and armed with sufficient learning, united to keen and sarcastic wit, our author attacked most of the living dramatic writers, from Dryden to Durfey, with a degree of force and dexterity which the power and skill of the ablest of them who ventured to meet him in the field were unable to resist. Collier completely triumphed, not only in the judgment of the wise and pious, but in the public opinion ; and is entitled to the merit of having contributed, by his animadversions, to produce considerable reformation in the sentiments and language of the theatre."—*Rose's Biographical Dictionary.*

William Law was an able and pious divine, born in 1686, and educated at Cambridge. He was tutor to the father of Gibbon the Historian. He wrote several works ; by one

The Rev. J. Newton—

The theatre is the very last of all places to which I would allow a child of mine to go.

Some men do not see the evil of these places. But let such men ask themselves, Is this *doing all to the glory of God?* Is it *redeeming the time?*

Tragedies are usually full of blasphemies. Comedies tend to defend and promote what is called gallantry. They not only dissipate, but they tend to impregnate the mind with evil.

The matter is so plain to me, that I wonder at Christians questioning it, as much as I should if they questioned the sin of swearing.

The Rev. B. Woodd—

Plays may be considered as to their intrinsic and extrinsic evil.

I. The intrinsic evil of the Theatre.

1. This is seen in the garnish of vice with which the theatre abounds. Bad characters are often there represented as examples of benevolence.

2. The theatre often exhibits false representations of Providence. Things end well to the wicked.

3. Profaneness is found there. The songs of libertines are sung with approbation and applause. A swearer is often the hero of the play.

4. The theatre exhibits fascinating representations of sin. If any one will say that the tendency is to degrade sin, yet let us remember that youth look more at the representation than at the moral.

5. It keeps up dissipation, and indisposes to religion.

6. It introduces to evil company.

II. The extrinsic evil of the Theatre.

1. This is seen in the number of bad characters which frequent the theatre.

2. The theatre supports a profligate society.

3. It corrupts the servants who attend.

4. It begets a taste for domestic amusements.

Tillotson says, the play-house is as much the temple of the devil, as the Church is the temple of Jesus Christ.

Gambold has done injury by writing *Ignatius.** Mrs More's sacred dramas have done injury. They have associated an idea of innocence with the drama. I know two young men now on the stage, in consequence of being taught to act Mrs M.'s sacred dramas.

The Rev. J. Venn—

If Vice were to come in person and take up her residence in London, she would naturally visit the play-house.

of which his name is well known—*A Serious Call to a Devout and Holy Life*. This work Dr Johnson declared to have been the first that led him to think seriously about religion. Another of the various works published by Law was, the Unlawfulness of Stage Entertainments.

John Witherspoon was an eminent divine in Scotland and America, and a lineal descendant of Knox, the celebrated Scotch Reformer. He was born in 1722. Among other subjects, he wrote on the Nature and Effects of the Stage.

* Gambold was a Bishop among the Moravians, born in Wales, and educated at Oxford, and an excellent man. In 1740 he wrote a tragedy, called the "Martyrdom of Ignatius," which was published after his death, and is alluded to above. He wrote other works, and died in 1771.

What kind of people are the actors ? — this is an important question.

Moral persons of the old school, who could see no great harm in attending the theatre, would yet deem it the greatest misfortune if one of their children turned player.

Who attend ?—this is another question.

All who are on the road to Tyburn. Must there not be, then, something congenial to the devil and sin ?

In the plays themselves is there not that which is directly opposed to our baptismal vow and covenant ?

The most dangerous plays are not the most gross. The most dangerous are those which diminish in the mind the abhorrence of vice. Those are dangerous which people are disposed to applaud, because they think they have but a moderate portion of vice.

We must not consider merely the mischief which is got from a single play. We must regard it in a larger view—as maintaining a system. In countenancing theatrical amusements, we are doing all in our power to keep up a system which works evil in many ways.

What use is generally made of plays ?

If any attempt is to be made against religion, the play-house is made use of.

If we desired to establish infidelity, nothing has a stronger hold upon the mind for this end than the theatre. The theatre is the great support of the Devil's Kingdom. No doubt he has a prime motive to regulate the play.

A great danger of plays arises from the fascination of vice.

The Rev. G. Pattrick—

Caution is necessary in warning people against the play, lest we should irritate them to try what it is.

The Rev. W. J. Abdy—

I once saw a play acted which impressed me at the time with the idea, that suicide was not evil to the degree I had been taught. It begot in me a fondness, moreover, for plays.

There is something of lewdness or profaneness in almost every play.

Jane Shore invoking God to witness that her soul shall never more know pollution, in the mouth of perhaps a bad character, is horrible.

The imitation of thunder and other such works of the Almighty, as in the witch-scene in Macbeth, I think objectionable.

I have thought going to the play a breach of the second great commandment of the law—*Thou shalt love thy neighbour as thyself.* If I would not wish my own children to imbibe a fondness for the play, how can I contribute to keep up a system which may ensnare the child of my neighbour ?

Plays tend to unfit young people for the business of life. They set young men above the business of their station ; and young women above domestic duties. They bring young people into the company of those who are worse than themselves.

The Rev. H. Foster—

Frequenting plays affords a proof of the depravity of human nature beyond most other things.

Even sober sort of men will go and gratify passions there, which they would be ashamed to have to do with in a private room.

The theatre is to be preached against with humility. We are apt to be angry when people are fond of what we would have them part with.

The Rev. J. Pratt began by relating the circumstance of his having once passed the Circus Theatre on his way to Newington, and his overhearing a man who was standing opposite the building, denouncing the play-house in language more true than polished, but awfully descriptive, as Mr P. thought, of the end to which it leads multitudes. He then proceeded—

The theatre makes a strong attack on the senses. It takes this advantage over religion, which appeals to the reason and conscience. So is it with Popery, the main hold is on the senses.

The theatre appeals forcibly to the principle of *association*. It uses this for the corruption of the judgment, both as to character and sentiment.

See a sermon by the Rev. W. Jones on the Imagination, in which are many just remarks on the right use of the imagination, with the dangers of abusing it.

Look at the present state of France. The Revolution was fostered and supplied by the theatre.

It is necessary to bring out these things in detail in preaching.

Johnson's not daring to frequent the Green-room, and his motive, shews what danger there is. But, nevertheless, his decided attachment to the theatre has done harm.

A sermon is the essence of dulness after a play : this shews the evil of the play-house.

[He here made some illustrative allusion to the Rev. W. Jesse, under whom he had recently served as Curate, and his family. The allusion we cannot interpret.]

The Rev. R. Cecil—

I don't give people credit for either piety or good sense, who pretend to justify the play and yet hold religion. *They have chosen idols, and after them they will go.*

Collier is not now so forcible as in his own day, nor is Law ; for Vice hides herself more than she did, though only covertly. Wither-spoon is best.

We must meet vice in all its forms.

I have been an old play-goer, and I know what the atmosphere is. Men go much less for the play than to act their own play.

It is nonsense to talk of the play-house being made a school of morality. As Law says, in order to keep the system up, they must meet the taste of the town.

The whole system of sentiment is directly opposed to that of the

Gospel. For a man to say, " I'll die rather than submit," that's a fine spirit ! For a man to rage like a tiger, that's being a hero !

As to comedies, they trick out vice in its most fascinating forms.

But the atmosphere of the play-house is poisonous. I remember how it was with myself. I've looked at my watch. The play's almost done. I must go to my dungeon. There's my father groaning with his infirmities. There's my mother with her Bible. What can I do ? Is there any other place open ? Why, if I've a shilling in my pocket, I'll find out that place.

As to *serious* people—it's impudent hypocrisy for them to attend plays, if they know what we mean by spiritual religion. Here's an accumulation of all that's bad.

I've not felt much less at Vauxhall.

Some pious people will not go to a play, but they will go to an oratorio at the play-house ; this is bad. So Jesus Christ is to be the amusement of the night ! A much more profane business is this than a play ! A parcel of profane people are collected together to entertain another parcel of profane people.

In preaching against the theatre, let us take care not to *bind up* vice in the play and card-table. They are branches of a great tree. Let us go to the root—" *the course of this world.*"

Plays have a tendency to give a romantic turn of mind.

The taste generated in the play-house is as opposed as possible to the taste of Jesus Christ. As you build up a young man in the taste of the play-house, you fit him for nothing but players or highwaymen. Even business becomes irksome ; family prayer the " abomination of desolation."

As to a parent letting his child see *one* play, how foolish and blind ! Why, old people forget what they were when young. [Here he told a story of his own youth.]

I've a good deal to do with my people in this neighbourhood who put these sorts of questions.

The Rev. Thomas Scott—

Some say the "play is a school." If so, the devil is the head schoolmaster.

People talk of *reforming* the play. These reforms of the play are most injurious to the age. They only teach the rogue how to become more plausible.

I know of no play, the principle of which, if brought into common life, would not unfit men for their relative duties.

The bad part of plays is the best done. This is the devil's contrivance. You could not poison vermin, but by mixing the poison with sweeter ingredients. What is bad sticks like burrs to one's stocking ; what is good slips off the mind like water from a duck's back.

Some say, there is no express prohibition of plays in Scripture. There is great wisdom in this absence of express prohibition of specific practices. Religion is uniform, one, and simple. The Church follows the Church from age to age. But vice is a Proteus. If a *few* of its forms had been mentioned, it would have assumed others, and so have escaped rebuke.

The spirit of these things is so strongly marked, as to be utterly inconsistent with the spirit of the Gospel. Mr Wilberforce has very strong and forcible remarks on this in the fifth section of his " Practical View of Christianity."

MARCH 31, 1800.

IN WHAT RESPECTS ARE MINISTERS WARRANTED TO EXPECT DIVINE INFLUENCE ON THE EXERCISE OF THEIR MINISTRY?—Proposed by the Rev. J. Davies.

Mr Davies—

In all respects are we warranted to expect a divine influence on our ministry. It is our duty to be expecting it. *Lo, I am with you alway,* said the Saviour, *even unto the end of the world.*

But I proposed this question more with reference to preaching, in particular. That promise is generally applicable—*I will give you a mouth and wisdom which none of your adversaries shall be able to withstand.*

Two extremes are to be avoided in applying this promise—(1.) Presumption. (2.) Unbelief.

Presumption, in expecting more than is promised ; or in a way different to the way promised. This generates idleness and reacts upon ourselves.

Unbelief, when, for want of suitable dependence, we should shrink from entering the pulpit, except when precisely, as we imagine, in the right frame.

The truth lies between these extremes. When we have prayed, studied, and thus fitted ourselves, we may safely enter the pulpit in full dependence on Christ's influence.

The Rev. J. Clayton—

Divine influence is peculiarly the glory of the New Testament dispensation. Christian ministers are warranted to expect in ministerial duties peculiar assistances, distinct from sanctifying influences.

These are not to be expected by the indolent. *Meditate on these things; give thyself wholly to them.* The Spirit of God loathes an indolent minister. Diligence should be a prominent feature in a minister's character. By diligence, I mean in prayer, as well as study.

There must be a congeniality with his subject. When so prepared, the Spirit often raises him above himself.

It is sometimes hard to distinguish between the Spirit's influences and Satan's temptations.

I have sometimes thrown aside a chosen subject for a new one, which something has suddenly suggested to me, and have found lively assistance. But, moreover, I have often found on these occasions that it was a trick of Satan.

If self-indulgence or indolence be at the bottom, then it is wicked trifling with God to be depending on expected influences.

Old sermons need not be abandoned, because we fancy that the special circumstances under which they were written have passed away.

The Rev. J. Newton—

Choosing a text is, in me, like a contested election.

When I have got a text, I try if it will bite. If not, I throw it away for another.

I got what is said to be the best sermon I ever printed, in a moment ; it came like a flash of lightning.

A minister need not be idle, though he is not composing sermons. An observing traveller is gathering knowledge and materials for future use, even though he does not set himself to write.

The Rev. B. Woodd—

1. Divine Influences—what are they ?

They are not a revelation of new truth ; nor a supernatural illustration of truth.   They are an impression of truth already revealed, but yet applicable in a new light to the person receiving them.

2. What influences are ministers authorised to expect ?

What other Christians are to expect.   But *as* other Christians may expect them, viz., in *means* and *diligence.*

Ministers are not authorised to expect more—

(1.) Because serious preparation is strongly enforced upon us.

(2.) Because the promise, *I will give thee a mouth and wisdom which none of thine adversaries shall be able to withstand,* is *confined* to times of persecution.

(3.) Because the varieties in ministers are reducible to the varieties in their natural talents.

(4.) Because varieties of natural talents are discernible even in divine writers.

It is a questionable point how far occasional elevations prove divine influences.   Cicero says—*Nemo sine multitudine unquam disertus fuit.*

We are creatures of habit and mechanism so far, that this must be taken into the account.

I do not deny divine influences, but I think much is assigned to them, which is merely the natural result of circumstances.

The safest way for a minister is to give God the glory for all he feels comfortable ; but to take to himself the shame of all he feels to be defective.

There is no encouragement to expect personal assistance from that passage—*Lo, I am with you alway, even unto the end of the world.*   It relates to the general prosperity of the Church.

In the exercise of our ministry, we should—

(1.) Understand the subject we are treating of.

(2.) Be particularly prepared, when possible.

We must not make too much of feelings, though it is certainly desirable to feel comfortably.   But we should leave all with God, however we feel.

The Rev. W. J. Abdy—

It is a dangerous thing to trust too much to feelings, for we often think God with us, when he is far from us, and far from us when he is near.

The Rev. J. Venn—

Our question depends much on the more general one—In what way does the Spirit usually influence man?

The Spirit generally works on the affections. These, when once moved, influence the man's views, and his modes of exhibiting his views. The varieties you see in ministers are also to be seen in other men in the common affairs of life; though there is this difference, that the Spirit has wrought in the minister these affections by giving his faculties a direction towards the great subject of the Gospel.

There is danger in entertaining wrong views of this subject, lest they lead to idleness and presumption, which have had a worse influence in the Church than almost any other evils.

A minister may be attributing to the Spirit what has arisen from his own vanity.

On the contrary, many men have been very useful when many have said they appeared to have no assistance of the Spirit.

The Rev. W. Goode—

What Woodd has said, goes further than he intended. It amounts to this: Because effects are sometimes produced by natural feelings, therefore no other mode is to be looked for.

I think there is danger in restricting the promise, *Lo, I am with you, &c.*, to the Apostolic times. All the promises which refer to assistance in the ministry, are as applicable to us as to the Apostles.

I have felt myself set at liberty often when low and dull. This is quite contrary to the animal feelings. But there is a mixture of the animal part in all that comes from man. But this does not prove that the Spirit is not peculiarly present with him.

The Rev. Mr Lloyd—

This is one of the deepest questions in theology. I should say it is not designed to be ascertained.

Woodd attributes much of what we feel to natural causes; but this does not preclude the co-operation of the Spirit, who works with such natural causes.

Whitfield and Wesley distinguish spiritual influences from natural causes. Enthusiasm cannot do so.

I find the preaching of Jesus Christ excite enmity on all hands. The intellectual part of fallen man rises as much against the doctrines of the Gospel, as the sensual part against the perceptive parts.

The Rev. H. Foster—

The subject is dark, and not much light has been thrown upon it; so it would be arrogant in me to attempt to do so. I will only add, every Christian has the promise of divine influence. The promise to a minister is, no doubt, suited to his duties, which are higher than those of any other man, and therefore the Spirit's influences may be looked for in proportion.

The Rev. R. Cecil—

A sufficiency in *all things* is promised. What does the minister require ?—for in these respects the promise applies to him. For example, a minister often needs courage. He may expect, then, that the Spirit will give him the courage he needs, and he may look for the divine influence in this way.

A minister may expect more elevation, more superintendence than a hearer.

It can hardly be questioned that a minister ought to pray to be thus influenced.

As to constitutional qualifications, I am of the same opinion with Owen. When a man furbishes up his understanding and thinks to shew off, God takes him and uses him for a particular purpose.

Unction is often present where learning is absent.

This results from a combination of the truth with grace and gifts. Nothing in nature will do, but as the Spirit works in and by the means.

I was cured of expecting the Spirit's influence without due preparation, by observing how men talked who took up that sentiment. I have heard men talk nonsense by the hour, as the "Spirit enabled them."

Combine St Paul with Luther. *" Give attendance to reading,"* &c., and, *Bene orasse est bene studuisse.*

One errs who says—" I will preach a reputable sermon, and please my hearers." Another errs who says—" I need not prepare, but will leave all to the Spirit, who is able to help me as I need help."

The Rev. Thomas Scott—

Our question has been lost sight of as it has gone round. The question is not, How are we to distinguish natural feelings from the Spirit's influences ? but a very different one, How far a minister is to expect divine influence in his ministry ?

When we consider what he has to do, and what he is, *Who is sufficient for these things?*

The danger of idleness and presumption have been well asserted ; but there is equal danger of self-dependence and pride.

APRIL 14, 1800.

Is REDEMPTION GENERAL OR PARTICULAR ?—Proposed by the Rev. B. Woodd.

Mr Woodd—

Redemption is both General and Particular ; but in different senses.

It is not general, so as to be available to all. But it is so far general, that the ransom-price is sufficient to save the whole world, and even fallen spirits. Also, by this means, a general grant, or offer of pardon, can be made to all mankind. In consequence of Christ's sacrifice, there is a general placability in God to man. This is the sentiment of Calvin, who distinguishes between sufficient and effective grace.

See also Musculus, Hall, Zanchius, Davenant, Assembly of Divines, and Daille. So Heb. ii. 9; John i. 29; iii. 16; 1 Tim. iv. 10; 2 Cor. v. 14; 2 Pet. iii. 9; 1 John ii. 1, 2.

The idea of general redemption is connected with the infinite sufficiency of the ransom. The benefit which accrues from general redemption is this, that the covenant of redemption was made with all mankind in Christ. But the covenant of grace is only with those who will be saved.

As to Particular Redemption.

This is analogous to God's general dispensations. There is, for instance, a Church visible, and a Church spiritual.

All are in a general sense redeemed, but none but the elect are actually redeemed.

Particular redemption, then, is the effectual application of general redemption.

I would illustrate this by the decree of Cyrus: all were free to go back from the captivity; but some only did so. (See *Ambrose* on Ps. cxviii.)

It is objected, upon the view of redemption being considered general, that, as to the greater part of men, Christ shed his blood in vain. I answer, this cannot be said, if it answered, as it did, the end designed by it.

General Redemption, then, consists in this—(1.) The sufficiency of the death of Christ for all; (2.) The offer being made to all. Particular Redemption is this—that the effectual application of the redemption is to the elect.

Election is the free act of God effectually applying redemption to men equally sinful in themselves with those who are not so brought to Him. Yet all is the result of wisdom and justice.

The Rev. H. Foster—

One great objection I have to state against redemption being considered general, is, that Scripture represents the substitution of Christ for sinners as the greatest possible act of love to His *children*.

The Rev. Josiah Pratt—

I assent to all Woodd has said. But he has thrown no real light on the question. The Crux Theologica remains; and he never can remove it.

As to general redemption, God has done all to make man inexcusable, and to shew us that it is our bounden duty to make offers of salvation to all.

As to particular redemption, God has taken all *glorying* to Himself. How is this? what is the rationale?—none can say.

The Rev. Thomas Scott referred the members to his sermon on election: and then said—

In answer to Foster I would say, 'Tis for Regeneration I feel gratitude; that is, for the effectual application of Redemption to my soul.

APRIL 28, 1800.

WHAT ARE THE ORDER AND ASSOCIATION OF CHRISTIAN GRACES?— Proposed by the Rev. B. Woodd.

The only remark of Mr Woodd's recorded in our Note-book is the following quotation from Baxter—*In velle, in posse, in actu*—which, we suppose, he made the text of his observations.

The Rev. W. Goode—

Faith in God precedes repentance. Faith in Christ, as a personal act for salvation, follows repentance.

Repentance, as a sorrow for sin in general, precedes saving faith. Repentance, as a melting sorrow for sin, follows saving faith.

The Rev. R. Cecil—

There's a good deal in taste. I have no taste for philosophical divinity. I have seldom found any distinct attainments in those who have.

It satisfies me to lay hold on the plain letter of Scripture. Whether I can fully comprehend and account for it or not, is nothing to me.

The Rev. J. Pratt made 2 Pet. i. 5, 6, the ground of his remarks— *Add to your faith virtue, &c.*

The Rev. Thomas Scott—

That is a beautiful character, where everything is in order : in which, for example, we see boldness, but meekness—meekness, but courage : in which a man is seen penitent, but believing—believing, but penitent.

The true character blends colours as the rainbow. Jesus Christ is the only perfect example of this. St Paul is the most wonderful among fallible men.

The Rev. J. Clayton—

All the Christian graces must be resolved into the divine life, or regeneration, from which they spring. In this we are passive, and God only works. In repentance and faith we are active, and work from life.

Conviction is not the warrant for a sinner to come to God ; but the free, unhampered invitation of the Gospel, is the warrant. Conviction is, however, a *motive.*

MAY 12, 1800.

WHAT IS THE PRACTICAL APPLICATION OF THAT SCRIPTURE IN-
JUNCTION, " LET EVERY ONE PLEASE HIS NEIGHBOUR FOR HIS GOOD TO
EDIFICATION " ?—Proposed by the Rev. J. Goode.

The Rev. H. Jowett, Rector of Little Dunham, Norfolk, a visitor
for the evening—

The passage must be, of course, limited in its application.   One main
point is, that it is opposed to seeking our own good and edification at
the expense of our neighbour.   It requires us to forego our own good,
when it interferes with that of others.   Scripture is very copious and
strong on this point.

The Rev. H. Foster—

St Paul was an example of his own precept.   He accommodated
himself to the weaknesses of men : he comes down to them to raise
them to himself.   See this most remarkably exemplified in his Epistle
to Philemon.

The practical application of the injunction is extensive.

Man should be in the spirit which it enforces wherever he goes.
He will meet with a variety of characters in his walk through life, and
many occasions of calling it into action.

A disposition which should be avoided is this—To please others and
ourselves for *no* good, but to get a good opinion of ourselves.

The Rev. Dr Gilbee, a visitor—

In pleasing others, we should be careful not to displease our Master.
We should please our neighbour in the same spirit as we would rebuke
him.

The Rev. J. Pratt—

The application of the injunction depends upon man's constitution of
mind.   The morose should guard against a want of kindness; the
amiable against an excess.

Sacrifice and self-government are as necessary on the one side as on
the other.

If I were to preach a sermon upon the passage, I should notice—
(1.) The Act—*Let every one please his neighbour;* (2.) The Motive—
for his good; (3.) The Qualification—*to edification.*

The Rev. T. Scott—

There is more danger of our being too much men-pleasers, than of
being too little so.   The fable of the man, the boy, and the ass, shews
us how useless it is to aim at pleasing man too much.

To please God should be our aim : and we may be sure, that if we
please not our neighbour " to edification," we please not God.

A loose-living preacher will always be a man-pleasing preacher.   We
must therefore make God's Word, not our own experience, the standard
of preaching.

We may indeed set St Paul's example before us, as a most instructive application of his own injunction.

A minister, in his own concerns, should be like a pliant willow; but in the concerns of truth, like a rock.

I wish I had more of the *suaviter in modo,* and I wish some had more of the *fortiter in re.* But *non omnia possumus omnes.*

The Rev. J. Clayton—

If we desired to please men on their own principles, we should be obliged to displease them often. If, rather than displease our neighbour, we withhold the truth, the man will nevertheless be displeased, if he should get it in any other way.

Whatever draws the thoughts towards God in His sovereignty, Christ in His cross, the Holy Spirit in His operations, will be displeasing to man, till he be called by grace. Therefore, if we cannot prevail upon ourselves to displease Him with these thoughts now, we shall displease Him to all eternity.

Men have different characters, and these furnish different handles, which we may use to their edification. And we ourselves, also, have different characters and dispositions; the rough should study to become smooth, and the smooth to be faithful.

It is more difficult for the amiable man to make a sacrifice of that amiableness, which is universally popular, than for the rough to sacrifice that roughness, which is universally unpopular.

We should seize opportunities of pleasing our neighbour for his good to edification.

The mariner avails himself with promptitude of every favourable gale. We should imitate this in a wise accommodation of all the occasions and opportunities which offer themselves.

The Rev. J. Newton—

The great point I would aim at is this—that whether people will accede to what I say or not, they may have a full persuasion that I mean them well. A young minister's exordium is too often in this spirit—" I know you all hate me."

I have been forty years in acquiring my present views. I reject some things I thought valuable; and receive some I before hesitated at. Now, why should I expect any man to receive my sentiments in half-an-hour, which I have been forty years in acquiring?

It was a common saying with Mr Whitfield—" If I am faithful, you'll either fall out with me or with yourselves."

A lady once found fault with my speaking too loud in preaching. Mr Thornton said afterwards—" Don't mind that; she was cut by what you said, and must say something. If she had not found fault with your speaking, she would have done so with your buttons."

The Rev. B. Woodd—

The common view of pleasing our neighbour is wrong. It's a sacrifice to self. Regeneration of heart restores the desire to please on right principles.

The natural character of man produces self-will towards God, and selfishness towards our neighbour. Regeneration removes both these.

The text has a reference to the preceding chapters, which shew that we should accommodate ourselves to the prejudices of our neighbour.

We please our neighbour not to edification, when we flatter our neighbour's vices, or abet his self-flattering, or repeat encomiums to him, or when we administer to his self-indulgences and undue compliance with the world : when we bear not an unequivocal testimony against sin and the world : when we administer reproof in such a way that it proves itself to be the most artfully covered flattery.

Lord Chesterfield's whole system is despicable. True Christianity is true gentility.

Yet we may displease our neighbour without doing him good.

We may please him to his good for edification, by exhibiting a consistent and respectful deportment ; by exercising the social affections under Divine grace ; by adapting an inoffensive, affable, courteous conduct ; by giving important truths their due weight ; by not laying undue stress on unnecessary points ; by accommodating ourselves to our neighbour's weakness, so far as conscience permits ; by maintaining Christian truth in the spirit of love ; by shewing to all men that respect which is man's just due ; by reproving him in that spirit which becomes a fellow-sinner.

A general rule in our ministry is this :—Avoid all offence, which is not the offence of the Gospel ; yet let the Gospel give its full offence.

On what principles should we act in endeavouring to please our neighbour ?

From duty to God ; love to Christ ; and the good of our neighbour.

To please our neighbour to edification, is a practice eminently endeared and recommended to the believer by the example of Christ. The apostle adds—" *For even Christ pleased not himself.*"

The Rev. R. Cecil—

A healthy man has good blood, and in circulation : it reaches to his toes and his fingers, and all is healthy.

So the man who has *the mind that was in Christ* has everything in proper tone. He is the man who succeeds in pleasing his neighbour for his good to edification.

He who truly aims at pleasing his neighbour for his edification, acts towards him as one who feels himself to be a sinner trying to help a sinner.

What different effects should we see if this spirit prevailed ! If Dissenters were like Watts, and Doddridge, and Henry; and if Churchmen were like Leighton !

The man who goes out into active life may expect to be found fault with. One will call him harsh, another a trimmer.

Men may reverence a hard man ; but they like him best at a distance. He's an iron man ; he is not like Jesus Christ.

Christ might have said to Thomas—" You won't believe, clear as the evidence has been ! Depart, you are unfit for my service ! "—but not so ! It is as though he had said, " I'll come down to thy weakness. If you can't believe without thrusting thy hand into my side, why, then, thrust in thy hand ! "

I would avoid all cant phrases in endeavouring to please. But yet I have found out from my own experience what I should not have suspected. I try to preach the Gospel, and preach it faithfully. Yet there are many among my people who can't see *much* distinction between me and others. *They* preach Christ as God. *They* do " this and that." Now, I want to make them feel the distinction. I would even use *cant* phrases, if I could do it in no other way.

A feeble, kind, tender man can do more than a genius, in whose manner there is anything of artifice or roughness. For example, compare Brewer and Saurin—one a most pious, diligent, and humble-minded dissenting minister, and the other an eminent and eloquent preacher. Which do you suppose did most good ?

There is a danger on the other hand of humouring others. I felt this myself when I was in what I thought a dying state.

The man that sticks his elbows a-kimbo along Cheapside, bruises everybody he passes.

Two goats met on a bridge too narrow for them to pass each other. The goat that lay down for the other to step over him was a finer gentleman than Lord Chesterfield.

MAY 26, 1800.

HOW SHALL WE DISTINGUISH BETWEEN TRUE AND COUNTERFEIT CHRISTIAN EXPERIENCE ?—Proposed by the Rev. B. Woodd.

The Rev. Thomas Scott—

The word " experience " is rarely used in the New Testament ; indeed only twice—once in Rom. v. 4 :—*For patience worketh experience, and experience hope,* &c. ; and once in Heb. v. 13, according to the marginal reading, *For every one that useth milk hath no experience in the word.*

No objection, however, exists to a right use of it. But an unscriptural use of it we must avoid. It is too often made a test of truth, when scripture is the only test.

Experience is the power of truth on the judgment and affections, the mind and heart. A man supposes that medicine will do him good. If it *do* so, this is experience. If it *do not* so, still it is experience.

There is no man in the world who ever thought of religion, but has something which may be called experience.

Truth may produce some great effect, and yet not a saving effect. I do not speak of tares, these spring from false doctrine.

What ought the effect of truth to be ? If it be what it ought, then the experience it works is genuine ; if it be not what it should be, the experience is counterfeit.

Man may not be a *hypocrite* to himself. He has his feelings, and he knows when his feelings are not right.

What is the experience of a true Christian ?—Humiliation, self-abhorrence, self-abasement ; not merely being frighted ; not comfort always ; not confidence.

Scripture lays weight on three things—
(1.) Humiliation before God and submission to His righteousness;
(2.) Hatred and dread of sin; and (3.) Love to Christ.

The Rev. J. Clayton—

1. True and false experience are essentially different in principle.
False experience must be the *various modifications of nature,* with an approbation of religion without.
True experience is derived from a spiritual life, derived from Christ by the Holy Spirit.
2. They differ as connected with truth.
False experience is connected with false ideas of truth in one way or other.
3. They differ as to visible display.
False experience is defective as to the commands of God. If the heart be not sound, man is not sound in God's statutes: True experience quarrels with self for coming short.
4. They differ in permanency.
False experience is soon dissipated; like a land-flood, it soon dries up. True experience will endure; it is a *well of water springing up unto everlasting life.*

The Rev. J. Newton—

The magicians of Egypt were at length baffled. This is the favour of God.
Is there some *infallible criterion* not to be counterfeited? I have one in the government of the tongue. I have observed a great difference in professors in this respect, whether they speak (1.) of God, (2.) of themselves, or (3.) of others.
True experience leads a man to a reverence of God, meekness toward others, and humbleness in himself.

The Rev. G. Pattrick—

I have observed that the most suspicious characters are most loquacious, and most forward in the exercise of their gifts.
False experience is of an ostentatious nature, making *self* its object.
Factitious experience is made up of *current phrases.*
False experience is partial in its disclosures. Enough is communicated to procure the character of humility, but not to lose the good opinion of friends.
True experience is silent; prefers perhaps conferring with God in private, to conferring with a friend.

The Rev. J. Goode—

When experience on the whole is genuine, yet it is often defective.
There is a want of due proportion in views of Divine things and corresponding affections towards them. An arch from its symmetry defies the stream; but let one stone be out of place, and the whole falls and is swept away.

The Rev. Mr Lloyd—

Edwards makes this a leading feature of the Christian character—an evangelical humiliation for sin.

A great variety of motives operate on man.   It is hard to ascertain from what motive a man acts.   In nature, heterogeneous principles destroy each other ; not so in *man !*

A bending of the will to God in the midst of numerous infirmities is a striking feature.

Men may adopt some great principle in religion, while it stands in the mind without its proper combinations, and therefore their experience is unsound.

The Rev. J. Venn—

It is commonly said, that experience is the process a man goes through in becoming a Christian.   But in this definition, the means are put for the end.   If an alchymist could produce *gold,* he would not say it was gold, because he had taken it through the process.

Scripture generally dwells on effects.   Men in error generally dwell on means, and substitute feelings for holiness.

Experience is liable to infinite delusions.   If comfort is all that is sought for, the question is not of so much consequence ; but if it goes to establish a test whether Christ has been received by us, it becomes of the utmost moment.

Many are in sorrow, because they think they have not passed through the right experience, though they are full of anxious desires to please God.

Let us place experience where it ought to stand.

The Rev. J. Pratt—

There is danger on *both* sides.   Venn has pointed out the danger on *one.*

But Pharisees are in as much danger of building holiness on a wrong foundation, or measuring it by an imperfect standard, as enthusiasts are of being deluded by feelings without holiness.

True experience must be run into holiness, and true holiness must be run up into sound experience.

The great turning-point of distinction between true and false experience is *a struggle;* not the mere reluctancies of natural conscience, but the efforts of a renewed nature directed against the whole body and being of sin.   The devil cannot imitate this.

True experience in a weak or ill-taught man may be very like false experience in a wicked man ; but the genuine character will be borne through all his blunders, while Judas is left to hang himself.

June 9, 1800.

Are known Seals of a Minister's Labours necessary to evince the Acceptableness of his Ministry to the Lord ; and how far ?—Proposed by the Rev. Josiah Pratt.

Mr Pratt—

Known seals of a minister's labours are an evidence of the acceptableness of his ministry.

I. This is NATURAL. It is in the order of things.

II. It is USUAL.

III. It is DESIRABLE—

For a minister feels it a great and comfortable evidence of his calling and his acceptableness, if such be found in his congregation. He feels his ground. He speaks with confidence. It gives a new set of feelings to a minister—a parent's affections. He knows that all he says is received in love and kindness. How we see this in St Paul's epistles to Philemon and to the Corinthians. Yet it is not to be made too much the object of desire, for—

IV. This kind of evidence is NOT UNEQUIVOCAL.

The Lord sometimes, to honour truth, will give bad men success. I do not speak of pretended seals—the deluded are often made the means of confounding the deluders.

V. This evidence is NOT NECESSARY.

The Lord reduces us sometimes to hold to bare duty, while He retains effects and events in His hands.

The apostle, in writing to Timothy and Titus, nowhere speaks of the *visible fruits* of their ministry. He says much of their spirit, aim, character, doctrine, labours. When he speaks of the Deacon being proved, and having used his office well, he does not make success necessary.

On the contrary—in 1 Tim. iv. 6, 16, and 2 Tim. ii. 15—his being approved of God depends on his *character*. Do thy duty towards those committed to you, but (ver. 25) it is *then* a "peradventure" whether God will give them repentance.

VI. Yet the WANT of this evidence is a CAUSE OF INQUIRY.

1. Is there any obstacle in my *matter?* Do I exhibit God's remedy? Do I preach a free and holy gospel?

2. Is there any obstacle in my *manner?* Is it unsuitable or offensive?

3. Is there any obstacle in my *spirit?* The Lord may be teaching me self-renunciation hereby, and the difference between gifts and graces?

A minister may be under a cloud, like B——, or he may move from a successful to an unsuccessful situation, like R——.

He may have a different talent, and be called to other work.

He may be a writer, and, when dead, may speak with effect, and may so become the instrument of converting the yet unborn.

He may not know how far in reality he is successful. [This he illustrated in some way by alluding to Mr Robinson of Leicester.]

VII. Yet the WANT of this evidence is also a CAUSE OF HUMILITY.

A great and good end is gained if we lie in God's hands.

It is a high honour to be an instrument of turning many to righteousness; and if God see me to be such a man as not to be so employed, then I learn humility.

Even where He grants seals, He will often teach a man humility. [Mr Romaine was here mentioned in illustration, but what the allusion is we cannot discover.]

It is a great work to be brought to do WHAT, WHEN, WHERE, God pleases.

The Rev. J. Davies—

If this be a necessary kind of evidence, it would seem that a minister is acceptable *in proportion* to the number of seals he has. But this is disproved by the case of our Lord himself—whose ministry, moreover, was less successful than that of some of his Apostles.

A minister may have many *unknown* seals. If by *known* seals is meant converted persons, this is not necessary, because many ministers may be appointed to *edify* the Church.

A minister may be *useful*, yet not acceptable.

The Rev. J. Clayton—

Our brethren seem to confound the acceptableness of a man's person with the acceptableness of his ministry. Success is not the rule of duty.

If so, a good minister may be tempted to give up, and a bad minister may seem to be true. [Wheatly of Norwich was referred to for illustration.]

As to success, we must wait patiently.

Many will not speak of the influence of the Word upon their hearts.

The Rev. J. Newton—

A single seal is worth a life of suffering.

It is said that Harvey had no certain evidence that he had any one seal in the parish of Weston Flavel. So also of Mr Adam of Wintringham [whose " Private Thoughts on Religion," published after his death, has since been so eminently useful.] But good seed was sown, and sprang after his death.

Children are sometimes as much or more attached to nurses than to parents.

Christ's charge to Peter is about feeding, rather than gathering— *Feed my sheep—my lambs.*

Many faithful men have but little visible success. How true was this of the prophet Jeremiah : " *Run ye to and fro,*" he cries, "*through the streets of Jerusalem, and see now, and know, and seek in the broad places thereof, if ye can find a man, if there be any, that executeth judgment, that seeketh the truth.*"

Yet is a minister useful in doing what God sent him for.

We might be proud if we knew our seals.

We preach not a single right-hearted sermon, but it produces a proportionate effect.

The Rev. B. Woodd—

The Apostles had a discernment of spirits which we have not. They could speak of their seals with more certainty. It is difficult for us to say who are seals and who not. Itinerant ministers are in peculiar danger of mistaking. Their novelty, too, often induces people to listen to the Gospel.

I do not think even the greatest *apparent* success is an absolute proof of the acceptableness of the minister. There is a sovereignty in God's dealings in this respect.

The Rev. J. Goode—

There are seals of different kinds : Paul plants, and Apollos waters, but God giveth the increase ; and yet both Paul and Apollos in some sense has a seal of his ministry ; and each may take comfort from his success.

Seals are necessary more for the comfort of the minister than for his acceptableness.

The Rev. J. Venn—

The idea that success is necessary to acceptableness arises from two false suppositions. It supposes (1.) That God will never use any instrument but a good one ; (2.) That this instrument shall know of his success. Bunyan's first serious impressions were from a wicked woman's telling her child she would soon be as bad as John Bunyan.

A great principle which God lays down in his moral government is, that man shall do everything with a right aim. We perpetually run into the mistake of preferring the glaring and the splendid.

We make too much of the ministry in thinking it *necessary* to the work of God. Give the glory to God ; and place men as instruments brought in to do the work as he pleases : and then he directs this or that providential circumstance to let us know our seals or not, as he sees fit. Ministers are as pipes—if they convey the water, it matters not whether they are wooden or leaden.

A faithful minister, if not successful, is acceptable even as a *sweet savour in them that perish.*

A great deal of *little good* is done by some men.

God generally works in a *calm, silent* way. His kingdom *cometh not with observation.* The good is often not perceived for a long time.

The Rev. W. J. Abdy—

A most difficult thing it is, especially in London, to put our hand on a person and say, this is my seal.

There are extremes on both sides in this question.

There is danger of something like a mercenary spirit. You must let me *know* that some good is done in return for my labour. Ministers have sometimes made want of success a pretext for leaving places. On the other hand, a minister may be careless and indifferent. The Apostle speaks of *travailing in birth* with his converts. This should not be a feeling peculiar to an Apostle.

Yet, after all, a minister's acceptableness does not depend on seals. He may satisfy himself without them whether his ministry is acceptable.

It is a great point gained if we keep some knowledge and conviction of divine truth alive. Perhaps the chief end attained by the Christian minister in this day is to keep alive a conviction that religion is a *great reality.*

We have no great outpouring of the Spirit in these days.

The Rev. E. Edwards, a visitor—

A distinction is to be made in the seals themselves. A man's having conviction of sin does not render him a seal. Men may be brought from a self-righteous spirit to accept of Gospel truth ; but if they go no further, they are not seals.

I would feel more humbled on account of the *willing* not being built up, than the *wicked* not being called.

It may please God to leave a minister a long time ignorant of his success, in order to *wring* pride out of his soul.

The Rev. H. Foster—

It is desirable to a minister as a *man*, to have known seals to his ministry. And generally he *will*, if he be honest, find success. The case of Jeremiah is against this ; yet it is generally true.

It requires an uncommon degree of grace for a minister to go on in the face of want of success. God must be pouring in great grace to keep a man alive against such occasions of deadness.

Want of success is a temptation tending to divert a man to other pursuits. I have seen some turned away in this manner : because they are not attracting notice, they have turned away and fallen into deadness.

That text, *We are a sweet savour of Christ in them that are saved and in them that perish,* is a great comfort to me. Preaching Christ, whether successful or not, is our duty ; and he who does preach Christ, may rest satisfied he will have His blessing.

The Rev. R. Cecil—

The Gospel is a net which brings up rubbish with the fish. A man can never estimate acceptableness by the degree of his success.

The sun shines on some places, not on others.

He did not many mighty works, because of their unbelief. So in these days. Yet Christ's minister is as acceptable there as elsewhere.

There is much, we must remember, in the *ground*, whoever is the sower.

There may be reasons for *withholding* seals, or at least the knowledge of them, to check presumption.

There may be reasons for *disclosing* them, in order to cheer the sinking spirit of a minister.

The Apostles were ordered to shake the dust off their feet if the Word was not received. *They* were *accepted* in their Ministry, though *not sealed.*

Conversion is so much God's work, that He will take the whole business into His own hand.

Well done, good and FAITHFUL *servant*—this commendation does *not depend on visible seals.*

Yet I think with Pratt that it is a matter of inquiry, when we have not known seals to our ministry.

It is very easy to say why such and such men meet not with success. A sleepy preacher or a man of a hard disposition—it is no wonder if such men meet with no visible success. Our *temper* is much

G

more of an obstacle than is generally thought of.   The Spirit of Christ commends itself to the heart.

Man is made up of conceits—and God deals with him accordingly. An impatience to have seals may be a reason for God's withholding seals.   There is hardly anything we set our hearts upon, which God, in a dispensation of mercy towards us, will not withhold from us for our good.   Others may see the necessity of this; but not we ourselves.

A right disposition is the right kind of seal to the acceptableness of our ministry.

JUNE 23, 1800.

HOW SHALL A MINISTER BEST PRESERVE HIS PEOPLE FROM THE INFLUENCE OF SECTARIAN TEACHERS?—Proposed by the Rev. W. J. Abdy.

The Rev. H. Foster—

Several who are called Gospel-preachers have lost their people from not preaching the Gospel in its proper fulness.   It is painful to hear the charge, that a sermon may be preached without the name of Jesus being mentioned in it.   No wonder that people with a sense of sin go away offended.   But when a Minister *does* preach the Gospel, we leave God to manage.   If one leaves us, another will come.

But here I speak not with the experience of a *parochial* minister. With him I acknowledge it is different.

The most troublesome Sectarians are the Baptists.   I wish some short pithy tract were written against them.

The Rev. R. Cecil—

The Sectarian proselyting spirit is deeper than it pretends.   Baptism among the Baptists is made much of a stalking-horse.   "You must come to our place, and we'll keep you"—that's the intention—"and therefore we fasten this point on you."   [This he illustrated by the case of a Meeting-house at Lewes, his own parish, in past years.]   It is therefore a question of importance as to the *agenda*.

A Minister should store his mind with right views on the subject. Let him consider—

1. That it is in *human nature* to desire to draw others over to our way of thinking.

2. What it is which has so much increased Sectarianism.

(1.) It is the want of more faithful Gospel-ministers amongst us.

If the Minister is drowsy, Sectarianism is fervent.

If the Minister is not evangelical, Sectarianism is evangelical.

If the Minister be vexatious or idle, Sectarianism is all alive.

Whitfield's maxim is excellent—"Outpreach and outlive them."

Let us keep the room warm.   We want warmth in our ministrations.   The Clergy of the Church of England have been the great cause of Sectarianism.

Let us by our zeal produce a high interest, and Sectarianism will go

down. We have advantages above the Sectarians, in point of *education*
and in other ways.

The common people, it has been said, love a daub better than a
painting. But I differ. The common people love *to be interested.*
They can't distinguish nicely between *doctrine* and *practice*, but
excellence will always attract them. They have an eye for excellence,
because excellence is an appeal to nature. No instance can be
quoted of a diligent and laborious Minister possessing talents being
slighted. Was not this said of Jesus Christ?—" *The common people
heard him gladly.*"

(2.) But mere whim is the cause too often.

There is a time when any man will follow pretenders.

When a man's conscience is uneasy, though the Minister be orderly,
" Go to the Baptists," says a friend. With little light, and with an
uneasy conscience, a man may be thus easily led away.

When a man, too, is dead from the influence of the world, the fault
is thrown on his Minister, and the man goes to seek comfort elsewhere.

Begin, then, in *prevention.*

The Sectarians seize a raw Christian. We have been throwing out
generalities. The man is attacked and is unarmed.

Shew the people the difference between essential and non-essential
truth.

The particular notion of a Sectarian is often advanced into the rank
of a *first-rate* truth.

Shew a *superior* spirit. Get them out of a niggling spirit. Shew
them that you would carry them to heaven by Christ, rather than pin
them to your sleeve.

If our people are really made to taste of the old wine, they won't
like the new, but some will come back again.

Yet use no unfair means.

Get an acquaintance with the people.

In almost all Sectarianism, there is a wrong spirit :—violent, hard
uncandid, conceited. Shew the people, then, how this spirit uncovers
the evil.

The Rev. J. Pratt—

1. Make much of essentials ; 2. Little of non-essentials ; 3. Beget
a sound mind. Especially labour to bring the people to a *sound mind*
[He exemplified this in several eminent Ministers.] Sectarian teachers
operate as a trial of the state of a Christian. They detect the beginning of a wandering spirit. [This was illustrated by a reference to
Seager.] They present a temptation to test the stability of an established spirit. I tell them that a tender conscience is not a fit judge of
such points.

Establish a Christian community and society. [The advantages of
this were shewn by a reference to St Mary's, Birmingham, the Church
where Mr Pratt attended in his early years.]

It will not do to stand on Roman Catholic ground, viz., " You can
be saved only in *the Church.*"

The Rev. Thomas Scott—

A distinction should have been made among Sectarians, in the remarks made by the brethren.

The real Sectarian spirit is the spirit which would at all rates get men over to their party.

Our honest brethren of the Baptists should not be confounded with others.

In my sphere at Olney, I have had some experience. I find it well to preach on the subject. My brethren, I think, are too backward to controversy. The Baptists have some weighty things to say, which require a solid answer.

However, they don't catch people by their weighty things, but by their frivolous ones.

For instance, they harp upon the *word* Baptism, and gather from it, that immersion is absolutely *necessary*. Why, we might as well say, that we must be actually *crucified* with Christ, if we come to the exact and literal meaning of words. These metaphors are not intended to instruct us in an outward ordinance.

We should ground the people in the Scripture truth. It is a most dangerous thing to bring such points before newly-awakened consciences. It is like giving the sacrament to a dying wretch, who puts the sign for the thing signified. It is the spirit of Popery.

We should labour to give the people no just ground of complaint against our preaching as to its evangelical nature.

We should explain the ordinance of Baptism, shewing our own view of its importance and the obligations it lays on all parties concerned.

As to *all* Sectarians, not Baptists only, let us preach the WHOLE GOSPEL in its generalities and particularities.

The Rev. J. Clayton—

I generally preach a sermon on Baptism when we have children baptised.

As to repressing a Sectarian spirit, the method of *prevention* has often succeeded. We never receive men who want to be considered of consequence. As to you of the Church of England, if you cut off all your trappings, &c., many would come over to you.

The Rev. J. Newton—

A Sectarian spirit is the spirit of a man who would disturb a united congregation, to whatever community of Christians it might belong. We are all brother-journeymen in one shop.

The Rev. B. Woodd—

I should define a Sectarian to be one who separated himself from the Church of Christ in his neighbourhood.

I conceive all the Dissenters, therefore, to be such. I should think the man so in the neighbourhood of a Dissenting Minister.

But then I am obliged to say—" Is there not a cause ?" So then I enlarge my definition.

Our National Establishment is merely the Church of Christ under the protection of the State.

Dissenters are certainly aggrieved. Human impositions may be expedient, yet should not be binding on the conscience. Nothing should be binding but Scripture.

The Act of Uniformity inflicted a deep wound. The Act of Toleration applied a poor plaster.

I would have the doors of the Church so open, as to admit all conscientious Baptists and others.

JULY 7, 1800.

How is the Duty of Abstaining from the Reproof of Sin to be Distinguished from the Temptation?—Proposed by the Rev. J. Pratt.

The Rev. T. Scott—

There is no reproving by receipt. Times and circumstances must determine as to the mode.

I. Something may be collected from the character of the person to be reproved.

1. There is a desperate kind of profaneness which is but provoked by admonition. Serious solemn silence does best then. Mr Hey used to say in such cases—" Answer him not."

2. On the other hand, there is an insidious plausible way of sinning. This is a dangerous case. An insidious specious enmity to the Gospel should be met and exposed, if we can do it.

3. When a man who, in another situation, would wish to be looked on as a religious man, does and says things evil. There, no quarter is to be given. *Is this thy kindness to thy friend?*

II. We may learn something on this subject from our own character and relations.

1. With some persons, boldness seems the only Christian grace.

There should be great delicacy and deference on the part of inferiors, if ever they are called to reprove superiors. In general, silence is best. Few things dishonour the Gospel more than the boldness of young professors towards their superiors.

I would always inculcate that, though it is a duty to reprove sin, yet the spirit of reproof should be in harmony with other Christian duties.

2. We should consider our own character.

Do we see no sore place there?

Elijah and John the Baptist could reprove with authority, because of their own personal character, as well as their commission.

Many things become aged, which do not look well in young Christians and ministers.

As a minister, I may be bound to reprove what, as a private Christian, I may not be called to notice. For a minister should regard himself as a champion for the truth by profession. He is a Shepherd's dog, and *must* bark.

3. We should consider our situation, and what the effect is likely to be.

For instance, we might often see it right to reprove a companion, though not a man in the street.

4. We should consider what the thing to be reproved is.

For instance, don't enter into an argument upon a secondary topic with a fellow-passenger in a passing journey in a coach. But I would always reprove the reviler of the Bible and the Truth.

5. We should look at the spirit and motive which actuate us.

Do we abstain from reproving men who send us presents ?

There is but little credit for boldness to him who reproves gross sin in others and connives at infirmities in himself. Something above nature is necessary in reproving rightly.

6. We must consider what we are capable of in this difficult duty.

If we cannot do it without passion, then we should not do it at all.

The Rev. J. Davies—

There are few cases in which it is not a duty to reprove sin.

Cowardice generally lies at the bottom of our abstaining.

The chief case in which it would be right to abstain is when we have to do with a person who is incorrigible, and we are with him alone, without others being present. When in company, if *he* get no good, others may.

The Rev. J. Clayton—

I would add another view to Brother Scott's.

Never reprove a man for sin before men who are in the same spirit. This will awaken his pride. But get him alone, and *then* reprove him.

As I often ride in a stage-coach, I know the trials to be met with and the difficulty of undertaking to be a reprover; sometimes one is almost obliged to infringe on the usual civilities of life.

Good is done if we can but dam up the evil.

There are some people in whom there is no handle that you can take hold of.

None are more impenetrable than those who are under a delusive religious system.

The Rev. J. Newton—

There are diversities of gifts, but the same Spirit. It seems to me that some have a *gift* for reproving. Some are so prompt, wise, gentle, winning in their manner of administering reproof. A friend of mine had this, who used sometimes to stop and reprove swearing by saying, " Sir, give me leave to swear next."

Yet, where it is our duty to abstain from *speaking* in reproof, we should nevertheless shew it by *looks*.

There is a good deal in tempers and dispositions. I am phlegmatic and not impetuous. If I feel inclination to reprove, I am not likely to do wrong. But the impetuous may be wrong in following their feelings.

I tell infidels that I don't believe them. They try to carry a bold face, but they are wretched at heart.

If a gross thing pass in company, I would either reprove or leave the room.

Reproof should be IN SEASON, IN SECRET, and IN LOVE.

I knew a minister who used to reprove swearing by taking off his hat when he heard it.

[Dr Gifford in the British Museum, and Mr Wesley in a coffee-house, were brought forward as examples of reproving.]

The Rev. G. Pattrick—

In company, an ingenious man might do some good in the parabolic way.

The Rev. H. Foster—

As to the streets, I feel myself easy in being quiet. I feel no duty in it. If I did, I could do nothing.

There is a great difference between those who commit themselves in any way to our care, and strangers.

Every man must consider his talent, and each should consider it with sobriety.

It may be one man's duty to do what it is not another's. My own temperament is to be silent. Sometimes I have felt compelled from conscience to reprove; but yet have come off so ill, as to shew me how little good I could do. The duty of reproving is one of those things which God has left in a large and general way. God has not bound the conscience to particulars in this matter.

The Rev. R. Cecil—

I don't know that I ever had, or am likely to have, much success in this matter. I feel with Foster that I have nothing to do with the blackguards in the street.

I don't feel myself called in a parish to shut up ale-houses, and to do things of that sort, as Grimshaw does. I have no talent for it. I don't think it is because I am disposed to shrink from the duty. I am discouraged in the street from seeing greater sins allowed—such as taverns and gaming-houses.

I once tried in a stage-coach, but not with success. I once worked a clergyman so up by reproving him, as almost to lead him to strike me. On another occasion I encountered a young man who pleaded it was the fashion, and got the company on his side.

But the great difficulty is reproving, not out of doors, but those who are your friends.

I should never have thought a man's religion so much depended on the circulation of his blood as it does, if I had not experienced it.

The zeal of reproving is, in a young man, a questionable thing altogether.

Twenty years ago, I would have taken a man by the collar and preached four sermons a-day to him. Now I am glad if circumstances bring on an excuse.

One case I feel important:—That of a young man, a good man, drawn out too much into the world, his wife leading and urging him.

He should not be content to say—" My wife or my daughter likes it."
But he should be faithful and reprove, as the case may require.

A more urgent case still;—the case of ministers. Here is a man
who is a captain, an officer in the regiment; or some one else whose
errors we are afraid to point out. This ought not to be the case. All
are to be blamed in not stating to a brother what we say of him to
others. Man is so blind that he can't see in his own case. And
although he be so touchy that he won't bear it; why, it is to be
lamented, yet we should venture.

Now if the minister is a flaring man, and one wishing to lead a
party, he will seldom meddle with such a case. This man is wrong
at bottom. But if the minister be a godly man, the person reproved
will take it well *afterwards*, if not at the time, if he is a true man.

It should be a subject of examination in one's own mind—" Why
do I abstain from reproving?" Where I don't see it to be my duty,
I answer to myself accordingly. But if I find that I am indisposed
to the labour, or to the consequence of it, then it is a temptation to
sluggishness, selfishness, and want of zeal.

And when we feel this temper of mind—"I am not in the right
frame for it "—why, here's a *sin*, then; that I am not in a frame to do
my duty.

When in company with our own people, it is often difficult to
reprove.

The conversation is, perhaps, poor and worldly. Somehow or other,
one becomes all one with them. They come to Church on Sunday,
and we preach. The week comes round again, and the nonsense with
it. This disease is not a putrid fever, but a consumption, and grows
worse slowly. Yet something must be done. Now, if I am what I
should be, the people would feel it. They would not attempt to
introduce this dawdling, chattering, diurnal stuff. I have really
thought since I was ill, that I have done more good by staying at
home than I did before by going out.

Moreover, there is this evil. It looks like this—" On the Sunday, I
am ready to do *my* business; and in the week, you may do *yours*." It
lowers the tone of what I say on the Sabbath. It is a sad comment
on my preaching. Though I can't bring out what Grimshaw could,
yet I might shew them, and tell them, and make them feel, that there
is a higher and more holy thing. He used to abstain, in his visits to
his people, from commenting on the Bible, but would pray with them.
But commenting might give an opportunity of glancing at the thing
which one can't well openly reprove. What is said in this way should
be said with caution; but there is a great deal in having a talent
for the thing. I feel myself no more called on to *bear down sin*, as
Mr Venn did, than a barn-door fowl to fly like the hawk. There is a
felicity and success about some, which is a real talent. Yet we should
be cautious not to be saying this to excuse ourselves, when we ought
really to act.

I have traced a little the root of this shrinking from difficult duties.
We are more concerned to be thought gentlemen, than to be felt as
ministers.

Being willing to be thought of as a man who has kept good company, cuts at the root of that rough work which is often required of us in bringing God into His own world. It is rough and hard work to bring God into His world. To talk of a Creator, and Preserver, and Redeemer, is an outrage and violence on the feelings of people.

There is something of truth in what Mr Wesley said to his preachers, though I have heard it much ridiculed :—" You have no more to do with being gentlemen, than being dancing-masters." The character of a minister is a great deal above the character of a gentleman. It takes a higher walk. I would not have a man rude, and disdain to learn how to handle his knife and fork ; but to be a gentleman, should not be his chief aim.

When the religious character is well sustained, the Minister feels himself strengthened ; his loins are girt up ; and a reproof falls from such a man with authority.

Another thing I've found a snare. The drawing one out into conversation upon the stocks, or the news of the day, largely. If you can be got to give twenty opinions on this and that of politics or literature, it places you at disadvantage. A man of sense feels something violent in the transition from such conversation to the Bible and Prayer.

If you go to a dinner, it is a very unprofitable opportunity. The company are so occupied in mangling and slaying, that nothing is to be done.

The most we are able to do to any purpose in the way of reproof, is in PRIVATE, with our FRIENDS.

JULY 21, 1800.

HOW FAR IS IT EXPEDIENT TO ENCOURAGE RELIGIOUS SOCIETIES, AND WHAT IS THE BEST METHOD OF CONDUCTING THEM ?— Proposed by the Rev. J. Davies.

The Rev. J. Davies—

The advantage of forming societies for religious intercourse arises from the fact, that man is a social being : therefore, much good may be expected from them.

Their disadvantages are as follows :—

1. They tend to promote spiritual pride.

2. They tend to produce a spirit of religious dissipation.

3. They tend to produce hypocrisy.

But no plan is to be abandoned, because evil may result from it.

As religious societies are at present formed, the evil generally preponderates.

But probably they may be so constituted, that the good should preponderate.

The best method of conducting them—

1. These societies should be formed out of one community.

2. One member should not be set over another : personal superintendence should be avoided in these meetings.

3. The meetings should not be too frequent.

4. The objects should be prayer, perhaps discussion on religious subjects, or reading religious books, or, though it is a tender point, consulting each other on religious subjects.

5. The minister should have such a connexion with the society as would be profitable both to him and them.

The Rev. J. Clayton—

We want something more than preaching among us. We want a nearer approach, a faster hold of our people.

I have found great difficulties in prayer meetings, though I have kept them up for twenty-one years. Yet these meetings have many advantages.

1. They accustom young men to pray with ease with the sick, &c.

2. If they be conducted in a proper spirit, they encourage the minister.

3. They promote brotherly love and a knowledge of each other's circumstances.

• The Rev. Mr Vansittart, a visitor—

There is ground for the general expediency of these meetings.

But the question of expediency arises from the state of the place where they should be introduced. If the people are only just beginning to hear the Gospel, they should be taught, rather than encouraged, to indulge in a conferring spirit among themselves.

The Rev. W. J. Abdy—

Religious societies are consistent with—(1.) the nature of man, (2.) Christianity, (3.) the Holy Scriptures.

We have found the benefits of them in *this* Society.

But I've found it very difficult in my parish to maintain them.

The Rev. J. Venn—

There is little or no positive evidence from scripture or ecclesiastical history, that such societies were ever formed. Dr Woodward's were the first sort we read of. They might have existed to this day, had not Mr Wesley's arisen.

They were of great* influence, and were felt to be so during the French Revolution, when infidel principles were spreading in this country.

The difficulties are great, especially in the Church of England.

I. Consider the Church as divided, and tending to form parties.

If we imitate Mr Wesley's method, a minister may be the means of hindering his own work, and inducing the better part of his flock to listen to such enticing hints as these :—" You should be more perfect," &c.—" We have so and so."—" Come with us."

But circumstances must govern. In a confined and limited sphere, as in a small island, it would be well perhaps to form such societies as Mr Wesley's.*

* The following notice of Mr Wesley's Religious Societies is taken from Chalmers's *Biographical Dictionary* :—

" The first division of the society is a *class*. All those hearers who wish to be considered

In a parish, we must consider circumstances.

2. Consider the nature of man : the pride of his heart.

3. Consider, again, the want of talent for taking a part in such meetings. My society at Little Dunham, Norfolk, dropped away from this cause. This was in a country place.

4. Consider the heterogeneous materials of which such societies may be composed. It does not do to mix ranks, nor sexes.

In forming such societies, we should attend to these things :—

(1.) Should the minister attend or not ? If he does, things may go on well. This I have seen in societies of this kind at Hull.

(2.) Circumstances may render them highly useful. If God vouchsafe a great outpouring of the Spirit, and if new congregations are formed in consequence of them (as has been the case), then the blessing is seen.

(3.) The meetings should not be large, but have few in number.

(4.) Each should consist only of intimate friends, and those of equal rank.

(5.) The minister should be the director. The societies at Lynn, also Mr Walker's, might be taken as examples.

There are great advantages attending these religious societies ; but great judgment is required in conducting them.

The Rev. J. Goode—

I am a friend to religious societies.

When the soil is unfavourable, what does the husbandman do ? He would bestow more labour on it. So we, as spiritual husbandmen.

We are too apt to give way to difficulties perhaps. We could do more, if we attempted it.

The Rev. Josiah Pratt—

I. These religious societies are not expedient, if they cannot be kept up.

If we have to retrace our steps by giving up, consequences are worse than if they had not been undertaken. The London spirit is against them. Nor are they expedient, if they are not of sufficient number to embrace a large number of persons.

as members, must join a class. This is composed of such as profess to be seeking their salvation. About twelve form a class, at the head of which is the most experienced person, called a *class-leader*, whose business Mr Wesley thus defines : ' To see each person in his class once a week at least, in order to inquire how their souls prosper ; to advise, reprove, comfort, or exhort, as occasion may require ; to receive what they may be willing to give to the poor ; to meet the minister and the stewards of the society, to inform the minister of any that are sick, or disorderly, and will not be reproved, and to pay to the stewards what they have received of the several classes in the week preceding.' These classes, according to the present custom, meet together, once a week, usually in the place of worship, when each one tells his experience, as it is called, gives a penny a week towards the funds of the society, and the leader concludes the meeting with prayer. The next step is to gain admission into the *bands*, the business of which seems to be much the same with the other ; but there is more ample confession of secret sins here, and consequently admission into these *bands* implies the members having gone through a higher degree of probation. They have also *watch-nights* and *love-feasts*, which are merely meetings for prayer, exhortation, and singing, and are more general, as to admission, than the preceding. Against the classes and the bands, as far as confession of secret sins and temptations to sin are concerned, very serious objections have been urged, but they are too obvious to be specified. Wesley had always great difficulty in preventing this from being considered as equivalent to Popish confession."

II. The advantages are as follows :—

1. They form a line of distinction.

2. This, therefore, raises the question—" Why am I not a member of one ?"

3. They afford means of training up young Christians, as they are brought in contact with older ones.

4. They afford means, also, of preserving them from falling back.

5. They knit together in love those who are in earnest.

6. They encourage us to rely upon the promise, *If two of you shall agree on earth, as touching anything that they shall ask, it shall be done for them of my Father which is in heaven.*

III. On the disadvantages, Davies has spoken well.

IV. The rules I would propose are these :—

1. The societies must be under the control of the minister.

2. The minister should not meet his people in these societies as on an equal footing with them.

3. Care should be taken to have grave men in each ; not one only, but several.

4. Less good can be gained by these societies in conversation on each other's experience, than in studying the Holy Scriptures together.

5. There should be but one denomination of Christians in each society.

[He referred, in conclusion, to Mr Wesley's classes and bands ; to the St Mary's Societies, Birmingham ; to the Truro Society, and Mr Woodwards ; also to his own at St John's Chapel, Bedford Row.]

The Rev. Thomas Scott—

I agree with Brother Venn in this, that there is no absolute command in Scripture for the formation of such societies.

It must be left to circumstances. These are to form the grand criterion of determining whether it is expedient or not.

Man is capable of neglecting opportunities of doing good from indolence.

But if we are doing all we can in our sphere, and we judge such societies to be inexpedient on the whole, then we do right in not having them.

It seems to be inexpedient in London, from the general spirit of religious professors. At Olney, the societies turned out ill. The reason of this was, that they were not well conducted.

They *may* be the means of bringing out modest young men, who might afterward become useful ministers. But I should say they are rather calculated to act as a hot-bed. Let the sun bring them out rather than a hot-bed. They will otherwise grow up and become puny in their knowledge. A little bit and scrap of Christianity will be preached about the country—something about grace and Christ—but little which enters deeply into Christian truth and the Christian life.

Then there is this danger. These young men are more acceptable to those of our people who are not truly alive to God than we are. They tell them more pleasant things, a shorter way to peace. In fact, their knowledge and experience are both meagre and shallow.

These societies have a great tendency, as I know they have been conducted, to nurse such Christians.

I have a great objection to "experience meetings." They are a short sermon upon the little word "*I.*"

Then, as to expounding meetings. None would I have, but under the sanction of the minister.

I have nothing to say against the plan at Birmingham, of which Brother Pratt has spoken ; but I am much against *heterogeneous* meetings.

I should make these fundamental rules—

1. That the pastor should be *generalissimo.*

2. That the members of the society should be a select company.

3. That no one should take part in the meeting but those of some considerable standing.

The Rev. H. Foster—

In London, it appears to me to be ambiguous whether these societies are desirable or not.

In country places, I should not much think of forming them, unless it were to guard against the danger of some of my people being drawn away from me for want of them.

AUGUST 4, 1800.

WHAT IS THE BEST METHOD OF COMFORTING AFFLICTED CONSCIENCES ? —Proposed by the Rev. Josiah Pratt.

Mr Pratt—

I. This is an important question. The physician should cure, and not kill. So the minister.

II. Yet it is also a difficult one.

1. It is difficult to be *faithful.* Our people are too often like those who said of old *to the seers, See not, and to the prophets, Prophesy not unto us right things, speak unto us smooth things, prophesy deceit.* (Isa. xxx. 10, 11.) When interest comes in, and natural affection opposes, it is difficult to see clearly and be *faithful.*

2. It is also difficult to know how to act so as not to wound where God would not wound, and *vice versâ.*

III. It is frequently attempted in a mistaken manner.

See Jer. vi. 14, and viii. 11—*They have healed the hurt of the daughter of my people slightly, saying, Peace, peace, where there is no peace.* So also Ezek. xiii. 10, 16, 22—the "untempered mortar."

IV. The leading error is this. The unseasonable application of consolation to the *unbroken* in heart.

The Law must wound before the Gospel can cure.

Unwounded consciences have nothing to do with the blood of Christ or the promises of the Gospel.

We should carry home, then, the Law to every conscience.

V. A second error is this. Indiscreet application of consolation to those who are not wounded aright.

1. The grief of such does not arise from *sin*, but from outward trouble. We should endeavour to turn the torrent of worldly tears on *sin*.

2. Grief may arise in such, not from *sin*, but from a melancholy habit of body.

The doctor is here needed. But still our advice should be to employ the soul's sorrow, from whatever it springs, on *sin*.

3. Grief may arise from a *general* view of sin only.

The truly healed must have (1.) Illumination ; (2.) A seeking for consolation ; (3.) A high prizing of Jesus Christ; (4.) A parting with all for Christ ; (5.) A casting of themselves on Christ in all his characters.

The antidotes for an afflicted conscience are—

(1.) The infinitude of Divine mercy ; (2.) The invaluable blessing of Christ's blood ; (3.) The promises ; (4.) The freeness of Divine love ; (5.) The open invitations of the Gospel. (*See* Bolton.)

The Rev. Thomas Scott—

Visiting sick persons a little frightened, is very different from the general business of comforting afflicted consciences.

The most difficult case to deal with, is a sick person in such a state, with a family around at the time of the minister's visit.

Nothing stands in the way of our success more than to be thought cruel.

To lodge a prejudice in the minds of all around leads to evil.

It is however worse, perhaps, to flatter.

On one occasion I went on the idea of being faithful, but carried it too far, and did harm to survivors, and no good followed that I know.

There is no precept in Scripture for visiting every sick person. We should go in some instances as a *witness*, not so much as a *minister*.

It is good sometimes not to say anything to a man about his past life, except in asking a few questions which will make him *feel* his state.

If we find the man unhumbled, we should reason with him as a professor. In such cases, I often advert to my own case.* I quote Beveridge.† Then I talk of regeneration, and its necessity. I come to the point in prayer.

* See this related in Scott's " Force of Truth ; " or in the " Memoir of the Rev. Thomas Scott."

† No doubt pointing out the following well-known passage in his " Private Thoughts:" —" For my own part, I am resolved, by the grace of God, never to go about to confute that by wilful arguments, which I find so true by woful experience. If there be not a bitter root in my heart, whence proceeds so much bitter fruit in my life and conversation ? Alas ! I can neither set my hand nor heart about anything, but I still shew myself to be the sinful offspring of sinful parents, by being the sinful parent of a sinful offspring. Nay, I do not only betray the inbred venom of my heart, by poisoning my common actions, but even my most religious performances also, with sin. I cannot pray, but I sin ; nay, I cannot hear, or preach a sermon, but I sin ; I cannot give an alms, or receive the sacrament, but I sin ; nay, I cannot so much as confess my sins, but my very confessions are still aggravations of them. My repentance needs to be repented of, my tears want washing, and the very washing of my tears needs still to be washed over again with the blood of my Redeemer. Thus, not only the worst of my sins, but even the best of my duties, speak me a child of Adam ; insomuch that, whensoever I reflect upon my past actions, methinks I cannot but look upon my whole life, from the time of my conception to this very moment, to be but as one continued act of sin.

" And whence can such a continued stream of corruption flow, but from the corrupt

If the patient is in a burning fever, it is terrible work ! The man may want a cordial, though he really needs something to arouse him.

He will catch at a twig. He will watch and wait for a word from us. And if he can but catch *one*, he is lulled.

I know it seems hard not to speak soothingly; but no motive should influence us to hide the truth, or leave men in their delusion.

There may be reasons why we should not wound, yet reasons also why we should not give cordials.

The thought of a soul deceiving itself should swallow up every idea of dealing out cordials, where something else is required.

So much for *sick* persons, as a separate case.

There is a most important distinction between being frightened and being humbled.

I would lay no stress on any affliction of conscience which does not include—

(1.) Humiliation for sin ; (2.) Abhorrence of sin.

When these exist in any measure, I would pour in the balm of the Gospel.

The best way of doing this is to pour in more and more light. No man is discouraged because he knows too much of his disease, but too little of his remedy. Come with the Law in one hand and the Gospel in the other.

Be not afraid of looking at the disease. Know the depth of the disease, but point to the adequateness of the remedy. This will give steadiness. I would do this, except in nervous cases.

There are many *ifs* in the Bible : none, to be sure, as to our being in a meritorious condition. But—" If you desire so and so, then (we may say) depend on it He will cast none such out." Hold out all these encouraging declarations—IF *you seek, you shall find.* I have often told men, " Don't tell me you do seek. *If* you seek, you find. Go on, persevere, you shall obtain."

" Did you always feel as you do now ? " I ask.—" No."—" Who put you on it ? "

" I'll tell you—this is the Spirit of God. Don't quench him."

The discovery of difficulty in prayer is a thing which is repeatedly felt by afflicted consciences. But I say to them, " Why you felt not this before ?—who wrought it ? This implies life."

But I always hold out these things on the idea that the persons inquiring are what they *profess* themselves to be.

Remember the difference between an *incipient* and a *mature* state of grace, when you are endeavouring to comfort afflicted consciences.

cistern of my heart? And whence can that corrupt cistern of my heart be filled, but from the corrupt fountain of my nature ? Cease, therefore, O my soul, to gainsay the power of original sin within thee, and labour now to subdue it under thee. But why do I speak of my subduing this sin myself? Surely this would be both an argument of it, and an addition to it. ' It is to thee, O my God, who art both the searcher and cleanser of hearts, that I desire to make my moan ! It is to thee I cry out in the bitterness of my soul, *O wretched man that I am, who shall deliver me from the body of this death?* Who shall ? Oh ! Who can do it but thyself. Arise thou, therefore, O my God, and shew thyself as infinitely merciful in the pardoning, as thou are infinitely powerful in the purging away, of my sins ! ' "

The question very seldom concerns the will and power of Christ, but whether they come to Him aright. All crowded upon Christ: but one only touched him with the hand of faith.

I then aim at shewing what it is for a sinner, as a sinner, to come and put his trust in Christ.

The plan of some is to persuade such persons, that they *have been* with Christ. But this leaves them, as a man waking from a dream—all is past and an illusion.

We shall certainly be counteracting the very end at which we are aiming, if we comfort without appealing to *evidences*.

The man that was healed, took up his bed and walked.

The distinction between *promises* and *invitations* is important. Promises are invitations with reasons attached to them.

The Rev. W. Goode—

Where *terror* and *conviction* are mingled, there is some difficulty in distinguishing them.

The Rev. W. J. Abdy—

I have more to do in my parish in trying to awaken stupid consciences than to comfort afflicted ones.

It is a great business, if we find men under worldly sorrow, to divert that sorrow into a right channel.

Many will acknowledge sin, but not in reality. I ask such, "Do you feel, then, yourself to be a sinner to that degree, that you deserve condemnation?" They then frequently fly off, and to all intents and purposes say—"No."

My method generally is to probe very deep. This is because I have found such little success.

I have been discouraged in visiting sick persons. And, whether from the spread of infidelity or whatever cause, I am seldom *sent for* now.

I appeal sometimes to bystanders against the sick person, when he is difficult to move. But I would do it always with all possible tenderness. In general cases, the simple way is the best.

To pour in light, is the most solid way in the end. A certain process they must go through.

Some good persons have little comfort. In this case, I appeal to their change in character. Here cure is more wanted than comfort. When I fail, I add, "Well, if you cannot *feel* so and so, go on, and you will get comfort in heaven."

Few persons have less comfort in religion, of a sensible nature, than I have. But if God give me grace to overcome my corruptions, I am willing to wait for consolation till I get to heaven.

The Rev. B. Woodd—

I would not expect a person to *feel* that their sin is deserving of hell: but to *see and acknowledge* it.

Here Mr Scott interposed—

On that very ground I differ from the American Divines."

No subjects were discussed at the next two meetings—August 18, and September 1.

SEPTEMBER 15, 1800.

WHICH IS THE MOST PROFITABLE METHOD OF STUDYING THE SCRIPTURES IN PRIVATE, AND BRINGING THEM BEFORE THE FAMILY?—Proposed by the Rev. Josiah Pratt.

The Rev. R. Cecil—

It is easy to keep up the attention of a congregation, in comparison of that of my family.

I have found most attention by bringing the truth of Scripture into comparison with *facts* which pass before us. More stimulus is thus put into family expositions. I never found a fact lost ; the current news of the day always comes into aid—" How does the Bible account for *that* fact ? That man murdered his father : that happened in our house to-day—what says the Scripture of that ? "

If I have no fact to illustrate Scripture, I bring the Scripture to illustrate facts.

It is a hard thing to fix and quiet the family. The servants want to go and stew the walnuts. There's perhaps a fume between the mistress and servants. Catch the opportunity. Don't drive them at the time ; but do not let the matter slip by.

It is a great matter to keep regularity. If certain hours are not observed, you are sure to find all in a bustle.

Religious truth should be cautiously applied to a family.

The old dissenters wore their children to death. Jacob reasoned well about his cattle.

There should be something little, gentle, quiet. We should not scold ; all should be pleasant and sweet.

I would not have a uniform mode of proceeding. There is something bad in uniformity, if carried too far : but eccentricity is still worse. The human mind, however, revolts at uniformity. Sometimes I make remarks: at others, none.

Make it as *natural* as possible. And let the feeling be—" We are a religious family—how natural it is that we should thus meet together."

It should not be a superstitious thing; nor should it be looked on as indispensable. If it were ordered, as the Jews were commanded to bring a lamb, why, it must be absolute. But this is my *liberty*, not my *task*.

I don't mean the contrary, however. Servants and children should see—*I will speak of thy testimonies before kings*.

Whatever great man happens to be there, let them see I deem him nothing before the Bible.

The Rev. J. Clayton—

In private, I read through some commentary—as Horne, Orton, and Doddridge—morning and evening.

I have endeavoured, in doing this, to combine the devotional and ministerial.

In my family, I read Brown, Orton, and Doddridge, selecting the reflections.

Though I ought to expound, I don't seem to have the gift. I never exceed a quarter of an hour.

The Rev. B. Woodd—

I have before me, in the family, Baxter or Ostewald; but I don't confine myself to them. I dislike extempore, long comments. I would sooner hear a commentary read, unless the extempore exposition be something superior.

The Rev. W. Goode—

In private, I have found difficulties in deciding what is the best plan to adopt.

I read the Scriptures through, and endeavour to make my own remarks.

At other times I read them in the original, and at others with commentators. There is a constant danger of degenerating from the devotional into the critical.

In the family, I read Brown. Quesnell seems calculated to be helpful. I read the Old Testament in the morning, and the New at night. I read as much as makes a complete sense—about twenty minutes in all; ten reading, ten prayer.

The Rev. J. Venn—

What will affect permanently, must be the effect of study.

There is a flimsiness and superficiality in unprepared, unpremeditated expositions, which leave no impression. We may read Henry in private; but bring it before the family in our own way. The servants should bring their Bibles. Be plain and simple. Study the sense, and be as plain as possible in commenting upon it.

Take a short passage. If it is a passage likely to be misunderstood, give the sense in which they are likely to take it, and then say—this is not the sense, the following is the meaning, and the true interpretation will be more deeply impressed.

SEPTEMBER 29, 1800.

HOW SHALL WE DISTINGUISH BETWEEN THE WORKINGS OF NATURAL CONSCIENCE AND THE CHRISTIAN CONFLICT?—Proposed by the Rev. B. Woodd.

The Rev. B. Woodd—

Natural conscience is that intuitive judgment by which a man approves or condemns his own actions. See Rom. ii. 14, 15.

Whether it is derived from nature or tradition, yet such a feeling exists in all. See it even in Cain, Saul, and Judas.

A man may act according to his conscience, and yet be wrong. For example, Paul before his conversion.

Conscience, then, is a capacity of knowing our duty and of judging accordingly; but it must be informed, or we shall judge wrong.

The light of natural conscience is improved by Scripture. We see this by comparing Christian nations and heathens.

The renewed soul is convinced; repents; receives Christ as Saviour and Lord. Here is a new creature. Yet only in part. Sin is subdued, but not destroyed : hence the conflict.

Now natural conscience warns and remonstrates; but how different is this to the workings of grace.

(1.) They differ as to their efficacy. The natural conscience remonstrates, grace triumphs.

(2.) They differ as to information and the object of pursuit.

Natural conscience is satisfied with general views, and general acts.

Not so the renewed. Grace receives the Divine Law in its spirit. It is so far from being satisfied, that it seeks new convictions and a renewed conscience.

It is a criterion of true religion, that the man prays to be *searched*.

(3.) They differ as to the causes and objects of self-upbraiding and remonstrance.

Natural conscience upbraids for public, debasing sins. Grace remonstrates, not only for evil words and actions, but for heart-sins and defects.

(4.) They differ as to their refuge and relief.

Natural conscience is easily appeased. If public censure is removed, all is at rest. Grace is, however, slow to admit palliating considerations. It takes all shame. It is cautious of admitting excuses. While it is candid to others, it is severe to itself.

(5.) They differ as to their determined and persevering opposition to evil.

Natural conscience soon quits the field. Habit reconciles to evil. It knows nothing of determined and persevering opposition to sin.

Grace sets a man against himself, and urges him to persevere. It never justifies him to yield from difficulties.

1. Mistake not struggles of natural conscience for grace.

2. Wait upon God in the means of grace.

3. Every attainment and conquest ascribe to the grace of God, and be encouraged to look forward to the day of complete victory.

4. If spiritual conflict requires so much exertion, how awful the state of those who oppose even natural conscience !

The Rev. W. Goode—

In natural conscience, there is something required.

Man gains everything by *instruction*. There would be no natural conscience if a man were shut up from society.

The difference between nature and grace is this :—In the struggle between passion and reason, the sinner laments he cannot commit what he loves and is bound to what he dislikes. But in the struggle between grace and nature, the believer laments if he cannot do what he loves, and is bound to do what he dislikes.

The Rev. H. Foster—

As to the origin of natural conscience, I think with Goode.

In the beginning of a man's profession, one can scarcely distinguish between natural conscience and grace.　As he goes forward, things will probably grow clearer.

Natural conscience has more to do with the punishment than the criminality of sin.

A man that has grace, has likewise nature.　He feels the same things, but something *more*.

Where it's mere natural conscience, it will terminate in wickedness.

Where there is a real spiritual conflict, natural conscience acts in part, grace universally.

The Rev. J. Venn—

There is a distinction in natural conscience between its capability and its exercise.　Though we find natures differ, yet all have some idea of *something* being right and wrong.

As to what the difference is between the workings of natural conscience and grace, Can the question be answered ?　Should it be ?

It may be of use, that men should have alarm.

The Rev. T. Scott—

Natural conscience is a capacity of self-reflection.　We are born with this capacity, but depravity makes us use it perversely.

As to the difference between natural conscience and grace.　(1.) Natural conscience judges by some defective rule ; grace by Scripture. (2.) Humiliation marks grace, not nature.　(3.) Low attainments satisfy the one ; perfection only the other.　(4.) They are, in short, two natures.

The Rev. J. Goode—

Nature looks to nature, grace to God.　Sin is an enemy to us—are we to Sin ?

OCTOBER 13, 1800.

IS THERE ANY FOUNDATION IN SCRIPTURE FOR THE DISTINCTION BETWEEN COMMON AND SPECIAL GRACE, AND WHEREIN DOES IT CONSIST ? —Proposed by the Rev. B. Woodd.

The Rev. B. Woodd—

I. The following are the common benefits of the covenant of grace to *all* men.

1. No man is born under the covenant of works ; but under that of grace.

2. In consequence of redemption, man is not left in a hopeless state, but under probation.

3. Common grace is extended to all men, as to a grant of temporal mercies.

4. Common grace is given to all as to the restraining influence of grace.

5. Common grace is granted to every man in natural and moral ability to use means for his salvation.

6. Grace that cherishes every moral and spiritual exercise, in the lowest degree of it, is granted.

II. Special grace.

This is grace issuing in eternal salvation. I know not whether there is a special difference between common and special grace, or whether the one is only carried further than the other.

All the elect are under a covenant which secures their salvation.

Here is the difference—

1. All men are under a remedial dispensation by the covenant of grace ; but all the elect are under a dispensation of covenanted mercy by the covenant of redemption.

2. All men have mercies as to this world, but all the elect for another world.

3. All men have grace ; but in the wicked it is amissible, in the elect not.

4. All men are in a state of possible salvation, but all the elect are in perfect security.

The Rev. H. Foster—

I have been obliged to give up all *system*. My aim is to be borne out by the Bible in all I try to say.

These distinctions rather confuse me, than assist me. I begin, indeed, to be satisfied more than ever with being a sort of inconsistent man.

The Rev. J. Venn—

No system suits me. They who insist on having one, are either *dry*, *e. g.*, High Calvinists ; or they are reduced to a state in which they contradict themselves.

Free-will pushed to extremes, passes into Atheism.

This is one of the questions which have ever agitated the world, and ever will ; and I know not whether we shall fully know it in a future state.

The Rev. Josiah Pratt—

Common grace is all *special* as it respects the believer.

Common grace is all punishment to the impenitent. God works in órder.

Though He sees that the impenitent will abuse common grace to his greater destruction, yet He gives it, because He will prove his condemnation to be just.

But seeking after accurate views on such subjects, is becoming " dark with excess of light."

The Rev. J. Newton—

As the heavens are high above the earth, so great is his mercy towards them that fear him.

The fault is in the will, not in the ability.

OCTOBER 27, 1800.

ON WHAT GROUNDS MAY THE PRACTICE OF FAMILY PRAYER BE
ENFORCED ?—Proposed by the Rev. J. Venn.

Mr Venn—

There is no positive injunction in Scripture on this subject.   The
Christian dispensation is one of liberty.   It is *supposed* that Christians
would embrace every opportunity of honouring Christ.

The chief ground is that of expediency.

The Rev. J. Pratt—

The argument for family worship seems to rest rather on inference
than command.   It grows out of the very constitution of Christian
families.

Christian families are societies consecrated to God.   Hence their
duty to worship Him.   For things consecrated to God must be used
for Him to the utmost.

The Rev. Mr Simons, a visitor—

There are some things, like this, which are common, obvious,. self-
evident truths.

The Rev. J. Clayton—

Whatever can be fairly inferred from Scripture, may be considered
as a truth or duty.   For example, the baptism of infants ; women
coming to the Sacrament ; and so Family Worship.

Whence is the obligation to *closet* worship ?—from our *personal*
wants.   Whence to *family* worship ?—our *family* wants.

It is strongly implied in the commands given to Masters, in the
Epistles.

Then as it respects the *tendency*—everything may be said.   What
softens the little rancours and ill-tempers in a family ?—Family
Worship.   It is the grand palladium against the devil.   Let God be
worshipped, and worshipped fervently and spiritually.

Then if we look to the *effect*.

I know no family where worship has been conducted aright without
some blessing.

One I know, in which, during thirty years, many of the *servants*
were born of God through this means.

I feel it so strongly a duty by way of inference, that to me it is as
plain as if delivered from Sinai.

The Rev. H. Foster—

God has manifested His wisdom and goodness in not prescribing on
this subject.

Some have it not in their power to enjoy Family Worship.   And
they would have no peace, if it were expressly enjoined.

For myself, it is the pleasantest part of my life.   Here is no room
for pride to work, which mars all our public services.

Whitfield and Wesley would perhaps have told their preachers, how often they should preach, &c. But God has left all things at large, which must be left at large.

The advantages of Family Worship are without number.

The Rev. Thomas Scott—

If man truly loves God, can he do too much for Him ?

Relative duty—this is another and a good ground.

It is a talent given us for improvement. *Whatsoever ye do, do all to the glory of God.*

My happiest moments are during Family Worship.

I have more comfort at home than anywhere else.

I rest this duty on these three things—

1. A spiritual mind will delight in it. 2. Relative duty requires it. 3. It is a talent given us.

NOVEMBER 10, 1800.

WHAT IS THE PROPER TEST OF RELIGIOUS SINCERITY, BOTH TO OURSELVES AND OTHERS ?—Proposed by the Rev. J. Pratt.

The Rev. J. Pratt—

I. What is the test whereby we may judge of our own sincerity ?

The heart is deceitful above all things, and desperately wicked. This is less known to others than to one's self. *What man knoweth the things of a man, save the spirit of man which is in him ?*

There may be an affectation of religion with a disaffection of the thing. But though the artist may hide himself under the veil from others, yet he cannot from himself.

Ignorance and delusion make many conclude well of themselves, who are *in the gall of bitterness and the bond of iniquity.*

Plutarch says, " a man is the first and principal flatterer of himself."

But if he will take "the candle of the Lord," he will see little in himself to flatter him.

1. Anxiety about our own state, we may take as a test of sincerity. There is a moral use in anxiety. It implies diligence in self-examination, and humility.

2. Our aim in all our pursuits and desires is a good test.

3. Our willingness to discover and crucify the bosom sin is another.

The bosom sin may differ from our besetting sin. Our callings, states, companies, and times have their besetting sins. If a man judges of his sincerity by considering his besetting sins, he may be judging wrong.

What, then, is a bosom sin ? That which is easily committed, and with difficulty detected ; which engrosses the thoughts.

Now willingness to discover this bosom sin, is a great evidence of sincerity.

Keep your eye on your spirit : record its workings : say, *Search me, O God, and see if there be any wicked way in me.*

If a man indulge in those very things which are his temptation, he has no sincerity.

4.. A universal regard to God's commandments, is a test.

5. Cleaving to God in difficulties and darkness, is another. What Hooker calls "the certainty of adherence." *

6. A man's recovery from his falls, is a sixth test.

II. What is the test whereby others may judge of our sincerity?

1. A sincere man is not to despise the opinion of others. Job was in danger of this.

2. Yet he must be content to rest sometimes under unjust suspicions—as Job did.

It is rare that a sincere man does not live to see his sincerity acknowledged.

And as rare that an insincere man is not in the end unmasked.

3. The Church and the World have a right to expect a holy consistency. The guilt of unbelief in part rests on the head of inconsistent professors.

The Rev. Thomas Scott—

What is to shew our sincerity?

I. To ONE'S SELF.

1. Consciousness. *Our rejoicing is this, the testimony of our conscience, that in simplicity and godly sincerity, not with fleshly wisdom, but by the grace of God, we have had our conversation in the world, and more abundantly to you-ward.*

We must have a *right* rule before conscience can be a test.

I like what Pratt said of *anxiety*. If a man have a title-deed to an estate, he is anxious to see that it is clear and undoubted. So the Christian.

Our very *limping* in God's ways calls us to inquire into our sincerity; this is not, however, inconsistent with sincerity.

The wisdom of God is seen in this, that where love does not constrain, fear may restrain.

I like, too, what Pratt said of a universal regard to God's commands; but I would carry it into all God's revelation, as well as his commands.

But after all, gloomy hours come over us, and then we must look to—

* See his Sermon on Habak. i. 4, from which the following is an extract :—
" If the things which we believe be considered in themselves, it may truly be said that Faith is more certain than any science. That which we know either by sense, or by infallible demonstration, is not so certain as the principles, articles, and conclusions of Christian Faith. Concerning which we must note, that there is a Certainty of Evidence, and a Certainty of Adherence.   .   .   .   .   .   .
" The Certainty of Adherence is when the heart doth cleave and stick unto that which it doth believe. This certainty is greater in us than the other. The reason is this : the Faith of a Christian doth apprehend the words of the Law, the promises of God, not only as true, but also as good ; and therefore even then, when the evidence which he hath of the truth is so small that it grieveth him to feel his weakness in assenting thereto, yet is there in him such a sure adherence unto that which he doth but faintly and fearfully believe, that his spirit having once truly tasted the heavenly sweetness thereof, all the world is not able quite and clean to remove him from it ; but he striveth with himself to hope against all reason of believing, being settled with Job upon this unmoveable resolution, ' Though God kill me, I will not give over trusting in him.' For why? this lesson remaineth for ever imprinted in him, ' It is good for me to cleave unto God.'"

2. The witness of the Spirit with our spirit. *The Spirit witnesseth with our spirit, that we are the children of God.*

II. To OTHERS.

In this also I approve of all that Pratt has said.

It is also a good evidence of sincerity, if we desire others to sift our character.

1. The best evidence to others is found in consistency.

2. When a man is willing to own wrong when he has done it—this is a convincing evidence to others. It has amazing weight with people around.

The Rev. J. Davies—

This is an evidence whereby we may test our own sincerity—In what degree do we take pleasure in those exercises which are purely of a spiritual nature ?

In proportion as we feel sin, heart-sins are a burden. Evidences satisfactory to others are—(1.) humility, (2.) consistency.

The Rev. J. Newton—

I. The anxiety Pratt speaks of grows out of a want of a simple view of the Gospel.

I have as little sensible comfort as most people who would be thought sincere; but I know the Scripture is true, that Christ is able and willing, and that God has promised : and here I rest my soul.

II. Colonel Gardner's memoir furnishes some admirable tests by which to judge of sincerity.

St Paul thus speaks, *Ye are witnesses and God also.*

The world is borne down by an inward conviction, though they won't confess it, when they see a man consistent : and there are occasions when they will shew their preference for such persons.

The Rev. B. Woodd—

I. We must judge of our disposition by external effects.

For example, the test of *friendship* is the exertion a man will make for his friends. So the existence of parental regard is shewn by parental care.

So in judging of ourselves as to our disposition toward God, we must judge by fruits.

Noah's faith led him to build an ark to the saving of his house. The evidence of faith is its overcoming the world and being dissatisfied with self.

There is evidence of sincerity when a man perseveres in the face of discouragement.

A difficulty in ascertaining sincerity arises from insincerity being in everything.

We may judge of our sincerity from our general character. What do we aspire after ? When we look at particular dispositions and actions in others, what do we feel regarding them ?

We have an evidence of our sincerity when we mourn in secret over what the world applauds.

Another evidence is, if, when afflicted, we are willing to be so.

II. Zeal for the Gospel, consistency in our walk, are evidences of sincerity.

Baxter says, " What a man *wills*, that a man *is*."

The Rev. W. J. Abdy—

I am sometimes afraid that my anxiety itself may be false—merely mechanical. Why does it not produce more activity ?

The testimony of the Spirit of God is a difficult point to ascertain. Does it precede, or accompany, or follow evidences ?

There are times when no evidence can bring relief. We come to Scripture tests, and all fail, except that great one, *Him that cometh to me, I will in no wise cast out.* I then feel disposed to cry, " Lord, if I never yet believed, *now* give faith."

I wait a little while, and there is but little growth. I must have recourse to Jesus again.

But I must not be always laying the foundation. For then, where is the growth ? And yet if I am believing, there must be an increase.

It seems that, in general, God's dispensation respecting his children is, that they shall not have that evidence which some lay claim to.

The Rev. H. Foster—

I. The more sincere a man is, the more he'll find out sin.

I have been driven out of all hope in myself. All other ways are blocked up; I must come to Christ.

I am conscious of these two things—

1. Distress that such a mass of sin is found in me. 2. That I come to Jesus.

On these two points, God knows that I am sincere. I have been driven round and round for forty years, and at last am come to these two points.

But what fruits are there ?

Such infirmity, such a devil—that I am driven again to Christ.

When I preach, I talk of Scripture marks; but how little do I exhibit them myself !

I don't know, however, how to doubt about getting to heaven, when I think of the glorious object, Christ the Saviour of sinners.

II. If we are sincere, people will see a marked character in us, corresponding with this.

The Rev. R. Cecil—

I would add a third point to Foster's—I *am not* what *I was*. Limping I may be ; but yet I am *going on*. I am a soldier in Christ's, not in Diabolus' army.

Things are denominated from the *greater mass* to which they belong. Thus copper and gold are copper and gold, however small the quantity.

I once went with the current, like a dead fish : now I strive against the stream—here I find an evidence of sincerity.

November 24, 1800.

What was the Degree of Light Enjoyed under the Old Testament Dispensation ?—Proposed by the Rev. J. Venn.

Mr Venn—

Too much has been said on both sides.

God's usual way of communicating light is gradually.

Man, had *he* had the ordering of events, might have sent Christ
sooner into the world.

But there was a " fulness of time " for the great event.

In the meanwhile, notices gradually rise.

The antediluvian knowledge was uncertain.

After the deluge, there was darkness till Abraham.   From Abraham
to Moses, revelation was very general and dark.   The Mosaic dispensation was not much clearer on great gospel doctrines.   Even the future
state, as Warburton proves, was not among the sanctions of the
Mosaic dispensation.

At the same time, though gospel doctrines are not distinctly
revealed, as you proceed the light grows clearer, *e. g.*, in the prophets.
The Psalms seem to convey a clear revelation of a future state.
Habakkuk speaks of faith.

But all is obscure.   This was the dispensation of " beggarly elements."

When Christ came, the body of Jews (1.) believed in a future state,
and (2.) had a knowledge of the coming of Messiah, though confused.

The knowledge of Simeon, and other truly good men, was higher
than that of the generality of the Jews.   With those who meditated
continually on the prophecies, this was a natural consequence.   The
light, however, which they had was, nevertheless, a light which required
to be searched out.

The Jews were taught in types and shadows.   They who could
penetrate these types and shadows, would see gospel truths.

But in the gospel, everything is clearly pointed out : and the vast
difference between the light under the Old Testament and under the
New, is as great as the blaze of the meridian sun is brighter than the
twinkling of the midnight stars.

The Rev. H. Foster—

I think the Jews had much more light than Venn allows.   Every
gospel doctrine was known to spiritually-minded Jews, though darkly.
Even carnal people are now ignorant of what believing Jews then
knew.

The promise to Adam was the acorn of the gospel.   The Apostle
says, *The gospel was preached to us, as well as unto them.*   Again, *These
all died in faith, not having received the promises, but having seen them afar
off.*

The doctrine of the resurrection was one chosen for the prophetic
illustration of the restoration of the Jews.

Manna, the brazen serpent, &c. &c., form a whole system of shadows, which must have given the pious among them some insight into gospel truths.

Their inferiority appears more in their *morals* than in their doctrine.

The carnal ideas of Christ's disciples arose not so much from want of sufficient means, as from a carnal mind.

When they came to be illuminated, 'twas no new light, but light cast on the Old Testament Scriptures.

David, Solomon, &c., were figures of Christ. Spiritual men saw this: carnal men saw it not.

As a general view, I would say, every gospel doctrine was known to the spiritual among them, but not so clearly as to us.

The Rev. R. Cecil—

I have made up my mind by my low system. I don't think so much light is necessary to make a Christian. I have found very well-squared men quarrelsome.

I don't think it necessary to make everything out.

The Jews, I conceive, had a few spiritual people among them; but the mob of the Jews, like the mob of Christians, had no religion.

The Spirit of God gave the spiritual man sufficient to enable him to walk with God.

The spiritual Jew had—

1. Ground to walk on.

This we see in Jacob's ladder. They had not such a view of the Cross as we have, but yet *Abraham rejoiced to see my day, and was glad.*

There was light enough to lead men to follow God: see this in the histories of Noah, Moses, &c.

That Old Testament saints saw not beyond this world, I reprobate the sentiment; *they looked for a city which hath foundations, whose builder and maker is God.*

2. A spirit of holiness was put into his heart that he should choose this ground.

We see the actings of spiritual life in the book of Psalms. There can be no such actings without a foundation. David and others must have seen means of reconciliation and recovery.

We see no man now having a stronger hold on these great points than David had.

Christians may give more reasons than he for their hope, I have no doubt; but believers died in evangelical faith. I think that faith mentioned in the Hebrews meant rather a general reliance on God.

The Rev. J. Pratt spoke next, and commented on the views of Warburton in his *Divine Legation.*

The Rev. T. Scott—

Pratt's distinction is solid, in saying that the Mosaic dispensation was not an *enlargement,* as many learned men suppose, but a *contraction* of the Abrahamic covenant. St Paul argues this point in Gal. iii. I differ from Pratt in this: temporal promises did not respect *individuals.*

I think they only respected the *nation*. Warburton goes entirely on this mistake in his notions of an equal providence.

The Sinai covenant made no alteration in the Abrahamic covenant. Every believer under the Mosaic covenant was accepted as a partaker in Abraham's faith: all unbelievers, as to their state under the covenant of works. The Mosaic covenant altered not their state at all.

The Mosaic covenant was a hedge in the nation to keep them from idolatry, &c.

To the believing Jew, the shadows taught Christ. To the unbelieving Jew, they were the mere *opus operatum*.

It is plain that the Sinai covenant was not a covenant of works, for a covenant of works has nothing to do with sacrifices.

They had not so much light as we, but yet enough to lead them. They saw but a little way, therefore at the death of Christ the veil of the temple was rent because the way was now opened.

Knowledge was according to diligence then, as now.

The Apostles and Disciples knew not so much as Simeon.

It was the want of a right state of heart.

The Jews were as men before sun-rise.

Read 1 Peter i. 10–12.

I cannot but think that Messiah is clearly revealed in the Old Testament, in his person, offices, &c., independently of the argument for his divinity from the divine names.

I can't go all the lengths with the Hutchinsonians on this subject, yet something may be learned from them.

Why did not the carnal Jews understand the Scriptures ? For the same reasons as carnal Christians. They searched them not, were too proud ; and Warburton himself is an instance of this operation of pride.

The greatest of ancient believers knew not so much, doctrinely and explicitly, as the meanest believer under the gospel.

The man of a false system is like a dead corpse with perfect limbs.

The man of a true system is like a living man with limbs perfect.

The man of a true system generally, but who holds some doctrines imperfectly, is like a living man without a leg or arm. He finds the want of it.

All believers under the Old Testament went as far as, *If thou, Lord, shouldest mark iniquities, O Lord, who shall stand ? But there is forgiveness with thee, that thou mayest be feared.*

What redemption was, was not clearly understood.

To sum up all, they had every ground and reason to look for just such a system as the gospel to be revealed proved to be.

The Rev. J. Newton—

Mr Law swept away Warburton's cobweb at one brush.

Abel is said to have pleased God. The next news is, that he was killed by Cain. Now, if they knew of no future state, the plain inference by a common Jew would be, that it was the worst thing a man could do to please God.

When the soul is most deeply exercised, no words are more suitable than the Psalms.

The testimony of Jesus is the spirit of prophecy.

Many things which the prophets said were not understood by themselves; *e. g.*, no doubt Zechariah's of the potter's field.

The Rev. J. Clayton—

Regeneration was taught by circumcision : the Atonement by sacrifices.

DECEMBER 8, 1800.

WHAT ARE THE MAIN POINTS OF INSTRUCTION TO BE DERIVED FROM THE BOOK OF JOB ?—Proposed by the Rev. J. Venn.

Mr Venn—

As to the time of its composition. It was written between the times of Abraham and Moses. The length of Job's life is an argument for this : 210 years, or upwards. One of the speakers alluded to the shortening of man's life, which, probably, took place just before he wrote, and this soon after the. Flood.

If it be so old, it is the oldest book in the world.

It affords an illustration, too, of the Patriarchal religion ; and shews how far man degenerated ; for how different the state of religion, as shewn in this book, from Pagan corruptions.

A great object of the book is to answer the objection, that there is no good in serving God.

Job's objection is answered by this simple argument—Are you to judge what is right ?

His acknowledgment, *I abhor myself, and repent in dust and ashes ;* means, " I ought not to have murmured at any of thy dispensations."

The Rev. H. Foster—

When we consider Satan's power over Job, to do everything but kill him, he must have had prodigious power over the spirit of Job. Probably, then, many of Job's sayings are to be considered as uttered in a state of temptation, and not as the settled sentiments of his heart.

Job was scandalously used by his so-called friends. He was represented to be as proud as a Pharisee.

But does God say anything of or to him which justifies this ? On the contrary : while all self-righteousness is abomination to the Lord, no allusion to Job's being guilty of it occurs in the Almighty's address.

It is a comfortable truth which we learn, that our enemies are under control. If they bring an increase of trouble, He gives an increase of support. *Who shall separate us from the love of Christ ? shall tribulation, or distress, or persecution, &c.*

The Rev. R. Cecil—

No spirit is more prevalent in man than a Sadducean spirit. To those who combat present things with a mere idea, the life of faith is proportionably hard.

The book of Job is important as drawing the veil from the invisible world. Satan's agency is made prominent.

He is seen to be busy not only in revolutions and great affairs, but he condescends to the concerns of a *single man*.

That such a transaction should take place between God and Satan, is wonderful! It lifts up man into importance. As Pascal says, intellect is of more consequence than all material worlds.

If we have anything to do with souls, it is of infinite importance. For this book shews a controversy about a soul.

This brings the subject down to our ministry. If so much is said about one soul, then how puny all our efforts, which concern so many.

Ogden admirably touches another point—the design of Job's temptation was *to silence man*.

It shews God's mode of treating man. It is opposed to all modern rational ways.

A question may be started, how far the speeches of Job's friends are of authority? Answer—" They might be abstractedly true, but false as applied to Job's case."

They have authority, then, so far as they agree with other parts of divine revelation, but they do not rest on their own simple authority as the other parts do.

It shews an instance of deep malignity in Satan, that he should wish to harass such a character as Job.

The case of Job helps us to feel that no man's opinion is sufficient to move us off a ground we have considerately taken.

There is something so nice in our case, that it is not a man's pronouncing dogmatically that will determine it. I should be glad of an opinion. Well, here it is; weigh it. We should suspect ourselves, especially in what we are fond of, against that opinion.

Judge not from appearances. Job's friends thought themselves the wise ones, yet they were not.

Here is a check even for wise and good men. For there is a pride in man which thinks, that if *he* goes down, I *must* go up. "If all the world is blind, I shall be the one-eyed monarch of the blind."

The Rev. T. Scott—

The grand outlines of our holy religion are here.

Job and his friends agree on the main points of religion, while they jangle on other points.

This book proves that the Christian's blessings are not to be attained here.

No human creature bears every suffering equally, his Lord excepted.

Job is a striking *type of Christ*. Not least in his interceding for his friends.

We talk of his passionate expressions. But what can we say, then, of ourselves?

He seems to have been at last wrought up to a pitch where the powers of darkness were let loose: then everything was dark: "*horribilia* de Deo."

He nowhere asserted his innocence before God. But in asserting his innocence before man, under this dark view, he was provoked in some instances to irreverent and unadvised expressions.

He had the best of the argument all along.

His confession, I *abhor myself, &c.*, as Venn says, was not an acknowledgment of hypocrisy, but of his unadvised and irreverent speaking of God.

We are not to judge of the measure of grace by the measure of trial, as though Christian improvement was in proportion to the measure of trial.

Often is trial great as an *honour*, to illustrate the strength of the grace given.

It was the means, in Job's case, to exhibit an evidence to the Church of divine mercy. How many have gathered strength from his trials!

Job did not suspect this. Therefore there are many reasons connected with our suffering which, if we could see them, would make them to be no sufferings; but then they would not answer their end, for we *must* suffer in the dark, in order to illustrate the divine mercy.

We see how indebted we are to divine care, for the safety and blessings of our persons and families, from evil spirits.

Judge of man not as what he is under temptation, but *when he is himself.*

It is not enough for us to preach sound doctrines, but the conduct of Job's friends shews it is of the last importance how we *apply* them.

Another thing we learn is, carefully to watch our spirit in religious controversy.

Lastly, consider " *the end of the Lord.*" (Jas. chap. v., v. 11.) Give God credit for designing mercy in all his dealings.

The Rev. C. Simeon, a visitor—

This book is a poem. Part of it may be allegorical; as Satan's appearance before God. [Mr Cecil objected to this, as unhinging things.]

God made chastisement a subject of *promise*, and that it should be in measure.

Now we are apt to think God afflicts us *out of measure.* Could Job have seen God measuring out his trials, he would never have been betrayed into impatience. We should endeavour to feel all trial as the subject *of promise*, and *in measure.*

The Rev. Mr Simons, a visitor—

There seems no reason to call it an allegory. For God and Satan are always together. Satan is always attacking me: God, I hope, always defending me.

This book is a great store-house of all fine poetry. It was, no doubt, David's manual when in such troubles as described in Psalms xxxviii., civ., &c.

Dr Jackson proves that Job was a type of Christ.

The judgments Job's friends describe as coming on the wicked, are all aimed at him.

The Rev. J. Davies—

We may learn that the best of God's people are defective in that very grace in which they excelled.

So Abraham in faith, Moses in meekness, Peter in courage. Scripture notices these defects to shew us that there is no perfect man, but the man Christ Jesus.

The Rev. J. Newton—

As to allegory, the whole Scripture is allegorical in one sense.

There is not an idea there of the eternal world, but is represented to us under the image of sensible things.

We are not to suppose a *personal conference* between God and Satan.

The Scripture teaches us, that the whole sum of earthly good cannot make us happy. See this in Solomon and in Job.

They that go down to the sea in ships, see the works of the Lord, and his wonders in the deep. There are *land-men* and *sea-men* in the school of Christ. Some go down into the depths of trial and experience, and they know more of the power and grace of God than the land-men.

I have learned from this book the unprofitableness of controversy. If God had not interposed, and Job and his friends had lived to this day, they would have disputed till now.

Some have supposed from that passage, *I have heard of thee by the hearing of the ear, but now mine eye seeth thee,* that all Job's knowledge before was *head* knowledge. But he speaks comparatively ; and we all know what difference is made in our knowledge of God by our trials.

December 22, 1800.

Is there anything in Christian Experience which a mere Pretended Experience cannot Imitate without Detection ?—Proposed by the Rev. J. Newton.

Mr Newton—

The Egyptian Magicians could not imitate all the miracles of Moses.

St James says, " He who bridleth not *his tongue,* this man's *religion is vain.*" Very much is said in Scripture about the tongue. I have thought, therefore, that the true Christian has a way of speaking—1. of God ; 2. to God ; 3. of the brethren—which hypocrites cannot imitate.

God's dealings with man are strikingly illustrated in Ezekiel, chap. xvi., under the image of an outcast infant. Whoever has felt the mercy of God's recovery of him, will have his mouth shut from :—1. Complaining ; 2. Boasting ; 3. Censuring.

The Rev. J. Venn—

A man's real character is not to be ascertained by one thing.

Consistency is difficult, perhaps impossible, to be imitated.

Private duties may be performed, true humility be feigned, heavenly-mindedness imitated ; but not consistency.

The Rev. J. Goode—

Perseverance is a fair test.

H

The Rev. H. Foster—

I doubt whether such a thing can be.

Godliness is life in the soul. I may make the arm of a dead man move, but this is not life.

We may learn much of a man from his falls: by seeing how he feels after having done amiss.

God never meant us to have certain evidence concerning others.

For ourselves, we must try the matter over and over again.

I accept of Christ day after day, and there I am obliged to rest.

The Rev. R. Cecil—

Thirty years ago, I should have said there was: now, I should say there was none. I have been so often deceived.

As to any particular point of character that can be brought forward, that thing may be shewn to have been imitated, yea perhaps excelled, by one hypocrite, and another by another.

We should consider as to opportunity. We must live with a man to know all. We must make great allowance for constitutions. A sanguine would destroy a phlegmatic man.

I could name a man who, though good, is more unguarded in his tongue than many immoral people. Shall I condemn him? He breaks down here, and almost here only. He starts off, and one knows not where he goes. On the other hand, many are so mild and bland as to make one wonder how such a thing could be brought out without true grace.

Every man will have his criterion in passing his judgment on others. I consider how a man comes out of the furnace of affliction. Gold may be for a month in the furnace without losing a grain.

It must be a judgment of time. We must take into account a collection of things.

Cudworth says we may paint a rose, but not its scent.

The Rev. J. Pratt—

Man may cheat himself. All hope is gone, if we are to judge by perfect freedom from evil. Christian and Hopeful judged differently of Talkative at first. Let us see how a man acts after *falls*. David affords some light on this. Some men are known and read of all men.

The Rev. T. Scott—

I believe all my brethren here are *true*, yet they *may* all be hypocrites. I think it is not God's intention that we should certainly know the character of others.

There are rules in Scripture enough to ascertain how far we are to govern ourselves in our conduct towards others.

It has done mischief in the study of divinity, that this has been so much insisted on.

When a man falls into sin, we are apt to make allowance for him, if supposed to have been a Christian, if we are Calvinists. We argue against final perseverance, if we are Arminians. I should say we know not whether he ever had grace, or whether he was a man not recovered.

We are physicians judging from symptoms. We must do all we can to ascertain the truth, and then leave the rest to God.

If we give to a hypocrite as a Christian, though we be deceived, yet shall we be accepted, if we are diligent in investigating. You meant it to be to one of the *household of faith*. *It was well that it was in thy heart.*

We should lean to the favourable side, and be as the judge, an advocate for the prisoner. If we are too determined, we may strengthen the hypocrite in his hypocrisy, and wound in a way God has not wounded. We might have thought Judas a more unexceptionable man than Peter. Perhaps not one of the Apostles suspected who was meant when our Lord said, *I have chosen you twelve, and one of you is a devil.*

As to SELF—a man may cheat himself; he may be ignorant of conversion, and yet be subtle on every point. Scripture says more of self-deception than of the deception of others. The general cause why true men have less satisfaction on this point is, that they seek it from some other quarter. Scripture charges us to *make our calling and election sure.* If we are right, then *the Spirit of God witnesseth with our spirit that we are the children of God.* God would have us *judge ourselves, that we be not judged of the Lord.*

And for OTHERS, He would have us judge them no further than our duty with them is concerned. As some one says, when we get to heaven we shall wonder at three things :—

1. Some will be there whom we should not have expected. 2. Some not there whom we expected. 3. We shall wonder to find ourselves there.

The Rev. J. Davies—

There must always be some nice touches in a master-painting which distinguish it from a copy, however artfully done, though, perhaps, no man's eyes may be sufficiently accurate to discover the fraud.

The Rev. J. Clayton—

What are the faculties for discovering copies from originals in God's works in nature ?   Let us use them here.

I think *growth* may be a criterion.

It has been said, " The hypocrite grows only in one way—in his head." But the true man grows every way.

Christ has a *savour* in a true man.

Openness to conviction ; a coincidence between heart and words, and between words and actions ; uniformity ; humility ; affection. These give means of testing.

JANUARY 19, 1801.

WHAT KIND OF PREACHING IS BEST CALCULATED TO GUARD A PEOPLE AGAINST DECLENSION IN RELIGION ?—Proposed by the Rev. J. Pratt.

Mr Pratt—

As to the DUTY of preaching thus little need be said here.   It rests on the fundamental truth, that the means are ordained in order to the end.

There is not a whit of difference in the madness and enthusiasm of either extreme. We are equally wrong if we deal with men as beyond hope on the one hand, or as without doubt certain of salvation on the other.

Though I firmly believe that the man once in Christ is never out of Christ, yet *this* man is to be treated as a *reasonable* creature, even if I could put my finger upon him and be assured that he was in a state of salvation. He is to be kept firm, and recovered from declensions and falls. By just the same motives I should urge watchfulness upon him as if his salvation depended wholly on himself.

But, then, there is not a man on earth of whom I dare to affirm that he is certainly in a state of salvation. Scripture leaves us to judge only from appearances and effects. Wherever we see sin, we must call it sin, and treat it as sin, and the man as a sinner.

What conjectures and hopes we may form of a man, overtaken in sin, from our knowledge of his past state, is out of the question. We have no right to call him a child, even though dealt with as a child, while he is notoriously behaving as a prodigal. David for twelve months, and Peter for an hour or two, had the signatures of hell upon them.

We must do as the Scriptures do. And let any man find me a book in them which treats at all on the subject, which does not abound in strong, warm, pathetic, and awful reasonings and remonstrances and exhortations.

Then as to the DISCHARGE OF THIS DUTY.

Our difficulties lie not in speaking as the Scriptures speak :—yet this condemns very many ; but in saying what the Scriptures do, *in season* and *in measure.*

The application of Scripture is our main difficulty, and here is abundant room for diligence, prayer, dependence, wisdom, and everything rare.

Give a fair view of things, of what Christianity costs : the sacrifices and self-denial necessary. Tell the cheering, but the self-denying part also. Tell them of the Hill Difficulty, the Valley of Humiliation. But do this *in reason.* A harsh man is apt to dwell on this side, and a mild one to pass it over lightly.

The Rev. J. Clayton—

That preaching which is calculated to preserve in health the spiritual constitution, is the kind we should aim at in endeavouring to keep our people from declension.

As they began the divine life in the knowledge of the Father, the Son, and the Holy Spirit, so constantly bring this forward.

The doctrine of the Cross must be prominent, Christ is to be used every day. If he lives in us, he will take care to keep us to the end.

But as these are things which gradually impair, we must not rest in generals. Disease comes on by symptoms.

A ministry, then, which is specific, and comes down into particulars, is what is wanted. Retirement, real prayer, meditation, we must much insist on. If we live much in company, we soon begin to borrow motives from men. Retirement will be the detector of borrowed motives. The things which buoy up another in an impaired state, will be seen by us in their nullity.

The doctrine of Divine Influence is hardly dwelt on enough. When we read the Epistles, we particularly find it there. Christ, the great promise of the Old Testament, is the spirit of the New.

The Rev. J. Newton—

I generally aim at the four classes of the parable of the sower. The great thing is to preach CHRIST. I preach, also, the deceitfulness of the heart, the snares of the world.

Privilege is generally connected with comfortable doctrines, but I endeavour to state it as the believer's privilege to walk with God. A man who has walked well forty years, if he once relaxes and declines, God may see it needful to bring breach upon breach upon him.

We should insist upon prayer. Prayer is said to be the key of the morning, and the lock of the evening. Go out every day with this spirit—*Hold thou me up, and I shall be safe.*

Circumspection should be urged. Persons of ill-health should not go into *contagious* places : nor neat persons into *dirty* places. When the conscience is once struck, go *immediately* to the blood of sprinkling. Don't say I shall be better disposed soon. Some other difficulty will aggravate the case. *Haud ignara ac non incauta futuri*, may be the Christian's motto.

The Rev. B. Woodd—

Election and such doctrines are to be treated delicately.

There is a great analogy between the animal and spiritual economy. Yesterday's food supports us not to-day. It arises from the very nature of the system. So daily life, and renewal of it in Christ, must be given us.

We must impress upon our people the necessity—(1.) Of seeking happiness in God. (2.) Of applying daily to the Redeemer for grace. (3.) Of walking in the Spirit. (4.) Devotional employments must be insisted on. Many evangelical people overlook this. There is much of doctrine, experience, and practice ; but the devotional character is left out too much. (5.) We must stir up the active principle in man. (6.) Point out the avenues of danger. (7.) Occasionally enter into the detail of vices and virtues—*e. g.*, the influence and actings of covetousness, pride, &c. These kind of sermons seem to have laid hold on my hearers most.

I by no means speak against giving general views of the Gospel. The Gospel is the glory of our preaching. But the more we enter into details of life and Christian character, the more likely are we to arrest the conscience and heart. If I preach against any vice, I would shew its contrariety to the holy law of God, and the redemption which is in Christ ; and rouse the sinner to escape by Gospel motives.

The Rev. J. Goode—

Our own ministerial defects may be a cause of the declension of others. It is better not to tell them to the people; but to mourn over them in secret, and correct them. For people under declension will be able to buoy themselves up by this.

An excess of comfort has an ill effect, and an excess of alarm will not let the people thrive. A minister may be under temptation to encourage a false taste, which he should rather correct.

He should address himself to the grace, rather than to the reason and passions of his hearers.

1. That kind of preaching which presents Christ as *all in all*, is what we should follow. 2. That which honours the Divine Spirit. 3. That which has much to do with the heart and the working of the mind. 4. That which comprehends the whole of revelation, unites doctrine and precept, duty and privilege.

The Rev. W. J. Abdy—

The preaching of the Cross is the grand remedy for all the sins and sorrows of man—*He hath anointed me to preach the Gospel to the poor, he hath sent me to heal the broken-hearted, to preach deliverance to the captives, &c.*

Declensions take place under all descriptions of preaching. Men may have a way of turning off the most heart-searching preaching.

The general character of even good men is, that they are too much in the world. Is anything to be done to counteract this spirit? Perhaps we are too tenacious of some sentiments, which are good to a few, but evil to many.

Election and final perseverance are to be treated cautiously.

A minister should always have in view the false applications which may be made of our preaching, and so far as we can without sacrificing the truth, we should prevent these applications; *e. g.,* I once spoke of " guarding the Gospel." A friend resisted the expression. " Sir, the Gospel will guard itself ; " I meant the Gospel should be guarded by itself, and one truth connected and explained by another.

The Rev. H. Foster—

A man who thinks he can so preach, that there shall be no declensions among his people, does not understand his Bible. We cannot be wiser than Christ, or St Paul.

I much disapprove some things Brothers Woodd and Abdy said. It would starve me and the people. I approve what Pratt and J. Goode said.

A great means of preserving from declensions is the example of ministers. It is marvellous what strict scrutiny people make into our characters: they sift, tempt, invite a minister in order to make him a glutton, &c., and, if he is off his guard, find out he does not mean anything by his doctrine. But let him go before his people an example of humility, of deadness to the world, &c., and a great cause of stumbling will be prevented. If it be not thus, sad effects follow.

I marvel to hear friends say, that election and perseverance make not a prominent feature in the New Testament. There is, I know, a bad way of stating these truths ; but, then, they are real and important, and should be brought forward. I hold no man to be a godly man who does not virtually hold the doctrine of gratuitous election, ascribing all to free grace. And if these doctrines are scriptural and good *for me,* why must I be wiser than God ? They may be abused, but that is not my business.

The Rev. R. Cecil—

The question is how to keep a piece of meat, which has a tendency to putrefaction, from putrefying. None deny that some kinds of preaching have a greater tendency to preserve from declension than others.

As to preaching election and perseverance, it seems a bad attempt among some men. They neutralise everything by it. It's like mixing acid and alkali. The soundest thing I ever saw on this subject is our Seventeenth Article.

Keep up a lively sense of the whole truth upon the mind. " Guarding the Gospel " is an injudicious mode of stating the thing.

The statement should be sound in matter and manner. The matter, the whole counsel of God ; the manner, not studied and stiff.

It is not a very judicious mode of preaching which will let the thoughts run wild, and set the man ruminating about the stocks, and his wife about the pudding, the daughter's eyes upon the next cap, the young fellow looking at his boots.

A holy application of doctrine is what Foster meant. He took the idea from one who says, " Such a thing shews *holy.*" Holy preaching takes hold of the conscience.

Our preaching must not be general but particular. *It is not lawful for thee to have her to wife.* This was John the Baptist's style. We must *collar* men. *Thou art the man!* I mean you, sir ! We are not half enough convinced of the evil of *general* preaching.

On the other hand, we must take broad ground. There will be no need then of " guarding the Gospel."

The beef must have the salt of truth, and the saltpetre of life ; but it must be rubbed in by particular application ; and rubbed into every part by a comprehensive view ; and rubbed in by clean hands.

As to contagion. A minister must have general knowledge. Many professors won't go to the theatre, but will to oratorios. We can here detect the *spirit* of the thing. Bye-path Meadow catches such.

We ought continually to remember that 'tis nothing but the Spirit of God that can raise the spring higher. I agree with Clayton, that we have not sufficiently honoured the Spirit. We ought to enter the pulpit every day with this spirit—" I am going to work miracles ; and how ? Why, God, by his Word, will." Instead of which, I've often gone into the pulpit, saying, " This argument shall strike such, and this such," &c. But I have over and over again been bitterly taught that it is not of man.

The subject on the next occasion of meeting, viz., on February 2, 1801, was, How SHALL WE BEST IMPROVE THE APPROACHING FAST ?—and was proposed by the Rev. W. J. Abdy. No notes were taken, as only a general conversation ensued. The opening of the nineteenth century was dark and threatening ; war abroad, and distress among the poor at home, called for a national humiliation. About this time, too, the King (George the Third) was threatened with a return of his malady, which appears to have been endangered by his reasonable agitation at the attempt of Mr Pitt to urge upon His Majesty the admission of Roman Catholics into the British Parliament—so just were the King's apprehensions for the nation, should the door once be opened for the emissaries of the Pope ! He repelled the suggestion with indignation, and is said to have added, " I shall reckon any man my personal enemy who proposes any such measure." Happy had it been for England had succeeding Sovereigns been as firm !

FEBRUARY 16, 1801.

WHEREIN CONSISTS THE DIFFERENCE BETWEEN THAT KNOWLEDGE WHICH A NATURAL MAN MAY RECEIVE FROM THE GOSPEL, AND THAT WHICH A SPIRITUAL MAN RECEIVES ?—Proposed by the Rev. H. Foster.

Mr Foster—

It is a most difficult question. Perhaps the difficulty is of great use, as it brings true Christians to try themselves more ; and this brings growing evidences.

The difference lies in—

1. The clearness with which the mind perceives the things revealed. It is not in the knowledge, but in the spiritual perception of it, that the difference lies. Sanderson, in giving his lectures on optics, might communicate more scientific information to those about him than a countryman possesses, who yet would have by his sight more true enjoyment of the things described than they. There is an *inwardness* in the knowledge which the spiritual man has :—*When it pleased God to reveal his Son* in *me*—*Knowing* in yourselves *that ye have in heaven a better and an enduring substance.* This is a matter of experience, rather than one to be explained.

2. The relish and delight which the spiritual man has in the things revealed. The natural faculties have a relish ; so have the spiritual. *Oh taste and see that the Lord is good !* (Psalm xxxiv. 8.) *I sat down under his shadow with great delight, and his fruit was sweet to my taste.* (Cant. ii. 3.) A difficulty arises here ; for the stony-ground hearers had some delight. So again experience alone can point out the difference in this case. *Herod heard John gladly.*

3. Its extent as to divine truth. *Then shall I not be ashamed, when I have respect to all thy commandments.*

4. Bringing home the things of the gospel to themselves, and claiming an interest in them.

5. The humbling tendency of the gospel. The natural man is proud, and cannot bear this humbling tendency of the gospel of the grace of God. Isaiah was a spiritual man, as we see from his self-abasement.

6. Its transforming efficacy.

7. The steadiness of its influence.

8. Saving knowledge leads us to detect heart evils.

9. Saving knowledge is satisfying, yet never satisfies.

10. Saving knowledge leads us to admire God's glory in the gospel, rather than as a system by which we may escape hell.

The Rev. Mr Simons, a visitor—

Balaam was an illustrious Doctor of Divinity!
True men know the truth *as it is in Jesus*. How is this? Because there is a conformity to him. See Eph. iii., 17–19. Knowledge is a sceptre to the wise, but a rattle to a fool. The spiritual man admires the glory within the temple; the natural, the sublime and beautiful. The spiritual man enters *into detail*; the natural rests in *general* truth. There is no communion with a natural man; no unction. The natural man is a journeyman; the spiritual builds for himself: thus Noah and his assistants. The natural man would bring Christ into the mind; the spiritual into the heart. *Omnis sensus denotat affectus.*

The Rev. J. Davies—

They differ in their source. The natural man's knowledge is from his own understanding; the spiritual man's from the Divine Spirit.

The Rev. J. Clayton—

The difference is not in the *matter* of knowledge, but in the *manner*. The natural man, as to *matter*, may know all that the spiritual does. The natural man seems to have all his knowledge, but not in relation to Christ. Owen says all knowledge is like a ray cut off from the sun. Or it is like a stream cut off from the fountain.

The Rev. B. Woodd—

There is no difference as to the knowledge. Nay, sometimes the knowledge of the natural man exceeds that of the spiritual. That a man may have great knowledge without corresponding grace, appears from 1 Cor. xiii. 1, 2, and Heb. vi. 1–8. The effect of saving knowledge is to be looked for in its influence on the will and affections. For man is what his will is.

We should look for the effect of religion in man's faculties—in his understanding, will, affections, and all his powers. The natural man has much religion in his understanding, but not elsewhere.

There is a difference (1.) In interest; the spiritual man has an interest in the success of truth. (2.) In sympathy; this is felt by us in the Psalms, though written 3000 years ago.

The shades of influence are so various, that we must wait for the establishment of religion.

The specific difference is perseverance.

The Rev. W. Goode—

The difference lies in—

1. The sources. The natural man knows spiritual only as he knows other things.

2. The things known. The natural man knows nothing of sin, self, Christ, &c.

3. The manner. In the natural man, all is theory. In the spiritual, all is with reference to himself.

4. The object. In the spiritual man, the reference is to the glory of God.

5. The effect. One enlightens the mind. The other sanctifies the heart.

The Rev. S. Crowther—

Natural men may be employed about spiritual things ; but there is no savour. Spiritual men may be employed about natural things ; but there is not the same interest. When a man is able to apply the passages of Scripture to himself, there is some sign of spirituality.

The Rev. W. J. Abdy—

Blessed art thou, Simon Barjona, for flesh and blood hath not revealed it unto thee. With the outward revelation of the Word, an inward revelation of the Spirit is necessary. The difference we are considering lies in the operation in the time of trial and of sin.

The Rev. J. Goode—

There is an essential difference ; but it is difficult to distinguish. *I will give them a heart to know me.*

The Rev. R. Cecil—

How this knowledge will operate, has been largely spoken to. But then the question goes deeper. I think it may be more simplified.

There is (1) knowledge of the head ; (2) knowledge of the heart.

I have gained most light from Owen's work on the Spirit. I was rather confused in my mind, till I read that book, about men being enlightened for special purposes. It proves to my mind that natural men, for special purposes, sometimes know even more than spiritual men.

I don't think with Baxter, who makes the difference to consist in degree and permanence. There are two suns—one has light, warmth, &c. ; the other only light.

A musician who knows but hates his science, answers to the natural man's attainments in spiritual things. While another man who plays but little, and yet has a savour, may represent the spiritual man with less attainments of knowledge.

The natural man can never have that knowledge which is drawn in from experience. There is all the difference between a traveller, and the compiler of travels. The one is the produce of sagacity, &c.; the other has a *savoury thing*.

MARCH 2, 1801.

THE NATURE AND CRIMINALITY OF PRECIPITATION.—Proposed by the Rev. J. Clayton.

The Rev. J. Clayton—

I. The nature of Precipitation.

There is a difference between hasty conduct and irresolute conduct. And this may be applied to things of time and of eternity : to God, our neighbour, and ourselves.

II. The criminality of Precipitation.

There is much : and great evils are brought on persons, families, and nations by it ; *e. g.*, Rehoboam's counsels.

The Rev. S. Crowther—

Criminality is often incurred rather in judging than in acting ; *e. g.*, Jacob—*All these things are against me.*

The Rev. J. Venn—

Precipitation consists in forming a determination without the use of reason. God gave us reason to counteract the passions.

Passion first leads us in most of our undertakings. In precipitation, we abandon this guide. This is a great evil. Most of the miseries of mankind flow from it.

In judging of character, in embracing doctrines, rashness should be guarded against. All enthusiasts are rash.

In judging of providences, too. See the *Life of Lady Huntingdon.*

The Rev. R. Cecil—

Precipitation is shewn in acting without sufficient ground of action. There is much in constitution. A cool man cannot well conceive the springs in warmer minds. We don't allow enough for constitution on either side. Youth is particularly the season of precipitation. His motto is " Onward."

There is no such case as when experience teaches, where we are made to feel in mind and body. God only can bring a man acquainted with himself.

There is a self-blindness in precipitation. A precipitate man is, at that time, a blind man. Thus St Peter : *This shall not happen to thee.* Also David : *The man that hath done this shall surely die.*

A precipitate man is continually tempted to take God's work out of His hand. It is not a state of *creature-ship.*

Man is not a creature that can afford to exercise precipitation.

Want of patience with respect to God, want of faith, is shewn by the precipitate man. *I shall one day perish by the hand of Saul.*

Pride is seen in precipitation. In rash moments, pride and precipitation have led us to do an injury to our neighbour that we never can repair.

Want of charity is also manifest in it. Man would feel the injury and cruelty of his own precipitation if against himself. There are few that have not felt how they have smarted themselves through life by their precipitation. *He that trusteth his own heart is a fool.*

Precipitation is frequently the means of man's committing himself for life. It would be good if we could say in precipitate moments, "Now, at this time you cannot do this."

The weakness of human nature is seen most in a wise man when he indulges this precipitate spirit. Everybody sees it in a fool. It renders a man unteachable.

Sanguine men are in continual temptation to be precipitate, and therefore it is their bounden duty to guard against it.

MARCH 16, 1801.

WHAT IS THE SCRIPTURAL NATURE OF THE ASSURANCE OF HOPE?— Proposed by the Rev. B. Woodd.

The Rev. S. Crowther—

A fire will burn variously, according to the materials it acts upon. A stream will flow variously, according to the depths and shallows.

The assurance of hope has a cleansing efficacy : *He that hath this hope in him purifieth himself even as he is pure.*

The Rev. H. Foster —

Constitution has much to do with this question. It enters every day into a godly man's experience. He deals with God about the salvation of his soul. He begins with a self-righteous spirit. The process goes on from time to time, till he is stripped of all self-dependence ; and, from looking at self, he learns to look to Christ entirely, and an assurance springs up.

The Rev. J. Davies—

There is a difference between the assurance of hope, and absolute assurance. Assurance of hope is a moral certainty. Absolute assurance is an absolute certainty.

The Rev. J. Clayton—

Scripture speaks of—

(1.) Assurance of the *Understanding*. (2.) Assurance of *Faith*. (3.) Assurance of *Hope*.

In these respects we see a difference even in our brethren in the degree of their hope. So in such men as Baxter and Owen, what a difference is manifest on this point.

The assurance of this hope flows from—(1.) The purpose of God ; that is my ground. (2.) The purchase of Christ ; that is my title. (3.) The power of the Spirit ; that is my power.

It is connected with all concomitant graces ; and is obtained in the diligent exercise of means.

The Rev. J. Newton—

What is *now* thought *so uncommon,* in early days was spoken of as *the common portion of Christians.*

MARCH 30, 1801.

WHAT SHOULD BE THE CONDUCT OF A MINISTER TOWARDS PERSONS WHO APPEAR TO BE FALLING AWAY FROM THE SPIRIT OF THE GOSPEL?— Proposed by the Rev. R. Cecil.

Mr Cecil—

Some who seemed to be awakened and to run well, and to be approved, go to another part of the town, and hear other things, and forsake their former guide, and fall away.   Now the question is, whether these should be dropped, because they are willing to drop me? They want a lift.   Now, should they not have this lift?   I recommend plain-dealing and simplicity.

The Rev. T. Scott—

It is true that London has peculiar difficulties.   But ministers have carved out this evil for themselves.   I could write a letter best in such a case; and should in that way be likely to do most good.

The Rev. J. Clayton—

There is a caste among religious professors who are against this subject. The Methodists have struck at the root of the pastoral office.

There are peculiar difficulties in London, as has been said, and even among us.   The Methodist caste has stolen on the mind of our people.

Neglecting the distinction between the true and the false, tends to annihilate the visible Church of Christ on earth.

As to *members,* we [of the Independents] have a regular discipline. As to *hearers,* though I am the minister, I can't be the acquaintance of the whole congregation.

The state of the heart is, indeed, as has been said, of vast importance ; and a minister should be as anxious, and as much in business for souls, as a man is for his gain.

The Rev. J. Newton—

In the country, it is easy to lift up the leather latch, and walk in and converse.   In town, one has to wipe one's shoes, send up one's name, and speak as if afraid to be understood.

The Rev. S. Crowther—

The difficulty arises much from a spirit of insubordination.   We are to watch for souls ; to seize the *mollia tempora fandi.*

There is much in the situation of a minister himself—his age, the length of time he has been in his present post.

We are not to wait for opportunities, but to watch for them.

The Rev. W. J. Abdy—

After all apology, none of us have done all we should or might have done.

The Rev. J. Venn—

This condemns me. How much more in earnest should we be. What strong expressions the Apostle uses—*Of whom I travail in birth again, until Christ be formed in you—now we live if ye stand fast—we were gentle among you, even as a nurse cherisheth her children—watching as those that must give account.*

I would not consider what a minister is merely bound to do, but what he may do. Fletcher of Madeley sets us an eminent example of zeal, boldness, and tenderness in this matter.

A capability for meeting such cases implies great zeal and affection. Where this affection is, it will dictate a manner. A minister should consider himself as a father of his flock.

It is esteemed friendly to warn of bodily health. How much more should we minister to spiritual health. Two reasons, for the endeavour being made, are—(1.) to satisfy conscience; (2.) to do good to the party concerned.

The office of a minister as a shepherd is beautifully described in Ezekiel.

Our kind endeavours may fix a *dart*, though they may seem only to excite resentment. A shower of affliction may come and water this seed.

Much must depend on a minister's ability to speak. At all events, we may *pray* for such. They may get good and know not from what quarter the intercession that prevailed came.

The Rev. H. Foster—

Pray for the *principle* of zeal and love. As to the *exercise* of this, we must depend upon circumstances.

APRIL 13, 1801.

UPON WHAT GROUNDS DO WE INVITE UNCONVERTED SINNERS TO BELIEVE IN THE LORD JESUS CHRIST?—Proposed by the Rev. J. Newton.

The Rev. T. Scott—

God's designs are beyond man. The sailor uses his plumb-line only near shore, not at sea. A great part of heavenly wisdom is to learn when we are out of our depth. There are many writers whose arguments I cannot answer: as a philosopher, perhaps, I should think with them, but as a divine, I have nothing to do with them; *for* God has said thus and thus.

Strong things may be said against man's speculations; but not against God's declarations. Had men confined themselves to God's declarations, the chief occasion of exception against predestination and such doctrines would be cut off.

With reference to the question in hand—

1. There is the Lord's express command—*Go ye into all the world, and preach the gospel to every creature.*

2. It is the means by which God works. It was on this ground that Whitfield went, and was so successful. The Apostle gives express direction to Timothy (2 Tim. ii. 24–26) to meet the *unawakened.*

3. It is adapted to have effect upon men.

The Rev. Mr Simons, a visitor—

Christ invites all—*Ye will not come unto me that ye might have life.*

The Rev. J. Davies—

Success shews that we ought to invite all ; so does the example of the Apostles—*Repent ye therefore and be converted, &c.* So Peter to Simon Magus—*Repent therefore of this thy wickedness, &c.* So also the prophet addresses his people—*whether they will hear or whether they will forbear.*

The Rev. B. Woodd—

The following are arguments for invitation :—

(1.) The general statement of Scripture respecting the purpose of the death of Christ (John iii. 16 ; 1 John xxii.) (2.) God's command (Acts xvii. 30). (3.) The will of God, as expressed in Scripture (1 Tim. ii. 4). (4.) God's invitation (Isa. lv. 7, 8 ; John vi. 37). (5.) The divine expostulation (2 Cor. v. 19). (6.) The divine commission (Mark xvi. 15 ; Col. i. 28). (7.) Christ's example — *Repent, for the kingdom of heaven is at hand* (Matt. vi. 17). *Except ye repent, ye shall all likewise perish.* (8.) The divine influence and operations. (9.) The procedure of God in judgment (Prov. i. 24, &c. ; 2 Thess. i. 8, 9). (10.) Analogy of God's dispensations.

The difficulty vanishes by distinguishing between the governing and decretive will of God.

There are instances in Scripture in which the governing and decretive appear to be contradictory to each other ; but they are not ; *e. g.,* Abraham sacrificing Isaac. So the salvation of individuals will appear thus in the end.

(1.) All who *will* come *may* come. (2.) All who come not, do not through pride. (3.) The elect *will come.*

The Rev. W. Goode—

Christ did not give himself for the world in the sense which he did for the elect : *God is the Saviour of all men, especially of those that believe* (1 Tim. iv. 10). He died for the *sheep. The good Shepherd giveth his life* for the sheep (John x. 11). Christ gave himself *for the church* (Eph. v. 25).

But the question does not depend on this. What warrant has a sinner to believe ? This will depend—(1.) On the nature of faith. (2.) On the warrant which the Scripture gives to a sinner to believe. The strongest passage is, *Him that cometh unto me I will in no wise cast out.*

The arguments for inviting all are :—(1.) This is God's means of bringing to himself even the elect. (2.) We know not who are the elect. (3.) It is the duty of men to believe. (4.) We are commanded to invite. (5.) We have the example of John the Baptist, of Christ, and of the Apostles. (6.) The effect of this practice.

The Rev. H. Jowett, a visitor—

Guard against specious difficulties and objections. Some have even restrained prayer by such arguments. It is unnecessary, say they, to inform God of our wants. And thus they forget that God has commanded, *Ask, and ye shall receive*, &c.

So as to this subject. God declares his will ; and we are simply to follow it. If we could know who were to be finally rejected, a serious question might arise, how we should treat such ; but of this we are left in ignorance ; and therefore have to invite all alike. What would have been the state of the world, when the Gospel was first preached, if this had been the case? No. This is the Apostle's method to all — *We beseech you, in Christ's stead, be ye reconciled to God* — *The Spirit and the bride say, Come!*

The Rev. H. Foster—

Fuller's *Gospel Worthy of All Acceptation*, is a work of great use. Hussey was the first who started this question. The Old Calvinists never thought of it.

The Rev. J. Venn—

The Methodists sometimes carry invitation to excess.

You must define what you mean by faith. If to believe the truth of the Gospel is enough, then all may be saved. If it be to believe savingly, then the range is more limited.

APRIL 27, 1801.

THE NATURE OF THAT FAITH MENTIONED IN THE ELEVENTH CHAPTER OF THE EPISTLE TO THE HEBREWS.—Proposed by the Rev. J. Goode.

The Rev. J. Clayton—

I would ask whether there are not two kinds of faith here mentioned ?

1. A faith with which is connected eternal salvation.
2. A faith of *privilege* as descendants of Abraham.

There seem to be some crooked characters, of whom greater things are spoken than their characters would seem to lead us to expect.

The Rev. J. Davies—

In some parts of this chapter, faith seems to mean nothing more than credit given to the testimony of God.

It varies in different parts of the chapter.

The Rev. J. Newton—

Faith is credit given to the testimony of God with the heart.

The Apostle groups Abel and the truly spiritual with Samson and others of his class. He knew more of them than we can, and therefore we should hope, notwithstanding their eccentricities, that they were yet pardoned.

The Rev. T. Scott—

The connexion with the tenth chapter seems to indicate clearly that it is the faith which is connected with salvation : the same faith which *we* exercise, *mutatis mutandis*.   Many things in Scripture are explicitly revealed, many *implicitly*.

David did not see things so fully as Paul.   It is the *nature* of faith, not the *quantity*, which determines the character.   There are some who know not the tenth part of what is contained in Scripture, and yet are more truly believers than most others.   The faith in this chapter, then, is the faith which these worthies exercised, according to what was revealed to them.   All believed the great truth of Christ to come.   The Apostle chiefly aims to shew the difference between *dead* and *living* faith.

True faith is a principle which sets in motion.   Samson was a riddle to me, till I unriddled myself—he was an inconsistent believer.   As to Rahab, I look upon her as a *first-rate* believer.

The Rev. W. Goode—

There is an admirable definition of faith in verse thirteen :—*These all died in faith, not having received the promises, but having seen them afar off, and were persuaded of them, and embraced them, and confessed that they were strangers and pilgrims on the earth.*

The Rev. S. Crowther—

The Apostle in this chapter gives a *twofold* view—(1.) That all men are saved by faith.   (2.) That this faith is an active principle.

The Rev. W. J. Abdy—

This faith is not simply a credit given to God.   Ahab and the Ninevites did this, and yet they come not under this chapter.

The Rev. J. Venn—

What is the precise point the Apostle had in view ?   The Hebrews were under severe persecution.   The Apostle is now animating them to cleave to the Gospel.   In this he takes occasion to tell them how they are to stand.   They are to stand by faith.

He first defines faith, and then shews from the Old Testament History that all great acts sprang from faith.   It is not the Apostle's object to shew who believes with a saving faith, and who not ; but that all great acts spring from faith.   If you won't extend the idea of saving faith to *all*, why imagine it is meant to apply to *any* in the list ?

The Rev. R. Cecil—

How does it appear improbable that a powerful act of faith, and that in a public person, might not be brought forward for encouragement without any reference to the safe state of the character ?

I am not of Trail's opinion, who gets over the difficulty of Samson's character, by saying he is found in this chapter.   The Apostle says, a man may have a faith that may remove mountains, and yet not have love. I don't deny Samson was in a safe state, yet I don't see it proved here.

The Apostle speaks of saving faith in the tenth chapter, but in the eleventh he seems to go off to the *abstract view* of faith. He is speaking of the activity of the principle. This power is connected with a reliance on God.

MAY 11, 1801.

WHAT IS THE NATURE OF THE STRIVING OF THE HOLY SPIRIT WITH UNCONVERTED PERSONS ?—Proposed by the Rev. B. Woodd.

The Rev. T. Scott—

Many, and some judicious, divines think there is no such striving. They put another sense on the passages usually brought forward. But I am not satisfied with their interpretations.

The striving of the Spirit with unconverted persons is different from his communications to the converted. It is different, too, from miraculous gifts. The ordinary gifts of ministers are different from converting grace, and from the strivings of the Spirit.

Ministers are bound seriously to sift this matter : for the exercise of gifts without grace tends to stupify. We may learn somewhat of this striving from Satan's seductions of evil men. Where he finds evil, he works on that evil. He does not plant new principles.

The Holy Spirit, in converted persons, gives new principles. But in unconverted persons, Satan works on old principles; *i. e.*, natural principles, the remaining part of what God made man.

We must bring in the *decrees* here. No reason can be given by us why the Spirit leaves one and goes on with another.

Sometimes the Spirit sets home an appeal to the unconverted, although without saving effect : for example, in the case of Herod, Agrippa, and Felix. It does not work a saving change, but such a strong feeling is excited that they are seriously affected : fears and hopes interchange. This working on *natural* principles is often the step taken by the Spirit to conversion in real converts, as well as *all* he does in unconverted.

Men sometimes feel that Christians are happier, and yet do not embrace the truth. Sometimes, when they hear a sermon on the love of Christ, they are bathed in tears; but only as they would in hearing of any great character on the stage.

In these, and a hundred other things which might be mentioned, the Spirit sets home with strivings on the unconverted, by working upon the natural principles and affections remaining of what God made us. This resembles Satan's method of working on natural principles and affections. For nearly fourteen years I had convictions of this kind, which I cannot but think were supernatural.

The Rev. S. Crowther—

That the Spirit does strive with unconverted persons is evident from

Scripture and experience, and he uses both external means, and internal, such as the conscience.

The mouths of the ungodly will be stopped at the last day. Our inability is no excuse, when the almighty power of God is considered, and also the invitations given them to ask and seek it.

The Rev. H. Foster—

God contends with men, as the American divines say, not only by raising up prophets, &c., but by *an energy accompanying the Word.*

God seems to work out the character of man as a sinner in the case of the man who finally resists and rejects this energy. This is what the evil spirits are not capable of. I don't like to say the Spirit would convert you and you refuse, but you resist and refuse his influence.

The Rev. R. Cecil—

There are reasons for this, though we see them not. The Spirit. of God is represented as having a wider sphere of influence than merely in conversion. He is a Suggestor, an Elevator : the Instructor even in arts, *e. g.*, Aholiab and Bezaleel : see Ex. xxxi. 3. He will be a Judge at the last day.

The working of the Holy Spirit in unconverted persons is like the influence of the sun and rain on bad ground.

———

MAY 25, 1801.

WHAT IS IT TO GLORY IN TRIBULATION ?—Proposed by the Rev. R. Cecil.

Mr Cecil—

Vanity will help a man even on his death-bed : while the good people think it all genuine.

Watch over the *motive* in bearing tribulation. Yet be not careless to neglect a duty because of the infirmity which may cleave to it. It is of great use to consider what our character requires. Take Nehemiah's spirit :—*Should such a man as I flee ?*

Trouble is a trial, a battle. Now skill in a battle often gains it. [This was illustrated by an account of a French general turning with address the defection of a part of his troops to his own advantage. Also Ezra refusing the king's guards.]

We must take care in glorying in tribulation, that man glories in nothing in *self.* *Let him that glorieth glory in the Lord.*

The Rev. W. Goode—

Reasons why we should not glory in tribulation :—1. Fear of not being in a right state. 2. It may be looking at things temporal and not eternal.

The Rev. T. Scott—

The thought of dishonouring God before my children has done more to restrain me from acts of desperation than any other consideration.

We are not called to tell our family and those around us all the trials that pass within—nor our people.

Glorying *in the Lord* bears a greater proportion in the Scriptures than in our experience or preaching.

There is no one thing that more recommends religion than cheerfulness, in a consistent character.

The Rev. J. Davies—

Is there any among you afflicted, let him PRAY. This is rather different from an outward expression of glorying.

The Apostle, in Romans, v. 3, &c., gives a reason for his inward glorying, as working patience, &c. Tribulation should be considered as a chastisement.

The Rev. J. Goode—

Glorying in tribulation is a fruit of justifying faith. In St Paul, tribulation wrought patience; the love of God was shed abroad in his heart ; and he rejoiced in the hope of the glory of God. Glorying is justifying God, approving his conduct, giving up ourselves to him.

The Rev. S. Crowther—

Christians, particularly ministers, draw the eye of the world on them in affliction. There is a medium. They should not over-act their part, nor conceal their feelings. They should not be anxious to recommend themselves in this way to those about them, and so be a show. We may embrace such circumstances, but not anxiously seek them.

The Rev. J. Pratt—

There is—1. A negative glorying. By *silence.*
This is directly opposed—(1.) To sinking under tribulation. *Where is now thy God?* (2.) To murmuring, fretting, and repining. Now the thing comes to the test. (3.) To impatience for the severity or length of trial.

2. A positive glorying. Since tribulation is the subject of promise, glorying in it may signify—(1.) Glorying in it as the means of ripening for heaven. (Rom. v. 3, &c.) (2.) Rejoicing in it as an evidence (Rom. v. 5) that God cares for his children. Tribulation proves the relationship. (See Matt. v. 10, 11, 12).

3. Rejoicing in the comfort accorded to us in tribulation. (See 2 Cor. vii.) So Paul and Silas singing psalms in prison.

The Rev. H. Foster—

A man should be cheerful, it is true ; but there's another side. If a man does not tell his trials and weaknesses, it will distress God's people.

I have perhaps prayed God to raise up ministers. But when I have heard of talents or success, I have felt such envy, that though a saint on my knees, yet I have been more like a devil elsewhere.

June 8, 1801.

WHAT DOES THE SCRIPTURE TEACH US CONCERNING THE DUTY OF INTERCESSION ?—Proposed by the Rev. W. J. Abdy.

The Rev. J. Pratt—

It rests on Scripture precepts and example. We must not merely follow our natural feelings, but cultivate the *practice* of intercession.

What can be done at any time, will be done at no time. Once a week, I would make a practice of it. Dealing in generals is not interceding. Peculiar cases should be brought forward.

The Missionary Societies afford means of stirring up intercession.

The Rev. J. Venn—

Intercession strengthens the bond of natural affection. It sanctifies this affection.

My father used to retire at noon with such of the family as were at leisure. He prayed for absent members and afflicted friends.

The benefit of intercession goes further than we suspect.

As benefits are conferred on men through a Mediator, so God, by the prevalence of our intercession for each other, would perpetually remind men of this.

Berridge said that he supposed that not one prayer made in faith ever fell to the ground.

None know what evil is prevented. None know what prayers are answered.

The Rev. T. Scott—

Intercession is a means of keeping down natural selfishness.

It has an enlarging tendency, bringing the heart into a right frame, a forgiving frame, &c.

If we ministers prayed more for one another, we should feel less envy, and not care to what journeyman in the shop the customer goes, so that he go to their shop.

The Rev. J. Davies—

We see the benefit of intercession in the case of Peter in prison.

The Syro-Phœnician woman was answered *at last.* So that prayer which seems not answered, yet will be so in time.

The Rev. J. Clayton—

I have felt an inward condemnation, while my brethren have been speaking.

The extent of this duty of intercession is as wide as God's government.

There are promises. If we are not pleading these, we are not opening the sluices of divine favour.

As objects approach us, the duty strengthens.

Promises, commands, experiences, examples—all urge it.

Intercession particularly cherishes benevolence and charity.

He that prays for his family, does not go down and find fault with his wife, and scold his children.

So for his people, if he be a minister. We can tell on Saturday night what sort of state we shall be in on Sunday. Is there more tenderness ?

As to enemies, we may pray for them to get rid of bad feelings.

The Rev. J. Newton—

The use of prayer is wholly for one's self, not for God. He knows all ; but the exercise is for *our* good.

As to success in intercession. This I have often experienced myself. Remember Austin's mother.

None so little prayed for, and yet need it more than Ministers *ex-officio*—who have neither heart, nor skill, nor care for the flock.

I go round the world sometimes, and intercede for all who know the Lord, at the places on which my thoughts alight.

I go round England, and pray for all I have seen and known.

The Rev. B. Woodd—

I use some sweeping clauses : " All who desire my prayers "—" All who pray for me."

June 22, 1801.

What is the Proper Province of Reason in the Reception of Christianity ?—Proposed by the Rev. S. Crowther.

The Rev. W. J. Abdy—

It lies with reason to judge of the evidence of doctrines. There is nothing in divine truth contrary to reason, though there is *above* it.

The Rev. J. Venn—

The proper province of reason in religion is twofold—

1. In judging the evidence of a revelation pretending to be divine. (1.) In determining the external evidence. (2.) In inquiring into internal evidence. Here I should assign to reason only a negative power ; that is, not to invent what should be there, but determine the fitness of what is there.

2. In examining in what sense this revelation is to be understood. But here it is to act by comparing spiritual things with spiritual. The proper province of reason here is to determine the meaning of Scripture, as we would of a classic author. The danger is of squaring divine truth to our reason, rather than forming reason upon its statements.

Grace works upon the heart chiefly. It makes many a man of little understanding a better Christian than the most learned. We must not make divine truths too rational.

The Rev. H. Foster—

The proper province of reason is to go in Scripture as far as God leads, to understand what he says : but to go no further than God leads ; for all beyond is that imagination which ought to be cast down.

The Rev. R. Cecil—

We apply reason to the evidence, the Socinians to the doctrine.

Man is a rational creature, however depraved; and is capable of reasoning upon the evidence of revelation. But the question is not what man can do, as he *now stands* with his *improved* reason on the evidences of Christianity, but what is his nature, what could he find out of himself.

How puny are our powers! My eye may examine a guinea, but not the ring of Saturn.

To this day I feel shakes, from my own thoughts, or something I've read. I find it well to take my rush-light, and go into the cellar, and examine the foundations. I may be hippish. But I could do nothing so proper and suitable. I come up-stairs well and satisfied. It is troublesome to go and examine the vaults, but then there is always at hand the powerful feeling of what there is in the word. I feel as a diseased creature, and here is my *medicina mentis.* To the present hour nothing can combat the obligations, and keep from turning to the right hand or the left but this rule.

The *moral* evidence is with me overwhelming. What a prodigious thing to pull down the great foe of the soul! Besides, what are those doing who idolise reason? They are like blind men wandering among the tombs. So it appears that if men will not believe God, He scourges them by their own lie. Keep off metaphysical ground.

The Rev. J. Pratt—

The question rather respects the province of reason in *conversion.* It respects the personal reception of Christianity.

God affects the conscience and the heart, and through them the reason. He proposes nothing but what reason, as grace grows, will yield to.

The Rev. T. Scott—

I take the question much as Venn does. I do not oppose reason and revelation. Reason is the eye, revelation the sun. Reason is a plumb-line.

Almost all the business of the world is conducted by faith. Why, then, not believe God? Proud creatures cannot believe such humbling truths: nor carnal creatures such spiritual truths. Reason in corrupted man is blinded by the fumes which passion sends up : its eye is jaundiced by sin. Fuller distinguishes admirably between reason and vain reasonings.

Locke says, one great cause of men's not advancing further in knowledge is, that they do not distinguish between what *can* and *cannot* be known.

The Rev. J. Clayton—

The reason which is to judge of evidence must be *right.* If reason be not sanctified, man will find reasons for the position in which he stands.

In Scripture, there are trials for the will—for the passions; shall there be none for the understanding?

The Rev. J. Newton—

There is sufficient of external evidence to fix guilt on every man who rejects revelation.

In sinful man reason can do nothing till it is brought and baptised at the foot of the cross.

What the gospel proposes is highly reasonable, and will appear so to the man who is taught of God.

———

On the subject for July 6, 1801, viz., WHEREIN CONSISTS THE EVIL OF READING NOVELS, PLAYS, AND ROMANCES, &c.? proposed by the Rev. J. Clayton, we have no notes.

———

JULY 20, 1801.

WHAT ARE THE NATURE AND MARKS OF HYPOCRISY IN RELIGION ?— Proposed by the Rev. Josiah Pratt.

Mr Pratt—

I. The NATURE of Hypocrisy.

Hypocrisy is acting a part, putting on a mask, seeming other than we are, with an ill intention.

1. Official hypocrisy—

Where a man takes upon himself a character which obliges him to a religious profession, but he has not, nor ever had, any serious views of it, nor any concern about it—e. g., the Scribes and Pharisees ; and so also the majority of priests throughout the world.

2. Hypocrisy of self-condemning professors.

Where a man voluntarily took up a religious profession for sinister views ; or, where he set out under the goadings of natural conscience and fear of punishment, but has turned aside, "like a dog to his vomit," and yet keeps up the appearance from habit, from interest, and from shame, and is conscious to himself that he does this. For example—Judas, Simon Magus, Ananias and Sapphira. In this class for a time is to be ranked the true man under the power of sin—e. g., David and Peter.

3. Hypocrisy of self-deceiving professors—

Where a man set out with what he supposed a religious and honest motive, but this motive was fear, or some partial approbation of the gospel, or the unobserved influence of friends and connexions, or such like cause. He made a fair profession, went on seemingly well for a time, but his heart is departed from the Lord. Generally he has fallen into no notorious sins. The Devil knows he has him as sure as if he did, and can do more mischief by him as he is. The man pushes aside all self-inquiry. He is actually given up to a state of self-deception—e. g., the Church of Sardis : *Thou hast a name to live, but art dead.* This is the most affecting of all the characters ; the most difficult to distinguish from the true man ; one which it concerns us as Ministers most to know, that we may unmask such characters to themselves, while we neither cry peace when the Lord saith not peace ; nor, on the other hand, wound them whom the Lord hath not wounded.

II. What are the MARKS for detecting the hypocrite ?

As to the official and the self-condemning hypocrite, they are generally known and read of all men. And as to the self-deceiving hypocrite, I don't ask for marks which distinguish him to observers, but to *himself.*

How shall we teach such a man to *detect himself?* How shall we teach *the true man*, in his lowest frames, to hope that he is *not* such a one.

1. The hypocrite suspects not himself of hypocrisy. 2. He has little jealousy about motives ; and 3. Little anxiety about his state. 4. He feels shame for detection in sin, but no sorrow for sin. 5. He is sparing of the bosom sin.

The Rev. T. Scott—

I. On the nature of Hypocrisy.

There is a striking class of hypocrites, who use our Liturgy and go home and deny the doctrines of the gospel.

Another set in the class of self-deceiving hypocrites are those who make an Antinomian pillow of the gospel.

David was, for the season of his fall, a self-condemning hypocrite. We are sometimes in this case. Some short or long parenthesis occurs in our experience. We keep up appearances. Some great sin is committed. This produces a lethargy.

We should die if Christ did not intercede. It is not the nature of spiritual life to return and recover, but all depends upon the renewal of grace through Christ's intercession. David and Peter would have perished but for this.

A general definition of Hypocrisy is this—It is a form without life. A man pretending to be what he is not, and sometimes thinking himself what he is not. He won't look into things. He is a bankrupt through ignorance of his books.

The most difficult thing in the Ministry is, to draw the line between the most which Nature can do, and the least which Divine grace does.

Sometimes by our judgment we shall afflict the true man ; but God will over-rule.

It is never God's purpose that true grace shall always make a man happy. As to the hypocrite, no views can make a false man happy, for happiness results from health of body and soul.

I hope most from preventing people, when first setting out, from deceiving themselves. 'Tis a most critical time when a man is crying out, *What shall I do ?* Give him no comfort till he proves himself to be a true man. It is an awful thing to see a man so self-deceiving as to reject what is intended for him.

II. Marks of Hypocrisy.

Neglect of self-examination. A text comes on covetousness ; and he goes to the promises.

When a man quarrels with his Minister, rather than with himself, this is a bad sign.

Indifference about their state and the end to which they are moving.

A want of fears and doubts—these are both bad signs.   Fears and
doubts are so far from springing from unbelief, that they are often
the offspring of faith.   They are a sign of life, though not of health.

Take two characters—One man's conscientiousness exceeds his confidence.   Another's confidence exceeds his conscientiousness.   The first
is true : the last is bad.

If a man is in health, he feels comfortably ; if sick, uncomfortably ;
but if dead, he feels *nothing.*

Observe his behaviour after sin.   The weak Christian is not strengthened till his constitution is mended.

The Rev. J. Clayton—

The hypocrite is a stage-player.   The character of Hypocrisy is, that
it is ostentatious (Matt. xxiii. 5, 7); censorious (Matt. vii. 3); dis-
proportioned in zeal, *Ye tithe mint and cummin;* want of perseverance ;
begins unscripturally ; exercises false graces.   Such are assisted in
their hypocrisy by the flattery of dependents ; the imperfections of
others ; sophistry influenced by logic.

The Rev. J. Newton—

Though we may hope we are not hypocrites, yet there is hypocrisy
in us all.

The Rev. W. Goode—

The chief evidence of hypocrisy is an unwillingness to be searched,
especially on those points where we are likely to fall.

Hypocrites are loud and clamorous against the sins of which they
are guilty.

The Rev. W. J. Abdy—

There are generally some indications before a hypocrite discovers
himself fully to others.

The Rev. B. Woodd—

We are not to judge ourselves so much by frames as by the general
tenor of our pursuit.

The Rev. H. Foster—

We are all born in the element of sin.   An essential difference
between the regenerate and unregenerate is, that one is labouring to
get out of this element, and the other is not.

Though David and Peter would never have recovered but through
Christ, yet there is an essential difference between them under their
fall, and Judas under his.   The very nature of the divine life seems to
me to be immortal.   But it was suspended in them; and it did not,
nor would revive, but through Christ.

Wherever spiritual life is, it will operate throughout, and meet a
man's sins in his closet and everywhere.   Where no life is, there may
be some motion, or something like motion, in a leg or an arm, but
it's not the life which lives.

The Meetings were adjourned till September 28, 1801, when the subject was, THE USE AND ABUSE OF IMPRESSIONS FROM PASSAGES OF SCRIPTURE, proposed by the Rev. B. Woodd. On the 12th October, the question was, IN WHAT CIRCUMSTANCES, AND HOW FAR, ARE THE THREATENINGS AND PROPHECIES OF SCRIPTURE TO BE CONSIDERED AS FORMING THE RULE OF OUR CONDUCT TOWARDS OTHERS? proposed by the Rev. J. Goode. On neither of these have we any notes.

The subject of the next evening was suggested by the Peace, which was happily concluded with France about this time—the preliminaries having been signed October 1, 1801, and the final treaty at Amiens on the 27th of the following March.

During the long struggle which thus terminated in a tempo-rary peace, many had been the marks of the Divine favour to England. The principles of the French Revolution, which threat-ened to bring ruin upon all constitutional Governments, were not suffered to cast their deadly shade upon our happy land. God raised up instruments equal to the emergency, and blasted all the malicious efforts of the enemies of England and of England's liberty. Towards the close of this fearful crisis, England was left single-handed in the struggle. Italy and Switzerland had been subdued by the French arms, Austria had been compelled to retire exhausted from the contest, and to treat for peace more in the posture of a suppliant than of an equal; and Russia, with Sweden, Denmark, Holland, Spain—in short, nearly all the powers of Europe—enlisted themselves under the banner of France against us. England stood alone. A deadly blow was aimed especially at her naval strength—that bulwark to which, under Providence, she owed not merely her greatness and prosperity, but her safety, and almost her very existence as a nation.

Combined with all this, a national calamity was feared in the threatened insanity of the king. The deepest distress, too, was felt by the agricultural classes from the failure of the crops during two successive seasons. Scarcity and discontent were working upon the masses of the people. So gloomy were England's pros-pects at the commencement of this year (1801), that a day of national humiliation before God was appointed and observed throughout the land.

It was in this crisis that God interposed, and fought for Eng-land. By a series of wonderful victories by land and by sea, the strength of France was broken, the war terminated, and peace restored.

The people of God should ever watch the signs of the times, that they may trace the footsteps of Him whose never-failing providence ordereth all things in heaven and earth. This did the members of the Eclectic Society, and we find them, on the first

occasion after the happy issue of the struggle was known, proposing for discussion at their following meeting this subject:—

OCTOBER 26, 1801.

WHAT HAVE BEEN THE SIGNAL INTERPOSITIONS OF PROVIDENCE IN
FAVOUR OF BRITAIN DURING THE LATE WAR?—Proposed by the Rev.
J. Clayton.

The Rev. J. Clayton—

I wish the question to be considered in two views. 1. The interposition of Providence in favour of us as a nation. 2. The interposition
of Providence in favour of the Church of God in the nation.

The Rev. J. Newton—

The threatened invasion of Ireland we have been saved from. God
has raised up hopeful young men for the ministry during this period.

The Rev. B. Woodd—

1. Moral.

Providence has exposed in France the misery of anarchy and
irreligion. We are shewn what a nation is when stripped of all its
finesse and artifice. We learn the uncertainty of all human grandeur.
The history of these times is a comment on that passage—*Boast not
thyself of to-morrow, for thou knowest not what a day may bring forth.*

2. Political.

Providence has shewn us the blessing of a wise Government; the
duty of men to uphold authority; the danger of attempting changes;
the wisdom of bearing partial burdens. The abating of the seditious
spirit in this country—great naval victories off Ireland—the removal
of mutiny in the fleet—the preservation of the King—the dissolution
of the northern coalition—the destruction of the French fleet off
Egypt—the fidelity of our Government to treaties—all these furnish
topics of gratitude to God.

3. Religious.

There has been a bursting forth of infidelity, but it has been overruled to the weakening of Satan's kingdom. Advances have been
made towards the abolition of Popery. We have learned that a nation
cannot do without religion. The missionary spirit has been promoted.
There has been an increase of religious feeling and moral reform. We
have learned what the spirit of man is when left to itself, particularly
as delighting in blood. Lastly, we see what a blessing true religion is.

The Rev. W. J. Abdy—

We have been blessed in the last harvest. The wisdom with which
the treaties have been kept up is a cause of thankfulness.

The Rev. S. Crowther—

In raising up such a man as Bonaparte as the scourge of Europe,
there were many *unkown* interpositions in behalf of Britain. *God
passeth by, and we see him not.* The death of the Emperor Paul, when,
from being the vehement enemy of France, he had become one of its
warmest friends, was a wonderful interposition.

The Rev. H. Foster—

The exciting a spirit of hearing the Gospel and prayer has been one happy result of these troubles. The war has been the means of preserving this kingdom from confusion.

The Rev. J. Venn—

Quasi Deus dicat, "I am now going to punish the world, and the island of Great Britain shall fear and feel, but I will preserve it."

The recovery of the King in his first illness has been a great blessing. Providences are to be judged of by future circumstances.

War has been forced upon us ; and yet it was necessary (1.) to put a stop to French intercourse, and (2.) to keep us aloof to wait and see the issue of French principles.

It has been a signal blessing, that men of such firmness as Mr Pitt were at the head of affairs. Democracy prevailed only among a few of the lower orders. When the Duke of Bedford and Fox countenanced it at all, Burke is raised up to shew how far this spirit would go.

In the sea victories, particularly in that of Lord Howe, on 1st June 1794, we see the hand of God.

God always made the means equal to the expenses.

The protecting influence of Providence over England was extended all over the globe—*e. g.,* over the West India Islands.

Many particular interpositions of God in favour of Ireland came out on the trial of O'Connor.

Defensive operations were favoured ; offensive defeated—Egypt excepted, as a barrier to India.

The French were the means of aggrandising us in India by exciting Tippoo Sahib.

The battle of Copenhagen and the death of the Emperor Paul were signal interpositions.

Those before whom Europe fell, God allowed not to inflict a stroke on this island.

Whenever our country is visited with similar difficulties and dangers, we may learn from the past how soon He who sitteth above may put forth His power, and change the whole aspect of things at His will, when, as a people, we humble ourselves for our sins and implore the Divine mercy.

NOVEMBER 9, 1801.

THE NATURE AND SINFULNESS OF SPIRITUAL PRIDE, AND THE BEST MEANS OF REPRESSING IT ?—Proposed by the Rev. J. Goode.

The Rev. T. Scott—

I. Natural pride occupies itself about birth, wealth, talents, &c. Spiritual pride about *spiritualia.* Spiritual pride is a hard feeder. It will grow where everything else starves. It is a sacrilegious collector of the revenue. It robs God and the treasury of what is their due. It has given birth to all the heresies and sects in the world. It never does anything without a corrupt mixture, yet it pretends not to do anything which is not perfect.

II. Spiritual pride is one of the greatest of evils. The man takes to himself the merit of what is no more his than the sun. Natural pride is like a glow-worm in the dark ; but spiritual pride like opposing the sun. While spiritual pride acknowledges that gifts are from God, it is yet proud of them.

Man is a poor judge of what is evil in the sight of God, though he may be a good judge of what is evil as to society. It is a strange thing to make a law to establish humility. The pride of self-wisdom is as evil as the pride of self-righteousness. Humility does not require a man to undervalue anything he has received. Let him remember the *source* of all. Remember, the more gifts we have, the more we have to answer for.

The Rev. J. Clayton—

I. Spiritual pride consists in withdrawing our dependence. Man sets up for himself. " *I* " is the signature to everything. It consists in obstinacy. Hence such caution is necessary in reproving it. Our Saviour therefore spake in parables. It is an universal disease, and appearing in different forms. It is a foul feeder on virtues and vices.

Spiritual Pride shews itself in the Minister in this—when he cannot rejoice in the success of others ; and when he imputes his own success to himself. The spiritually proud are great pilferers, they pick jewels out of the Saviour's crown, till they leave him only a crown of thorns.

II. Its sinfulness appears in this, that it is God's rival in the world. It takes from him what is his due. It prevents repentance. It shuts out divine assistances. It breaks the tenderest ties. Its criminality appears from what God has said and done regarding it.

III. The remedies of spiritual pride are :—1. Regeneration. 2. Forming a true estimate of things. 3. Contemplating the character of God. The angels have no time to contemplate their own excellencies. 4. Remembering from whom we have received what we have, and for what end. 5. Mortifying providences.

The Rev. S. Crowther—

Pride and ignorance are twin-sisters. Pride is often left to cure itself. Man is often wounded in that of which he is proud. Guard against it in the poor. We are apt to be proud of a little knowledge.

NOVEMBER 23, 1801.

How shall we best Treat Malignant Opposers of the Gospel, with whom we are Constrained to have Intercourse ?—Proposed by the Rev. R. Cecil.

The Rev. R. Cecil—

A notion I had of late was this, that almost everything can be done by *benevolence ;* it was a kind of nostrum with me.

I imputed much of the complaints of the brethren to a want of this. But what is good in the closet, will often not do in practice. I think I carried the matter too far.

I have met with a case of this sort :—A man is very civil to your face, and will curse you behind your back: and when he meets you again, he is as friendly as ever. Now when a private man meets with this, the question is easy : but when a Minister, who has the charge of this man's soul, has to deal with such a man, it becomes a question whether he is not bound to deal with him openly. All this is quite agreeable with kindness and benevolence. But whether civility should be kept up with a man who thus acts, rather than coming to the point —this is the question.

The Rev. J. Pratt—

A man must be well aware of his own disposition, and know how to manage it, in reproving such a character. Temper may lead to reprove too soon, and a cowardly spirit too late.

Example and character, right judgment, a single eye, a courageous spirit, a humble heart—these are the qualifications for the minister who could manage such a character.

The Rev. J. Goode—

Much depends on the abilities of the man who is to manage this affair. Consider the rank, character, and education of the person to be admonished. Unite courage with tenderness. Harp not always on the persecuting spirit of the world ; this will irritate.

The Rev. W. Goode—

Imitate the conduct of Christ in kindness and gentleness. If this will not answer, faithfulness of reproof must be resorted to. This depends on our situation and circumstances.

The Rev. Mr Storry, a visitor—

I have tried to soften a man by shewing tenderness to his children.

Rev. S. Crowther—

Embrace opportunity ; but go not out of the way to do it. Visit them in sickness and sorrow. Private expostulation is useful. Many who are civil, yet hate the truth.

DECEMBER 7, 1801.

IN WHAT SENSE ARE WE TO UNDERSTAND THOSE WORDS OF OUR LORD, " IF YE SHALL ASK ANYTHING IN MY NAME, I WILL DO IT?"—Proposed by the Rev. J. Newton.

The Rev. J. Newton—

Many things are asked and not done. Yet all things asked rightly in Christ's name are done. What is it to ask thus ? We must ask with right views of the character and office of Christ.

The Rev. W. Goode—

There are two questions.

1. What is it to ask in the name of Christ ?   It is to ask as a sinner, on account of Christ.

2. The extent of the promise ?   Another passage explains this—*Whatsoever ye ask according to his will*, that is, his revealed will ; but since there is no express promise of earthly things, we have no right to look for any certain thing.

Yet in some cases very extraordinary circumstances occur as to earthly things in answer to prayer.

The Rev. J. Pratt—

There is little difficulty to us in this matter.   There was more to the disciples, as they had never asked in Christ's name.

There was now an explicit command to do this.   The Church had obtained everything through Him ; but had not asked *in His name*. Now a new era begins.

Even the Lord's Prayer had not mentioned the name of Christ explicitly.

DECEMBER 21, 1801.

THE EXPEDIENCY OF THE ACCOMMODATION OF SCRIPTURE ?—Proposed by the Rev. H. Foster.

The Rev. H. Foster—

Types are not accommodations.   The Old Testament is full of typical meaning.

I would rather lean to the excess of finding Christ where he is not, than pass him by where he is.

Accommodation is the embodying of truth from some historic or other passages.

Its use is regarded by some as rather an indication of weakness in the cause of truth.

The Rev. R. Cecil—

Accommodation, if sober, gives some variety ; it embodies.   The Apostles do this so far as to shew it may be done with propriety.

It must not be taken as ground-work, but allusions may thus be thrown out.   Weakness and youth most abound herein.   Whether weak or young, I know not, but I know that I set out thus.

But why should we go to questionable passages when the same things are clearly said elsewhere ?   For instance : *There is a friend that sticketh closer than a brother.*   This may be used as an allusion ; but should never be made the ground-work of our setting forth the love of Christ.

We should grapple with the conscience of the hearers, and give them no hold upon us in these things.   Mr Romaine should have preached upon the imputed righteousness of Christ before the university from a plain passage.*

* " William Romaine, an English divine and writer of great popularity, was born September 25, 1714.   Besides other sermons before the university, he preached one in 1757, entitled ' The Lord our Righteousness,' in consequence of which he was refused any future admission into the university pulpit.   He interpreted the articles of the

I had not preached more than six months before I had worn out the Bible. I could have done something with a new Bible. What was I to do? I went to accommodation. If, however, I had been disposed *to dig*, I could have found treasures beneath, without this keeping at the surface.

Consider your people. It is rash to set out with accommodation among unconverted persons. A man is glad to find a loophole, and to get out of your reach. You must grapple with him—*What shall a man give in exchange for his soul?*

On the whole, it is lawful, with caution and care, to use accommodation ; but in proportion to his seriousness and diligence, a preacher does not want it, especially as a body and ground-work.

The Rev. Mr Johnson, a visitor—

I explain passages literally first, and then accommodate. Thus I treat the miracles and historical events.

The Rev. J. Clayton—

Bishop Atterbury is a fine example of allusion. Lord Bacon's illustration of the right mode of using Scripture is admirable. Press the grape tenderly, the wine is fine ; press it hard, it tastes of the husk.

The Rev. J. Pratt—

Accommodation is taking a passage out of its proper use and applying it to an improper one. This may be done—
1. By explaining figuratively what should be taken literally. For example, drawing some spiritual and hidden meaning out of the statement, that *the snuffers were of pure gold.*
2. Doing the reverse of this ; 3. Drawing unfair inferences ; and, 4. Illustrations not obvious.
Accommodation, as thus explained, is never to be allowed.

The Rev. B. Woodd—

Drawing practical observations from historical passages is accommodation. For example, the Apostle's comment upon Hagar and Mount Sinai.

Texts may be used as mottoes ; *e. g., Is there not a cause?* may be used without any reference to the actual connexion of the words.

But accommodation is bad, when we strain and force the sense of Scripture. Dr Gill exceeded everybody in accommodation.

The Rev. J. Goode—

We should distinguish between illustration and proof.

The Rev. W. Goode—

Accommodation is not applying figures to the things meant by them. Nor is it drawing inferences from historical passages.

Church in the strict Calvinistic sense, which at this time gave great offence."—*Chalmers's Biographical Dictionary.* We understand that Mr Romaine selected a highly figurative text in setting forth this doctrine, viz., Isaiah xlv. 8. It is to this that Mr Cecil alludes.

I

But it is endeavouring to derive some instruction from a passage which was not meant by the Holy Spirit in that passage.

On the next occasion, in January 4, 1802, there was no question discussed; but Country Members and Visitors were chosen for the new year.

The subject on January 18, 1802, was—WHAT ARE THE PRINCIPAL ERRORS OF THE QUAKERS, AND WHAT IS THE INFLUENCE OF THOSE ERRORS UPON THEIR GENERAL CHARACTER?—It was proposed by the Rev. J. Venn, who brought forward sixteen propositions from Barclay.*

On February 1, 1802, the subject was—IN WHAT RESPECTS DOES THE INFLUENCE OF THE HOLYSPIRIT ACCOMPANY THE WORD?—Proposed by the Rev. B. Woodd. We have no notes on either of these subjects.

FEBRUARY 15, 1802.

THE CAUSES OF NOT PROFITING UNDER THE WORD PREACHED, BOTH AS IT RESPECTS MINISTERS AND THEIR HEARERS?—Proposed by the Rev. J. Goode.

The Rev. J. Goode—

Some have often profited when they think not.

We are not to look exclusively for comfort.

I. Hindrances to usefulness in the Minister :—

1. An awkward manner. 2. A low character. 3. Using vulgar phrases. 4. An undue attention to composition and delivery. 5. Being a man of fashion. 6. A want of affection and tenderness.

II. Hindrances in hearers :—

1. Unbelief. 2. Want of affection to the Minister. 3. Inattention. 4. Having itching ears. 5. Too much hearing. 6. Neglect of previous prayer. 7. Want of self-denial on the Sabbath. 8. Speaking too freely of a Minister's foibles often lodges a prejudice in the minds of young persons.

The Rev. Mr Vansittart, a visitor—

Ministers should choose the best subjects. There should be a manifest love in the manner of preaching.

The Rev. S. Crowther—

Want of prayer in the Minister, I would add to what Goode said. In hearers, want of subsequent prayer.

The Rev. J. Venn—

We should have a clear idea of what profit is. Large congregations are not always a test of profit. We should not expect the same visible effects after some time as at first. To know how far people really do profit, follow them to the sick-bed or into their families. The true

----

* Robert Barclay, the celebrated apologist for the Quakers in the reign of Charles II.

place to discover profit is not in Church, but at home. Consider, too, how far a man is capable of profiting, according to his talents. The proper question, therefore, is, what prevents a Minister from profiting so much as he might do?

I. Means of profiting in a Minister:—

1. Heavenly-mindedness.

A minister's frame of mind is of infinite importance. There is much in the word *unction*. My father used to pray for an hour before entering the pulpit. His hearers could generally tell whether he had been near with God. When it was so, he almost always preached well.

2. The truth of a Minister's doctrine.

Many even shed tears, but there may be little profit; unless the truth is really felt, and made to sink into the heart.

3. Study.

Study both your subject and simplicity in setting it forth. A Minister infuses the taste into his hearers. He should therefore ground them in such a taste that they should disrelish what is unsound.

4. Abstaining from disputing.

5. Being free from prejudices.

6. Conversation out of the pulpit. If a Minister feels that he is not profiting, he should examine himself. In this light, the subject is a very useful one. It sometimes pleases God to withhold his favour, that we may thus be led to look into ourselves.

II. Means of profiting in hearers.

Great business is unfavourable to profiting.

The Rev. H. Foster—

If a Minister be everything that he should be, yet there will be certain classes who do not profit. There will be wayside and such like hearers, even if Jesus Christ preaches. There may be much to blame in ourselves, but still these sorts of people will come.

A Minister often exerts himself to little purpose, when he dwells upon circumstantials. We should bring things forward in the due proportion in which the Bible brings them forward. Much depends on the spirit and character.

The Rev. R. Cecil—

There are two sorts of preachers who take the road in which they are not likely to do good. 1. Speculatists. 2. Rhapsodists.

It is hardly possible to make too much of what has been said of a Minister's *spirit*. He should be a man of business and a man of God, doing the work of God! There is much in the spirit of a particular day: for example, hearing, in this day.

We are often seduced to feel satisfaction in a sermon that keeps up our reputation, rather than to seek the profit of the hearers and the glory of God. While we hold in theory that the Holy Spirit must work miracles, we still go out as if *we* were to persuade this and that person. I don't always find that I can honour the Holy Ghost. I know I ought to do so, but I find it difficult.

The Rev. Mr Ring, a visitor—

Attention to dress is a hindrance in hearers. Late attendance on worship, another. Careless attendance, a third.

The Rev. T. Scott—

He who profits the people is—1. A converter of sinners. 2. An edifier of the Church.

Hindrances to a Minister are—1. Want of simplicity of intention. 2. Want of simplicity of dependence. 3. Want of " *the word of the kingdom*." 4. Want of study.

In hearers—1. Late visits. 2. Want of prayer.

The Rev. J. Clayton—

1. The character of the times operates on both preacher and hearer. We have no sacrifice to make for Christ, none.

2. Want of personal religion in a minister is against the hearers.

3. Want of right instruction in the great fundamentals—Christ, regeneration, &c.

4. Want of judgment in the application. This requires a knowledge of the flock, and of the temptations arising from their various callings.

5. The devil is our great hinderer.

6. The character of those with whom we associate and whom we hold up as our converts, has a most important influence upon our usefulness.

MARCH 1, 1802.

HOW SHALL WE DISCOVER THE IMPRESSION WHICH OUR CHARACTERS MAKE UPON OTHERS, AND HOW FAR IS THE INQUIRY IMPORTANT?— Proposed by the Rev. H. Foster.

The Rev. H. Foster—

Hints come out in this way. For want of a disposition to learn, hints are lost. *Thou art the man* is generally too abrupt, and seldom does good.

This is a very important inquiry.

The Rev. R. Cecil—

There are many sorts of characters known and read of all men except themselves. Much delusion arises from a man listening only to his favourites—his own circle.

In discovering the impression our character makes—1. We must not indulge self in listening to the people who admire us. 2. We should consult men of different complexion to ourselves. 3. Ask the common people what they think. They have not learned *finesse*.

The question is vastly important, since God employs character as well as truth in carrying on His purposes.

Character gives an irresistible force to what is otherwise of little weight. We are not officiously to search for hints, but to lay wait and learn if anything is likely to be said against us. We may take hints even from anonymous letters. Saurin has a Sermon upon *Whom do men say that I am?* See his application.

The Rev. J. Pratt—

The inquiry will be somewhat dangerous if made of set purpose : and perhaps it is hardly right to make it. We should pick up hints.

Guard against vanity. There is danger of aiming at making an impression. For some it is dangerous to find out that their character makes a great impression.

Impression is sometimes made not by single acts, but by a series. There may be many aberrations, but yet the character good in the main. All this shews how necessary caution is in judging.

In discovering the impression made—

1. Lay it down that something is to be discovered in us that ought to be amended.

2. Take the most likely method. Look out of your own circle— look at similar companies.

3. Give it its due weight. Do I ever get good ? have I ever changed my conduct with a view of improving ?

The Rev. T. Scott—

We are exhorted *to avoid all appearance of evil—to provide things honest in the sight of all men—to take care that our good be not evil spoken of.* Yet we are not to do evil in order to avoid the appearance of doing it.

Sometimes we cannot do right without appearing to do what's wrong. Every man's conscience is at last the rule. Our brethren condemn us : we have, then, no method, but studying the Word of God.

If a favourer gives hints, we may be confident that something wants correcting, or looks as if it did. [Here he made some allusions to his own character and history.] It has been said, that in matters of conscience, man should be unbending as an oak ; but in those of his taste or humour, pliable as a willow.

The Rev. J. Davies—

This matter is important as a means of self-knowledge. Mason, in his book on Self-Knowledge, speaks of this in this light. Plutarch says, the reproaches of enemies cause us to see the worst side of our character.

It is important also as to others, because much usefulness depends thereon. It is important as it respects our duty to God that we may *adorn the doctrine of God our Saviour in all things.*

How far are we to carry the inquiry ? Pay not undue regard to what others say, and attend to the general character rather than to particular acts.

The Rev. J. Clayton—

All impression worth anything must arise from our nearness to the Saviour and from our conformity to him.

We may learn much of ourselves from—1. Self-converse; 2. The malice of enemies; 3. The faithfulness of friends.

The Rev. J. Newton—

If we could hear all that is said of us, it would not flatter us much

The Rev. J. Venn—

It is well in many cases that we do not know all that people think of us.

There are two extremes to be avoided :—

1. Caring too much what people think of us. It is the duty of some to avoid this.

2. Caring too little. For others are proud and supercilious. *To the pure, all things are pure.* The desire of praise is often at the bottom of this kind of inquiry.

[Mr Venn here referred to some custom of Mr Walker of Truro and his friends ; and we refer our readers to Mr Sydney's " Life of Mr Walker," published in 1835, in the third chapter of which is some account of his religious societies, and rules which bear in part on the present subject.]

MARCH 15, 1802.

WHAT WERE THE INFLUENCES OF THE HOLY SPIRIT IN THE CHURCH PREVIOUS TO THE DAY OF PENTECOST ?—Proposed by the Rev. J. Venn.

Mr Venn—

Scripture often speaks of the influence of the Holy Spirit as being new under the New Testament Dispensation. The Gospel is often called the Dispensation of the Spirit.

On the other hand, we cannot suppose that this influence of the Spirit was not received in the Old Dispensation.

The question, then, seems to be—What particular difference was there in the influences of the Holy Spirit after the day of Pentecost ? Some light may be got from the terms of the New Covenant as enumerated by St Paul in Heb. viii. 10–12 : *This is the covenant that I will make with the house of Israel after those days, &c.* Here this influence is classed with what certainly the Church under the Old Testament had. I infer, therefore, that only a greater measure of this influence was received under the New Testament. Consider the ardent breathings of the Old Testament saints.

What, then, is new in this influence under the New Testament ?

1. Clearer views of the distinct person and offices of the Holy Spirit.

2. What relates to the peculiar mode of the acceptance of a sinner.

3. The spirit of adoption. God revealed himself under the Old Testament rather as a Lawgiver than a Father.

4. The consolations given.

5. The ordinances and means of grace.

In a word, there is a great difference under the New Testament with respect to light and knowledge, and the means of attaining this light and knowledge.

The Rev. H. Foster—

There is great difficulty about the subject. If under the Old Testament human nature was as evil, spiritual enemies the same, the difficulties of getting to heaven the same, the spiritual influence must have been much the same from the beginning as now.

Prophets were miraculously inspired for their ends. But I have little apprehension of difference in the saving operations of the Holy Spirit.

The Rev. R. Cecil—

The New Testament Dispensation always appeared to me like a thing made out of another thing. More clarified; more enlarged; the same story told more fully; placed in stronger light; unrolled more fully.

All saving influence under the Old Testament was from the Holy Spirit; but there is more liberty under the New Testament.

The Rev. T. Scott—

Believers one with another have not more of the influence of the Spirit under the New Testament than under the Old Testament.

God from Mount Sinai spake as a righteous Judge; but from the mercy-seat as a Father.

There seems almost as much spiritual life and devotion under the Old Testament as under the New; not so much explicit light. Paul seems not more elevated in devotion than David.

The Christian Dispensation is portable; and is adapted, not for a nation, but the world. The ordinances, therefore, are more spiritual, less burdensome.

One very perceptible view of the difference of this influence under the two Testaments, is that of the Holy Spirit as the purchase of Christ, and given to glorify him. Another is, the expressness of the promise of the Holy Spirit: *If ye, being evil, &c.* Freedom of access to the Father is another. The wider range of this influence—the world —is a fourth.

The Rev. Mr Simons, a visitor—

There is some evidence of even a superior strength of influence for consolation upon the Old Testament saints above that upon the New; for they express themselves, even under a darker view of the object, with as much or more warmth. The chief difference is in *extent.*

The Rev. J. Clayton—

In the Scriptures, the New Testament Dispensation is constantly represented as a Dispensation of greater privilege. John the Baptist was greater than all who preceded him, yet the least in the kingdom of heaven is greater than he.

The superiority of the Gospel Dispensation lies—(1.) In the greater light. (2.) The greater extent. *He shall convince the world of sin, &c.* (3.) In worship. *The hour cometh, and now is, when the true worshipper shall worship the Father in spirit and in truth.* John iv. 23. (4.) In gifts to ministers. (5.) In duration.

The Rev. B. Woodd—

The influence of the Spirit has always in its nature been the same.

We have instances of the power of faith in Old Testament saints in Hebrews xi.; of heroic courage for God in Daniel, Shadrach, Meshach, and Abed-nego. The views of the Church are now more explicit, distinct, unfolded, and general. The New Testament is spoken of as a veil removed—a restraint taken off—a shadow substantiated—a prophecy accomplished.

Under the New Testament, we have superior light on—(1.) The Doctrine of the Trinity. (2.) Justification by Faith. (3.) The Person of Christ. (4.) The love of Christ as a motive of conduct. (5.) The love of the brethren.

The Rev. W. Goode—

That the same sanctifying influence existed under the Old Testament is proved from the Great Example of faith being under the Old Dispensation.

We enjoy superior light in—(1.) The clearness of the New Testament Dispensation. (2.) The extent of this Dispensation.

Though there are high examples of faith in the Old Testament, these are *individuals*. Yet the Church generally came short more so than now.

The promises in God refer to the whole extent of the New Testament Dispensation; so that the day of Pentecost is in part only a fulfilment; subsequent revivals are so, in part, also.

On the next subject—How SHALL WE BEST IMPROVE THE EVENT OF PUBLIC PEACE?—there was only a general conversation.

APRIL 12, 1802.

How SHALL WE DETECT THE ENMITY OF THE HUMAN HEART AGAINST GOD, IN AMIABLE MORAL CHARACTERS?—Proposed by the Rev. B. Woodd.

The Rev. B. Woodd—

Consider the disposition of such persons with regard to the Divine Government, the Law, and the Gospel. Do they discover any true regard to true believers as believers? Any interest in the honour of God in the world? They are offended, if a friend becomes truly religious. They are in a state of friendship with that world which is at enmity with God. Pride is often at the bottom. Religion is with them a compound of self-righteousness and ceremonial formality.

The Rev. H. Foster—

There are two ways to discover such characters—(1.) Holding up the standard of purity. (2.) Insisting upon the gospel ground of justification. To this may be added the doctrine of election. God bestows *paribus imparia*.

The Rev. R. Cecil—

There are many truly spiritual men, who, from prejudices of education and books, object from the head, rather than from the heart, to our statement of election. Those people do not come out. They study to speak softly. Old writers compare them to a *fine peach.* Much of this is in constitution.

Adding morality to amiableness rather hardens. Sometimes the lie comes out in some inconsistencies. The truth is, whatever such have, there is no reference to the God of the Scriptures, or to the sinner-like spirit. The only difference between them and open enemies is, that their enmity is not coarse.

Some have taken up the matter as a politician—" Why ! you'd save trouble by being amiable." Nature, honest nature, sometimes suddenly betrays itself. They don't believe the Bible. Such men, if Ministers, read in the desk, *Strait is the gate and narrow is the way, which leadeth unto life, and few there be that find it:*—but meet them in the parlour, and they would brand such a sentiment, uttered there, as harsh and uncharitable.

The Rev. J. Pratt—

The heart of every man is equally removed from God. Some seem to have a kind of morality and amiableness founded in their blood. The moral man's concupiscible passions, and the amiable man's irascible passions, are not strong enough to overcome their natural self-command, which in the eyes of so many is mistaken for something higher than it is.

All predisposition to the Gospel is from an operation of the Spirit of God.

One way, not yet mentioned, in which these men shew their enmity, is, that they are listless, indifferent, and gape and turn away when spiritual things are entered upon.

The Rev. T. Scott—

St Paul was an ardent man. Your *quidque vult valde vult* men are seldom amiable men. To be amiable in such a world as this, in the sense of Lord Chesterfield, is not to be like Jesus Christ. Eli was an example of weak amiableness. Jehoshaphat wanted spirit and activity. We must detect the enmity by shewing that such are in an habitual state of enmity against God.

The Rev. J. Clayton—

The following appearances mark such characters :—(1.) They form a Deity of their own. (2.) They are intolerant against the Gospel-view of God. (3.) They are at war with the doctrine of motives. (4.) They object to what they think the intolerance of the Gospel.

The Rev. J. Newton—

This child is set for the fall and rising again of many in Israel, and that the thoughts of many hearts may be revealed.

The Gospel is Ithuriel's spear.*

* *Paradise Lost,* book iv., 799–814.

" Him there they found
Squat like a toad, close at the ear of Eve,

APRIL 26, 1802.

WHAT JUDGMENT SHALL WE FORM CONCERNING THE DEGREE OF SANC-
TIFICATION POSSESSED BY THE OLD TESTAMENT SAINTS ?—Proposed by the
Rev. J. Venn.

The Rev. T. Scott—

We have more knowledge and light, but these, like money, do not
enrich unless in circulation.

Some saints under the Old Testament were much higher than saints
now, and nearly equal to apostolic days. For example, Enoch, David,
Hezekiah, Josiah, Daniel. The *omnium* were rather lower than that of
the apostolic days.

As to David, God condemned not his polygamy. He winked at these
things. His repentance was deep for his adultery. His humility,
meekness, and patience, under conviction, were deep and sincere.
Abraham and Job are also eminent for their graces.

Consider the faithfulness of the historian recording all the defects of
his subject. It had not been known that Isaiah and Daniel were
sinners, if they had not told us so themselves.

The Rev. J. Davies—

The New Testament holds out Old Testament saints as striking
examples of faith. And as faith is in proportion to sanctification, it
follows that sanctification must be high in them.

The Rev. J. Clayton—

Religion in substance is the same in every age. Jesus Christ exe-
cuted his office then as now. Yet I consider the Old Testament saints
as inferior to the New. I am led to think many things said by David
and others were said by them as prophets.

The very eminent saints under the Gospel are not chargeable with
the defects of those of the Old Dispensation.

There was a malignity and ferocity among those of the Old. There
was very little religion among the Judges. They were rough heroes
raised up for the defence of an external system. The spirit of benevolence and love were little known and exercised.

The Rev. J. Newton—

There was a roughness in the Dispensation of the Old Testament:
for example, Elijah and John the Baptist. If holiness consists in de-

> Assaying, by his devilish art, to reach
> The organs of her fancy, and with them forge
> Illusions, as he list, phantasms and dreams;
> Or if, inspiring venom, he might taint
> The animal spirits, that from pure blood arise
> Like gentle breaths from rivers pure, thence raise
> At least distemper'd, discontented thoughts,
> Vain hopes, vain aims, inordinate desires,
> Blown up with high conceits engendering pride.
> Him thus intent Ithuriel with his spear
> Touch'd lightly ; for no falsehood can endure
> Touch of celestial temper, but returns
> Of force to its own likeness : up he starts
> Discover'd and surprised."

votedness to God, obedience, submission, and faith, few surpass Abraham.

The Rev. B. Woodd—

The difference between Old and New Testament saints is, that they had equal degrees of sanctification, but less degrees of knowledge under the Old Testament.

The Rev. H. Foster—

The Old Testament saints are set before us as models in the New to a high degree.

If our secret history were published, we must stand upon a level with the Old Testament saints.

The Rev. J. Venn—

When we speak of Old Testament saints, we use a very vague expression. It comprehends multitudes of men for nearly 4000 years. A few are selected, and the account given of them is such as is connected with the history of the Church. An account of this kind is very different from what their private history would give. What is objected to in David, is very much to be accounted for by considering him to be a King. Much allowance is to be made for the age. So with the early fathers. In Calvin and Cranmer, we have to excuse some of their acts by remembering the spirit of the age they lived in.

The New Testament does not approve in the mass of what is said of saints in the Old Testament. The Old Testament relates things as facts which occurred ; as Jacob's lie. The New Testament selects some striking feature, as Job's patience, Abraham's faith, and brings this forward with high commendation.

To consider David as not concerned in his personal experience in what he says, is dangerous indeed. A man of a devout spirit like David, most people will suppose furthest from the danger of impurity, when perhaps he is most likely to fall into it.

The Rev. R. Cecil—

If Christ raised the standard of morals, was not this with effect ? Something more eminent, therefore, in general sanctification, is to be expected. To bring forward Abraham, or any other eminent saint, is not to the point.

Make the question wider. The New Testament raised the standard of purity. In the New Testament, there is a greater degree of abstaining from the borders of evil.

MAY 10, 1802.

WHAT IS THE BEST WAY OF DEFENDING THE TRUTH ?—Proposed by the Rev. H. Foster.

The Rev. H. Foster—

This question arose in my mind from reading Overton. What he did was well done, but such a mode will irritate. It is a question whether more good is not ultimately done by living the truth, and displaying its spirit.

Yet Christ exposed the wickedness of his enemies, though he knew it would irritate. So did St Paul. It is, I think, a lawful and useful way of defending the truth, to use the press. But the occasion should be plain and palpable. Not " He has knocked me, and I'll knock him again."

The Rev. R. Cecil—

There is a rational, and also a scriptural way of defending the truth. *Be ready always to give an answer to every man that asketh you a reason of the hope that is in you.* Christ and his Apostles did this.

But a man should consider his talent. It follows not, that because the truth is to be defended in every way, that therefore every man is to defend it in every way. It is to be done in a holy way. *Michael the archangel, when, contending with the devil, he disputed about the body of Moses, durst not bring against him a railing accusation, but said, The Lord rebuke thee.*

Let us shew that we are men of a different spirit, as well as of diffe rent doctrines. In defending the truth with any one, we should have the good of the man's soul in view. We should avoid litigiousness. This was too much the spirit of Baxter. Oswald wisely suggests that we must insist upon first principles.

The Rev. J. Pratt—

That might have been the best way, if none had been taken which may not be the best in the present state of the Church. Had the Church agreed, as a standing law, that no defence but that of the *spirit and life* should be given, it might have been well. But other methods have been taken : and the question is, which is the best according to circumstances ?

Repetition wears sentiments into the mind. Local circumstances may call a man out. There is a disadvantage in attacking men— personalities do mischief. There is advantage in holiness. The force of our arguments is diminished by generals.

The Rev. T. Scott—

Every man is bound to exercise his talent.

The Apostles had not the press : but I doubt not if they had had it, they would have used it.

We are not sufficiently distinguishing between the defence of the truth, and the defence of ourselves. Unless attacks on ourselves involve attacks on truth, we should rather pass them by. If specific charges are brought against a man, he is called upon to defend himself ; if general railing, let it pass.

The Rev. J. Clayton—

It is no question with me that the truth ought to be defended. The various Apologies in the early days of the Church were useful.

1. Decline human authorities.   2. There should be a fair call. Consult the end, and the temper.   3. We should use preaching.   And here we should use not dead arguments, but living.   4. Writing also should be used.   5. And prayer and a holy life.   It is astonishing how much is carried on upon the theatre of the mind.   A prodigious conflict is carried on in the invisible world of spirits.   6. We should not call in the aid of those who hold not the truth.

MAY 24, 1802.

WHAT RULES CAN BE GIVEN FOR TREATING ALL SUBJECTS EVANGELI-CALLY ?—Proposed by the Rev. Josiah Pratt.

The Rev. J. Pratt—

I would premise what is—

I. The NATURE of evangelical preaching.   It is *according to the proportion of faith;* that is, we should—

1. Bring forward the features peculiar to Christianity, not as a Jew, nor as a philosopher, but as a Christian.   The work of Christ, the influence of the Spirit, Christian motives, a high measure of holiness : these should be prominent.

2. Assign everything its due place.   We should begin at the right end : distinguish between the duties of the unregenerate and the regenerate.

3. Assign everything its due proportion.   Dwell neither on doctrines nor duties disproportionately ; either is equally contrary to real evangelical preaching.

II. The IMPORTANCE of this method—

1. It is important to the preacher.   *Principiis obsta.*   Error generates error.

2. To the hearer—there is no real edification but by the truth.

3. To the brethren—we thus shew them who err a more excellent way.

III. The DIFFICULTY of it.

Scripture is written so as to exercise our diligence.   The great and saving truths are so plain, that he *who runs may read;* but there are many subordinate parts not to be reconciled with the leading truths, but by a large and comprehensive and well-studied view of the matter. The frequent failures herein prove the difficulty.

1. Choose manageable subjects.

If you cannot introduce Christ without violence, change your subject.   There is a great difference in men here : one can do it with *naiveté;* not so, another.   Lay it down as a rule, that all subjects are not fit for the pulpit.   And many perhaps may be fit for another preacher, but not for me ; because he can manage them " *according to the proportion of faith,*" but I cannot.

2. Choose appropriate subjects.

I mean appropriate to our own turn of mind ; so as to counteract by the very subject, if possible, any tendency we may have to a disproportionate view and representation of Divine truths. For example, R. should lean to the close of the Romans; C. to the beginning; because R. will be sure to treat a practical subject doctrinally, and C. a doctrinal subject practically.

3. Habituate them to view the simplicity of the Divine dispensations. There has been one way of salvation from the beginning.

Privileges and duties have borne the same relation to man since the Fall.

He is the same character as a sinner, the way of salvation is the same, the necessity of Divine influences, the obligation to holiness—all the same.

The Rev. J. Clayton—

I would enter into detail. I have preached single sermons upon single vices and duties, and have got great attention.

The Rev. J. Davies—

No subject can be treated evangelically, unless the great truths are brought in.

The general rule is, doctrines should be treated practically, and duties treated doctrinally.

The Rev. J. Newton—

There are various instructors, but the same Spirit. I have no notion but of preaching *Jesus Christ and him crucified.* There should be doctrinal, experimental, and practical matter in every sermon. There is no effectual teacher but the Spirit of God.

The Rev. B. Woodd—

That ministry is defective which does not occasionally treat upon particular duties. All subjects are naturally connected with the Gospel. Every practical subject shews the effect of the Gospel when rightly received. Suppose envy is the subject. What an instance of the Fall is envy! What an instance of the need of mercy! What a proof of the necessity of sanctifying grace! How can this be most effectually rooted out, and the contrary impressed, but by the love of Jesus Christ shed abroad in the heart?

The Rev. W. Goode—

In order to treat every subject evangelically, we must endeavour to view it evangelically.

Pratt's views are liable to exception. 1. They would incline me to idleness, by making me think a subject in which I found any difficulty was not manageable. 2. If I think in any particular way, I shall hardly think that wrong.

The Rev. S. Crowther—

We are generally agreed, that all subjects should be treated evangelically. Our duty to do this springs from the effects of such preaching. Whenever the Son of Man is lifted up, he will draw all men unto him.

The Rev. Mr Robinson, a visitor—

The subject has taken a wider scope than I expected it would. The question is, what rules can be given? Not whether we should do this or that, which is *supposed* in the question.

Do we preach according to the great scheme of redemption? Every man should go away with a knowledge of what the Gospel is.

I have gone through most of the Epistles in part, in order to force myself upon all subjects. This has brought me into more difficulties than any other, and has driven me more to my knees.

A question with me is, what have I not insisted on? On Sunday mornings and Tuesday evenings, I follow generally in some course, in order to compel myself to take all subjects. With God's help, every hearer shall know how he is to be saved. Men have different tendencies; but if we take the Word of God and expound it verse by verse, we shall counteract this tendency, if wrong.

The Rev. J. Venn—

We shall preach evangelically when we preach like the Apostles. They prescribed, like physcians, for the disease of the people to whom they wrote.

So did our Lord, *e. g.*, in the Sermon on the Mount. In John vi. he preached the Gospel. He kept close to his subject whatever it was. So did the Apostles. Though they did not always enlarge upon the topics of the Gospel, yet they introduced them.

We are preaching evangelical when we are aiming against the particular faults and hindrances of our people. Some men cannot wander from a subject. Some cannot cleave to one.

There is a danger and an evil to the Church from persons endeavouring to treat *every* subject, as they call it, evangelically. This leads to spiritualising every subject. Cocceius began this; Huntington completed it. Great mischief arises from this, which we should guard against. Would not most men say St James did not preach evangelically? But he knew the state of the people. Walker of Truro has given an excellent example of preaching evangelically.

My reverence for truth will not allow me to say anything beyond what I find in the text.

But a man should be judged of from the course of his ministry, not from separate sermons.

The religious world is ill-instructed upon particular duties.

The Rev. R. Cecil—

Put this question closely—Are the religious world sufficiently instructed in duties?

I say not this to damp an evangelical exhibition of truth. I am persuaded that if any extreme is to be preferred, a leaning to the evangelical will have the best effect. The sun must be above the horizon. No other sort of sermons do me good.

I consider evangelical preaching to be the connecting of every subject with the great points of truth. The nostrum of every man, who drags in his favourite topic on every point, is not to be regarded.

I knew a man who brought in the five points on every subject. He had but two subjects—Baptism and the five points.

Now, covetousness, for instance, would be so essayed upon, that he would appear not even like a spiritual Jew, much less like a man who lives after the religion of Jesus Christ. " There has been no Gospel ordinance for me to-day," one might feel.

1. A man must endeavour to cultivate an evangelical mind. If not labouring to live by the faith of the Son of God, he won't mix these things with savour; he must force it in, but then it loses its virtue.

2. Cultivate also a practical, holy habit. Two men may treat the same subject with equal weight, yet there may be a vast difference in the holy savour.

3. Though all points have a certain proportion, yet there is one thing which God means to lift up and glorify.

4. Care not to overstep the modesty of nature. I dislike the expression, " Bringing it in head and shoulders." It need not be so : it ought not to be so. Blunder not on texts. With all the teaching of the Spirit that was promised, yet Timothy was *to give himself wholly to these things*.

JUNE 7, 1802.

WHAT FOUNDATION IS THERE IN SCRIPTURE FOR THE DOCTRINE OF THE MILLENNIUM; OF WHAT NATURE WILL THE MILLENNIUM BE; AND TO WHAT USE MAY THE DOCTRINE BE APPLIED ?—Proposed by the Rev. J. Venn.

The Rev. J. Venn—

It is clear in Scripture that there is to be a long period of peace and glory in the Church, such as has never yet been known.

The Rev. T. Scott—

I could not say much of the foundation of the Scripture doctrine of the Millennium, unless we are first agreed upon its nature. There are differences of opinion upon its reality; and these arise generally from representations of its nature.

There will be, I think, no visible appearance of Christ, but a peculiar outpouring of the Spirit. By the resurrection of the souls of the Martyrs, I suppose men coming in the spirit and power of the Martyrs.

A Millennium is the grand subject of prophecy of the latter ages of the world, almost as much as Christ was of the middle ages. Almost 4000 years the world was left to see what it could do without a general revelation. It is now left to see what it can do with a revelation, without much of the Spirit.

Icy fetters at present bind up the earth. It wants but the Holy Spirit to make men feel sin, and to take of Christ and glorify him, to make men *beat their swords into plowshares and their spears into pruning-hooks*. Have the large promises of the Old Testament ever yet been fulfilled ?

More will in the end be saved than will perish.   Diseases, wars, passions, will all be subdued.

In the New Testament, the Apocalypse is a prophetic history of the Church.

As to the practical uses of a belief in the Millennium, we should do as Daniel did, who set himself to seek the Lord ; and as David, who, though he was not to build the temple, yet collected materials.   Our preaching and writing may be some of the little stones used in this building.   A man with a family should think that his descendants will live therein, though not himself.   A man who plants an acorn expects not to enjoy the tree, but leaves it to posterity.

The Rev. C. Simeon, a visitor—

Some Scriptures intimate the *universality* of the change.   *In that day, they shall be all righteous.   Holiness shall be written upon the bells of the horses.*

The Rev. J. Clayton—

It will not be so universal as to exclude evil men from the world, though it will be very extensive.

The Jews, in their dispersion, knowing the languages of the respective countries where they are, and maintained, so separated in their dispersion, when converted, may become preachers of the Gospel, and lead to a repetition of the Pentecostal miracle.   Then that text may be fulfilled—*In those days it shall come to pass, that ten men shall take hold out of all languages of the nations, even shall take hold of the skirt of him that is a Jew, saying, We will go with you, for we have heard that God is with you* (Zech. viii. 23).

Its use.   It gives encouragement in the Church and the family.   It is a comfort to me and my wife, that we are training up children who will bring on the Millennium.   Then will begin the great Sabbatical year.   Date the Papacy from 666 [this is probably a mistake in the MS. for 606], and then we have data to proceed on from that period.

The Rev. H. Foster—

I have considered the Jews as kept distinct for a punishment in rejecting Christ.

Mr C.'s statement is new, probable, and pleasant.

The Rev. R. Cecil—

Difficulties, as Scott observed, have arisen from exaggerations on the subject.   The Scripture representations of the Millennium are a reasonable and expected thing.

Christ is not honoured in the world yet, in a manner worthy of him and his undertaking.   But is the thing to be left here ?   No !   God will honour His Son !   Why does not the Gospel travel over the world ?   Indisposition to it.   A book detailing a new *pleasure* would speedily find its way through all languages.

If a man be surrounded by a repulsive spirit in his parish, he is apt to withdraw in discouragement.   But if he consider, that he is sowing seed which shall spring up in blessed fruits hereafter, he cheerfully perseveres. This is a practical, animating idea.

JUNE 21, 1802.

WHAT IS THE BEST METHOD OF FORTIFYING THE MINDS OF YOUTH IN SCHOOLS AGAINST INFIDELITY?—Proposed by the Rev. B. Woodd.

The Rev. B. Woodd—

I recommend Scott's Essays, particularly the first.

The Rev. W. Goode—

Doddridge's three Sermons are excellent.

The Rev. S. Crowther—

It is a mistake to put controversial books into the hands of young persons.

Tell children the lives, and spirit, and death of infidels. Point out the deficiency of their standard of morals.

Get at the minds and habits of their parents. Endeavour to bring them to evangelical preaching.

Stackhouse's "Body of Divinity" is a dangerous book, as the objections are stated with more strength than the replies.

The Rev. H. Foster—

Some good extracts may be gathered from Pascal's "Provincial Letters." He shews the importance of the business, and states arguments which are of great weight with my mind.

That part of Scott's Essays which relates to the divinity of the Scriptures is of great use.

Doddridge's plan with his pupils was of sad effect.

Catechise children on the truth of Christianity.

The Rev. R. Cecil—

I never picked up from infidel writers, when a professed infidel myself, any solid objections, which were not brought to mind by a child of my own of four years old. This proves to me that it is the growth of fallen nature, and that Satan works this way as in all others.

Why was sin allowed?—How insignificant a world is this for redemption!—How few are saved!—these are all the innocent questions of a child, as well as the dark insinuations of the unbelieving man.

The nurse of infidelity is sensuality. By this youth are decoyed. The Bible stands in their way. *The lust of the flesh, and the lust of the eyes, and the pride of life, is not of the Father, but is of the world.* But the young mind loves them. It hates the Bible, therefore, which condemns them. "If any, then, will bring me arguments," such a mind says, "I'll thank them. If not, I'll invent them."

As to the infidel's arguments, there is nothing in them; they are all *jéjune.* Infidels are not convinced by themselves.

In combating these things, we must remember the old proverb, that a man may bring his horse to the water, but can't make him drink. The mind is pre-occupied, and won't listen.

Yet a crisis comes. All this goes on to a certain time. Then they will stop and bethink themselves.

1. One method is, appealing to facts. What sort of men are these infidels? and what their understandings? They are for the most part loose, fierce, overbearing men. Nothing like sober, serious inquirers. They are the grossest fanatics on earth. Have they agreed on their own scheme?

2. Another method is, to dwell on the need and necessities of men. What will these infidel schemes do for you in death? Every pain tells man he needs a helper, but infidelity provides him none.

3. Point them to the character of true believers.

4. Appeal to their conscience. Why is it that you listen to infidelity? Is it not a low, carnal, wicked game? Is it not the picture of the prodigal? *Father, give me the portion of goods that falleth to me.* The question, Why is infidelity received? exposes and shews it to the light. *Why* will a man be an infidel? They bring difficulties. But tell them that inexplicable difficulties surround us all. They are forced to believe, whether they will or not, in ninety-nine cases out of a hundred, in the ordinary concerns of life. Then, if forced from necessity to be a believer in ninety-nine cases, won't you be a believer in the hundredth from choice?

5. Impress them with a sense of ignorance. I silence myself many times a day by a sense of my own ignorance. Arguments addressed to the heart press stronger than those addressed to the head. When a child, and a very wicked one, too, one of Dr Watts' hymns set me crying in a corner. The lives in " Janeway's Token "—the triumph of faith in suffering believers—the conduct of Samuel—come home when perhaps least expected.

The daily use of diurnal facts is important. For example, the death of the Duke of Bedford.

Draw out a map of the road of infidelity. It will lead to such stages at length as man never suspected. One thing is of more weight than all these put together, and that is, the spirit and tone of the house where they live. This fastens a conviction on their mind, though become ever so wicked. This was true in my own case : I felt—" My father's right, and I am wrong." *Let me die the death of the righteous, and let my last end be like his,* is not seldom in an infidel's mind. The bye-conversations in a family are of unspeakable importance.

The Rev. J. Davies—

Encourage in children industry and humility. Inculcate early habits of reverence for Scripture.

The Rev. J. Clayton—

All are born in sin, and dislike all rule. The times give a particular direction to this disposition. So in the present time. Children early imbibe influence.

1. Keep corrupted children out of schools. It is astonishing how much is done with children in a short time. I have seen an effect on my own children from half-an-hour's conversation, which has put my

own character upon a sort of balance, whenever the parents are not wrong.

2. Convince children that all disposition to enter into what leads them to err is a symptom of fallen nature. Do the objections you state come from the principle you feel when most serious, when a friend is dead, when you have heard an awakening sermon ? No! therefore they are all fruits of our fallen nature.

3. Children will listen to the advantages of religion. The tranquillity of soul : the Bible-plan being a plan of blessedness.

4. Bible maxims produce right dispositions towards all relations.

5. Let these things have the uppermost place in the family.

6. Send youths to meet God alone in the closet.

The Rev. J. Newton—

Explain " Bunyan's Pilgrim's Progress." Get hold on conscience. Send youths such books as " Baxter's Call," and " Alleine's Alarm."

The next evening, July 5, 1802, the writer of the Notes was absent.

JULY 19, 1802.

WHAT CAN BE SAID RESPECTING THE SALVATION OF INFANTS, AND VIRTUOUS HEATHEN ?—Proposed by the Rev. J. Pratt.

Mr Pratt—

Arguments for the salvation of INFANTS.

1. Sinners are always represented in Scripture as condemned for actual transgression. (2 Cor. v. 10 ; John v. 28, 29 ; Rev. xx. 12, 13.) *Small and great*, in the last passage, refers to station, &c. Compare with xi. 18, where the same terms are used of intelligent agents. But infants have committed no personal sin.

2. Infants are not capable of remorse and anguish of conscience. There is reason to believe that future punishment will consist chiefly in this.   This is most likely *the worm that never dies, and the fire which never shall be quenched.*   But as infants commit no actual sin, so there is no consciousness of it : nor can it be conveyed to them by any imputed guilt from Adam.

3. Infants are not capable of a sense of divine dereliction. For it might be said, that though not capable of remorse, yet they might have a sense of the loss of the divine favour.   But as they have acquired in a state of probation no ideas of a God, a creature, a law, obedience and disobedience, sin and duty, the favour and the anger of God, they could not acquire these but by the immediate impression of God upon their minds, and it is not to be imagined that God would give them these ideas purposely to punish them.

4. Many draw an argument from part of Romans v. This passage represents Christ as removing and cancelling the effects of Adam's sin.

With regard to HEATHENS :—Faith in Christ is universally required to salvation—say some. But it is answered, that this regards such only as hear the Gospel.   The truth seems to be, that none of the heathen will be condemned for not believing the Gospel ; but they are liable to condemnation for the breach of that law which they have.

Yet if in any there be a prevailing love to God, and a care in the practice of virtue, they may be accepted through Christ.   Particularly if we consider that many of the ancient Jews, and even the Apostles of Christ, before the Ascension, knew but little of those truths generally thought fundamental.   Compare Rom. ii. 10 and 26 ; Acts x. 34, 35 ; Matt. viii. 11, 12 ; 1 John ii. 2 ; John i. 29.

The Rev. T. Scott—

I. As to HEATHEN :—No heathen will be saved as a heathen.   This would damp our ardour in saving them.   It is not uncharitable to believe this, but charitable.   Little is said in Scripture concerning the heathen.   Four things determine my mind against the salvation of heathen as such—

1. *They who sin without law, perish without law.*   Every man knows more than he practises.   No doubt, great indeed will be the difference in the state of heathen in the next world from that of the unbelieving Christian.

2. *When they knew God, they glorified him not as God.*   The Bible says these are *without excuse.*   Rom. i. 20.

3. *Without Christ, without hope, without God.*

4. *Except a man be born again, he cannot see the kingdom of heaven.*   I will not say they are not saved because they have not explicit faith in Christ, but because they have no marks of a regenerate nature. " Heaven is a prepared place for a prepared people."

II. As to INFANTS :—The case is quite different with children. There is no doubt of the salvation of the children of believers.   Persons who doubt of their own salvation, will doubt, perhaps, of their children's salvation.   But doubts, in such, of their own salvation arise either from unbelief or low walking.   Perhaps it is a privilege attached to faithful walking, which others are deprived of, that they are confident of the salvation of their children.   Besides, our part is to submit to the divine sovereignty with respect to the state of dead relations.

We are not upon so firm ground with respect to the salvation of other children.   But there is much in Scripture that favours the idea. *Of such is the kingdom of heaven,* carries much weight.   When I think that two-thirds of the human race are infants, there is a great relief to my mind in this.   This text cannot mean merely that of such as are *similar* to children : this would be expressed in other language.

There is something in analogy.   If they partake of Adam's punishment without actual sin, why not of the Second Adam's merit without it ?   There is not the objection to their salvation which there is against that of the heathen.   No infants will be saved but as regenerated. But infants offer no opposition to it.

Some say we must be first accepted in our persons, before our prayers can be accepted ; but I would say—WHATEVER COMES FROM THE SPIRIT OF CHRIST WILL BE ACCEPTED THROUGH CHRIST.

My idea, then, is, that all who have not actual sin, will be partakers of regenerating grace.

Christians, in general, mistake in one point. They do not think children so early capable of repentance and obedience as they really are—they think that at three or four years old they are not; but I think that as soon as they know what a lie is, they are capable of these graces of the Spirit.

We may be satisfied if we prayed for our infants who are gone. But most pain about young children arises from the idea and fear that we have not done all for them which might have been done.

The Rev. J. Newton—

We can't keep this question out of our minds. We ought to do so, for we have nothing to do with it. *Shall mortal man be more just than God?*

I believe that God's election extends to all children.

If any heathen can be brought who sees the vanity of the world, &c., and says from his heart, " Ens Entium miserere me !" I believe he would be heard. But I never found one such, though I have known many heathen.

The Rev. B. Woodd—

The moral attributes of the Deity seem to contradict the idea of the salvation of all infants. Yet there are other things which appear to be reconciled with these attributes with so much difficulty, that perhaps this ground is not tenable. *I shall go to him, but he shall not return to me.—In Ramah was there a voice heard, lamentation and weeping, and great mourning, Rachel weeping for her children, and would not be comforted because they are not.—As by the offence of one judgment came upon all men to condemnation, even so by the righteousness of one the free gift came upon all men unto justification of life.*

As infants are included in the effects of Adam's sin without actual concurrence of their own, why should they not be included in the salvation of Christ without actual concurrence ?

As to heathen :—They are amenable to the light they have. I have taken hope from this circumstance, that wherever the Gospel comes, it may in this knowledge find some people in a prepared state.

The Rev. S. Crowther—

All is gathered by analogy and inference. There is little sure ground. Charity and hope should lead us. It is not contrary to Scripture to suppose infants to be in grace.

It is more clear with regard to heathen. There is much direct to the point of their being lost. A contrary opinion would relax our efforts, and make us undervalue our own privileges.

The Rev. W. J. Abdy—

Resolve the whole into the holy and wise will of God. I should suppose children of believing and unbelieving parents to be on the same ground. I suppose all infants saved. I argue from analogy, as Scott and Woodd have done. *In heaven their angels do always behold the face of my Father.*

As to heathen :—Though we cannot say, perhaps absolutely, that all heathen are condemned, we certainly cannot say absolutely that one is saved.

The Rev. W. Goode—

I have no doubt of the salvation of all infants. That passage is to be understood literally, *Of such is the kingdom of heaven.* The fact must be true, or no allusion can be drawn from it. *A multitude that no man could number,* is not to be understood of all that we suppose saved who come to years of discretion. The great majority of mankind are not saved unless infants are ; and if not this majority, the strong expressions of Scripture are not to be understood. Some argument may be drawn from Christ's becoming a child. Children may be considered as the first martyrs of Christ, and we cannot suppose these 2000 sent to hell. David's case is conclusive as to the children of believers. The close of the second commandment implies that the covenant may extend beyond the immediate descendants.

As to heathen :—Scripture never speaks of the condition of infants, but does of heathen.

On the 27th September 1802, there was a general conversation.

OCTOBER 11, 1802.

HOW SHALL WE DISTINGUISH BETWEEN UNBELIEVING FEARS AND THOSE DOUBTS CONCERNING OUR STATE WHICH ARE SALUTARY AND SCRIPTURAL ? —Proposed by the Rev. J. Goode.

The Rev. J. Goode—

This question arose in my mind from a passage in Jay.

The Rev. H. Foster—

Perplexities increase on a serious man in proportion to his seriousness, till he sees the Gospel as a constitution of grace.

An increasing view of this object, and an increasing application to this, generates what is called assurance.

When a believer has been coming to this object for thirty or forty years, he cannot well doubt that he has come.

The Rev. J. Pratt—

I. Unbelieving fears are these—1. Fear of the adequacy of the provisions of the Gospel. 2. Fear of the truth and faithfulness of God.

II. Salutary fears are, as Jay points out, such as flow from—1. The greatness of the affair. 2. The deceitfulness of the heart. 3. The shipwreck of others. What fairly arises out of these are salutary fears ; what not fairly, arise chiefly from constitution.

The Rev. T. Scott—

The question implies that there *are* Scriptural and salutary fears and doubts. Many speak as though all fear was un-Scriptural. Yet there is much in Scripture on this subject. Some have endeavoured to establish a distinction between the assurance of faith, and the assurance of hope. It is sin in any case to doubt the testimony of God, or the promise of God.

Ill-grounded confidence is great unbelief. For example, God says, the malicious shall not enter into heaven, yet men live in malice, and expect to go there!

But there is another description of persons very different indeed. Every one sees their sincerity but themselves. They labour under a confusedness of judgment rather than unbelief. They confound what *is to be aimed at* with what is *attainable*.

A partial conscience occasions fears. A torpid conscience on some points grieves the Spirit. Fears that are Scriptural and salutary have a salutary *effect*. If fear lead a man to abuse the free grace of the Gospel, it is not Scriptural; if it lead to humility, it is Scriptural. It is well that a man fairly meet the question. Dwell on the lower evidences—*hungering and thirsting after righteousness*, &c.

OCTOBER 25, 1802.

WHAT IS THE SCRIPTURAL IDEA OF THE TERM "MYSTERY?"—Proposed by the Rev. H. Foster.

The Rev. H. Foster—

The mysteries of Revelation are the great truths which God has set before us for our faith. The *modus* is not the object of faith.

Mysteries are what can only be understood by revelation, and can be understood only so far as revealed. It is commonly said, that mysteries are not to be understood.

I think we understand the mystery so far as revealed. [He here quoted several passages, to prove that mystery in the Scriptural sense is what may be *understood*.]

The Rev. J. Pratt—

1. Mystery denotes, in general, somewhat hidden, or not fully manifest, *e. g.*, 2 Thess. ii. 7. *The* MYSTERY *of iniquity doth already work.* It began to work in secret, and was not then completely disclosed.

2. Some sacred thing hidden or secret, which is naturally unknown to human reason, is only known by the revelation of God, nor then always comprehended fully; intelligible as facts, though not as to the mode.

For example, 1 Tim. iii. 16—*Great is the* MYSTERY *of godliness; God was manifest in the flesh, justified in the Spirit, seen of angels, preached unto the Gentiles, believed on in the world, received up into glory.* The mystery of the Gospel consisted in the several particulars here enumerated by the Apostle, particulars which it would never have entered into the heart of man to conceive, had not God accomplished them in fact, and published them by the preaching of his Gospel; but which being thus *manifested*, are intelligible as facts to the meanest understanding. Rom. xi. 25—*I would not, brethren, that ye should be ignorant of this*

MYSTERY . . . . *that blindness in part is happened unto Israel, until the fulness of the Gentiles be come in.* Eph. v. 32—*This is a great* MYSTERY, *but I speak concerning Christ and the Church.* 1 Cor. xv. 51—*Behold, I shew you a* MYSTERY. *We shall not all sleep, but we shall all be changed.* 1 Cor. xiii. 2—*Though I understand all* MYSTERIES . . . . *and have not charity, I am nothing.* 1 Tim. iii. 9—*Holding the* MYSTERY *of the faith in a pure conscience.* In all these places it means what was hidden or unknown till revealed, but then intelligible as facts.

1 Cor. xiv. 2.—Of him who spoke in an unknown tongue, it is said, *in the spirit he speaketh* MYSTERIES. But though these mysteries were unintelligible to others on account of the *language* in which they were spoken, yet were they understood by himself, for he is said (v. 4) to edify himself thereby.

1 Cor. ii. 7, 8.—The Apostle says, *We speak the wisdom of God in a* MYSTERY, *even the hidden wisdom which God ordained before the world ; . . . . . which none of the princes of this world knew.* He says, "we speak" or declare this wisdom : and he observes, that God had "revealed" the particulars whereof it consisted to them by his Spirit. This passage is a clear and full account of the word in this second sense of it.

1 Cor. iv. 1.—*Stewards of the* MYSTERIES *of God,* cannot refer to what was unknown to the Apostles, because to them it was given *to know the* MYSTERIES *of the kingdom of God.* (Matt. xiii. 11); and the very character of stewards implies they were to dispense these mysteries or make them known to others. In Col. ii. 2, St Paul mentions his praying for his converts, that *their hearts might be comforted to . . . . . the acknowledgment of the* MYSTERY *of God and of the Father and of Christ.* Of this mystery they must have that knowledge at least which is included in what our Lord says, John xvii. 3, *That they might know thee the only true God, and Jesus Christ, whom thou hast sent.*

Rev. x. 7—*The* MYSTERY *of God should be finished.* Now whatever this may mean, yet it was something which he "declared to his servants the Prophets."

3. The term mystery is applied by St Paul in a peculiar sense to the calling of the Gentiles.—(Rom. xvi. 25. Eph. i. 9 ; iii. 3, 4, 9 ; vi. 19. Col. i. 26, 27 ; iv. 3.) This MYSTERY he speaks of as hid before, but now made known.

4. Mystery denotes a spiritual truth couched under an external representation or similitude, and concealed or hidden thereby unless some explanation be given. Rev. i. 20—*The* MYSTERY, *that is, the spiritual meaning of the seven stars. . . . . The seven stars are the angels of the seven Churches.* Rev. xvii. 5—*And upon her forehead was a name written,* MYSTERY, *Babylon the Great: i.e.,* Babylon in a spiritual sense. Rev. xvii. 7—*I will tell thee the* MYSTERY, *or spiritual signification, of the woman.* In several places in *Theodotian's* Greek translation of Daniel, and in the Apocrypha, this word is used for a thing secret, but not unintelligible.

It appears, then, to be a great though a common mistake, to suppose this word means *something absolutely unintelligible and incomprehensible.*

So un-Scriptural is this sense, that in every passage where it is used, it is mentioned as something which is *revealed, declared, shewn, spoken,* or which *may be known* or *understood.* See *Parkhurst, in verbum.*

The Rev. T. Scott—

The veil must be taken from the *heart,* as well as from the *book.* A man will not understand divine truths, unless the Spirit open his mind.

In other things we know things to exist, connected even with which there is something inexplicable ; for example, God's existence. I would not call this unintelligible, but *I* am a child and understand not, because I am a child, while superior beings may fully comprehend.

Mind moving matter : Mysteries of Trade and Science are also illustrations of this. In these, however, the more a man knows, the less he wonders. Not so in the works of God : the more His works are examined, the more they are wondered at. Just so (in the Scripture sense of mystery) of the Resurrection. It is utterly incomprehensible to man as to its manner. Again, the Providence of God affords an illustration.

Many think the Calvinistic creed particularly clogged with difficulties. But they equally press upon a Socinian's creed. The grand difficulty is the origin of evil. Here we go on this ground. We *know* by experience that these things are, but there are difficulties connected with them which we do not understand, and here I say I am a child.

As to Scriptural mysteries, I agree with what has been said, except that I think a part of the mystery arises from that which is not revealed ; it is no object of our faith, but yet it is a part of the mystery.

There is nothing contrary to reason in divine mysteries, though above it. Scripture mysteries are not like Transubstantiation, which *is* contrary to reason.

Things are not commonly called mystery in Scripture, unless there is something difficult and deep, and likely to raise objections—such as would not be understood unless revealed; but understood when revealed, by all diligent inquirers, by the Spirit's teaching—and that which is not intelligible remains with the humble mind as in the secrets which it inquires not into.

Distinguish between *mysteries* and *absurdities.*

The Rev. J. Newton—

The Deity is not only above our comprehension, but above that of all his creatures.

A revelation was made from the beginning in the person of Him who is *the express image of His person.* Through Him the angelic world knows God.

All the truths we can savingly understand are through divine revelation. But there is another revelation necessary, the teaching of the Spirit : *Blessed art thou, Simon Barjona; for flesh and blood hath not revealed it unto thee, but my Father which is in heaven.*

The Rev. J. Davies—

I have considered mystery as referring both to the fact and the *modus*. When a thing is revealed, it can no longer be said to be mystery as to the fact. Some things may be mystery as to the *modus*, which have no mystery as to the fact; as the existence of God.

In many places in Scripture, mystery is applied to what was once a mystery, but is so no longer.

The Rev. J. Pratt—

Scripture nowhere proposes mysteries but as the objects of faith.

NOVEMBER 8, 1802.

WHAT ARE THE SEASONS IN A CHRISTIAN'S EXPERIENCE WHICH MAY BE CONSIDERED CRITICAL?—Proposed by the Rev. H. Foster.

The Rev. H. Foster—

It is of consequence how a man who commences a profession of religion obtains peace. There is much wildness on this subject. If it be through dreams and fancies, much hindrance arises. The man is likely to be unstable, and come to ill-founded conclusions. Into what connexions he comes is of importance. If they be loose, and he be tenacious of them, it is of sad consequence.

The death of a minister is a critical season to his hearers.

Coming into the ministry is a critical season. If he has to do with persons of small talents, he is tempted to vanity : if of great talents, to despondency.

When a man comes to an alteration in his religious sentiments, he has begun in error to a certain degree : when he gets out of the mistake, there is danger lest he should think he cannot go to excess in the opposite extreme.

When persons who have had weight with us turn aside to error—this is a critical season to us.

An entrance upon new connexions is another. So also a sudden change from narrowness of circumstances to affluence.

The Rev. R. Cecil—

No man can have an adequate idea of the effect that a *change of circumstances* has upon the mind. When five shillings come into the pocket of a poor man, it goes out, and another comes in, and all goes on right; but when principal and interest come in together, he is altogether thrown out.

In a rise of circumstances, too, the man becomes a " wiser " man, a " greater " man, and pride stands in his way.

And so *poverty* has its trials. Christian stumbled in going down the hill.

Marriage is a critical season. My brother F. " being high priest that same year, he prophesied;" but like the high priest he did not enter into some important circumstances. If my wife be delicate; if this, and if that.   Consider, too, the different circumstances marriage brings a man into as to his family.   Avoid the first error of entering into imprudent connexions.   Men tempt the devil to tempt them.

Coming under a particular ministry is sometimes a critical season.

There are special temptations and trials.   Joseph, and David, and Peter afford examples.

I cannot look through my past life without trembling : a change of circumstances, I have seen, is attended with such consequences. We should use particular prayer against sudden attacks.

Nothing is so repelling to the bringing up a son to the ministry as the danger he is thereby placed in.   One of his greatest dangers is popularity.

To come under a new dispensation of pain and sickness is, I know by experience, a critical season.   There is danger of a kind of despond-ency, ill-temper, spiritual incapacity.   Prayer does not necessarily come with affliction.   Like a beast wounded, the stricken man skulks to his den and growls there.

The Rev. J. Pratt—

Those very points which are the means of trial to real Christians, are the means of destruction to hypocrites.   God will educate his children.   His children must be educated by this very means.   They *must* come; but then He'll bear them through.   *The turning away of the simple shall slay them: and the prosperity of fools shall destroy them.* Prov. i. 32.

The discovery of the holy, self-denying spirit of the Gospel—the broaching of plausible error—the failures of others—times of persecu-tion—these are critical seasons.

The Rev. Mr Simons, a visitor—

Coming to this room—going out to dinner—having a great man come to your house—acquaintance with men you love and who love you—these are critical circumstances.

The Rev. J. Clayton—

Every day brings critical circumstances.   And a circumstance is critical according to the temper of mind we are in.

A time of contention is a critical time, when discord enters our circle *offences will come;* but it requires great wisdom to manage them.

When children are to be introduced into life.   I have seen some Christians, who, through their children, seem to have had an extinguisher put upon their character.   What with extenuating the gaiety of the daughter, and the extravagance of the son, they seem themselves to have lost their principles.

Retiring from a life of activity to one of leisure, is a critical season.

When a man has fallen into sin, is another.   If rebuked, he perhaps vindicates himself, till he apologises for downright sin.   Another is broken-hearted—walks softly all his days.

The Rev. J. Newton—

I know not one hour of my life that is not critical.   If the Lord were to leave me one hour, I should fall into gross evil. I can only say, *Hold thou me up, and I shall be safe!*

I am like a child, who dares not go across Cheapside, unless some one hold his hand.

These critical times are to teach the soul. We believe, on the authority of the words, *Without me ye can do nothing:* but we know nothing of this till we practically enter into it. To humble and prove His people, has been God's design respecting them, from first to last. *These things*, says the Apostle, *I write to you, that ye sin not.* If we have been at Gethsemane and Golgotha, and seen what it cost the Redeemer to expiate sin, we should feel its guilt and danger, and live accordingly.

The Rev. Mr Mayor, a visitor—

These critical times are intended to draw out what is in us; *e. g.*, Job. When children are untoward—this is a critical time.

The Rev. B. Woodd—

Forming a new acquaintance—when a young man goes to the University—when a minister changes one sphere for another—these are critical seasons.

The Rev. W. J. Abdy—

When a minister is brought out into public life, he is in danger. The loss of a parent—this is a critical event.

NOVEMBER 22, 1802.

WILL NATURAL CONSTITUTION IN ANY DEGREE EXTENUATE GUILT ?— Proposed by the Rev. B. Woodd.

Mr Woodd—

There is variety of disposition in the human character. The cause is physical in most cases. A child is stubborn, or tractable, or humble, often from education, from society, from disorders, from affliction.

This difference in the natural character makes a difference in the spiritual. This is seen in St Peter and St John ; also in St Paul and St Barnabas. So, too, in Luther and Calvin.

Two questions arise—1. What allowance ought WE to make for one another in this view ? As to bearing and forbearing, great allowance should be made. As to our judgment of others also.

2. What allowance is it probable that GOD will make on this account ? *As a father pitieth his children, so the Lord pitieth them that fear him; for he knoweth our frame, he remembereth that we are dust.*

There is danger in applying this to ourselves ; but no danger in severity towards ourselves. As to others, provided we tolerate not sin, we cannot be too lenient.

The Rev. Mr Mayor, a visitor—

It is sin that is condemned in a man. This sin will break out at the weakest part. Eminent Scripture characters failed most in that grace

in which they most excelled : as Job, Peter, &c.   Perhaps because men
watch most closely against their besetting sins, and sin less in that
respect than in any other way.

Natural constitution seems only the discovery of guilt, and therefore
not an extenuation.   This is the weak part through which sin breaks
out.

The Rev. W. Goode—

The question turns much on what is meant by natural constitution.
I suppose Brother Woodd means innocent nature, such as might have
existed in uncorrupted man.   It is variety of constitution which leads
to variety of temptation.   If we allow that there are different degrees
of guilt, though the natural constitution do not take away the guilt,
yet we may allow that it extenuates.

The Rev. S. Crowther—

This question calls for great caution.   It is one which I should
never broach in public.   Kindness towards others should lead us to
judge of them as favourably as possible.

The Rev. J. Goode—

This is a dangerous question for a man to ask concerning himself.
As to others, *if a man be overtaken in a fault, ye which are spiritual restore
such an one in the spirit of meekness, considering thyself lest thou also be
tempted.*

The Rev. R. Cecil—

By natural constitution, I mean corporeal organisation.   By extenuation, I mean some allowance, so that a man does not stand equally
chargeable with guilt, as one of a natural constitution ; for as to sins
before God, they are equally breaches of his law.

Consider two characters of different propensities committing the
same crime.

I have no question as to our treating others.

I would never broach this subject in public.   There is nothing in
Scripture about *corporeal organisation*.   The best account of insanity is
to be found in "Rasselas."

Paley is an unsound casuist respecting the extenuation of drunkenness.   Multiply the crime of getting drunk into the consequences, and
you have the sum-total of a drunken man's guilt.

The Rev. J. Pratt—

This is a question of comparison between the different sins of the
same man, or between his sins and those of another.

Natural constitution is an incentive and a strong temptation.•   God
will view man as tempted or not.   A sin without temptation is malignant *per se ;* a sin committed under strong temptation is comparatively
less guilty.

Scripture gives no countenance to this subject.   Why ?   Because
the helps offered are sufficient, and man's heart is deceitful.   Scripture
penitents plead no self-extenuation : see David, Psalm li.

There is a difference between natural constitution and invincible difficulties.

Scripture abounds in injunctions as to others.

We are in danger of a want of caution of the evil effects of entertaining such questions.

The Rev. T. Scott—

That text, *The spirit truly is willing, but the flesh is weak*, is not an extenuation, but a warning.

We must allow for others more than ourselves—not because their case is different, but because *there may be circumstances* in them which exist not in ourselves.

We might administer the same comfort in *despair* to ourselves as to others, were it not for the deceitfulness of the heart.

The Rev. J. Clayton—

Antinomianism is flowing into the Church through the plea of extenuation.

As to others—take care of making allowance for relations and those whom it is our duty to counsel.

The Rev. H. Foster—

God's Word does not notice this subject. Therefore we ought not. It provides remedies, but it says nothing of difference of constitution.

I should view natural constitution as aggravating sin, rather than extenuating it. I question whether any temptation can extenuate guilt.

December 6, 1802.

WHEREIN LIES THE SPECIFIC DIFFERENCE BETWEEN AN ANTINOMIAN AND A REAL CHRISTIAN ?—Proposed by the Rev. B. Woodd.

The Rev. Mr Mayor, a visitor—

The difference lies chiefly in *views*.

The Rev. S. Crowther—

There is as great a difference in their *practice* as their *views*. A real Christian has all an Antinomian has, but an Antinomian only a part of what the Christian has. There is a specific difference, as it concerns HIMSELF. Religion is a mere science with the Antinomian : it has nothing to the glory of God. He places an unwarranted trust in God. There is also a specific difference as it concerns OTHERS.

The Rev. W. J. Abdy—

A distinction should be made between practical Antinomianism and men who hold tenets of an Antinomian cast. Some men's practice is better than their system. Some men's hearts better than their heads.

The Antinomian here meant is a lover of sin. There is a difference in views, and in the temper of their hearts towards God, their neighbour, and themselves. The Antinomian's wickedness is discernible in his ideas of God's power. He connects no ideas of holiness, wisdom, and truth, and mercy with power.

The grand specific difference between the Antinomian and Christian, is the doctrine of *Regeneration*.

The Rev. H. Foster—

Consider that there *will be* Antinomians. Bad men will come to hear, and they will turn out Antinomians. If I think I can so preach as to turn them, I mistake. There are bad men of all sorts under the New Testament. We must take all pains so that there be nothing to lay to our charge.

Experience begins often in the fear of hell. The possibility of salvation strikes with new feelings. Humble reverential delight in seeing Christ is the result. Now I suppose many people have views of hell, which excite fear. A turning-point comes ; not being *regenerated*—for that is the turning-point—a lust gets hold of them, they fear hell ; they hear of the Antinomian system, they get hold of it. In turning-points, the regenerated man will shew he is so, and the unregenerate that he is not regenerate.

The specific difference is this, the Christian sees in the Gospel a system which glorifies God, but the Antinomian one which is to save him from hell.

We must take care that we keep not the truth from our people. In order to keep men from Antinomianism, preach the Gospel in its fulness and freedom. Press the truth into their tempers and life ; and this is the way to bring out the difference between the two characters.

The Rev. R. Cecil—

The matter turns on this point—The Holy Spirit makes one man alive, and he uses the doctrines of the Gospel to holy purposes ; another man is dead, and he uses the Gospel to unholy purposes. The question is, therefore, between an *opiniated* and a *true* hearer. Huntington himself says, " Christ crucified in a broken heart is the Gospel." Now this is true indeed. Something one gathers from experience. I hardly know any sin on earth into which circumstances are not able to enter. *My heart sheweth me the wickedness of the ungodly.* (Ps. xxxvi. 1., Prayer Book.) I have felt myself getting down into a carnal frame. And then I reason—" Well! but I preach the Gospel." But I have felt disposed to preach but one part of the Gospel at that time. I could preach that part easily ; but not so every part. If I can get such views as will consist with my passions, how natural is it that corrupt nature should fall into them ! Hell cannot fashion a deeper scheme. 'Tis being saved, and yet remaining a sinner. 'Tis belonging to the kingdom of heaven, and yet a citizen of the kingdom of hell !

Distinguish between men who are Antinomians and those who are microscopic men. Their field of view is small. They see nothing but that. Like a quack with his panacea. Distinguish, therefore, between Rayleigh and Crisp.* No doubt Crisp meant to promote

---

* Tobias Crisp was a Puritan writer of considerable eminence, born in 1600. His preaching was accused of leaning to Antinomianism, and involved him with many of his brethren in a controversy. He was baited, says his biographer, by fifty-two opponents,

holiness. I myself have felt exhilaration in particular states, after reading a sermon of Crisp's. But he was a microscopic man.

Antinomianism errs rather in defect as a system. What can an Antinomian say which we cannot? Like a piece of music, he stops short : the parts taken separately are fine, but there is a want of congruity. The effect which generally follows brings out the evil of this thing.

The Antinomian is heady, blustering, sinking other people—*great swelling words of vanity, &c.* The Antinomian does not love a great part of the Scriptures. He gets rid of the spirit of them. I know no worse symptom in a man, than to be shy of one part of the Scriptures. The Christian loves the very part that condemns him, and humbles himself under the word which lays him low.

In first setting out in the ministry, I was taken in through my ignorance. I was sent for to people who represented themselves to me as in distress. I administered the full grace of the Gospel, and determined that they should have peace ; but found that I had been administering wrong medicine. They needed strong cathartics. They wished to be comforted by evangelical arguments in the love of some sin.

Antinomianism is contradictory to the mystics, *e. g.*, Law.† His system is—that you are to be wrought up to a pitch of self-annihilation. The cross of Christ is all within him. Now, the Antinomian seeing this, says, " Christ came with blood ;" no, says the other, " with water." But Christ came with " water and blood."

Do not obscure the Gospel. For this rivets the Antinomian in his notion. He says, " I at least have a part of the truth."

The Rev. J. Pratt—

There are several sorts of Antinomians.

1. Perfectionists. 2. Holders of a remedial law. 3. Men who make Christ the minister of sin. The difference is in the state of the heart—regenerate or unregenerate. [He here made some reference to the Cheshunt Academy.] There is more in the feelings and state than in views.

---

in a grand dispute concerning the freeness of the grace of God in Jesus Christ. He appears not to have published anything in his lifetime ; but, after his death, three quarto volumes of his sermons were printed by his son, under the title of " Christ Alone Exalted," containing in all forty-two sermons. These led to further discussion. " The truth appears to have been, that Crisp was extremely unguarded in many of his expressions, but was as far as the fiercest of his antagonists from intending to support any doctrine that tended to licentiousness."—See *Chalmers's Biographical Dictionary.*

† Edmund Law, Bishop of Carlisle, born in 1703. During his residence, as Fellow of Christ's College, Cambridge, he became known to the public by a translation of Archbishop King's " Essay upon the Origin of Evil," with copious notes, in which many metaphysical subjects, curious and interesting in their own nature, are treated of with great ingenuity, learning, and novelty. Among other works, he published *Considerations on the Theory of Religion.* The life of Dr Law was a life of incessant reading and thought, almost entirely directed to metaphysical and religious inquiries ; but the tenet by which his name and writings are principally distinguished is, " that Jesus Christ, at his second coming, will, by an act of his power, restore to life and consciousness the dead of the human species ; who, by their own nature, and without this interposition, would remain in a state of insensibility to which the death brought upon mankind by the sin of Adam had reduced them."—See *Chalmers's Biographical Dictionary.*

K

The Rev. Mr Simons, a visitor—

The Gospel produces in unsanctified minds depths of guilt and sin : in sanctified minds, heights of holiness.

The Rev. J. Clayton—

Heads of difference.

1. Doctrinal. The Antinomian denies all subjective work. The Christian has already repented, prayed, trusted, &c. All is now turned to the *objective* work of Christ.

2. Experience. This is a carnal heart indulging itself in speculative views of Scripture, but with the will unsanctified. His spirit and practice are not that of the Bible. Follow him into the undress of life. you'll find him entangled in his notions.

December 20, 1802.

How does the Gospel Establish the Law?—Proposed by the Rev. J. Goode.

The Rev. J. Goode—

The Moral Law is established by the Gospel in all its authority and requisitions. It is established in the mediatorial undertaking of Jesus Christ. He has "magnified the law" and made it honourable :—its precepts in his life ; its penalties in his sufferings.

The Rev. T. Scott—

There is a sense in which the ceremonial law is established by the Gospel. Established in the view which God designed it for. It is established as a bond which is fulfilled by Jesus Christ.

But here the Moral Law is meant. Whatever requires absolute perfection in the person, or the acceptance of imperfection through the infinite perfection of Christ, establishes the Law.

The Rev. J. Davies—

The Gospel requires of those who receive it all that the Law required, and therefore establishes it. The Gospel enforces the Law more clearly than the Law did itself. See the Sermon on the Mount. The Gospel gives the strongest possible proof of the excellence of the Law. The cross of Christ is necessary for its vindication : the Gospel directs us to the only source from whence grace is to be derived, by which grace alone we can obey the Law.

The design of the ministration of the Spirit under the Gospel is the establishment of the Law. *I will put my Spirit within you, and cause you to walk in my statutes, and ye shall keep my judgments, and do them.* Ezek. xxxvi. 27. The Gospel establishes the Law as a rule of life.

The Rev. J. Clayton—

The Gospel establishes the Law in the merit of Christ, in the preceptive authority and penal sanction of the law. The Gospel establishes the Law by implanting the principles which lead to keeping the Law. The energy of Gospel motives promotes the keeping of the Law.

The life of Christ throws everything into the shade, but obedience to God.

The Rev. J. Newton—

Christ's sufferings shew the horrible nature of sin more than it could have been otherwise shewn. Sin cannot be hated for itself, till we have seen the malignity of it in Christ's sufferings.

The Rev. B. Woodd—

The Gospel harmonises with the design of the Law. Both require obedience, point out sin, the necessity of a Saviour, &c. *The law is our schoolmaster to bring us to Christ.*

The Law is God's eternal rule of moral government. The Gospel is the display of God's government of fallen creatures.

The Law in its tenor is established under the Gospel, by exhibiting Jesus Christ as bearing the curse for us, and by his obedience constituting his people righteous.

The Gospel displays the moral excellence of the Law. The Gospel punishes the guilty and protects the righteous. The Gospel requires and inspires the obedience which the Law requires as a rule. not a condition, of life.

The Rev. W. Goode—

The Gospel establishes the Law in the person and atonement of Christ — in the gift of repentance — in the gift of faith — by the renovation of the Spirit upon the heart—and as the rule of conduct to a believer.

The Rev. Mr Mayor, a visitor—

Whatever prevents men from disobeying the Law and secures obedience to it, establishes it. This is done by the Gospel.

The Rev. S. Crowther—

The Gospel establishes the Law in its extent, universality, and spirituality.

JANUARY 17, 1803.

IN WHAT SENSE IS THE SIN OF THE BELIEVER IMPUTED TO CHRIST, AND THE RIGHTEOUSNESS OF CHRIST IMPUTED TO THE BELIEVER?— Proposed by the Rev. J. Clayton.

The Rev. J. Clayton—

The sin of a believer is imputed to Christ as a substitute, a surety ; not nominally, but really. In his temporary sufferings, Christ endured all that the sinner could have endured throughout eternity. This is from the dignity of his person.

As to the imputation of Christ's righteousness to us, it depends on the nature of the imputation of Adam's sin to us. This was a real imputation of Adam's act to his posterity. Righteousness is placed to our account on believing.

The Rev. C. Simeon, a visitor—

This matter is best understood, perhaps, from the ceremonial law. Mutual light is reflected between the ceremonial law and the Gospel. The scapegoat, and Joshua the high priest, are apt illustrations.

The imputation of Christ's righteousness is rather too much wire-drawn by some—by Mr Harvey, for instance.

The Rev. B. Woodd—

The sin of Adam is imputed to his posterity ; but not so imputed as that his posterity are considered to have personally committed his sin. Christ is the restorer of the human race. By the righteousness of Christ, I understand the whole of his obedience, from his conception to his glorification. I would make no distinction between active and passive obedience. His righteousness is his submission to the law of his mediation. *This* righteousness of Christ cannot be imputed to believers.

The Rev. R. Cecil—

There are two ways of knowing these things—

1. The scientifical. Then we go to Baxter. It was charged upon me, in the beginning of my ministry, by a female, to study one of Baxter's works.* I did so, and got but one idea—that we know little of anything beyond the more obvious truths of Scripture. A proper punishment for persons who contend for excessive views, is to be obliged to digest that book. Baxter shews, indeed, that the intemperate men on either side know little how far their tenets would go. So Dr Owen no more satisfies one from his exabundant attempts to shew things too accurately. The Bible will not be treated scientifically. After all their accuracy, you will be left aground.

The Bible does not come round and ask our opinion of its contents. This is a construction I must receive, though I do not comprehend it. I must take a great deal for granted, even of what respects myself. And this is agreeable to analogy. So it is between me and my child.

2. The simple method. Take Scripture simply as it speaks in every passage ; nothing else will answer. The schoolmen can make nothing out. Then there are the Dominicans and the Jansenists—and there is the *de re*, the *de nomine*, &c. The accurate and very clear men cannot agree, and they only puzzle other people.

The Rev. J. Pratt—

The great point of difference among good men, with regard to the doctrine of imputation, is, whether it mean the imputation of sin and righteousness in *themselves* or in their *effects*.

They who hold imputation in the most rigid sense, *i. e.*, of our sin

* The name of the work we cannot decipher : the only mark is " C. Th." ·

to Christ in *itself,* and of Christ's righteousness to us in *itself,* suppose that Christ became the *same person* in a *law-sense* with all the elect; that God reckons to him the sins of the elect as though they were really his own ; and to the elect the righteousness of Christ as though the several acts of it were personally performed by them. See Crisp, Gill, &c.

They who hold the doctrine of imputation in the less rigid sense, *i. e.,* of sin and righteousness in their *effects,* suppose that believers are dealt with as righteous persons, out of regard to Christ's having, though perfectly holy, submitted to be dealt with as unrighteous, whereas they would not otherwise have been so treated.

See Doddridge, Watts, Boyse, Riccaltown, &c.

January 31, 1803.

WHAT ARE THE GROUNDS AND TENDENCY OF THE OPINION THAT CHRISTIANS MUST LOSE THEIR FIRST LOVE ?—Proposed by the Rev. J. Pratt.

Mr Pratt—

I. What is the Scripture meaning of *losing first love?* A good deal depends on ascertaining this. Some take it too high and some too low.

Some consider it the loss of those warm emotions which some believers experience on first believing. But these may decay and yet not imply the loss of first love. Others make it to mean a total departure from God. The expression is taken from the Epistle to the angel of the Church of Ephesus. (Rev. ii. 4.) By considering the whole of that Epistle, we may infer that the loss of first love is much more than the loss of first fervour, and yet much short of total departure, and, I think, of any allowed and wilful sin.

1. It is a fall : *remember from whence thou art* FALLEN.

2. It is to be repented of : *and* REPENT.

3. It implies a departure from the first spirit and efforts of a Christian : *do the* FIRST WORKS.

4. It incurs the loss of spiritual privileges : *I will* REMOVE THY CANDLESTICK OUT OF ITS PLACE.

It may be judged of by the following symptoms :—

It is a loss (1.) of the singleness and entireness that first accompanied the Christian; (2.) of the simplicity of affiance; (3.) of the especial tenderness; (4.) of the peculiar delight in ordinances; (5.) of the great tenderness toward the brethren, and (6.) of that abounding fruitfulness—which often mark the Christian's character on his heart being first won to Christ. See Gal. iv. 9–15.

II. The grounds of the opinion that Christians must lose their first love.

1. A mistake of its meaning. Christians in the enjoyment of their first love do rarely expect to lose it, as I have described it. But they take it to signify first fervour, and this they do expect to lose, and the ground of this is the state and circumstances of man in this world.

The steps, however, from one to the other, are imperceptible, for want perhaps of more clearly distinguishing them from each other.

2. Those who have lost their first love, properly so called, seek an extenuation for themselves on the same grounds—the state and circumstances of man in this world. They are willing to think it was inevitable. They flattered themselves for a long time that it was nothing but the natural decay of early fervour. But now they cannot but feel it is much worse with them, and that then *singleness* and *simplicity* of affection and faithfulness are greatly decayed. Yet they seek a reason for this in the frailty of man, and the infinite difficulties and temptations around him. And these *facts* glare before their eyes. They find every one almost with whom they converse, and whose spirit they closely observe, sunk down like themselves. And it becomes a business of mutual flattery. And so a general sentiment is propagated, and if they look at a young Christian walking in nearness with Christ, they say, or they think, " Ah, it will not be long ! "

But what should hinder it from being so ? No stinting in the Divine promises. No straitness in the Divine provisions. No unsuitableness to all possible cases in Christ's declarations. No inability, no unwillingness, no unfaithfulness on his part. Not the least countenance is given in Scripture sentiments or characters to the loss of first love. Christians are spoken of as in a state of nearness, friendship, devotedness, and absolute oneness and fellowship with their Lord.

I therefore fix the ground of this expectation of the loss of first love upon our own loss of it—and our own loss of it upon our unbelief, negligence, and unfaithfulness.

III. The tendency of this false opinion.

1. It leads to the establishment of a lower standard of the Christian life than is Scriptural. There is no one thing of which Christians are more in danger than lowering their standard. They say—" It is, and it will be, my duty to become and to continue that sort of character, though I feel it is almost impossible, and see not one man come up to it ! "

2. This renders us satisfied with low attainments. He who aims highest will shoot highest.

3. It diminishes humility. The higher the standard, the greater the deviation. And the more the deviation is seen, the deeper the humility.

4. It dishonours Christ and the Holy Spirit. John the Baptist said, *Out of his fulness have all we received, and grace for grace.* And Christ himself, *My grace is* SUFFICIENT *for thee.* It is a practical disbelief of these things which leads to the loss.

5. It relaxes vigilance.

6. It opens a door to temptation.

The Rev. J. Clayton—

What persons have called their first love is often seated merely in the passions—and this must decay. The opinion that we must lose that first love which is founded in a right view operating upon the affections, is unscriptural and pernicious.

Why do the Scriptures exhort so strongly to *grow in grace?* We should repel, therefore, the idea as a thing of course. Many persons who begin to decay in heart-religion multiply outward duties, and persuade themselves that this is the thing. Such are pernicious to all around them as well as to themselves.

The Rev. W. Goode—

We are exhorted that our *love should abound yet more and more.* We are to *forget those things which are behind and press forward.*

The grounds of this false notion are chiefly in a mistake of the nature of first love. The tendency is bad indeed.

The Rev. S. Crowther—

Vital religion is represented as progressive. Therefore the idea that we must lose our first love is wholly unscriptural. A distinction may be made—love may abate, but not be lost. I should suspect negligence in the use of means in those who complain of the loss of first love. *Be watchful, and strengthen the things that remain.*

The Rev. R. Cecil—

To say that first love, as stated in Scripture, must needs fail, is an Antinomian and wicked thing. It is as much as to say that man must go back in vital religion.

The ground of this opinion is to be traced to the Tabernacle. It is a cant term growing out of this connexion. The mere froth of first setting out and the heat and excitement over, is made a grievous sin : and a passage of Scripture is thus perverted, for they say all this is the loss of first love.

People are taken, children especially are exceedingly taken, with blossoms ; with what meets the eye. But that which comes after the flower, is what the proprietor of the orchard looks for and rejoices in. It takes *deep root downwards, and bears fruit upward.* There is, *first the blade, then the ear, then the full corn in the ear.* Injudicious people will decide upon a character who yet is grown in patience, submission, quietness, &c.

There is no question that there is such a thing as a decay in the divine life. But the tendency of the opinion that a Church must lose its divine life is abominable. The thing, properly stated, is an answer to itself. " What are the grounds and tendency of the opinion that a Church or an individual must spiritually decay?"

There is nothing plainer in Scripture than that what is worthy of being called religion—viz., the life of faith, the life of hope, and the life of love—ought to be urged upon us.

———

FEBRUARY 14, 1803.

HOW MAY WE WITH PROPRIETY IMITATE THE EXAMPLE OF ST PAUL IN BECOMING " ALL THINGS TO ALL MEN."—Proposed by the Rev. J. Pratt.

The Rev. J. Pratt—

There are three main rules to settle this accommodation.

1. The end must be holy.   2. The means lawful.   3. The manner becoming.

I. The END. This passage is not seldom made a cover for cowardice, indifference, and disaffection. The end is often selfish. To conciliate esteem—to gain some low end—to indulge a natural feeling. But the Apostle's end was to "*gain*" men for Christ. (1 Cor. ix. 19–23.) He repeats this in each verse as though he felt it important to impress it. Now, if selfish and sinister purposes are put out of the way; if our end be well purged from these, and be high and holy for the real edification of others, this will go a great way to remove difficulties upon the matter. A vast number of our casuistical difficulties arise from want of real integrity and simplicity.

II. The MEANS. It is in things *lawful* only that we can accommodate this passage. No sacrifice must be made of essential truth, nor of Scripture statements. The Apostle's own conduct is to be thus understood in the above quotation. We have the same example in Romans xiv. and xv. 1–3. It is remarkable that the Apostle immediately refers to Scripture for example and guidance on this very head. (Romans xv. 4.)

Difficulties will arise on this subject to a conscientious man, and they are perhaps best removed by examples. The Old Testament examples are not so unequivocal as the New. The standard of purity and truth is not so high. The history does not mark the divine displeasure against many sins in the way the New does. The standard in the New is very high, and held up continually. No favour is shewn to the greatest friends or the greatest character; for example, the rebuke of the sons of Zebedee and Peter. Besides, there is not so much conciliation in the Old Testament saints. Love was little understood in its extent. An exclusive and appropriating spirit in the system was the occasion of calling out a selfish spirit in the evil heart.

CHRIST is the great pattern. *He shall feed his flock like a shepherd, he shall gather the lambs with his arm, and carry them in his bosom, and shall gently lead those that are with young. A bruised reed shall he not break, nor quench the smoking flax.*—See, too, Ezekiel xxxiv. 11, &c. St Paul's example descends most to particulars. For example, his circumcising Timothy, (Acts xvi. 1–3): his shaving his head—(Acts xx. 20, &c.): his blaming Peter, (Gal. ii. 11, &c.)

III. The MANNER. This must be suited to our character, situation, and circumstances. Much of our duty lies herein. Seize times, occasions, the *mollia tempora fandi*. New wine must not be put into old bottles.

The Rev. T. Scott—

Read the context from the 8th to the end of chapter 10th of the Epistle of 1st Corinthians, and you see St Paul's spirit.

A false man would accommodate where his maintenance, his comfort, and his profit were concerned—not the truth. The more determined a man is for truth, the more yielding he is in all personal concerns, and *vice versâ*. St Paul and the Corinthians both illustrate this. In truth itself, the Apostle's example teaches us sometimes to wave a question in accommodation to others, though not to sacrifice it. A man is not to *give up* what yet at times he may *suspend*.

The Rev. J. Clayton—

The Apostle in this passage opposes a high, proud, unbending spirit. In everything in which he can consistently with his grand points, he will be all things to all men that he may gain some.

The Rev. J. Newton—

Calvinism should be diffused through our ministry as sugar is in tea ; it should be tasted everywhere, though prominent nowhere.

The Rev. J. Goode—

It is written again, *If I yet pleased men, I should not be the servant of Christ.* Gal. i. 10. St Paul sharply rebuked Peter, *I withstood him to the face, because he was to be blamed.* Gal. ii. 11. St Paul, therefore, in being "all things to all men," did not himself what he condemned in others.   His accommodation contained nothing contrary to his con- science, the moral law, or the Gospel.   It was a noble example of boldness for the truth ; of condescension to men for the Gospel's sake. There is great difference in natural dispositions ; between a bold man and a timid man.

The Rev. R. Cecil—

St Paul's spirit here shews a fine combination of zeal and love.   There are three characters.

1. A ferocious, unbending, haughty character ; which has the letter of the truth, but he gets up into the pulpit like a prize-fighter.   He is a scolding character—a Gospel reproach.   This is not the spirit of Jesus Christ, who seems to have laboured to *meet* men.

2. The very opposite of this.   He has so much milk, and so much manners, and so much delicacy, and so much fastidiousness !   Touches with such tenderness ! and if the patient shrinks, will touch no more ! The times are too flagrant for this sort.   The Gospel is sometimes preached in this way by a man, till all the people agree with him.   He gives no offence, and does no good.

3. St Paul unites both these.   Here is the hand of a lady with the heart of a lion.   He *must* win souls, but will labour all sorts of contrivances.   Men of the world are determined on their point, but yet labour with all possible discretion, tact, and wisdom.   So St Paul exhibits a grand combination of zeal and love.   Zeal alone may be ferocious and brutal ; love alone fastidious   The true method is *fortiter in re, suaviter in modo.*

FEBRUARY 28, 1803.

WHAT IS THE DIFFERENCE BETWEEN ACCURACY IN STATING SCRIPTURE DOCTRINE, AND MERE SPECULATION ?—Proposed by the Rev. T. Scott.

The Rev. T. Scott—

An objection to full Scripture statements has arisen among the enemies to the great truths of the Gospel. And this has crept in too much among those who are better.

Some think the world may be put into good humour by not so explicitly stating the doctrines of the Gospel. Ignatius Loyola had a great maxim, that he who would do anything in the world must not aim at doing it in the way which will be universally called wise.

We ought to explain *every doctrine* at one time or other, in the connexion and relation in which it occurs in Scripture—and *every duty*. Like anatomists, we should exhibit, not disjointed bones only, but a skeleton.

Every doctrine should have a holy stamp upon it; and every duty its foundation. State, apply, and proportion every truth in a Scriptural manner. Go as far as Scripture goes; but stop there. Assign no causes which Scripture does not; nor run truth into any consequences into which Scripture does not run it.

In Calvin, Witsius, Toplady, &c., may be many things perhaps philosophically true; but they form no part of my creed as a divine, because they are not to be found in Scripture.

The Rev. J. Clayton—

They who object to the investigation of truth, are either indolent persons, or persons to be suspected.

The difference between accuracy of statement and speculation lies :—

1. In the motive of a man's mind. He who means to set himself off by his shew of skill, is a speculator; he whose intention is holy, is not speculating.

2. In the means employed. This is, whether theoretical writers, or the Scriptures, are chiefly used.

3. In the effect on the man's own mind. Speculation obtains no peace, humility, nor hatred of sin. A contrary effect to this proves it not speculation.

4. In the effect on others. Like will beget its like, speculation will generate speculative persons. The other character will form men of sound judgment.

The Rev. B. Woodd—

Speculation is entertaining : but it is endless. Sin, election, grace, &c., afford abundant scope for a speculative mind. But our duty is to ascertain and to maintain the truth. We must be careful how we draw inferences even from Scripture statements.

Most divines and Churches go beyond Scripture ; on such topics, for instance, as Church Government, Baptism, the Lord's Supper. The Calvinists and Arminians have had their differences widened by this spirit of speculation.

The Rev. S. Crowther—

The difference is exemplified in the Apostles' characters of the Bereans and Thessalonians.

The Rev. H. Foster—

A plain and godly man will state the truth and its use, and will bring forward the substance of the thing ; but beyond this, will not attempt anything. Every Scripture doctrine has " its meat in its mouth."

The Rev. R. Cecil—

The difference is that which lies between *a scribe well instructed in the kingdom of God*, who has *compared spiritual things with spiritual,* and another who runs into the " fitness of things " and other grounds of human reasoning. Owen and such men knew the bearing and relations of Scripture truth. Watts, Hopkins Hutchinson, gave way to speculation ;—Watts on the Trinity, Hopkins about hell, Hutchinson in his Principles of Scripture Philosophy. Part of their speculations might be true, but speculation is hazardous.

The difference between the two is somewhat like the difference between one traveller who follows the lantern of a guide, and one who would follow this guide in general, but will yet go down this lane and over that bridge, to see that he is guiding right. The difference lies in a humble and teachable spirit, searching out not only the general truths, but their relations ; and the man who runs into what he thinks clear, &c.

March 14, 1803.

What is the Scripture Doctrine of the Trinity, and what are those Deviations from it which Tend to Heresy ?—Proposed by the Rev. H. Foster.

Mr Foster—

God is one, yet He is exhibited in Scripture in one sense as three. In the 14th, 15th, and 16th chapters of St John, personal characteristics are ascribed to each. The character of the Father is begetting ; that of the Son, begotten ; that of the Holy Ghost, proceeding. Any account of the modes of generation and proceeding is wrong. Dr Gill has erred here.

Deviations from this doctrine.

1. Denying the proper Sonship of Jesus Christ. This, for instance, Ridgeley, and also the Hutchinsonians, were in danger of.

2. The supposition, that they are merely names of office, and that there is no real distinction in the characters assumed. Upon this plan the Father might have been the Son, and the Son the Father, &c.

3. Denying the proper personal distinction of the three. The great evil of this plan is, that it makes the Mediator only a man.

4. Denying the proper Deity of the Son.

The Rev. R. Cecil—

The Doctrine of the Trinity is a matter of pure revelation. Repel, therefore, anything like help. I am a sceptic as to all help in such matters. If Beveridge tells me of a river as a simile, or Mr Hutchinson of the sun, or any one else of a simile, much less an appointed simile, I ask, " Does the Word of God state this ? " Watts' thoughts are striking ; he was humble and supplicant, while misled. He had received great injury, and was likely to convey great injury. His book on " The Redeemer and Sanctifier " is a very dangerous book, but this came from his dabbling.

One thing struck me in reading *Milner's Church History :* that in proportion as the Church left the doctrine of the Trinity, it began to lose its life.

The wisdom of a creature like man is to cease from reasoning on the subject. The first deviation from the truth in this appears to me to be, to make any attempts at explaining the matter. The primitive Churches went on with more peace than the moderns ; because they rested in general grounds. On the Hutchinsonian plan, we can make nothing of those passages which represent God as giving His *only begotten Son* to the world.

The Rev. J. Clayton—

Though the word Trinity is not in Scripture, yet the doctrine is. Though the word " person " is not there, yet " subsistence " is : see Heb. i. 3. I have found none reject the term " person " who are not inimical to the doctrine itself.

The doctrine of the Trinity is essential to all Divine Revelation. The whole plan of Redemption is intimately and essentially involved in the doctrine. It is not, therefore, a speculative doctrine, on which we may indulge conjectures. Separate from the truth of the Gospel, we are not to expect the grace of the Gospel.

Deviations. The statement, that if you hold the eternal generation of Christ, you concede so much to a high Arian, that you cannot stand your ground. As to Sabellianism, and the indwelling scheme, they are gross departures. Every deviation from the doctrine of three Divine persons in one Deity, designing, purchasing, and applying redemption, is dangerous in the extreme.

Where there are any departures from this doctrine, God's providence is a comment upon His Word, and He writes *Ichabod* upon such places of worship.

The Rev. B. Woodd—

Son of God has appeared to me a name of Christ in his nature, not his office.

The Rev. W. Goode—

The great error has been the endeavouring to explain the filiation of the Son. This conducts to high Arianism. There are difficulties on both sides. I incline to the Hutchinsonians. The word " Son " is never applied to Christ, but with reference to his office ; nor the procession of the Holy Ghost, but as economical in the work of Redemption. The love of the Father in giving the Son may thus be understood as infinitely great, though the relation of Father and Son be not considered.

But, then, here is a danger attending the view of these names being *merely* official, that it leads to Sabellianism. I think, therefore, that there is a distinction in the divine nature on which the distinction of office in redemption is grounded. And thus far, perhaps, I differ from the Hutchinsonians. And this is all I think that sound men mean by " eternal generation."

The power of vital religion rises or falls with the doctrine.

The Rev. S. Crowther—

Deviations spring from the exalting of one person of the Trinity to the exclusion or denial of the other.

The more we pray, and the more humble we are, the more disposed we shall be to receive and hold this doctrine.

MARCH 28, 1803.

WHAT ARE THOSE EXERCISES OF GRACE WHICH BRING WITH THEM THE COMPLETEST EVIDENCE THAT THEY ARE GRACIOUS?—Proposed by the Rev. H. Foster.

Mr Foster—

If you ask me of the fruits of the Spirit, I feel so little of them and so much of the contrary, that I doubt. If you ask of self-abhorrence, I think that I cannot doubt that I have *this*. So of believing on Christ—I am conscious of *this*. I am conscious of such evil, that I feel God can look into HIMSELF only for motives of making me differ from others. So in gratitude for mercies—I cannot but feel that I have this.

Not so in the simplicity of my views in going about my ministerial duties. I come to loathe myself for this: and I pray to be humble and simple. But why? " Because you know it will make you more acceptable "—I say to myself. Then I bless myself for my sagacity in finding out this working of pride!

The Rev. R. Cecil—

This question much depends on constitution. Several men may have distinct consciousnesses. For example, our brother, he has his: [and he mentioned another person of whom we have no account.]

I think I could not rest much on Foster's grounds. I have a consciousness that I can sometimes stand upon precarious rather than good ground. I have got much from a consciousness of change in my own breast, and mixed with a consciousness of integrity. I dreamed that I was in heaven, and Peter kept the door according to the Popish legend. I saw some walking there that I thought ought not to be there: I went and scolded Peter. Even a foolish dream may teach us how over-ready we are to judge others.

I have two evidences. (1.) A consciousness of approbation of God's plan of government in the Gospel. (2.) A consciousness that in trouble I run to God as a child.

The Rev. J. Pratt—

Mr Cecil and Mr Foster yet agree more than they seem. Though

Mr Cecil dwells on the great change, yet that would give him no satisfaction without an adverting to the present state of the mind. Let a man set the picture of his ungodly state by the side of the picture of his present state, and he must say, " *This hath God wrought !* " And as to present evidence in general, man can trust no acting of the mind, which has a reference to other men ; but the most unequivocal actings are those which are between God and the soul, where no eye can see nor any ear hear. [He here referred to the Rev. Joseph Milner's experience.] There is a wide difference between self-consciousness and self-abhorrence.

The Rev. J. Clayton—

When praying alone, I have felt that I should have been assisted if any one were hearing me. Therefore, the exercise of grace in public men is difficult to be discovered.

I have felt two symptoms of the exercise of real grace.—(1.) When I have prayed earnestly against *resentment* so as to overcome it. (2.) In time of affliction, a consciousness that it has led me to God.

The Rev. J. Newton—

I am as a pardoned rebel wearing a fetter.

And in preaching, the upper part of the score, which the people hear, runs off well. But there is an under part full of discord. If the people heard this, I should be ready to jump out of the pulpit.

The Rev. W. J. Abdy—

Several things that have been mentioned are truly gracious. There are these other—

1. The knowledge of sin in the consciousness of the working of a depraved nature, in our besetting sin, and a deliverance from its dominion.

2. Entire and absolute dependence on Christ.

3. Desire of heaven as a state of complete holiness.

The Rev. W. Goode—

It is not what evidences we really have, but what evidences we can take hold of. A desire of deliverance from sin, and of victory over it, is an evidence ; though a desire of heaven may not be. Another evidence is when we can look with gratitude upon the success of the Gospel by other instruments than ourselves.

The Rev. S. Crowther—

The general desires and affections of the soul are an evidence of the exercise of grace.

The Rev. J. Goode—

Acknowledgment of the divine sovereignty is an important evidence.

April 11, 1803.

WHAT IS THE SCRIPTURE ACCOUNT OF THE NEW COVENANT ?—Proposed by the Rev. B. Woodd.

Mr Woodd—

The " covenant of grace " and " covenant of redemption," are not Scriptural expressions, and therefore not to have too much stress laid upon them. I have generally taken the New Covenant to be the revelation of the Gospel. These subjects are all mysterious. We agree in this and in some other points ; that all is summed up in this, that the sinner's salvation, from first to last, is of grace.

As to our differences, I think they may be generally traced to this, that we call the different stages of the sinner's conversion and progress by different names. The covenant of grace is the universal offer of mercy to man. The decree of predestination is God's secret decree kept behind the scenes. The covenant of grace is the same thing as the covenant of baptism. He engages to become to us a Saviour, if we renounce the world, the flesh, and the devil. What my brethren call the covenant of grace, I call the covenant of redemption; and herein we quite agree. I confine the new covenant, or covenant of grace, to the offer of mercy made to all men, upon condition of faith and repentance, but think that it does not include the promise of faith and repentance which the covenant of redemption secures to the elect.

The Rev. W. Goode—

I see but two covenants in the Scripture—the covenant of works, and that of grace. I see no covenant made with man under the new dispensation, but one made with Christ for his people. What Brother Woodd calls the covenant of redemption, I call the covenant of grace. I see no grounds in Scripture for what is called the covenant of baptism.

With regard to the universality of Christ's redemption—as to its *sufficiency*, this is clear. The term " covenant " never is, I think, applied to the *offer* of grace, but to the *gift*. *If thou believe, thou shalt be saved*, is not proposed as a condition, but as the only means of obtaining this blessing. See Heb. x. 16, 17, quoted from Jeremiah.

The new covenant in the Gospel takes two aspects :—(1.) A proposal. (2.) A gift. I question whether there is any exhortation in Scripture to man to make a covenant with God, but rather to enter into God's covenant

The Rev. J. Goode—

There is no ground in Scripture for a distinction between the covenant of redemption and the covenant of grace, though many great divines make the distinction ; but they explain them differently from Brother Woodd.

They consider the covenant of grace as that made with Christ on behalf of his people, and the covenant of redemption as that made with Christ in executing the work of redemption.

The Rev. H. Foster—

There are but two covenants—that of works, and that of grace. In the covenant of works, man was to fulfil the law ; if he fulfilled it, he was to live ; if not, to die.　He did not fulfil it, and incurred the penalty.　In the covenant of grace, Christ suffered what man should have suffered, and did what man should have done ; and upon believing on him, the penitent believer is saved.　In the gospel, God publishes this salvation ; and it is the duty of every man to believe, and he will be condemned for not repenting and believing, and yet it is God's sole work in the hearts of his people.　How to reconcile these things together, I know not.

The Rev. W. J. Abdy—

The dispensation of divine mercy comes down so much to the hearts and consciences of men, that it is not necessary for them to understand terms and distinctions.

The subject of covenants, as it runs through the Word of God, is a matter of difficulty to me.　The covenant of redemption seems to me to precede the covenant of grace.　The covenant of grace proceeds upon something of the mutual engagements between man and man ; though I fully allow that every act of repentance and faith is only by the grace of God.

The Rev. J. Newton—

A covenant that has not yet been mentioned, is a *covenant with the day and with the night*. (See Jeremiah xxxiii. 20.) I consider a covenant then as a *grant*.　If believing and repenting are *proper conditions* of my salvation, I can no more fulfil them than I can touch the stars.

The Rev. J. Pratt—

There are but two covenants—that of works and that of grace.　If you imply in the word " covenant " under this dispensation, anything else than an acceptance of God's proposal and provision, and that by His own grace, it is inconsistent with the honour of God and the incapacity of man.

The covenant of redemption is an integral part of the covenant of grace.　The covenant of grace, as Brother Woodd interprets it, brings no grace to those who perish, for the Gospel is a savour of death to them.

The Rev. J. Clayton—

These terms, covenant of redemption and covenant of grace, are invented by those divines who opposed those who established a remedial law.

There have been various covenants.　As the covenant of safety with Noah ; and of peculiarity and property with Abraham.　But there are only two covenants with regard to the eternal state of man.

The objects of the administration of the covenant of grace are all mankind.　Brother Woodd construes terms universally which are to be understood *distributively*.　Repentance and faith are secured in the covenant.

April 26, 1803.

WHAT ARE THE SCRIPTURE EVIDENCES OF A STATE OF SALVATION?—
Proposed by the Rev. J. Pratt.

The Rev. T. Scott—

There cannot be any true love of God and man in us, without its proving that we are in a state of salvation. It is easier to add the truth to this partial statement, than to explain it so as to avoid error.

The question is not whether the Christian is a perfect creature in the way to heaven, but a sinner in that way.

1. Having a proper view of our guilt and depravity leading the man to submit to God's righteousness—this is an evidence. *To this man will I look, even to him that is poor and of a contrite spirit, and trembleth at my word.* (Isa. lxvi. 2.) *Thus saith the high and lofty One that inhabiteth eternity, whose name is Holy; I dwell in the high and holy place, with him also that is of a contrite and humble spirit, to revive the spirit of the humble, and to revive the heart of the contrite ones.* (Isa. lvii. 15.)

2. A consciousness of acquiescence in the Scripture representations and views. *God forbid that I should glory, save in the cross of our Lord Jesus Christ.*

3. A hatred of sin, and desire of deliverance. *I delight in the law of God after the inward man.*

4. Love of God and man is a fourth evidence we may rely upon.

The Rev. J. Davies—

Evidences of being in a state of salvation are—

1. When the Holy Spirit subdues pride and self-righteousness. *When he is come, he shall convince the world of sin.*

2. Approbation of the law, though it condemns. *I consent unto the law that it is good.*

3. A perfect acquiescence in the plan of salvation.

4. Connected with this, the fruits of the Spirit manifested in us.

The Rev. J. Clayton—

A STATE OF SALVATION—what is this? A state of acceptance with God. Justified by the righteousness of the Great Surety. Renewed by the Holy Spirit.

EVIDENCES—what are these? The Scriptures lay a great stress upon *believing*. *He that believeth shall be saved.* There are many other graces as evidences of the saved, but "believing" is a prominent one. As to the evidences to *ourselves*, there may be the life of Christ in us, yet we live in a state of distressing uncertainty. And therefore we shall not have the evidence without that witnessing of the Spirit which the Scriptures lay much stress upon. In these varying states, we are like the dial without the sun and with the sun. And this evidence is in general acquired gradually. In cases of extraordinary trial, there may be, and often is, a particular communication; but in ordinary cases, this results from a course of holy activity and self-denial. But this may and does decay, and it is renewed again, and therefore the grand evidence is *perseverance*.

The Rev. J. Newton—

The moment a child is born, he has all the rudiments of a perfect man, and is as much entitled to his father's estate as he ever will be, though he is to be unfolded gradually and to acquire knowledge gradually.

The Rev. B. Woodd—

Evidences of real grace will appear in the judgment, the will, and the affections. Negative evidences are morality, integrity, benevolence, &c. Positive evidences are love to God and man, zeal, hatred of sin, self-abhorrence. *He that believeth hath the witness in himself*—consisting in a perception of the harmony of the divine character with the state of man and his wants. *The Spirit beareth witness that we are the children of God.*

The Rev. W. J. Abdy—

Christ has established the love of God and of man as the sum of religion. *Upon these two commandments hang the law and the prophets.* The Gospel has indeed added motives.

The Rev. W. Goode—

Our Lord did not design to shew the scribe what are the evidences of a state of salvation, but to shew him that he was not in a state of salvation. For if it had been his design, it follows that the evidences are a perfect conformity to the law of God. I would not say that the love of God and man is a false evidence, but it is an imperfect and partial one. It may be so explained as to include all the right views; but it may be so as to be false.

The evidence, then, is—the disposition of the Christian's mind towards the truth of God. 1. Humility. 2. Concurrence with the plan of salvation. 3. A reliance upon Christ for all. 4. A determination of heart for God. 5. The Spirit's sealing his own work.

May 9, 1803.

How may we Discover and Correct the Defects of our Characters ?—Proposed by the Rev. H. Foster.

Mr Foster—

Proud man is indisposed to be put out of conceit of himself—therefore he does not discipline himself. Those defective habits which form defective characters are difficult to be discovered and corrected. We should continually suspect ourselves of defects. We should examine our characters by the proper standard. We should associate with the excellent and look at their excellencies.

" *My* sermon, *my* books, &c."—how odious is this language ! But how frequent ! and how little we know it ! A perfect mimic would be of great use to us. Jocular hints will help us. Open enemies can teach us much. We should frown upon all flatterers. Excellence of character is of vast weight in a preacher.

The Rev. C. Simeon, a visitor—

We are lost too much in generals.   Every action has (1.) MATTER, (2.) MANNER, (3.) END.

1. The matter must be conformed to the Scriptures.

2. The manner must be fitting.   David bringing up the ark will shew us this.

3. The end we have in view is most important.   Jehu is cursed for the very act for which he was rewarded to the fourth generation.   See Hosea i. 4.   This should be our prayer—*Search me, O God, and know my heart,* &c.   Psalm cxxxix. 23, 24.

In little things, not great, we shall most truly discern our own character.   There may be something in our characters, not occasional, but habitual, which needs correcting; like a defective warp into which the woof is continually woven.   For correcting these defects, the love of God must be wrought into the heart.   Mr Atkinson said to me many years since, "Lean on the side opposite to your constitutional bias."

The Rev. Mr Simons, a visitor—

The pure and perfect example of Christ we should always keep before us to correct our characters.

Confess to God: conceal not sin.   Run over your sins in prayer at night before others; though you do not say, "I am this man," it will put you on your guard next day.   Trust not yourself.   Go to your friends for their hints.

The Rev. J. Davies—

Self-inspection is of the last importance.   Guard against self-love.   Attend to the opinions of others.   Cultivate an openness to conviction.

The Rev. J. Newton—

God only can give a desire of knowing our true characters.   Where He gives that desire, He will in His own time answer it.   Crosses, difficulties, and affliction will come, and be in God's hand the great instruments.

(1.) Attention to the Word of God, (2.) Prayer, (3.) The teaching of the Holy Spirit—are means of learning our defects.

The Rev. B. Woodd—

The importance of the question is seen from this, that few people know their defects.   Anonymous letters may be made useful to us.   Many defects are little in their beginnings, and not known by us until they break out into greater evils.   Men sometimes are left to fall into sin, in order to discover them to themselves.   There are defects that attach to different periods of life, therefore never grow secure.

The Rev. R. Cecil—

Willingness is the great means, under God, of detecting our defects.   We are very willing to do this for others.   Why is there such continual shifting off from ourselves, extenuating, palliating?   The man would not be without the information, but wishes he had received it in some other way than from *you.*

Let me lay it to heart that I have faults. Temptations follow temperaments. Little is to be got from friends. If you do not pocket up what you get from enemies, you are a loser indeed. Though their criticisms may be exaggerated, yet there is some foundation; at least the appearance of some.

Sometimes a man pays very dear for his errors. Let him not regard the expense only, but the lesson. There is a prodigious source of deception in plausible names for things. We may see ourselves in others. Temptations discover the man. Take as examples, Balaam, Achan, David, Peter.

In correcting these, *willingness* is still useful.

The Rev. Mr Atkinson, a visitor—

A deep conviction that we are exposed to the judgment and wrath of God, will lead a man to watch with godly jealousy over himself. In proportion as a man sees this, in that proportion will he be self-jealous.

The finding out errors is of chief value to us, as it drives us to Christ.

The Rev. J. Pratt—

A deep and practical conviction that we have defects, is a great help in detecting them. The *silence* of friends may teach us something. Our own prayers at most ingenuous times, when compared with our life, may teach us. A man is often one thing on his knees, and another in the world. Mix retirement with intercourse with others. Consult not the *first* feelings after reproof.

MAY 23, 1803.

WHAT ARE THE SYMPTOMS, EXTERNAL AND INTERNAL, WHICH DENOTE MAN TO BE IN A DANGEROUS PREDICAMENT?—Proposed by the Rev. R. Cecil.

Mr Cecil—

Dangerous predicaments are the brinks of temptation. Man often gives evidence of being giddy, and yet perhaps is not aware of it. He, however, who has been in danger, will make a shrewd guess.

The following are signs :—

1. A haughty spirit.

2. Presumptuous carelessness. "Who fears?" This is to be feared, that there seems nothing to fear. Remember Peter—*Though all men forsake thee, yet will not I.*

3. A man being in power and relishing it.

4. An accession of wealth. At first, he is stunned; he is very humble and grateful. Then begins to speak a little louder. People think him more sensible, and he soon thinks so himself.

5. Venturing upon the borders of danger. Men do pretty well till they get within the atmosphere of danger. The atmosphere makes him sick. They become like a ship in a whirlpool, which will not obey the helm.

6. Popularity. Waterland and the idiot.

7. When, in suspicious circumstances, disposed to equivocate; *e. g.*, Abraham and Abimelech.

8. Self-indulgence.

9. Gadding; *e. g.*, Dinah.

10. Stupidity of conscience, so as to resist strokes.

The Rev. J. Davies—

1. A spirit of curiosity.   2. An indolent spirit.   Both these are symptoms of danger.

The Rev. J. Clayton—

Look into Scripture history, and inquire what have been the situations most dangerous to good men.   If we see any individuals placed in situations that have been dangerous, we may look for symptoms, for human nature is true to itself.

1. Careless discharge of closet duties.   2. A frivolous spirit, especially with females.   3. When vain of our prudence.   4. When we cannot bear to hear of the symptom—these are symptoms of danger.

The Rev. W. Goode—

1. A reasoning spirit; 2. Great prospects—are dangerous.

The Rev. S. Crowther—

1. Neglect of want of fervour in prayer.   2. Too much converse with the world.   3. Casting off the fear of God.   *So did not I, because of the fear of the Lord.*   4. Parleying with temptation; *e. g.*, Eve. 5. Self-confidence—are all warning symptoms.

The Rev. J. Goode—

1. Where the heart is much set upon anything.   2. When we are ready to listen to the enemy.

The Rev. J. Pratt—

1. Want of guard over the senses.   For example, Achan, pictures, &c.   2. Cold and formal in official exercises.   3. Disproportionate fondness for parts of truth.   4. A speculative turn of mind ; *e. g.*, Zaccheus and the sycamore-tree.   5. Undue fondness for accuracy. 6. Listening to conversation and party.   7. Pursuing some favourite topic that is foreign to the direct duty.   8. The spirit of egotism.   9. Secular employments.   These are all occasions of danger.

JUNE 6, 1803.

WHAT IS THE DISTINCTION BETWEEN EVANGELICAL DEVOTION AND ENTHUSIASM ?—Proposed by the Rev. J. Clayton.

Mr Clayton—

Devotion is sometimes introduced with a view to set aside the truth.   Others plead for rapturous devotion, who appear not to be members of Christ, betraying a waspish disposition.   Some make this devotion and retirement stand instead of public means.   I therefore ask the question.

The Rev. J. Newton—

True devotion originates in deep humiliation of heart.

The Rev. W. J. Abdy—

Devotion depends upon the cast of the mind.

The Rev. B. Woodd—

There are two kinds of rapturous devotion or enthusiasm—
1. One combined with true religion, and is genuine.
2. The other, animal satisfaction built on ignorance and presumption.

There is a distinction between evangelical devotion and enthusiasm in two respects :—
1. In views of the Divine Law and the Gospel. Enthusiasts know not the spirituality of these.
2. In views of safety and views of holiness. The devotional character wishes to be safe.

The Rev. J. Goode—

Evangelical devotion is founded in the knowledge of ourselves and of Christ. Enthusiasm is founded in ignorance ; evangelical devotion in knowledge. Evangelical devotion is spiritual ; by the Spirit and from the Spirit : not so of enthusiasm. Evangelical devotion is humble : enthusiasm is self-pleased.

The Rev. S. Crowther—

Evangelical devotion is uniform in its exercise : enthusiasm varies : enthusiasm confounds gifts with graces.

We must be careful in condemning as enthusiasm what the world calls such. Enthusiasm, as it is called, is allowed in every art and science.

The Rev. H. Foster—

Enthusiasm has life in the exercise, but goes no further : devotion goes into the life. When the enthusiast's devotion is over, his religion is over. Genuine devotion is grounded upon revelation : the enthusiast goes on wild imaginations. The enthusiast is satisfied in his devotion : the devotional man is dissatisfied.

The Rev. J. Pratt—

This is a constitutional question. There is a distinction between evangelical devotion and enthusiasm—(1.) in their nature, (2.) in their object, (3.) in the means by which they are exercised, and (4.) in their issue.

The Rev. R. Cecil—

Enthusiasm is an unscriptural heat, however generated. If, therefore, enthusiasm fixes upon a scriptural truth, it distorts it, and makes it an error. [This was illustrated by the case of Quakers exalting the Spirit, but depreciating Christ : also Antinomians exalting Christ, but leaving out the Spirit.]

As to the mind being inflamed, instances of this are seen in a bacchanalian, an actor, a fop; and Archimedes exclaiming, 'Εὑρήκα, 'Εὑρηκα.

Evangelical devotion and enthusiasm differ essentially in their humiliation. Evangelical devotion is the life of faith. See Habakkuk.

I have seen a whole congregation of Papists fall down on the elevation of the host. What is this?—Irritation on the nerves. Much is to be attributed to constitution : in women, for instance. Some melt at everything. Some are case-hardened, though they have principle.

Evangelical devotion is a holy impression of God's Spirit on the heart, discovering itself according to circumstances. We see this in David, in different frames. It is the same religious principle, tending God-ward, and according to God's Word, but directed by circumstances.

Evangelical devotion is that which is common to the Church in all ages. The devotion of the enthusiast is peculiar to his sect ; it cannot be taken up by the Church at large. It is not found in the Psalms, it is not found in the Scriptures.

The enthusiast swells in his devotion : the Christian sinks. The enthusiast boasts like the Pharisee : the Christian, like the Publican, smites his breast. The enthusiast rests in the exercise of devotion : the Christian looks beyond, and is dissatisfied with it.

June 20, 1803.

Does St Paul, in the 7th Chapter to the Romans, speak in the Person of a Regenerate or Unregenerate Man ?—Proposed by the Rev. H. Foster.

Mr Foster—

St Paul describes, in the former part of the chapter, the manner in which he passed from a state of nature to a state of grace. When married to the law, the issue was death. When new-married to Christ, the first husband being dead, the issue is life. He clears the law from any blame of sin being the fruit of that union between the law and the sinner. He speaks what every man feels in the working of sin and the law. The words " carnal, sold under sin," present the chief difficulty. But if he speaks not of himself here, neither does he in the whole chapter. That the word " carnal" is used of persons professedly regenerate, is plain from what is said to the Corinthians. *Are ye not carnal?* The words are, *sold under sin* ; not " I sell myself," but *sold* under sin.

I may appeal to my own experience as a confirmation of the view that St Paul here speaks in the person of a regenerate man.

The Rev. Mr Simons, a visitor—

The Apostle is led to this subject by a question in chap. vi. 1. *Shall we continue in sin that grace may abound?* He has a constant regard to the opinion of the Jews. A Jew objects, vii. 7. " *Is the law sin?*" This he answers. The Jew objects again, vii. 13. " *Was then that which is good made death unto me?*" This he answers in the rest of the chapter. He proves to the Jew that the law is not sin, nor of itself death ; and also points out the difference between serving in newness of the spirit, and oldness of the letter. Chapter viii. 23, proves that these things are said of the regenerate.

The Rev. W. Fry—

1. An acknowledgment of the righteousness and holiness of the law is found here which no unregenerate man feels.

2. The law shewing him the sinfulness of sin, convinces me that the speaker is not an unregenerate person.

3. The state of the affections, *I delight in the law of God after the inward man* (v. 22), shews the same.

The Rev. R. Cecil—

If a regenerate man cannot speak thus, then I am not a regenerate man ; but if he may, then I take hope, though under captivity.

Indeed the other expressions, *I delight in the law of God; I consent unto the law that it is good,* cannot be put into the mouth of an unregenerate man ; but the expressions indicating sin may be put into the regenerate man's mouth.

Scripture in other parts speaks the same thing. The substance of this passage is in Galatians : *The flesh lusteth against the spirit, and the spirit against the flesh,* and this is evidence addressed to Christians.

The Rev. B. Woodd—

1. Many expressions in this context must be understood in a qualified sense. The metaphors may be here taken so. Rom. vi. 14, 18, 22. Eph. ii. 1. 1 John iii. 9.

2. Some passages apply only to a regenerate man. For example, vs. 4, 6, 9.

3. None have a clear idea of the spirituality of the law, but the regenerate.

4. Verse 17 describes two distinct natures which exist only in the regenerate.

5. Verse 18 describes a self-knowledge peculiar to the regenerate.

6. This is more or less the experience of all Christians.

7. Passages which none but the regenerate can adopt, are vs. 16, 22, 25.

8. None but the spiritual know what the difficulties of the spiritual contest are.

9. It is analogous to the whole Scripture. *The flesh lusteth against the spirit, &c.*

This is the view of such men as Bishop Beveridge, Bishop Hopkins, Archbishop Usher, and Bradford.

The Rev. W. Goode—

The writer in the *Christian Observer* notices no expression in the whole chapter which is the ground of the opposite opinion.

The expressions, as Mr Cecil said, which are the ground of the opinion that the Apostle speaks of an unregenerate man, *may* be true of the regenerate, but the opposite expressions *cannot* be true of the unregenerate.

JULY 4, 1803.

IS THERE ANY GROUND FOR THE DISTINCTION BETWEEN BAPTISMAL AND SPIRITUAL REGENERATION ?—Proposed by the Rev. B. Woodd.

Mr Woodd—

Nothing more is meant by baptism by many of the ancients than an admission into the Christian Church. Irenœus says that Christ was regenerated by John in the river Jordan ; meaning, no doubt, the external rite of Church membership.

No objection whatever can be urged to the office for adult baptism in the Church of England—such as offer themselves for baptism are considered to be true converts. With regard to the service for infants, there are objections. Mr Baxter has given me light. He grounds the right of children on the covenant relation of the Christian parent. See 1 Cor. vii. 14. The Church of England goes on this ground, presuming every child offered for baptism to be a child of a Christian parent.

There is danger of making too much or too little of the ordinance.

The Rev. H. Foster—

There is a vast difference indeed. Baptismal regeneration is nothing ; spiritual regeneration is all in all. Baptism answers the same end in the Christian Church, that circumcision did in the Jewish.

The Scriptures, speaking of the Sacraments, speak of the outward signs as if they were the things signified : *This is my body: this is my blood :* that is, signs. And if the Bible means no more than this, our Church may be allowed to mean no more by these expressions than the signs of grace. But because the expressions have stumbled thousands, I wish them altered.

As to actual communication of grace in baptism in all cases, experience shews there is nothing in it. For example, Simon Magus. And yet I have sometimes doubted whether I have made enough of the ordinance. Some serious things are said about children, that they that are not circumcised should be cut off ; but I know not whether this is is not to be limited to outward things. There are some things which hang about this subject which I do not fully understand. I can go no further positively than considering Baptism an ordinance which I take up in obedience to a Divine command.

The Rev. W. Fry—

Scripture uses baptism nowhere in the sense of regeneration. 1 Peter iii. 2, so seems ; but 'tis only in the expression. I see no objection to connecting spiritual regeneration with baptism—that is, that God connects them as he pleases, not necessarily. The primitive fathers never used the term regeneration in the sense of spiritual change.

The Church services are composed throughout under the idea of all being Christians who participate in them. "To be born of God," "born of the Spirit," are distinct in their use from "regeneration," and mean the spiritual change.

On the next subject—WHAT ARE THE DUTIES WHICH THE PRE-

SENT TIMES PARTICULARLY REQUIRE OF US?—we have no remarks. The meetings were adjourned to September.

SEPTEMBER 26, 1803.

How shall we know whether our Convictions are from Natural Conscience or the Spirit of God?—Proposed by the Rev. S. Crowther.

Mr Crowther—

Conscience is common to Christians and unbelievers; natural conscience may lead to various things. From the Spirit of God, the guilt and filth of sin is discovered.

Distinguish these by these marks—

1. The convictions of natural conscience reach only to external sins: those of the Spirit of God to the sins of the heart.

2. Natural conscience leads men to fear punishment; but those of the Spirit of God to fear the evil of sin, rather than the punishment.

3. Natural conscience leads men to silence conviction, rather than to a change of nature and a removal of guilt.

4. Natural conscience renders men particular in their obedience; but not with that liberty which the Spirit of God gives.

5. Natural conscience leads men to pride themselves in the performance of their duties; but the Spirit of God humbles them under their best efforts.

6. Natural conscience is not durable in its working, but the Spirit of God carries on his work to the end.

The Rev. J. Clayton—

Natural conscience does not exist in any shade of its operation, independent of the Spirit of God. Wherever, therefore, there be an operation of conscience, there must be a fragment at least of revelation.

The Spirit of God acts in different degrees and proportions according to the degree of light. But we may distinguish between the common operations of the Spirit of God on the conscience and his gracious operations. This is Dr John Owen's view. The great characteristic of a gracious operation is a conviction of the soul of unbelief in Christ. Permanence of conviction is the grand proof of a gracious operation.

The Rev. H. Foster—

I have known men anxious to ascertain whether they were children of God; but when once they have got this persuasion, they have gone off into sin. They have merely used Christ and election to help them into hell.

I have known a man make the chair and floor tremble under him while relating his sins, who, as soon as he got comfort, from that moment relaxed, and is now, though persuaded of his being a child of God, yet living in notorious sin.

The following subject was proposed at the time that an invasion of Britain by Bonaparte was expected; a National Fast having been appointed by the King on the 19th October, to deprecate the divine wrath, and implore the divine aid, at this momentous crisis.

OCTOBER 10, 1803.

WHAT ARE THE LEADING POINTS TO WHICH THE ATTENTION OF THE PUBLIC SHOULD BE DIRECTED ON THE APPROACHING FAST?—Proposed by the Rev. J. Clayton.

Mr Clayton—

There is a disposition in the people to receive impressions. They are alarmed. This is like wind and tide, which we must take at their time. We ought to be more impressed with the evil of sin, than with our danger. Bonaparte is God's instrument. If we are in a suitable frame of mind for deliverance, then we may expect it.

We should lead them to the encouragements we have—unanimity, courage. "The men of might have found their hands." Then the natural and political means. But the spiritual means are our great encouragements, at home and on the continent.

Lead them to reflect on the particular sins which the French Revolution introduced :—Alienation of mind from civil governments; disregard to domestic authority ; disrespect for the marriage duties ; infidelity.

The Rev. Mr Simons, a visitor—

God is the defence of Britain. Is there, then, a spirit of prayer? The one sin which will sink any nation is unbelief in Christ. *Kiss, then, the Son, lest he be angry, and ye perish from the way.* It is discouraging that there is a deadly antipathy in many of our governors against evangelical religion.

The Rev. H. Foster—

Tremble at the abuse of the peace. It seems as though it must be, if there be a God upon the earth, that he must be avenged on such a nation as this. That there are praying people abroad is encouraging. I am afraid to depend upon feelings. We may pray earnestly ; but perhaps through fear of a Frenchman's bayonet. Yet I go before God, and tell him I have offended him, and get some quiet.

I cannot think he will give us up to ruin, though he may chastise us deeply. I feel great anxiety from the want of a godly spirit among ministers and people. There are great scandals which call aloud for punishment.

The Rev. Mr Gilbert, a visitor—

The sins of our nation and Church are such as to excite the greatest apprehension. Yet favourable circumstances are predominant in my mind. The abuse of peace filled every one who is accustomed to mark the providential government of God with dismay. The flocking of persons to France was a bad symptom.

The Rev. W. Goode—

Let us consider—(1.) The cause of our present troubles—sin. (2.) The means of our preservation—turning to God. (3.) The encouraging circumstances—God's interference.

The greatest discouragement is in the professing Church ; not in the nation. Yet the people of God always have been a remnant. When deliverance has been given to a nation, it has been in answer to the intercessions of the remnant. This is ground of encouragement to expect we shall not be ruined, though chastised. It seems as though the Lord meant to honour this nation. Wickliffe gave birth to the Reformation.

The Rev. B. Woodd—

Encouragement may be gathered from the great exertions made by all classes for the instruction of the rising generation. It rather appears to me, that the honour of God is concerned for the preservation of this nation.

The Rev. J. Davies—

We should guard religious persons from a dependence upon their prayers, or upon the efforts of this nation for God's cause.

The Rev. R. Lloyd, a visitor—

In a comparative view, we stand high as a nation in religion, morality, and loyalty. The French Revolution enlightened men concerning false philanthropy, philosophy, and infidelity. Men are now better prepared to judge. The volunteering spirit is an answer to prayer. A Jacobin would live on tumult.

OCTOBER 24, 1803.

IS IT IN ANY CASE LAWFUL TO DEVIATE FROM TRUTH ?—Proposed by the Rev. J. Clayton.

Mr Clayton—

I feel it unlawful to deny myself to others. If nothing more is understood by the frequent intimation to callers, " Not at home," than that we are engaged, and that is known, something may be said in excuse. I would not rigidly condemn.

If the French come and demand money, it is better to trust God and tell the truth. The honesty of the avowal may lodge conviction.

I incline to think that in *all* cases truth should be spoken ; there is such majesty and grandeur in truth.

The Rev. Mr Gilbee, a visitor—

Our Lord's command is, *Let your communication be Yea, yea; Nay, nay:* implying the necessity of simplicity and truth. Our Lord was a volunteer for truth even where life was concerned—*I am he.*

If it be lawful to deviate from truth, we might in some cases be reduced to this dilemma ; that if the end justify the means, we might be drawn into sin.

The Rev. H. Foster—

Abraham was guilty of base equivocation, when he said Sarah was his sister. Elisha in Dothan, I am not clear about. The standard should be kept up in purity. We should ask what Christ would do in such cases. Madmen are perhaps not entitled to truth.

We are all dishonest with ourselves. With regard to the income-tax, I find more difficulty to be honest than to ascertain the amount.

The Rev. W. J. Abdy—

A most difficult case would be when one in pursuit of a person under your protection should demand of you whether you knew anything of him : or when the life or character of your friends are in question.

Though I agree to the thing in general, yet I feel difficulties. Jacob's case is difficult, so is Rahab's ; because the Scriptures commend them. It seems as though God had left good men to act much from the exigencies of the occasion.

The Rev. Mr Fry—

In no case is it right to deviate from the truth. Question not the consequences, but consider the will of God.

I did not scruple to deny myself * when I came to town ; since it was customarily understood in the sense intended, and having considered that I should offend many if I did not. But I now see it to be wrong, because some may come to my door who do not understand the words in the sense generally understood, and I may give an evil impression. My servants, too, may infer from it the lawfulness of lying. It may, too, offend the brethren ; and says the Apostle, *If meat make my brother to offend, I will eat no meat while the world standeth.* I used to consider it in the same view as signing a letter, " I am," &c., to a man whom you despise ; but that phrase is universally understood, not so the other.

We should carry truth into our whole spirit and character. We ought to pay more respect to a poor Christian than to a rich worldling. It is a deviation from truth, if we do not treat all persons in proportion to their holiness. Truth also respects our raising expectations in others.

David's case with the king of Gath is not censured. But I have observed that those believers who were eminent for any particular grace were left to feel their weakness.

The Rev. S. Crowther—

The method in which the Society for the Suppression of Vice detects the sellers of obscene prints is painful.

The Rev. J. Davies—

One is not bound to truth with a robber or assassin. Physicians will give hopes when they see none—they justify it on the idea of keeping up the spirits.

* By this phrase is apparently meant " denying I was at home ; " or allowing the servant to say, " Not at home."

The Rev. J. Goode—

We are not always obliged to tell the whole truth. We should say nothing but truth; but are not obliged to tell all. David, in the thirty-fourth Psalm, ascribes his deliverance to God; though in the case of Achish he appears to have departed from truth. Jeremiah did not tell the whole truth in the case of presenting his petition.

There is a good sermon of Dr Evans's on truth. He says that it is not unlawful to use a stratagem in war, though unlawful to tell a falsehood.

The Rev. W. Goode—

When a person has two motives of his actions, he is not bound to acknowledge both. Samuel, in going to anoint David, told the people he went to sacrifice, which was true, but was only part of the truth, and seems to have been said to deceive the people. There is no necessity, therefore, to tell the whole truth, though it may deceive.

NOVEMBER 7, 1803.

IS THERE ANYTHING OF APPROPRIATION IN THE NATURE OF JUSTIFYING FAITH?—Proposed by the Rev. H. Foster.

Mr Foster—

I think there is. The blessings of the covenant of grace are in Jesus Christ; without him, we are wretched. The Scriptures set him forth as the object of our faith. The images which are used in Scripture imply application. By application, I do not mean assurance; for there may be application in the midst of doubts and perplexities.

Yet there is something of appropriation in receiving him; in looking to him, as to the serpent in the wilderness; in eating his flesh and his blood, which conveys the idea of appropriation most strongly; in coming to him. An evil growing among some of us is, to allow that we must go on in a degree of uncertainty.

The Rev. J. Newton—

There are three things attributed to faith—(1.) It works by love; (2.) it purifies the heart; (3.) it overcomes the world.

The Rev. B. Woodd—

The difficulties on this subject appear to me to arise from the figurative language of Scripture. Receiving Christ, looking to him, coming to him, all come to one and the same thing: *i.e.*, credit given to the divine testimony, and the comforts consequent thereon.

Appropriation is involved in the very nature of justifying faith. The gospel is a general grant; faith appropriates this to myself. This appropriation appears in three instances:—

(1.) It exists in the first act of faith.

(2.) It exists in the covenant grant of the gospel: it is the tenor of the covenant of grace that a sinner should appropriate. *Hear, and your soul shall live. All that the Father giveth me, shall come to me.*

(3.) It exists in the effects of faith.

Appropriation as an act of faith is distinct from its comfort. Comfort arises—

(1.) From the fruits of faith in the heart.

(2.) From growing views of the Divine mercy, &c.

(3.) From God the Spirit's shining upon his own work. Wherever there is a real reliance upon Christ, there is the appropriation of faith; though there may not be comfort and assurance.

The Rev. J. Davies—

What is the faith of that man who has no appropriation? A mere belief of the truth of the gospel.

The Rev. W. Fry—

If by appropriation he meant nothing more than application, I cannot see any question. But if it means assurance, it is dangerous. I am not to look into the Scriptures to search if Christ died for *me*. This is searching for a revelation distinct from that which God has given. The promises of God are made to particular characters. If I feel I have the marks of these characters, I can claim the promises and comfort. Faith is receiving Christ, and appropriating him, though not in the sense of the followers of Mr Wesley; or Mr Hervey, if he means that I must look into the Scriptures to find that Christ died for me.

The Rev. J. Goode—

The Scripture account of faith is more simple than most writers make of it.

The Rev. J. Clayton—

Christ is the object of faith; the Word of God is the warrant. I must approve of this. I cannot without appropriation. An exercise of the understanding, will, and affections unite in faith. Brother Fry states the matter, as appears to me, unscripturally. For he changes the warrant of faith. Instead of making the divine declaration the warrant, he makes it what is done in us. Assurance is distinct. It is nearly connected with the advance of sanctification. If we associate with God's enemies, we cannot feel ourselves his friends.

The Rev. Mr Simons, a visitor—

Appropriation is not a careless, bold thing. It is accompanied with tears of joy and gratitude, and a sense of unworthiness. The more of application there is in one sense, the more is there of doubt. The more we can realise the astonishing blessings offered, the more amazed we are that such as we are should be the subjects of them.

The Rev. C. Cecil—

Coming to Christ, receiving him, &c., appear to me not to express the effect of faith, but the thing itself. Though metaphorical, yet they express the thing itself. If joy, &c., be spoken of, this I allow is the effect of faith.

NOVEMBER 21, 1803.

HOW ARE WE TO UNDERSTAND OUR LORD'S WORDS, "EVERY IDLE WORD THAT MEN SHALL SPEAK, THEY SHALL GIVE ACCOUNT THEREOF IN THE DAY OF JUDGMENT?"—Proposed by the Rev. Mr Fry.

Mr Fry—

Some suppose "idle" words to be synonymous with *wicked* words. This may be disproved. (1.) From the definition of the word. (2.) From the context. Our Lord had reproved the Pharisees for blasphemy. He goes on to shew that other words which they thought not sinful were culpable. Idle words are such as do not aim at the glory of God, and are unprofitable to those who hear. For example—(1.) Unmeaning compliments. (2.) Sallies of humour and wit. Wit is dangerous even when chastened. But when not, it is most destructive of all vital godliness. Ludicrous tales to amuse spring from a love of self. They are *foolish talking and jesting*, which are not convenient. (3.) Garrulity. *In a multitude of words, there shall not want sin.*

The Rev. R. Cecil—

Our Lord was continually preaching the extent and spirituality of the Law; and that in opposition to the gross and carnal views of the Jews. For example—"You have counted that only adultery, which consisted in the act; but I say that the thought even is sin. You count blasphemous words to be evil; but I condemn idle words also." So that it is an explanation of the spirituality of the Law. If *whatever we do in word or deed, we are to do all in the name of the Lord Jesus;* and if we are bought with a price, we are accountable to our Master for everything we speak or do. When a man comes to appear before the judgment-seat, if he have not an atonement for this as well as all other sins, he will sink.

But when you come to enter into particulars, what are sins under this view, I feel some difficulties. With regard to COMPLIMENTS, we must remember St Paul's address, *Most Noble Festus!* We should cultivate a clement and civil spirit, but abstain from the frothy habits of the world. As to SALLIES OF HUMOUR. These are dangerous indeed, and pernicious. They often do mischief, and never do good. But then if we would banish wit entirely from the system, it is a question whether we should gain anything. One very strong thing against wit and humour is, that it is nowhere employed in Scripture. Elijah's sarcasm is the nearest, but he had a set of abandoned villains to deal with.

TALKATIVE people are to be pitied, if old. It is quite an infirmity of old age.

This passage of Scripture wants to be brought forward much in the Church, and home to our own consciences. For how can we look on the words of one day without confusion? What is the intercourse among Christians? It shews little more care, except in point of decency, than among others.

The Rev. H. Foster—

This passage most forcibly discovers our guilty and lost condition. Hammond, Whitby, &c., consider it to relate only to criminal words. But they see not the spirituality of the Law. The right view does not exclude that conversation between a father and a child which is suited to circumstances. We must keep up the standard, and, in all our conscious fallings short, fly to the blood of sprinkling.

NOVEMBER 21, 1803.

WHAT ARE THE ADVANTAGES AND DISADVANTAGES OF KEEPING A DIARY ?—Proposed by the Rev. Josiah Pratt.

Mr Pratt—

I. ADVANTAGES.

1. To the WRITER.

(1.) The practice of keeping a diary would promote vigilance. The lives of many are spent at a sort of hazard. They fall into certain religious habits : and are perhaps under no strong temptations. They are regular at church and sacrament, and in their families. They read the Bible and pray daily in secret. But here it ends. They know little of the progress or decline of the inner man. They are Christians, therefore, of very low attainments. The workings of sin are not noticed as they should be, and therefore grace is not sought against them : and the genial emotions of grace are not noticed, and therefore not fostered and cultivated. Now, a diary would have a tendency to raise the standard to such persons by exciting vigilance.

There is another class to whom a diary answers the same end. Not so smooth, plausible, equable, and undeviating as the other class. Passions are stronger. Temptations more violent. And yet grace more vigorous. They sin the more grievously, yet have more fervour and meaning in prayer. They are rash, incautious, heedless, presumptuous; though honest men, like Peter. Now, a diary would put them on their guard :—" *Here* I fell. *There* I fell. Let me watch."

To the insipid and the rash Christian, a diary, therefore, would be useful in exciting vigilance.

(2.) It would promote humility. A faithful record would be very humbling. Our wounds heal too soon. Our sins are too easily forgotten. The facts themselves—atrocious facts perhaps, that, when they came home first to the conscience, made us tremble—are seldom thought of, and seldom mentioned before God in humiliation. If we do name them, it is with very little compunction. The custom of naming them has worn away all remembrance of the circumstances, the detail, the aggravations that accompanied them. Now, a diary would promote humility if it recorded these aggravations and the impressions made by them on the conscience while lively.

(3.) It would excite gratitude. Ebenezers raised in the memory only, soon become illegible. *Litera scripta manet.* The grateful feelings recorded in their full vigour and exercise, chide us for our coldness and insensibility.

L

(4.) It would teach us spiritual wisdom. *Set thee up way-marks.* Jer. xxxi. 21.

2. To the CHRISTIAN WORLD. Without diaries there would have been no Pascal's Thoughts, no Baxter's Life, no Adam's Private Thoughts, no Williams' Diary, no Milner's Memoranda, no Austin's Confessions; and, I think I may say, no Rom. vii. 14, &c.; and no such instructive monuments of egregious vanity as Gibbon's Memoir of himself.

The history of mind is the true history of man. All else is the man disguised and acting a part before the world. But so far as diaries may be supposed free from the disadvantages that seem closely connected with them, so far they form a fair and true history of human nature.

II. DISADVANTAGES.

These are perhaps wholly to be confined to the writer. For I do not know that there can be any bad result, on the whole, to the Christian world. There is an after-judgment exercised by friends upon a diary before it is published; and though these, from partiality to the deceased or to a party, may publish crude or erroneous matter, yet it will find its own level and cure itself. Such diaries are not merely the abuse of a good thing, but they enter in some measure of necessity into it.

The practice of writing diaries tends to—

(1.) Self-deception; (2.) Formality; (3.) Hypocrisy.

On the whole, I strongly incline to favour diaries. But then much of the good depends on the *kind*. And much of the evil may perhaps be avoided by adopting a sort suited to the man and his circumstances.*

The Rev. B. Woodd—

On the whole, I approve of diaries. I kept one till fifteen years old, and then burned it, and have been sorry since for it. Yet one is unwilling to put on paper a faithful delineation of experience. There is an advantage in its helping us to be more grateful and cautious. It helps self-examination.

The Rev. Mr Fry—

I have left off a diary because it was troublesome to keep it. For this I am sorry, for I am sure it was advantageous to me. In darkness I could look back with satisfaction on the workings of grace. The advantages are such as to make it desirable that it should be pressed on Christians.

The Rev. R. Cecil—

A distinction is necessary. There is a dissenting diary which some of the dissenting writers advise persons to keep.

If a man keeps a record of leading features, it is useful; I am

---

* Mr Pratt's opinion in his maturer years may be gathered from the following extract from the Preface to his Memoir :—" Mr Pratt left no diary behind him, and very few papers exhibiting his sentiments on particular topics, or illustrative of his Christian experience. One of the few memoranda which have been discovered, expressly states : ' I occasionally kept records of the workings of my mind, but I have destroyed them all.'"

altogether for it. I have for many years made it my practice, and for this reason :—If you walk under a church, it is grand; if you view it at a few miles' distance, it is scarcely seen. So in the affairs of the mind. The thing seen near is grand and interesting—at a distance, cold and dull.

There is a duty, too, involved :—*Thou shalt remember all the way which the Lord thy God led thee.* It is of vast importance that we should not lose the benefit of the lesson through the treachery of the memory. Making a record, therefore, of our journey, is a useful and important thing. But a wise man will leave an order to burn it, because other characters are often involved. Things are sometimes very improperly introduced. [Here he referred to Madame Roland's Memoirs.] Prudence should be exercised. A well-managed diary is a most important thing. An ill-managed one, like other things, is pernicious.

DECEMBER 19, 1803.

WHAT IS THE DIFFERENCE BETWEEN THE JEWISH AND CHRISTIAN SABBATH ?—Proposed by the Rev. H. Foster.

Mr Foster—

It is plain that the Jewish Sabbath is not obligatory on us in all points. The Jews were not to light fires ; not to gather sticks. The Sabbath among them was in a considerable degree typical. The introduction, *I am the Lord thy God,* &c., applies, therefore, peculiarly to them.

There was, however, a Sabbath before. Owen has written a laborious treatise on the subject. The original Sabbath was made for God to rest in from all His work. Man is to look at God, and rest in Him. Christ entered into *his* rest after the work of redemption, as the Father after creation. Christians observe, therefore, the Sabbath in resting in Christ's work, and keep the day in memorial of that. Our Lord went to a Pharisee's house on the Sabbath, who *made him a great feast.* He would not have done this if it were *malum per se.*

He said, *The Sabbath was made for man, not man for the Sabbath.* This implies, that though it should be properly kept, yet there is a degree of liberty which man may use according to circumstances. Slaves, when converted, would probably serve their masters in the usual way, if they had the liberty of attending the public worship of Christians. There would have arisen a considerable objection to Christianity, if the slaves had been compelled to refuse all such service. Among ourselves, servants in families will consider it their privilege to attend worship, and not feel called to do what is not really necessary.

But I wish for more satisfaction on this subject. Perhaps it is left thus not to burden the conscience, so that honest men in all circumstances may serve God.

The Rev. J. Davies—

How was the Sabbath observed before the Mosaic institution of it?
That is the rule for Christians as to the *manner;* with the additional
sentiment of Christ's resurrection.

If the spirit be right, I feel but little difficulty as to ourselves. I
feel it a privilege. There is some difficulty in directing others.

The Rev. B. Woodd—

Works of duty, of necessity, and of mercy might be performed under
the Jewish Sabbath, much more under the Christian. Secular reflection, conversation, and business are to be avoided.

Should hair-dressers be employed? Leave it to a man's conscience.
Bakers? One at home will prevent many from being detained from
worship. Coaches? I have great misgivings.

The Rev. Mr Fry—

I have always looked upon the Sabbath as of the same obligation on
us as on the Jews. It is placed in the Decalogue for that purpose.
The spirit of the command I conceive to be, that we do no unnecessary
work. If we lived, therefore, where Jews did, when the command was
given, we should not light a fire; but we should catch cold if we did
it not here. The man who gathers sticks is not now stoned; neither
the adulterer put to death; but in the other world will have to give
account.

The Sabbath is now to yield, as it was under the old dispensation,
where it is called to do so. Our Lord only explained the extent of
obligation, and removed the Jewish misinterpretations; but did not
lay down any new views of it, different from those which entered into
the original institution.

JANUARY 16, 1804.

WHAT IS THAT ASSISTANCE WHICH WE HAVE REASON TO EXPECT IN OUR
MINISTERIAL WORK?—Proposed by the Rev. W. Goode.

Mr Goode—

This question arose from a paper in the *Christian Observer,* for
November, on the use of the term, " The people of God." There is
much crudeness in the paper. Read the last paragraph.

The Rev. W. J. Abdy—

The minister's work is—(1.) Preaching. (2.) Visiting the sick.
(3.) Occasional duties : always in the spirit of our profession : always
labouring to do good.

Some confine the minister's work to the pulpit. Some look for
more influence than it is right to expect. We cannot look for that
which the Apostles enjoyed. Yet for some assistance, without which
all is hopeless, we may look.

The Rev. H. Foster—

Not that assistance which will secure us from *error.* Remember that, even after the outpouring of the Spirit, Peter fell into error. Nor that assistance which will secure us from *falls*. Here Peter again affords an example, though at an earlier period. If a man be devoted, he shall have such reflections on his mistakes in sentiment and practice, as will do him good, and enable him to preach better.

On the whole, we may expect this :—To be led to take those kind of subjects which will most benefit the people. A minister knows but few of his people's cares. God knows them all. God will make him one of the people by leading him through trials. Peculiar light is thus often thrown on a passage : people see it. God brought it to him for their sakes.

Well for the poor that it does not depend on us where the influence shall take place from our ministry. The rich, the great, the learned, the amiable, would be aimed at too much. God will therefore direct the truth where and when He pleases ; so that ultimately we shall be made a blessing to God's chosen, scattered through the world. There is the same miraculous influence *on souls* as in the days of the Apostles. On the whole, the assistance will be given such as God will carry a man forward with in His gracious purposes, and say at last, *Well done, good and faithful servant.*

The Rev. R. Cecil—

This matter has been carried to extremes. The enthusiastic part of the ministry have stumbled : the dry part also. Enthusiasts have said that learning, and studying, and writing sermons, have checked the Divine influence. The others say, " Go and hear one of those men hold forth. Such meagre stuff ! "

Both classes are useful. Let each do his work in his own way. Yorkshiremen seem to think every man wrong who does not read. Some men set up exorbitant notions about accuracy. But exquisite accuracy is totally lost. Most see no such connexion as you do.

I should advise a young man to break through all such cobwebs, which those half-witted men would surround him with. An humble, modest man is silenced, if he sees one of these men sit before him. He should say, nevertheless, " I am God's servant as well as you." We are particularly taught in the New Testament to glorify the Spirit of God. We are nearer the Apostles' time than we choose to think ourselves. All this is consistent with a man's being a labourer in the vineyard, not a rhapsodist. It matters not that idle men can be brought forth. What cannot be abused ? After all, we must expect a special blessing to accompany the truth, not to *supersede* labour, but *upon* labour.

The minister is to be in season and out of season ; and, therefore, everywhere a minister. He will not be writing histories, discoveries in mathematics. He will labour directly ; but in a vast variety of ways, as he may be enabled.

God may bless the Word in private, when it has been long heard in vain in public. A man should satisfy himself in saying, " It matters not what men say of my talents ; am I doing what I can ?" for there is much in that—*she did what she could.*

It is bad to say, " If I had done it in such and such a way, I should have succeeded." This is carnal. If God bless the simple way you spoke in, that will do it ; if not, no manner would have done good.

I would go forth in preaching to work miracles. What is the calling forth the dead body of Lazarus to the raising of a dead soul ?

There is such a thing in the religious world as a cold carnal wisdom : holding the scales : working by rule. The question is, whether this is not worse in its effects than the enthusiasm which it opposes. Both are bad, but this is the worst of the two. I hardly ever knew such a preacher, or such a writer, who did much good.

We must go forth, therefore, expecting the excellence of God's power, while we are such frail vessels ; and if, in the Apostles' days, diligence was necessary, how much more now ?

The Rev. Josiah Pratt—

I would not consider ministers so much as a *privileged order*, as though they had peculiar assistance which was withheld from others. The assistance of the Divine Spirit is promised to every Christian, according to his wants and difficulties. Generally speaking, the minister's work and duties are greater than those of any other man ; and, therefore, he will receive, IN THE HUMBLE AND DILIGENT USE OF ALL MEANS, the help required. I say, in the humble and diligent use of all means, because without this, his expectation of peculiar assistance is PRESUMPTION and INDOLENCE ; and God marks his abhorrence of this presumption, by leaving men to talk in such a way as clearly demonstrates, to a capable judge, that they are not in the proper state. " Meditate on these things." *Bene orasse est bene studuisse.*

It must be in the humble as well as diligent use of means. Beware of self-deception and pride. Consider *what* is to be done, and *who* is to do it, and cry out—*Who is sufficient for these things?* When well prepared, we are apt to be self-confident. Frequently there is most effectual help when we feel the least pleasant in ourselves. If we be humble and diligent, we should endeavour to feel a simplicity of affiance in the Spirit's aid ; and bring it down to particulars.

The Rev. J. Goode—

In the diligent and humble use of means we do not expect enough.

JANUARY 30, 1804.

How far is Comfort necessarily Connected with Sanctification ?—Proposed by the Rev. J. Pratt.

Mr Pratt—

This question is of considerable importance in dealing with afflicted consciences.

There are two errors—

1. Of a self-righteous spirit, which says, " In proportion as you are holy, you will feel happy."

2. Of an Antinomian spirit, which says, " Your comfort is independent of all holiness in yourself."

I. There can be no Solid Comfort independent of Conscious Integrity.

Our rejoicing is this, the testimony of our conscience, that in simplicity and godly sincerity . . . . we had our conversation in the world. (2 Cor. ii. 12.) *I know nothing by myself; yet am I not hereby justified: but he that judgeth me is the Lord.* (1 Cor. iv. 4.) *Herein do I exercise myself, to have always a conscience void of offence towards God and towards men.* (Acts xxiv. 16.) Not that conscious integrity is anywhere spoken of as the meritorious cause of comfort, but the *sine qua non.* Comfort cannot be sought in Christ by a man conscious of dishonouring him, without making him the minister of sin. And, therefore, all real Christians, however they may scruple to insist on the evidence of sanctification, and sometimes talk as though they despised evidences of all kinds, yet will lay down such marks of their own, as clearly suppose honour and integrity in every man who seeks comfort of Christ. (Here Romaine was referred to.)

II. A Christian may be actually in a Sanctified State, though he judges otherwise of Himself.

1. Through the prevalence of a *melancholy habit,* he always takes the *black side;* not in its spiritual affairs only, but in common affairs.

2. Through the want of the Spirit's evidences to his own work. The Church (Isa. lxiii. 17) complains that God had hardened their hearts from his fear; and yet his fear was there, for they complain of the want of it. Graces in us shine with a borrowed light. Our spirits, that is, our graces, never witness alone. The Spirit of God witnesseth with our spirit, that we are the sons of God. If we would bear to see our graces without pride, the Spirit would more often witness with our spirit, and we should consequently have more comfort. Few men can bear to see more of his work, without immediate pride of spirit, than that they are not hypocrites, but are conscious of integrity. Without *this,* they would be absolutely wretched, and driven to despair. And where there is much more than this, yet the man is kept low often by a *general dissatisfaction* spread over his view of himself.

3. Through increased increase of spiritual discernment. A Christian is sometimes unable to realise the comfort which he is entitled to, by comparing his present state with what he recollects of his graces and attainments years before. He now more fully understands that for which *he has been apprehended of Christ Jesus.* He has now his spiritual senses better exercised in discovering good and evil. The standard is raised; the prospect widened; he feels more of the infection and malignity and universality of sin. But he recollects less of his former ignorance of these things, than he does of his graces and comforts; and now judges himself lower, though in reality much higher in the scale.

III. Though, from these or other causes, a Christian may not be able to perceive his graces, yet *wherever* there is real comfort, there is actual corresponding sanctification.

One man speaks exultingly of his views of the Gospel—*e. g.,* of God's sovereignty; Christ's glory and fulness; God's electing love, &c., &c. But these exulting views are delusions of the devil, if not attended with corresponding satisfaction. *There is no peace, saith my God, to the wicked.* Solid comfort is the work of THE COMFORTER. And he dwells in that heart only which he sanctifies, and will leave the heart which grieves him. True, some who are scrupulously jealous in appealing to personal evidences, and who talk as though they looked to Christ for comfort, without any respect whatever to their own state and character, are yet holy men. But yet they put themselves in Satan's way hereby, and give him an advantage over them.

IV. THE WANT OF COMFORT IS GENERALLY THE CONSEQUENCE OF WANT OF SANCTIFICATION.

1. In case of carnal confidence. David was in carnal confidence— *In my prosperity I said, I shall never be moved.*

(1.) Carnal confidence leads a man to trust to *false* signs, together with true. God, to discover to him which are false and which true, leaves a man, and then he will find all his false signs, like flatterers, to leave him.

(2.) Carnal confidence leads a man to repose too much on signs, though true. He trusts in comforts and graces, and the witness of the Spirit too much, which are all but acts of God on us and in us. When, therefore, we stay ourselves almost wholly on these, God often makes us feel that *no flesh shall glory in his presence.*

(3.) Carnal confidence leads a man to neglect going to Christ for upholding his graces. He thinks graces and comforts so rooted in him that he neglects this. And then God withdraws the light of those graces, that we may have recourse to the Fountain. Peter is an example.

2. In case of negligence of means. *I sleep, but my heart waketh.* (Cant. v. 2.) Performing holy duties, with the inward man half awake and half asleep. Doing the work of the Lord negligently. God is thus provoked to absent himself. *I opened to my beloved, but my beloved had withdrawn himself.* (Cant. v. 6.) God complains (Isa. lxiv. 7) that there was none that stirred up himself *to take hold* of him ; and therefore he was *wroth :* whereas (v. 5), *Thou meetest him that rejoiceth and worketh righteousness, those that remember thee in thy ways. He that walketh according to this rule, peace be on them*—not otherwise.

3. In case of gross sin.

(1.) Against light. As David's lying to Achish. So Ps. cxix. 25–28, he is very low. *My soul cleaveth unto the dust ; my soul melteth for heaviness.* But the cause is at hand (v. 29)—*Remove from me the way of lying.* God will make a man feel his sin, however he may think circumstances may excuse him.

(2.) When sin is not thoroughly humbled for. David's sin, see Ps. xxxii., li. The incestuous person, till humbled, was to be delivered to Satan ; but when humbled was to be comforted. See also Job xxxvi. 8–9. If we grieve the Spirit, he will grieve us. If we rebel against him, he turns to be our enemy, and fights against us. Isa. lxiii. 10.

4. In case of a stubborn spirit under trials.

For the iniquity of his covetousness was I wroth, and smote him ; I hid me, and was wroth, and he went on frowardly in the way of his heart.

(Isa. lvii. 17.) When lighter and outward strokes will not make us stoop, God deserts and wounds the spirit. This yoke will tame any man. *The spirit of a man will sustain his infirmity; but a wounded spirit who can bear?* (Prov. xviii. 14.)

5. In case of deserting the truth when called to profess it.

Jonah in the whale's belly. Cranmer and Spira. When we will not witness for God, it is fit that his Spirit should not witness for us.

6. In case of UNTHANKFULNESS for former comforts. See Hos. ii. 9.

V. THE WANT OF COMFORT IS SOMETIMES TO BE CONSIDERED AS THE SOVEREIGN ACT OF GOD FOR GRACIOUS ENDS.

Who is among you that feareth the Lord, that obeyeth the voice of his servant, that walketh in darkness, and hath no light? Let him trust in the name of the Lord, and stay upon his God. (Isa. l. 10.)

1. When he intends to qualify a man for arduous service. Heman —Ps. lxxxviii. compared with 1 Kings iv. 31. St Paul "buffeted," &c., in order to, 2 Cor. i. 4–5; *That we may be able,* as he says, *to comfort them which are in any trouble by the comfort wherewith we are comforted of God.* That comfort which answered one man's temptation answers all. Temptation was one of Luther's masters.

2. In case of abundant revelations and consolations. Christ, after the testimony to him at his baptism, is led into the wilderness. St Paul had the thorn in the flesh sent him, lest he should be exalted above measure by his revelations. But in all these things, it pleases God to act very variously.

He has wise and gracious ENDS in view.

1. To illustrate his own power and faithfulness.

2. To make his children partakers in the fellowship of Christ's sufferings.

3. To shew the different state of his children here and hereafter, and to quicken their desires after a better world, *where their sun shall no more go down.*

4. To manifest to us the spring of all spiritual comforts, and our absolute dependence on him.

5. For the trial and perfecting of our graces.

6. For the destruction of our corruptions.

On the whole, let us conclude, that COMFORT in general is connected with SANCTIFICATION. Yet not always, since God may and does deal as a Sovereign for wise and gracious ends.

The Rev. J. Davies—

Some are unhappy who appear to others to be sanctified; while others are happy who are manifestly not sanctified.

What are the causes of want of comfort? God's sovereignty, though he acts with wise ends in view. Constant light is not of advantage to us. Storms are useful in nature; so in grace. Sometimes there is a sort of comfort which seems independent of sanctification. Yet solid comfort must be connected with evidences of grace.

The Rev. J. Goode—

Comfort is either true or false. Suspect that comfort which is not connected with sanctification ; for unholy comfort is not the consolation of the Gospel. *They walked in the fear of the Lord and in the comfort of the Holy Ghost.* But though comfort is connected with sanctification, it does not follow that it springs from holiness. Luther says, " To comfort a heart is more than to make a world." It is God's prerogative. *I, even I, am he that comforteth thee.* Christ was anointed *to comfort those that mourn.* The minister is to cry, *Comfort ye, comfort ye, my people, saith your God.*

Though there is no solid comfort which does not lead to holiness, yet there are many holy persons uncomforted. Our sanctification may discover itself in different ways, as in greater discernment of sin.

I doubt whether God ever withdraws comfort merely as a sovereign. Many divines state this, but I have not seen them prove it.

The Rev. B. Woodd—

God may withdraw comfort in the same view with which he afflicts his people in other respects.

Comfort—what is it ? Not the quieting the rising clamours of conscience : for that a Papist can do in *his* way.

1. It is either that tranquillity of mind which arises from assurance of acceptance in Christ.

2. Or holy tranquillity enjoyed in walking in God's way. Many enjoy much of the last, though if pressed on the point of personal evidence of interest in Christ, would fear to speak positively. This last species of comfort is necessarily connected with sanctification.

The first kind arises, (1.) from the *direct act* of faith ; (2.) from the *reflex act* of faith.

We should judge of personal sanctification in the aggregate, rather than in particular, when we look at it as any evidence.

God vouchsafes his comfort in very various ways. There is peculiar comfort at first conversion, in particular tribulation, at the hour of death.

The Rev. W. Goode—

The comfort of a believer arises from a sense of the favour of God. Another kind of comfort which arises from a confiding of the heart with God.

Sanctification is not the ground of our comfort. The work of Christ is the only ground of comfort. Sanctification is an evidence.

Never lose sight of the idea that comfort cannot exist without conscious integrity.

It is a question whether there are not persons of a lower degree of sanctification who have more comfort than those of a higher : for example, young converts. Those who pretend to comfort while they commit sin, yet perhaps persuade themselves, on the whole, that they are right.

The comfort of a Christian does not always depend on the *most regular* walk—this may lead to a self-righteous spirit.

There may be times when God withdraws himself from his people, though not for this or that particular sin, yet for sin in general ; and therefore He means to humble the heart.

The Rev. Mr Fry—

I am not very anxious for comfort, because I have found that I have suffered for it ; and therefore I am comfortable without comfort, because I find it the best state for me.

The Rev. H. G. Watkins—

Comfort is the work of the Spirit, enabling the judgment to conclude our interest in Christ by the graces.

The Rev. W. J. Abdy—

I feel much as Mr Fry. Many look for more comfort than is consistent with our state and character in this world. A soldier must look forward to difficulties.

The Rev. D. Wilson, a visitor—

Simple country people seem to have more comfort than I and others. Perhaps it is that they come more as children to Christ, coming to him to be fed.

Comfort is not only connected with sanctification, but is a means of sanctification. *The joy of the Lord is your strength.*

You invigorate your child by speaking lovingly to him. I cannot do so much for God when my habit of mind is in an uncomfortable frame, as when cheerful.

Comfort may be distinguished into habitual and occasional.

The Rev. J. Clayton—

Owen says, " The Christian must either be rejoicing in the love of God, or mourning for the absence of it. To undervalue comfort is to withhold from God the *whole* man, which we owe to him—not the judgment only, but the *heart.*

Of holy comfort the Father is the fountain, Christ is the purchaser, the Holy Ghost the applier.

There is no comfort independent of sanctification.

February 13, 1804.

What is that Peculiar Blessing which we may expect to attend the Preaching of the Gospel ?—Proposed by the Rev. W. Goode.

Mr Goode—

This question arose from a passage in the *Christian Observer* in Nov. last, pp. 658, 659.

The Rev. J. Davies—

Lo, I am with you always, even to the end of the world. Particular promises are given to the ministers of the gospel. Particular effects are pointed out as accompanying the ministry. Conversion is a miraculous work ; calling the dead to life.

The Rev. J. Clayton—

This is an interesting question to us all when we stand up to preach.

No idea can be gathered from analogy of any result being produced, but by adequate means. Rain and dew are as necessary as ever to the productiveness of the earth. Divine influence is as necessary as ever for the forming of Christians. 'Tis the production of miracles still, though seen only by the eye of faith.

An ordinary influence of the Spirit is annexed to truth, which is never connected with error. Further than this, there is an influence which *convinces* men, and carries the truth home to the conscience. There is an equal effect in relieving the oppressed conscience.

An influence is annexed in meeting persons under temptation. The minister is led to lay the temptation open. The convert may be getting into bye-path meadow, and is thus stopped. In various ways the old man is weakened, and the new man strengthened.

The Rev. B. Woodd—

We may judge of the effect of the ministry by St Paul's commission to the Gentiles, which was *to open their eyes, and to turn them from darkness to light,* &c. Those passages, too—*Is not my word . . . like a hammer, that breaketh the rock in pieces?* (Jer. xxiii. 29.) *The word of God is quick and powerful, and sharper than any two-edged sword,* &c. (Heb. iv. 12.) *Do not my words do good to him that walketh uprightly?* (Micah ii. 7)—shew the effects of preaching the truth. The effects are also seen in Acts ii. These effects always attend evangelical preaching, and none other.

There is an effect on the minister himself. Delight in his work ; frequent seals to his ministry. Another effect is, the world will take offence.

The Rev. W. Fry—

There is no converted man who does not ascribe his change to the mighty power of God. The enmity of Satan against preaching the efficacious grace of the Spirit, is an argument for the truth. The way in which the Spirit operates, shews that the effect is from Him. When our efforts are studied much, often but little good follows. The means which the Spirit uses are not adequate, in any natural point of view, to the conversion of sinners. Comparatively weak instruments are often made the power of God to salvation.

There is an error, in hearers looking up to a minister in a manner which is not scriptural. The minister has no new revelation. It is an error to expect a minister to speak the gospel as an Apostle. This leads hearers to lay more stress on the emotions, than on solid effects on the soul.

The Rev. H. G. Watkins—

It is a question whether anything is done by the ministry of the Word, which God does not do by other means at times ; *e.g.*, by sickness, &c.

The Rev. S. Crowther—

The gospel came to you not in word only, but in power, and in much assurance. This is the very same power which attended the preaching of St Peter.

The Rev. H. Foster —

Man is represented in Scripture as wretched by every image. The gospel is a remedy for every malady. Ministers are like medical men; physic may give pain, convulsions, &c., but these are necessary for the cure. One patient has bad eyes, he sees; another dropsy, this subsides. Even *gout*, that scandal of physic, can be relieved. There is no malady which we, as ministers, cannot reach, under God. *The blind shall see; the lame shall walk*, &c. It will be efficacious on all whom God purposes to save; and when all the saved are gathered home, then the work will be shut up for ever. The rest of men will be an awful example to eternity of the consequence of resisting the gospel.

Miracles never converted a man. They have corrected him, and turned his attention to truth; but it was the *truth* which changed him. Some men are converted by reading, but still it is the *truth*. Preaching is the usual means. *The weapons of our warfare are not carnal*, &c.

The consideration of what God is, and what God has promised to do, has sometimes strengthened me in a moment.

The Rev. J. Goode—

What has God promised? *that* we may expect, be it what it may. God has promised to be with his ministers to the end of the world.

The Word of God does not work as physical causes do. The effect does not always follow the cause here.

Afflictions may turn the attention to the Word. Remember Manasseh.

The Rev. J. Pratt—

All success is from the divine influence : not *without* labour, manner, men, suitable means; but *by* these, and sometimes without what we should deem suitable. *No* success is *by* these, *without* the Spirit. *Who then is Paul?* &c. (1 Cor. iii. 5.)

This influence is exclusively confined to the *word read or ministered*. Meditation, self-denial, &c., are means of growth, not of conversion, though God may use anything.

What is this influence?

I. As to the DEGREE of it.

Suppose the man simple, diligent, praying, devoted. Suppose him a man of *one aim*, viz., to save souls. If this is made out, then he may rest satisfied that all the influence is secured to his ministry which is consistent with the will of God.

God acts as a sovereign in the distribution of gifts. His are our appointments to such and such stations, large or small spheres.

He acts also a sovereign in the success he gives. We have no reason to believe that success corresponds to the grace bestowed. Two men of equal devotedness may have very different gifts, and very different opportunities; and even in stations of the same apparent importance, and probability of usefulness, may yet have very different success.

When I say God acts as a sovereign herein, I do not mean that he acts without motive, but that he acts above and beside our views and natural expectations. He may deny the influence which is necessary to usefulness in judgment on the people for long despising the gospel; in judgment on the man for past falls, for an unhumbled spirit, for a spirit of self-conceit, for indolence, for want of devotedness : or to keep the man low, as severe discipline is sometimes necessary. In all cases where it is withheld, there is ground of self-inquiry and of self-abasement.

We should mourn its absence, and wait in prayer. And in all cases where it is granted, there is a call for self-jealousy, lest we should forget that it arises solely and exclusively from the Spirit of God.

II. The OPERATION of this influence.

(1.) It is suited to the instrument. It is sometimes adapted to awaken men ; at others to convince, or melt, or build up, or plant, or water. A minister should not be dejected, because that sort of work is little seen under his ministry to which his gifts are but little suited.

Mr Wesley's plan was admirable, so far as it consulted the qualifications of most of his preachers, but not as to the edification of his hearers ; therefore his people were more *jejune* than other classes. It would have been an improvement on the plan to have made one able minister stationary for life, or many years, in each considerable circuit. He would have built up those who are now always dwelling on first principles.

(2.) This influence is various. It is sometimes *sensible*—a man struck with sudden conviction. Sometimes *insensible*, like dew distilled. This is true, both as to first turning to God and as to subsequent growth.

(3.) It is efficacious. *Ye received the word of God . . . . . which effectually worketh in you that believe.* And this, not new notions, but change of heart and spiritual growth.

(4.) It is abiding. There is a degree of influence which may be said to accompany the minister, which is frustrated in its results. But all efficacious influence is abiding, in its main effects.

FEBRUARY 27, 1804.

WHAT IS THE PRECISE EXTENT OF THE APOSTLE'S MEANING WHEN HE SAYS—" I COUNT ALL THINGS BUT LOSS FOR THE EXCELLENCY OF THE KNOWLEDGE OF CHRIST JESUS, MY LORD ?" (Phil. iii. 8.)—Proposed by the Rev. H. Foster.

Mr Foster—

All our righteousnesses are but as filthy rags. I think the Apostle excludes all his attainments, of whatever kind, and looks to Christ.

The weight of commentators is against me. They consider the Apostle as looking back to works wrought in him as a Jew, and not to graces wrought in him by the Holy Ghost.

The Rev. R. Cecil—

The Apostle seems to speak here, not of justification, but of salvation in general. *All things* can only include those things which are opposed to the knowledge of Christ. Now, the graces of the Spirit are not opposed to, but a part of, the knowledge of Christ.

The Rev. Thomas Scott—

In point of justification, he excludes all works. *I count all things as loss*, in the present tense. Knowledge is used here as in Isaiah liii.: *By his knowledge shall my righteous servant justify many.*

I count all things loss for Christ, (v. 8), *i. e.*, my worldly prospects, &c. *I counted* (v. 7), all works, &c., in point of justification. There is a disposition among some good men to forget the great truth, that the best works of the best men need forgiveness. I do not say that the Apostle counts the graces of the Spirit loss, *as* they are the graces of the Spirit, but as they are exercised by an imperfect creature. These graces might be evidence of his justification; but he could never be perfect in holiness.

The Rev. J. Davies—

The changes of tense, as it appears to me, are not by way of including more, but by way of answering an objection, and asserting that his opinion *is* as it *was*. I cannot think that in that passage he meant anything more than what he mentioned before, viz., the advantages which he enjoyed over his countrymen. It might be objected to him, " You repent of the sacrifice you made." He replies, " No."

The Rev. W. Goode—

I have been accustomed to look upon it always as Brother Davies always did *not* look upon it. His loss was—(1.) All his legal righteousness ; (2.) All his privileges ; (3.) All his Christian graces.

The Rev. J. Venn—

This is not a question of doctrine, but of the meaning of a particular passage. Of the doctrine, there can be no question, that works have no share in justification. But it depends, I think, on other passages, and not on this.

We must take care not to extend the meaning of this expression, *all things*, beyond the rest of the passage. There is a very material difference between the works wrought *before* and *after* justification. The particulars enumerated before do not warrant the extending of the term, *all things*, to works after conversion. Nor what he mentions afterwards. He would not use such a degrading expression as *dung* to describe the works wrought by the Spirit. Since his great end was to attain the power of the Spirit on him, is it likely that he would count the Spirit's graces, though wrought in him imperfectly, so low ?

The Rev. H. G. Watkins—

I hardly think the Apostle would use so degrading a word to denote the works of the Spirit. *The excellence of the knowledge of Christ Jesus* must include the works of the Spirit in him. The Apostle was not so refined in his expressions as to admit of this extension.

The Rev. W. J. Abdy—

I think the Apostle did not include here the works wrought by the Spirit, though in point of justification there can be no doubt that he did.

MARCH 12, 1804.

WHAT ARE THE MOST SATISFACTORY EVIDENCES OF A DEATH-BED REPENTANCE?—Proposed by the Rev. W. Goode.

Mr Goode—

When persons consent to all you say, there is no certainty in this. If you let them speak *their own* sentiments, perhaps they shew ignorance, and you have some hold. I never knew but two of which I had much opinion. They were a change from a self-righteous spirit to an apparently contrite spirit.

The Rev. H. G. Watkins—

I have the best hopes of those who are most earnest for information. An anxiety to know more of what they then seemed first to hear. When they are open and candid as to their former state. When they complain they cannot see sin as they wish.

The Rev. W. J. Abdy—

The longer I live, the more reluctant I become to form an opinion upon subjects of this nature. Some people there are whom you may work up to say such things as would appear well in print, who yet betray in other ways that they are not right. Religion is the business of life. It is hopeless where they do not see the evil of sin.

The Rev. J. Goode—

I don't know that anything can be absolutely satisfactory. Saurin says, that if we judge of those who are gone by those who survive, after having discovered apparent symptoms of repentance, the result is unfavourable. An honest man was satisfied as to his wife, but wished it not to be reported, lest others should take encouragement to defer as she had done.

The Rev. H. Foster—

The evidences of repentance are the same on a death-bed as in health. Appearances which in health look well, we live to see come to nothing. Nothing but perseverance will ascertain. A variety of trials will shew the unsoundness of the rotten foundation. I do not know that I was ever concerned in one case in which I found real satisfaction. My chief hope is of bystanders.

The Rev. R. Cecil—

A change from a Pharisaic spirit is the most satisfactory. As to their acquiescing with what you say, this is nothing. And yet it is upon that on which most of what we have read is founded. Great fears prove nothing. Nor can anything be inferred from apparent peace and joy in one who has not lived as he ought. In real cases, a man is not easily satisfied.

There is something judicial in the death-bed of those who have lived in a parish where the Gospel has been preached to them without effect. The example of the thief on the Cross is not parallel to such cases. This is a ground of encouragement to us, but of presumption to none.

The Rev. J. Pratt—

It is important in the minister to hold out the uncertainty of a death-bed repentance. Mr Venn knew of but two cases, and one only good. There is only one in Scripture. A death-bed is of vast importance to us as ministers, to demonstrate the whole work of God. If we knew of any certain case, we should bring it forward to God's glory.

The Rev. W. Fry—

I have generally thought more favourably of a death-bed repentance than most of my brethren. I have had no hope of those who had heard the gospel ; but have had of those who never heard it before. A sense of weakness is a good evidence.

March 26, 1804.

What are the Signs of a Minister's Preaching Himself in Contradistinction to Preaching Christ Jesus the Lord ?—Proposed by the Rev. J. Pratt.

Mr Pratt—

I. What is the END the minister looks to ?

The minister who does not make the glory of Christ his supreme end and aim, opposes self to Christ in the most criminal sense.

The minister who proposes the glory of Christ as his chief end, may yet have such indistinct views of truth, as not clearly to discern what his avowed end requires of him ; and so be led often to oppose self to Christ.

The minister who has the glory of Christ as his settled and approved principle of conduct, may be liable to the temptation of forgetting his end, and so far will oppose self to Christ.

II. The MEANS by which he preaches himself.

1. An improper indulgence of one's own peculiar manner.

2. Withholding truth through fear or interest, instead of declaring the whole counsel of God boldly and impartially. It is not requisite, indeed, that a man should bring forward prominently Calvinistic views.

3. Self shews itself perhaps as much, too, in stating truth offensively, instead of labouring *to find out acceptable words*.

4. And self again will push this labouring-to-be-acceptable into *craft*, in opposition to simplicity. An oratorical *finesse* is dangerous.

5. An undue use of curiosity. There is a due use of it. An undue use generates a dissatisfaction with plain food. It begets an Athenian spirit. It sets the minister hunting for striking, more than useful, thoughts.

III. What is the SPIRIT of such a man?

1. Of self-dependence, in opposition to dependence on the Spirit of Christ.

2. Of presumption, in opposition to diligence.

3. Of impatience with Christ, instead of patient waiting for him. Such men want *more* success than appears, *quicker* success, *other* success.

4. Of impatience with hearers, instead of pity and prayer.   An imperious spirit, a scolding spirit, shews itself.   Self may appear in a mild spirit, but more in the contrary mind.

5. Of self-importance and self-abounding, instead of a lowly preference of the brethren.   " *My* way; *my* congregation; *my* books; *my* schools."   Somewhat less offensive, but equally selfish, is the plural—" *Our* this and that:" " *we* do so and so."

Such a man gets to think himself of some importance to Christ. He has lost the abiding, practical influence of the recollection that he is an earthen vessel.   This leads to a spirit—

6. Of self-gratulation, instead of giving all the glory to Christ.

7. Of envy of the success of others, instead of rejoicing in it.   Self has too much influence if we cannot rejoice as much in others' success as our own.

In short, the whole evil originates in a feeble hold on Christ ; too little concern for his glory ; little real love to him.   SELF is the grand enemy of the Christian and the minister.   It dodges and meets him in a thousand guises.   At the very moment that he is, in the simplicity of his heart, shouting victory over self, it is self that makes the loudest noise.

And the scriptural remedy for this desperate malady is the *love of Christ shed abroad in the heart by the Holy Ghost.*   A swallowing up of the soul in the contemplation of the amazing love which the Saviour has shewn.   An expanding of the heart beyond the narrow bounds which self prescribes by the force of this grand principle.

The Rev. J. Clayton—

Tests of preaching Christ and not himself are—

1. A willingness to sacrifice everything which may be gratifying to him, if he will not preach Christ.

2. The prevailing disposition of the heart in solitude—Is it sloth? is it self-indulgence?   Does he look upon a subject as difficult or easy?

3. The manner in which he will consider the subject.

4. The satisfaction which a minister feels in accomplishing his end. When he is as glad the poor man is called as the rich.   When he considers the end answered—not in having a large congregation, or a great revenue, but in real good being done.   A minister may have a crowded auditory, who sit in the spirit of people at the theatre.

5. When a minister feels happy in coadjutors.   Some may love coadjutors, perhaps, in the next county, but not in the next street. Ministers should feel themselves as journeymen serving at the same counter.   The revenue is all for the Master.—*Newton.*

The Rev. B. Woodd—

I feel all the evil spoken of; and, I hope, some of the good. Sincerity would go into a small compass. God has respect to a little sincerity.

The Rev. J. Goode—

Self is subtle and importunate. It sparkles in the preacher's eye ; it forms the muscles of his face.

The Rev. S. Crowther—

A man may be preaching himself, while he appears to be, and thinks he is, preaching Christ. He may be useful at this time, since there is a sort of fashion in attending the preaching of Christ. But he should watch lest he is gratifying the itching ear. The effect on his own heart of what he hears of his own preaching forms a good test.

The Rev. H. Foster—

When we are conscious what *self* is, and what Christ Jesus the Lord is, it would surprise us that there should be any kind of opposition between them. This affords a marvellous instance of our depravity. If weighed in a balance, I fear more will be found for self in our ministry than for Christ. There is, no doubt, a reality in our regard to Christ : but if we look at our minds *before* preaching, *while* we preach, and *after* preaching, there is even then too much of self. We are disgusted with ourselves, and *with God* too, when we think we have so preached as to sink ourselves before the people.

Bishop Hall says that " our attainments here consist rather in lamenting what we are, than in being what we should be." This remark has helped me. I am taught to see the value of the Gospel by this influence, and the constitution of grace. It is only in such ways as this that we can *really* see and feel the glory and suitableness of justification by Christ. There are moments in which the Christian thus learns the truths of the Gospel in a way he cannot otherwise. I was disappointed much in my early expectations. I feel now more of the working of sin than before. Jealousy of coadjutors or neighbours was my bane. Once I wished I had for a time done with preaching, while this spirit lasted. I heard Berridge on *My name is Legion.* Envy was one of the evil spirits. He described himself envious at Everton. This helped me much to go on ; though it did not, I hope, quiet me in a wrong way.

If we could get to be in the business *vox et praeterea nihil*, it would be right and pleasant. We should be like Abraham's servant when he went to get a wife for his master's son : he set his master and his master's son forth.

A good impression is produced when a congregation does not talk about the preacher, but about the Saviour. I once preached on scripture words at Spitalfields. " Mediator" was one night the subject. Coming home, I heard a man say, " Oh, what a blessed Mediator we have !" and I was pleased. We must be glad to lie in the dust, and that there is a fountain opened for sin and uncleanness.

The Rev. R. Cecil—

The text points out two ends. One of these, the carnal nature always proposes to itself. The other, a great mind will propose to itself. It would be a strange sight to see a man on the hustings proposing himself.

I was struck with Clayton's remark, that when a man can rejoice in coadjutors, 'tis a good symptom. Yet this must be with some limitation. For a man may be justly displeased with any attempt to set up post against post. I have seen some instances of this in my own case. " This is a good spot. Better than the wilderness. Good pasturage is here."

I was struck also with Clayton's remark, that there may be something antichristian in zeal for evangelical truth. Huntington shewed this sometimes.

Naming Christ over and over again is not preaching Christ. Preaching Christ is setting forth the kingdom of Christ.

April 9, 1804.

WHEN MAY A PEOPLE BE CONSIDERED THE JOY AND GLORY OF THEIR MINISTER ?—Proposed by the Rev. J. Goode.

Mr J. Goode—

The minister will have to weep for many: *I tell you, even weeping, that they are the enemies of the cross of Christ.* He stands in doubt of others.

A people are the joy and glory of their minister when they give clear evidence of their conversion. Some are our converts, but not our joy. When we can congratulate our people on their safety, they are our joy. When ministers can trace the progress of the divine life; when their people are in love with holiness; when they are in judgment not children; clothed in humility; sanctified through the truth; regular in devoutly attending the divine ordinances. This more than compensates the minister's toil. Our people are then Christ's epistle, our best letters-testimonial.

A people are the joy of their minister when they studiously avoid what would bring the Gospel into disrepute, and are careful to cultivate what is amiable. By what would bring the Gospel into disrepute, I mean little fretfulnesses, &c., not gross sins.

The Rev. H. G. Watkins—

Affection for ministers is an equivocal ground of joy. Regularity of attendance upon their ministry is the same. Inquiring after further religious knowledge is a good sign; also when religion is made an affair of conscience; and when a man considers himself, rather than the minister. In London, we must be satisfied with few instances.

The Rev. H. Foster—

The Apostle calls the Corinthians his epistle, and yet there were such things among them that he seems broken-hearted. Perhaps we sometimes pitch things too high. There may be marks of humiliation and self-loathing, and grounds of rejoicing, though also much evil among the people.

The Rev. W. Fry—
Do we know our congregations enough in London?

The Rev. J. Clayton—
When people are steadfast in the faith in trying times; when the bond of union among them seems to promise permanence; when they demean themselves suitably in affliction; when they shew a forwardness to discountenance sin :—these are grounds of rejoicing.

The poorer people in my congregation are my joy, and I hope will be my crown. Some rich would give, as though they would bribe to silence.

The Rev. W. Goode—
What is a minister's joy? When God is glorified—Christ exalted—the Gospel honoured.

Our hearers are our joy and glory when they are sound in the faith; *wherefore I also, after I heard of your faith in the Lord Jesus, and love unto all the saints, cease not to give thanks for you :* when they shew a conduct becoming the Gospel; acting with integrity in private concerns; shewing a deadness to worldly pleasures.

APRIL 23, 1804.

How far does the Word of God encourage Christians to expect Consolation in the Present Life?—Proposed by the Rev. W. Goode.

Mr Goode—
There is a danger of making *too much* of consolation, and *too little.* Consolation may rest on a false ground; yet that is no argument against scriptural consolation. Scriptural consolation is an incitement to duty. It is lawful, therefore, to seek consolation. It is, indeed, a duty to seek consolation. *God, willing more abundantly to shew unto the heirs of promise the immutability of his counsel, confirmed it by an oath; that . . . we might have a strong consolation.*

Consolation is stated to be the peculiar work and office of the Spirit. It is his *to seal;* to give the *earnest;* to *shed abroad the love of God in our hearts.* The manner in which this is communicated is intricate : it is by his shining on his own work.

There is a danger of giving consolation an improper importance. Some make it the main end; and yet too easily sit down without having marks of the Spirit's work. There is as great danger, perhaps, of undervaluing it.

The Rev. H. G. Watkins—
The whole tenor of Scripture is consolatory, as directing mortals to the prospect of immortality. As sinners, dying, afflicted, hopeless, it

meets us. It is full of promises, precepts, to remove evils. The names of God are full of comfort : *Gracious and merciful : God of love—of hope—of comfort.* There may be much real, though not sensible consolation, such as a staying upon God in a dark day.

The Rev. H. Foster—

We are differently made in our animal frames. Religion, acting through the animal frame, will be coloured. The word of God is our ground of consolation. The object of consolation is Christ. If a man looks at this object only through the medium of his sanctification, he will always have hesitation and fears. Yet there is danger on the other side. Remember the stony-ground hearers, who *hear the word, and anon with joy receive it.* In one view, I wonder we have not more consolation. In another view, that we have any at all.

The Rev. J. Pratt—

The primitive Church dealt more simply with this subject. They were more holy. Consolation is connected with near-walking with God.

The Rev. Mr Simons, a visitor—

The best consolation is in the actings of faith.

The Rev. J. Davies—

There is a great difference between having ground for consolation, and enjoying consolation. Sanctification may be promoted by a change of dispensation. Clouds are as needful as sunshine.

The Rev. J. Goode—

Christ—the character of God—the oath of God—his ordinances— the charge of God to ministers, are all grounds of consolation.

The Rev. B. Woodd—

I think the word of God holds out unlimited consolation.

MAY 7, 1804.

IS THERE AN ESSENTIAL DIFFERENCE BETWEEN THE WARFARE OF THE FLESH WITH THE SPIRIT IN BELIEVERS, AND THOSE WARRINGS OF CON- SCIENCE WITH THE PASSIONS FELT BY SINNERS IN GENERAL : AND WHEREIN DOES THE DIFFERENCE CONSIST ?—Proposed by the Rev. H. Foster.

Mr Foster—

I premise that the difference is essential ; but the operations are so intermixed as to be perplexed. The unregenerate does not partake with the believer in *his* warfare, but the righteous partakes with the unrege- nerate in *his.* The workings of conscience in the unregenerate *may* lead to the work of the Spirit. God often makes use of this kind of fears to lead to conversion.

The difference is this. The warrings of conscience come and go with outward circumstances. Pharaoh and Judas afford examples. The warfare of believers is more permanent.

The one is like a spring ; the other like a land flood. The one deals with sin, as it exposes men to wrath ; the other as it is filthy. The one quiets itself by false remedies : prayers, vows, tears ; the other only by the blood of atonement. *O wretched man that I am ! . . . . thanks be unto God through Jesus Christ our Lord.* The assurances of forgiveness strengthen one to sin again ; but arm the other against sin. The one springs from terror ; the other from love. An ungodly man may be led through fear to many things for relief ; but a godly man is chiefly influenced by love in the pain he feels from sin. The one lives through the struggle ; the other dies in it. The one is altogether selfish ; the other respects God.

They differ as to the universality of the contest. The unregenerate holds fast some evils ; making a sort of bargain : for example, Herod and John Baptist. The warfare in the regenerate may operate at first in particular sins, but it will go on to *right hands* and *right eyes.* It is of the essential nature of grace to enter into contest with one sin after another, while there is a Philistine remaining. The one deals with the interior workings of sin ; the other respects chiefly the outward conduct. A godly man is often distressed at the motives of actions which others admire. For example, in giving to public charities.

The one, by prevailing, sees little need of Christ ; the other all the more. The unregenerate does not sift his motives, and, therefore, is satisfied with himself ; but the spiritual man, the more progress he makes, the more deeply does he see the corruption of his motives, and the more need of Christ. The one gives up the contest so far as he dares ; the other yields to no conditions. The one seeks the glory of God, as David in attacking Goliath ; the other, his own.

The one asks how far he may follow sin, and yet be safe, and the other how far he may profess to godliness, and yet be nothing.

The Rev. Mr Simons, a visitor—

A man may approve of what is excellent from its being of good report. There is, too, a fearful looking for of wrath. There is a *delight* in the godly man, not merely an *assent.*

The Rev. J. Clayton—

1. They differ in principle. The Holy Spirit is the author of the new life, and, therefore, there is a universal struggle. The natural conscience is the operation of the mind called into action by light thrown in upon it.

2. They differ in the strength in which the warfare is carried on. Natural conscience acts by its own resources ; the regenerate mind by its dependence on Christ.

3. The one is temporary and transient ; the other is constant and permanent. Natural conscience is quieted when it gets the victory over a particular sin. The regenerate mind sees an increased host of enemies in proportion as he obtains victory.

4. Whatever originates with self, tends to self-exaltation ; but the more victories a believer achieves, the more humble he is, and grateful to Christ.

The Rev. J. Davies—

They differ (1.) in their nature. In the unregenerate it is not a conflict between sin and grace, but between one sin and another ; or one faculty and another ; light in the understanding against lust in the will. But the conflict in the regenerate is between the divine and natural principles in the same faculty.

(2.) In their origin.

(3.) In their extent and influence. The warrings of the passions are partial ; the warfare of the regenerate man is against the whole body of sin.

(4.) In their end.

The Rev. B. Woodd—

In the regenerate man, the warfare is against sin in the soul : the unregenerate man glosses over his sins. There is no warfare.

Therefore in the unregenerate man as to the natural man. Self-will as to God, and selfishness as to man, are the ruling principles in the natural man, though he knows it not. But the Christian opposes sin as in the heart.

There is a difference between the sins of the regenerate and un-regenerate man, as to the manner in which sin gains the master. In the regenerate man, there are sins of surprise : for example, Peter ; but Peter *wept bitterly.* After sin, there is an essential difference between the men. The unregenerate man labours to reconcile his conscience to it, the regenerate man is the last to receive comfort.

The Rev. Charles Simeon, a visitor—

They differ—1. In the occasion of the struggle. In the unre-generate man, it is from shame before the world : but the regenerate man is against all sin ; particularly his master sin.

2. In the means by which the struggle is carried on. The unre-generate acts in the way of resolutions, self-righteous endeavours, mortification. The regenerate has learned to implore help of God alone : a way which none but a regenerate man can understand. *Stand still, and see the salvation of God.* I do not mean indolence, but dependent waiting. No human being could have conceived of things as the Word represents them. *God hath given to us exceeding great and precious promises, that by these ye might be partakers of the divine nature.* But the unregenerate say, " No, become partakers of a renewed nature, and then claim the promise." But let us remember—*Having therefore these promises, let us cleanse ourselves,* &c. Here is the power in the promises, of looking to Christ.

3. In the end in view. The unregenerate man seeks to conquer something which lowers him in his own and others' approbation. The regenerate desires, indeed, the testimony of a good conscience as the sublimest joy, but not as a ground of self-satisfaction. He hates the smallest sin, as a wedge to which Satan will give blow after blow.

The Rev. W. Goode—

The sinner grieves, because he dare not commit the sin which he loves; the believer, because he cannot be free from the sin which he hates.

The Rev. H. G. Watkins—

What is called natural conscience, is little else than a sort of calculation of consequences. Where, indeed, it ends in conversion, it may be considered as the incipient work of the Holy Spirit.

The Rev. J. Pratt—

This question has nothing to do with *outward* sins.

The Rev. R. Cecil—

There is a principle in a godly man which *can* be in none but a godly man, with respect to this struggle. Between a true husband and wife, a parent and child, if anything arises to create a suspicion of their friendship, it needs nothing else to make them miserable.

A Christian feels in sin that his strength, his hold of God, is gone : *know that it is a bitter thing that thou hast forsaken the Lord.* The unregenerate man never had such a hold of God ; never did walk with God; and therefore this cannot be interrupted. " I was made with passions," he says ; whereas the language of the other is, " I repent, and abhor myself." He has no idea of this cold and wintry state. This is a grand and essential difference.

MAY 21, 1804.

BY WHAT ARGUMENTS SHALL WE PLEAD WITH GOD TO DELIVER US FROM THE FRENCH ?—Proposed by the Rev. H. Foster.

Mr Foster—

Prussia, Holland, and Switzerland have fallen, though they have many pious.

The Rev. C. Simeon, a visitor—

The great argument of Scripture, is the glory of God's own name.

The Rev. J. Davies—

Even among religious people there is too much of a self-righteous spirit in comparing ourselves with the French. We should try to pull down this spirit, lest God punish us. Yet much of the work of God is going on in the nation. We may justifiably plead with God that He would bless this work. Let us take Hezekiah as an example.

The Rev. J. Clayton—

Mercy already received is an argument for deliverance from the French.

Public institutions would be destroyed if France prevailed. Take Nehemiah : *Remember me for good.* There are many who are praying, and understand the influence of the Spirit. God has given us the means of defence.

The Rev. B. Woodd—

The first argument is, that we have *nothing to plead.* All our mercies are forfeited as individuals, and therefore as a nation. The main argument is from God himself. We have a God to go to. The war engaged in is not a war of ambition. There is a public stand for God here. Britain is a grand medium of diffusing truth. In schools, an immense number of children are being instructed.

Particular interpositions have already been shewn in our favour. The destruction of this constitution would lead to the advance of Infidelity. There is more true religion in this nation than in any other ; more humanity, public decency, public faith. God, in His dealings with individuals and nations, adopts a system of present rewards and punishments.

We may plead the character and object of those who come against us.

The Rev. J. Newton—

Considering our advantages, we are worse than any nation under the sun.

The Rev. W. Goode—

We are not to look for any *certain* arguments which *must prevail.* There is no absolute promise. Yet we may inquire what will most encourage our hopes? The character of our King. But that text has struck me with fear : *I will not bring the evil in his days, but in his son's days.* The people of God abroad view the success of this nation as important to the success of the Gospel. This will not go as an argument against correction, yet against destruction. *You only have I known of all the families of the earth, therefore I will punish you for all your iniquities* (Amos iii. 2). The goodness of our cause is an argument.

There are two ways of pleading these things—(1.) in a self-righteous spirit : (2.) viewing it as God's work.

The Rev. S. Crowther—

A sense of unworthiness will encourage us to plead. The continuance of our public worship is a ground of thankfulness ; also the consolation and support of God's people in the land.

The Rev. H. G. Watkins—

Our prayers should be general, not particular. It may please God to disperse Christian ministers by persecution, that they may diffuse good. God is acting upon a grand scale, far beyond our comprehension. We must submit to God. We should pray that our sins increase not upon us. From hundreds of schools the Bible is excluded. This is a great evil.

The Rev. W. J. Abdy—

I agree with Brother Watkins. We should pray that God would prepare us for all issues. Our danger is great, our fears great, and our hopes great. We must labour to counteract the love of ease and the world.

The Rev. J. Venn—

Why do we use arguments at all in preaching? Not to persuade God ; but to cultivate right feelings in ourselves.

What, then, tends not to this? When we presume to consider what God may do hereafter ; or what God will do by these events. We have to do with present events and duties, and not remote consequences.

If France prevail, everything great and good will be extinguished. You might as well hesitate about praying against a body of lions and tigers as against the French. *Arise, O God, and maintain thine own cause!*

Every man had better die at once than come under their sway. Bonaparte is Satan personified, and his legions.

Therefore, when you set forth in preaching the excellence of our land, of its institutions particularly, and pray for them, you are in a right spirit of thankfulness. When timid in pleading thus, in a wrong spirit.

There are many reasons common to all nations—God's mercy, &c.

One argument is the Fathers' and Martyrs' sake ; Cranmer and all our Reformers. Where is there any nation which can boast such a host of great men?

We should plead for the generations yet unborn. What father would not rather follow his children to the grave, than leave them to such rulers as the French would be? The morals of Holland are ruined ; and so might ours be. There is a relative goodness and an absolute goodness.

If ever there is a time when we could plead the honour of God's name, it is now. If the French prevailed, I should consider it the death of the two witnesses.

The Rev. J. Goode—

We should seek for the spirit of prayer. *Pray not for this people for their good*, has not yet been said. If God gives the spirit of prayer, we may plead with God on his faithfulness to his promises.

The Rev. R. Cecil—

God's own glory was a motive used of old. The character of our enemies was also so used. What does a man mean when he says, *Deliver us from evil, for thine is the kingdom, the power, and the glory?* And what is evil, if that is not evil which Bonaparte would bring on this land? When the enemy begins to boast and blaspheme, we may well look up and plead. Ours is a war purely defensive.

The Rev. J. Pratt—

One grand argument is—" If our deliverance may promote Thy glory." One argument has not been mentioned— Bonaparte, as it were, claiming God to be on his side. *Am I come up without the Lord?* (2 Kings xviii. 23).

The Rev. Mr Gilbert, a visitor—

We should be accustomed to identify our cause with that of God. David so pleaded : we should *à fortiori.*

This appears to have been the last meeting which Mr Newton attended.   His increasing years henceforth deprived his brethren of the advantage of his presence.   He lived till the end of 1807, and was buried on the last day of that year, " in sure and certain hope" of a joyful "resurrection to eternal life" through that REDEEMER whose blessed gospel he had so long and faithfully preached.   He was one of those instances in the history of the Christian Church, which at once illustrate, in the most remarkable degree, the DIVINE SOVEREIGNTY, and the power of DIVINE GRACE ; having been called in maturer years from a life of reckless infidelity into a state of light, peace, holiness, and joy in Christ. His memoir, written by the Rev. Richard Cecil, one of his companions in the Eclectic, relates a story which redounds in a wonderful manner to the glory of the grace of God.   He was constantly in the habit of referring back with shame and contrition to the days of his youth, and of magnifying the grace of God, which had effected so vast a change.   After he was turned eighty, some of his friends, fearing he might continue his ministrations too long, recommended, through his friend Mr Cecil, that he should " consider his work done, and that he should stop before he should evidently discover that he could speak no more."   " I cannot stop," said he, raising his voice—" What ! shall the old African blasphemer stop while he can speak ?"   He left a solemn injunction upon his executors, that if any epitaph were put up to his memory in his church, none should be erected but the following :—

JOHN NEWTON, CLERK,
ONCE AN INFIDEL AND LIBERTINE,
A SERVANT OF SLAVES IN AFRICA,
WAS, BY THE RICH MERCY OF OUR LORD AND SAVIOUR
JESUS CHRIST
PRESERVED, RESTORED, PARDONED,
AND APPOINTED TO PREACH THE FAITH
HE HAD LONG LABOURED TO DESTROY,
NEAR SIXTEEN YEARS AT OLNEY, IN BUCKS,
AND —— YEARS IN THIS CHURCH.

JUNE 4, 1804.

HOW FAR IS IT OUR DUTY TO VISIT OUR PEOPLE IN PRIVATE, AND THE BEST METHODS ?—Proposed by the Rev. W. Fry.

Mr Fry—

The minister is the father of a large family ; and is bound to labour to improve them.

Visiting the people is an essential part of the minister's duty :— (1.) To learn their state, and so how to preach; (2.) To remove obstructions from my ministry.

In the country, I have visited all, invited or uninvited. Those who would have opposed if asked, are silenced by a visit.

Preach the Gospel in the pulpit. But when with enemies, we should labour to soften prejudices, by shewing that we are like other men. We must not, however, make wrong concessions.

In town, I have found talk about religion not profitable ; I then take up the Bible, and pray, and away. This is not useful.

I have determined, therefore—(1.) that I would have societies; and (2.) visit once a-year the families, address parents, children, &c.

If I preach from my own heart and experience, I shall not reach all the hearers. Many circumstances exist among them of which I have no idea from my own experience. When I speak of such while warm in the subject, the impression upon them is most efficacious. Visiting single families when expected, therefore, appears to me my duty.

The Rev. B. Woodd—

Neglect and decay of pastoral duty is one of the crying sins of the time. See "Baxter's Reformed Pastor." He gave two days a-week to visit his parish.

Visiting sometimes removes the prejudices of the minister as well as of the people. It furnishes matter for discourses. It discovers the difficulties, trials, wants of the Christian. It is humbling to a minister, by shewing how ignorant our admirers may be; and the little effect of favourite discourses. It is endless to visit all in a London parish. We must do what we can.

The Rev. W. Goode—

My parish is divided into rich and poor. The rich are out of town; the poor are out getting a living. I visit when my people are sick, for then they are at home.

The Rev. H. G. Watkins—

Jones carried books to give away. Some would say, " Just come in time; I wanted to boil my pot." Yet you have done your duty.

It is not so necessary for composing sermons. We know enough from sick persons for this purpose. I am afraid of being too personal if I call too much, and, as it were, pry into the private concerns and ways of my people.

The Rev. H. Foster—

London and the country are essentially different in this respect.

JUNE 18, 1804.

WHAT IS THE IMPORT AND APPLICATION OF THAT PASSAGE, " WISDOM IS JUSTIFIED OF HER CHILDREN ? "—Proposed by the Rev. B. Woodd.

Mr Woodd—

As much as to say, "You, children of wisdom, understand my conduct ;" or, all true disciples, by their rectitude, prove religion to be divine.

The Rev. W. Goode—

Wisdom's children are satisfied with her ways.

The Rev. S. Crowther—

Whatever the multitude may think, wisdom is justified by the conduct of both John and myself.

The Rev. H. G. Watkins—

Real Christians justify their profession.

The Rev. H. Foster—

Men hate the thing in *any* aspect. God's children approve it in both—in any.

The Rev. J. Pratt—

I rather fall into Crowther's sense.

The Rev. R. Cecil—

He that is spiritual judgeth all things. I like Foster's sense.

———

On July 2, 1804, we have no notes.

———

JULY 16, 1804.

WHAT LIMITS OUGHT TO BE PUT BY MINISTERS TO THE INDULGENCE OF CURIOSITY WITH REGARD TO PUBLIC EXHIBITIONS?—Proposed by the Rev. R. Cecil—

Mr Cecil—

There is an extreme to be avoided. Some would condemn all rational curiosity; even going to see the rattlesnake. But the *works of the Lord are great, sought out of all them that have pleasure therein.* (Ps. cxi. 2.) Thus I go to the Museum; or to see views of cities, and panoramas. But I am not to be running after every sight; I am to use my liberty in selecting. I would therefore avoid these extremes.

On the other hand, there are some who come to town and are found everywhere. But a *scribe of the kingdom* is not to be found everywhere. A man who is *seeking a country* must shew the spirit of one whose *conversation is in heaven.*

There is something in religion, when rightly apprehended, which is masculine and grand. It removes those little desires which are "the constant hectic of a fool."

Music is a proper pursuit. Yet a man must deny himself if he finds it carrying him away. He must not be running after concerts. He must, moreover, to this end deny himself in private. Anything dramatic is to be avoided; and whatever is according to *the course of this world.* If a minister take one step, his hearers take two. Much is to be learned from the sentiments of the carnal world. If a hearer of mine meet me, and say, "Why, I did not expect to see you here:" then I might well feel, you ought not to have seen me here.

The arts and sciences may be followed, but with proper caution.

Why, were not these the idols of the heathen world ? And what are they who now pursue them at the expense of better things, but like children who are charmed with the sparkling of a rocket, and yet see nothing in the sun ?

Yet we must not be sour. If I go through a gentleman's gallery of pictures, I would say, " This is an admirable Claude !" but would take occasion to drop a hint of something larger, and higher, and better, and that I fell in with these things rather incidentally than purposely, and, moreover, not in a proud spirit. " I tread on the pride of Plato," said Diogenes, as he walked over Plato's carpet. " Yes, and with more pride," said Plato. " They pass best over the world," said Queen Elizabeth, " who pass quickly, for it is but a bog. If we stop, we sink." *God forbid that I should glory save in the cross of our Lord Jesus Christ, by whom the world is crucified unto me, and I unto the world* —this is our motto. " The whole world is one great impertinence to the cross of Christ," says Leighton.

I would not say, " Christ would not come here ;" I must take a lower standard in these things ; I am a poor creature, and must be contented to learn, as Christ needed not to learn. St Paul did not frequent such places, some may say ; but he might perhaps have no taste for music or painting.

The Rev. W. Fry—

The introduction of music into private parties of Christians is a device of Satan to waste time. In what is called sacred music, there is often much profanation.

The Rev. J. Goode—

Much depends on circumstances and disposition. A man must inquire what effect the indulgence has on his own mind. Time is precious, and not to be thrown away. If these things are used for relaxation only, it is well ; but if they unfit us for our main work, it is evil. But besides this, we should yet inquire what influence the opinion of others should have upon us.

The Rev. S. Crowther—

We must ask ourselves, " Do I feel these things to be consistent with duty, principle, and the hopes of a Christian ?" *After all these things do the Gentiles seek*—may be said of many. We must not too generally and too strongly condemn these things in others.

The Rev. H. G. Watkins—

There are many sorts of public exhibitions. Some tend to illustrate the works of God—these are lawful and expedient : *e. g.*, anatomical lectures ; many of which we can sufficiently form an idea of at home ; as reviews, &c.—others from which no knowledge is to be collected ; as phantasmagoria.

The Rev. W. J. Abdy—

Religious parents should gratify their children in all in which they can lawfully do so, because they must necessarily keep them from much. I would not speak of public exhibitions contemptuously in public. I would follow the Apostle's example with respect to the Olympic games : though he would wish them abolished, yet he used their terms to stimulate the Christian in his race.

The Rev. J. Venn—

It is a minister's duty to see all public ceremonials of religion, though these do not come under the question.

One of the first indications of a man becoming a Christian in the primitive Church, was his absenting himself from the theatres.

Pay great regard to the sentiments of the world. The world will allow themselves what they deny to clergymen : as the playhouse and cards. This should much determine us. Though I would not implicitly follow it, yet I would reverence it.

We must take all circumstances into account, and make them bear upon every particular question. Yet even in all lawful sights, we should remember *Perimus licitis.* There may be no absolute evil, perhaps, in my playing at cards with my friend ; yet it should be considered, as it affects the world, unlawful. Forty or fifty years since, there was less danger in attending public music, because it was much less in the spirit of the world. What in one age is lawful, may thus become in another unlawful.

Limit not innocent amusements : the pursuits of natural history, of botany. Go to the glass-house. Many of the works of man are beneath our notice : *e. g.*, the chariot drawn by six fleas ! Treat such as Alexander did nobly, when he rewarded the skilful artist who could fix a pea upon a point with a bushel of peas.

July 30, 1804.

How far does the apparent state of many, supposed to be real Christians, consist with the Scriptural Idea of the New Birth ? —Proposed by the Rev. J. Venn.

Mr Venn—

In many writings we meet with such high ideas of the New Birth, as seem inconsistent with the general state of the Christian Church ; so that we must unchristianise a great part of the Church, if we insist on this view.

The question then is, What is Regeneration ? Some say, Faith in Christ and its results.

The Rev. R. Cecil—

There is not much difficulty. I cannot say that I mind much what old writers say on this system : they are respectable, and shew the prevalent opinions. But there is not much comparison of Scripture with fact. I hold this point much as predestination. Calvinists and Arminians talk too boldly. Scripture speaks analogically ; not intending to give accurate ideas on some subjects. The dialogue between God and Satan concerning Job never took place, but some-

thing as like it as men can conceive, or as one man can represent to
another. So with respect to Divine Decrees, the Covenants, the New
Birth. Mr Howe's *Carnality of Religious Contentions* set me off in my
way of thinking on these subjects. I don't think that this figurative
mode of representation reduces things to that reality which marks
the Jew becoming a Christian. But the New Birth is like a child
being born into the world : one is a dwarf, and grows up stunted or
deformed ; another a giant, with well-strung nerves.

But it is a real change—it is a new life. The understanding, will,
affections are all renewed. This man is quite another man from what
he was : quite another thing from the man that wraps himself up in
his virtue.

Regeneration is a moral change—essential, though imperfect—in
the understanding, will, and affections. There is much in this contrary to systematic views of regeneration—to views drawn in the closet
without outward observation.

Analogical views are necessarily imperfect. Ice may be compared
to slates ; but a man who would cover his house with frozen water
would find himself in a pretty predicament.

There is no one adequate characteristic of Regeneration in Scripture.
You may find a key with twenty wards which will fit the lock, but it
will not turn because it wants the twenty-first. Hypocrites meet
many points—yet not all. Scripture, therefore, speaks of Christians
as trusting the Lord ; believing him ; walking, yet standing, &c., &c.

The Rev. B. Woodd—

Animal life is like spiritual life : some creatures fly, some run,
creep, rest, &c. Yet even in the oyster there is animal life.

The Rev. W. Goode—

Walker's *Christian* appears in the end to build up the Law at the
latter end, which he had thrown down at the beginning—he is not a
Christian, unless he attains to this and to that. There is as great a
difficulty in the state of believers, as recorded in Scripture on this
subject, as in that of Christians in the present day.

The Rev. J. Venn—

Much depends on the nature of the " flesh," as opposed to the
" Spirit."

" Flesh " is used in the sense of (1.) Carnal descent—*e. g.*, Jews
being descended of Abraham. (2.) Outward ceremonies : *If any other
man thinketh that he hath whereof he might trust in the flesh, I more;* &c.
(3.) The fleshly principle, or corrupt nature. The New Birth is
opposed to all these.

Another point with our Lord was, to shew that this great change
was to be effected only by the Holy Spirit. Many passages in Scripture speak of the distinction between the flesh and the Spirit.

On the next subject, we have no notes.

M

OCTOBER 8, 1804.

ADVANTAGES AND DISADVANTAGES OF FORMS OF PRAYER IN PUBLIC WORSHIP.—Proposed by the Rev. H. Foster.

The Rev. H. Foster—

The best way is having a form with liberty. "Sometimes," said a hearer, " I pray as a Socinian, sometimes as a Calvinist, sometimes against a neighbour," according to the character of the one praying. When the Dissenters present a petition to the king, they like to have it written that they may know whether they can unite with it or not. It is important that we should fully acquiesce in the matter of prayer. There is a great difference between acquiescing in a prayer and making it our own petition.

There is something due to the surrounding nations, that the world may see what sort of people we profess to be : this is done by a Liturgy.

When a minister's power of speaking decays, though hearers cannot fully hear, yet they can join, if he use a form.

There is danger, no doubt, that a form should lead to formality. Yet we should be cautious of charging the evil upon the form, which originates in the mind.

The Rev. J. Pratt—

I. ADVANTAGES.

1. Security in erroneous times.

2. Security against the effects of weakness, indolence, or unsoundness of the minister.

3. Security against a factious, passionate, personal, bitter spirit in a minister.

4. It diffuses concord throughout the worship of the Churches.

5. The prayers are more exact—suitable—full, than they otherwise would be.

6. They are previously assented to, and, therefore, readily and fully concurred in.

II. DISADVANTAGES.

1. It may encourage idleness and ignorance in a minister.

2. It may require greater exertion to keep up the spirit of worship, and so lead to deadness and formality.

On the whole, perhaps, Baxter's middle way is best. To have so much of Scripture form as to avoid the inconvenience of a total exclusion of forms and to attain their acknowledgedly desirable ends, and so much of freedom in prayer as is necessary to its ends, and to avoid the inconvenience of forms. (See Baxter's *Works*, vol. i. pp. 671, 672.)

The Rev. J. Davies—

Scripture and antiquity warrant the use of forms.

1. As to Scripture, see Num. vi. 22–27, Deut. xxi. 7, 8. Also there were Psalms used in public worship. Hezekiah and Ezra enjoined their use. The Lord's Prayer also ; *When ye pray, say, Our Father*. Forms were used by the Jews in Christ's time. They were not reproved

by Christ for this.   So far from it, that Christ took his prayer from the Jewish rituals.

2. So of antiquity.   There are the Liturgies of St Peter and St Mark.

A minister is helped by forms ; because he has only to attend to the spirit, and not to the words.   He can, therefore, fix his devotion.

Sometimes it is said that a form of prayer limits the spirit of prayer. But there is no promise of the Spirit as to the manner and words of prayer.   It respects the spirit and temper of the mind.

It is objected to a form of prayer, that it is a neglect of the ministerial gift of prayer.   But no such gift is promised.   It is objected that the common cases and wants of Christians are not so well expressed in any form as in extempore prayer.   But common cases are all alike. Public prayer should not descend lower than what a form will well express.

The advantages of forms are these :—

Persons may consider the form, and become affected beforehand. It is generally better comprehended.   We are satisfied beforehand that the form is good.   Forms do not divert the attention so much as extempore prayer—*e. g.*, if blunders are made ; if a person be too fluent.   The decency and solemnity of public worship are better secured by forms than by extempore prayer.   Those who join in a form may be better assured of their devotion.   Extempore prayer is said to have been introduced by one Friar Cumming, in Elizabeth's days, to draw men off from the Church of England.

The Rev. J. Clayton—

In some cases forms are necessary.   Many men are ignorant. Others have not a command of words in public.   Even able persons are ruffled. In distracted times, it is a difficulty.

As to hesitation of assent.   The whole Church is of one mind. Religion is the same in doctrine, experience, and practice throughout the Church.

Forms are good to restrain vagrant teachers.   The Head of the Church bestows gifts.   The pastoral office is set aside by vagrant teachers.   We may well suspend assent to such.

Forms much hinder the free exercise of the heart.   They cramp the powers which God has given.   They lead to hypocrisy and lip-service.

Extempore prayer is a test to myself of my spiritual state.   Our communion with God is contracted and limited by forms.   Extempore prayer gives scope for diversified exercises of the mind arising from our mutable state.

The Rev. S. Crowther—

A great advantage of forms is, that they present a barrier against the intrusion of error.

Disturbance of mind, indisposition, and other hindrances, are not felt so much in forms as in extempore prayer.

I increasingly feel the Church of England service.

The Rev. W. Fry—

I am more inclined, on the whole, towards committing the office of prayer to the minister than to forms.

There is no argument in favour of forms from antiquity. None earlier than A.D. 150. Those which bear apostolic names are not genuine. Jewish rituals are not binding upon a more enlightened dispensation.

Ministers, as well as private Christians, should be taught to consider the spirit of prayer as a privilege.

The advantage of forms, such as ours, is great, in the interspersing parts for the people and parts for the minister. There is so much of Scripture, too, in our service.

The Rev. W. J. Abdy—

Setting aside the Liturgy would shew its importance. What would go with the nation if we were to lose it ?

OCTOBER 22, 1804.

IN WHAT SENSE DID CHRIST LEARN OBEDIENCE BY THE THINGS WHICH HE SUFFERED ? AND IN WHAT RESPECTS IS HE A FIT EXAMPLE FOR US IN SUFFERING ?—Proposed by the Rev. J. Pratt.

Mr Pratt—

The first question I ask in order to answer the second. The reason of asking them is this—I have urged Christ's example, and his acquired sympathy as Mediator, to tempted persons, but have found them repelling the benefit of these views by the notion, that Christ, as God and man inseparably united, and absolutely sinless, never could have been subject to temptation and suffering in the sense in which we are, and therefore could never, as Mediator, have acquired a proper sympathy with us. This seems to me to be a common snare to minds of a refined and metaphysical turn when under trials ; and it strikes me as important to be noticed in our ministry. The epistle to the Hebrews asserts both points fully : e. g., ii. 17, 18 ; iv. 15 ; v. 7, 8. That expression, chap. ii. 10, *To make the Captain of their salvation perfect through suffering*, seems rather to mean, that he became, through suffering, a perfect accomplisher of the work which he had undertaken.

I. The first difficulty is taken from the inseparable union of the Godhead with the manhood. But the proper resolution is, to insist upon the real and absolute distinction of the two natures, while they existed in mysterious union. The Athanasian Creed expresses this distinction and this union admirably well :—" Perfect God and perfect man, of a reasonable soul and human flesh subsisting. Who, although he be God and man, yet is he not two, but one Christ : one, not by conversion of the Godhead into flesh, but by taking of the manhood into God ; one altogether, not by confusion of substance, but by unity of person. For as the reasonable soul and flesh is one man, so God and man is one Christ." We are not to understand by this last expression that the Godhead supplied the place of the human soul to

Christ—that is an old heresy; but that the union between the human nature of Christ and the Godhead was as intimate as that of the soul with the body.

It seems to me, then, that the just way of representing this matter is, that Christ, in his temptations and sufferings, felt only in the human nature which he had assumed ; and that this nature received aid from his divine exactly in the way in which the Christian receives aid; and that, as man, he was subject to withdrawments and derelictions—not in the way of chastisements, but that he might acquire, by his own experience, the knowledge of all the trials incident to his brethren. I leave out of the present question another great end of this dereliction—that is, that he might accomplish his mediatorial work of satisfaction for sin.

We must not extenuate the Saviour's sufferings by attributing human passions to him figuratively, as they are frequently in Scripture to God. In John xii. 27, we see the actings of Christ's human soul, as separate and independent of divine influence from his Godhead, as the soul of a Christian from divine influence in similar circumstances. See, too, Heb. v. 7, 8. So in his agony, Matt. xxvi. 36–44 ; Luke xxii. 39–44.

The two natures must throughout be considered as retaining their incommunicable properties. Bishop Jeremy Taylor remarks—" Christ, as God, is not subject to sufferings; as a man, he is a subject of miseries. As God, he is eternal ; as man, mortal and commensurable by time. As God, the supreme Lawgiver ; as man, most humble and obedient to the law. And, therefore, that the human nature was united to the divine, it does not infer that it must in all instants partake of the divine felicities—which in God are essential ; to man, communicated without necessity, and by an arbitrary dispensation."

II. The second difficulty is taken from the sinless perfection of our Lord's human soul.

I think the best answer to this is, that though our Lord did not endure all our temptations and sufferings in *kind*, yet he endured infinitely more in *degree*; and what he has not acquired by experience as man in this particular respect, is more than supplied by the infinite knowledge he possesses as God. *The prince of this world cometh, and hath nothing in me.* The sentiment is ambiguous. It may mean, hath nothing of victory to allege against me ; or, hath nothing whereon to ground his attack, and to get an advantage from. Allowing that he had no temptations *ab intra*, as we have, yet his temptations *ab extra* were greater beyond comparison ; and the reluctance and horror of his soul must have been great, in proportion as his perfection exceeds our sinfulness. He suffered all the afflictions which we can suffer in this world, in a far higher degree than we can suffer them. He was more strongly tempted to sin, whether by fear of evil or hope of good, than we can be. He had a more distinct view of all the forces and terrors of hell—a more full experience of their active attempts, than any man in this life can have. If we consider only the attempt, assault, or active force by which Satan tempts us, and not the impression of his temptation on us as sinful men, there was no kind of temptation to which Christ did not submit, that he might have full experience or perfect notice, as man, of all the dangers to which we are exposed. By that which was done against the green tree, he knows what will become of the dry, if it be exposed to the same fiery trial.

He has obtained, then, by experience, as the great Captain of God's warfare against Satan and of our salvation, a perfect view of all the forces which fight against us, that he may be a faithful intercessor for succour to those who call on him, with strong crying and tears, as he called on the Father.

To the second question I answer—Christ is a fit example to us in suffering :—

1. In his submitting as a SERVANT throughout the whole of his mediatorial undertaking.

2. In his LEARNING OBEDIENCE, though a son. In his passive obedience—patiently suffering what was enjoined. He at all times submitted his human will to his Father's will, and always undertook with alacrity whatever his Father appointed him to suffer or undertake. This obedience increased as the severity of his sufferings increased.

The Rev. J. Clayton—

The human nature of Christ, as the receptacle of the divine graces, was capable of suffering and improvement. He is an example in suffering—(1.) In the end proposed; (2.) In the submission exercised; (3.) In meekness towards enemies; (4.) In love to the Church in suffering.

He ought to be so considered, because he has destined us to be conformed to him. By looking to Christ, we have the curse taken out of sufferings.

The Rev. W. Goode—

Commentators take the passage in another view; not that Christ had to *learn* obedience, but that he practically *exercised* it. See Gill, Brown, and Guyse.

He partook of all our infirmities, felt them as man. He endured sufferings in their general nature, though not every particular temptation.

The same objection might be made as to our Lord's *active* obedience as has been made to his *passive*.

The Rev. Dr Gilby, a visitor—

There is more importance in the subject than I have seen before.

Christ is our example in sufferings, to rejoice in them; because the time is coming when we shall have no opportunity of so glorifying him.

Sufferings are the school for Christ's children.

The Rev. W. Fry—

I have generally taken those passages in Hebrews to refer to Christ's sufferings outwardly ; and the writer is by that view comforting the early Christians under the loss of earthly good.

The Rev. H. G. Watkins—

By sufferings, Christ's love to his work increased. Christ might in the wilderness be placed as the first Adam in paradise ; but did not, like him, fail, but persevered. Christ's example is inimitable, yet is it to be proposed to ourselves as we set a copy before a boy.

The Rev. S. Crowther—

I view the subject much as Fry.

The Rev. W. J. Abdy—

I do not agree with Fry and Crowther. Outward afflictions are dangerous from the temptations which they present to our minds. I feel the difficulty of the question how Christ could feel a temptation when no party to it within.

The Rev. Mr Mayor, a visitor—

Our sufferings under temptation are in exact proportion to the reluctance we feel. If I were tempted to murder my child, my suffering in being so tried would be in proportion to my affection and consequent reluctance. If I have any inclination to the sin to which I am tempted, there is a pleasure to be resisted ; if none, an abhorrence. If tempted to murder my enemy, the struggle could not be so violent as in the other case.

The Rev. H. Foster—

There are difficulties still about the subject, which, probably, are not removeable. We must come to a willingness to be, and to feel ourselves poor ignorant creatures. We may get the comfort of what we do not fully understand. I have felt myself the difficulty stated ; but have come to this, that Christ went through a scene of suffering to learn to succour us. Owen, a great man with me, makes nothing more of it than that Christ learned the thing experimentally. As to the sins to which we are tempted, no sin is greater than that to which he was tempted. But still there are difficulties, and so I acquiesce in God's statements, and leave them there.

The Rev. J. Goode—

Christ's being perfect seems the reason of his being a proper example, because he may be fully followed.

The promises given to Christ as Mediator for his support imply that he would meet with difficulties and discouragements.

November 5, 1804.

How shall we Know when we are in the Path of Duty ?—Proposed by the Rev. H. Foster.

Mr Foster began by stating the difficulties he had in his own parish, Clerkenwell.

The Rev. R. Cecil—

If light come afterwards, a man is not dissatisfied at a step taken by him in less light. He may hereafter see still more light than he now has, and see what he now thinks best not to have been so.

It is enough if we are conscious that at the time we had an adequate motive. If we are conscious of having a wrong motive, then we must suffer for it.

There is a way that God leads his ministers *per ardua ad astra.* We should be in danger if every one cried, " Hosanna ! "

We are not in the way of duty if we are plainly acting contrary to any other known duty.

We are short-sighted, like raw chess-players, who take the next man, while old players will wait and not sacrifice it so soon.

He who sees through everything will appoint the most unaccountable way for us.

Joseph was put in the pit that he might become governor of Egypt.

We are in the way when we do not run into our own will. The Israelites were with difficulty convinced that they were in the way when they were shut in at the Red Sea.

Man must be quiet in the path, from which he cannot recede without danger and evil. Man wants to know too soon and too much. He wants the light of to-morrow, but it will not come till to-morrow. And perhaps a slight turn will throw much light that he will be astonished he did not see before. " I can wait," says Lavater.

The Rev. Mr Gambier, a visitor—

Distinguish between actions—good, bad, and indifferent. Repentance is to be exercised for imprudence.

The Rev. J. Pratt—

This is one of the most difficult questions in casuistry. It is easier to say when we are not in the path of duty, than when we are.

There is no proof that we are—(1.) that we have comfort of mind, because this is often fallacious ; nor (2.) that we see coincidences of circumstances.

Consciousness of integrity of purpose, and that we have made use of all means, is the best security.

The Rev. B. Woodd—

I am rather disposed to waive the inquiry as too difficult.

If we are following the *preceptive* will of God is the main point, in my view, as to the morality of the case : we have nothing to do with the *governing* will of God.

I should take difficulties rather as a token of future success. " When God designs a mercy to a man, he puts for a time the sentence of death upon that mercy."—Brydges.

The Rev. J. Clayton—

It is important to be *willing to know* the path of duty. *Lord, what wilt thou have me to do ?*

We are not to judge of the path of duty by the aspect of Providence, but by the Word of God.   Where there is a want of express testimony we may draw inferences.

We may collect hints from the debates of our own conscience, from the " dry light " of other minds, from the expediency of the case, from what the impression is on others.

The Rev. C. Simeon, a visitor—

Singleness and simplicity of mind are excellent tests.   Where our natural disposition is thwarted, and yet we feel a willingness to acquiesce in the Lord's will, we have intimation we are right.

November 19, 1804.

The Use and Expediency of Anonymous Letters ?—Proposed by the Rev. B. Woodd.

Mr Woodd—

The use of them.   Few give or take reproof well.   Few ever cordially like the man who reproves him.   Pusillanimity is the check in most. They cannot muster courage to reprove.   The use of anonymous letters is like that of fables.   They convey instruction while they avoid offence.   Anonymous letters point out what friends feel not enough ; little things which friends think not worth noticing.   They inform a man of circumstances which would be never otherwise known.

If things are pointed out of which a man is not guilty, then anonymous letters furnish an opportunity for the exercise of charity.   Anonymous letters acquaint us sometimes with the ignorance of our people ; sometimes they lower our crest, by shewing a minister that he is not so high in the estimation of his people as he thought.

The expediency of anonymous letters is seen in this.   There are some persons whom it is of importance to approach, and yet we can do so in no other way.

The use a minister should make of anonymous letters is this :— " Here is an occasion given me from God's permission to examine myself—to walk humbly with him," &c., &c.

The Rev. J. Goode—

Use them without letting it be known : for they generally proceed from a wrong principle.

The Rev. H. G. Watkins—

They are generally the effect of cowardice.   Unless they are peculiarly modest and sensible, they should be treated with suspicion. I would treat them as a general would a spy : take their information, and then hang them up.   Their expediency, however, is considerable. For instance, when a modest hearer is troubled, and wishes a subject discussed.

The Rev. H. Foster—

I once received a series of letters from a hearer at Spitalfields, almost every week ; many were bitter, but some good.   Another I received from a friend, in printed words, about descending too much into circumstances in a case of delicacy.

The Rev. R. Cecil—

It depends on the motive for which the letter is written. If a man's motive is right in sending it, we should be willing to get all the good we can. It may be the means of conveying information to persons who would be glad of it, but who have no means of otherwise getting it. A writer may find access, who as a speaker would be considered prejudiced. Some can write who can't speak. Like Mr Addison, they have a good pen, but when they attempt to speak, they conceive, but can't bring forth anything.

To a superior, facts may be usefully brought forward by anonymous letters which could not be by speaking.

The Rev. W. Fry—

I should think it rather my duty to reprove openly than write anonymous letters, wherever there might be reason for writing such.

The Rev. J. Pratt—

They are of vast use in addressing superiors and equals. But we should not substitute them for reproof, where that is a duty.

The Rev. S. Crowther—

Inquire into—(1.) the motive ; (2.) the spirit ; (3.) the subject of the writer.

DECEMBER 3, 1804.

WHAT RULES SHOULD A MINISTER OBSERVE FOR HIS HEALTH IN THE DISCHARGE OF HIS DUTY ?—Proposed by the Rev. R. Cecil.

Mr Cecil—

A minister is not called to go where a physician may. It is the physician's *sole* calling. But the minister has other duties.

We must not refuse cases as *hopeless;* for we may get more good ourselves than the sick.

I have visited a man who cursed with the rattle in his throat. I felt, what a blessing the Gospel is in fitting such a wretch as I am for eternity!

Avoid anxiety. Nothing pulls a man down more than this. People *will* find fault. George Herbert says, " Think not thy fame at every twitch will break."

A minister should do what is best on the whole. Let conscience say in what way. But care must be taken that he does not make a cloak of his health to cover idleness. There is danger on the side of sloth.

Sir William Temple says, " A man must be temperate, or use great labour, or take physic, or be sick."

The Rev. J. Clayton—

I have never refused to visit the sick when sent for. But I never visit infectious cases, if not sent for. But when I go, I take care.

The Rev. B. Woodd—

Avoid secular concerns.   Early to bed, and early to rise.   Avoid interruptions.   Beware of acquaintances.

Many ministers have caught their death in visiting the sick.   The pulpit is of the first importance.   Visiting the sick is subordinate.

On the next occasion we have no notes.

DECEMBER 31, 1804.

WHAT CONSTITUTES CHRISTIAN UNITY?—Proposed by the Rev. W. J. Abdy.

The Rev. D. Wilson, a visitor—

Christian unity consists in having one heart: renewed, guided, sanctified by the same Spirit.   Uniformity is not necessary.

The Rev. R. Cecil—

I have printed my thoughts on this subject in my Life of Bacon. What constitutes gold?   Not the working up of a piece of brass, however exquisitely.   Gold is gold in whatever form.   Unity consists in sentiment, in affection.   It is like electric attraction.   There is a common sense and feeling among Christians.   We agree in the theory. But in the practice I find difficulties.   Stillingfleet is of great weight in his *Irenicum.*   If the Church of England is to be defended, on that ground it must be.

Difficulties in practice arise thus.   There must be order in everything.   This does not touch the Dissenters, strictly as such.   *They* are men of order.

But there is such a thing as disorder in the Church.   There is a fanatical love of order.   I cannot meet the disorderly men.   They call this bigotry : I can't help it.   They may have communion of spirit with such men as Pascal, and Hale, &c., but they seem to me disorderly.   An army consisting of different corps is still united.

The Rev. J. Davies—

We may be united in—(1.) main doctrines, (2.) subjection to Christ, (3.) Christian graces, (4.) mutual love, (5.) privileges.

The subject of Roman Catholic emancipation from political disabilities was again brought before the attention of the public about this time; and the members of the Eclectic took up the subject, as we see, on the following occasion.   It was reserved, as we know, for a later day for Parliament to open their doors to these enemies of our Protestant Church—a step for the consequences of which we are suffering to the present day.   At the period, however, to which the following notes refer, the feeling was strong against such a measure.

On the 10th May 1805, Lord Granville moved that the Roman Catholic petition should be referred to a Committee of the whole

House. The debate was closed on the 13th, and there appeared for the measure 49, against it 178. Mr Fox brought it before the House of Commons on the 13th; and after two days' debate, the division was 124 for the question, and 336 against it.

JANUARY 28, 1805.

SHOULD ANY ENCOURAGEMENT BE GIVEN TO POPERY BY A PROTESTANT GOVERNMENT?—Proposed by the Rev. H. G. Watkins.

Mr Watkins—

TOLERATION is wise and good; and it ought to extend to Papists, though they give it not to Protestants. It is the bulwark of true religion.

As to the PRINCIPLES OF POPERY. "No faith to be kept with heretics," is one. Everything is lawful with them to aggrandise *their* Church—Popish absolutions and indulgences; not to speak of their nonsensical speculations about Transubstantiation and the Idolatry of the Host. One grand error in their system is *salvation by merit*—a damnable doctrine. If we are not to wish such God speed, are we to give our money to support such tenets?

As to the POLICY OF POPERY. This system is congenial with man's carnal nature. Much show and parade is a cheap religion, and likely to increase as a sect, and to overthrow other sects. All that is bad in Popery is likely to grow. No toleration is allowed by them. We see how intolerant some idolisers of merit are in the Church of England already. The bad in one Church will conglomerate with the bad in the other, and Popery may again rear its head in this island. The indifference to all religion is like *fuel* for such an endeavour as is now being made.

Surely all Protestant Dissenting ministers are as deserving of our pay as avowed enemies to our system; and if *all* were paid, what a tax upon society, and on the liberties of Dissenters! If the pay of Government be used to support its measures, what a vast addition would be given to the executive power! It might become an engine subversive of civil liberty, if it were worked proportionally to the strength of its materials. Would not such a measure increase the number of Popish priests in England and Scotland? For Government to encourage Popery, would be contrary to the stipulations at the accession of the House of Hanover.

Protestants have not done what they could to remove the ignorance of the Irish. Money will not alter men's principles.

The Rev. S. Crowther—

It would be a fatal error in Church and State. To what *extent* we ought to go, would be a difficult point. What would satisfy them? Every concession would make way for fresh demands. Is it benevolence or fear that works upon those who advocate such a measure?— FEAR. Encouragement and toleration are very different. Our poor Church clergy deserve encouragement first.

The Rev. H. Foster—

As to opinions, every man ought to have his own. But it is one thing to tolerate and another to support. No coercive measures should be used. It is a serious question, if FEAR has given rise to it.

The Rev. R. Cecil—

How far can political considerations set aside religious obligations ? They ought in no respect to do so ; it would be irreligious indifference, not liberality. So Gifford calls adultery an " amiable weakness." But no liberality is shewn towards truly good men, only an atheistic indifference. Enthusiasm is allowed in statuary, music, and such things, but not in religion. Some would say, " Give a crust to a surly dog to quiet him." But this is, after all, not a good political measure. This is Antichrist. Every priest swears he will use the utmost of his power to extirpate heresy. A conscientious man will despise the policy. A bad man will be bad still. No political consideration can sanction a bad thing.

The Rev. J. Davies—

We are *not to do evil that good may come.* Popery is a lamb when inferior, a fox in equality, and a wolf when superior.

As to some early Protestants having been cruel, it is to be observed that the remains of Popery produced this. They had conceived some early prejudice that the true Church was to be supported by coercion. The irritation, too, on their minds at the time was another cause.

FEBRUARY 11, 1805.

WHAT IS THE BEST METHOD OF ADDRESSING A CONGREGATION FROM THE PULPIT ?—Proposed by the Rev. J. Davies.

Mr Davies—

An advantage of extempore preaching is, that the frame of mind is more dependent upon Divine help. Also the preacher thus cultivates a talent which will be useful to him on other occasions. The strong prejudice against extempore preaching is a disadvantage.

The best sermon is the one which is most studied but least written. This is not, indeed, my own plan ; for I write much, and then make an analysis, which I take into the pulpit.

The Rev. J. Clayton—

Writing at the beginning of a ministry is of great advantage. It promotes close reasoning and a good style.

The disadvantages are—dishonour to the Head of the Church ; we cannot be so impassioned ; and are not open to new light, nor amplification which the occasion might suggest.

The Rev. B. Woodd—

As to manner, &c. Cultivate a popular delivery : but avoid vulgarisms, incoherencies, monotony, insipidity, expletives, an affectation of accuracy, all abstract statements. Use frequent, plain, pertinent illustrations. Take our Lord's discourses as examples. Introduce anecdotes, particularly Scripture anecdotes. Bring forward prominent examples.

A mixed plan, as to writing and extempore, is preferable to any other.

FEBRUARY 25, 1805.

THE IMPORTANCE, USE, AND RESPONSIBILITY OF PERSONAL INFLUENCE. —Proposed by the Rev. John Clayton.

Mr Clayton—

Personal influence is a talent, of which a solemn account is to be given. Every man has such influence. Ministers particularly have, influence from sentiment, character, and habits.

The Rev. H. G. Watkins—

Parents have much personal influence: so masters of families.

The Rev. S. Crowther—

Manner gives to some a superior personal influence.

Nothing is unimportant which we either do or say as ministers.

The Rev. W. Goode—

Personal influence may turn either on our official character, or on a previously acquired character.

The Rev. H. Foster—

Consistency gives personal influence. A man should not affect to be a great man, if he be not one—a scrupulous one, if he be not scrupulous.

A minister's people are much like himself. Grace converts, but it works by suitable means.

The Rev. R. Cecil—

Influence is power, whether from money, or talents, or connexions. No person is so little but has much of this power. For example, the little maid in the case of Naaman.

Whoever neglects this power is the unprofitable servant.

Some suppose that they have more power than they have; but generally we think we have less than we really possess. Unbelief, timidity, delicacy, often damp the exertion of power. It becomes a man's duty to call himself out to the exertion of his power. See this in the account of Mordecai and Esther.

A man's duty is to watch against what hinders his influence.

Men of feeble public talents often have much personal influence from kindness, consistency.

Reputation is influence. It will indeed carry many into error. Who would not follow AARON in worshipping the calf?

Situations much promote influence. A tailor has more influence than a blacksmith. This is the reason why there are more preachers from tailors than blacksmiths.

Ministers are defective in resting their personal influence too much on their public ministry.

Bishop Butler justly observes, that man is capable of much more evil than good.

Time will give weight to a man's character. It is one advantage that a man be cast early into his situation, that he may earn a character.

The Rev. J. Pratt—

Ministers in town have less advantage than in the country in exercising personal influence.

Much depends upon the spirit and temper of ministers. We search the characters of others to justify ourselves.

We are often more influenced by the presence of our fellow-creatures than by a sense of duty to God.

Our Lord had this personal influence in perfection. See the account of his visits to the Temple, and of his presence among the Scribes and Pharisees. St Paul was jealous over his personal influence.

The Rev. B. Woodd—

Let us see—(1.) that we are right in ourselves; (2.) that our influence is right; (3.) that our manner is kind.

March 11, 1805.

Is it Lawful to Use Artifice to Promote a Good End ?—Proposed by the Rev. H. Foster.

Mr Foster—

The question seems to mean, " Is it lawful to do evil that good may come ? " If this be the meaning, we must at once say " No ! "

But there are difficulties. For we have Scripture examples. Jehu's artifice in destroying Baal's prophets. He is rewarded, for executing God's commands, to the eleventh generation. God, however, appointed him to destroy the house of Ahab, but not the *method*. He took his own wicked way. God approved the obedience, but not the mode.

We may use sagacity, but not artifice. Jacob and his mother obtaining the blessing afford another example. God had decreed this. But they proposed sinful methods; and God punished Jacob in subsequent life.

Again, our Lord going to Emmaus: *He made as though he would go further.* But he acted as a stranger. He tried their earnestness. So the angels in Sodom.

Pious frauds in the Church have degraded the Church in the opinion of men.

The Rev. R. Cecil—

The question turns on the meaning of ARTIFICE. If it mean equivocation, the act of lying, then any instance brought from Scripture of *that*, as of any other sin, is for our avoiding, and not imitating it.

If Abraham or Jacob tell lies to carry their points, this is no warrant for me to do the same.

If any part of the truth which I am *bound* to communicate be concealed, it is sin. Jesuits in China giving out that 'twas a lie of the Jews that Christ was crucified, is something of this kind; but they were punished. This, perhaps, is to be held up as a sign to all missionaries, that they will carry no end by tampering with truth to meet men's prejudices. David's lie about Goliath's sword argued distrust of God. Pious frauds bring all signs and wonders into contempt.

But then the question is not answered thus. If by artifice you mean ADDRESS, it is no sin. There is no falsity, deception, or equivocation in this. I don't hold St Paul a sinner in setting the Sadducees and Pharisees at variance. He made use of an argument to turn the Pharisees in his favour. This was great *address*, but was not criminal. Monro saved himself at Edinburgh by appealing to the mob, "Is there no widow's son among you?" A hundred freemasons stepped out to rescue him. There was nothing wrong in Joshua's ambushes for the men of Ai. It was a stratagem in war. It would have been unlawful to have told the men of Ai that there was no ambush; but they knew they came out liable to such ambushes.

Christ's conduct at Emmaus, and that of the angels at Sodom, were trials of the regard of those they were with.

As to Scripture examples, they do not bear unless you can shew that they were commended. For instance, Jeremiah's case when the king sent for him.

The Rev. J. Pratt—

There is a difference between voluntary and involuntary artifice. The Society for the Suppression of Vice voluntarily put themselves into a situation in which they must use artifice. Involuntary artifice is illustrated by misdirecting an intentional murderer.

There is danger in morals and politics of drawing extreme cases into general rules.

The Old Testament examples were under less light. For example, Rahab and Jael. The New Testament produces us clear examples. In an involuntary case, we could hardly refuse artifice. For example, Samuel when he went to anoint David.

The Rev. Mr Simons, a visitor—

If our skill fails, remember God's does not.

The Rev. B. Woodd—

Children are to be dealt with in perfect truth. Not so, perhaps, madmen.

The Rev. H. G. Watkins—

We are not to consider Deborah's commendation of Jael as altering the character of her conduct in the sight of God. The commendation of Rahab may be considered to refer to her faith.

If the Society for the Suppression of Vice could establish it as a general principle that any men, in their senses, would forfeit their right to truth, it would do more harm than any dissembling efforts of theirs to do good.

The Rev. S. Crowther—

I think the Society's conduct is most reprehensible.

MARCH 25, 1805.

WHAT ARE THE MOST IMPORTANT PARTS OF THE MINISTERIAL DUTY ? —Proposed by the Rev. B. Woodd.

Mr Woodd—

Pulpit duties I consider to be the most important.

The Rev. W. Goode—

It is difficult to say what is most comparatively important in a minister's duty.

The Rev. S. Crowther—

Our duties are either (1.) public or (2.) private. Most is expected from us in public duty.

The question depends much on circumstances. One person cannot lay down a plan for another. I could not accomplish my public duty in the short space in which others do.

The Rev. H. Foster—

Preaching is by far the most important part of a minister's duty. It is the grand instrument in the hand of the Spirit. Catechising is also important.

Something depends on *success*. If a man finds the nail will go, let him drive it.

The Rev. R. Cecil—

We have to build a house—a spiritual house. The mason must not say what the carpenter should do. We are in different circumstances with our different talents. Let each do what he can. Two equally acceptable may be exceedingly distinct in the account they will give of their work.

Our grand aim as ministers must be, the exhibition of Gospel-truth. Mr Pitt may make the greatest blunders in the world ; but that's not *my* affair. Like a messenger, we must not stop to care for a person fallen down. If he *can*, consistently with his duty, it is well ; if not, he must prefer his office.

Eight hours, on an average, I take for every sermon. Notes, if properly done, require more stuff than written sermons. Written sermons want no devotional spirit, as *necessary*.

It is most important in us ministers—(1.) to secure time for our sermons, and (2.) to cultivate our spirit. If we cultivate our spirit so as to carry unction, we have far more weight than all other gifts will bestow. This is the result of a devotional spirit. To affect feeling in our manners is seen through.

Seeing a young minister call an old minister out of his study only to ask him how he did, once hurt me much. There is a tone, an intimation that may be given to an idler, " This is not the house." Refuse secular affairs. *No man that warreth entangleth himself with the affairs of this life, that he may please Him who hath chosen him to be a soldier.*

What can I do most to the purpose? Perhaps more by sitting quiet than by being active and about. "They also serve who only stand and wait." Watch against a dozing away of time. Though the clock weight goes down slowly, yet it pulls everything after it. A man may sit with his wife too long by the fire. He may enjoy little tales that should be resisted. Keep under the body. The Newmarket groom sweats himself thin. The Church of England is defective in this. We want inferior officers. *Give attendance to reading, to exhortation, to doctrine. . . . . Meditate upon these things, give thyself wholly to them; that thy profiting may appear to all.*

The Rev. J. Pratt—

All this implies that a minister has command of his time. But some have to take pupils, and this is no part of the ministerial duty. I would lay down the following gradation of a minister's duties :—(1.) personal religion, (2.) the pulpit, (3.) his family, (4.) his health, (5.) the spiritual wants of his people, (6.) schools, (7.) authorship, (8.) public societies, (9.) secular affairs of his people, (10.) secular affairs of his friends. It is good to have a rule.

He should write one original sermon a week.

The Rev. J. Davies—

We should give ourselves to reading in order to preaching; and should cultivate all that the people expect to meet in a *preacher.*

APRIL 8, 1805.

WHAT IS TO BE UNDERSTOOD BY THE SEALING OF THE SPIRIT?—Proposed by the Rev. J. Pratt.

Mr Pratt—

The Epistle to the Ephesians is particularly full on this point—see i. 13–18; iii. 14–19; iv. 30. Now, the influence of which the Apostle speaks in these passages rests on those who *already believe and love,* and must therefore be regarded as a corroborating, confirming, enlarging, sealing influence, carrying to the heart a pledge and a foretaste of eternal glory. See also Rom. viii. 15, 16; 2 Cor. i. 21, 22.

From these passages I collect that the sealing of the Spirit is an influence—

1. Peculiar to those who have believed;

2. Distinguishable from his ordinary operations of a sanctifying and comforting nature : though also sanctifying and comforting; but in a more eminent degree, and possessing something of a peculiar nature.

3. Its chief characteristics are—(1.) Assuring us of our interest in Christ. (2.) Enlarging the conceptions and sacred sensibilities of the Christian. (3.) Bestowing a filial spirit as the spirit of adoption.

(4.) Enabling the Christian to feel what he possesses as earnests and pledges of future glory.

The idea of SEALING seems to be—(1.) Distinguishing from others as the Lord's own. (2.) Maturing for heaven. (3.) Securing for heaven. (4.) Giving foretastes of heaven.

The work of the Spirit is represented by many divines as the immediate operation of the Spirit without the intervention of common means. I see not why. It may: it may not be.

It is various as to seasons. It is generally under trials, or to prepare for services to come. See Mr Howe's Life (p. 75). See Watt's 12th Ev. Disc.

We are not to dismiss *all* impressions, because many are fanciful. The Spirit is too little acknowledged in this work. Attention is too little called to it in preaching. The expectations of Christians are too low in consequence. Therefore there is less of this enlarged and elevating influence than there otherwise would be.

The Rev. W. Fry—

I agree with Pratt, that there are not such enlarged views among us as there should be of Christian privileges.

Mr Wesley's people made much of the spirit of adoption, perhaps somewhat fancifully; but we have probably substituted complaint for pursuit.

The Rev. J. Clayton—

We have not honoured the work of the Spirit so much as we should.

The Spirit acts as a seal when he softens the heart. Afterwards the form is improved by changing into the same image from glory to glory.

The design of this operation is—(1.) to distinguish Christians as the Lord's property : *The foundation of God standeth sure, having this seal,* &c.—(2.) to secure them. Eph. i. 13. It is a dangerous thing to touch sealed property. *Touch none on whom is the mark.*

Particular seasons when this sealing operation is felt, are—(1.) Times of *eminent intercession* with God. For example, at the Lord's Supper, which is a *sealing* ordinance. (2.) Times of *suffering*. (3.) The season of *death*.

The Rev. B. Woodd—

There are—(1.) extraordinary influences of the Spirit, (2.) ordinary, (3.) especial. Here I agree with Pratt.

In Eph. i. 13, the same participle is used throughout. The sealing of the Spirit is a comprehensive term for the whole gradual work of the Spirit : *Having* HEARD *the word, and having* BELIEVED, *ye were sealed.*

Grace, as Mr Newton says, is like a sun-dial—no hour is shewn unless the sun shines. The Spirit must shine on his work.

Times of overwhelming feeling are—(1.) Conversion. (2.) Trials. (3.) Death.

The Rev. W. Goode—

The sealing of the Spirit implies—(1.) Performing a certain work on the heart ; (2.) Bearing his own testimony to his own work. Both are necessary : the first, for the *being* of a Christian ; the second, for the *comfort* of a Christian.

The design of sealing was—(1.) Appropriation ; (2.) Security.

Ye were sealed, Eph. i. 13, is in the same tense as the participles ; implying a consequent, but an immediate consequent.

There are three ways in which the Spirit bears testimony to his own work—(1.) By bearing witness with our spirit, opening the mind to discern and apprehend Christ. Some have this who cannot believe they have. (2.) By applying the promises of *the Gospel* to our hearts. (3.) By special and peculiar manifestation of divine love to the soul. It is generally under trial, or as a preparation for trial, that these sealing seasons come.

The Rev. W. J. Abdy—

The Methodists speak of a threefold gradation of the influences of the Spirit—(1.) awakening ; (2.) giving a sense of justification ; (3.) bringing perfection.

The sealing of the Spirit is generally through the medium of sanctification.

The Rev. J. Goode—

Some old writers distinguish the sealing of the Spirit as—(1.) The seal of demonstration ; (2.) the seal of confirmation.

The impression at first is faint ; but gradually grows deeper, and is the fruit of strong faith, and a high measure of holiness.

The end of sealing is—(1.) to distinguish, (2.) to denote property, (3.) to mark high esteem, (4.) to give security.

The effects are—(1.) humility, (2.) gratitude, (3.) superiority to the world.

The Rev. H. Foster—

The sealing is universal. All that are children of God have it, and at all times. If so, it cannot mean those comforts and impressions which are superior to ordinary blessings.

Sealing is the confirmation of a regular state. That is the simple meaning. God thus sets his confirmation to the Christian. Regeneration is the *epistle written.* Sealing is the confirmation of the soul in that state. My idea may be illustrated by what the Apostle means when he says of his own Apostleship, *The seal of mine apostleship are ye in the Lord.* Sealing is always the same as an act of God, however we can see it or not. Great comforts are given in peculiar times, but this is not *sealing,* and should not be confounded with it.

The Rev. R. Cecil—

I object to Pratt's view. It carries the matter beyond the intention of the expression. I object to Foster's view. It is not sufficiently explicit. I could not preach on this view. My idea is that of an impression. An impression carries the mark of the seal to the thing sealed. I agree with Foster that it is certain and universal ; and would not make it depend on feelings. Mr Wesley's people talk fanatically of sealed times, hours, sermons, &c.

Under the first operations of the Spirit, the heart is softened ; under the second, the impression of the seal is made. Sealed, not by any purpose of God, as Foster speaks, but by an evident act on him. This distinguishes the work of sealing from strong impressions.

Holiness is always a concomitant of sealing. Softened wax takes an impression. When the wax is cold, or the affections are not alive, yet it retains the impression.

I am always of the opinion that we have not sufficiently spoken of the work of the Spirit. Christ is the great promise of the Old Testament ; the Holy Spirit of the New. This is the reason that we are not sufficiently made up in our own minds. It is not proper to say to our congregations, " I am come to raise the dead, I come to work miracles," because it would not be understood ; but we must go fully made up with this view in our own mind ; and if we had our hearts full of this feeling, out of the abundance of the heart the mouth would speak.

APRIL 22, 1805.

IN WHAT CONSISTS THE SIN AGAINST THE HOLY GHOST ?—Proposed by the Rev. B. Woodd.

Mr Woodd—

Charging Christ with having a devil, and with working his miracles by Satan ; while they knew, in their consciences, that he wrought them by the finger of God. This is clear ; it is a great mercy that it is so clear. For the fear of it is a common temptation with which Satan assaults humble believers.

It is NOT—

1. Resistance of the Holy Spirit's influences. For of this we are all guilty, more or less so.

2. Nor falling into gross sin ; either *before* conversion, or *after* conversion. For never was there a greater sin than the Apostles' desertion of Christ.

3. Nor every presumptuous sin against conviction. For Peter's was such.

4. Nor rash and profane utterance of even blasphemous expressions. For Paul blasphemed, and compelled others to do so.

It IS a determined and malicious rejection of the Gospel of Christ, and attributing the miracles of Christ to Satan.

The practical lesson we learn is, caution to ourselves against slighting the Holy Spirit. We may thus make near approaches to the sin against the Holy Spirit. This sin may as easily be committed in the present day as in that of the Apostles.

The Rev. H. G. Watkins—

Deism is a near approach to this sin. Malignant opposition to a Christian's character is a near approximation.

Mr Romaine thought it could not be committed till death. Doddridge thinks God leaves some to a judicial state of alienation *before* they die.

The eternal punishment awaiting this sin seems not so much a punishment, by a special appointment of God threatened to the sin, as an inevitable consequence of the sin.   St John says, *There is a sin unto death, I do not say that ye shall pray for it.*   If we could know what the sin is, it might be sinful to pray ; but it is a mercy that we do not know.

What state is that man in who commits this sin ?   He is in determined opposition to the Gospel ; in a settled state of committing sin. The conscience is gradually hardened.   Stimuli must increase in strength, if they have any effect.

This sin is left, in some measure, undefined in wisdom and mercy. Something was needed to counterbalance the large and bountiful views and offers of the Gospel ; that we may escape presumption ; that we may awfully dread doing despite to the Spirit of God.

The Rev. W. J. Abdy—

I think, on the whole, with Woodd and Baxter, that the sin is defined ; yet what Watkins says has some weight.   There is a high probability that the sin lies in what Woodd and Baxter represent ; it is not absolutely certain, so that Woodd's views may be useful.

There may be many approximations to this sin.   Where there is a desire to escape this sin, that is an evidence that the man has not committed it ; for its punishment, as Watkins said, is a necessary consequence, rather than an annexed punishment.   Therefore, Spira's was not a lost case.

The Rev. J. Goode—

I don't expect to be applied to by any person who has committed the sin ; for such persons are not likely to feel the want of advice. When persons of tender conscience are disturbed, I generally relieve them by what Abdy says.

If we limit the sin to denying our Lord's miracles, we narrow the question.   And some have controverted that view ; see Whitby.

The Rev. H. Foster—

The *sin against the Son of Man* is, what Whitby says, blaspheming his person and work ; and for this, considering the Jewish prejudices, he seems to make allowance.   But the *sin against the Holy Ghost* would be a rejection of a full and clear display to be made after our Lord's ascension.   This sin, therefore, was a sinning against the dispensation of the Spirit after the day of Pentecost.   I have some hesitation whether the passages in the Hebrews and in St John's Epistle mean this sin.

The Rev. R. Cecil—

Old divines think this sin might be committed now.   They express it in few words—the light of Peter with the malice of Paul.

In my view, it is tantamount to *Hath done despite to the Spirit of grace.*

It is perfectly safe to say to tender consciences, that if they are anxious on the subject, there is no reason to fear that they had committed it.

There is a malignity and venom in some which indicate judicial hardness.

The Rev. J. Clayton—

It is illustrated by *Whoever stumbleth on this stone shall be broken, but on whomsoever it shall fall it shall grind him to powder.*

Sinning against the Holy Ghost is sinning against the terminating operations of the Holy Trinity.

The state of mind in the man renders it impossible that he can be forgiven. He rejects the means.

May 6, 1805.

The Nature and Extent of Filial Duty ?—Proposed by the Rev. W. J. Abdy.

The Rev. Mr Atkinson, a visitor—

It is a difficult question, in which we must be governed by circumstances. The Apostle enjoins obedience in *all* things. It cannot mean, however, anything sinful. Cards lead to irritation.

The Rev. H. Foster—

Whether it be right in the sight of God—that is the question. What appears criminal to any one *is* criminal to him. Even an erroneous conscience is to be followed. Cards at home with a parent must be left. The playhouse is an abomination. A child must determine not to sin.

The Rev. R. Cecil—

Parents' authority should never oppose the authority of God, so as to claim submission.

There is not equal authority in parents after age as before. The child owes *duty* to parents as long as they live, but is not so bound to the peculiarities of the parent, nor the parent so bound to cover the child in his mistakes, as in non-age.

A parent is not right to insist on a child going into danger; nor to make his son embark in a wild scheme, hurt his character, deprive his son of reasonable comfort, much less to touch the right of conscience.

In matrimonial connexions—the parent is prone to avarice, the son to passion.

There is a lax principle, however, with respect to parental authority, notwithstanding these exceptions. There ought to be a great reverence—in appearance, as well as in reality : patience to bear the parent's infirmities : affording all the support possible in trouble. Ham is an instance of profane sporting with a parent's infirmities. It is something like that when a young man says, " My father has got that odd way," &c.

A case frequently occurs difficult to determine. When young persons are restrained from hearing the truth. In some implacable instances, I should advise them to submit: not so perhaps in others. Children should often submit where a parent does not give his reasons. Children should never attempt to deceive a parent: no shirking, nor artifice.

There was a degree of incorrigibleness so sinful under the Jewish law, that there was a command to stone such : see Deut. xxi. 18–21.

The Rev. Mr Gambier, a visitor—

It is difficult to know how far to limit the general injunctions of Scripture. Things *mala per se* are not binding on children, notwithstanding a parent's word ; but those that are evil by consequence require perhaps obedience in many cases.

The Rev. J. Pratt—

Parental authority is of great importance. OBEY YOUR PARENTS is the *first command with promise.* The influence of parental authority is vast upon future life and social life. There are three views :—

(1.) In things indifferent, children should obey parents through life. This is grounded on the law of gratitude and kindness.

(2.) In things important to temporal interest, they are not to obey beyond age, or when they have separate establishments. Yet this must be with consideration and love.

(3.) In matters of conscience they should at no time go against it. There is danger, no doubt, that passions may misguide. But conscience must be kept sacred. Conscience is always to be followed ; yet do it *with the meekness and gentleness of Christ.*

In case of attending worship, I should advise a dissenter's child much more strongly than a churchman's.

The Rev. Mr Simons, a visitor—

Make a stand the moment you know the thing wrong. I dishonour my parent in complying with a parent's sinful suggestion.

MAY 20, 1805.

WHAT IS THE BEST METHOD OF RENDERING OUR SOCIAL INTERCOURSE PROFITABLE TO OURSELVES AND OUR FRIENDS ?—Proposed by the Rev. J. Goode.

The Rev. J. Venn—

Some persons possess the power eminently of improving social intercourse. This is a gift. My father had it ; so had Mr Fletcher of Madeley.

(1) A man should know his own talent. If he have not a happy turn, he may do more harm than good. His talent may lie another way. Yet some may have great power of improvement, though not so amiable : as Mr Milner. Talents are an appendage to the power of improving social intercourse. Yet God may give a man great influence, &c., without this power.

(2.) A man must appear to be sincere. For this end he must *be* sincere. A rule with my father was to pray before he entered company. He entered, therefore, with an intention to do good. He was upon the watch to improve opportunities.

(3.) Profitable subjects should be kept in store.

(4.) Take their subjects up from others. Consult the feelings of others.

(5.) Things said by the by, in a natural way, are most impressive.

(6.) Let people be impressed with the feeling of your benevolence. Remember the little trials of people. How they got out of them.

(7.) Make a decisive avowal of your sentiments : not obtrusively, however. In a stage-coach, for instance, take the first opportunity. Companies despise those suspected of trimming.

(8.) Shew simplicity. Some have great powers, but not for conversation. For example, Jonathan Edwards. The great difficulty is, to get our hearts into a right frame, and then to speak in all simplicity, *not with fleshly wisdom.*

The Rev. R. Cecil—

Leighton says justly of company, that it is either a *blank* or a *blot.* It is not necessarily so. If we made more *full proof of our ministry,* we might do more. I have seen companies not unwilling to be led, but nobody led them.

Man should not go where he has no prospect of usefulness. Perhaps his absence might do good. " Why is not this man to be found in trifling company ? "

But if there be a prospect of good, then let him go, and—

1. Shew benevolence. Imitate Mr Venn.

2. Condescend to capacity. Hurt no feelings.

3. Avoid litigation. A young amiable prig often spoils useful company.

4. Consider that the same opportunity may never return. Persons, rather than things, should be the general subject of conversation.

5. Remove mischievous prejudices. Exercise faith in the invisible world. Rules are proper, and men have talents ; but faith in the invisible world is the great thing.

The Rev. J. Clayton—

1. We should consider it as our duty to make social intercourse profitable.

2. We should cultivate a disposition to comply with this duty.

3. This will give ease and nature. This is like the spirit of a merchant—to make a good bargain.

4. We should add to our intellectual stores with this in view.

5. Start such subjects as will not disturb any.

6. Be vigilant in observing instructive occurrences. " Catch their manners living as they rise."

7. Prayer should be used for these ends.

The Rev. J. Pratt—

1. As to CASUAL intercourse. In a stage-coach, for example, we should not urge matters, so as to appear offensive.

2. As to SOCIAL intercourse: in the family, among relations and friends ; a minister and his people ; we should *make* opportunities, if none offer. " He *is* a minister! " one said ; " he never enters company but for good."

But PIETY will supersede all rules. A seraph communicates fire. A low carnal spirit seals the lips.

The Scriptures make much of the tongue. *Every idle word that men shall speak, they shall give account thereof in the day of judgment. I will praise God with the best member that I have. The tongue is a world of iniquity,* &c. If any man offend not in word, the same is a perfect man.

JUNE 3, 1805.

WHAT ARE THE PRESENT SIGNS OF THE TIMES WITH REGARD TO THIS NATION ?—Proposed by the Rev. H. Foster.

Mr Foster—

Bonaparte is the means of occupying those who would have persecuted religious persons. There is more bitterness in many against vital religion than against infidelity. There is a dreadful spirit of irreligion. The diffusion of religion amongst us is a promising sign. Bonaparte may be permitted to *humble* us.

The Rev. R. Cecil—

A determined opposition to piety ; a levelling principle ; frivolity ; violent cupidity, in order to extravagance ; more surface and noise in religion than spirit ; deterioration from the old English character ; Sabbath-breaking ; self-confidence ; indisposition to marry, except with political views—these are signs of the times.

The Rev. J. Pratt—

Providence seems to lead on to a decision between the church and the world.

1. There is an increase of ministers. Bishops cannot account for it. Some are alarmed at it.

2. Providence permits a bitter spirit. Now all is run down as Calvinism. Mrs H. More is so dubbed. There is an approximation of the High Church to Popery.

SATAN tries to counteract this—(1.) By impurity among professors ; (2.) By amusements.

There are vast efforts for education. Public committees too much displace *retirement*. Party spirit in public affairs is a great evil.

The Rev. Mr Simons, a visitor—

The enemies of the Church of Christ have chiefly suffered in this war. Trusting to an arm of flesh, and rejection of Christ, have been evil signs.

The Rev. J. Goode—

Servants professing religion have drunk into the levelling spirit of the age more than others.

Some one speaks of Popery as "a lamb in adversity, a fox in equality, and a ramping and ravening lion in prosperity."

The Rev. W. Goode—

The spirit of Popery is among High Churchmen. The time of slaying the witnesses seems to approach.

There has always been an opposition to the truth; but it is more systematic now.

The Rev. S. Crowther—

Insubordination; profligacy and extravagance in public schools; indifference towards religion; aversion to hear practical discourses—these are evil signs of the times.

The Rev. Henry Martyn, a visitor—

The extension of Gospel truth does not counterbalance our danger. Amongst younger men there is little spirituality. In the universities, there is not much zeal, nor prayer meetings.

There is less spirit among pious clergy than I expected to find. I am astonished at the low standard of conversation among them. If this be the case, the number of ministers is not of so much importance; for what influence can they have on their people?

The Jews had a zeal for God when the prophet was sent to reprove and threaten.

The Rev. H. G. Watkins—

Increase of circulating libraries; Sunday newspapers; conjugal infidelity in higher orders—are signs of the times.

JUNE 17, 1805.

THE MEASURE AND MEANS OF HUMAN HAPPINESS?—Proposed by the Rev. B. Woodd.

Mr Woodd—

As to the BODY—competence for the supply of its wants. *Your heavenly Father knoweth that ye have need of these things.* As to the MIND—a competence is necessary here; but regulated by the Word of God. Imagination is to be repressed when it becomes wild. As to the SOUL—*This is life eternal, to know Thee, the only true God, and Jesus Christ whom thou hast sent.* The passions are not sinful in their origin and principles, but disordered. Regeneration, producing repentance, rectifies these passions.

I. What detracts from happiness?

1. Some things do so necessarily: ill health; indolence; want of object.

2. There are others which dazzle, but detract from real enjoyment : as popularity ; patronage ; abundant gratification.   Paley's chapter on happiness is excellent.

II. What contributes to happiness ?

1. An object for the exercise of our faculties.   2. A moderate variety. 3. As to my own feelings—rural scenery.   4. Health.   5. Social affections.   6. Domestic life.   7. A degree of bustle, and of solitude. 8. To observe others' miseries.   9. To relieve others' wants.

III. What supremely constitutes happiness ?

Spiritual happiness :   *Return to thy rest, O my soul, for the Lord hath dealt bountifully with thee.*   It gives a spiritual enjoyment of temporal mercies.

The Rev. W. Goode—

Ricaltoun's Essay on Happiness is far better than Paley's.

The Rev. H. G. Watkins—

Temperance ; moral habits ; gospel hope ; reliance on God's overruling care—these give human happiness.

The Rev. J. Venn—

There are few happy.   Why ?   From various causes.

Happiness is the adaptation of man's mind to his circumstances.   A man must therefore bring his mind to his circumstances, or his circumstances to his mind.

Men may make themselves happier than they in general are.   Let them look on the bright side of circumstances.

Study happiness as a Christian.   Exercise self-denial.   Do not multiply the causes of happiness, lest you multiply disappointments.

The Rev. H. Foster—

We are miserable beings.   The Gospel is God's remedy for this misery.   Happiness is the application of God's remedies to man's miseries.

Christians having God with them in trouble are possessed of real happiness in that trouble.

Take St Paul's example.   As to his misery as a sinner, he has well described that, and its alleviations, in Rom. vii. ; such light seems to burst in on his mind, that he was probably happier than angels. Christians thus under temporal misery, and in the midst of temptations, may be happier than the very angels.   Arrowsmith, in the beginning of his *Chain of Principles*, says something like this ; that happiness is the fulness of the satisfying of the rational appetite with that which is durable.   When we see God settling everything we may be happy.

The Rev. J. Pratt—

I have no objection to what Mr Woodd and Mr Venn state as to the MEANS of happiness, when considered as *God's using them;* but I acquiesce in Mr Foster's resolution of all happiness into acquiescence in the will of God.   God can make us happy in the destitution of all outward good. This appears to be the Apostle's view. See Phil. iv. 11, 12 ; 2 Cor. vi. 4-10. Poverty or riches ; disease or health ; pain or ease ; reputation or infamy—are indifferent in *themselves* to happiness or misery.

The Rev. J. Clayton—

It is a fallacy to think that happiness consists in external things. Booth says, "Happiness does not consist in *things*, but in *thoughts*." Those who make happiness consist in external things go on the plan of making up an independence of God—*e. g.*, "My money is not all in one place, &c., and is therefore safe whatever calamities may come."

Maclaurin's definition of happiness is, "A clear perception of supreme goodness and beauty, and our interest in it." Happiness is reduction to order.

Howe says if you lay a man with broken bones on a bed of roses, he will not be at ease.

1. Personal happiness results from the degree of our sanctification. When sanctification is much advanced, we shall be taken up with *present* duty and *present* employment.

2. Some degree of usefulness is necessary to happiness. *It is more blessed to give than to receive.*

3. The order of our families is so also.

4. The possession, too, of intelligent and disinterested friends.

5. Expect little, and you will be the happier.

The Rev. J. Goode—

A man's life consisteth not in the abundance of the things which he possesseth.—Godliness hath the promise of this life, and of that which is to come. —A little that the righteous hath is better than great riches.

There is a happiness in godly sorrow, in the exercise of faith, in hope. Expect little from men, but much from God. Also in obedience : *Great peace have they that keep thy law.—In keeping of them is great reward.*

———

On July 1, 1805, the subject was, WHAT IS THE SPECIFIC DIF-FERENCE BETWEEN THE FAITH OF A NOMINAL CHRISTIAN AND OF A REAL BELIEVER ? We have no Notes.

———

JULY 15, 1805.

HOW HAS THE OFFENCE OF THE CROSS BEEN INCREASED BY EVAN-GELICAL PREACHERS ?—Proposed by the Rev. B. Woodd.

The Rev. S. Crowther—

It is impossible to remove the offence of the Cross. It is increased more by *manner* than by *matter*. Stories frequently increase it. The great way to avoid it is, *Take heed to thyself and the doctrine.*

The Rev. R. Cecil—

To suppose any way of preaching the Cross so as not to offend the world, is to know nothing of the subject.

But wherein has this offence been *unnecessarily* increased ?   By an imperious spirit.   By strange interpretations of Scripture.   By accommodation to the taste of a spoiled people ; ludicrous comparisons ; low transactions ; silly stories.   By loose and indiscreet conduct in life. The world look at a minister *out* of the pulpit to know what he means *in* it.   By an ostentatious spirit, *giving out that himself was some great one.*   Even a child will often detect our spirit when we think no one sees it.

Also by controversy; vulgarity and ill-manners; talking without thinking, " Such as the Lord gave me ! "

By the manner of conducting the devotional part of the service in a way perhaps as much as to say, " We don't mean anything by this. Have patience, and you shall hear *me*." By slighting the offence of irregularity.   It was a wise reply of a Spanish minister to the king : "Leave off the affair, it is but a ceremony."   " A ceremony ! why, the *king* is a *ceremony*."   By good men maintaining suspicious connexions.   There is a wide distinction between my not harassing and exposing a man, and endorsing and authenticating him.   By a contempt of men's prejudices and education : *I became all things to all men, that by all means I might save some.*   By a want of the spirit of the Cross ; of the humility, patience, and love to souls, which animated Christ.

The Rev. J. Goode—

Some are determined to take offence.   That is a selfish spirit, when a man is so full of himself, that he spills it, as Dr Watts says, on all the company.   Young men fond of preaching from Solomon's Song increase the offence.   So also by railing against human learning.

On July 29, 1805, the subject was, How far can we infer Future Events in this Life respecting Individuals from their Moral Conduct?   We have no notes.   The meetings were adjourned to September 23.   The writer of the notes was not present on that day.   On the next occasion, October 7, 1805, the subject was, On the Nature and Obligation of a Promise.   On this, also, we have no remarks.

October 21, 1805.

In what respects is the Present State of the World adapted to Promote our Moral Improvement ?—Proposed by the Rev. H. G. Watkins.

The Rev. J. Davies—

It shews us the depravity of man ; God's sovereignty ; the vanity of riches and honour ; the value of our civil and religious privileges.

The Rev. W. Goode—

The present state of the world tends to excite a spirit of dependence on God. It shews the necessity of bringing forward the evidence of Scripture to counteract infidelity; it illustrates the truth of God's word in the fulfilment of prophecy. It leads to an expectation of the approaching kingdom of Christ.

The Rev. S. Crowther—

View the times comparatively with other times. They were worse in Queen Anne's reign and George I. than now, particularly in dramatical entertainments and periodical papers. There is at present, however, a spirit of insubordination.

The Rev. W. J. Abdy—

In politics, we learn to cease from man. In morality, to study the grounds of evangelical morality. In religion, we learn its value.

The Rev. H. Foster—

We learn the vanity of boasted Liberty and Equality. A maxim among physicians is perhaps illustrated by the present times : *Malum benè positum maneat.* Let evils, but little troublesome, alone.

The Rev. J. Pratt—

The present times shew—1. The vanity of man : his distinctions, hopes, riches, power. 2. The folly of man. 3. His depravity. 4. They impose silence on curiosity. 5. Man is made the interpreter of Providence. 6. These times excite expectation of the fulfilment of Scripture and of Christ's kingdom. 7. They shew the value of early subordination ; 8. The importance of domestic religion ; 9. The value of national grounds of union. 10. They endear heaven to us.

The Rev. J. Goode—

They teach absolute dependence on God. *It is good that a man should both hope and quietly wait for the salvation of the Lord.* (Lam. iii. 26.)

The Rev. B. Woodd—

Thankfulness for present mercies ; the vanity and instability of earthly possessions and honours ; the depravity of human nature ; the blessings of the divine covenant, of heaven—are taught us, and the necessity of filling up our post of duty.

NOVEMBER 4, 1805.

DOES DIVINE TEACHING LEAD MORE TO THE DISCOVERY OF INTERNAL GRACE OR INTERNAL DEPRAVITY ?—Proposed by the Rev. H. Foster.

Mr Foster—

Man repents and believes; but the more he repents, the less will he look at it, and the more out of himself at Christ.

The Rev. R. Cecil—

If light be let into a dirty room, will it discover more dirt or cleanliness?

A Christian's growth will be rather, as Bishop Hall says, growing downward in a sense of depravity, than in any positive sense of attainment.

The Rev. B. Woodd—

The Holy Spirit discovers depravity, the glory of Christ, the consciousness of receiving Christ. *When he is come, he shall convince the world of sin, and of righteousness, and of judgment.*

The Rev. W. Goode—

The Apostle's experience in Rom. vii. is an answer to the question, where he shews his depravity. The design of grace is to produce gracious feelings; but the question is, how far it leads to the discernment of those feelings. Shaw, in his *Immanuel,* says, grace discovers itself more in *looking* and *longing* than in any positive attainments.

The Rev. J. Goode—

Divine teaching leads more to the discovery of depravity.

The Rev. H. G. Watkins—

The Spirit leads not so much to discover its own work as our hearts.

———

On November 1805 the recorder of the notes was not present; and on the next subject, How SHALL WE BEST IMPROVE THE APPROACHING DAY OF GENERAL THANKSGIVING? we have no remarks. This Thanksgiving Day was upon the occasion of the victory of Trafalgar: a victory so great in its results, though clouded by the death of Nelson.

———

DECEMBER 16, 1805.

WHAT EFFICACY MAY BE EXPECTED TO ATTEND BAPTISM, AND WHEREON DOES IT DEPEND?—Proposed by the Rev. W. Fry.

Mr Fry—

The Church of England teaches that grace is conferred in Baptism. A sacrament supposes a means of grace, when rightly used. See Articles 25, 27. Scripture and the Church consider Baptism as an institution for conveying over, signing, and sealing, as an estate. We pray for the "spiritual regeneration" of the child. Baptism is connected in Scripture with some saving grace.

I understand then by Spiritual Regeneration in Baptism, the commencement of a new and holy principle. I do not maintain that this necessarily takes place, for this could not have been the case with

Simon Magus ; nor usually, God is a Sovereign ; nor that there is any other way of regeneration.

But baptism is the USUAL way of commencing spiritual life. *Except a man be born of water and the Spirit. Having our hearts sprinkled from an evil conscience. The like figure whereunto baptism doth also now save us. That he might sanctify and cleanse it (the Church). Saved by the washing of regeneration, and renewing of the Holy Ghost.*

Scripture uses not regeneration to denote inward change. Renewing by the Holy Ghost is the expression used. The word Regeneration is only twice used. *Follow me in the regeneration; i. e.,* the gospel dispensation. *Saved us by the washing of regeneration.* If Baptism be only an external rite, how can it be a covenant ordinance ?

Objections chiefly arise from matters of fact. Many baptised are evidently not regenerated—even children of believers : but the ordinances of God bring blessings or not, as they are used. The prayer of faith, it is promised, shall prevail. Promises are made to believers.

Heathens' children are not to be baptised, as children, till the parents are converted. If a believer presents his child in baptism, disbelieving baptism to be a means of regeneration, so far he is an unbeliever. It may be said, that that would be making children's salvation dependent on the faith of parents. But if a child was not circumcised, he was cut off.

The Rev. R. Lloyd—

Baptism is a grand and especial means of regeneration. We should be particularly careful respecting godfathers and godmothers. If more were made of it by us, more efficacy might be expected.

The Rev. B. Woodd—

The Assembly's Confession admits efficacy in Baptism ; but limits it to the elect people of God, which, in due time, discovers itself. Usher has the same idea.

We shall not understand the subject till we understand the Divine covenant. God always taught by symbols—Sacrifices, Circumcision, Baptism. All teach the Covenant of Grace. The covenant was made with Abraham and his posterity ; therefore it is called *the adoption,* as our Church says, " Children of God."

Baptism is an exhibition of divine truth, an outward figure of the covenant of grace. It is not clear that the grace and the form always go together. Baptism is an investing ordinance on God's part—like the coronation of the king.

What is the EFFICACY of Baptism·? In the case of adults the Church of England presupposes faith. " Faith is confirmed, and grace increased."

The privileges of a child baptized are—That he is entered into covenant, the covenant of his parent with God ; that dying in infancy, he partakes of the benefit ; that living, if he depart from God, he forfeits all advantages. *Circumcision verily profiteth, if thou keep the law,* &c.

N

Baptism lays a peculiar obligation on us to holiness; especially if the covenant relation of our children depend on ourselves.

Children should be frequently reminded of the covenant and the promises made in their name.

The Rev. W. Goode—

It is a strange doctrine that a child's interest in the covenant depends on parents!

The two sacraments are meant to exhibit great doctrines—RENEWAL and ACCEPTANCE. That they are *means* of grace, no one denies; but he communicates it sovereignly. I see no ground for peculiar belief that my children shall be absolutely renewed and saved.

The Rev. H. Foster—

When I subscribe to the Liturgy, it is not in the same sense in which I do to Scripture. The Baptismal Service is unhappily drawn up. I think myself of the same sentiments as the Reformers, and therefore I subscribe. Sometimes I suspect my sentiments are too low concerning baptism, because they differ from many of the best writers.

St Paul says, *I thank God I baptized none of you, but Crispus and Gaius.* He could not thank God that he had not regenerated any one. The Scriptures speak of the thing signified : *That spiritual Rock that followed them . . . was Christ.*

The Rev. Josiah Pratt—

Titus iii. 5—*Saved us by the* WASHING OF REGENERATION, *and* RENEWING OF THE HOLY GHOST. John iii. 5—*Born of* WATER *and of the* SPIRIT. There are means, both EXTERNAL and INTERNAL, by which we are brought into a way of salvation. Baptism is the EXTERNAL SIGN and SEAL of the new covenant, and whereby we are admitted into the Church of Christ, and entitled to the assistance of the Holy Spirit, which is represented and sealed to us by baptism.

Christ makes both necessary to salvation; and St Paul makes them, accordingly, the means of salvation. Primitive writers usually styled baptism regeneration, and baptized persons regenerated.

The main question is,—IN WHAT SENSE is each of these a means of salvation? How are we saved by baptism? How by the renewing of the Holy Ghost? How the renewing of the Holy Spirit saves us, we need not here inquire.

BAPTISM *saves* us—

1. As it brings us into a state of salvation, being the appointed rite of admission into the Christian Church. The Church is a body taken out of the rest of the world. It is the peculiar care of the Redeemer. He affords it special means of salvation. It is compared, therefore, by St Peter (1 Pet. iii. 20, 21), to the ark. The ark saved those sent into it from the deluge which destroyed the world. They were *saved by water*; *i.e.*, in the ark, which was carried on the water. *The like figure whereunto, even baptism, doth also now save us.* For Christ has appointed

that all who will enter into the ark of his Church shall be admitted by the solemn rite of baptism.

2. As it is a sign of the cleansing of our souls from the pollution of sin, of the renewing of them by the Holy Spirit. The sign is used in the Old Testament as well as in the New (Ez. xxxvi. 25–27). It is a natural sign. And also by custom ; as new-born infants are cleansed by water.

3. As it is a seal of the covenant. So circumcision. Abraham *received the sign of circumcision, a* SEAL *of the righteousness of faith; i.e.,* a seal which God set to his covenant, that he would accept him as righteous, on his believing ; and · Abraham, by making this sign on himself and children, sealed the covenant on his part. So both sacraments—God acting with us, as men one with another—not only giving his word and promise, and receiving our vows, but, by visible signs, sealing and confirming his promises, and engaging our vows.

4. As it is a means of obtaining the blessings which it represents. In the Church Catechism we read—" An outward and visible SIGN of an inward and spiritual grace given us, ordained by Christ himself, as a MEANS whereby we receive the same, and a PLEDGE to assure us thereof." No institution was appointed by Christ in vain. God is not wanting to his Church in the use of such institutions. Therefore immediately after he commanded to disciple all nations by baptism, our Lord adds, *And, lo, I am with you alway, even to the end of the world.*

The Gospel is peculiarly the ministration of the Spirit : the Spirit is the peculiar promise of the Gospel. All the institutions of Christianity are represented as so many means, in the use of which the Spirit will be certainly communicated, if we use them aright. This is the true reason why baptism and regeneration are so frequently joined, as if inseparable,—as if convertible terms. See John, Titus, and also Peter in Acts ii. 38, 39.

Now if baptism be a means appointed for obtaining remission of sins and the influence of the Holy Spirit, we may certainly be said to be *saved* by it, or brought into a state of salvation. Especially when we add, that, being admitted into the Christian Church by this solemn rite, we are admitted to the use of all other means of salvation.

See now the meaning of the expressions in our Baptismal Office :— " That of his bounteous mercy he will grant to this child that thing which by nature he cannot have : " " Wash him and sanctify him with the Holy Ghost : " . . . " That he may receive remission of his sins by spiritual regeneration." " Give thy Holy Spirit to this infant, that he may be born again : " " Sanctify this water to the mystical washing away of sin : " " We yield thee hearty thanks . . . . that it hath pleased thee to regenerate this infant with thy Holy Spirit, to receive him for thine own child by adoption," &c. In the office for adults we pronounce that they are now " born again, and made heirs of everlasting salvation." All this is agreeable to the account given ; viz., that the baptised are incorporated into the visible Church of Christ, and thereby entitled to the pardon of sins, and received into the number of God's children through Christ, and have a right to expect the Spirit's influence so long as they do not wilfully violate their baptismal covenant.   They are born again or regenerated into a new state, have entered on new relations, are obliged to live new lives, are admitted into the body of which Christ is the head, and in which the Holy Spirit dwells.   This is baptismal regeneration, and what will be attended with the *renewing of the Holy Ghost*, where there is no obstruction to his sacred influence.

Why is baptism styled the WASHING OF REGENERATION ?   It is a way of speaking familiar among the Jews.   Those who are saved are admitted mostly by baptism.   Those baptized resembled such as were new-born ; they entered into a new state, were admitted to new relations, were obliged to live new lives, and to govern themselves by new laws and customs.   Christ and St Paul used the expression in the same sense. (See Bradford on *Bapt. and Sp. Reg.*)   The Church of England treats her members as true Christians.

DECEMBER 30, 1805.

HOW FAR MAY THE SACRED LANGUAGE BE CONSIDERED AS A PROPER MODEL FOR THE PHRASEOLOGY OF CHRISTIAN INSTRUCTIONS ?—Proposed by the Rev. J. Clayton.

Mr Clayton—

Foster says, and labours it, that Scripture phrases are improper for Christian instruction.   It is generally found that those who dislike Scripture phrases, dislike the just views of truth.   Scripture phrases generally come with more pleasure and weight on my own mind.

The Rev. B. Woodd—

The Scriptures are given us as a standard of TRUTH, of EXPRESSION.   The use of Scripture phraseology familiarises Scripture to us ; puts honour on Scripture.   Scripture phraseology is better than any that can be substituted.   Where Christians differ, they differ where they depart from Scripture phrases.   They may, indeed, be the vehicle of error, but only when used partially.

The Rev. W. Fry—

I have observed error on both sides.   Some so use Scripture phraseology as rather to disgrace themselves.

Some Scripture phrases convey no ideas to common minds, and displease the refined.   For example, *Held in the galleries—A nail in a sure place—Pins of the tabernacle*.   These are Scripture expressions ; but as they are allusions to habits and manners quite foreign to ours, they should not be used.

No phrases should be used which tend to the ludicrous.   Some, however, reject the chaste and just use of Scripture phrases.

Prove every point of doctrine and practice by Scripture phrases. I have heard too much of the accommodating use of Scripture phrases.

They may be chastely used, when they are meant for illustration only, not for proof. We must not use Scripture phrases merely to prevent controversy, but should give the *sense* in which we use them.

The Rev. W. Goode—

Those who object to the use of Scripture phraseology, yet use it in creeds and confessions. In defining or stating the doctrines of the Gospel, or in confessions of faith, it is not right to use Scripture phraseology, because you are there to give the *sense* of Scripture. But in *preaching*, it is useful and effective.

The Rev. S. Crowther—

Sydney Smith reprobates the use of Scripture phraseology, as discovering a barrenness of invention. Man is a sinner. Scripture phrases were always as suited to him as now.

The Rev. H. G. Watkins—

Scripture phrases are of great use to preachers. The English translation is not certainly of the same authority as the original. It is useless to introduce Scripture phrases which need to be explained. It is better to use such words as carry the scriptural idea. I have heard improper Scripture phrases in prayer.

The Rev. W. Goode—

All Scripture is given by inspiration of God. The sacred language is peculiarly beautiful. It comes as a kind of *clencher* to what we say. Some use Scripture phrases, and hide doubtful or false sentiments under them. They do not mean by them what you do. I have no scruple to leave out or alter some phrases, because some expressions convey now a secondary idea.

I know a minister who established every head of his sermon with two or three passages of Scripture, that *out of the mouth of two or three witnesses every word might be established.*

The Rev. R. Cecil—

"Barrenness" does not apply to such a subject. Smith might have said, it was fanatical, &c. The last age, which was eminent for its divinity, was eminent also for its Scripture quotations and Scripture phraseology. The grand desideratum here is, GOOD SENSE. Give a blockhead good rules, and he will ruin all by a bad use of them, but good sense will guide a man to a wise use.

By transferring the Hebraisms of Scripture into equivalent expressions in English, I use in reality Scripture phraseology.

The disuse of Scripture phraseology tends to the loss of the Scripture sense, and to make men clearer than Scripture! Clearly make out the doctrine of the Trinity, also draw inferences from the doctrine of predestination from the Scripture language—because they are so deep.

There may be so much *ex abundanti*, as to become unscriptural.

Deviation is dangerous without absolute necessity. The danger is with respect to the temper and turn of the age. We are not so virtuous as our ancestors, but more fastidious. We have the fastidiousness of a corrupt age, refined *without*, but debauched *within*.

We must resist this. Not like a new edition of the *Whole Duty of Man*, which was lately advertised as "accommodated to the present age."

Every science has its proper terms. The Holy Spirit used most suitable phrases. Explain these terms, but use them not thoughtlessly. We should not use Scripture phrases which convey no idea to an English understanding, without explaining them. For example, *I am like a bottle in the smoke—Put new wine into old bottles—Lift up thy head from off thee*.

The least touch will alter essentially a portrait. It is dangerous to touch in religion.

Avoid cant phrases. There is nothing untrue in the phrase, "the blood-bought throng;" but I would not use it. The same idea is conveyed in "purchased or bought by his blood."

It is right to alter Scripture phrases with the limitation above mentioned; but utterly wrong to *omit* any portion.

Christ and his Apostles constantly used Scripture phrases. They carry an authority—a holy authority—likely to arrest the conscience in those who even dislike our sentiments.

The Rev. J. Pratt—

Heaping together passages, without using them with intelligence and force, is uninteresting; not so, if introduced wisely. I have seen this in preachers. Some carry their hearers' mind on—some not.

Scripture phrases are the language of Canaan.

The Rev. H. Foster—

We can't mend God's way of stating truth.

The Rev. Mr Simons, a visitor—

Which things we speak, not in the words which man's wisdom teacheth, but which the Holy Ghost teacheth. Scripture phraseology savours of the cross.

The Rev. H. Stewart, a visitor—

Apollos was *mighty in the Scriptures*.

JANUARY 27, 1806.

THE DUTY AND IMPORTANCE OF PUNCTUALITY IN ALL OUR ENGAGEMENTS—Proposed by the Rev. W. J. Abdy.

The Rev. H. Foster—

Want of punctuality is often the occasion of unpunctuality in others. If a man fails he should apologise, because that will contribute to make him more punctual, for he will not like to be always making apologies.

The Rev. R. Cecil—

Lavater says that there is no end of the evils which attend want of punctuality. Mrs More says that method is the very hinge of business ; and there is no method without punctuality.

The importance of punctuality is great, as it is *gaining time*. It is like packing things in a box, where a good packer will get in half as much again as a bad one.

The calmness of mind which it produces is another evidence of the importance of punctuality. A disorderly man is always in a hurry. He has no time to speak with you, because he is going elsewhere ; and when he gets there, he has no time, because he is coming away. The Duke of Newcastle said, " I do one thing at a time."

Want of punctuality runs through a man's whole affairs. A man lost an estate by telling his uncle, that he did *nothing* with his razor after shaving.

Punctuality is important, because it subserves the peace and good temper of a family. Want of punctuality not only infringes on necessary duty, but sometimes excludes this duty.

The world has given us the nickname of Methodists. I wish we deserved it. The misfortune is, that it seems to be ironical. Punctuality gives a weight to character. " Such a man has made an appointment. Then I know he'll keep it." And this generates punctuality in you. Like other virtues, it generates itself. It makes servants and children punctual.

Appointment is a debt. I owe you punctuality. I have therefore no right to throw away *your* time, if I do my own.

Most men do not sufficiently estimate the importance of punctuality.

The Rev. J. Pratt—

A man must be judged by his habit, not by a single act. [Here he made some reference to himself, and an instance, a rare one, of unpunctuality to an engagement at Blackfriars.] It may be useful to even an habitually punctual man once in his life to make a grievous mistake.

Arithmetic gives early habits of punctuality. Constitution does much.

There is nothing in Scripture on punctuality but what is very general.

The Rev. J. Clayton—

1. The importance of punctuality is great as to our personal plans.
2. It is important in the family. Keep punctual, especially with your wife. " It is only my wife," one would say—only your wife ! Cherish the delicacy of affection.
3. It is important in intercourse with friends.
4. It is important in the worship of God.
5. It sets forth the value we put on time.
6. It produces calmness of mind.
7. It gives a likeness to God.

The Rev. S. Crowther—

Every man *may* be punctual. Some men are too soon. Punctuality is being neither too soon nor too late.

On the next subject, WHAT IS MEANT BY OUR LORD'S DESCENDING INTO HELL? we have no notes.

FEBRUARY 24, 1806.

HOW MAY WE BEST IMPROVE THE APPROACHING FAST?—Proposed by the Rev. W. Goode.

Mr Goode—

We should acknowledge particular circumstances of humiliation.

1. The nations of Europe are awake to a sense of danger; and have formed a strong combination. There is reason to augur well. Yet they are wholly broken. They have been destroyed by (1.) rapidity, (2.) the treachery of the enemy, (3.) misconduct, (4.) famine. However it has been done, yet the hand of God is in it. It has given a new state of things on the Continent. Its tendency is to humble the chief supporters of Popery.

2. The great victory of Trafalgar is a ground of encouragement.

3. The death of Nelson, Pitt, and Cornwallis,* are events which call for reflection, and the introduction of a new order of things at home.

4. The Continental powers are still jealous of one another.

5. The distresses in Germany in consequence of Bonaparte's mad career should shew us *our* blessings.

We might divide our sermons into—

1. Judgments under which we labour. 2. Causes of fear under those judgments. 3. The true spirit and temper to be cultivated. 4. Ground of hope under humiliation.

The Rev. R. Lloyd—

We should call on our people to be prepared for a better world, and lead them from the gloomy instability of human events to a better hope of infinite realities.

The Rev. H. Foster—

It is a new sort of thing which God is doing in the earth. He is now long come out of his place to punish. We have escaped comparatively. But we may shudder when we think what sufferings would follow the enemy's prevailing against us. Yet why should not God allow it? We have nothing to say.

I don't feel so much on God's dishonour as I should do. I've a selfish feeling for ease. I often feel thus before God. I *know* nothing. I *can do* nothing. I *deserve* nothing, and there I leave it with God.

---

* Nelson died in September 1805; Cornwallis, in India, October 5, 1805; Pitt, November 23, 1805.

The Rev. R. Cecil—

Since the last Fast, we have had a further proof of the weakness of man. Nothing is to be depended on in the strongest armies, or the wisdom or valour of man. If successful—Pitt was idolised.

There has been a want of feeling among the people in the progress of the war.

Here is a caution. Whatever we treat on, we should treat it spiritually. There is no objection to mention the victory of Trafalgar, but we should not enter into the matter so as to appear politicians.

The Rev. J. Pratt—

A child-like simplicity is pre-eminently called for. Everything demonstrates our ignorance, and that we are altogether in God's hands.

On the next subject, THE CAUSES AND CURE OF INDECENCY AND IRREVERENCE IN PUBLIC WORSHIP, we have no notes.

MARCH 24, 1806.

HOW FAR IS IT THE DUTY OF CHRISTIANS TO ASSOCIATE WITH WORLDLY PEOPLE, IN ORDER TO PROMOTE THEIR SPIRITUAL PROFIT ?—Proposed by the Rev. H. G. Watkins.

Mr Watkins—

If we are not likely to gain such influence as to reprove, we should not form such connexions. It is improper to associate with the immoral. Intercourse should take place by the advances of the worldly persons themselves. If such advances are made, a Christian should attend to them.

Intercourse among relations should be maintained by a Christian ; there is such influence from a truly godly man ! In every family almost there is a grain of salt. An old uncle or aunt in a corner. Good books thus creep in.

In marriage it is dangerous to form unbelieving connexions. It is more dangerous, however, to a woman than a man, because women are likely to take the colour of the man's mind, more than the man the woman's. No marriage, perhaps, was ever undertaken from the pure motive of converting the other party : subordinate motives intervene.

The Rev. H. Foster—

I object to acceding to the advances of worldly people. I should soon find it unprofitable. But it is a question of circumstances. Some have talents to control and influence the worldly ; others not. I have heard of a clergyman, separated from the world, who was seduced to bowl with worldly companions : he drank till intoxicated, and did not go to bed sober for four years : afterwards he was so terrified at himself, that he was recovered, I hope, at last.

Some people ought to go into the world. They can do it, and do it in simplicity. But they will generally soon grow tired. If we can't carry our religion into the world, one absolute duty is to keep out of it. If the worldly see us like them, it will encourage them in their own ways.

The Rev. R. Cecil—

Christ is an example for going into society of all kinds. But there is no absolute rule. It admits of restrictions. A public man must keep out of danger. If any one could go into society as Christ did, let him go. Let him attend marriage feasts and Pharisees' houses.

Much depends on a man observing his call, and an opening. It is not enough for a minister to say he goes to a public company to hang on the wheel. It is not sufficient to justify his going. Many evangelical ministers dawdle away a day, and wrap it up by a little expounding. Every minister must be a man of business. It is not sufficiently considered how great is the sin of idleness. We talk in the pulpit of the value of time, but too little act on what we say.

People of the world should be treated kindly, tenderly, with feeling and compassion. They should be helped, if they ask it. But if you meet with a mere worldling, it must be like the meeting of two persons in rain, who will part as soon as they can.

If a man loves the company of worldly people, it is an ill symptom. But a minister who withdraws himself much, must satisfy himself that he has a good reason. If reproached for not visiting his flock so much as they wish, let him have a reason. For example, a man at work for his children may say that he has as much love for them as his wife has, though she is always with them.

I fell into a mistake when a young man. I thought I could talk with the world on my own ground; could win them thus over to mine. I was fond of painting, and so I talked with them on that subject. I pleased them ; but did not consider that I gave a consequence to their pursuits which does not belong to them. I ought to have raised them above their level. I did not see this at the time ; but now I see it to be a great error. A man builds a fine house, and has fine prospects, he wants you to see them, for he is sick of them himself—and particularly if he can get the parson. Then they draw you into their schemes. A man has got ten thousand pounds. You congratulate him on it. Now you may tell him in the pulpit in vain that riches are nothing worth, while you tell him out of it that they are.

Romaine and Newton are both profitable in conversation, though both differently. Romaine is short, prophetical rather than evangelical ; but he is not to be trifled with. It is Christ and faith, but it has left its savour. Newton *came eating and drinking*, full of story and of figure, kind and tender ; but all told for good.

Lord Chesterfield says a man's character is lowered when he is *to be had*. A minister ought never *to be had*.

A minister should shew the *value of time*. It is a sad thing when people begin to yawn.

Venn * would sing a solo, if worldly people would not sing with him.

* The Rev. Henry Venn, whose valuable Memoir and Letters is so well known, the father of the member of the Eclectic at this time.

But he was never fanatical, never gave himself spiritual airs. For this is death to all usefulness. He had a beaming benevolence ; a thorough satisfaction in himself of the value of divine things. They thought him a *character*, but let him go on, and gave him up in despair.

The Christian should be careful not to be drawn off his ground on things not unlawful in themselves. Time may be consumed by a political event, just as the most carnal man would spend it.

The Rev. B. Woodd—

Worldly people will not wish our society if we keep up our character. Keeping up a general acquaintance keeps open the door for the time of adversity.

The Rev. Mr Simons, a visitor—

I have heard of a minister who resolved to enter no company but in his Master's livery ; nor to let an hour pass without introducing the great things of the kingdom. Much good might be done if such were the universal resolution.

The Rev. J. Clayton—

In the world's advances to us, let us ask, What do they make their advances to ? This will determine whether it becomes a *duty* to meet their advances. If they ask light and help, we are bound to give it.

With respect to the general question. The Scriptures require separation. And this we should obey unless duty calls us with a hope of raising children to the Church. All the gregarious animals associate with their kind. In the operation of the gracious principle, there will be a conformity to the rule. When the disciples were let go, they went to their *own company*. Scripture examples all bear the same testimony. John Baptist went to court, but to reprove sin. A painter went into a field of battle to realise the scene he wanted to depict : but a ball took off his hand !

We lessen our influence by losing our decision of character. The jackdaw is seen in all companies. This separation is calculated to do good to others. It is a specimen of the future and eternal separation. An anticipation of that eternal separation. It is calculated to set men thinking. A scriptural separation encourages young beginners.

The Rev. W. Goode—

The question has been considered as relating to the duty of separation from the world. Of this there can be no doubt. But the question is, How far is it the duty of Christians to associate with worldly people *for their good?* This is a more delicate and difficult question than the other. Much must depend on the call in providence, the introduction, and the prospect of doing good.

The Rev. J. Goode—

Relative obligations are to be considered ; and the motives for going into worldly company are to be thoroughly sifted. The world has no charms for some, but a thousand for others : the danger of the one is, therefore, far beyond that of the other. Certainly there would not be so many cautions in Scripture on this subject, if the danger were not great.

The Rev. S. Crowther—

It is difficult to lay down rules for others on this question ; but not for ourselves, if we study our own character.   The first consideration must be, what the effect of going into the world is on *ourselves*, before we consider its effect on *others*.   " No man," said Louis XIV., " is a hero to his own valet."   So shall we easily lose our character.

The Rev. Mr Lloyd—

The man who *has* the talent for going into the world with advantage, should mind the proportion of time given to this.

April 7, 1806.

THE NATURE AND SPECIFIC EFFECTS OF UNION WITH CHRIST.—Proposed by the Rev. Mr Simons.

Mr Simons—

Sin only excepted, we are wholly like the man Christ Jesus.   The renewed Christian then, as such, is wholly like Christ.   The difference between them is such only as between a fountain and the stream. Christ emptied himself not of his essential divinity, but of the glory due to him as Divine.

The blood of Christ is the source and cement of this union.

Our notes on this subject, as well as on several others, are scanty, as the recorder of them, now deeply engaged in the affairs of the Church Missionary Society, of which he was secretary, had to attend its Committee Meetings, which, at that period of its history, were held in the evening.

April 21, 1806.

IN WHAT WAY MAY WE BEST ASCERTAIN THE MOTIVES OF OUR CONDUCT, AND THE USES WHICH OUGHT TO BE MADE OF THE DISCOVERY ?—Proposed by the Rev. H. Foster.

Mr Foster—

An examination of our motives is, of all other inquiries, the best adapted to humble us.   The Scripture is full of statements of false motives.   For example, Dinah's brothers ; false apostles in preaching Christ.   The whole world, Christians excepted, is corrupt in motives. With ourselves, our motives are, no doubt, the conversion of sinners ; and the glory of God in this, through Christ.   Something of this is in every true minister.   Yet I come to this after examination—That my attainments consist more in shame for sin than in any actual acquirement.

We may pray for humility and spirituality, and yet our motive be

abominable—to be highly esteemed as ministers. Unless *we* are to
have some hand in the good done, there is little zeal. Not to think
of ourselves one way or the other, is the best proof of being freed from
sinful motives.

The Rev. R. Cecil—

Being willing to know the truth is a proof that our motives are
good. But it is seldom so. Man can't deny that he has imperfect
motives; but he is vexed that another should find it out.

If a man would encourage another to tell the truth, he would hear
what he did not suspect. But nobody will tell anybody. There is so
much self-love that we abhor to be lowered. In any *worldly* pursuit
we can suffer in order to gain, but not *here.*

Put cases. Suppose I have ascertained that I should do so much
more good by being a blundering preacher: it would go hard with
many a one of us to give up our own way. We don't like good to be
done in certain ways which are contrary to our notions : *Master, we
saw one casting out devils in thy name, and he followeth not us ; and we
forbade him, because he followeth not us.*

I dreamed once that I was in heaven, and saw there a man whom I
had always thought a hypocrite ; and I fell into a passion with Peter,
who kept the keys, and told him that he ought not to have let him in.

We are not to be discouraged at this discovery. We might be
prevented from attempting anything. Consider, if the bye-ends of all
the active men who do much were taken away, what dead and cold
hard work it would be.

Another use of this discovery of our motives is—It's a paltry thing.
You'll be in the dust to-morrow.

Again, a man will be found out. His character will lose its
weight. *He that exalteth himself shall be abased.*

The Rev. Mr Storry, a visitor—

We are sometimes tempted to accommodate the representation of
evangelical truth to great hearers. But—*I am the voice of one crying
in the wilderness.* My business is with the middle and the poor. Again,
this should be our aim—*I have set the Lord alway before me.*

The Rev. J. Goode—

It is difficult to ascertain motives where various motives combine.
In seeking the things of Christ, we still seek our own. Everything
that passes through our hands is contaminated. We seldom have a
pure motive. Few, like St Paul, can *rejoice* in the work of others,
(Phil. i. 14–18) ; or with John the Baptist, that Christ should increase,
though he decreased.

The Rev. W. Fry—

Where natural affection goes with a duty, we are willing to discharge
it. If a husband love his wife, he is willing to make a good husband;
otherwise, not so.

One who pressed me to preach *practical* sermons was not aware that

I was to come into *his* family. After a few sermons, he thought I had better not .get *so dry*, but give them a little more of the Gospel. When I have most tried to please, I have succeeded least. Balaam is an example of motives. I have ascertained my motives most easily, when duty and inclination are opposed to each other.

The use of ascertaining our motives is to teach us charity in judging others.

The Rev. S. Crowther—

The means of ascertaining our motives are self-examination and listening to others.

The use of ascertaining them is to produce humility, and prayer for greater sincerity.

The Rev. R. Lloyd—

All our conduct takes its complexion, in the sight of God, from our motives. It is most difficult in a conflict of motives to ascertain which is the predominant motive. Circumstances, at one time, make a man far different from himself at other times. Vanity is at the bottom of envy, rather than malignity. Men will often shew esteem for the poor man when in retirement, while they slight him before others.

MAY 19, 1806.

WHETHER THE TRUE FERVOUR OF DEVOTION BE NOT NECESSARILY IN PROPORTION TO TRUE LIGHT IN THE UNDERSTANDING ?—Proposed by the Rev. R. Lloyd.

Mr Lloyd—

Ignorance is not the mother of devotion. It is through the *truth* that we must be sanctified : the truth, as the instrumental cause ; the Spirit, the efficient. Where there is profound ignorance, there cannot be true fervour. An *ignis fatuus* shines only in the dark. It is light without heat ; that from below—not from above.

An infidel position is, Where mystery begins, religion ends. Though there is much falsehood here, yet there is some truth. Zeal, like other passions, is indifferent. It is good or bad according to its object, and the degree in which it is pursued is proportioned to its importance. " Zeal is fit," says Tillotson, " for wise men only ; but flourishes chiefly among fools." True fervour will improve according as we live up to the light we have.

The Rev. H. G. Watkins—

There is a difficulty in discovering the proportion between devotion and light, they being such different things. Mary Magdalene and the disciples had much love, though they were vastly ignorant concerning Christ's kingdom. There was light on the main points, and the heart sincere. Many even violent Calvinists and Arminians are right men ; and yet their judgments must act very differently on the subjects before them.

The Rev. H. Foster—

I agree in general with what Mr Lloyd states, as a speculative view. Yet, as grace exists in human nature, it works in an eccentric being. The old saying has much truth, *Ignoti nulla cupido.* We have no real desire for what we are ignorant of.

The Rev. R. Cecil—

The position is true in the abstract; but man is so complicated a creature that we cannot apply it too closely.

I'll take Leighton, Pascal, and Toplady. There is no doubt but Pascal was more devoted than Toplady, though running about Paris after scientific matters.

Leighton is a standard, so far as man can go : the light of his understanding and the devotion of his heart bore such a just proportion.

Much emphasis is to be laid on the word " true " fervour. There may be much religion in it, but not *true* fervour. It may lapse into superstition.

The Rev. J. Pratt—

I rather differ. Scripture makes knowledge and love convertible terms : Eph. i. 17, &c. ; iii. 17, &c. ; iv. 13, &c.

Thousands are substantially right who are formally wrong. Can the *heart* be right while the head is comparatively dark ? Yes. I grant devotion may be wild, yet it may be true at the same time.

There is no necessary connexion between light and love. Nay, there is no *tendency* in light, in itself, to love. The Spirit of God may use it to produce love. There is a sense in which *great accuracy* is adverse to warm affections.

The Rev. S. Crowther—

There is a sort of difference between light and love, which makes it important for us to ascertain how far love may or may not exceed light.

The Rev. J. Clayton—

Brother Lloyd's philosophical religion is not meant for the poor. The understanding is the seat of light ; the will, the seat of holiness; the affections, of love. Many poor unlettered men have a holiness of will, which excites a degree of fervour which is thoroughly genuine. If we deny this, we shall speak against the generation of the righteous. I lay stress on the fervour being grounded on the holiness of the will.

The Rev. W. Goode—

Our brethren do not, I think, differ so much as they seem to do. There is a distinction between light and knowledge. Light is a simple apprehension of the great truths of the gospel: knowledge is an acquaintance with the connexion and harmony of these truths. A man may have the grand points of light—and this is necessary to true fervour—but not knowledge.

June 2, 1806.

WHAT ARE THE PRIVILEGES AND OBLIGATIONS OF THE CHILDREN OF GODLY PEOPLE, AND ESPECIALLY OF MINISTERS ?—Proposed by the Rev. B. Woodd.

Mr Woodd—

They have a federal interest in the covenant of grace. The advantage of early initiation in Christian habits : the bias of education and prejudice in favour of religion. They derive a general acquaintance with Christian doctrines and obligations.

[The question was enlarged and deferred to the next meeting.]

June 16, 1806.

WHAT ARE THE PECULIAR OBLIGATIONS OF CHRISTIAN PARENTS, AND ESPECIALLY OF MINISTERS, IN BRINGING UP THEIR CHILDREN, AND WHAT ARE THE CONSEQUENT PRIVILEGES AND OBLIGATIONS OF THEIR CHILDREN ? —Proposed by the Rev. B. Woodd.

Mr Woodd—

Adam, if sinless, would have peopled heaven. Sin ruined this glorious plan. Families are too often the scene of discord and irreligion.

The obligation of parents towards children is great :—

1. On the ground of natural relation. There are mutual advantages and disadvantages through parents and children. The parents have been the means of bringing into being rational and immortal beings.

2. From the example of God. God included children in the covenant with Abraham.

3. From the example of Christ. He shewed great regard towards children.

OUR OBLIGATIONS AS PARENTS lie in these particulars :—

1. To have personal religion. If we are not in covenant with God, our children are not naturally in covenant with him.

2. To shew that they themselves are not of the world. We must consider our families as to be trained for heaven.

3. To set up the honour of God as the governing principle of the family. Suffer not parental government to degenerate into a petty tyranny. " Maintain God's authority more carefully," says Baxter, " than your own, and God will maintain yours." Shew children that truth is important, because God enjoins it.

4. To shew that this world is not the grand object, but the world to come.

5. To endeavour that our children be not of the world. For this end—

(1.) Frequently point out the common occurrences which shew the emptiness of the world. Point to God.

(2.) Make home happy, and let your child feel it is religion that makes it so. I detest the severe system. Punishment is never to be resorted to, if anything will do besides.   I would have him feel, if a prodigal, *I will return to my Father.*

(3.) Be as little as possible in the society of the world.   We shall perhaps be obliged to sink the characters of some of our acquaintances in the opinion of our children.

(4.) Keep out of the habits of the world.   Dress, indulgences, amusements.   Music should be devoted and hallowed.   No improper songs admitted.

(5.) Occupy the time and the mind.   The study of the Bible comprises everything—fine taste—maxims—providences.   Study history, science.   Make all these handmaids to lead to God.

(6.) Benevolent engagements.   Act like Dorcas, instead of drawing strings across to imitate engravings.

The Privileges of Children are—

1. A federal interest in the covenant.
2. Initiation in good habits.
3. A bias of educational prejudices in favour of the gospel.
4. A general acquaintance with Christian doctrines and obligations.

The Obligations of our Children are—

1. They should know more than others.
2. They should promote their parents' plans : (1.) by prayer, (2.) by submission to their authority, (3.) by cultivating spiritual dispositions, (4.) by directing others.
3. They should cultivate that spirit and character which will enable them to glorify God when their parents are carried to another world.   This will almost raise enthusiasm.   We have spent our day, and have one foot in the grave.   But if our offspring carry on the work and glorify God, what an expansion does it give to our view !

The Rev. S. Crowther—

Early subjugation of the will is most important.   Speaking of vice as vice on every opportunity.   Manifest moderation in the acquisition of wealth.   Vigilance over our temper and spirit.   Just severity, but not in anger.   These are all important.   We should not expect too much from children.   There is much in federal union.   But often there is no influence to shew that all is of *grace.*

The Rev. H. G. Watkins—

Regularity, particularly in religious concerns, is our duty as parents. This gives an impression.

The Rev. R. Lloyd—

Picture to your children the world in a *true* manner.   Not as all without pleasure.   Give vice its animal pleas.   But confront true and spiritual pleasures with this.   Worldly men recede from such overcharged representations.   I would shew children the theatre if I could with safety.   Fancy throws up such images that they conceive what is not true.

The Rev. Mr Shaw, a visitor—

Children are creatures of sense.   Nothing is so dangerous as venturing them on the territories of Satan. Their feelings overwhelm all their ideas of spiritual pleasures. Young people should be deeply instructed in the fallacy and danger of sensual representations.

Where there is an inclination to dress like the world, there is an inclination to be where that dress will be seen and admired. The anxiety of dress intrudes on the hours and spirit of prayer. Lay, therefore, as much restraint as possible on whatever will carry children into the spirit of the world.

If the will be subdued, they will easily take up the cross as to outward things. There is much foundation laid for self-will in indulging early infancy. Spend much time in prayer. Pray as much as if your children's salvation depended altogether on your prayers.

Ministers are to be pitied. I have found the children of ministers disposed to charge their parents with hypocrisy. Ministers are obliged to hold up the standard of perfect holiness; but, alas! they are not themselves wholly conformed. And children cannot reason and see that *the flesh lusteth against the Spirit, and the Spirit against the flesh.*

Quakers shew us what can be done by discipline. No people are lower in religious knowledge except Jews. Yet we see what they have done.

The Rev. H. Foster—

One minister's wife takes a glass to church. Another says her husband does not speak against dress, and leaves people to follow their own conscience, and she dresses.

The Rev. J. Pratt—

An old angel might train up a young one in Brother Lloyd's way ; but not an old sinner a young one.

The Rev. R. Cecil—

The duty of a Christian is never to despair. The seed may be buried and seem lost, but it will spring up. The privileged child cannot *un*know what it has heard ; it can't sin like other children.

Dr Owen's severity towards his son overwhelmed him, and made nothing of him. But there are more like Eli.

There is a distinction between us and the world as to music. Put songs in the fire.

The Rev. J. Clayton—

Strictness has succeeded. Fondness generates fondness ; but, as the judgment has matured, it has generated contempt. Correction is an ordinance ; to be used with prayer. *Thou shalt beat him with a rod, and shalt deliver his soul from hell.* I have always delayed correction for a time. Children feel this.

Give your children social consequence as they grow up. Draw out their absurdities. Don't then thwart them by saying, "Don't talk foolishly." Sap it the next time, and overturn it all. Your child then becomes your friend.

On the next topic, WHAT ARE THE CAUSES OF THE PREVAILING BODILY INFIRMITIES OF MANY MINISTERS OF THE PRESENT DAY, AND HOW MAY THEY BEST BE PREVENTED ? we have no notes.

JULY 14, 1806.

DOES THE SPIRIT OF GOD BY THE GOSPEL OPERATE ON THE MINDS OF MEN IN PRODUCING MORAL EFFECTS SHORT OF SOUND CONVERSION ?— Proposed by the Rev. H. G. Watkins.

The Rev. W. Goode—
All influence to good is from the Spirit of God.

The Rev. R. Lloyd—
Bishop Hopkins's *Almost Christian* is an alarming sermon.   The conscience may be greatly alarmed by it.
A mariner in a storm will throw all his goods overboard ; but when it is over, will do all he can to collect them again.   Remember Felix, Judas, and stony-ground hearers.   Nothing short of the whole heart given to God is sound conversion.

The Rev. B. Woodd—
The preaching of the Gospel produces *restraint*.   The sight of a minister does too.   The sound of a bell, also, calling to worship.
Moral reformation, from drunkenness, profaneness, Sabbath-breaking, may be produced.   Moral virtues may be produced ; the tone of morality raised ; more accurate ideas of forgiveness, mercy, &c.
We are accustomed to these things, and, therefore, do not remark them ; but recall the Saxon times, and what a change you see, though short of true conversion.
Herod did many things.   Agrippa said unto Paul, Almost thou persuadest me to be a Christian.   Multitudes who heard John the Baptist must have been deeply touched.   There were multitudes who followed Christ for a time.
Parishes where the Gospel has been preached, become civilised. Nations where the Gospel is preached purely, are more moral than others—England, America, Holland, beyond Italy, Spain, and France. Conviction and approbation may take place without real conversion.

The Rev. R. Cecil—
Bezaleel and Aholiah, also Balaam, were under the divine influence of the Spirit.

The Rev. J. Pratt—
Influence to real good is from the Spirit *directly*.   But the Gospel's natural tendency is to raise the standard.

The Rev. J. Clayton—
There is no ground for the distinction of *direct* influence.   1. A clear knowledge ; 2. A fuller assent, from greater degree of evidence ; 3. A transient joy ; 4. Gifts ; 5. Reformation of life—may all be pro-

duced without real conversion. Illumination is not always attended with renewal of will.

———

On the two following occasions, a general conversation took place, and the meetings were adjourned till October. On the first topic, How far is it Expedient for Ministers to Encourage Private Meetings for Religious Exercises? we have no notes.

———

November 3, 1806.

What may we infer of the Designs of God from the Dispensations of his Providence?—Proposed by the Rev. B. Woodd.

Mr Woodd—

1. To expose the evils of the human heart, and thereby to confirm the truth of the Scriptures. This is done by withdrawing the restraints of Providence. As in the cases of Cain, Pharaoh, Hazael, and the fall of David, the fall of Solomon—what is human wisdom when not upheld?—and Judas Iscariot.

2. To humble the pride of the heart. *Let not the mighty man glory in his might,* &c. So Pharaoh, *I will pursue, I will overtake,* &c. Nebuchadnezzar. Herod, *eaten of worms.* Recantation of Cranmer, which speaks to us thus, " See by whose power, not man's, this great work is accomplished!"

There is some one respect or other in which every man breaks down. Sometimes this is known to the world; sometimes is the subject of private consciousness only.

3. To display Divine wisdom, by providential interposition. For example, Joseph, the preservation of Moses, of David against Saul, of the Jews by Esther, of Daniel, and the deliverance of Peter.

4. To shew the manifest justice of God, in rewards and punishments.

(1.) Punishments. A system of retribution is often shewn, as on Joseph's brethren; the tenth plague; cutting off the first-born, as Pharaoh decreed the destruction of the Hebrew children; the sword not departing from the house of David, because he had slain Uriah; the accusers of Daniel; the protracted punishment of the Jewish nation.

(2.) Rewards. Joseph again. We cannot trace individual rewards and punishments to individual sins or exertions; but this is true in the general tenor. Sir M. Hale observed, that he found the week prosper or otherwise, in proportion to the strictness or laxness with which he observed the Sabbath-day. God is exercising this retribution in the communication or withdrawal of grace continually. " He who observes providences will never want a Providence to observe."

5. To display the triumphs of Divine grace. The genealogy of Christ runs through such names as Thamar, Bathsheba, &c. The conversion of Saul, of the jailor; the recovery of David from his sin; the forbearance of God with Jonah; the recovery of Peter—all illustrate this. Every individual reads this in his own case.

NOVEMBER 17, 1806.

How far is Success attending any Ministry a Criterion of its Authority, the Truth of the Doctrine, and the Divine Approbation?—Proposed by the Rev. J. Pratt.

The Rev. W. Goode—

The internal call to the ministry may be confounded with the effectual call of grace in the heart. But God *may* call a man both internally and externally to the ministry for special ends, without enduing him with grace.

The Rev. J. Venn—

This is a branch of a wide question—How far we are to judge of the will of God by events? I answer, In no case. It would lead us to vain curiosity; it would turn the mind off gracious dispositions. St Paul, with his opponents, never pointed to success as his evidence; but to his divine call, and to the truth of his doctrine.

Success may be considered in respect of EDIFICATION as well as CONVERSION. A word may be the instrument of conversion; but diligence and information are requisite for edification.

God may bless the work of a bad man. Perhaps Judas was chosen to shew that God will use any instrument.

On the next subject, CAN POLITICAL REASONS JUSTIFY THE LAYING OF ANY GENERAL RESTRAINTS ON MARRIAGE? no remarks are recorded.

DECEMBER 15, 1806.

What Effect should the Present Posture of Public Affairs have on Us as Christians and Ministers?—Proposed by the Rev. H. Foster.

Mr Foster—

The times are awful. In such times Scripture characters fasted and prayed. The old Puritans did so. I have not. Yet I think we ought to do. We have long had mercies, of which we shew little sense. " Have I said and done everything I can?" we may well ask ourselves. I feel now that prayer is more of a *business* with God. I spend double the time morning and evening in prayer which I used to do.

We can judge nothing from the aspect of public affairs of what God is about to do.

The Rev. J. Clayton—

The evil of sin is taught by the state of public affairs.

The Rev. S. Crowther—

Point to God as the Author of all events: to sin as the cause of suffering. Consider God's design in afflicting us; what improvement the rod has had on us. Administer consolation to God's people.

The Rev. R. Lloyd—

The profligate conduct of the princes is a dark feature.

Six great men have fallen—Nelson, Pitt, Fox, Thurlow, Horsley, Cornwallis.

DECEMBER 29, 1806.

WHEN A MINISTER SEEMS TO HIMSELF TO HAVE EXHAUSTED ALL THE SUBJECTS OF THE CHRISTIAN MINISTRY, WHAT CONCLUSION OUGHT HE TO DRAW FROM SUCH A STATE OF MIND, AND HOW OUGHT HE TO PROCEED UNDER IT?—Proposed by the Rev. J. Clayton.

Mr Clayton—

Preaching to the same people for many years; decay of animal spirits; decay of the spirit of the office, of simplicity of mind—these are causes of this feeling.

I have recurred to old sermons. But have yet felt an abjectness in preaching old sermons: feelings have altered, though not doctrines, since they were written.

This state may be used—

1. To purify one's motives. One may correct, and commence again.

2. To prevent a mechanical making of sermons. We cannot make sermons without God. We are perpetually convinced of the necessity of the operations of the Holy Ghost anew.

3. To beget humility, to lower one's ideas. If my auditory keep up, I may be tempted to think myself somebody; but this state convinces me that I am nothing.

4. To trust God for the future. Not to be agitated and fluttered by these and other various circumstances.

The Rev. B. Woodd—

I have been twenty years minister of the same place; and have preached about two thousand sermons. I have made about sixteen hundred. I make one new one a-week, and preach one old one.

If brought to a stand, I have thought I would go over the old ground again. I have found much ease and pleasure in preaching my old sermons.

The Rev. H. G. Watkins—

I have written nine hundred skeletons, three hundred and seventy wholly written sermons. I fail in handling *practical* subjects.

The Rev. W. J. Abdy—

My easiest sermons cost me twelve hours. My brethren have seemed to me prodigies. I am not averse to preaching old sermons.

There are three sorts of hearers:—1. Those who never heard the sermon. 2. Those who have totally forgotten it. 3. Those who wish to hear the sermon again.

The Rev. R. Lloyd—

Dr Milner used to say, that if a man has no ideas he may talk for ever. Colloquial preachers are of this kind. They can go from a conversation on the stocks to a conversation in the same tone in the pulpit. But this is wholly reprehensible.

The Rev. R. Cecil—

I have written between two and three thousand skeletons.

Remedy of the evil we are considering may be found in the following points :—

1. Recollect that that state of mind is wrong: it is a bad atmosphere : it carnalises the mind.

2. Let a man work to his point : not lounge and trifle in his study. Ministers are an idle set of men. It is said of Mrs Siddons, that she declined many invitations from noblemen, on the plea, " My public occupation is such that I cannot come."

3. Consider not so much what he has done, as what he has not done. I have found some of my most useful sermons made when I thought I could make none. Perhaps when I feel myself to be in such a dry, emptied state of mind, I am most fit to preach usefully.

4. Call in common occasions. We preach too abstractedly. People can receive nothing abstracted. A great thing is to employ familiar images : particularly the affairs of the family, servants and children. When you tell people it is so and so at home, they, even country people, feel and remember this. Ability and necessity dwell near each other. Necessity does the business. Pump or drown.

5. Let a man preach to himself. Let him study his own experience. Whatever you do, don't work on a Saturday. You exhaust and fatigue your spirit. Begin earlier in the week. Some are too fastidious about old sermons, particularly skeletons.

The Rev. J. Pratt—

I would preach on relative duties, and on leading Christian doctrines ; but not distinct sermons on vices or duties. I would take passages including such topics, in the way of exposition.

The Rev. J. Goode—

I have often found a walk remove the feeling of difficulty. The conclusions I would draw are—

1. Guard against intrusions. Say " No " when your time of preparation and thought is invaded.

2. The frame of mind for study is a delicate thing, and not to be trifled with when we have it.

3. Our sufficiency is of God. A quarter of an hour's prayer has often done more than two hours' study.

4. Remember that something must be said. Every Sabbath the call is " Bread ! "

We have no notes on the next topic — THE EXPEDIENCY OF MAKING PARTICULAR DUTIES THE BASIS OF SINGLE SERMONS.

FEBRUARY 9, 1807.

WHAT IS THE BEST WAY OF IMPROVING THE APPROACHING FAST?—Proposed by the Rev. B. Woodd.

The Rev. S. Crowther—

Point out the hand of God more particularly. *When thy hand is lifted up, they will not see; but they shall see, and be ashamed.*

The Rev. H. Foster—

Bless God there is a prospect of the Abolition of the Slave Trade; bless Him for the efforts to stop vice, and educate youth.

The nation at large are just what they were. We cannot expect much till God arise to do a great work. If God destroy us because we are wicked, he must soon do it, and wholly. But after the flood, God said he would no more destroy the earth with a flood, *because* man was evil; as if there could be no cessation of destruction, if it were always according to the wickedness of man.

We must repeat the old thing. *Line upon line, precept upon precept.* It will have a double operation. And we must repeat, till God either harden the sinner, or convert him.

The Rev. W. Goode—

We have a peculiar thankfulness to God for preservation, while others have suffered who as little expected it as we.

The Rev. J. Clayton—

I have generally preached two sermons in preparation for each Fast Day, and one after. I have preached thirty or thirty-five sermons during the contest with the Gauls. I have conscientiously fasted in my family.

We have had new proofs that God is angry, and will visit sin.

———

On February 23, 1807, the topic was, WHAT DO THE SCRIPTURES REVEAL CONCERNING THE FUTURE RESTORATION OF THE JEWS? But the writer of the notes was absent at the debate on the Slave Trade. The debate on this question had ended in the House of Lords on the 5th, and terminated with a division of 100 against 36. This night the triumph in the Commons was still greater, being 283 against 16! It was decreed that the slave trade was "contrary to justice, humanity, and sound policy;" and that, after the 1st May, no vessel should clear out from any port or place under the dominion of the king, for the purpose of carrying slaves; and that, after the 1st January, the British slave trade should cease for ever. Such was the triumph of the friends of liberty over this nefarious traffic!—a triumph, however, as we know, which may be said to have been eclipsed by a still greater one, in the abolition of slavery itself within every part of the British possessions, and the payment of twenty millions sterling in compensation to the West India planters.

MARCH 9, 1807.

WHAT ARE THE JUST BOUNDS OF TYPICAL INTERPRETATIONS OF THE SCRIPTURE ?—Proposed by the Rev. W. Goode.

Mr Goode—

The principal facts of the Old Testament appear to be designedly typical. They seem to have been selected from a variety of other facts, which must have occurred, for this purpose ; and to be particularly intended to be typical of the person and work of Christ, and of the Gospel-church. There were different ways of accomplishing this end.

1. Enigmatical. The seed of the woman to bruise the serpent's head.

2. Hieroglyphical. The cherubim and the flaming sword to preserve the way into the garden.

3. Figures. The ark, and preservation by it ; the rainbow ; Hagar and Sarah ; Abraham sacrificing Isaac ; the history of Joseph ; the Jewish nation ; the ceremonial law ; David, his very name and kingdom.

Many instances of moral and spiritual instruction may be derived from these figurative actions, besides the figurative purpose. But they seem designed to be figurative, not to be used so but by way of accommodation.

The proper bounds of this mode of interpretation. Many of the trivial circumstances ought not to be spiritualised, though they are necessary for filling up the chain of events. Psalms typical of Christ should be considered personally and mystically as to his Church. I cannot consider the 21st Psalm as referring to Christ's person. Almost all the actions of the Prophets are figurative. I think we cannot understand the Old Testament without this view. To ascertain the proper bounds is the difficulty. Much of the New Testament is typical. The miracles and parables—if there be nothing typical in them, when we have illustrated by them the power and grace of Christ, we have said all. For example, the good Samaritan ; if there be nothing typical in this, it merely, though most beautifully, commends brotherly love. But if it be typical, even the primary, or at least the moral, end of the parable is most enforced by supposing it has a figurative reference to Christ. If it be mere history, then its object was limited to moral instruction. If it be parable—implying a sense beyond the mere historical fact—it must refer to Christ. So the prodigal son.

The Rev. T. Robinson, a visitor—

In public instruction, I would go no further than Scripture leads me, except by way of accommodation. In my private meditations, I might dwell on typical thoughts with delight for my own edification.

There is a manifest difference between the parables of the good Samaritan and that of the prodigal son. The good Samaritan is particularly introduced to illustrate brotherly love—the prodigal son to illustrate the love of the Saviour in receiving sinners. *This man receiveth sinners.*

The Rev. H. G. Watkins—

Much of the Old Testament would seem barren history if it be not typical. *All Scripture is profitable for instruction,* &c. I would consider how far the quotations from the Old Testament in the New, which actually authorise a typical interpretation of it, counteract a further interpretation of other parts ; and intimate how far our Saviour and his Apostles would have so referred to those parts had they thought proper to refer to them. An analogical mode of interpreting the Old Testament enables us to illustrate the harmony of the divine dispensations, and to furnish our discourses with variety.

Extremes are to be avoided. To treat the manna in a dry and unfigurative way is absurd. So, on the other hand, the context will often limit the typical application. A frequent use of typical interpretation, and especially extravagant applications, tend to beget a wish to hear all subjects so treated. Huntington was extravagant. *Honour thy father,* that is, God ; *and thy mother,* that is, the Church ! Children would thus forget to honour their parents.

The Rev. W. J. Abdy—

The Epistle to the Hebrews is a development of the whole Levitical dispensation. Jones, in his lectures on this Epistle, is excellent. In one place the Apostle says, *The Holy Ghost this signifying ;* but when there is no scriptural authority like this, we must be cautious.

The Rev. R. Lloyd—

The Jewish religion is the Christian in its infancy—the outline, the shadow of the substance. The Epistle to the Hebrews is a wonderful key. It gives a certain latitude, which, independent of its Divine authority, we should fear to adopt. Good common sense must be brought to the typical interpretation of Scripture.

The Rev. J. Venn—

Avoid two extremes. Give not up this truth, that all along, from the beginning, there is a continued reference to Jesus Christ. He is brought forward again and again, in every variety of manner. Some types are so plain that we should almost inevitably apply them without Scripture authority ; as the brazen serpent. But avoid falling into the absurdity and folly of forcing applications, as some do.

The use of types is chiefly these :—

1. To the age in which they were delivered. Those healed by the brazen serpent might not know its typical reference to Jesus Christ. God might accept a faith analogous to that which was afterwards to be clearly exercised on Jesus Christ. Their faith was in God's appointed way, without any distinct reference to Jesus Christ.

2. The grand use of them is the same as that of prophecy. Not to instruct those who were under it, so much as to reflect evidence on the events when they took place. When, therefore, Christ came, there was a body of evidence ready to demonstrate the authority of Christ. This was a principal means of leading to Christ. For example, the two disciples going to Emmaus.

Shocking effects may follow from the abuse of typical interpretation. For as much as you add to the undue interpretation of Scripture in a typical manner, you detract from the majesty and dignity of truth. I once heard a good man expound the 119th Psalm, who declared that the Psalm belonged to Christ, and only to Christ !

The following are rules :—

1. *Nec Deus intersit nisi dignus vindice nodus*
   Inciderit.

This cuts off all the trivial applications about the pomegranates, &c.

2. Types are in no cases proofs, though they may be illustrations. Those, indeed, which are plainly authorised in Scripture amount to proofs ; but not such as *we* think we can apply. I would keep close to what Scripture has said, and go nowhere beyond it, except in the way of illustration.

3. Types and prophecies are to be interpreted broadly and generally, not minutely.

The Rev. R. Cecil—

It might be supposed *à priori*, that when God had determined to send his Son into the world, there would be a train and concatenation of circumstances preparatory to his coming. And that the history which declared his coming should exhibit many persons and things—though not so many as an absurd fancy would find—that should form a grand preparation for the event. A certain class of persons wish to get rid of the type. Sykes insists on the brazen serpent being called in by way of illustration, not as a designed type. Robinson of Cambridge, when he began to verge towards Socinianism, began to ridicule the types, the pomegranates, and the bells. Hagar and Sarah is a singular passage : *Which things are an allegory.* At all events, the typical method should not be treated lightly and with irreverence. It deserves serious reflection.

As to the expediency of employing this mode in the pulpit, that is another question. I seldom employ it. I want to get hold of the conscience. The typical seems rather a round-about way. Many of my people might think it fanciful.

I find my people cannot enter into the *reasons* of the cross. They adopt what I think Butler's grand defect on this subject. He speaks of the cross as an *appointment of God*, and therefore to be submitted to. But I think God has said a great deal of the reasons : *That he might be just, and yet the justifier of him that believeth.*

A minister should avoid as much as possible having his judgment called in question. Many watch for this, and will avail themselves of it. Gill considers the parable of Dives and Lazarus as, in its primary sense, referring to Christ.

The Rev. J. Pratt—

Whitby's book, *De Interpretatione*, shews the Fathers to be unsafe guides.

Typical interpretation is useful, as giving an interest, embodying truth, and fixing it in the memory.

All the leading types of the Old Testament are clearly established by the New. Quotations from the Old Testament do much in this way.

I hesitate about the *personal* types, as Joseph. I would commend my good sense to my hearers by employing no types which are not on Scripture authority. I would never use accommodation, except, indeed, by way of occasional illustration in a sermon.

Calvin has harmonised the law in a masterly manner. He is the wisest of commentators.

The Rev. J. Clayton—

Persons, places, and things are taken hold of in the New Testament, and applied to illustrate salvation by Christ.

The Rev. J. Goode—

Use caution. We should not hunt for types. Let us value truth and its sanctions. Typical preachers may be followed, but they are not useful.

Some parts of the Psalms are applicable to David, and some to Christ.

" By too much drawing, allegorisers bring blood instead of milk," says Archbishop Leighton.

The good Samaritan, I think, is not typical of Christ. *Go thou and do likewise*, is applicable to the moral use of the parable ; but we are not called to go, as Christ did, and redeem sinners.

The Rev. C. Simeon, a visitor—

What bounds shall we put ? We must not take *words*, but the *thing*, as typical. The ark, the altar are not typical of Christ. Thus not the ark, but the salvation of Noah and his family, is typical of Christ and his salvation : not the altar, but the offerings on the altar are typical of Christ. Even the snuffers, &c., are typical, not in the *word*, but in the *thing*, so that the whole service of the tabernacle was so in the mind of God ; though I cannot find it out, yet that does not alter the nature of the thing.

Typical things are graphical exhibitions of divine truth. They will give many clear views of truth to those who would not otherwise comprehend it. While the Gospel illustrates the types, the types illustrate the Gospel. For example, repentance is better understood, and more felt, when the penitent is represented as confessing his sins over the sacrifice he offers, than if abstractedly represented.

MARCH 23, 1807.

WHAT ARE THE TEMPTATIONS PECULIAR TO MINISTERS, AND THE BEST WAY OF RESISTING THEM ?—Proposed by the Rev. H. G. Watkins.

Mr Watkins—

Ministers are apt to preach to others, without preaching to themselves. It is taken for granted that they are converted men. They

stand on high ground. They should make the doctrines an affair of
their own.

The fear of man is a temptation. We should use great delicacy
with regard to others, but exercise great jealousy over ourselves.

The pride of talents is another. Also indifference in the minister is
a temptation. "There are many more popular," he is apt to say;
"Christ can do without me." A man of property is exposed to this
temptation.

If diligent, he is tempted to think it self-seeking. This may produce a torpor.

Indolence, under the garb of doing themselves no harm, is another
temptation.

The Rev. R. Lloyd—

The Scylla and Charybdis against which to guard is, presumption
and despair. Much duty leads to dulness. Our ministerial acts are
not vivified—not lighted up.

There is a temptation not to consider the importance of character.
Many a villain would give ten thousand pounds for a character, and
make thirty thousand of it. Character is of great weight in spiritual
concerns. *Blessed are ye when men shall speak all manner of evil against
you falsely for my sake.* It leads a minister to difficulties. He has
much prejudice to preach through.

They are sometimes tempted to do too much work, and yet in a
wrong spirit, so much as to injure their health, and are then apt to
look for the assistance of the Divine Spirit in an enthusiastic manner.

Another temptation is to catch a bad spirit 'from the spirit of
opposers. A malignant spirit towards men who oppose them. The
Church of England acting at this day on the defensive is in danger of
this. Gospel ministers throw down the gauntlet.

Gospel ministers assume too much. They speak too much in a
party spirit against those who differ from them. Sermons on the
times are too much of an *imperium in imperio*. We give ourselves too
much prominence, and then this prominence is not supported by
sufficient ability. Vanity, envy, extempore preaching, schism—all
these are temptations. We introduce into our congregations an ecclesiastical piety, an enlightened attachment to order.

The grand cure is to have a single eye to God's glory.

The Rev. W. Goode—

Ministers have the same corruptions as others. They are tempted
to abuse that passage, *Becoming all things to all men.*

Temptation arises from conversing with the female part of his congregation.

Another is to make his own sentiments a standard for others. The
remedy is—Be humble, be everything.

The Rev. H. Foster—

A peculiar temptation is that which puts a man into a situation
where he sees none like him. When St Paul returned from the third

heavens, God saw him in danger from this, and He gave him a thorn. Pride is the most prevalent and universal temptation. Intercourse with women too. Covetousness also; this leads to cringing to benefactors, disgust towards those who are not.

The cure is, an examination of motives. " Why do I visit here and there? Why do I preach thus and thus?" We should be low in the dust, while others applaud. The doctrine of motives· is the doctrine of humiliation.

The Rev. R. Cecil—

The danger is not generally covetousness. Many might have been high in the world who are contented with being low. Evangelical ministers, in general, are poor men. Sloth is a temptation. We connive at little hindrances—doing little jobs, lounging in bed. Levity is a snare. The irritation also we are likely to suffer from objections of little nibbling minds. Self-preference. *My* notions are the standard.

The Rev. W. Fry—

Want of unity and brotherly kindness; proneness to corrupt imitation; and many such-like temptations we are obnoxious to as ministers.

Saying feeling things when we feel them not; cultivating a spirit in order to popularity; neglect of stated seasons of prayer and examination, without regard to our ministry; to run in debt, if the income be strait—these are all temptations peculiar to us.

In town we have not time for retirement; yet we may be too recluse. Let people see what you are. Know them in their domestic circles. Beget in them a conviction of the reality and sincerity of your character. I do not preach and pray in private, but endeavour to introduce useful topics.

The Rev. J. Pratt—

Our situation as evangelical ministers of the Church is peculiar and difficult, as we are members of a Church of which many ministers possess not the reality of religion.

There is an *esprit du corps* among us. A great difficulty is, not to stand off from blind brethren, and yet not to accommodate ourselves to their wrong notions.

The Rev. J. Davies—

Our temptation is to measure usefulness by popularity.

The Rev. C. Simeon, a visitor—

Our temptations as ministers are these—

Not improving our conversation with one another. What is the reason? We do not pray in secret for the divine presence. The neglect of children and servants. We ought to be incessantly endeavouring their good.

Not endeavouring to bring into action the faculties of our people.

We do not sufficiently inculcate the necessity of parents' care of children, of visiting the sick, &c.

While cultivating the vineyard of the Lord, not sufficiently attentive to our own vineyard.

Having respect to character. There is a proper medium between too much and too little attention to character.

The Rev. J. Clayton—

Our temptations as ministers are to pride—*not a novice, lest being lifted up with pride he fall into the condemnation of the devil;* covetousness, *filthy lucre,* which is only so called in reference to ministers ; a dictating, overbearing spirit—*not as lords over God's heritage, but as ensamples to the flock;* envy ; sloth ; being superficial in private prayer.

The remedy for all is PRAYER.

The opposite virtues are here : 1 Tim. vi. 11, *But thou, O man of God, flee these things; and follow after righteousness, godliness, faith, love, patience, meekness, &c.*

The Rev. B. Woodd—

I have numbered the temptations which I have heard to-night, and they amount to thirty-four. There is another—the danger of not reproving those evils which we are conscious of carrying about with us.

On the next topic, BY WHAT MEANS MAY PIOUS WOMEN BEST SUBSERVE THE INTERESTS OF RELIGION ? we have no notes.

APRIL 20, 1807.

MAY EMULATION BE EMPLOYED AS A STIMULUS IN THE EDUCATION OF CHILDREN ?—Proposed by the Rev. C. Simeon.

The Rev. W. J. Abdy—

In Rom. xi. 14, emulation is spoken of in a good sense. In Gal. v. 20, in a bad sense.

The Rev. H. Budd—

If it be for the attainment of excellence, it is just : if for the elevation of self, it is evil. Whence does it spring ? From pride. What its operation ? To create jealousy. What its effects ? In gain—exaltation, insult, triumph of self: in loss—envy, jealousy, hatred.

Let us remember John and James calling down fire from heaven. Our Lord's words, *Take my yoke,* &c., *for I am meek and lowly of heart.* He bids us elsewhere to be *as little children.*

In 1 Cor. ix. 24, *Know ye not that they which run in a race run all, but one receiveth the prize? so run that ye may obtain.* But it is the object to be aimed at that is here spoken of rather than the excelling of others. So again, *I press towards the mark.* It is the object, *the high calling of God,* which he aims at, and not the surpassing of others in emulation. In Eph. iv. there is much against emulation : so also in 2 Cor. xii. 20.

Reputation is not to be sought for *itself*, but as the *means of good*.

The Rev. J. Venn—

The desire of excellence is not to be confounded with emulation. The desire of reward is sometimes confounded with emulation : so also is the desire of approbation. So long as this is the approval of persons capable of judging, it is laudable. We may seek the approval first of GOD, then of angels, then of the Church, then of the good sense of the world. *Whatsoever things are of good report, think on these things.*

Emulation is rivalry. In emulation we must come in contact with some person, and may envy his superior talent. Emulation must be employed about things within our reach. The evil of emulation is that you rise by depressing your neighbour. How contrary this is to Christianity ! *Let each esteem other better than himself.* We are to be lowest of all, and servants of all.

Emulation is only a species of vanity directed to certain objects.

Can, then, emulation be allowed in Christian education ? Man is naturally torpid, slothful, sensual. He must apply strong stimuli. But are there no motives but such as are contrary to the Christian system ? True it is, that there are no motives so ready, so energetical, as corrupt motives. Touch a man's vanity, and the idlest drone will be roused. Yet in the end, the most really efficacious motives are the most virtuous. If vanity excite to exertion, you will fail in the end. This emulation works but for the moment. This is sometimes exemplified in Cambridge men.

The system of education is totally depraved. It is not to make Christians, but accomplished men, learned ; accomplished women. Pagan principles exclude Christian.

The operation of habit is mistaken. Constraining to do a thing merely will not make a man delight in it, and persevere therein. But continued repeated action, with the concurrence of the will, this only forms permanent habit. Men will get thus into the habit of chewing tobacco, but never into the love of chastisement.

Substitute the LOVE OF EXCELLENCE. Teach children to love knowledge, not to strive to surpass others. This will *wear well.* This will operate when the object that might rouse emulation is away.

A SENSE OF DUTY is to be ever inculcated. Point out the use of health, riches, opportunities.

NEVER VIOLATE CONSCIENCE. A sense of reward is not excluded. But be careful not, by these rewards, to stir up emulation. Imitation has nothing to do with emulation. We may set Christ before us and to others as an example to be followed.

There is nothing which *true principles* would not lead a man to do at least as well as any *false principle*. If not, how shall we consider GOD as a wise governor of the world ?

Nelson and Cicero had other motives. But how contemptible is their vanity !

The Rev. R. Cecil—

The pursuit of good is to be distinguished from rivalry. There is nothing wrong in a man saying, "I'll be the best shoe-black in the city :" not, better than *that man* on the other side of the street.

The Apostle excites to excellence, not to emulation : *Covet earnestly the best gifts.*

To my son I would say, " Try to preach with *reputation ;*" but not, " Try to preach better than *such a one.*"

" Becoming pride " is but a gilded devil.

The Rev. J. Pratt—

The Apostle in 2 Cor. viii. ix. points to persons only to excite *shame* in not possessing the good ourselves.

The next topic was, BY WHAT MEANS MAY INDIVIDUALS PROMOTE THE OBSERVANCE OF THE CHRISTIAN SABBATH? We have no notes on it.

MAY 18, 1807.

WHAT ARE THE BEST EVIDENCES OF A SCRIPTURAL ATTACHMENT TO A CHRISTIAN MINISTER ?—Proposed by the Rev. J. Clayton.

Mr Clayton—

Evidences of Scriptural attachment to ministers are—

1. Regard to Him whose authority gives them their commission.
2. A cordial reception of the message.
3. Imbibing the spirit so as to exemplify it in their life and conversation.

Much attachment is far different from this. Manner, connexions, kindness, apart from the vital point, create attachment. Such will go away if they do not see their favourite minister.

The Rev. W. J. Abdy—

Regular attendance on the minister established in the place, is a first evidence of Scriptural attachment to the Christian ministry. For I consider the attachment to be rather to the Christian ministry than to ministers.

The Rev. R. Cecil—

Scriptural motives may be combined with personal attachment, and may exist together. We should not sweep away the motives because there is this mixture.

Spiritual children will understand and feel their father better than even an abler man. When the preaching has a tendency to work most on the *heart*—to do *business*—then there is an attachment. There may be constitutional attachment to a minister. Where a great idea is formed of a minister's piety and experience, an attachment follows. If a person is willing to *bear the seasons all round* with a minister ; to go with him not only when comforted, but when adverse circumstances and trials arise—this is an evidence of attachment of the right kind. If attachment take place only for the Shibboleth of his party, this is

o

a proof of a bad mind. If a person came to a minister, not saying with Ahab, *I hate that man, for he prophesieth not good but evil concerning me;* but in this tone of mind, *I will hear what the Lord God will say concerning me*—there is evidence of attachment of the right kind.

The Rev. T. Scott—

Unscriptural attachment to a minister is—

1. Such as leads men to put the sentiments of their minister in the place of the Word of God. Mr Wesley's and Mr Romaine's people commonly do this.

2. Such as arises primarily from the eloquence of a minister.

3. When there is something soothing in the minister, which puts the hearer into good humour with himself.

I have thought concerning popular preachers, " A popular preacher is a thing I could not be, if I would; nor would be, if I could."

Grounds of scriptural attachment to a minister are—

1. When he is a tried and proved character. The pursuit of popularity, as such, is as bad as the pursuit of money. Let popularity be the shadow that follows us; not that which we pursue. Go not out of the way to pursue it.

2. Conviction that the ministry is scriptural.

3. Benefit received under him.

4. Conviction that the minister is the pastor whom God hath appointed me.

Effects of a scriptural attachment are—

1. Constant and earnest prayer for the minister.

2. His people seek their minister's comfort.

3. Constant endeavours to strengthen the minister's hands.

4. Regular attendance on his services.

5. Consistent lives.

The Rev. Thomas Scott ceases to appear as an attendant at the Eclectic after this meeting. His name had been transferred from the list of members to that of country members and visitors as far back as 1803, when he left London for Aston. But he continued up to the present date to attend occasionally.

JUNE 1, 1807.

IS INGRATITUDE A CHARACTERISTIC OF THE POOR?—Proposed by the Rev. R. Lloyd.

Mr Lloyd—

How far poverty exposes to irritability is a question.

So far as this is true, it may lead the poor to ingratitude. On the other hand, prosperity may tend to render us insensible to favours. Perhaps it is difficult to strike the balance. It is a question whether gratitude is not instinctive—a part of the moral sense.

The poor have not been studied till of late years. The Society for Bettering the Condition of the Poor led the way. They were fed—

grossly fed—but not treated as human beings or intelligent creatures. The means of conferring favours often removes all obligation. Where the poor are studied, and treated as intelligent creatures, I believe they will be found not to be ungrateful, and that ingratitude is not their characteristic. I never knew a country gentleman who lived on his estate, and was kind to the poor, but he was adored by them. A poor man has his family around him, and then is happy : only enable him to live in this state, and to rear his family, and he will be grateful.

The Rev. H. Foster—

Ingratitude is the characteristic of man, whether poor or rich. If the rich were poor, and the poor rich, they would be just what they are, according to circumstances.

With respect to God, the rich are more ungrateful than the poor. The godly man, with his infinitely superior benefits and obligations, is the most ungrateful of men. When he comes to a right feeling, he has a genuine sense of this ingratitude, which makes him feel the greatest wretch of mankind.

JUNE 15, 1807.

HOW FAR IS IT THE DUTY OF CHRISTIANS IN GENERAL TO STUDY THE PROPHECIES ?—Proposed by the Rev. S. Crowther.

Mr Crowther—

It gives enlarged views of the divine government. Yet it has not necessarily a tendency to piety.

The Rev. J. Clayton—

It arrests the attention unduly. Mr Reader was always preaching from the Revelation. It tempts to a disproportionate attention to the Scriptures. Bicheno's ministry was comparatively barren in consequence. It alienates the minds of private Christians from the Word of God as the rule of conduct, and makes events the rule.

The Rev. B. Woodd—

Ministers who have an active sphere of duty should not enter into these discussions. If withdrawn from duty in providence, it may be expedient. Occasional illustrations are important, but on the broad ground.

The Rev. H. Budd—

Much good may result from it ; it is therefore a duty. But the difficulty is to know how to proportion the study. I question whether students of prophecy are spiritual men. Newton's book is dry. So is Fleming's, though more spiritual.

The Rev. Mr Shaw, a visitor—

The Church of Rome would exclude the study of the prophecies. She grounds her influence on this ignorance. It tends to enlarge and elevate the mind. Applying it to the present day is unprofitable.

The Rev. J. Venn—

Circumstances should determine our study of prophecy.

1. There should be a natural aptitude. It is generally dry, contemplative people that take it up. Any study has a great tendency to dry up the soul. My father, in writing the " Duty of Man," felt this. In general it may be said, that such men would have omitted other duties, or have ill performed them.

2. Consider the design. If it be to open the book of Fate, we might as well study the Sortes of Virgil. If it be to mark the dealings of God, it is well.

Be not particular as to events of the present times. God purposely covered the beginning of the 1260 years with a veil. At such, or such, or such a time, it began. We wait to see, by the openings of providence, which of these is true.

The Rev. R. Cecil—

The prophecies were dictated by the Spirit of God. Paley writes very judiciously on the Evidence of Prophecy. He makes a preamble, but puts down Isa. liii. In proportion as the thing is important, it is evidence.

JUNE 29, 1807.

WHAT MANAGEMENT SHOULD MINISTERS ADOPT TOWARDS PERSONS WHO PLEAD THE WEAKNESS OF THEIR NERVES IN RELAXATION OF CHRISTIAN TEMPERS AND DUTIES, AND HOW FAR IS SUCH A PLEA TO BE ADMITTED? —Proposed by the Rev. H. Budd.

Mr Budd—

Such shew irregularity in temper towards God ; selfishness towards men. I know a lady who is unwilling to allow the same degree of nervousness in others that she pleads for in herself. An apology for this spirit is, in a case I know of, nervous irritability.

God, however, who knows our frame, remembers we are but dust. If the state be real, God will allow the plea of nervous irritability. How should such act ?—

1. Lay the case before God.

2. Use natural means : air, exercise, change of place, medicine.

3. Other persons should perhaps never argue with them. It rouses up the mind to acute opposition.

The Rev. J. Goode—

The question, how to manage nervous persons, is almost like— " How shall we manage Proteus ? "

The Rev. J. Clayton—

It is important to determine how far temper and how far distemper play their parts. Vicious habits often grow tyrannical by indulgence. How shall these vicious habits be *baptised?* A chief remedy is, avoiding idleness.

The Rev. B. Woodd—

As to yourself, allow *no* plea. We are so partial, that if we admit plea for infirmities, we soon admit plea for sin. Allow every candid plea for others. Some persons view *every* subject in connexion with fear. Some have an extreme of feeling, both of pleasure and pain. Bile, gout, small-pox, will deeply affect the system.

Remedies: first, spiritual—study the Law and the Gospel ; natural —good hours, washing, bathing, external compulsion.

The Rev. S. Crowther—

Obsta principiis. If disease be confirmed, it is hopeless.

The Rev. H. G. Watkins—

Diseases altering the system borders on Materialism. Afflictions will affect the temper ; but the temper is generally the same in health as in sickness.

The Rev. R. Lloyd—

Mind, body, mutual influence—all is wonderful ; and yet they can bear much. I have laboured to impress nervous persons with the persuasion, that it is not *they*, who judge of themselves, but their *disease*. I do not wholly agree with Woodd that no plea should be allowed for ourselves. Nervous persons are generally low-spirited, rather than presumptuous. I would rather put encouraging books into their hands, than those on duties. A spirit of self-righteousness is common to them, rather than the contrary. Nervousness sometimes urges to too much activity. Mr Wilberforce affords an example. On the other hand, to listlessness.

I should be inclined to make allowances for nervous persons in relaxation of *tempers*, rather than of *duties*. In duties, a man may ask, " *Quid valeant humani?* " Don't oppose such persons. Go down the stream with them. As you go, vary the course. They will find themselves in port before they are aware.

Good men should study themselves. A pressure of duty often brings on nervous diseases. They run themselves out of breath.

The Rev. W. J. Abdy—

It is a mistake to laugh nervous persons out of their habits. It irritates, or drives to despair.

The Rev. H. Foster—

A man threw his wife into the water and cured her of nervousness.

In Scripture there is but one rule for a man with good nerves and bad nerves. All deviations are evil : they are to be avoided and re-pented of. If persons offend without subsequent humiliation, I should have but a low idea of their religion.

The Rev. R. Cecil—

What is the real state of the case ? Is it, on the whole, physical or moral ? If physical, it is to be treated with entire tenderness ; if moral, with faithfulness.

An inactive life may be punished with inability. They have said, " I will do nothing." God says, " You *shall* do nothing."

Such a man as Watts is to be allowed to scream at going through the door. He had worn out the machine. These pleas are often a cloak to cover weak piety and half-heartedness in religion. We shall daub the wall with untempered mortar if we allow this plea.

So much prejudice was lodged in my mind against Dr Grosvenor, my mother's uncle, from stories she told me of him, that I could not open one of his books till after I was in the ministry.

Great strokes of calamity are often advantageous in such cases.

The Rev. J. Pratt—

We may in general suspect the sincerity of people who plead nervous influence in excuse for moral evils.

Nervousness seems to be a disease of modern times. Perhaps tea-drinking has been one cause of it.

July 13, 1807.

How shall Ministers best Excite and Direct the Active Services of their respective Congregations ?—Proposed by the Rev. J. Pratt.

The Rev. W. J. Abdy—

When thou art converted, strengthen thy brethren, &c., applies to all Christians. *Freely thou hast received, freely give.*

Make not the sphere too wide.

The Rev. H. Budd—

I fear my congregation know little of the principles, means, subject, or object of true charity. Personal visiting is, perhaps, the most efficient way of exciting and directing their active services. We may meet with frequent rebuffs, but shall be amply repaid. Have the young people at your own house ; know them ; class them ; repress what is erroneous, and encourage what is good.

The Rev. B. Woodd—

General principles may be laid down in the pulpit. Preach discourses on the management of time, family arrangements, &c. Appropriate districts may be given to particular persons, to visit the sick, schools, &c.

There is a danger in calling out the energies, especially in the way of association. It feeds vanity, self-importance, envy.

I urge again and again the appropriating a portion of income to charitable objects—a tenth where it can be afforded. This is the secret of the large collections made at Bentinck Chapel.

Urge the good ordering of families ; looking after children or the poor. Have useful persons in your eye. Send such persons on particular cases.

July 27, 1807.

How far may an Unregenerate Man be said to see Spiritual Objects?—Proposed by the Rev. H. Foster.

Mr Foster—

A difficulty lies here. *Except a man be born again, he cannot see the kingdom of God.* On the contrary, *Seeing they shall see, and not perceive.*

There may be something of wise appointment in this to put men on diligence.

An unregenerate man may desire heaven, and fear hell. But what he sees is rather the consequence than the means. He sees not the Gospel, which leads to holiness and the enjoyment of spiritual and heavenly things. Some are said *to have* KNOWN *the way of righteousness,* and afterwards to turn again like a sow to her wallowing in the mire. An unregenerate man cannot see the beauty of any spiritual objects, though he may talk as if he saw them. See Sanderson's Lectures on Light and Colours.

The Rev. J. Davies—

The natural man receiveth not the things of the Spirit of God; neither can he know them, because they are spiritually discerned.

The Rev. B. Woodd—

No new faculties are communicated in regeneration ; but a new direction given to the faculties.

It is impossible for those who are once enlightened . . . . to renew them again unto repentance.—They on the rock are they which, when they hear, receive the word with joy. Such passages seem to imply that unregenerate men may see spiritual objects. The history of the Church shews many men who have preached the Gospel with light and energy, and yet have fallen away.

The Rev. W. Goode—

There is a specific difference between the sight of regenerate and unregenerate man ; as much as between life and death. The unregenerate man may seem to *us* to see things as the regenerate man does, but not so in the sight of God.

The Rev. W. J. Abdy—

Unregenerate man may see spiritual objects. But the question is, how far ? Perhaps it is not to be determined.

A great difference appears to be in what the two men consider those spiritual objects to be. An unregenerate man cannot enter into that passage, *We all, with open face beholding as in a glass the glory of the Lord, are changed into the same image from glory to glory, even as by the Spirit of the Lord.* The unregenerate man does not see the necessity of a holy nature, and, consequently, does not desire it. He has a dread of the consequences of sin, not a hatred of sin.

The Rev. J. Pratt—

I differ from most of my brethren. The fall seems to have injured the understanding but little, but wholly to have perverted the will and affections. I think the unregenerate man may *see* the necessity and the beauty of every truth; but the great difference is, that his will never chooses them, nor are his affections raised to embrace them.

How does Satan see truth? Many ignorant Christians have far less apparent discernment of truth than others not Christians. But they embrace it.

The Rev. R. Cecil—

A musician may play admirably, but have no right perception, no taste of the beauty of what he plays.

Baxter thinks there is no difference between the light and knowledge of the regenerate and unregenerate man for the time. Owen thinks them different. Milner considers the Holy Spirit as illuminating the understanding, independent of His influence on the affections. Ludlam thinks otherwise.

Two seeds before being sown may have no apparent difference; but when grown, they are manifestly different. Balaam and the Ethiopian eunuch are examples—the one, of light without regeneration; the other, of regeneration with feeble light.

The meetings were adjourned to October. On the first subject, What is the Ground of that Dissatisfaction which so universally Prevails among Mankind? we have no notes.

OCTOBER 19, 1807.

What are the Best Means of bringing a Congregation acquainted with the Scriptures?—Proposed by the Rev. J. Pratt.

Mr Pratt—

I would premise—

1. That a thorough acquaintance with the Scriptures is necessary to the stability and growth of a people.

2. That there is a general and lamentable deficiency in this respect among religious professors.

3. That the ministry is in some measure chargeable with this evil.

How may ministers remedy the evil?

1. By shewing a great and habitual regard to the Scriptures themselves, in the frame and material of their sermons.

2. By resting their discourses on half-a-dozen passages of some length, and quoting these with deliberation and emphasis.

3. By contriving to make some large portion, as a chapter or a history, come in as illustrations of their discourse; and urging the study of that portion at home.

4. By frequent and explicit statements of the duty, benefit, and manner of privately studying the Scriptures.

5. By frequent expositions of large portions, and sometimes of whole books.

6. By setting the children and young persons portions to commit to memory, and other portions to read, in their knowledge of which they are to be examined at an appointed time.

The Rev. H. G. Watkins—

Courses of sermons are good. Ministers themselves preach, some on the *credenda*, and others on the *agenda*. It is wrong to take up a set of texts. The latter part of the Epistle to the Romans is very little dwelt on. The fruits of the Spirit are spoken of generally at the end of sermons ; but, for want of sufficiently particularising, every professor easily persuades himself that he does what is urged. Many professors are seemingly anxious to hear, who do not open the Scriptures from Sunday to Sunday.

The Rev. H. Budd—

The means of making Scripture known are public and private.

Public.—Frequent incidental mention of the necessity of reading the Scriptures. Shew the difference of the knowledge of God derived from His works, that is, Philosophy ; and from His Word, that is, Religion.

Shew the great privileges of the knowledge derived from the Scriptures ; it is certain, fixed, not fluctuating—grace and glory. Shew explicitly the connexion between sound preaching in the ministry, and sound hearing in the people. Recommend in each subject some particular chapters which treat on those subjects : for example, on justification, Rom. iii., iv., v.

When Usher asserts anything in his sermon, he begins by a passage of Scripture, in a very forcible manner.

Private.—In visits. The gift of Bibles. Pointing out the authority on which the Scriptures rest.

The Rev. W. J. Abdy—

Serious working people are much pressed for want of time. Little tradesmen, too, must be great economists of time, if they redeem a good portion to spend on the Scriptures. So mothers, and mistresses of families.

It is not easy, though very important, to take up large portions of Scripture.

The Rev. H. Foster—

Search the Scriptures, is our Saviour's injunction. This implies an exact, serious, diligent search. Search, as an heir his title-deeds.

1. WHY we should search them. (1.) Because they come from God. (2.) As it is the command of Christ and his Apostles. (3.) As they are a *light and lamp to our feet.* (4.) Because they testify of Christ. What a blessing to have such a testimony ! (5.) They make us *wise to salvation.* (6.) They contain wonderful things: *Open thou mine eyes that I may behold the wondrous things in thy law,* &c.—Wonderful things as to doctrines, prophecies, &c. (7.) They are the seed of

regeneration and the food of the soul. (8.) They are the *sword of the Spirit.* We cannot meet the enemy without them. Christ thus met the enemy. (9.) The wisest and best of men have made this their practice. Joshua, the Bereans, the Prophets. (10.) They warn us of our dangers, enemies, and sins. (11.) They are the rule of our future and final judgment. We feel the importance of the judgment to come. We can carry our case to counsel, and know the issue before the day, by having these Scriptures in our hand.

ADVICE as to searching the Scriptures.

(1.) Let your search be impartial. Search the precepts and threatenings, as well as the promises.

(2.) Search them from passage to passage, that one may explain another. Compare *The seed of the woman* with *A virgin shall conceive;* and with, *When the fulness of time was come, God sent forth his Son, born of a woman.* Compare the account of the Passover with *Christ our Passover is sacrificed for us.*

(3.) Search them to obey them. Not as a man searches the writings of an enemy, to find out where he can object; but as a subject searches acts of Parliament, willing to obey them.

(4.) Search them with prayer, that God the Spirit would write them on the heart.

(5.) In searching, expect depths unfathomable and difficulties insurmountable. *Oh the depth of the riches both of the wisdom and knowledge of God! how unsearchable are his judgments, and his ways past finding out!*

(6.) Digest, rather than devour them.

The USES. The Holy Scriptures are a ground of—

1. *Congratulation,* to Britons, as dwelling in a land of Bibles.

2. *Alarm,* to such as are reading anything or everything rather than the Bible.

3. *Caution,* to such as read to cavil and oppose.

The Rev. J. Goode—

There are some good directions in *Bennett's Christian Oratory* respecting the private reading of the Scriptures.

In congratulating Britons, we might well introduce what Tillotson says of the Church of Rome, That she allows no salvation out of her pale, and deprives those within it of the best means of salvation.

We might shew how holy men have felt. Job : *I have esteemed the words of his mouth more than my necessary food.* David : *The law of the Lord is perfect, converting the soul.* Jeremiah : *Thy words were found, and I did eat them; and thy word was unto me the joy and rejoicing of my heart.*

The Rev. J. Clayton—

Hindrances in the way of a thorough knowledge of the Scriptures :

1. The practice of Dissenters in conducting their worship, in some cases without reading the Scriptures at all.

2. Much occupation; which keeps people in ignorance of their

Bible. Reading magazines, Bogatzky, and such like excellent books, instead of the Bible itself.

3. Allowing people to rest in systematic attainments regarding doctrines, the fall, election, adoption, regeneration.

4. Not honouring the Divine Spirit by dependence on Him when they do read, and in prayer for His illumination.

NOVEMBER 2, 1807.

HOW MAY A MINISTER ASCERTAIN THE PATH OF DUTY WITH RESPECT TO CALLS TO OCCASIONAL SERVICES?—Proposed by the Rev. H. G. Watkins.

The Rev. H. Budd—

When called on to pray in company by the master of the house, who shews—(1.) A trifling spirit, (2.) a curious spirit, (3.) a self-righteous spirit, (4.) an ostentatious spirit, or (5.) a kind of challenge,—we may consider whether it will not have a good effect on the company, though the master be wrong. There is a call, when we think people who wish it are in the main honest.

The Rev. H. Foster—

I should in such cases intimate that expounding and praying will not prove the company to be Christians. A bad system has crept in —a worldly spirit is patched up by concluding in prayer. I would protest against this.

A minister should go nowhere, perhaps, where it is not natural and easy to pray and expound. He *may* be where he had better omit prayer and exposition.

The Rev. Mr Simons, a visitor—

Go nowhere but as a minister of the Gospel. Be in no company half-an-hour without delivering your Master's message.

NOVEMBER 16, 1807.

WHAT INSTRUCTION MAY BE DERIVED FROM THE SUPPOSED SENSIBLE INTERPOSITIONS OF SPIRITUAL AGENTS?—Proposed by the Rev. H. Foster.

Mr Foster—

There can be no doubt of the reality of the appearances of spiritual agents. There may be false relations; but they are grounded on true appearances. Their end is to silence and alarm.

We are in the midst of a world of good and evil spirits—perhaps ten times the number of mankind. We have no certain account of the number; probably it is surprisingly great. A legion possessed one man; and a legion consisted of at least 2000; and from his entrance into the swine, it appears to have been 2000: see Mark v. 13. Taking a view of the whole, we are in the midst of a wonderful scene of

NOTES OF THE ECLECTIC SOCIETY, LONDON.

invisible agents. All are under God's control, and that is our comfort. This concurs to help our faith in the Scripture account of things.

The Rev. J. Pratt—

Ours is a spiritual dispensation. God has in some sense withdrawn from the world as to sensible interpositions.

I think, with Addison, that the general evidence of spirits is incontrovertible; but that particular stories are suspicious. No new truth, no new revelation, no particular direction in duty, is, I think, to be expected. This would lead men from God's Word. The effect is intended to be only of a general kind, that there is an invisible world, that our thoughts may be directed generally and not particularly. It is not intended, probably, that we should have clear intimations of any particular interpositions. *If they hear not Moses and the prophets, neither will they be persuaded though one rose from the dead.* Christ's mission, the truth of God, are all fully evidenced : if men will not hear and receive this evidence, neither will any interposition of spiritual agents help them. They may be frighted, but not permanently impressed. Doddridge's story of Colonel Gardiner seems counter to this. But it is a rare case. Anything that leads to serious thought on realities and the Scripture statements must be so far good.

The Rev. B. Woodd—

Our family is remarkable for intimations previous to death. [He gave many surprising instances, which, unhappily, are not recorded in the notes.]

The Rev. J. Clayton—

All the apprehensions raised from the supposed sensible interpositions of invisible agents lead to God, and are therefore useful. They renew a practical impression of an existing Deity. This is a salutary operation.

There may possibly be a designed obscurity left over the sensible interposition, that man's mind may not be weaned from the sure Word of God.

The Rev. S. Crowther—

Formerly, too much credit used to be given to narrations of this nature. At present there is too great incredulity.

There is always some end worthy of God in these interpositions.
Nec Deus intersit nisi dignus vindice nodus
Inciderit.
Yet we may not know what this end is.

The Rev. R. Lloyd—

There is a difficulty of ascertaining the influence of the body on the mind. The laws of their union are beyond our comprehension. This should make us jealous of allowing supposed interpositions.

The Rev. J. Venn—

Supposing the interposition to be true, what INFERENCES are to be drawn ?

The former was a credulous age : this is a sceptical age. We must set ourselves against the error of the age. If we had lived in a former age, we should have resisted.

The aim of Satan *then* was to multiply stories, to throw the whole into discredit. In discrediting these instances, he discredits divine revelation, its miracles. There is a kind of masked battery here.

There has been an impression all over the world, in every age, of the invisible world. Satan brings ridiculous stories, in order to make all this ridiculous.

In the present age, I would resist the scepticism. Though twenty stories proved false, if the twenty-first cannot be so proved, it should have more weight with me than all the rest to discredit real interpositions. All this is consistent with the analogy of what is recorded in Scripture. The miracles of Moses were imitated by the magicians of Pharaoh. The outpouring of the Spirit was imitated on the wicked (Acts xix. 13–15). I am afraid then when I hear many ridiculous stories on the subject ; they tend to weaken a forcible and important argument.

The LIMITS are not difficult to be determined.

So far as they tend to confirm the existence of an invisible world, they are just and useful : but when they go to reveal new doctrines, they are not to be received. Swedenborg therefore ought to be rejected.

A lying spirit may be permitted to make discoveries, to blind those who will not believe the Scriptures. The grand stumbling-block to the reception of revelation is the rejection of spiritual agency. The diabolical possessions and the miracles of Scripture are the ground of the rejection of Scripture among multitudes.

Much must be allowed in the stories we hear to imagination. But imagination cannot account for multitudes of authentic relations. The number of well-authenticated narrations is much greater than is generally believed. There is scarcely any person who has not himself seen, or has some relation or friend who has seen, some such appearances.

[Here he referred to Lord Teignmouth's dream of his daughter ; Lord Lyttelton's story ; Blumberg, prebendary of Bristol ; General Wynward's brother laying down his sword. Most of the well-authenticated appearances have been to persons perfectly calm, and in the day-time.]

November 30, 1807.

WHAT ARE THE CHIEF DUTIES OF CHRISTIAN MINISTERS WITH RESPECT TO ONE ANOTHER ?—Proposed by the Rev. W. Fry.

Mr Fry—

A spirit of unity should prevail among ministers. This is the case among the Bristol ministers : and the people are accordingly united.

There should be special and occasional seasons of intercession among ministers for one another. This would guard them against occasions of disunion. It would lead them to rejoice in each others' success.

They should guard against mutual jealousies. We should view a brother minister with much candour. We should guard against occasions and subjects of offence.

We should be jealous of one another's character and reputation. People will prefer you to others.

There is danger of being more attached to little points of difference, than to the great work of saving their souls. Resist this. Be jealous of the moral character of one another.

Represent to one another what is thought exceptionable. Cherish a spirit of willingness to receive such intimations.

Raise the fallen. Do not countenance sin. But some are lost to the Christian world by want of tenderness.

Do not act immediately on the judgment of others, nor yet refuse due weight to such judgment.

The Rev. J. Clayton—

Suppress a spirit of envy. The indolent envy the active. The aged have a propensity to envy the young. It is a difficult thing to rise with humility, and to decline without repining.

We should not receive any accusation but before two or three witnesses. Consider every solitary testimony against a minister to be scandal, till proved.

Allow the right of private judgment to ministers.

Mention in love whatever may operate against usefulness. Many little things do this. Bear witness against what is wrong; and, if in vain, separate.

PRAYER. I pray every Saturday evening preparatory to the Lord's day for all ministers within my knowledge.

The Rev. J. Goode—

All the law is fulfilled in one duty—LOVE. Speak with caution of ministers before our families. Regard the rule of equity: *As ye would that men should do unto you, so do ye unto them.*

The Rev. Mr Sheppard—

Exhort one another. Defend one another, so far as possible. Rejoice in one another's success. Mention the names of ministers in prayer.

The Rev. W. J. Abdy—

We should not cover evil in our brother, because he is one of our party; though we should defend him to the utmost. We should take much pains to sift evil reports against a brother to the bottom.

The Rev. R. Lloyd—

Enlighten one another. Converse on the constitution of the human mind. Trace prevailing opinions. Truth is paramount to every thing.

No fallen man perhaps was ever fully under divine influence.

Prejudice is actuating us continually. Guard against a spirit of intolerance.

Many ministers have a circle of flatterers. They are popes in this circle. Cultivate a catholic spirit. This does not involve latitudinarianism. Preserve the principle of catholicism from the varied expression of it.

The Rev. H. Budd—

Prayer should extend to every description of ministers—the indolent, the carnal, and the heretical.

The Rev. H. Foster—

The principle actuating should be love. The rule is, *As ye would that men should do unto you, so do ye unto them.*

The Rev. J. Pratt—

Diffuse the faults of ministers as little as possible.

The first business a minister has is with himself. There is something flattering when he thinks of doing this and that for his brethren. If he have dissension with any, he should be ready to forgive ; but it should be sealed in silence. We should guard against abounding in our own sense, which is the natural danger of age and activity.

Guard against flattery. Flattery is founded on a preference of us to others.

———

DECEMBER 14, 1807.

How far is it True that the Christian Life consists rather in Desires and Aims than in Actual Attainments ?—Proposed by the Rev. W. Fry—

Mr Fry—

Scripture describes the Christian state as an actual attainment: *I can do all things.* Though there is not freedom from sin, yet there is ability.

Desire alone, however vehement and sincere, is no proof of a gracious state. We may remember the young man in the Gospel.

We are apt to allow too much to desires. We cannot judge of ourselves or others but by actual attainments.

Men seek Christ rather because they cannot do without him, than for anything they really desire of him.

The perfection of Methodism, however, is not warranted by Scripture. I have read much and conversed much with the Methodists. Their perfection is a wild tumult of passions. It fixes their view on particular objects. It proceeds from an unbottomed view of human corruption.

As to outward circumstances, the Christian life consists in attainments. As to the inward state, in desires, though there are actual attainments.

The Rev. B. Woodd—

The Christian character consists in what the Christian approves and pursues.

The Rev. Mr Sheppard—

Every Christian has every grace in a measure.

The Rev. W. J. Abdy—

Liberation from actual sin as a habit is the character of a true Christian, though he may be overcome by an *act* of sin. But real attainment might be much more than it is. There are great promises. *We have not, because we ask not.—The very God of peace sanctify you wholly, and I pray God your whole spirit and soul and body be preserved blameless unto the coming of our Lord Jesus Christ.*

The Rev. R. Lloyd—

Christians in their highest attainments are in an infantine state. There is no ground for the distinction between desires and attainments. For as a Christian grows he gets deeper views.

The Rev. H. Foster—

I am not out of Rom. vii. I have stuck there for forty years.
The more a man grows, the more will he bewail his depravity.

The Rev. R. Cecil—

I die daily, is a matter of experience. *Lord, what wait I for? Truly my hope is in Thee.—First the blade, then the ear, then the full corn in the ear.*

The Rev. J. Pratt—

There is a difference between actual and perceived attainments. A man cannot perceive his attainments without pride.

Conscious attainments are not to be acquired, because the standard advances as the Christian grows.

DECEMBER 28, 1807.

How should a Christian Act to Induce his Friends and Connexions to the Practice of Vital Christianity?—Proposed by the Rev. H. Budd.

Mr Budd—

1. By conciliation.

We must be *all things to all men*, so far as consistent with our profession. It is difficult to divest ourselves of the irritability occasioned by constant opposition.

2. Avoid controversy.
3. Avoid needless singularity.

Comply in all indifferent matters. Christian sentiment and practice are sufficiently singular to draw down opposition.

4. Talk not continually on the subject.

Fervent affection to relatives may urge to unseasonable attempts, which we should guard against.

5. We should not press the admissions or conclusions which our friends may make, so as to irritate them.

6. Bear with opposition without availing yourselves of every opportunity of answering again.

Forbear under evil tempers. Shew your Christianity indeed by bearing such evil tempers.

7. Where conciliation avails not, warn gently and mildly.

How should a *son* speak to a father in such a case? Perhaps ask an audience, and solemnly and affectionately and delicately discover to him your feelings.

8. Let example speak.

Shew that your religion is more than words. If you have been disobedient in times past, shew that religion changes the man. Seek to reconcile family differences. The true Christian is the *pivot* on which his family turns. There is something which forces their approbation, though not their accord.

9. Remember prayer for them.

General, and personal. Lay each person's case before God.

The Rev. H. Foster—

The Apostles Peter and Paul seem much to insist on kindness: *What knowest thou, O wife, whether thou shalt save thy husband? or how knowest thou, O man, whether thou shalt save thy wife?* (1 Cor. vi. 16.) *That they also may, without the word, be won by the conversation of the wives.* (1 Peter iii. 1.)

Let our relatives see that we are happy in our religion.

The Rev. R. Cecil—

Duly appreciate the state of your friends. Perhaps they cannot see, feel, taste our enjoyments. They must accommodate themselves to you, and you to them. It is much a matter of accommodation on both sides.

[Here he referred to a story of Franklin's about some missionaries and the Indians.]

Avoid disgusting friends unnecessarily. The precise man must be humoured. They set down religion as a case of humour. Pity is sometimes exasperating. We must be delicate in our management of such cases.

Cultivate good sense. If they perceive you weak in one part, your friends will think you weak in others.

Avoid vain jangling. There is a disposition to shirk important and pinching truths. Such persons are very fond of talking on predestination. They will ask too, " What think you of the salvation of infants and of heathen ?" This is meant to throw the great question out.

Seize occasions. Not only the *mollia tempora fundi*, but touch upon public characters, public events, public fears and plans. Of some great men we might say, " Poor creature ! that he should on the greatest subjects have the ignorance of a child, and the inconsideration of a brute !"

Bring before them the extreme childishness of an unconverted state.

People of fashion are sick at heart of their very pleasures. Treat cards as *childish* things.

A minister should go as a minister, or not at all.

The Rev. J. Pratt—

Relatives are committed to us as a charge. We cannot justly leave them to themselves. Professing relatives are to be animated and warned. The spiritual life should be for this end vigorous in ourselves. Intercourse should be more improved. We are not to limit God and prescribe to him. We are not to grow indifferent on not seeing success.

The Rev. Mr Simons, a visitor—

We must bring our relations to hear the Gospel.

The Rev. W. Fry—

Whatever we do should be done in character. Simons and Simeon might do what I could not. The aged can do what the young cannot. It is common to say, " What would Christ do, or St Paul ?" But Christ or St Paul might do what would be improper for us.

Much depends on the relation. The spirit in which advice or reproof is administered is important. Dropping hints is more successful than long conversations.

The Rev. B. Woodd—

Offices of kindness win the way.

The Rev. Mr Sheppard—

Allure relations by philosophical experiments, or in any way, and let them then feel your holy example in incidentals. Recommend books. Use correspondence by letters. *Nulla dies sine linea. Nullæ literæ sine Christo.*

Make lawful compliances. Hear their preachers sometimes, if they hear yours.

———

At the next meeting, the country members and visitors for the new year were chosen, and no subject was discussed. On the following occasion, the topic had reference to Missions in India, and to the new opposition they were beginning to encounter.

The Rev. Dr Claudius Buchanan, a chaplain of the East India Company, and well known for his zeal and exertions in behalf of India, had recently published an important *Memoir*, dedicated to his Grace the Archbishop of Canterbury, upon the necessity of an Ecclesiastical Establishment for India, " both as a means of perpetuating the Christian religion among our countrymen, and as a foundation for the ultimate civilisation of the natives." An appendix to the *Memoir* contained a variety of information on the superstitions of the Hindoos, tending powerfully to correct erroneous opinions entertained of their character and condition. It had a wide circulation, and the eyes of the public were turned towards India and its wants.

About this time pamphlets appeared from the pens of two Bengal officers, calling the attention of the public to what was regarded the danger to which our empire in India was exposed, by the attempts of missionaries to convert the Hindoos to Christianity. One of these productions opened with a bold avowal of the extraordinary sentiment, that it is very doubtful whether Christians of the present day are under any obligation to promote the diffusion of Christianity, even where to diffuse it is practicable. And the other, designedly pointed against Dr Buchanan's work, proceeded upon the untenable ground of the "excellence of the moral system of the Hindoos." These pamphlets attracted much attention; and the Directors of the East India Company partook, as a body, of the general alarm, and of the bitter spirit of opposition against missionary efforts, which so disgraced those days. The Eclectic Society, as we have seen, had already taken a lively interest in the spread of the Gospel in heathen lands, and in fact had given birth to the CHURCH MISSIONARY SOCIETY. It was natural, therefore, that they should watch with an anxious eye these attempts to crush a work in which they were so deeply concerned.

This spirit of opposition, however, turned rather to the furtherance of the good cause. Attention was roused; a mass of information was accumulated; and arguments were multiplied to shew the groundlessness of the apprehensions of these half-hearted Christians, and the duty and importance of placing the Gospel within the reach of the benighted millions of Hindostan. Soon after, in 1813, when the East India Company's Charter expired, and the discussion came on in Parliament for its renewal, India, with its teeming population, was thrown open to missionary enterprise, and, at the same time, the Indian Episcopate was erected. No convulsions have followed; but, on the other hand, repeated expressions of wonder have passed the lips of the Hindoos themselves, that their rulers should have been so shy in keeping their religion in the background, as if ashamed to produce it.

We live, thank God, in more promising days. The Indian army, as well as the Civil Service, abounds in men who are zealous for the work of conversion; and who shrink not, even when holding the highest and most responsible posts, from avowing their attachment to the missionary cause. Upon the discussion of the India Bill, three years ago, evidence was given before the Committees of both Houses of Parliament, by secretaries to Government, and other officials, strongly in favour of Christian education, and speaking in high terms of the successful result of missionary effort. Such is the progress and triumph of truth!

The proposer of the following question felt a personal interest in this subject, as he had recently parted with his friend and fellow-labourer at Cambridge, HENRY MARTYN, who had devoted himself to India, first in the service of the Church Missionary Society, but eventually as a chaplain of the East India Company, having received that appointment from Charles Grant, Esq., at the recommendation of Mr Simeon. Mr Pratt was not present at this meeting of the Eclectic Society. The following notes were taken by another member, the Rev. H. G. Watkins.

———

JANUARY 25, 1808.

WHAT IS THAT LINE OF CONDUCT WHICH THE PRESENT IRRITATED STATE OF MANY OF THE INDIA PROPRIETORS RENDERS PROPER TO BE FOLLOWED BY THE PIOUS MINISTERS IN THE EAST INDIES, WHETHER MISSIONARIES OR CHAPLAINS, IN RELATION TO THE DIFFUSION OF THE SCRIPTURES OR THE EXERCISE OF THEIR MINISTRY?—Proposed by the Rev. Charles Simeon.

Mr Simeon—

Difficulties now lie in the way of both chaplains and missionaries. All are there either by the appointment or by the connivance of the East India Company. And, therefore, the question is an important and delicate one.

The Rev. Mr Sheppard—

Let them go on and preach the Gospel.

The Rev. S. Crowther—

The duty of chaplains and missionaries is the same under this question as it was before. The spirit of opposition to the conversion of the heathen was to be expected.

The labourers should exercise the same zeal as hitherto, because their time may be short, or this hostile spirit may drive them from the country.

The Rev. H. G. Watkins—

They should follow the same exact line they have hitherto pursued. They are judicious men. They have already with judgment preached the Gospel.

The hearts of the Directors are in God's hand. Nothing we can advise can alter their conduct before the question is settled.

The chaplains and missionaries are best able to judge what they should do. Difficulties are best known and met by the persons themselves.

Ignorance of what may happen should teach us to go on and leave events to God. This opposition to the Gospel may prelude Bonaparte's obtaining the East!

The Rev. W. J. Abdy—

Buchanan had laboured long and with little effect, and it was time to write. It might be indiscreet to publish names.

The Rev. H. Budd—

We have no data. We know not the ground of offence.

The Rev. H. Foster —

Let them go on. Do not talk about it.

The Rev. R. Cecil—

A good conscience is the best casuist. Sir William Jones recommended a calm ardour. Silent energy is most effective. A little cur in a house makes more noise than a great dog. *Suaviter in modo, fortiter in re.*

"How shall I best carry the point for which I came?" each of them should ask himself. Whatever the Company is doing, what ought *he* to do? Business, and not bustle. Avoid all sorts of duplicity. If entangled with a noisy, bustling brother, separate from him. Every man cannot do as Samson, who slew a lion, and did not tell his father of it. Men, it seems, must blazon things abroad.

The Rev. W. Goode—

Buchanan's Memoir was written during the Marquis Wellesley's administration as Governor-General, when all went on swimmingly.

FEBRUARY 8, 1804.

HOW SHALL WE BEST IMPROVE THE APPROACHING FAST ?—Proposed by the Rev. J. Clayton.

Mr Clayton—

Look at the mitigations of the evils we have suffered from.

The Rev. Mr Sheppard—

Look at—(1.) Our danger; (2.) our sins. Let us (3.) exhort to repentance, and (4.) urge to prayer.

The Rev. H. G. Watkins—

We should labour ourselves to be more spiritually-minded on that day.

The Rev. W. J. Abdy—

Candour with reference to the Government is our duty.
We should pray for forgiveness if there be anything wrong.

The Rev. H. Budd—

Our text may be : *Let no man deceive you with vain words, for because of these things cometh the wrath of God upon the children of disobedience.* Introduction : Vindicate the pulpit from the charge of interfering in politics. Take it for granted that the congregation acknowledge the government of God.

1. Give instances of man's vain words :—" We are better than other nations." "We are as good as ever we were." "Look at the superiority of our fleets and armies."

2. Shew that because of these things wrath comes on the children of disobedience.

3. Take a rapid and general view of the decay of the world.

4. Take a view of society in Europe for the last eighteen years.

5. Point out the changes of nations before our own eyes. Mention remarkable circumstances. The withdrawing of the Court of Portugal.

6. Bring the matter home in shewing what is calculated to draw down the wrath of God upon us. The sins of the land, especially those which are sanctioned by the statute-book. That the slave-trade is abolished we may indeed congratulate ourselves. Oppression in distant colonies. The fomenting of political dissensions in India. The extension of our commerce and vices throughout the world, and neglecting the favourable opportunity of diffusing the Gospel. Exposing the Gospel to contempt among heathen nations. The profanation of the Sabbath. The neglect of ordinances and means of grace. Gin-shops; distilleries; lotteries; oaths. Disregard of judgments for eighteen years. Disregard of mercies. The particular defects of our particular congregations. Let us press repentance and prayer.

The Rev. H. Foster—

My text will be, *Neither know we what to do, but our eyes are upon thee.* (2 Chron. xx. 12.)

On the former fast days we had *some* arm of flesh to look to; but now all is cut away.

The plan of the sermon—

I. Consider the awful perplexity of our case.

II. The means of deliverance.

III. The issue from the distress when the means are used.

I. Our awful perplexity : *Neither know we what to do.*

1. The number and complexity of our enemies.

2. The ruin of the nations around.

3. The depth of the misery into which our enemies mean to bring us.

4. The burden of taxes and decay of trade.

5. The want of a mediator.

6. The aggravations of our sins.

I have nourished and brought up children, and they have rebelled against me.—What could I have done more for my vineyard, that I have not done in it?

II. The means of deliverance : *Our eyes are upon thee.*

1. We see THY HAND in our perplexities : *Shall there be evil in the city, and the Lord hath not done it? The word of the Lord came to Shemaiah, the man of God, saying, Ye shall not go up, . . . for this thing is done of me.* (2 Chron. xi. 1–4.)

2. We feel our own insufficiency : *O our God, wilt thou not judge them? for we have no might against this great company.* (2 Chron. xx. 12.)

3. We turn not to arms of flesh.

4. We believe and apply to THEE as able to help us in this perplexing case.

5. We confess our unworthiness of the blessing which we ask.

III. The issue.

King Jehoshaphat quieted the people's minds. Their enemies were destroyed. They were enriched with the spoils of their enemies. They were piously thankful for deliverance. The realm had rest from its calamities.

The Rev. Mr Marsden, a visitor—

Urge the comparative privileges and mercies of England.

The Rev. Josiah Pratt—

It is the duty of ministers to search out the peculiar and appropriate circumstances of the times.

Urge confidence in the King's ministers doing their best with regard to peace.

Urge the awful prospect if harvest should fail, and the consequent call for intercession for the country.

Urge the prospect of permanent peace being impracticable while Bonaparte lives.

Sin is accumulated upon us by the way in which our Fasts are observed.

FEBRUARY 22, 1808.

WHAT MEANS CAN AND OUGHT AN UNREGENERATE MAN TO USE, IN ORDER TO SPIRITUAL LIFE?—Proposed by the Rev. R. Lloyd.

The Rev. H. Foster—

Every man ought to obey God. Therefore, every man who hears *ought* to come to Christ for life. *Labour not for the meat which perisheth, but for that meat which endureth unto everlasting life,* was addressed to wicked men. It is the duty of every man to keep the law. If he *attempt* it, he will learn his inability, and be brought to Christ.

The Rev. R. Cecil—

An unregenerate man can do nothing in order to spiritual life, without the RENEWING OF THE HOLY GHOST. He can no more give himself spiritual life, than raise himself from the dead. Yet man is called to AIM AND ENDEAVOUR all he can.

The Rev. J. Pratt—

As a question pointing out ministerial duty, it is easy to answer. I would call on every man to do everything. I will leave it to God to make the call effectual or not. I will also leave it to God to judge the world righteously. I know He will condemn no man without just cause. I would urge every man's conscience with the neglect of what he knows he *could* do.

As a METAPHYSICAL QUESTION, it is impossible to be answered till we can fathom the depths of God. As to the phrases, "We are not to work *in order* to life, but to work from life," they may be generally used in a sound sense : "We are not to work *meritoriously* in order to life, though we are to work in the order of divine appointment." But as these aphoristic expressions are liable to be misunderstood, it may be prudent rather to use Scripture language.

The Rev. J. Clayton—

Explain the Law. Hold up the standard. Your inability to obey it does not deprive God of His authority.

But here are MEANS. All *meritorious* means are centred in Christ. All instituted means, as rational creatures, we are called on to use. These means we are to call on men to use, in conformity to the eternal decree of election. We know not whom the Holy Spirit may create anew, but WE are to call upon all. By this system of means, God fulfils his great decree.

The first principle of life may be communicated independently of the Word. Why does man receive the Word? Because God has implanted a principle of belief in his heart—a principle which is the fruit of God's electing love.

Human industry is not connected with JUSTIFICATION, but it is with SANCTIFICATION. Whoever works for justification is in a damnable error; but whoever, in the use of instituted means, works for sanctification, is a vigorous saint.

The Rev. B. Woodd—

While we implicitly follow the directions and examples of the Bible, we must wait for the light of another world.

Man ought to set apart time for consideration; he ought to study the Scriptures, to pray, to avoid bad company, to practise moral duties, to frequent public ordinances.

The Rev. H. G. Watkins—

We must use MEANS, as we use food.

This meeting possesses an affecting interest in being the last when the members of the Eclectic were allowed to enjoy the presence of the most original and gifted of their body—the Rev. RICHARD CECIL.

During this month he was seized with paralysis, which deprived him of the use of his right side, and totally disabled him from further exertions in public. He lingered for more than two years, and departed on August 15th, 1810. In this last illness his friends were deprived of that rich vein of reflections with which they were privileged during his confinement in 1798, which we have noticed, p. 88. Though torn then with pain, yet his MIND retained its full vigour; but in his last illness his mind became emaciated as well as his body.

"The energy, and decision, and grandeur of his natural powers," says the present Bishop of Calcutta, in one of his funeral sermons on the occasion of his death, "gradually gave way, and a morbid feebleness succeeded. But . . . . the spiritual dispositions of his heart displayed themselves in a very remarkable manner. He appeared great

in the ruins of nature ; and his eminently religious character manifested itself, to the honour of divine grace, in a manner which surprised
all who were acquainted with the ordinary effects of paralytic complaints. . . . . . The real character of the man could only appear,
when disease allowed it to appear at all, according to the grand leading
habits of his life. If his habits had been ambitious, or sensual, or
covetous, or worldly, these tendencies, if any, would have displayed
themselves; but as his soul had long been established in grace, and
spiritual religion had been incorporated with all his trains of sentiment
and affection, and had become like a second nature, the holy dispositions of his heart acted with remarkable constancy under all the varia-
tions of his illness : so that one of his oldest friends observed to me,
that if he had to choose the portion of his life, since he first knew
him, in which the evidences of a state of salvation were most decisive,
he should, without a moment's hesitation, select the period of his last
distressing malady.

" Throughout his illness his whole mind . . . was riveted on spiritual
objects.   Every other topic was so uninteresting to him, and even burdensome, that he could with reluctance allow it to be introduced. The
value of his soul, the emptiness of the world, the nearness and solemnity of death, were ever on his lips.   He spent his whole time in reading
the Scriptures, and one or two old divines, particularly Archbishop
Leighton.   All he said and did was as a man on the brink of an eternal
state."

Among the various interesting testimonies to the spiritual and
devoted state of his heart we will mention one, though at the risk
of being charged with repetition, as we have already noticed it in
our sketch of Mr Cecil as a preacher, in an earlier part of the
volume.   A short time before his decease he requested one of his
family to write down for him in a book the following sentence :
" NONE BUT CHRIST, NONE BUT CHRIST, said Lambert dying at a
stake : the same in dying circumstances, with his whole heart,
saith Richard Cecil."   The name was signed by himself, with his
left hand, in a manner hardly legible through infirmity.

The last sentiment he uttered, as it proved to be, in the Eclectic
meetings, is a counterpart of the Apostle's inspired words : *Work
out your own salvation with fear and trembling ; for it is* GOD
THAT WORKETH IN YOU *to will and to do of his good pleasure.*

MARCH 7, 1808.

WHAT ARE THE PROMINENT ERRORS OF THE DAY, AND THE BEST MEANS
OF COUNTERACTING THEM ?—Proposed by the Rev. B. Woodd.

Mr Woodd—

The shades of error are diversified and complex.   The prominent
errors of the present day are of an Antinomian tendency.   There is an
erroneous idea abroad of what constitutes FAITH.   The Calvinistic
Methodists think it a persuasion of an interest in the Gospel—" a

belief that I am a believer." The writings of Henry, Marshall, and Romaine, rather favour this idea.

A practical error of the day is a lax idea of church government. Evangelical congregations are much infected with this.

An undue depreciation of the forms of religion is another. It is true that the forms of religion are but the shell ; and that the outward form will never save a man. Yet a disregard of the forms of religion indicates a departure from the vital spirit of religion.

Remissness as to prayer and private duties is an evil of the day. Ministers have inadvertently encouraged this. We feel the wandering of our minds ; but should be careful of saying this in public. There is a danger of relaxing the form of the attitude of the body, and of the fixed time of prayer. Mr Newton and Dr Conyers gave too much allowance in this. We may be chasing a half-hour through the day, and never overtake it.

A bigoted attachment to certain ministers is an error. Christianity would soon look as if the Gospel were only the Gospel as ministered by certain persons.

An unhallowed mixture of the profession of godliness with the spirit of the world is an evil of the times.

The first remedy is, the minister's personal religion ; next, his family's religion ; next, the practical character of his discourses.

The Rev. H. G. Watkins—

One evil of the times is a careless, lukewarm priesthood. This drives men to another extreme—high doctrine without practical preaching.

The Rev. Mr Sheppard—

Infidelity is a great error of the day.

MARCH 21, 1808.

How far is the Cause just to which Crantz[*] ascribes the Success of the Greenland Missionaries—viz., the simple Declaration of the Love of God in sending his Son, after Preaching in vain concerning the General Attributes of God and the Doctrines of Natural Religion? and how far is it applicable to other Missions, or to the Preaching of Ministers in general?—Proposed by the Rev. J. Venn.

The Rev. Mr Simons, a visitor—

The wolf once went to school. His master said he never had so untoward a scholar. He got over *a* to *g*, and skipped to *n—u—s;* but never learned more.

The Rev. B. Woodd—

Do this and live, is the way to lead men to Christ. *Repent and believe*

---

[*] See *History of Greenland,* from the German of David Crantz, in two vols., chap. ii. of second volume.

the Gospel.   The way some preach the Gospel would seem to exclude repentance.

See St Paul's method at Athens, Acts xvii. ; also, *I have taught you publicly and from house to house, testifying . . . repentance towards God and faith towards our Lord Jesus Christ.* (Acts xx. 20, 21.)   REPENTANCE is the first point, therefore to be insisted on.

FAITH is next.   The jailer was already in a repentant state.   Therefore, says the Apostle, *Believe on the Lord Jesus Christ, and thou shalt be saved.*

The EFFECTS OF FAITH are next.   *This is a faithful saying, and these things I will that thou affirm constantly, that they which have believed in God might be careful to maintain good works.*

The Rev. W. Goode—

The Scriptures take the being of God for granted.   All the attempts at philosophical discourse on the perfections of God have no tendency to conversion.

There are natural obligations, but there is no natural consequence independent of divine revelation.

1. Aim to convince a sinner of his need of Christ.   This leads to repentance.

2. To excite faith, state the suitableness of Christ, the work of Christ, the benefits of Christ.

3. Enforce the work of the Spirit.

4. And urge the manifestation of this in the practice.

Take advantage of all the notices that may exist in the minds of the heathen.   In this view, the simple declaration of the love of God in sending his Son is the one grand instrument of converting the world.

The Rev. R. Lloyd—

I would stand in the centre of my subject.   I would take Christ as the sum and substance.   And I think I could reach the circumference all round with more efficacy from this position.

The Rev. Mr Marsden, a visitor—

You must first bring the heathen to think, and must find something to fix their vagrant attention.   Then you can bring the truths of religion before them.

The Esquimaux are better prepared for religion than the Otaheitans and New Hollanders, because the Esquimaux are obliged to provide for their sustenance by exertion.

———

We have no notes on the next subject, WHAT IS THE MEANING OF ST PAUL'S EXHORTATION TO THE HEBREWS, TO LEAVE THE PRINCIPLES OF THE DOCTRINES OF CHRIST, AND TO GO ON TO PERFECTION ? AND HOW FAR DOES IT APPLY TO PREACHERS OF THE PRESENT DAY ?

APRIL 18, 1808.

HOW MAY A MINISTER BEST RENDER HIS INTERCOURSE WITH HIS PEOPLE EDIFYING ?—Proposed by the Rev. J. Clayton.

Mr Clayton—

In intercourse, the people see our sermons ; they see whether they are to lower the strict things they hear in public. Intercourse is the key to public services.

1. We must intend to profit the people. Personal religion must, therefore, be cultivated.

2. Gravity of manners is our duty. We cannot kneel to pray, if we have indulged in levity.

3. A knowledge of the state and habits of the people is to be aimed at. In public, we cannot apply the chisel where the machine hitches.

4. Through the rising generation speak to the declining.

5. It is not good to make long visits.

By such rules we shall avoid flattery, mis-spending time, and neglect of our studies.

The Rev. B. Woodd—

Intercourse teaches ministers the ignorance of many of the people, and how to adapt his language to their comprehensions.

It is a means of enabling ministers to enter into the temptations of the people, and of guarding others against temptations.

There is need of prayer and dependence on God to give a mouth and wisdom, so many cases unfold themselves unexpectedly.

The Rev. H. Foster—

There is a very good paper in the *Christian Observer* on pastoral visits, as applicable to the country ; but this could not be done in London.

Unless a minister can go as a minister, and can manage the people, he had better stay away.

The Rev. J. Pratt—

Learn by studying characters and states. Make a favourable impression even on irreligious people. Hang on the wheels of evil. Convince people that you are friendly.

The Rev. J. Goode—

Some people are disposed to ask puzzling questions. Ask them questions in return, and so silence them.

Improve occasions as they arise.

On the next subject, WHAT MODE OF CONDUCTING PUBLIC WORSHIP IS LIKELY TO PRODUCE THE MOST SALUTARY EFFECT? there are no notes.

MAY 16, 1808.

WHAT IS THE SCRIPTURAL IDEA OF PERFECTION ?—Proposed by the Rev. W. Fry.

Mr Fry—

Perfection is not a sinless state, nor is it the highest possible state of Gospel obedience. St Paul says, *Not as though I had already attained, either were already perfect;* implying that he might become so. Again, *Let us therefore,* he says, *as many as be perfect, be thus minded.*

The idea of sinless perfection appears to arise from our ignorance of ourselves ; from a want of recollection of sin ; from a lowering of the standard of the law. This perfection consists in avoiding gross sin, and giving mild names to evil things.

What, then, is PERFECTION ? A maturity of age, in contradistinction to infancy ; and this by a figure is applied to the mind. Christian perfection, then, is the maturity of Christian graces.

1. A maturity of understanding in the things of God. *Till we all come in the unity of the faith, and of the knowledge of the Son of God, unto a perfect man, unto the measure of the stature of the fulness of Christ,* &c. It implies enlarged views of the Gospel in all its fulness.

2. Purity of motive. *I will walk in my house with a perfect heart :* with a single eye, and exalting Christ.

3. A more complete subjection of our besetting sin.

4. A cheerful and natural exercise of all holy dispositions. The soul is weak on first conversion, like the weakness of the body on first recovering from disease, but it afterwards becomes invigorated and strong.

5. A depth of humiliation. To *talk* humbly, and to *be* humble, are infinitely different.

6. A holy confidence, with which he looks up to God in Christ Jesus. The servility of fear gives place to the filial spirit of adoption. Perfect love casteth out fear.

7. The more perfect, the less is he thought to be so by himself. *Not as though I had already attained,* were the words of St Paul, so eminent for his Christian character. But the true believer discerns more keenly the remains of sin ; not that he is in reality more subject to sin, but he feels and perceives it more.

8. It is a gradual work. *The path of the just is as a shining light, shining more and more unto the perfect day.* In all God's works there is a beautiful progression.

9. The attainment of a perfect state depends on the use of means. *Of his fulness have all we received, and grace for grace.*

The Rev. Mr Sheppard—

The subject may be considered—

1. As we are perfect in CHRIST.

2. As we are perfect in OURSELVES ; the leading sense of which is sincerity. A further sense is that of maturity, of knowledge, of grace.

The Rev. W. J. Abdy—

Loving God with all our mind and heart is as near an approach to perfection as we can conceive.

The Rev. B. Woodd—

There was a perfection in the state of innocence ; another in the fallen state ; a third in future glory.

The Rev. R. Lloyd—

What Fry and Woodd said rather mark the *growth of piety* in the Christian, than the state of perfection. Perfection seems to be uprightness and sincerity. All the parts of a Christian, however, are unfolded. There may be a perfection of *principle*, though not of *attainment.*

This sweeps away Popish piety and the piety of the world. This is a piety of compensation, weighing what is good against what is evil. But the Christian is *full-orbed.* We are required to be absolutely perfect. There is no relaxation of this demand. The intellectual, moral, and animal system is to be wholly devoted to God.

The Rev. H. Budd—

There is a comparative perfection. This relates to the perfection of intention and of practice.

There is also a complete perfection, as we are found in Christ : *I in them, and thou in me. Presenting every man perfect in Christ Jesus.*

The Rev. H. Foster—

There is perfection as to justification on embracing Christ : *For by one offering he hath perfected for ever them that are sanctified.*

The word means sincerity, in opposition to all kinds of hypocrisy.

It means a perfection of parts. The Christian has life in his judgment, conscience, will, affections. The perfect man feels not perfect. The body is not felt when all its parts act well. It is rather an evidence of defect in the body, when the body is felt.

The Rev. J. Pratt—

Brother Lloyd makes perfection to consist of sincerity, which even the babe in Christ must possess. And yet says *absolute* perfection is required.

Perfection, as Brother Fry proposes the question, refers to the maturity of Christian graces. See 1 John ii. 13, 14.

General ideas regarding perfection are—

1. Quick discernment, keen sensibility, freedom from prejudice and selfish bias.

2. Actual conformity to such light and holy views.

3. Deep humiliation for deviations ; ready acknowledgment before men ; anxiety and care to avoid occasions of falling.

The Rev. C. Simeon, a visitor—

The perfection of Mr Wesley went on this :—Love is the fulfilling of the law ; therefore if your love be perfect, you are perfect.

These will look and wink hard till they find perfection ; *we* are looking for imperfection.   They are looking for ground of self-complacency ;
we for ground of *humiliation*.

Their views (1.) lead to looking for good in themselves, and (2.)
make their very gratitude pharisaical.

The Rev. T. Robinson, a visitor—

Perfection in point of justification admits not of degrees.   Perfection
as to sanctification is the work of the Spirit.   Christian perfection
is in regeneration.   Here he is τέλειος, perfect in all his parts.

The perfect in sanctification has his mind enlarged ; a gradual progress towards absolute perfection.   There may be awful suspensions
and witherings of the Christian life.

Satan tempts us according to our religious views.

MAY 30, 1808.

DOES PEACE OF MIND DEPEND UPON THE STRENGTH OR THE JUSTNESS
OF CONVICTION ?—Proposed by the Rev. R. Lloyd.

Mr Lloyd—

Peace is the prerogative of truth, and of truth alone.   It is
founded in knowledge—in a knowledge of Christianity.   It rests on a
stable foundation.

Yet heathens are heroic in suffering and death.   They do this
under some idea of religious duty and reward.   So high-flown Antinomians.

The Rev. H. Budd—

If it be *real* peace, it must depend on the *justness* of conviction ; for
a *false* peace can arise only from the *strength* of conviction.

There is a PEACE *which passeth all understanding*—a peace from
consciousness of having fled to Christ as a refuge from sin.   The
martyrs died under this peace.

But how to account for martyrs for falsehood is very difficult ;
because it is difficult to draw the line between a true and a false
peace.   Both kinds of peace appear to arise from sincerity of intention.
Paul going to Damascus was sincere, though wrong.

The Rev. H. Foster—

With respect to the strength of conviction, much seems to depend
on the animal frame. · Real peace depends most on the justness of
conviction.

The things on which peace is founded must be simply such as a
babe may be able to comprehend ; as a just sense of the evil of sin,
of our misery as sinners, of Christ as the Saviour, of our affiance in
Him.

The weak can't talk so well, nor think so justly on these points as
the wise, but they can and do as substantially live in the exercise of
these views.   Yet sanguine men will get peace sooner than doubting

and hesitating persons.   Mr Romaine doubted on no subject ; but others do on all.

The Rev. J. Pratt—

There is a difference between being entitled to peace on evangelical grounds, and being able to realise that peace.

Though strong conviction will mislead in proportion to its want of justness, yet such conviction will not quiet but in proportion to its strength.

Whence is it that there is so much more doubt and fear than one would expect to find from the New Testament.

Perhaps some degeneracy in the animal frame or a spirit of the world has crept in, or too little time given to converse with God. For if a man gives himself to public duties to the injury of private ones, peace cannot abound.   Christ will reveal himself only to those who cultivate his friendship.

I should vindicate Christianity by insisting on its *tendency* to produce peace to such beings as men are in such a world as this.

The Rev. J. Goode—

True peace depends more on the strength than the justness of conviction, because strong conviction I consider delusion, if not on just grounds.   Conviction is faith ; and the stronger this be, the more peace there is.

The Rev. J. Clayton—

The change from Paganism to Christianity is so great, that the change was decisive : there was more evidence therefore in the earlier days than there is now.   In the present day it is more honourable to profess Christianity, and therefore there is less conviction and evidence of a decisive work.

All true peace must arise from a sight of God being reconciled. This is objective peace.   This God of peace and Jesus the peace-maker must be known by the influence of the Spirit ; this is necessary to our subjective peace, which is the fruit of the Spirit.

The fruits of the Spirit, if we have these we—

(1.) Carry on war against all sin ;

(2.) Carry on the war in God's way ; apply to Christ for the removal of fresh guilt ; apply to the Spirit for renewals of strength and grace :

(3.) Are strict and conscientious in our obedience :

(4.) Shew a yielding submission to the providential will of God.

There is a Peace of Justification which is perfect, as we discern the ground of acceptance.   There is a Peace of Sanctification, which will always bear a proportion to our yielding to the Spirit.

The peace of an Enthusiast is in the passions ; of the Antinomian, in the objective view of the work within ; of the Pharisee, in his regard to outward duties.   This false peace will not bear examination on all sides.

The peace of many being lost, means only their good opinion of themselves has been disturbed.

Martyrs for falsehood have no humility in their spirit. Theirs is carnal heroism, not chastened with love to God and man—a sympathy merely with nature and the spirit of this world.

The Rev. B. Woodd—

Peace is grounded on—

1. A view of redemption.

2. A consciousness of complying with the terms of the Gospel covenant.

This evidence may be more or less distinct, and so peace more or less enjoyed. And this, on the one hand, may arise from a relaxation of self-government; and, on the other hand, will be in proportion as a man mortifies his besetting sin. *The work of righteousness shall be peace, and the effect of righteousness quietness and assurance for ever.—Then had the churches rest, . . . and were edified; and walking in the fear of the Lord, and in the comfort of the Holy Ghost, were multiplied.*

Attention to private duties and faithful walking with God lead to peace. Yet God may, to shew his own sovereignty, withhold peace.

There are often abundant grants of peace in EARLY CONVERSION, under AFFLICTIONS, and at DEATH.

The Rev. W. Goode—

This seems to be one of those questions which separate the things which in Christian experience are never distinguished. True peace must arise from the strength and justness of the conviction united. It flows from a witnessing or sealing of the Spirit—from an influx of light, which chiefly respects the object, rather than the conviction of that object being embraced by us. Yet this influx will bear all examination.

The Rev. H. G. Watkins—

Distinguish between a state of peace and a state of safety. There is a class of visitors of the sick who make it a leading question, " Do you believe that Christ died for *you?*" We are obliged to agree with many, that they may be in a state of salvation, though they cannot feel peace.

JUNE 13, 1808.

WHAT ADVANTAGE MAY A MINISTER OBTAIN, FOR THE CONDUCT OF HIS OWN MINISTRY, BY HEARING HIS BRETHREN?—Proposed by the Rev. J. Pratt.

Mr Pratt—

The advantages of a minister hearing his brethren are such as follow :—

1. The trial of his own spirit. How does he feel excellencies and defects?

2. The enlargement of his own views. He sees different gifts. He may learn new methods of exhibiting truth, or get a wider view of truth.

P

3. Comfort under discouragement. Though he is not to exult in the defects of others, nor to pride himself in being free from some of them, yet he may see that the best and most efficient have their respective peculiarities.

4. The correction of his own faults. He may see himself in others.

5. Guidance in difficulties. "How do *they* act in such and such cases ? "

6. The cultivation of affection and sympathy.

Caution. He should only correct the defects of his own ministry, and not model it on that of others.

The Rev. J. Goode—

We hear others, but do not hear ourselves. Without a third person to point things out, we shall not derive these advantages. Even when we have been told that we have such and such habits, yet we scarcely believe it. If we hear a bad tone, yet we do not believe *we* have such a tone. If we hear a man preach an hour and a half, and see the people wearied, we may learn not to weary them.

The Rev. Mr Sheppard—

We may gain advantage by avoiding *faults*—(1.) In *manner;* and (2.) In *mode of expression.*

By imitating excellencies. Henderson learned something from every man. We may profit, as private Christians, from the truths we hear.

The Rev. S. Crowther—

We are much more likely to profit by a brother's sermons than by our own. We are apt to rest too much in making our sermons. Our faith and love are kept up and strengthened by what we hear from others.

The Rev. W. J. Abdy—

In hearing popular preachers, one has a disposition to say what Simon Magus said, *Give me also this gift.* Yet, without making any minister a *model*, we may inquire whether there be not some points on which we may improve our ministry.

The Rev. H. Foster—

I was once encouraged at Blackfriars by the acceptance which another met with.

When we hear preachers of note, we may ask, " What is it that gains such attention ? "

If it be only a style or manner, we may see perhaps the vanity of popularity. We sometimes hear of preachers being very unpopular. We may try to find out and correct it in ourselves, and see whether it can be avoided. Very long sermons tire out congregations. This we learn from hearing others.

Berridge's sermon on, *My name is Legion*, profited me on the subject of envy. He spoke of Envy being one of the Legion, and a captain or colonel in the devil's service.

JUNE 27, 1808.

HOW FAR IS IT TRUE THAT GOD EVER WITHDRAWS HIS PEACE MERELY AS A SOVEREIGN?—Proposed by the Rev. B. Woodd.

Mr Woodd—

I am disposed to answer this question affirmatively. That God should do so, seems analogous to his usual course of proceeding. He has acted like a sovereign in the diffusion of the Gospel ; also in the Reformation, some countries having it not. God acts as a sovereign when his acts are not cognisable by human reason, as in individual experience. This is analogous to God's purpose in his various dealings —to humble man.

The Rev. W. Goode—

God would never withdraw his presence and favour from his creatures but for sin ; and therefore he never acts as a mere sovereign arbitrarily ; but he acts with sovereign wisdom—with sovereign goodness.

But there may be no *particular* cause for which God may at any time withdraw : nevertheless it may be to humble the believer more; and this implies that he needs humbling.

This seems, then, the idea of God's withdrawing as a sovereign— that there is no *particular* sin for which God withdraws ; but yet there is always a general cause in sin and its effects.

The Rev. S. Crowther—

He does it to teach us the value of the divine peace. Let us see, when peace is withdrawn, if we cannot trace it to some relaxation in ourselves.

The Rev. Mr Sheppard—

Some sin or other may probably be discovered in most cases. God's way may be designed for the exercise of grace, and to shew more of God's power in recovering.

The Rev. H. G. Watkins—

It may be intended for the benefit of a man's connexions, when no particular reason can be traced in himself.

Great peace have they who love thy law. So that, in general, the way of peace is that of close walking with God.

It may be as a winter season, to prepare for providences to come, though not arising from any particular cause past. Much lies in constitution.

We must be careful of speaking publicly of God's thus acting : it may induce a carelessness of walking.

The Rev. W. J. Abdy—

The fundamental blessing of the Gospel is peace with God through our Lord Jesus Christ.

The Psalmist says, *He will speak peace unto his people, and to his saints ;* but an important caution follows—*but let them not turn again to folly.* So that, in general, peace accompanies walking with God.

The Apostle's thorn in the flesh was sent, not for any particular sin, but in *prevention* of spiritual pride. So, under sudden or considerable temporal elevation, God may have prepared his people by his withdrawing his peace.

[He here referred to his own experience.]

God's withdrawing his peace is to admonish us of particular evils ; to prepare us for future trials ; to prove whether we will still cleave to God under such trials.

The Rev. H. Budd—

God withdraws his peace frequently in mercy. It induces a more absolute dependence on God.

The Rev. Dr Fearon, a visitor—

God draws his reasons from himself. I have no right to stand up and ask God why he deals thus and thus.

Conscientious men lose more of their peace from bodily infirmity than they can be aware of. Yet much depends on a close walking with God. Infirmity of body may lead to remissness of walking ; but if we can break through this infirmity, we shall have more peace than is generally enjoyed.

The Rev. H. Foster—

Who did sin, this man or his parents, that he was born blind ? Jesus answered, Neither hath this man sinned nor his parents, but that the works of God may be manifested in him. God acts as a sovereign, when there may be no particular reasons in the creature who suffers, but to manifest his own glory. But the sufferer will be the better for his sufferings. The man born blind gained unspeakably by his blindness. God has in view the confusion of the wicked one ; as in the case of Job.

The Rev. J. Goode—

Mental darkness is not meant in that passage, *Who is among you . . . that walketh in darkness, and hath no light ?* The darkness of affliction, or even of temptation, may be meant.

This doctrine is much abused. Persons of an Antinomian temper fly to it when under trouble.

The doctrine should be brought forward with caution. No passage of Scripture has been brought to prove it.

I understand by God's withdrawing his peace as a sovereign, when he shall do it without any reason in the walk of the creature towards himself. There *may* be reasons which we cannot discover. We should act as Christian did when he had lost his roll.

I doubt the point, and would mention it with great caution. A minister may address the *reason*, the *taste*, the *passions* of his people, rather than their *graces ;* and then they cannot truly and considerably prosper.

Witsius argues for the question from, *Shall I not do what I will with my own ?* But there is a great difference between the bestowing and the withdrawing of his favours. In bestowing his favours, God always acts sovereignly ; but I think not in withdrawing his favour.

Job does not appear to have lost his peace till he grew fretful.

The *man born blind* is no case in point. Afflictions are distinct from the loss of peace.

. It is not a mere sovereign act, when it is designed for either the discovery or the prevention of sin. St Paul's case does not apply.

Generally, the divine withdrawing arises from grieving the Holy Ghost. *He will speak peace to his people; but let them not turn again to folly;* which implies that they who had lost peace *had* turned to folly, and *so* had lost their peace.

Nervous feelings or physical causes have nothing to do with God's acting as a sovereign.

Often men may have acted evil out in their hearts, which God sees and visits. Most might answer that question affirmatively, *Hast thou not procured this to thyself?*

The Rev. J. Pratt—

I think with brother J. Goode.

The Rev. J. Davies—

Ministers are tried that they may be able to comfort others with the comfort wherewith they are comforted of God.

The Rev. J. Clayton—

The *state* of peace with God is always the same ; but our *sense* of peace varies. The work of the *surety* as the ground of peace is immoveable, but our sanctification is imperfect.

The first visitation of the soul is an act of pure sovereignty ; that is, God derives his motives purely from himself. But when united to Christ, we come under new laws ; nor do I know that God ever visits in withdrawing, without his children being in a state which requires such withdrawing.

JULY 11, 1808.

WHAT ARE THE BEST RULES BY WHICH SOME SEEMING INCONSISTENCIES IN THE OLD TESTAMENT MAY BE RECONCILED WITH THE MORAL PRECEPTS OF SCRIPTURE?—Proposed by the Rev. W. J. Abdy.

Mr Abdy—

This question arose in my mind from reading parts of the Old Testament in the family, particularly the books of Samuel and Kings, in which difficulties of this kind occur.

The Old Testament is a partial dispensation and imperfect. As our Lord observed to the Jews in respect to polygamy, that it was suffered because of their hardness of heart, so in other respects possibly. God may have suffered these things to be recorded, to try whether we will take things as he chooses to state them. CONSEQUENCES often prove God's displeasure, where that displeasure is not specially expressed.

The Old Testament dispensation was far inferior to ours. The Spirit of God was more limited in his influences than since the day of Pentecost. The number of wives taken by David and Solomon especially shewed unbounded sensuality. And yet God marks them as pious men.

Now, whether, in reading such passages, are we to pass them over or attempt any explanation ?

The Rev. B. Woodd—

There are errors in the best characters of the Old Testament. For example—Abraham's prevarication, his fear of man, want of faith. The grand design of God is to display the weakness of man and the necessity of Christ. He therefore suffered the father of the faithful to fail in want of faithfulness. Again, Noah's intoxication. He probably knew not the efficacy of wine. Then Lot's intoxication and incest ; Moses' irritation ; David's polygamy, adultery, and murder ; Solomon's polygamy and idolatry. What a lesson, that the wisest of men should fall into the most absurd sin ! Next, Jonah, what a strange, obstinate, self-willed being ! Yet, by examination, we feel somewhat of this in ourselves. These infirmities and sins are not reconcilable with the moral precepts of Scripture. They are designed as faithful discoveries of human depravity.

Such men are here set as on a pinnacle. Their history is read by tens of thousands—to debase man ; to magnify the riches of divine grace ; to admonish, and caution, and alarm—*These things were our examples, that we should not lust after evil things ;* to console the striving Christian. We read in Scripture what preserved them from despair.

Ministers should bring these things forward as they occur ; should point them out as instances of corruption in the best men ; urge from them humility, prayer, and watchfulness. *Watch and pray, lest ye enter into temptation.* Pray not only to be upheld in temptation, but to be preserved from it.

To guard against ABUSE, hold out prominently the graces of these saints. Mark David's groans, his *broken bones!* Ask, have you David's spirit ? have you David's deep self-abhorrence ?

Polygamy was allowed under the Old Testament. As to the number of David's and Solomon's wives, that must be rather considered as matters of state than of passion.

The Rev. J. Pratt—

Brother Woodd stated the USE of the inconsistencies in Scripture characters ; but difficulties arise from the consideration that such things appear, as it were, to be suffered, from the use made of them in God's providence. We may add some more instances to shew this :— Isaac's prevarication ; the falsehood of Rebecca and Jacob ; the incest of Judah and Tamar ; the destruction of the Canaanites ; Solomon's conduct to Shimei ; Samson ; Jael ; imprecations too by David.

There are things of another class—the serpent speaking ; the ass of Balaam ; the whale of Jonah—which surprise some. Yet these are recognised in the New Testament.

The interference of Divine Providence took place in a more sensible manner than under a more spiritual dispensation. The simplicity of the primitive ages is to be taken into account also.

Facts are recorded nakedly, and are to be looked at in their *consequences*.

Lot, after his incest, is heard of no more. Abraham and Isaac are exposed to shame. The falsehood of Rebecca and Jacob is visited in their sufferings. As to David's apparent sensuality, distinguish between indulged sensuality and the disposition.

The Rev. H. Budd—

Omnia munda mundis.

The Rev. J. Clayton—

With regard to the Canaanites, God dealt with them as the righteous governor of the world.

One precept seems to contradict another.

Moral-natural precepts result from the nature of God, and cannot be dispensed with : for example, that God is to be worshipped. Moral-positive precepts result from the will of God, and may be dispensed with : for example, that God is to be worshipped one day in seven. This distinction may serve to reconcile some seeming inconsistencies.

Scripture histories are never to be omitted in reading. Even the Scripture history of impure acts are related in so holy a manner as to excite no impure passions. Joseph and Potiphar's wife, compare it with Macgowan's and Mrs Rowe's relation of the same.

Look to the CONSEQUENCES of the bad conduct recorded. No intimation of the guilt of the sin is so impressive as the relation of the consequences. Dr Delany draws out such a relation of David's sufferings as to terrify. God seems to have furnished by design occasions of stumbling to evil men.

The Rev. W. Goode—

Consider the Scripture writers as speaking under divine direction, in cases where objections may seem to lie. Consider men as acting in a public capacity when their actions seem sometimes inconsistent with moral precepts. Actions are recorded, but not justified. Saints are left to fail in their distinguishing graces—Abraham in faith ; Noah and Lot, who are yet "righteous" men; meek Moses failed in irascibility ; David, the man after God's own heart, yet fell into sensuality ; Solomon the wisest, yet his crime is the most foolish. Samson is the most difficult character. Yet in most of the cases in which there is a difficulty, it is introduced by a notice that under the Spirit of God he was raised up as a judge. Rahab is praised. Samuel, in anointing David, seems to think he may tell only part of the truth.

The next meeting was immediately before the members dispersed for the autumn. A general conversation took place, of

which the following are some memoranda. A journey appears to
have been looked on as a far more serious affair than it is in these
days of railway travelling, though the hints given may still be
useful.

July 25, 1808.

WHAT IS THE BEST MODE OF IMPROVING A JOURNEY ?—Proposed by
the Rev. S. Crowther.

Disperse religious tracts.   Good tracts for the purpose are—" James
Covey," " Onesimus," " Cheapside Apprentice," " Charles Jones, "
"Shepherd of Salisbury Plain," " Vivian's Three Dialogues," "Serious
Considerations," " A Word from a Traveller," " A Word of Advice, "
" Short Sermons."

A journey should be considered as a serious affair, as not knowing
what may befall us, nor what occasions of usefulness may occur.

For imparting good, we must not neglect prayer for this end, watchfulness, courage, prudence.

We are not to consider a journey as a relaxation from all duty, but
as a means of varying duty, and strengthening us for the usual duties
of our station.

We get enlargement of mind by views of men and of nature.

We return content with the quiet repetition of the duties of our
station, from feeling the incapacity of constant variety to satisfy the
mind.

We learn to have our own business, as journeying through life, most
deeply impressed on our minds.

Let us cultivate a spiritual mind.   Always ready to do good.

———

On the re-assembling of the brethren, on October 3, 1808, the
following was the topic, WHAT USEFUL OBSERVATIONS HAVE THE
SEVERAL MEMBERS MADE DURING THE RECESS? We have no remarks.

———

October 17, 1808.

WHAT ARE THE EVIDENCES OF THE DIVINE INSPIRATION OF THE BOOK
OF CANTICLES ?—Proposed by the Rev. J. Pratt.

Mr Pratt—

1. Its admission into the canon.

It is generally admitted that the canon was closed by Ezra. If it were
a mere love-song, it could not have obtained a place among the Sacred
Books.   It formed a part, therefore, of the sacred volume, which, in
the time of Christ, was called THE SCRIPTURES, and THE ORACLES OF
GOD.

2. There was no question among the Jews on its canonical authority.

There have been controversies among them concerning Proverbs and

Ecclesiastes, but none concerning Canticles. "All the Scriptures are holy, but the Song of Songs is the Holy of Holies." (*Misnah, Tract Yadaim.*) The ancient Book Zohar asserts that Solomon composed it by the inspiration of the Holy Spirit. The Chaldee paraphrase has this title: "The Songs and Hymns which Solomon the prophet, King of Israel, uttered in the spirit of prophecy before the Lord."

3. It was admitted in all the translations and ancient versions of the Scriptures.

4. Perhaps it is not "expressly quoted" in the New Testament, but it derives great authority from the "coincidence of its general argument, and of particular sentiments, with many passages, in both the Old and New Testament." (*Scott.*) Take for example, Ps. xlv. Isa. liv. 5 ; lxi. 10 ; lxii. 4, 5. Hos. ii. 16–20. Matt. ix. 15 ; xx. 2 ; xxv. 1–11. John iii. 29. 2 Cor. xi. 2. Eph. v. 23–27. Rev. xix. 7–9 ; xxi. 2, 9 ; xxii. 17. Compare also—

Cant.　i. 4 with John vi. 44.	Cant.　vii.　1 with Isa. lii. 7 ; Eph. vi. 15.
,,　iv. 7 with Eph.　v. 27.	,,　viii. 11 with Isa. v. 1-7 ; Matt. xxi. 33, 43.
,,　v. 2 with Rev. iii. 20.	,,　viii. 14 with Rev. xxii. 20.

—*Scott.*

5. The passages usually considered most decisive of its not being a sacred allegory, are surpassed by Ezek. xvi. xxiii.

"The simplicity of the Eastern nations made some of the phrases much less shocking to them, than the delicacy, or perhaps the licentiousness, of these western parts make them to modest people among us." (*Doddridge.*) That it is a continual allegory is well argued by Lowth, Præl. xxx. xxxi.

Questions are—

1. How far, if it be divinely inspired, is it the duty of ministers to bring it forward ?

2. What is the most expedient way of doing this ?

"Who can read it with understanding, and not be transported from the world, from himself, and be any otherwhere save in heaven, before his time ? I would rather spend my time in admiration than apology. Surely, here is nothing that savours not of ecstasy and spiritual ravishment. Neither was there ever so high and passionate a speculation delivered by the Spirit of God to mankind ; which by how much more divine it is, by so much more difficult. It is well if these mysteries can be found out by searching. Two things make the Scripture hard—prophecies, allegories ; both are met in this ; but the latter so sensibly to the weakest eyes, that this whole pastoral marriage-song (for such it is) is no other than one allegory sweetly continued." (*Bp. Hall.*) Hall's is a very sound and sensible commentary.

The Rev. H. Foster—

I have preached from various independent texts in the Canticles. I once went through Ezekiel xvi., but dared not do it again.

The Rev. W. Goode—

So have I preached from it, but not of late years. One objection to preaching from it is, that it is so difficult to get at the right meaning.

The Rev. J. Clayton—

I have preached from it, but not of late years. It is a question whether edification is promoted by preaching on passages on which most differ in interpretation? There are texts in other parts of Scripture which I dare not preach from, though I do not therefore reject them.

The Rev. S. Crowther—

I never preached from the Book of Canticles; and have been disgusted with hearing Huntington.

There are some texts on which most preachers would be agreed, and on which we might preach without any inconvenience. I am inclined to preach from it occasionally from such passages, to remove any prejudice that might be supposed to exist in my mind, or to remove any prejudice against the book at large.

The Rev. H. G. Watkins—

It is wrong, in commenting on Scripture in order, to pass this book. I have preached occasionally from different passages of it.

The Rev. Mr Sheppard—

I have preached occasionally from it, but not at large.

The Rev. W. J. Abdy—

I have preached about four sermons from the Canticles. To obviate doubts, it might be right to preach occasionally from plain texts.

The few spiritually-minded people in our congregations, and the ridicule which the rest would throw on it, are damping considerations.

The Rev. H. Budd—

This is the only remaining one of the sacred songs said to have been composed by Solomon. It agrees in its allegory with the representations in other parts of Scripture; for example, Ps. xlv., lxxii., cx. It agrees with the believer's experience. It represents his joys and sorrows. There is no other book of a similar kind that can be interpreted so as to agree with the experience of a Christian.

It is improbable that it has any other than a spiritual sense. The opening of chapters iii. and v. is not applicable to Pharaoh's daughter, but is applicable allegorically to the coming of Christ in our nature, the abrogation of the moral dispensation, the calling of the Gentiles, the enlargement of the Church.

I never preached from it, but frequently introduce passages.

Its high-wrought language and images are generally objected to; but there are similar in other parts of Scripture.

The Rev. W. Goode—

Its having been admitted into the canon, and our Lord saying, *Search the Scriptures,* without exception to any part, gives it his sanction. If, therefore, it be a part of Scripture, it must be worthy of reverence, and must be of high and important use.

I have preached from the decisive and clear parts; and would from no other, for the same reason that I would decline preaching from other difficult parts of Scripture ; for I must understand what I bring forward.

On October 31, 1808, there was only a general conversation.

NOVEMBER 14, 1808.

WHAT ARE THE CHARACTERISTICS OF CHRISTIAN POLICY AS DISTINGUISHED FROM CARNAL ?—Proposed by the Rev. J. Clayton.

Mr Clayton—

Be wise as serpents, but harmless as doves.
The characteristics of Christian and carnal policy differ—
1. In the END proposed.
Self is the end of carnal policy, in interest, or distinction, or pleasure.   The glory of God the end of Christian policy.
2. In the RULE.   The Word of God is that of the Christian.
3. In the DEPENDENCE.   Carnal policy may pretend to call in God, but Christian policy will *really* depend on him.
4. By a wise application of particular truths to the Christian's advantage, but not so as to confirm any in error, Christian policy may be shewn, and will differ from carnal.   For example, St Paul dividing the council.
The advantages of Christian policy :—
1. It allays opposition.   *A fool uttereth all his mind ; but a wise man keepeth it in till afterward.*
2. It gives an opportunity of fairly retreating.
3. It may better discover to us the mind of others.

The Rev. Mr Simons, a visitor—

The sum-total of Christian policy consists in being as open and clear as daylight.
Keep back nothing of the truth.   Let the people be let into apartment after apartment in the temple of God.   The Jesuits in China denied that Christ was crucified, and were in the issue expelled from the country.

The Rev. J. Goode—

Prudence has been called "a rascally virtue ;" but the Scripture commends it ; and many men have lost themselves for want of it.
Carnal and Christian policy differ in the principle, the rule, and the end.   There is much cunning in carnal policy.

The Rev. B. Woodd—

Christian policy consists in hallowed motives, hallowed means, hallowed ends.
Ministers should adapt instruction to their subjects.   *I have many things to say unto you, but ye cannot bear them now.*

The Rev. S. Crowther—

The doctrine of expediency is a carnal policy. A carnal man would say, " Honesty is the best policy." But merely as *policy* it is carnal.

The Rev. H. G. Watkins—

A man may appear to act on carnal policy, when God sees he does not.

When a minister takes the cast of his preaching from his congregation, it is very likely to be carnal policy.

It is carnal policy when we bend to times and circumstances from wishing to be respected. Christian policy gains its ends by a union of habit and character.

The Rev. H. Budd—

It is easy to define, but difficult to apply. Casuists differ in the application. Bishop Hall allows a criminal to plead " not guilty."

There are many things common to carnal and Christian policy. In what cases may particular good give way to general, and general to particular !

Carnal policy is said to be " folly engendered on cunning."

The Rev. R. Lloyd—

Christian policy attaches more to the means than to the end ; for the man is not a Christian if his great end be not good. In respect of means, a vast difference exists between carnal and Christian policy. Lord Bacon says that a great man need not stoop to little means. Wickedness is narrow, and mean, and little in its views. There is a vast deal of irregularity and religious libertinism, as to means, in the Christian world.

NOVEMBER 28, 1808.

WHAT IS THE EXTENT OF THE DUTY OF VISITING THE SICK, AND THE BEST MODE OF CONDUCTING IT ?—Proposed by the Rev. J. Clayton.

Mr Clayton—

As to the EXTENT of the duty :

How far is it binding on a minister to visit his neighbourhood, as well as his congregation ?

A drop of oil of vitriol on a piece of nitre is a specific against contagion.

As to the MANNER :

One has felt a desire to do something *speedily ;* and perhaps, therefore, it has been done superficially.

It is requisite to have some previous information respecting the patients.

We should not be too ready to apply the promises.

The Rev. W. Goode—

As to the EXTENT :

To all in my parish. It is the duty of every Christian to visit the sick. I would, therefore, visit out of my parish, not as a minister, but as a Christian.

I would not administer the sacrament without the leave of the minister.

Bishop Hall thinks we are not called on to visit where contagion is.

As to the MANNER :

I would *preach* to them on sin and salvation.

The Rev. S. Crowther—

The EXTENT :

It would be remiss if we did not go to every sick parishioner, whether we are sent for or not. But if an ex-parishioner put up a paper for the prayers of the Church, I do not think myself bound to go.

If a person be suffering from a raging fever, I may be excused for not going ; but must be cautious of keeping back from every door where there is any infection.

The MANNER :

Ascertain the moral state and views of the patient. Scott on Repentance is one of the best books for awakening. We must not go disheartened with the idea of there being little probability of good, as this will dry up the feelings. Much good may be done on bystanders, when none on the patient.

Most sick persons wish comfort, but we must be careful not to administer comfort before they are prepared for it.

As to the frequency of visits : if the sickness be a chronic disorder, seldom ; if dangerous, daily.

The Rev. H. G. Watkins—

The EXTENT : I would rather go to irreligious than to religious persons, as being more urgent and important.

The MANNER : Conciliate, by talking of their illness. Preach a short sermon.

The Rev. Mr Sheppard—

I generally read a few verses. This furnishes matter for prayer.

The Rev. R. Lloyd—

Give the impression that you are come as a FRIEND and a BENEFACTOR. Sick people are apt to look on a minister with terror.

Impress upon them a sense of ingratitude to God, and rebellion against Him, if they are dark and blind. By vivacity of remark bearing on the main point, you may keep alive their attention.

The Rev. H. Budd—

The EXTENT of the duty is such, that I think I should scarcely consider anything as an intrusion. We are bound, as ministers of the Church of England, to private monition.

We should encourage every kind of intercourse that is innocent with our people, in order to facilitate access in sickness.

Frequently state in the pulpit how painful it would be to visit many, in their present state, on a death-bed.

As to MANNER : I have engaged attention by using and enlarging on the service for the visitation of the sick. A *direct* attack on the patient as a sinner might be repelled. But under the wing of our mother— "The Church has appointed this to be read"—they will listen with attention.

The Rev. J. Pratt—

The EXTENT :

The parish. The minister might send an address to every house, declaring his willingness to attend the sick when asked.

The MANNER :

Extract from the patient, by questions, his own views. I would always aim at impressing three points—SIN, THE SAVIOUR, the necessity of the HOLY SPIRIT'S assistance to make them feel sin and bring them to Christ.

Recommend them to read Psalm li. to open SIN, Isaiah liii. to display CHRIST, John iii. to shew the necessity of work of the SPIRIT.

Have in view the influence of what you say (1.) on the patient if he should *die;* (2.) if he should *recover;* (3.) on the bystanders.

The Rev. J. Goode—

Ecclesiasticus vii. 35, and James i. 27.

DECEMBER 12, 1808.

THE GROUND OF EXPECTING THE CONVERSION OF THE JEWS, AND THE MEANS BY WHICH IT MAY BE PROMOTED.—Proposed by the Rev. W. Fry.

Mr Fry—

That the Jews will at length be converted, may appear from their present dispersion and state, in which they are reserved for a signal display of the divine power.

It is a pleasing idea, that from their knowledge of languages they will be fit instruments of diffusing the Gospel.

The Scripture prophecies which point to their conversion are Hos. iii. 4, 5; Zech. viii. 8–23; there are fourteen or fifteen passages which speak strongly : Rom. xi. 15.

I think nothing will be done, upon a large scale, for the heathen, till God's ancient people are brought to the knowledge of the Gospel. And considering our obligations to them, we ought to rouse ourselves to help them.

There are difficulties doubtless.

They are more disposed to *hypocrisy* than the heathen.

They are circumscribed by their own people. No Jew is allowed to send his children to a Christian school.

The MEANS—

Provision should be made for supplying the temporal wants of the Jews, such as a House of Industry, or Workhouse. They should thus feel assured that, if turned out of their bread for the profession of Christianity, they will be provided for. A school also should be opened.

The mere effort to benefit the Jews must be highly acceptable in the sight of God.

If not now successful, it might be the ground of a future attempt, forty or fifty years hence, which might be successful.

At all events we seem highly remiss. Everybody acknowledges the wretched state of the Jews. They live in the midst of us, and we leave them without any effort of a general nature to enlighten them.

Not long after this date the LONDON SOCIETY FOR THE CONVERSION OF THE JEWS was established. Several papers on the subject will be found in the *Christian Observer* about this time. The conversion of the Jews has engaged a much larger share of attention of late years; the creation of the Jerusalem Bishopric and other events having very greatly promoted it.

DECEMBER 26, 1808.

WHAT ARE THE CHARACTERISTICS OF AN EVANGELICAL MINISTRY? AND WHAT CONDUCT OUGHT TO BE OBSERVED TOWARDS THOSE WHOSE MINISTRY IS OF AN APPARENTLY DIFFERENT DESCRIPTION?—Proposed by the Rev. J. Pratt.

Mr Pratt—

Distinguish between an evangelical ministry in the judgment of man and in the sight of God.

In the judgment of man, that is an evangelical ministry which combines truth with apparent piety. But in the sight of God, that only is such which combines truth with real piety.

Our question respects the ministry which *we* must account evangelical.

1. It must be the ministry of TRUTH—essential truth; the Scripture character of Jehovah; the guilt, pollution, and impotence of man; his acceptance only through the merits of Christ; renewal and sanctification by the Holy Spirit; the obligation of universal holiness.

Some chief points of essential truth are defined in the *Christian Observer*, vol. i. p. 10.

Salvation originates wholly in grace, applied through the instrumentality of that faith which is the gift of the Holy Ghost, and which brings the believer into a state of acceptance with God, by making him partaker of the merits of Christ, and prepares him for heaven by maturing him in love and obedience.

If these truths are unequivocally held and brought forward, so far there is an evangelical ministry.

There may be an undue proportion; obscurity in statement; hesitation in coming up to the full standard of orthodox expression; there may be subordinate errors.

But these things, though they detract from the perfection and the efficacy of the ministry, yet they do not deprive it of the character of evangelical, provided the essential truths be held and brought forward.

2. PIETY is of course essential.

3. ORDER must not be neglected.

The Episcopal is the primitive order. The Church of England is derived from this ; yet it is not essential to the Christian ministry. *Some* order is *necessary*.

The same rules should govern us as writers and preachers.

Rules :—

1. Candidly separate evangelical truth from the errors and infirmities of those who hold it.

2. Make no concessions which truth does not absolutely demand.

3. Insist on the paramount necessity of evangelical truth.

4. Insist on the comparative excellence and usefulness of evangelical men.

5. Avoid all offensive and party terms.

6. Make kind and candid allowances for misinformation, &c. Many would more clearly preach the Gospel, if we could annihilate the present body of evangelical ministers.

The Rev. S. Crowther—

As to DOCTRINE :—

We are rightly to divide the word of truth. Thus Quakers have not the character of evangelical ministers.

As to ORDER :—

This implies regularity and consistency with what the minister undertook when ordained. There is as much evangelical order in a consistent Dissenter as in a Churchman.

As to CONDUCT :—

If we be consistent, and preach consistently with the truth, we shall be generally avoided by those who differ. But where we meet, candour and humility should mark the conduct. We should not pride ourselves in names. Where ministers are of marked character and are ungodly, come out and be separate.

The Rev. Mr Sheppard—

If persons are disposed to listen, I would pay them every attention ; if not, seldom any good is done.

We must say in the *pulpit*, that whoever preaches contrary to essential truth misleads the people.

The Rev. H. G. Watkins—

Not a word should be spoken in the pulpit of disrespect or judgment concerning other ministers. I am preaching to *laymen*, who cannot correct evils in the Church, whatever they are. If preaching a Visitation Sermon, I would say, *Take heed to thyself, and to the doctrine.* But if to my congregation I preach against other ministers, I by implication declare myself a man peculiarly enlightened.

But great allowance is to be made for a man who preaches to

empty pews, while his neighbour's church is crowded. Such men are to be treated with great tenderness and humility. We should speak, however, of our fuller church with modesty, and rather assign it to causes independent of themselves personally.

The Rev. W. J. Abdy—

It is a duty for ourselves to form as exact views of truth as possible, and to enforce them with energy.

Looking round on others, we should exercise all the charity consistent with regard to truth.

Consider men's education, connexions, the kind of evangelical ministers with whom they have had intercourse.

Withdraw from bad men. Cultivate kind intercourse with all others. We owe them respect as members of the same establishment.

Be careful to do nothing which shall make us to appear desirous to make a gain of godliness.

The Rev. R. Lloyd—

Proclaim the glad tidings of salvation. Alarm the sinner. Lift the torch of Revelation to enlighten the people.

To *publish glad tidings of great joy,* is a brief character of an evangelical minister.

Consider the clergy of the Church of England in our relation to them. Many of the dignitaries of the Church are the great and learned defenders of many leading truths of Christianity. Besides, they purify society and raise the standard of morals.

The Rev. H. Budd—

I should like to hear a comparison between evangelical and orthodox ministers.

There is a set of orthodox men who want energy.

The Rev. H. Foster—

Conciliate every one as far as possible. Yet win them if you can ; but fall into no evil.

———

At the next meeting, January 9, 1809, country members and visitors were chosen for the new year.

The first subject, as appears to have been the case in previous years, was on an approaching fast. A series of Fast Days was kept throughout the period of the Peninsular War.

———

JANUARY 23, 1809.

HOW SHALL WE BEST IMPROVE THE APPROACHING FAST ?—Proposed by the Rev. H. G. Watkins.

The Rev. Mr Simons, a visitor—

I have pledged myself to my people always to preach on a fast day from—*Kiss the Son lest he be angry, and so ye perish from the way,* &c.

God seems to be pulling down antichrist. " Crush the wretch ! " was said by Voltaire, we may suppose with reference to the Christian religion as represented in the prevailing form, namely, in the Roman Church. She was crushed by the foot of God, as in a moment. *It is the vengeance of the Lord ; . . . as she hath done, do unto her.*

The Rev. J. Goode—

Proper texts are, *For all this his anger is not turned away, but his hand is stretched out still. Thou goest not forth with our armies, thou makest us to turn back from the enemy.* Also Ps. lx. 10 ; cviii.

The Rev. W. Fry—

We should consider not only how to *improve* the fast, but how to *prepare* the people to improve it.

For one of the national sins is the manner of observing the day. I have found, on questioning the people, that they have in general but little other regard to it than that of going to church, and that but once. I think it right, therefore, to insist on a consideration and public distinction in our families.

As to what respects we should carry it into private duties, *Let not our left hand know what our right hand doeth.* Make a distinction in the food. Improve the day in the family so as to call them to personal examination.

Inspire the people with an idea of the importance of a public expression of consent with the appointment. Set apart a portion for charity. Call attention to Ezek. ix. 4.

They thought scorn of that pleasant land, and gave no credence to his word. Indifference is the sin of this day. We should aim a blow at this sin. Christians are now conscientious rather than devout. There is but little of breathing after heaven, and of living above the world.

I wish to stir up my congregation, therefore, to rise above the world amidst all its distractions ; so that when death comes, they may not say it is a melancholy thing.

The Rev. Mr Sheppard—

Here is an excellent text :—*Seek ye the Lord, all ye meek of the earth, which have wrought his judgment ; seek righteousness, seek meekness ; it may be ye shall be hid in the day of the Lord's anger.* (Zeph. ii. 3.)

The Rev. S. Crowther—

What circumstances are peculiar to the approaching fast ? Increased danger. We must exercise caution against shewing dissatisfaction with the measures of government. *When mine arm is lifted up, they will not see; but they shall see.* This awakens to serious consideration, humiliation, and prayer.

The Rev. H. Foster—

On the Sunday before the fast, I would preach on the success of prayer. How God stopped the mouth of lions, &c. I would infuse hope that if duty is well regulated, success will follow.

The PLAN of a sermon from the text, *Wherefore glorify ye the Lord in the fires.* (Isa. xxiv. 15.)

I. Why afflictions are called fires?

1. As they give pain.
2. As their tendency is to destruction.
3. As they distinguish what is genuine from counterfeit.
4. As they purify and fit for use.

II. What is it to glorify God in the fires?

1. To see God in them.
2. To see and confess our sins as the cause : like the prodigal.
3. To speak well of God, and to cleave to God in them : like the Shunammite.
4. To prefer the fires to sinning: like Shadrach, Meshach, and Abed-nego.
5. To be earnest in prayer: like the Jews in Egypt.
6. To find out and forsake the sins which brought us into the fires : as the Jews in Babylon; Jonah in the whale's belly.
7. To act so as to win sinners to God: as Paul and Silas in prison; Christian at Vanity Fair.

III. Motives to glorify God in the fires.

1. He has gone through more severe fires for us. (Isa. lii.)
2. As he is the greatest and best of Beings.
3. As able to make bitterest things sweet, and hardest easy.
4. The great and eternal weight of glory for which afflictions prepare us.

The address should be—

1. To SINNERS, who never tremble at any fires.
2. To BRITONS, who tremble at the fires around.
3. To CHRISTIANS specially.

FEBRUARY 6, 1809.

IS THE SOUL GENERATED OR INFUSED?—Proposed by the Rev. W. Fry.

Mr Fry—

Some are puzzled that God should create pure souls to inhabit vile bodies. If the generation of souls were established, it would relieve the doctrine of original sin of most of its difficulties. It appears to consist with the analogy of God's works. Scripture is not opposed to it : *Adam begat a son in his* OWN LIKENESS, &c.

I mark sins in myself which are sins of the *mind,* independent of the *body.*

Flavel is the great opponent of the generation of the soul. His objections are as follows :—

Objection 1.—What is generated is *corruptible.* But then the body of Christ would have been corruptible. Also *spirit* may cease to be ; not being immortal in itself, but by the appointment of God.

Objection 2.—How can a soul be produced out of matter? But soul may produce soul.

In short, all his objections want proof. He uses several Scriptures in proof of his doctrine :—

Zech. xii. 1, *The Lord . . . which formeth the spirit of man within him.*

But this refers to the original formation of the spirit. And the same term is applied to the formation of the body, Ps. cxxxix. 15.

Eccl. xii. 7, *Then shall the dust return to the earth as it was; and the spirit shall return unto God who gave it.* This only implies that at death the two grand constituents of man's nature return to their first principles.

Heb. xii. 9, *The Father of spirits.* But Father here means only Creator. The Apostle is only making an antithesis between an earthly and heavenly Father. It is unlikely he should have any reference to a doctrine so far out of his way.

The USES of this doctrine, that the soul is generated :—

1. It extricates us from a perplexity, in which we can say and do nothing. There is a difficulty that the pure God should infuse spirit, that he should be the Father of the spirit generated in illicit connexion.

2. It is a useful consideration to parents. There is a kind of double corruption in children. Reigning and bosom corruptions running through families. This is over and above the common corruption of nature.

FEBRUARY 20, 1809.

WHAT IS THE MEANING OF THE SCRIPTURAL EXPRESSION, " THE PRESENCE OF GOD"? AND IN WHAT SENSE MAY CHRISTIANS USE IT, AS AN EXPRESSION OF GOOD-WILL TOWARD ONE ANOTHER?—Proposed by the Rev. B. Woodd.

Mr Woodd—

It is synonymous with, *Lift up the light of his countenance.* Exod. xxxiii. 14 is the first time where it is used.

The presence of God, in its highest state, is the perfection of heaven. It is the glory of Paradise. *Adam heard the voice of the Lord God walking in the garden.* It was symbolised by the Shechinah. It was realised in the manifestation of Christ in the flesh. The grand promise of Christ when he left the world was, *Lo I am with you alway, even unto the end of the world.*

Wherein His presence consists:—

1. IN COMMON TO ALL THE CHURCH.

The favour of God appears in reconciliation, God's approbation, protection (Job i. 9, 10), control over our hearts, giving life to graces, restraining evil, direction and guidance.

As we grow in years, we feel more the happiness of dependence. Especially with regard to children. Who can tell what God is doing? Pharaoh's daughter could have no conception that the child she saved would be the potent enemy of Egypt. Oliver Cromwell had taken his passage to America, when delayed by an embargo.

2. IN A LIVELY AND AFFECTING SENSE of the favour and guidance of God.

The light of God's countenance. *Oh, how great is thy goodness which thou hast laid up for them that fear thee. . . . Thou shalt hide them in the secret of thy presence.* Some think this may be open to enthusiasm.

But the Christian's wish is, for a lively sense of the favour and protection of his heavenly Father. The poor often have most of this enjoyment. *The secret of the Lord is with them that fear him.* It converts the trials of earth into anticipations of heaven.

In worship, how cold we are! His presence is the life of ordinances.

The desire of the presence of God is a test of our state. The believer has often special manifestations of this presence—in sickness and death.

There is no promise of this blessing but while we are walking with God in duty. There is no elevation of mind without corresponding corrections and suspensions. *The churches, . . . walking in the fear of the Lord and in the comfort of the Holy Ghost, were multiplied.* This is also recognised in the priestly benediction, Num. vi. 24, 25, 26.

The Rev. W. Goode—

The presence of God is the manifestation of the divine favour, and the conveying the sense of it to the heart.

The Rev. W. J. Abdy—

The Lord be with you and with thy spirit.

The Rev. Mr Sheppard—

The presence of God is not to be taken in the general sense of *Whither shall I flee from thy presence?* but it is used for God's *gracious* presence, His sanctifying presence.

The Rev. H. Foster—

It denotes—(1.) God's omnipresence. (2.) God's presence to comfort and direct. (3.) God's presence in heaven.

The Rev. J. Pratt—

There is also a dreadful presence of God as a consuming fire. 2 Thess. i. 9.

The Rev. W. Fry—

All enjoy a less degree of this presence than the Scriptures teach us to expect. What is the cause? The *great* are tempted to lukewarmness ; the *lower* to enthusiasm.

To divine worship, we should go with expectation.

The Rev. J. Goode—

Poverty of spirit is a better evidence of God's presence in general than exaltation.

The Rev. J. Clayton—

There is a presence of God which is inevitable. Also, a presence which is symbolical, in institutions. In this way he dwelt with the Jews.

The presence of God is the mode of operation peculiar to our dispensation.

There is a presence on a philosopher, a moralist; but there is a peculiar evangelical presence dispensed in Jesus Christ.

Impediments to this presence are—neglect of Christ in his offices and work, and of the Holy Spirit in his operations.

Helps to enjoy this presence are—attention to Christ and the Spirit, and to our hearts. Keep pure the habitation.

MARCH 6, 1809.

WHAT ARE THE RULES AND LIMITATIONS OF A CHRISTIAN'S DUTY TO ESTEEM OTHERS BETTER THAN HIMSELF?—Proposed by the Rev. J. Pratt.

Mr Pratt—

I. GENERAL REMARKS on the duty.

1. It is peculiar to Christianity. It is the glory of Christianity. It is unknown to heathen. Revenge, ambition, high thoughts of self, was with them a virtue.

2. It is frequently inculcated, and in various forms and connexions : Phil. ii. 3, *Let nothing be done through strife or vainglory; but in lowliness of mind, let each esteem others better than themselves.* Rom. xii. 10, *Be kindly affectioned one to another with brotherly love; in honour preferring one another.* Gal. v. 26, *Let us not be desirous of vainglory, provoking one another, envying one another.* 1 Pet. v. 5, *Likewise, ye younger, submit yourselves unto the elder. Yea, all of you be subject one to another, and be clothed with humility.* Eph. v. 21, *Submitting yourselves one to another in the fear of God.* See also Matt. xviii. 1–4, and Luke xiv. 7–11.

3. Examples—Abram and Lot (Gen. xiii. 8, 9); St Paul (1 Cor. xv. 9); also, Matt. xx. 20-28, and Phil. i. 15, &c.

4. It is a difficult duty.

5. It is grounded on the corruption and obligations of man.

II. RULES and LIMITATIONS.

1. So to esteem others as not to be indifferent to good report.

2. So as not to pervert the judgment concerning good and evil.

3. So as not to undervalue gifts or station. For example, when false apostles constrained St Paul to magnify his office, he asserts that he *was not a whit behind the very chiefest apostles;* and repeats it—*For in nothing am I behind the very chiefest apostles,* (2 Cor. xi. 5 ; xii. 11); though even then the spirit of the great Christian breaks out—*Though I be nothing,* &c.; and he glories not in his PERSON, but acknowledges his infirmities (ver. 5, 6).

4. To have humble views of our graces, and candid judgment of the state and attainments of others. These will not call us to trench on either of the preceding limitations. But they suppose a Christian conscious of more evil in himself than he can possibly know of that of any other man. He is afraid, therefore, of *thinking himself something when he is nothing.* Of the *vilest* we may say, " Without grace I should have been that man." " There goes John Bradford, but for the grace

of God ! " is the well-known exclamation of that reformer, on seeing a criminal led to execution. " Nay, *he* probably has not resisted light and strivings as I *have* done," we may add.

We may well feel that there are defects in us which are not in a brother, and may therefore esteem him better than ourselves. He may not be better in truth, but my heart is deceitful. I am bound to confess my own faults, and to cover his ; and it is my duty to prefer him who may have some hidden good, which I have not.

As to gifts, I may feel perhaps that I cannot deny them in myself ; but I feel so much inferior in the use of them, that I may well esteem others better than myself.

We can be full of ascriptions of praise to God, yet with much egotism. One symptom of this is, when we are not interested in the good done by others. It is all " I," " me," or " mine," &c., &c.

The Rev. J. Goode—

Even in seeking the things of Christ we may seek our own. *The heart is deceitful above all things.*

Judge according to truth. Yet we are even then in danger.

MARCH 20, 1809.

WHAT IS THE MEANING OF THE PASSAGE, " WISDOM IS JUSTIFIED OF ALL HER CHILDREN " ? (Matt. xi. 19 ; Luke vii. 35.)—Proposed by the Rev. B. Woodd—

Mr Woodd—

One sense : Christ was justified of the Jews, when they were condemned of their own consciences.

Another sense : The doctrine of the Gospel, though reviled, yet loses nothing of its excellence ; but by her natural children is vindicated and justified.

Calvin's is a third. Cruden says, some take the meaning to be this : —" I who am the Wisdom of God, am justified by you who truly believe on me. You know I am no glutton, no wine-bibber, no friend of publicans and sinners." Others, he says, render it thus :—" Religion, in all the branches and duties thereof, . . . is owned and acknowledged to be full of wisdom ; and is vindicated from . . . cavils . . . by those who have devoted themselves to its study and practice."

However the world may reproach the doctrine of Christ, yet Christians will acknowledge its harmony.

The Rev. W. Goode—

All who are taught of the Spirit of God, and are therefore the children of Wisdom, will approve of all God's ways and will.

The Rev. J. Pratt—

The context seems to shew the meaning to be, that the dispensations of God are justified by the children of God.

APRIL 17, 1809.

HOW SHALL WE DISTINGUISH BETWEEN A CONSCIOUSNESS OF GRACE AND A SPIRIT OF SELF-RIGHTEOUSNESS ?—Proposed by the Rev. B. Woodd.

Mr Woodd—

A man may assert his integrity. See the case of Samuel, 1 Sam. xii. 1–5. Of Hezekiah, 2 Kings xx. 3. Of Nehemiah, Neh. v. 15, 19. Of David, Ps. cxxxi. Of St Paul, Acts xx. 33; 2 Cor. i. 12; 1 Thess. ii. 10, 11, 12; 2 Tim. iv. 7.

This is not the language of boasting, as we find these very men confessing their frailties and sins. A real Christian, therefore, may maintain his integrity before God and man, and yet feel abased for his sins.

A distinguishing characteristic is to have a talent to do good, a will, and an opportunity.

The Rev. W. Fry—

It is a dangerous thing when religion begins in the head rather than in the heart. It is better to find our need of doctrines to meet the wants of the soul, rather than first to take up notions to which we have not corresponding feelings. Such characters often take up two or three leading notions, and square everything to them. The doctrines not growing out of experience are crudely applied.

1. HUMILITY is a principal distinction between a consciousness of grace, and a spirit of self-righteousness.

2. TENDERNESS AND MEEKNESS of spirit is another distinction, as opposed to a harsh spirit and a heady mind.

3. SPIRITUALITY is a characteristic of grace ; vehemence and activity, that of self-righteousness.

4. Ascribing everything to GRACE is another.

The Rev. W. Goode—

If it be of grace, there is no impropriety in a consciousness of it : there is no thankfulness to God without this consciousness.

In the instances produced from Scripture, most of the cases arose from accusations being brought against the persons.

1. An acknowledgment of the origin, as from God, is a characteristic of grace.

2. A renunciation of dependence before God is another.

The Rev. J. Crowther—

A consciousness of grace is attended with a dread of sin, but self-righteousness leads to fearlessness.

The Rev. H. G. Watkins—

A self-righteous spirit undervalues the attainments of others.

The Rev. Mr Sheppard—

1. Self-righteousness leads us to look at the act; grace at the motive.

2. Grace leads us to a sense of a change ; self-righteousness knows it not.

3. Grace will bear examination ; self-righteousness shrinks from it.

4. Grace leads us to ascribe all to God ; self-righteousness may say, "God, I thank thee," but *mean* it not.

The Rev. H. Budd—

Religion is a matter of feeling, therefore we must be conscious of it ; and a consciousness of grace will lead to a fear of self-righteousness.

A settled purpose to repress vanity will accompany grace, and also to repress pride of talent and self under every guise.

The Rev. J. Pratt—

Consider the question rather as respecting grace and self-righteousness in the *same* man, than in different men. The self-righteous man's mind is gross in its workings ; the self-righteousness of the Christian's mind is full of subtlety.

A principal characteristic is, unwillingness to speak even of our own consciousness of grace. *Let not thy left hand know what thy right hand doeth.*

Another characteristic is, the victory to which every discovery of self-righteousness leads.

The Rev. Mr Simons—

As to RULE. The self-righteous man will stop short of the whole system of doctrine : the man of grace embraces the whole. Grace leads a man to groan after full holiness : the self-righteous man is scanty in his measure.

As to PRINCIPLE. A gracious man looks to the glory of God : the self righteous man to the fear of hell and hope of heaven.

As to SPIRIT. The gracious man's best work leads him to Christ : self-righteousness drives him from Christ. Grace is contrite : self-righteousness is never so.

The Rev. J. Clayton—

Some of the Scriptures alleged are brought forward as arguments with God for future mercies.

The question is scarcely accurate in expression ; because consciousness of grace is the highest kind of evidence, and is of itself clearly distinguished from self-righteousness.

Points of difference :—

1. Grace always gives affectionate honour to Christ. Self-righteousness terminates in self-complacency.

2. Grace gives all due honour to the Holy Ghost.

3. Grace is not impatient to divulge good deeds.

4. Grace gives pity and compassion to sinners, and makes allowances for defects : not so self-righteousness.

5. Grace reflects on the alloys of what we hear commended.

6. Grace is satisfied that Christ should be magnified in troubles. Thus Paul, *I will glory in my infirmities, that the power of Christ may rest upon me.*

MAY 1, 1809.

How far is it Prudent and Safe for a Minister to Accommodate Himself to the Taste of his Hearers?—Proposed by the Rev. H. Foster.

Mr Foster—

There is a prudent and proper accommodation. But it is dangerous to go far.

There was something of this in our Lord, in directing his disciples to preach to the lost sheep of the house of Israel and not to the Gentiles; perhaps, that the prejudices of the Jews might not be stirred up. So in the Apostles, in first limiting their preaching to the Jews, that the Jews might hear without prejudice.

In introducing the gospel into a new place, we should preach first on points acknowledged, and lay the foundation on which to build other things. One would begin by proving the being of God. Another would preach Christ as fully at first as ever. The truth may lie between them.

The Rev. J. Pratt—

Accommodation may be required to—(1.) ignorance, (2.) prejudice, (3.) ill-will, (4.) error, (5.) fastidiousness.

Accommodation may be made—(1.) In manner. Make here entire accommodation in all indifferent matters—writing or not—long or short—so as to win your hearers. (2.) In matter; but here sacrifice no truth.

On May 15, 1809, a conversation took place on the duty and manner of addressing sinners, a subject proposed by Mr Pratt.

MAY 29, 1809.

What is the Nature of the Change which takes place in Regeneration, according to the Scripture Account? And what is the most Proper Mode of Stating it in Public?—Proposed by the Rev. H. Budd.

Mr Budd—

If faculty means talent and natural power, then Regeneration does not communicate it. If faculty means ability, then Regeneration may be said to communicate it. By ability, I understand new perceptions, new principles, new tempers.

For example, love, before regeneration, is directed to *sin;* after regeneration, is directed to *holiness.*

Regeneration communicates a new *subject* to work upon—a new *object* to work for.

As to the proper mode of stating the matter in public, state the whole truth, as free from metaphysical distinctions as may be, and applied to individual cases.

The Rev. J. Venn—

Faith and knowledge are sufficient for duty.   When we go beyond this, we are involved in inextricable difficulties.

We know not how the soul acts on the body.   Much less how the Divine Spirit acts on our spirit.   We can tell the *effects*, and these are clear in Scripture.

The Holy Spirit is the author of all good.   He enlightens the mind, sanctifies the heart.   But the precise mode of his operation is not to be understood.

I should hesitate to say that he merely directs the faculties to new objects.   For sometimes appearances are infinitely beyond this; there is a raising of the faculties themselves.

In our Lord's miracles he does not appear to communicate new powers.   He restored faculties which were lost.   In regeneration, then, there may be no communication of new faculties; but a restoration of faculties perverted by sin and the fall.   The objects of our hope, and love, and joy are different after regeneration; but those passions existed before.

We may dwell on EFFECTS.   Effects are manifest.

It is remarkable how little the Scripture writers talk as metaphysicians: they never talk as philosophers among the heathen.   They state things plainly.   *If any man be in Christ, he is a new creature.*   They tell us we must look to Christ for strength and ability.   I would not, therefore, pronounce positively as to the *mode*.

The Rev. H. Foster—

In regeneration the Holy Spirit directs the mind to new objects, and strengthens the mind to look at the objects; and both together form the new life.

The Rev. J. Pratt—

Strong figures in Scripture arose from the state of the heathen world.   They are not in the *same degree* applicable to Christian congregations.   Yet they must be allowed to have their full force, as implying a mighty change.   We must distinguish between the state of persons *now* and *then*.

The effects of regeneration are less discoverable in the understanding than in the will and affections.   A new taste, a new world, new feelings, a new hope is given.

Regeneration is not to be known but by its ISSUE.   There is every degree of approximation towards it in unregenerate men, but not the thing itself.

We must appeal to the state, the feelings, the effects, in calling attention to it.

The Rev. J. Goode—

Regeneration is passing from death to life.   Sanctification is passing from glory to glory.

We must be short in explaining the nature of regeneration in public ; but must call the people principally to regard its effects.

The Rev. B. Woodd—

REGENERATION is the existence of the child. CONVERSION is the bringing of the child forth. SANCTIFICATION is the education, growth, and maturing of the child to manhood.

Self - will and selfishness are the predominant motives of the unregenerated man. But in regeneration all is changed. The UNDERSTANDING receives TRUTH as its object ; the WILL embraces GOODNESS ; the AFFECTIONS are fixed on GOD AND HIS GLORY.

The Rev. W. Fry—

We are agreed as to the author of regeneration ; but shew our ignorance of the mode.

I have generally considered regeneration as influencing chiefly the understanding ; and that, according to the state of the understanding, so is each of the other faculties. Scripture speaks much of turning us out of *darkness* into *marvellous light*. When we see truth in its glory, the will embraces and the affections follow. The darkness of the understanding casts a veil on objects. The understanding is an organ of sight, but the Spirit gives light. The Spirit affords the understanding a medium of sight. The affections follow of course. *The natural man receiveth not the things of the Spirit of God ; for they are foolishness unto him, neither can he know them, because they are spiritually discerned.*

This subject needs to be more frequently impressed on our people.

1. Lay not too much stress on feelings and principles.

2. So urge it as not to distress many serious persons in whom the change may be gradual and imperceptible.

3. So as never to supersede the necessary use of means.

As tests, ask—

1. Can you say you have prevailing power over besetting sin ?

2. How do you feel and act under declensions ?

3. In what way do you receive counsel and reproof ?

4. Consider the effects of regeneration—viz., poverty of spirit, love, humbleness of mind.

The Rev. S. Crowther—

Insist on the necessity of regeneration : *Except a man be born again, he cannot see the kingdom of God.*

In such texts as, *Ye were dead in trespasses and sins*, explain how the language applies to heathens, and then how to professed Christians. This anticipates objections.

[Mr Pratt replied to Mr Fry, that his reducing the influence to that on the understanding made the will inevitably to follow the last conclusion of the understanding. This would take away the responsibility of man. Whereas, *Ye* WILL NOT *come unto me that ye may have life*, is the language of our Saviour. *God worketh with us* TO WILL *and to do.*]

Fry, in representing the understanding as discerning the loveliness of the object, only describes *how* the will is operated on.

JUNE 12, 1809.

WHAT ARE THE DISTINCTIONS BETWEEN GODLY SORROW AND THE SORROW OF THE WORLD ?—Proposed by the Rev. J. Pratt.

Mr Pratt—

This is a question of importance to the minister. It involves the right method of dealing with the afflicted. There are few subjects which require nicer discrimination.

Consider the sorrow of the world and godly sorrow—

1. As to their CAUSES.

There is not so much difference to be discovered herein as in their effects. The causes are—disappointment; bereavements; shame; punishment; conviction of sin.

The most unequivocal cause of godly sorrow is apprehension of the mercy of God in Christ.

2. As to their SYMPTOMS.

Here also there is much similarity between godly sorrow and worldly sorrow. They are distaste with the world; fear of wrath; sense of sin and weakness.

The most unequivocal are, when we feel sin an offence against a holy and gracious God. Thus David, *I have sinned against the Lord.* (2 Sam. xii. 13.) *Against thee, thee only, have I sinned.* (Ps. li. 4.) *The publican would not so much as lift up his eyes unto heaven, but smote upon his breast, saying, God be merciful to me a sinner.* So also Ephraim. (Jer. xxxi. 18, 19, 20.)

3. As to the EFFECTS.

Here, principally, these two kinds of sorrow are to be distinguished. Worldly sorrow tends to despair, hardens, "promotes spiritual death, prepares for eternal death, and even hastens natural death." (See Brown.) Thus Judas and Ahithophel.

Godly sorrow works a change of *mind, heart,* and *life.* It puts a man on serious and persevering endeavours. See 2 Cor. vii. 11, *Ye sorrowed after a godly sort, what carefulness it wrought in you, yea, what clearing of yourselves, yea, what indignation, yea, what fear, yea, what vehement desire, yea, what zeal, yea, what revenge !* It sends a man into retirement : for example, Peter.

There are some fine passages on this subject in *Bishop Hall,* vol. vii. pp. 156, 421, 422.

The Rev. J. Goode—

Sorrow which arises from worldly troubles, and that sorrow which a worldly man has for his sins, is the sorrow of the world.

This sorrow worketh death, because it leads men from God, rather than to him. It causes men to entertain hard thoughts of God. It puts men on self-righteous endeavours rather than genuine mourning. A favourable turn in worldly circumstances relieves such men.

Godly sorrow leads to an open and ingenuous confession of sin. It will lead us to justify God. It springs from faith in Christ, a view of the atonement. The more we see of HIM, the deeper is our mourning.

They shall look on him whom they pierced. It will be attended with a turning from sin, and a bringing forth fruits of repentance.

The Rev. S. Crowther—

Worldly sorrow arises almost invariably from apprehension of punishment. It is not accompanied with a sense of sin as against a just and holy God.

In godly sorrow, a sinner is grieved and humbled because God is offended ; his cause injured ; his own soul violated.

The Rev. Mr Storry, a visitor—

The most backward to promise reform and make resolutions are generally the most to be trusted. The loudest outcries are generally to be feared and distrusted.

The Rev. W. J. Abdy—

Sorrow is so little to be depended on as to the cause and symptoms, that we must wait to see the effects. And this not in the entrance of profession, but in perseverance.

A question struck me, whether there might not be much of godly sorrow wrought in cases where full and clear views of Christ are not held forth. I grant that views of him will deepen godly sorrow. It will ripen wonderfully under clearer apprehensions of him.

Mr Pratt said that he thought that a preparatory work might be thus carried on ; but not the full exercise of godly sorrow.

The Rev. Mr Sheppard—

Remember Cain, *My punishment is greater than I can bear.* Herod heard of John the Baptist, yet could not give up Herodias. Felix trembled. Hence worldly sorrow arises from fear of punishment, more than from sense of sin; it consists with allowed sin, and is transient. Godly sorrow is deep and lasting.

Mr Abdy quoted the following from Bishop Thomas Wilson :— " More men are ruined by their repentance than by their sins."

The Rev. H. Foster—

Worldly sorrow is like the dog that turns to his vomit again. Man gets ease, and then returns to his iniquity. And thus his repentance helps him to sin on.

Godly sorrow arises from views of Christ and our interest in him. And the more we view him, the more deep will be our sorrow.

Godly sorrow reaches to all sins, but worldly sorrow will part with some sins to hold others.

Godly sorrow will not drive a man to get rid of itself at any rate, but worldly sorrow wishes ease anyhow.

JUNE 26, 1809.

WHAT IS THE BEST METHOD OF STUDYING THE EPISTOLARY WRITINGS, AS TO THEIR GENERAL USE AND APPLICATION ?—Proposed by the Rev. H. G. Watkins.

Mr Watkins—

Like a sovereign, Christ touched on the topics of his kingdom, but left it to his servants to enter into details.

Thus on Predestination : the germ is found in, *No man can come unto me, except the Father . . . draw him.*

Socinians and others have fewer difficulties in the Gospels than in the Epistles, and therefore prefer them.

A subsequent dispensation was evidently intended by Christ. *I have yet many things to say unto you, but ye cannot bear them now; howbeit when he, the Spirit of truth, is come, he will guide you unto all truth.— It is expedient for you that I go away ; for if I go not away, the Comforter will not come unto you.*

In the USE of them, we must study the circumstances and objects of each Epistle.

The Rev. Dr Fearon, a visitor—

The proud heart is unwilling to receive the full blaze of the Epistles. The great difficulty is to get the heart brought into a right frame.

The Epistles are generally addressed to certain characters.

The Rev. H. Foster—

If you preach holiness as Scripture does, the Pharisee will hate your preaching. Preach a formal holiness, and he will be pleased.

The whole mind is enmity against godliness, whether doctrine or practice.

Christ could not enlarge on many things, because they had not taken place ; but he hinted at them.

The Rev. J. Pratt—

Scripture is constructed with wondrous wisdom. The Old Testament abounds in illustration ; the New Testament in truth ; the Gospels are adapted to seize the mind ; the Epistles to lead on the mind.

The Epistles were written early ; the Gospel of St John last.

In the Epistle to the Hebrews, the Apostle tells us that the great salvation was begun to be spoken by the Lord.

But in the nature of things, it could not be expected that our Lord could fully disclose the Gospel scheme. He was in humiliation. He was to die for sinners, to rise, to ascend, to give the Spirit.

The Rev. J. Goode—

Col. iv. 16, implies that the Epistles are of general use among the Churches.

The Epistles are addressed to persons in communion together, as members of a Christian Church.

The Rev. B. Woodd—

I have been lately struck with the arrangement of the Scriptures in our service. The Psalms shew the experience of the servants of God : the First Lesson, God's dispensation to his servants of old ; the Second Morning Lesson and Gospel, the life of Christ ; the Epistle and Second Evening Lesson, the spirit and temper of the servants of God.

The Epistles may be taken as a general model. In this view notice in them, that—

1. The deep points are not on the whole brought much forward.

2. A frequent reference is made to the glory and love of the Redeemer.

3. A frequent reference to the work of the Holy Spirit.

4. There is a large statement of practical duties. This occupies, on the whole, about one-third.

On the next occasion, a general conversation took place on the following topic:—How FAR IS IT EXPEDIENT TO ABSTAIN FROM THE USE OF TERMS, INDIFFERENT IN THEMSELVES, IN ACCOMMODATION TO THE PREJUDICES OF THE TIMES ?

JULY 24, 1809.

THE NATURE AND EXTENT OF SANCTIFICATION?—Proposed by the Rev. J. Goode.

Mr J. Goode—

Mr Newton speaks of sanctification as consisting chiefly in abasing views of self, and admiring views of Jesus as a complete Saviour. He says others *will* follow.

But we ought to inquire whether they *do* follow. Take not this for granted. Speak with the Bible.

He says, too, that the holiness of Angels and of Christians is not only different in degree, but in nature : angels having never sinned, nor tasted of redeeming love. I cannot agree to this.

See the definition of Sanctification in the Assembly's Catechism.

The Rev. J. Pratt—

There are justification divines, sanctification divines, and justification and sanctification divines.

This meeting resolved itself into one of general conversation ; and the members adjourned till October.

OCTOBER 2, 1809.

WHAT RULES MAY BE LAID DOWN FOR THE OBSERVATION OF THE
APOSTLE'S INJUNCTION, "BE INSTANT IN SEASON AND OUT OF SEASON"?—
Proposed by the Rev. J. Pratt.

Mr Pratt—

This text chiefly refers to preaching, but is applicable as a general
principle to all Christian duties.

Be instant—earnest, diligent, persevering.

In season—

1. Embrace occasions of duty. For example, 1 Tim. v. 20 ; Titus
i. 9, 11, 13 ; Acts xvi. 13.

2. Seize opportunities—the *mollia tempora fandi. A word fitly
spoken is like apples of gold in pictures of silver.— Warning every man and
teaching every man in all wisdom.*

Out of season. For example, Acts xx. 18, 21, 27, 31. Christ and
the Samaritan woman : also Paul and the jailor.

The Rev. D. Wilson—

Much stress is laid on being "*instant:* " it is not the seasons so
much as being instant in them ; to have the heart wholly engaged.
In preaching, in preparing, after preaching—to enter into the spirit of
the work.

Merchants are always in frame for their pursuits. If called from
dinner, or any occupation, it's all well. *Out of the abundance of the
heart the mouth speaketh,* and the feelings prompt.

John the Baptist, Christ, St Paul, are eminent illustrations.

We should be instant in prayer. A man may have an interest in
all the good schemes throughout the world by being INSTANT IN
PRAYER.

After this meeting, the names of the several speakers are frequently not distinguished in the notes. Mr Pratt was moreover so
occupied in his work at the Church Missionary House, that he
generally left before the discussions were over ; which will
account for the increasing brevity of the remarks as recorded by
him.

OCTOBER 16, 1809.

HOW SHALL WE IMPROVE THE APPROACHING FIFTIETH ANNIVERSARY
OF THE KING'S ACCESSION ?—Proposed by the Rev. J. Clayton.

His Majesty's adherence to the principles which seated him on the
throne is a matter of great thankfulness. It is said, that the king, on
his accession, charged those who were to preach before him, that they
should forbear all flattering speeches, and deliver their Great Master's
message with the spirit, force, and freedom of the Gospel.

Q

Let us improve the subject as patriots and Christian ministers. Our congregations should understand our principles on government matters. In common, it is unsuitable to say a word on political subjects. But now we are called on, especially under the circumstances of the times, to lay open our attachment to government.

Point out what might have been the probable consequences had it pleased God to remove the king at any former period of his reign. Toleration to all Christian denominations is a blessing.

Suitable texts are—*Because the Lord loved you . . . hath the Lord brought you out with a mighty hand? By me kings reign and princes decree justice. Render unto Cesar the things that are Cesar's, and unto God the things that are God's.* Also Ps. lxi. 6, 7, 8, *Thou wilt prolong the king's life,* &c. *What mean ye by this service?*

Read Warburton's anecdotes of the king in his letters, quoted in the last *Christian Observer.*

The king's decided opposition to the Colonial Assemblies' schemes against missionary exertions, is admirable.

His conduct may be well contrasted with the temptations which surround him.

The king is not to be made responsible for the evils which the course of Providence has brought on.

Touch lightly on topics on which wise and good men may consistently differ : for example, Catholic emancipation. So speak as not to cast reflections on the heir-apparent.

Decry the incendiary spirit which would impute the weight of taxes, the high price of provisions, &c., to the king.

Waithman's scandalous speeches in the Common Council on the Jubilee, will supply many hints for topics to be by *implication* refuted. There is a peculiar call at this season to lay down sound principles of obedience.

Remember the king's conduct on the Duke of York's affair.

The king has a serious and solemn regard to God's authority, and of his own subjection to Him.

The Court of St James's is the purest in Europe. No person of suspected character is noticed by the king and queen. As a father, husband, &c., his conduct is exemplary.

Improvements in temporal things should not be touched on any further than they are owing personally to the king, any more than the evils.

The state of the administration of justice is a blessing.

The king's first speech in the Annual Register for 1760 is striking, as stating his principles—to which he has adhered.

The king's moral and intellectual character, and the long continuance of his reign, during the most convulsed period of the civilised world, is a special mark of Divine forbearance towards this nation, and the special means whereby it has pleased God to preserve this nation.

Make allusion to the Christian Jubilee, by way of evangelising the occasion. Also to the king's public acknowledgment of God on his recovery, and after the victories.

Improve the celebration.   Our king must die; the Great King liveth for ever.   Our king is imperfect at best; the Great King is infinite in all His attributes.

In respect to Infidelity, and Popery, and Toleration—the king has been uninfected by the first, opposed to the second, and a supporter of the third.

Henry III., Edward III., George III., reigned upwards of fifty years.

Compare in the last Literary Panorama, Sir Isaac Newton's estimate of different kings' reigns.

October 30, 1809.

What Influence have our Sinful Passions one on the other, and what Use can be made of such Influence?—Proposed by the Rev. H. Foster.

Consider every passion in the class of sinful which is not governed and directed by right principles.   In this view we may consider God as, in a great degree, governing the world of sinful men, by causing one affection of the mind to counteract another.

Christian ministers can make no use of one passion to counteract another, simply considered, but must ever inculcate a supreme regard to the glory of God.

Many preachers urge to benevolence by vanity, but the Christian minister must do it by a grateful regard to God.

Self, in one shape or other, is the grand object of human actions. Pride, fear, and self-love actuate men.   If the actions of men which render society tolerable were analysed, it would be found to have no virtue whatever.

We may act on fear, and all the *natural* passions, though not on the *sinful.*   But in doing this we should aim at leading man to seek the glory of God.

Shame may be worked on for the good of society.

It is not right in Christian ministers to press the *means* or *grandeur* of a thing, but in subordination to higher views.

Man's heart is occupied by a legion, but it is a kingdom divided against itself, so that the world is saved from becoming a howling wilderness.   Thus covetousness against indolence.   *Humility* may be learned from this view of man.   Want of gracious motive is sinful in a servant of God.   Watchfulness is inculcated by this view of man. Heaven is endeared to us thereby.

The counteraction of the passions, one on the other, may often, even in a Christian, restrain from sin, when higher motives do not avail. "What would the Church say?"   "What the world?"   Grace may be in exercise in stirring us up to counteract sin by motives inferior, though not in themselves sinful.

NOVEMBER 13, 1809.

WHAT RULES CAN BE LAID DOWN FOR ASCERTAINING THE INTERFERENCE OF A SPECIAL PROVIDENCE ?—Proposed by the Rev. J. Pratt.

Mr Pratt's remarks are alone recorded.

What is the right notion of a SPECIAL PROVIDENCE ?

By a GENERAL PROVIDENCE I understand the government of the world by that influence of second causes which God has connected with them. That is, when all creatures act according to the appointed law of their nature ; *e. g.*, that fire should burn, water flow, lions devour their prey.

By SPECIAL PROVIDENCE I understand an effect produced by the appointment of God.

(1.) Contrary to natural causes : for example, when the three children escape the fire ; when Jordan divides ; when Daniel is left unhurt by the lions.

(2.) Above natural causes.

(3.) By the extraordinary combination of natural causes.

General and special providences have something in common.

Whether second causes are left to produce their usual effects, or effects are produced contrary to or beyond these second causes, yet all *good* is from the ordinary and concurring will of God ; and all *evil* from His permissive will ; and everything, whether good or evil, is from His overruling will, guiding it to His own ends. See Hopkins, iv. 235.

The special providence of God is often not to be distinguished from the general. In His infinite wisdom He seems to produce the far greater part of events according to general laws. And these laws extend to the minutest objects. " Not a dust," says Bishop Hopkins, " flies in a beaten road, but God raises it, conducts its uncertain motion, and by His particular care conveys it to the certain place which He had before appointed for it, nor shall the most fierce and tempestuous wind hurry it any further."—Vol. iv. 234. Every hair is numbered. Every sparrow is known.

Many acts of Providence may appear special to us which really take place in the common course of general providence.

And this leads to the RULES.

1. Caution.—Gratitude may seem an excuse for a readiness to interpret providences as specially in our favour. But if rightly considered, we owe as much gratitude for the working of the usual course of things into our interests, as for the turning aside that course. For all is of God, and second causes have no influence but by his perpetual energy in and by them.

Besides, we should be aware how much the idea of special providences in our favour or against our interests may spring from, and in its turn foster, bad passions ; as pride, party-spirit, revenge.

2. Sometimes events take place manifestly contrary to or above the course of nature. See Flavel. The Scriptures are full of such events. They should be admitted now with the most rigid suspicion.

Sometimes natural causes unite and associate in a strange and wonderful manner. The history of Joseph shews twelve remarkable steps of providence. In the deliverance from the plot of Haman, seven acts of providence wonderfully concurred. See Flavel again.

We are not to infer a special providence merely from its subserving or opposing our wishes. Protestants are too ready to mark the judgments of God on Popish persecutors ; Presbyterians on Prelates, &c. See Eccl. ix. 1, 2.

3. We are not to act because a special providence seems to ascertain our line of duty, when it runs contrary to the Word.

4. It is never to be admitted but when its tendency is to *sanctify.*

EVENTS must be waited for in order to ascertain special providences. " I have been out this morning, and have great cause of thankfulness, for I have been almost miraculously preserved from imminent danger." " I," replied his friend, " have more cause of thankfulness than you, for I have been preserved from danger even threatening."

A providence adverse to our wishes may be special and more important in its consequences than one correspondent to them. The *worm* was from God as well as the *gourd.*

NOVEMBER 27, 1809.

WHAT ARE THE EXTERNAL (CHURCH) PRIVILEGES CONFERRED BY THE CHRISTIAN DISPENSATION, AND WHAT USE MAY BE MADE OF THEM IN THE DISCHARGE OF THEIR OFFICE ?—Proposed by the Rev. Basil Woodd.

Extension of the truth. Extension of the pale of the visible Church of Christ, in contradistinction to the limited nature of the Mosaic dispensation. Extension of divine influence. General beneficial effect on human happiness. The honour and benefit of being admitted a member of the Christian dispensation by baptism. This furnishes a ground for addressing men's consciences. " You were surrendered to God in your infancy." This is the ground of sponsors. Sponsors confer no additional obligation on the party. But they are an embodied exhibition of the obligations under which baptism has laid him.

The object of the two Sacraments is to embody before the world the two grand doctrines of the Christian Church—REGENERATION and REDEMPTION. This furnishes the strongest ground for infant baptism, which alone can properly and fully exhibit the necessity of regeneration.

The communion of saints ; order, discipline, and authority ; preservation of the truth in articles of faith—these are other external benefits.

DECEMBER 11, 1809.

WHAT IS THE DUTY OF A MEMBER OF THE ESTABLISHED CHURCH, IF THE PREACHING OF THE GOSPEL IS OCCASIONALLY SUSPENDED, OR ALTOGETHER CEASES, IN HIS PARISH CHURCH ?—Proposed by the Rev. H. Budd.

Serious men, who are seeking the truth in much darkness, will be greatly discouraged if deserted.

Q2

Where it is occasionally suspended, as at a charity sermon, it shews a want of patience, rather than zeal, to forsake the Church.   Patience is one of the brightest of Christian graces.   And it is far easier to go zealously with the bias of nature, than to wait with patient submission for the blessing and interference of God.

From occasional sermons mixed with error, a master of a family might take occasion to distinguish to his family between truth and error.

If conscience compels a man to leave a minister, it should be done with the utmost tenderness and consideration.

If a man thought it right to stay under a minister, *for a time,* who preached error, he ought to inform his family why he did it, lest they should imbibe the errors of his ministry.

The next time of meeting would have fallen on Christmas Day. and was therefore passed by.   On the two following Mr Pratt was absent.

FEBRUARY 5, 1810.

WHAT ARE THE CHARACTERISTICS OF THE DIVINE INFLUENCE WHICH CHRISTIANS ARE AUTHORISED TO EXPECT IN THE PRESENT DAY ?—Proposed by the Rev. B. Woodd.

The influence of the Spirit is not a revelation of any new truth, but a practical application of truth already revealed.

The influence of the Holy Spirit is not distinguishable from the acting of the mind, but by the effect.   It is not to be expected in the way of sensible perception, but in the gradual practical influence.

Are we to expect any other influence than that which gradually accompanies the use of means ?

If we admit the perceptible influence of mind on mind, why deny this to the Spirit of God ?

The first distinguishing characteristic of the influence of the Holy Spirit relates to SIN.   If there be a lively influence regarding the nature and evil of sin, it will lead the heart to the REMEDY, and thus to honour divine revelation.

Another character of this influence will be IDENTITY.   Permanence also distinguishes this influence.

Christ is present with his ministers and people, not as the king is present in his legislative capacity, with all his subjects throughout the empire, but sensibly present to give energy to his legislation.

FEBRUARY 19, 1810.

HOW SHALL WE BEST IMPROVE THE APPROACHING FAST ?

Kiss the Son lest he be angry, and ye perish from the way.   The Son has his rod in his hand in these times, and it is a rod of iron.

Let us be cautious not to make too much of secular things.   If the world goes, the world is nothing.   Let us mind our main work.

Another caution is, not to count that a calamity which is no calamity. Popery is falling, and *must* fall.

" What have *I* done ? " is a question to be above all others inculcated.

Alarm rather than comfort is needed in the present day, *lest coming suddenly he find thee sleeping.*

Seek ye the Lord, all ye meek of the earth. (Zeph. ii. 3.)

The EVILS of the day are—the prostitution of oaths ; lotteries ; distilleries ; concubinage and adultery ; Sunday travelling ; want of family worship and domestic instruction ; fast days neglected ; slur on the Gospel among the heathen.

ENCOURAGEMENTS.—The Bible Society ; applications have been made from the Navy and Army to the Naval and Military Bible Society.

The design of God seems to be to ruin antichrist. *We* seem to be building him up. Yet the *design* of God is not our rule of duty. We must do what appears right, and leave to Him the result. *The nations which will not serve thee shall perish.*

Humiliation should be inculcated and practised : personal and national. Many feel, " What have I to do with other men's sins ? " To them say, *Be not partakers of other men's sins.*

Thy kingdom come—let this be our real wish.

Cowper's " Expostulation " is a good Fast sermon. Preparatory sermons are useful.

MARCH 5, 1810.

HOW SHALL WE BEST DISCIPLINE THE IMAGINATION ?—Proposed by the Rev. W. Fry.

" To think well is to act well." Imagination is the faculty of receiving an image or impression of an object. The imagination, then, is the repository of materials, which the memory recalls, and on which the judgment decides.

" Imagination presents to reason the materials of judgment," says Lord Bacon, " which sends them back to the imagination, that it may refer them to the will and affections."

The importance of disciplining this faculty appears, because—

1. It is a source and fountain of evil. See this in David and in Achan. How many longings, preparatives, and acts of mind there are before the commission of sin !

2. The extent and range of the imagination. By it man may commit sin a thousand miles off.

3. Its power of reacting by the memory.

4. Its intolerable tyranny over a man. In prayer, in preaching, still it's at work.

5. Its strengthening other corruptions.

6. Its wholly destroying the proper exercise of the other faculties.

7. Its conversion of objects not in themselves sinful into occasions of sin.

8. Its delusion practised on man in regard to their spiritual state.

9. Its being the grand instrument by which Satan deceives sinners. It can do nothing without the understanding, because its decisions are necessary. But the imagination is his stronghold. David's being tempted to number the people, and Peter tempting Christ not to suffer death, are instances of the working of the imagination.

The discipline of the imagination.

1. Unremitting diligence and vigilance.

2. Prompt and immediate attention. The spark may be extinguished, but it requires promptitude.

3. Avoid idleness. David on the house-top is perhaps an example of this.

4. Realise the presence of God.

5. Improve by past failures.

6. Habitually practise ejaculatory prayer.

7. Guard against hasty determinations.

8. Study the nature and quantity of your diet.

9. Attend to mathematics and logic.

Read the Spectator, No. 411, &c., on the Imagination; also Jones's sermon on the Imagination; Locke on the Understanding; Riccaltoun.

MARCH 19, 1810.

THE NATURE, OPERATION, AND CURE OF PREJUDICE?—Proposed by the Rev. W. J. Abdy.

Lay down as a principle that we are all liable to prejudice, and in a measure actually under it. Early associations, education, connections, society, all beget it.

In the cure of it, be careful not to sacrifice truth, or to grow indifferent to truth. Selfishness is the root of prejudice. Humility is the radical cure. Tracing the origin of our ideas would much help the cure. We must trace the origin of prejudice to our fallen state.

A variety of views of truth in good men are an evidence of the existence and operation of prejudice.

Watts, in his Logic, has an excellent chapter on prejudice, and in the second part of the Improvement of the Mind.

Prejudice may be mitigated, but never cured, in our fallen state. A use of prejudice in others may be made—to lead us to cultivate candour and forbearance.

Intercessory prayer—an enlarged acquaintance with Christians is a cure. Light and love are cures.

APRIL 2, 1810.

MAY WE SATISFY OURSELVES OF OUR PERSONAL INTEREST IN CHRIST ANY FURTHER THAN AS WE ARE CONSCIOUS OF OUR SANCTIFICATION?— Proposed by the Rev. H. Foster.

Hervey's statement is in general good in his Theron and Aspasio: it is encouraging to sinners.

Our warrant to look to Christ is the provision and invitation and promise of God. An assurance that we have come is connected with discerning the effect and influence of grace. Christians who doubt and hesitate about their personal interest in Christ, give to others a sufficient evidence in their anxiety and their earnest desire to assure an interest in him.

It is not safe to take comfort independent of sanctification. Look at sanctification as it respects desires, aims, and habits.

In examining any one grace or duty, we shall find it full of imperfection ; but we must judge of our character on the whole. Without conscious integrity, there can be no solid comfort. Dominion over besetting sins will, on the whole, be found in a Christian ; though he will, at times, be foiled. Progress, on the whole, must be looked for. Compared with years past, he must feel progress. With all, a man must still feel that he is an unprofitable servant.

What may be safely said for the comfort of the dejected sinner will be improper to be said to the less anxious and careful about their souls.

The sense put on the word "sanctification" will much influence the answer to the question. Desire after Christ is an evidence of sanctification.

April 16, 1810.

How are we to Distinguish between the Delusions of Satan and the Comforts of the Holy Spirit ?—Proposed by the Rev. H. Budd.

Sound comfort is accompanied by humility. It is connected with self-renunciation. See David in Ps. li. Sound comfort induces repentance and a determination to please God in a renewed life. Peter wept bitterly. It exalts the Saviour. It glorifies God in his justice and his mercy. *God be merciful to me a* SINNER. It induces a watchfulness against the delusions of Satan.

We may be under delusion when we take comfort from any religious exercise in which we have taken a leading and enlarged share, when comfort is not warranted by the Word of God ; as enthusiasts by dreams.

When comfort is the mere effect of a sanguine temper wrought on by novelty, like the stony-ground hearers, or Herod hearing John gladly, we are under delusion.

There is no solid source of comfort but the Cross of Christ. The work of Satan with the Christian is to shut out the Cross, to darken his views. Accepting Christ simply as a suffering Saviour is full of consolation.

Whence do Satan's delusions arise ? They are grounded on the temperament of the party he deludes. They are grounded, too, on partial views.

Delusions of Satan grow strong when we hold fast some iniquity ; and yet, through some unauthorised view of the promises, we go on with some comfort.

Satan is inconsistent in his delusions. The Holy Spirit is consistent in his consolations.

Sorrow always precedes true comfort. Much of the religion of this day is a selfish religion. Sermons are considered good in proportion as they administer consolation. Such persons want probing. The most painful opportunities would be the most profitable.

Consolation refers to SIN and SUFFERING.

As to SIN. Comfort arises from justification, and the sense of being acquitted for Christ's perfect righteousness. Comfort arises also from sanctification, and the evidence it gives that God the Spirit is at work.

As to SUFFERING. There is such a thing as repenting *in* sin, rather than *from* sin; that is, merely to get ease, with no determination to forsake sin. The one is Satan's delusion; the other is from the Holy Spirit.

If Satan comforts from the Bible, it is from the Bible misunderstood or partially represented. If the Holy Spirit comforts from the Bible, it is from the whole view of truth in the Scripture, according to the real import and meaning.

Satan comforts by ONE particular means. The minister by his preaching; the hearer by hearing. But the Holy Ghost comforts by the regular use of all means.

Satan will allow some peace with sin. The Holy Spirit will bear with NO sin. No small, no secret, no dubious, no profitable sins are allowed.

Satan's consolations puff up, and make the man *severe* against others. Those of the Holy Spirit are accompanied by softness and tenderness of spirit towards others.

The consolations of the Holy Spirit are permanent. Those of Satan will terminate in despair.

The consolations of the Holy Spirit are rational—we shall be able to give an account of them. Of Satan's, we cannot give a reasonable account.

APRIL 30, 1810.

IS PERSONAL PREACHING IN ANY CASE PROPER? AND IF IT BE, BY WHAT REGULATION SHOULD IT BE GOVERNED?—Proposed by the Rev. H. Godfrey.

What is personal preaching?

Not aiming to point out a man to others, but to HIMSELF. See 1 Cor. xiv. 24, 25.

We may also exemplify personal preaching by referring to Lavater's practice of selecting seven persons in his congregation as representative of classes, and so directing his address.

There is great advantage in personal preaching when thus limited. What points out one character will stand for many.

A rule to guide us is, to do it in perfect charity ; therefore, after reflection ; therefore, after much prayer.

Bishop Jeremy Taylor and Dr Doddridge were strongly against aiming at characters in personal attacks.

Carefully avoid personal feelings, so as to take any advantage, and to indulge a spirit of anger or revenge.

In matters of general interest in a congregation, so avoid personal preaching as yet to save harmless the dignity of the ministerial office.

A minister should consider his talent for reproof before he employs personal preaching.

A test of searching preaching is, when it makes men think the preacher means them.

A minister may take considerable liberties where a vice is known, and is great.

Personal preaching, in its right sense, of entering deeply into sins and duties, is of great use to the preacher, as it reproves and directs his own soul in preparing such discourses.

Let personal preaching be well-timed, properly measured ; a hint may sometimes do.

Take a Scripture character for the foundation of remarks.

Preaching may be sometimes supposed to be so personally aiming at individuals, that offence may be improperly taken. Mr Mead had three challenges. To the last he replied that he would try with the challenger the point of a sword ; and produced, at the place appointed, a POCKET BIBLE !

MAY 14, 1810.

THE EXPEDIENCY OF MINISTERS FORMING A THEOLOGICAL SYSTEM ?— Proposed by the Rev. T. Robinson of Leicester.

A minister must be consistent with the times if he would enlighten his hearers ; yet never be afraid of bringing out all the truths of God, through apprehension of inconsistency.

The fall, acceptance, and renewal of man, are ever to be clearly and consistently produced.

The Rev. J. Pratt—

Common-places of Scripture may be well digested, without reference to a system.

Some system is requisite for the stability and comfort of a minister's own mind. Without one, he may be often in confusion. The writings of the early Fathers want system. Avoid, however, refinement. Baxter is a warning to us. Scripture will not bend to refined systems. For example, pardon and justification are not so clearly distinguished in Scripture as in human systems.

Our Articles, and Homilies, and Liturgy are a proper model of a system.

The analogy of faith, Rom. xii. 6, must be observed. *All scripture is given by inspiration of God, and is profitable for* (1.) *doctrine, for*

(2.) *reproof, for* (3.) *correction, for* (4.) *instruction in righteousness; that the man of God may be perfect, thoroughly furnished unto every good work.* (2 Tim. iii. 16, 17.)

All Christians agree *in re*, though not *in formâ*.

In system, avoid those representations of doctrine in which Christians generally differ. The Assembly's Catechism, as a system, is admirable. Fuller's sermon on Systematic Theology is also admirable.

The system, before Christ's ascension, was very limited; afterwards, it was more extended.

The Scriptures are written on the plan and design of exercising the research, and judgment, and candour of man.

Other Members—

Truth is to be preached as it is found in the Word ; and is not to be cut, and clipped, and *espaliered* down.

We must be cautious in distinguishing between essential and non-essential truths ; for we know not how important in the divine plan those truths may be which may appear to some persons non-essential.

MAY 28, 1810.

HOW ARE WE TO DISTINGUISH BETWEEN CHRISTIAN DISCRIMINATION OF CHARACTER AND EVIL SURMISING ?—Proposed by the Rev. J. Clayton.

All are not called on to discriminate publicly on characters ; all are not possessed of the power of discrimination.

To discriminate accurately, and to maintain Christian charity, is the highest style of Christian wisdom.

Charity is so far beyond superiority in discrimination, that it is better to excel in charity than in discrimination, if we cannot excel in both.

The motive and the manner will be the principal means of distinguishing between Christian discrimination and evil surmising.

In Christian discrimination, we must have regard to Christian principles, and not merely discern the man.

Envy is so interwoven in our nature, that we are in immense danger of being actuated by it in our discriminations. *The spirit that is in us lusteth to envy.* There is nothing so acceptable to us as satire.

Evil surmising is judging evil without adequate evidence. Evil surmising is the prevalent evil of the Church in the present day.

JUNE 11, 1810.

WHAT ARE THE PRESENT APPEARANCES OF TRUE RELIGION IN THE WORLD ?—Proposed by the Rev. T. Robinson.

We live in an uncommon day. Schools established ; the rapid way of instruction ; Missionary exertions ; Bible Societies ; the course of Providence. This and that method and plan may fail, yet the thing will proceed.

In the Church of England, things are in a good state. Opposition is strong, but this is no bad symptom. God is raising up in the Church of England an increased number of pious ministers.

The great call for faithful ministers is another extraordinary symptom. It is the most astonishing change in the public mind ever known.

Yet there is a sinking of the tone in many places. This is to be deeply lamented, while God is so greatly at work in the world.

It is to be feared that there has been too much accommodation— " How will this bear ? How will that be taken ? "

There was a good paper in the *Evangelical Magazine* some months since, on the causes which operated in bringing persons to church to hear the Gospel.

The Rev. J. Pratt—

Vital godliness cannot long flourish in the smiles of the world. The *proportion* of real religion, therefore, to its profession, is far less than in earlier and dangerous times. But the *quantity* of real religion is far greater. God raises his instruments suited to his work. The first Reformers are always regarded as a kind of Christian heroes or giants. Now he has raised up Whitfield, Wesley, Venn, &c.

The present state of religion is just what might be expected, under its present extension. Its present extension is owing to Divine Providence ; but its state such as might be expected. And this extension might be looked for when we consider what God is doing in the world, and has promised to do. The temple is to be built, and there must be materials and workmen. Disappointments are to be looked for.

But what is the tendency ?

1. To mere unmeaning profession.

Amiable children follow their parents. Self-interest operates widely on profession. It is even disgraceful in some places not to profess religion.

2. To superficiality in real Christians.

There is so much *action*—committees, &c.—as to impede reflection. A low tone is infectious.

3. To infidelity, in enemies.

They see much evil in professors, and they impute it to religion itself.

What is the remedy ?

1. Thought. 2. Prayer. 3. Separation from the world.

London and other large towns are peculiarly unfavourable to vital godliness.

Baxter says, " There is a great deal more good in evil men, and more evil in good men, than I supposed ; and, therefore, I have learned to judge more candidly of all men."

There were as evil things, and even worse, in the apostolic days, as we can find now.

JUNE 25, 1810.

WHAT IS THE SCRIPTURE DOCTRINE OF FUTURE REWARDS ?—Proposed
by the Rev. Mr Simons and Rev. J. Pratt.

The Rev. J. Pratt—

1. The Scriptures PROPOSE REWARDS.

Self-interest, in its highest and noblest sense, is the great duty of
man. The Scriptures never call us to sacrifice our real interest, even
for the glory of God. The glory of God may require an entire
surrender of our own will, even in lawful things ; but then it is for our
real good. The glory and will of God never run counter to our true
felicity and interest.

It is idle, then, to lay it down as a test of a right state of mind, that
we should be willing to be eternally miserable if it were for the glory
of God : it never *can* be for his glory that a soul which desires to be
happy in him should be eternally miserable.

The Scriptures, therefore, continually address themselves to man on
the ground of promoting his real felicity. They propose gratitude to
God, love to God, and a consequent desire to promote the glory of
God, as the direct ends of our actions : but all this is supposed to be,
and even stated and urged as being, consistent with our real interest
and happiness. We are called and urged to every step of the Christian
life on this very ground.

The Scripture is full, from beginning to end, of the proposals of
reward. And the greatest characters have acted on this expectation.
Moses chose *rather to suffer affliction, . . . for he had respect unto the
recompense of the reward.* St Paul endured affliction on this ground,
that *it worked out an eternal weight of glory.* St James says, *Blessed is
the man that endureth temptation, for when he is tried he shall receive the
crown of life.* Christ himself *endured the cross, despising the shame;* and
for this reason, *for the joy that was set before him.*

The Scriptures address the conscience and the heart : the conscience
through the understanding, and the heart through its hopes and fears.

The parable of the labourers cannot be urged against this view; for
that only respects the principles of merit, not the different degrees of
reward.

2. The Scriptures propose rewards, not of merit, but of GRACE and
of CONGRUITY.

(1.) Of GRACE. No degree of obedience and suffering can *merit*
anything at God's hand. It is by a constitution of grace, that where
such a state is attained, such a degree of blessedness shall be connected
with it.

(2.) Of CONGRUITY. There is an actual *suitableness* between the degree
of grace and the degree of glory. The rank attained in the school
indicates that for which we shall be qualified in the family.

3. The rewards bestowed WILL NOT BE FELT BUT AS OF GRACE by
those who receive them.

*Lord, when saw we thee an hungered, and fed thee? or thirsty, and gave
thee drink?* &c.

There is nothing in this derogatory of our title to heaven, which is wholly in the merit of Christ. Nor anything derogatory of divine grace; because these qualifications are from him Yet this touches on that inexplicable question of the compatibility of the freeness of grace with the accountableness of man. Man will be condemned for not working, though not rewarded for his works, as of merit.

This view is proved from the DIFFERENCES OF REWARDS proposed in Scripture.

1 Cor. xv. 42–44, *So also is the resurrection of the dead: it is sown in corruption, it is raised in incorruption; it is sown in dishonour, it is raised in glory; it is sown in weakness, it is raised in power; it is sown a natural body, it is raised a spiritual body.* This, however, does not refer to the words immediately before, *for one star differeth from another star in glory,* but to ver. 35, that as the wheat dies in order to life, so must the body. This text is, therefore, hardly in point.

2 Tim. ii. 20, *In a great house there are not only vessels of gold and of silver, but also of wood and of earth; and some to honour and some to dishonour.*

Then the talents in Matt. xxv. The two which gained two, and the five which gained five, are not distinguished as to particular measures of reward. But in Luke xix., the parties who gained from one pound—ten in one case, and five in another—were rewarded with ten and five cities.

The distinction of orders in the Angelic world, by analogy, illustrates this point. Also the difference of honour in the members of Christ's body. The sovereignty of God is thus illustrated in heaven.

The ground on which we are rewardable is the work of Christ wrought in us, and done by us. Samson and St Paul cannot be ranked together: nor the penitent malefactor and Timothy.

JULY 9, 1810.

WHAT ARE THE LIMITS OF SCRIPTURAL INQUIRY AS IT RELATES TO MINISTERS?—Proposed by the Rev. H. G. Watkins.

The Rev. J. Pratt—

Lay it down as *governing maxims*—

1. That the *modus* of many things is not to be understood by us.

2. That the relation and harmony of truth, in its various parts, admit of growing discernment, and must govern all inquiries.

3. That the vivid views and impressions of truth should be chiefly aimed at.

4. That the Scriptures should be allowed their full meaning, however that may bear on any preconceived system.

5. That the colouring which our fancy may give to Scripture, should be diligently guarded against.

The Scriptures are wonderfully formed, in the providence of God, to employ men of every capacity and acquisition.

Remarks of other members—

Ministers of speculative minds should have a guard on themselves, lest they waste their time in fruitless inquiries.

So far as any researches may answer the ends of the ministry, so far are they to be pursued, and no further.

Prophecies, in their fulfilment, will probably be accomplished by many circumstances not detailed in the prophecy. They are like enigmatical writing through holes in a paper, filled up with supplementary words, which becomes intelligible when the corresponding paper is applied.

Ministers should study their talents and their situations, and act according to their inquiries. Self-knowledge is an important qualification.

Utility is to be kept continually in view.

Opportunity should limit inquiry.

Local circumstances must be weighed; for instance, as our sphere is in town or the country. The razor may be needed for one place, the axe for another.

Boyle says, "Distinguish between what is said *in* the Scriptures, and what the Scriptures say."

Inquire into the evidence of Scripture; into *all* the truths of Scripture; into whatever illustrates those truths.

On July 23, 1810, the subject was, WHAT WAS THE MORAL CHARACTER OF THE PHARISEES? We have no notes. The meetings were adjourned till October.

OCTOBER 1, 1810.

WHAT IS THE NATURE OF SIMPLICITY AND GODLY SINCERITY, AND ITS INFLUENCE ON THE CHRISTIAN MINISTRY?—Proposed by the Rev. D. Wilson.

Simplicity is the principle: Sincerity the acting of that principle.

Simplicity is not rudeness nor uniformity of manner.

There is a beautiful picture of sincerity in Tillotson's sermon on the subject.

Simplicity is shewn in the intention, and sincerity in dependence.

Simplicity is a quality which runs through every grace of the Christian: thus faith must be unfeigned; love must be without dissimulation, &c.

OCTOBER 15, 1810.

WHAT IS THE DIFFERENCE BETWEEN CONSISTENCY AND BIGOTRY?—Proposed by the Rev. W. Fry.

Consistency is another word for integrity in morals; for beauty in the arts. It implies proportion, everything keeping its place.

Religious consistency is the conducting of ourselves according to the profession which we make. A proud, envious, passionate professor, for instance, is an inconsistent man.

" Unity in essentials ; moderation in circumstantials ; charity in all things," it has been admirably said by the Bishop of Gloucester.

OCTOBER 29, 1810.

HOW SHALL WE BEST OVERCOME THE FEARS WHICH HARASS US AS PREACHERS ?—Proposed by the Rev. J. Clayton

A fear of reverence towards GOD is to be cherished. And so a fear of respect towards our congregation.

Adequate preparation is a leading means of overcoming fear. Simple dependence on divine aid another.

We have perhaps fears regarding a personal interest in the blessings which we offer to others. The remedy here is simply prayer, and the maintenance of the divine life in us.

Our fears are of pride or avarice. The remedy is, Attend to motives. Let the leading concern be to glorify God.

There are fears of despondency in respect to success. The remedy is, Consider that success is visible or invisible, immediate or remote.

Faithfulness to God and souls is our great concern. Then leave success to Him.

Have we fears of bondage to some in the congregation ? *One is our Master.* Fears arising from conscious negligence ? Remedy, Be diligent in study.

Fears arise from offences and contentions ; from indecision. We have fears of anxiety from natural constitution or the state of our nervous system.

Habit and use help us. They remove the fear of man. But they have a tendency to injure us ; for they tend to weaken our fear of God.

Fears may arise from excess of preparation.

Fears respecting our call to the ministry may trouble us. Let us remember what Amos said, *I was no prophet, neither was I a prophet's son, but I was an herdman, . . and the* LORD *took me, . . and said, . . . Go, prophesy.*

Fears in preaching often arise from indevotion in previous prayers. Our remedy is to humble ourselves before God.

Fears arise from the immediate suggestion of Satan.

Remedies for some of these fears are—

1. Cherishing a holy indifference. 2. Humility. 3. Consideration of the dignity of the ministerial office. 4. Walking close with God. 5. To be much in prayer.

Other remedies are—

1. Natural : attending to health ; reading the prayers will animate the mind.

2. Spiritual : remembering the goodness of our cause ; the fidelity of the divine promise. The honour of Christ is committed to his am-

bassadors.   Let us encourage ourselves in our weakness.   God chooses *things that are not to bring to nought things that are.*   Let us be emptied of self.

On those doctrines which are most repugnant to human nature, let us commit ourselves at once ; and plainly state our views, without entering into explanations and qualifications.

Some fears are salutary—for example, fears that we have not been sufficiently plain and pointed.   This makes us jealous and watchful in future.

November 12, 1810.

WHAT ARE THE TEMPTATIONS PECULIAR TO A RELIGIOUS PROFESSION ?
—Proposed by the Rev. H. Godfrey.

The temptations are the following :—

1. To rest in the mere profession.
2. To feel spiritual and carnal pride.   Young people despising their parents, who, they think, do not come up to what they consider the standard.
3. To be censorious.   4. To be captious.
5. To neglect the Bible and private duties, and rest in the habit of hearing.   See a paper in *Christian Observer* about four months ago.
6. To be zealous for particular ministers.
7. To speak disrespectfully of other ministers.
8. To be zealous for particular doctrines.
9. To fall into schism ; and disregard of spiritual jurisdiction.
10. To hypocrisy.
11. To blasphemy.   The devil takes advantage, from the frequent contemplation of divine truths, to turn them to poison, and to infuse hard thoughts of God.
12. To irreverent use of the Scriptures.
13. To a misapplication of the Scriptures.
14. To a perverting of the ways of Providence.
15. To think ourselves right because formerly under religious impressions.
16. To rest in low attainments.
17. To rest in right principles.   Mistaking head knowledge for real conversion.
18. To Pharisaism.   19. To Antinomianism.   Shrinking at self-denial and mortification.
20. To the revival with increasing strength of besetting sins.   In a state of nature, one devil will cast out another.   In a state of grace, all sin must be mortified.
21. To impatience of contradiction.
22. To forget proprieties, in respect to the friendship of the sexes.
23. To waste time.
24. To lay too much stress on frames and feelings.
25. To make too much of hearing.

26. To a spirit of insubordination : not *submitting yourselves one to another in the fear of God. Speaking evil of dignities.*

27. To rest in a selection of our minister, and to think ourselves like the best of his hearers.

28. To advance worldly interests by religious profession.

29. To fear of the world.

30. To mistake our own spirit for Christian zeal.

31. To be intolerant of reproof. See Stukeley's *Gospel Glass.*

REMEDIES. — Self-examination ; closet-religion ; watchfulness and prayer ; self-suspicion and holy jealousy.

NOVEMBER 26, 1810.

IN WHAT SENSE DO THE SCRIPTURES AUTHORISE MINISTERS TO PREACH THAT THE DESIRE OF GRACE IS GRACE ?—Proposed by the Rev. H. Budd.

The sentiment is grounded on Rom. vii.

Desire of grace, whenever *sincere,* is grace. Where sincere, it is accompanied by (1) Love to God ; (2) Prayer, which is the language of desire to be accomplished ; (3) Praise, which is the language of desire gratified ; (4) Faith ; (5) Repentance ; (6) A desire of assurance ; (7) A consistent walk ; (8) An unceasing application to the means of grace.

The Christian life, as Ambrose says, is *Affectu magis quàm effectu.*

The Scriptures tell us of *groanings which cannot be uttered.*

Marks of a counterfeit desire of grace are—

1. Insincerity.   Mere fear of consequences—like the foolish virgins.

2. When the desire for spiritual things is for worldly ends : as with Simon Magus ; Judas with the bag ; Milton's Mammon.

3. When desire is unaccompanied by sincere efforts.

4. When no progress is made in satisfying our desire of grace.

5. When the desire ends in a mere profession, and there is no self-denial.

6. When the desire is not consistent with the proposals of the Gospel.

The doctrine cannot be properly preached in the general way stated in the question ; but when, in application, we are speaking to afflicted consciences, we may state it largely and fully.

On the next three occasions Mr Pratt was absent, and we have no notes.

JANUARY 21, 1811.

WHAT INSTRUCTION CAN BE GATHERED FROM THAT VARIETY OF SENTIMENT WHICH IS FOUND AMONG PIOUS PROFESSORS ?—Proposed by the Rev. H. Foster.

The Rev. J. Pratt—

It demonstrates the imbecility of the human mind.   It calls for mutual charity and forbearance.

Yet it should put us on our guard against the sacrifice of truth.

It is designed to inculcate teachableness. A wise man may gather new views and ideas from much more feeble men. *The eye cannot say to the hand, I have no need of thee; neither the head to the feet, I have no need of you.*

It teaches us to approve excellence in any form, though different from our views and habits.

It teaches us to abstain from all barren and fruitless discussions, and to regard these as temptations of Satan.

Remarks of other Members—

It casts no reflection on the sufficiency of Scripture. We all still hold that *all Scripture is given by inspiration of God, and is profitable for doctrine, for reproof,* &c.

It teaches us to pray for unanimity in the Church, according to the Apostle's words, *The God of peace himself give you peace always by all means.*

It distinguishes between unity of spirit and uniformity of sentiment. Unity in variety is the beauty of the Church.

It makes us more disposed to forbearance in respect of *actions* than of *sentiments.* This, therefore, is a higher exercise of grace.

Let us be careful, in looking for uniformity of sentiment, that we do not love our own image; but approve God's image, and love it wherever found.

It may lead us to think of heaven with more delight; and not to *despise the day of small things,* but to cherish the *babes in Christ.*

It contributes to establish the truth of divine revelation, inasmuch as persons entertaining a vast variety of sentiment all agree in the authority of Scripture.

On the next subject we have no notes.

FEBRUARY 18, 1811.

WHAT IS THE SCRIPTURAL IDEA OF THE SOVEREIGNTY OF GOD?— Proposed by the Rev. B. Woodd.

We should always associate our ideas of the sovereignty of God with infinite truth, wisdom, goodness, and mercy.

The sovereignty of God is principally displayed in his not revealing to us, in this present state of being, in what way these perfections are brought into action.

The sovereignty of God appears—

1. In the discriminations of his grace.

2. In the means by which he accomplishes his purposes. For examples—1 Cor. i. end ; the genealogy of Christ ; the Reformation in England.

3. In damping, at a stroke, all human expectations.

4. In delaying the accomplishment of the divine promises.

5. In the removal of apparently useful instruments.

6. In the effect of the ministry as to individuals.

Let us learn to submit ourselves in all things to God—to the dealings of his providence ; to the declarations of his word.

It is an encouraging truth, *The Lord reigneth, let the earth be glad!* and an argument against despair, *He will have mercy on whom he will have mercy.*

The Rev. J. Pratt—

The sovereignty of God consists in his not disclosing to us the particular reasons of his conduct.   General reasons he gives ; but they are all such as demand submission of mind ; *e. g.,* His own glory. But *particular* reasons he conceals.   Perhaps we shall never fully understand these.

Enthusiasm and fanaticism are the result of a want of acquiescence in the divine sovereignty.   Men will have God's reasons, where he does not disclose them.

Humility and sobriety of mind result from a real subjection to the divine sovereignty.

Submission to the divine sovereignty is the touchstone of true piety.   Every pious Arminian even submits to it, however his creed may seem to oppose it.

The Rev. H. Godfrey—

God is a sovereign from eternity.   He created, because he pleased ; He rules in providence as he pleases ; He gives grace as he pleases.

He asks no opinion.   We must, with a ready mind, bow down, and say, AMEN.

The Rev. J. Clayton—

Hardening the heart is to be considered as a judicial act of God. And it may be supposed to consist in withdrawing the fear of punishment from the mind.

The evils of abusing the doctrine of divine sovereignty are these—

1. Tracing up revealed truths to unrevealed causes.

2. Misstating the doctrines of election and perseverance ; separating election from its effects ; overlooking the principle in perseverance.

3. Declining expostulating with sinners.

4. Neglect of means.

5. Censuring the commendable actions of unregenerate men.

6. Censoriousness.

There are evils which—

1. Dishonour God the Father, and make him borrow the reasons of his conduct from his creatures.

2. Dishonour God the Son, and make the effect of his death dubious and uncertain.

3. Dishonour God the Spirit, and make his influence unnecessary.

4. Ministers are deprived of motives for diligence in their calling when they take a wrong view of this doctrine.

5. A wrong view of this doctrine cherishes in men the spirit of pride and self-dependence.

6. It confounds evangelical holiness with mere morality.

MARCH 4, 1811.

HOW SHALL WE IMPROVE THE APPROACHING FAST ?—Proposed by the Rev. J. Clayton.

Guard against weariness in this service.

What wilt thou do for thy great name ? does not seem to have taken possession of our minds so much as, How shall we meet our difficulties —how shall we bear the accumulated burdens ?

Present times are not common times. They are agitated by striking convulsions. They are marked by great events. We are now encountering almost all Europe, united under a most formidable leader —" nameless till the tempest brought him to the surface." The subjection of this yet independent country is his one aim. Here, then, we raise another Ebenezer, *Hitherto the Lord hath helped us.*

But much will depend on our improvement of this awful dispensation. That God has a controversy with this nation is too evident to be doubted. His voice cries aloud to the city—to the country—to the Church—to the world. Happy the man who *hears the rod, and him who hath appointed it.*

We should inquire what occasion we have given to God thus to contend with us. While some attribute our evils to this, and others to that, SIN must be acknowledged as the grand and radical cause of all our evils. Hence all our infidelity, worldliness, ungodliness.

But the grand inquiry should be, " Are there not iniquities with us —even with us against the Lord our God ? "

With regard to this, our families condemn us ; our hearts condemn us ; our closets condemn us.

We may be encouraged by reviewing what God hath done. Often have we been brought low, yet not given up.

When Moses prayed, when Joshua prayed, when Hezekiah prayed, when Israel prayed—God heard and answered their prayers.

Texts for our encouragement are—2 Chron. xii. 7 ; Titus iii. 1, first clause ; Gen. vii. 16, *And the Lord shut him in.*

We have subjects abundant for repentance, fear, supplication, hope, consolation, and thankfulness.

The illness of the king is a new feature this last year. It has been a stroke at the idol of this country. Our commerce has been threatened.

Be careful not to enter too much into particulars. For example, on this very topic, commerce ; then, again, on the conduct of the Regent.

The increase of evangelical men in the Established Church, the improvement in the general tone of divinity, are excellent tokens of good.

Censure the spirit of commercial speculations.

Advise the young not to attend debating societies.

Allude, in general terms, to the freethinking men. These men are encouraged by the presence of those who perhaps are themselves shocked at their impiety and recklessness.

Consider (1.) The state of the world. Wherever any remarkable event has taken place, notice it. Review every country as connected with Bonaparte ; as making diversions in our favour, though we cannot be much encouraged in this view now.

Consider (2.) The state of our own country. The slave trade is too much permitted. It is not sufficiently interfered with by our allies. Look at oppression in distant provinces.

Notice the misrepresentation of the gospel : by some, through treachery ; by others, through immoral habits—as intoxication.

The profanation of the Sabbath is a crying evil. The encouragement given by the state to lotteries, distilleries ; the perjuries which take place are dreadful.

Signs :—The disregard of judgments. Our wars of eighteen years ! Our abuse of mercies. The accumulation of everyday evil ; debates, deceit, fraud, &c., we should notice. They give a wonderful view of God's long-suffering.

The present mode of carrying on trade by fictitious papers, is an evil sign.

We should pray for the state of the army and navy.

We should mourn over the deficiency of our ministerial labours ; defects in magistrates ; the insensibility we shew for our sins.

Consider (3.) Our PERSONAL share in the crimes of our country. Have the Sacraments been attended as they should have been ? Have ordinances been used ? Is family prayer established in all our circles ? Have we increased in holiness ? Do our alms ascend to God as a memorial ?

Preach a preparatory sermon on this occasion. In the family and in private, lay the case before God, that he would cause the Fast to be rightly observed.

The scaffolding is now taking down ; we are in the midst of the noise and tumult. But we should wait to see the disclosing of the grand and magnificent temple which has been erecting for six thousand years.

On the next occasion the subject was, WHAT ARE SATISFAC-TORY EVIDENCES OF RELIGION IN CHILDREN? We have no notes.

APRIL 1, 1811.

HOW FAR ARE THE ORDER AND DISCIPLINE OF THE CHRISTIAN CHURCH CONNECTED WITH SALVATION ?—Proposed by the Rev. J. Pratt.

Mr Pratt—

The order and discipline of the Christian Church are not indispensable to salvation. Had they been so, doubtless they would have been clearly and unequivocally enjoined in Scripture.

The Church has power to decree rites, as Hooker largely establishes.

The Church may exist under different forms of order and discipline. Nay, the Church may be where there are no outward ordinances and discipline.   For we must distinguish between the INVISIBLE CHURCH and the VISIBLE.

Order and discipline are highly necessary to the extension and the edification of the Church.   But individual members, though profited by the order and discipline of the Church, will not perish for lack of them.

The order and discipline of the Church, therefore, promote the number of the saved, and their advance in holiness.   But it is possible to be saved without either.

As to any particular form of order and discipline, I, of course, judge Episcopacy to be of primitive institution; nay, of divine appointment, and of most eminent utility.   But I do not think God appointed Episcopacy as an exclusive form, though it is the most expedient form.

Had it been the *exclusive* form, God would have borne no testimony to other forms, by raising souls to life under them.   Living souls are of the Spirit's creation; and wherever he operates, he bears a testimony —a testimony never borne to radical and fatal error.

The attempt to confound UNITY with UNIFORMITY never can succeed. All that very high churchmen say of the Church is true only of the INVISIBLE CHURCH, but not of the VISIBLE in ANY form.

What is necessary to constitute a Church of Christ is a very difficult question : it is difficult to be neither too rigid nor too lax.

Other Speakers—

Distinguish between things morally right or wrong, and therefore circumstantially so.

Distinguish between things palpably right or wrong, and therefore doubtfully so.

Order and discipline are so far connected with salvation, as they appear true and obligatory to the mind.   For the man cannot be saved who rejects what his conscience tells him is obligatory on him. Remember St Paul's reasoning on meats.

Sabbaths and sacraments have kept up religion from the creation to this day.

Order is part of the system of Christianity, and contributes to the perfection of the whole.

Order and discipline form the visage of the Church, which the world is called to look at; and, by contemplating, to unite itself to her.

Where there is *real piety*, there order and discipline are of vast importance.   For in proportion to the energy of any principle is the importance of its right direction.

Milner says justly, that the primitive Church rather leaned to the excess of order and discipline ; but modern times lean to the opposite extreme.

The schism of the Ten Tribes was certainly contrary to the previous order of God, and was attended with consequences of extensive evil.

Yet they had prophets, and God blessed them. This should serve to lessen our attachment to any kind of order and discipline exclusively, under the New Testament; under which, by common consent, order and discipline of one particular kind are not so necessary as under the Old.

Order and discipline are means conducive to an end. If looked on in any other light, they lead to bigotry and superstition. They are necessary, therefore, circumstantially, not essentially.

***

APRIL 15, 1811.

WHAT USE MAY BE MADE OF THE DIFFICULTIES OCCURRING IN REVELATION?—Proposed by the Rev. D. Wilson.

The Rev. J. Pratt—

They are an evidence of the truth of revelation. Divine revelation must have difficulties. They urge upon us humility and diligent study.

They are the touchstone of the heart. St Paul was not ashamed of the Gospel; nor need we be with all the difficulties which may appear to beset it. *To the Jews it is a stumbling-block, and to the Greeks foolishness, but to us who are saved it is the wisdom of God and the power of God.*

The Rev. J. Clayton—

Beware of *Scepticism;* like opium, it produces palsy. A relaxed state of mind is pernicious to a Christian minister.

Devout admiration should fill us as we see what depths and mysteries the Scriptures reveal. This was the spirit of St Paul. It was not a conclusion of comprehension, but of admiration, which led him to exclaim, *O the depth of the riches both of the wisdom and knowledge of God: how unsearchable are his judgments, and his ways past finding out!*

Cultivate a spirit of dependence; particularly on the teaching of the Holy Spirit. None attain peace of conscience, purity of heart, conviction of mind, but by this coming to the Word.

We must shew forbearance towards our brethren, who find difficulties in revelation which we do not. Remember Newton's forbearance with Scott, as he was feeling his way.

But we must not tolerate error, and become indifferent to important truth.

Remarks of other Members—

Revelation does not propose to satisfy our curiosity; but to bring a remedy.

Always view revelation with reference to the state of the heart. If he meet it in a spirit of speculation, the man will, perhaps, have hard thoughts of God.

There is no doctrine of Scripture which is not corroborated by facts.

Anticipate the day when all difficulties will be cleared away.

Difficulties are calculated to exalt the mind, to raise its tone, and to make it look upward.

St Paul teaches us to state truth, but to avoid reasoning on statements. The American divines err here. They illustrate the divine legislation, not only from the excellencies, but even the imperfections of human legislation.

Infidels are more than a match for many of us on this ground.

APRIL 29, 1811.

IN WHAT WAY CAN A MINISTER MAINTAIN ORDER AND DISCIPLINE IN HIS CHURCH, SO AS BEST TO ANSWER THE ENDS OF GOD IN THE ORIGINAL APPOINTMENT OF THEM ?—Proposed by the Rev. C. Simeon.

Mr Simeon—

I have six societies, each of which I meet monthly. There is also a society of twelve, whom I call stewards, who have the management of our funds, and consist of the most serious and wise men in the congregation. By these stewards, who mix with all the members of the societies, I thoroughly know the affairs of each of them.

When persons are discovered to have received an impression under the ministry, he is spoken to on the matter, and deliberation takes place. This plan excites a great solicitude in persons awakened to unite themselves to our societies ; and a specific union is formed, and an intimate connexion is established, between me and them.

The stewards know and counteract, as far as is in their power, any danger of error or sin into which the members may seem to fall ; if they do not succeed, they bring the case to me.

By these means I have been enabled to preserve my people so much together, that, for twenty-eight years, I have scarcely lost one whom I would not have dismissed.

Some evils attending this system. During long absence, the stewards became rather too much their own masters, and not quite so humble and manageable as they were.

There are about one hundred and twenty persons in these societies.

Another Member—

The ends are two in such societies :—To build up the Church in faith and love ; to perpetuate the Church by the accession of new members.

Conciliate any who separate.

Make the points of separation apparently subordinate.

The next subject was, Is MORAL EVIL INCLUDED IN THE " ALL THINGS " WHICH WORK TOGETHER FOR GOOD ? On this, and on the next occasion, we have no notes.

JUNE 10, 1811.

HOW SHALL WE WALK IN WISDOM TOWARDS THEM THAT ARE WITHOUT ? —Proposed by the Rev. H. Godfrey.

Mr Godfrey—

1. Avoid sinful compliances with the world ; austerity of deport-

ment; levity and trifling; all religious affectation; needless singularity in dress. Avoid giving a loose to the tongue. Avoid political discussions; insubordination; party spirit; irregularity as Christians in the Church.

2. Render service to them that are without. Cultivate a general spirit of benevolence and generosity. Let integrity, punctuality, a disposition to concede, mark your behaviour.

Shew the cheerfulness of a Christian—the *contentment of a Christian*. Let them that are without see your purity of life and manners; your good temper and moderation; your consistency of conduct. *Provide things honest in the sight of all men. Whatever things are true,* . . . *honest,* . . . *just,* . . . *pure,* . . . *lovely,* . . . *of good report*—these are the things which will win.

The Rev. J. Pratt—

Study the character, station, circumstances, and prejudices of those with whom we have to do. We must accommodate ourselves to them in all things lawful. *I became all things to all men, that I might gain some.* We must accommodate ourselves especially to the capacity of others to receive the truth. *No man putteth a piece of new cloth on an old garment.* (Matt. ix. 16, 17.) *Cast not your pearls before swine.* Silence and yielding are very necessary at times.

Maintain charity entire.

Them that are without is spoken principally of the heathen. It is now used in a more restricted sense. We should guard against the arrogance of an exclusive system.

Beware of suspicious appearances, doubtful principles, selfishness, over-reaching.

Watch your temper; shew patience and forbearance.

Maintain a lively sense of this feeling—*What hast thou that thou hast not received?* And ever remember, *What do ye more than others?* Industry will do much. *Redeeming the time, because the days are evil.*

Remarks of other Members—

Guard against the contagion of the world, and so shew· wisdom toward yourselves.

Watch for opportunities of usefulness to the world. Let us aim *to please our neighbour for his good to edification.* Study to extract improvement from the world.

Deal, according to their character, with hypocrites, revilers, inquirers, &c.

JUNE 24, 1811.

WHAT IS THE BEST METHOD OF CULTIVATING A CONTEMPLATIVE SPIRIT?—Proposed by the Rev. B. Woodd.

Mr Woodd—

The subjects of contemplation are threefold : CREATION—see Ps. viii.; PROVIDENCE—see Ps. civ. ; and REDEMPTION.

Contemplation is highly conducive to personal edification and happiness.

Impress the mind with a view of the glory and goodness of God. Consider GOD as the portion of the soul. Cultivate the habit of contemplation. A familiar acquaintance with the Psalms is eminently conducive to this frame. So is a spirit of prayer. A deep sense of our unworthiness and dependence, a spiritual state of mind, and a habit of directing the mind to GOD, should be cultivated.

The Rev. J. Pratt—

Give a stated time to contemplation, and be firm in adhering to such time. Rise early. Make official and ministerial contemplation turn as much as possible into personal benefit. Beware of making official and ministerial contemplation a substitute for personal contemplation.

Have always a subject on the mind. Thoughts will grow out of the Scripture read in the morning ; take these as your helps. Beware of enthusiasm, and leaving the limits of the Word, as the mystics have done.

Remarks of others—

Ejaculatory prayer will promote this state. Watch that the subjects you choose are useful. Discipline the mind to this labour. Read books adapted to beget a spirit of contemplation in you.

July 8, 1811.

WHAT RULES CAN BE LAID DOWN FOR CHRISTIANS, AND PARTICULARLY FOR MINISTERS, IN ASSISTING IN THE CONDUCT OF PUBLIC SOCIETIES, SO AS NOT TO TRENCH ON PERSONAL RELIGION, OR TO COUNTENANCE ANY INDECORUM IN THE MANAGEMENT OF SUCH SOCIETIES?—Proposed by the Rev. W. J. Abdy.

The Rev. J. Pratt—

1. Lay down such rules for religious retirement as the conscience determines is necessary.
2. Make no engagements in frequenting and supporting public societies which will *habitually* trench in any material degree on these rules.
3. Let the time allotted to public societies be such as to leave to family, social, and ministerial duties—as well as private—their due proportion of time and care.
4. Protest against all indecorum in public meetings, either by future absence, by immediately quitting the company, or by a public appeal and remonstrance.

Remarks of other Members—

We should attach ourselves principally to one public society. We should not go where it is not a plain duty.

JULY 22, 1811.

IN WHAT WAY, AND TO WHAT EXTENT, SHOULD WE INSIST ON THE
WORK OF THE HOLY SPIRIT IN OUR PUBLIC MINISTRY?—Proposed by
the Rev. W. Goode.

The Rev. J. Pratt—

Take the Scripture model; look, for example, into the Epistle to
the Ephesians.

Occasional discourses might be preached on the personality, divinity,
offices, and work of the Holy Spirit.

Preach no discourse without *habitual* reference, expressed or implied,
to the work of the Spirit.

Be cautious of irreverent methods of speaking of Him and his
influences. Watch against unmeaning phrases.

Urge the expectation of his influence; prayer for that influence;
serious attention to his motions on the mind: when conscience is
speaking, it is his voice.

Lead your hearers to look for the Spirit's influences in respect of
illumination, consolation, and sanctification.

To insist effectually on this subject with our people, we should be
deeply imbued with it ourselves.

The Rev. D. Wilson—

1. In respect to the WAY of insisting on the work of the Holy Spirit.

(1.) It should be cautiously; feeling its importance; with a sense
of dependence; with reverence; considering the order of means in
which God works, giving, for instance, the full effect to alarms, &c.

(2.) With an adequate impression on our own minds.

2. In respect to the EXTENT.

(1.) Sermons should be preached expressly on the Spirit's work.

(2.) But not so as to exclude other great topics of the gospel.

On the next topic, WHAT IS THE PARTICULAR COURSE OF THIS
EVIL WORLD IN THE PRESENT DAY? we have no notes.

OCTOBER 28, 1811.

WHAT IS THE BEST METHOD OF APPLYING A SERMON?—Proposed by
the Rev. H. Budd.

Mr Budd—

This is to be decided much by the kind of sermon. In general, the
subject-matter of the sermon should be brought home to the heart.

There are two kinds of application : (1.) Current and occasional, as
the matter arises ; (2.) Collective, when the matter is collected at the
end.

Jay's *Life of Winter* enumerates six kinds of sermons. The Essay,
Expository, Observational, Characteristic, Topical, Textual. Experimental may be added.

It is well to catch the moment when the attention is excited, and not always to wait for the end.

In making applications, we may divide our hearers into classes. As to characters, careless, sensual, &c. ; attack the besetting sin ; as to condition ; as to profession ; with respect to tempers ; in respect of duties ; circumstances—as death, pestilence, &c.

Apply, by way of consolation, exhortation, instruction, warning, encouragement, caution, terror, supplication.

Apply practical subjects doctrinally in the way of motives ; as the love of the Father, &c.   Apply doctrinal subjects practically.

Draw out a scheme of application, and annex suitable Scriptures as they offer themselves.

All we can do is to use these means, but the Holy Spirit must effectually apply.   The most consolatory view of the ministry, is to view ourselves as mere instruments in the divine hands.

The Rev. J. Pratt—

Realise the idea of talking with an individual, will lead to an easy and natural mode of application.

The whole sermon should, in a sound sense, be application.

Doddridge advises a minister to choose, in application, a few powerful Scriptures, and to shoot them home to the heart.

The interrogatory style awakens attention.

There should be a constant endeavour to carry the hearers with us, to make them think as you think, to make them feel as you feel.

Keep your eye on the Scriptures read in the course of the service, and apply them to the illustration of your subject.

Remarks of other Members—

The mode of application should be varied.   If the habit were to apply each head separately, it would lose much of its effect.

Inferences should arise naturally out of *the subjects.   Flavel is excellent on this point ; his inferences are numerous and natural.

Ostewald has some good remarks on application.   So has Claude.

Saurin makes his hearers condemn themselves ; for example, in his application of " God's controversy with his people."

In doctrinal discussions, some thrusts at the conscience should be made by the way to awaken attention.

Enter into a minute detail of the operations of a gracious principle. Use similitudes.

All modes should be used for the sake of variety, and the best is that which is best adapted to the particular subject.

Application should be perspicuous ; requiring no effort to remember it ; affectionate ; pathetic, as our Lord's—*O Jerusalem, Jerusalem!* solemn.

Pitt said, whoever would make an impression on a popular audience must either *repeat* or *amplify.*   Fox repeated : Pitt amplified.

Examples of close Scripture application are—*Therefore thou art inexcusable, O man. . . . .—But who art thou, O man, that repliest against God?—Ye denied the Holy One and the True!—Ye stiff-necked and uncircumcised, ye do always resist the Holy Ghost.—Thou art in the gall of bitterness and the bond of iniquity.—I take you to record this day that I am free from the blood of all men.—King Agrippa, believest thou the prophets?—I charge thee, therefore, before God and the Lord Jesus Christ.*

Our Lord displayed divine address in application—*Simon, I have somewhat to say to thee.*

NOVEMBER 11, 1811.

WHAT INSTRUCTION MAY WE DERIVE FROM THE PRESENT APPEARANCE OF A MAGNIFICENT COMET IN THE HEAVENS?—Proposed by the Rev. J. Pratt.

Mr Pratt—

The works of the Lord are great, sought out of all them that have pleasure therein. We do not sufficiently bring forward God the Creator. This is done perpetually in Scripture.

This appearance may serve to awaken us from our insensibility to the settled course of Divine Providence.

It may rouse us to the recollection that the government of God is proceeding on determined laws, how much soever may be hid from our observation.

It may lead us to sure confidence in the fulfilment of the divine will, and accomplishment of all the divine promises.

It may serve to enlarge our views of the works of the Lord. It realises to us the unlimited power of God. Comets either have or have not extreme vicissitudes of temperature: if they have, and are inhabited, then those inhabitants are such as can bear these vicissitudes: if they have not, then the power of God is exemplified in preventing these vicissitudes, probably by the atmosphere.

It may serve to humble us on account of our ignorance.

It may serve to repress superstition; to repress also vain curiosity.

The Rev. D. Wilson—

God was displeased with some *who regarded not his works, neither the operation of his hands.*

Notice how hard is the heart of man! They who are called to investigate most narrowly the works of God, perhaps generally feel little of God's wisdom and power.

Enter into the Scriptural views of the providence of God as connected with the views of redemption. Isaiah, from chap. xl., lays the foundation of confidence in God's gracious providence in His sovereignty over His creatures.

Heavenly bodies are employed, particularly in Scripture, to demonstrate the stability of the covenant God makes with His people. See Jer. xxxiii. 20, 21, 22, *If ye can break my covenant of the day, and my covenant of the night, . . . then may also my covenant be broken with David my servant. . . .*

Draw an important analogy from the difficulties in the works of God in nature, to the difficulties which occur in Scripture and redemption.

We see in revelation, as much as in creation, only the part of a system.

Ask the modus and manner of the sun's existence : I am not to wait till I can resolve this difficulty before I enjoy his light and warmth— nor am I to wait till I can explain the modus of the divine existence before I enjoy the blessings He offers.

Our Lord made this use of the mysteries in nature around us :—*The wind bloweth where it listeth, and ye hear the sound thereof, but cannot tell whence it cometh or whither it goeth: so is every one that is born of the Spirit.*

Learn the littleness of man, and the consequent condescension of God in the work of redemption : *When I consider thy heavens, the work of thy fingers; the moon and the stars, which thou hast ordained; what is man, that thou art mindful of him? and the son of man, that thou visitest him?* Ps. viii.

The works of creation, wonderful as they are, are incapable of changing the heart ; but the heart, when changed, may derive abundant improvement from them. See Ps. xix.

November 25, 1811.

HOW FAR OUGHT THE EXPERIENCE OF A MINISTER TO BE THE RULE OF HIS PREACHING ?—Proposed by the Rev. S. Crowther.

The Rev. J. Pratt—

What is experience? The operation of truths, by grace, on our understanding, will, and affections.

Mr Cecil used to say, " Truth and sympathy are the grand instruments of the Christian ministry."

A minister is to aim at the most full and scriptural statements of truth. Though even in this, it should be made out to his own conviction. Even with some imperfect views of truth, he may meet the opening minds of his hearers.

With respect to the influence of truth upon our own will and affections — in general all Christians are hereon agreed ; but in particulars, and in degrees, we differ. In these respects we must preach only what we see to be scriptural, what we feel to be desirable, what will meet the object of preaching.

The danger of limiting a minister to experience is that of erecting a standard different from God's word, or short of it.

It is evidently not God's purpose that all his servants should preach truth in the same way, and with the same views and feelings. There is a beautiful variety in the order of all his works.

Nor is it possible to anticipate the maturity of experience ; nor the tone and character of sympathy.

An humble, diligent, praying minister is in no danger of preaching beyond his experience.

The man who is in danger is the merely educated, the conceited, the heady man.

The Rev. D. Wilson—

A minister cannot preach beyond his experience naturally. He cannot do it authoritatively. St Paul's language is—*Testifying both to the Jews and Greeks repentance toward God, and faith toward our Lord Jesus Christ.*

It may retard a minister's progress in the Divine life.

It would tend to increase the passive habits in religion.

Remarks of other Members—

Our congregations will be pigmies if we limit our ministry to our experience.

All that is said against preaching beyond experience is applicable to the minister who is not the subject of regeneration. But the truly regenerate minister will have the embryo of all experience in his mind.

If he be tempted, he will preach on the subject though he have not experienced the victory ; and that sermon will meet the feelings of many.

There are gradations of naturalness and authority in preaching—

1. Conviction of truth. 2. Conviction of its importance. 3. Conviction of its desirableness. 4. Feeling of its influence.

There are two species of naturalness : that of conviction, and that of feeling.

December 9, 1811.

WHAT ARE THE PRINCIPAL REFLECTIONS WHICH OUR EXPERIENCE IN THE MINISTRY HAS SUGGESTED ?—Proposed by the Rev. B. Woodd.

One of the most important ministerial attainments is, a knowledge of the world, of man, of the avenues of the heart.

It is important to know how to conciliate the good-will of our neighbour.

General knowledge is important, as it qualifies ministers to maintain intercourse with men.

Deep researches in doctrinal speculations answer no good end.

Obvious truths, plainly and affectionately urged, with a corresponding life, are a minister's best weapons.

A knowledge of medicine, especially in the country, is of great importance.

Seize occasions for subjects of preaching ; associations ; sick-bed suggestions ; conversations with the ignorant and poor.

Laborious and full preparation in the first years of the ministry are felt afterwards to have their high value.

It is good to limit ourselves, from the beginning to the end of our ministry, to one well-studied sermon per week. There is an advantage in having a constant subject of thought.

The Rev. J. Pratt—

Fight on with simplicity, self renunciation, and prayer through all discouragements, and God will appear in the end.

A minister's imperfections—his refractoriness, his vanity, &c.—may make him tender and forbearing towards others.

A minister should call in aid from his serious hearers in visiting the poor.

Pay special attention to children.

Watch for hints from all quarters. We should mark the excellencies of our brethren ; the failings of our brethren : note what has succeeded and what not.

It is important to embrace occasions of doing good.

There is necessity of watching against the deadening effect of ministerial occupations.

Deal largely with Scripture in the ministry, rather than be too topical.

The external Church appears much worse than young ministers apprehended, while the real Church is perhaps better.

Preaching the Gospel is now become rather a popular than an unpopular thing. If a minister loses one friend by preaching evangelically he gains more.

Non omnia possumus omnes, as Mr Scott used often to say. City ministers and country ministers have different experiences.

Religious societies among our people are inexpedient, unless the ministers can superintend them.

Experience in the ministry teaches us to admire the divine forbearance and mercy. A minister is but *the voice of one crying in the wilderness.*

A minister should be cautious of entangling himself with secular occupations. The committees of our religious societies are in some measure secular.

Experience teaches us the importance of strict regard to our engagements as ministers.

We learn, too, to be surprised at nothing ! What thin ice we have passed over, and yet escaped breaking through !

God's care of his Church is illustrated in much that we have seen. Useful and great ministers die ; but Christ lives !

The advantages and dangers of HABIT are impressed upon us by our experience of the past.

Let us labour and watch to become rather the *voluntary* than the *involuntary* instruments of doing the will of God. We may follow nature's bent too much ; God will use you, even then, for his glory. But follow rather the leadings of Providence and grace, though against nature.

DECEMBER 23, 1811.

THE QUESTION OF LAST EVENING RESUMED.

There is danger of our mistaking pulpit affections for spiritual affections. *Nemo sine multitudine disectus esse protest.*—Cicero.

There is danger of modelling our preaching on the peculiar views of some leading hearers, or of our own minds.

Those are the best seasons in the pulpit when there is the greatest fear of God and the least of man.

We are often more anxious to make a good sermon, than to deliver the simple message of the Gospel.

We may be suspicious where our congregation commends us for gifts. If his gifts be more prominent than grace, a minister should sink those gifts. A congregation is seldom advancing when they are apt to say, " How great you were to-day ! "

A minister should identify himself as much as possible with his congregation.

Beware of producing any impression on the congregation that you do not sympathise with them : for example, stand up in the pulpit and sing with the congregation before the sermon begins. The same spirit should prevail out of the Church, as well as in. Frequently ask for the congregation's prayers. Religious societies, at which the minister presides, keep up the sympathy.

We learn by experience the necessity and advantage of equanimity.

We are taught patience and charity under the petulance of lay-divinity.

We see the difficulty of submitting to the *means* by which God is bringing about the great ends for which we pray.

How much do we find in ourselves of a sad mixture of crooked policy ; of the workings of evil temper ; of the preaching of SELF !

One finds that every part of the ministry has gone on as the heart has prospered or not.

Sermons should smell more of the sweet incense of prayer than of the smoke of the lamp.

God's plan, we find, is to empty the man. This is done by His allowing sinkings of spirit, self-dissatisfaction, sickness, chagrin, &c.

There is a superintendence of Divine Providence in regulating our destination as to labour.

Degeneracy of motive is the chief cause of ministerial difficulties and embarrassments.

Jesus Christ, the Alpha and Omega of the whole ministry, and due honour to the Divine Spirit—these are master-keys !

Conversation with exercised souls is a great means of help to a minister. Work up your sentiments and experience thus gained into sermons.

Symptoms of decline are, when politics engross too much attention —when there is a want of family piety.

Using retirement to prepare for activity is an evidence of perseverance and usefulness.

Men of fixed principles are most useful.

Our ministry perpetually illustrates God's faithfulness ; *as a man sows, so shall he reap.*

JANUARY 20, 1812.

WHAT IS THE SCRIPTURE DOCTRINE OF ASSURANCE, AND HOW FAR SHOULD IT ENTER INTO OUR MINISTRY?—Proposed by the Rev. H. Budd.

Mr Budd—

There is an assurance of UNDERSTANDING (Col. ii. 2), when we perceive the harmony and consistency of the Gospel; of FAITH (Heb. x. 22), when we are convinced that this is the revelation of God, and that all his promises will be fulfilled; of HOPE (Heb. vi. 11), when beyond doubt or hesitation we are satisfied that we are true believers.

To be full of the assurance of faith, is the duty of every one. The assurance of hope is attained and preserved by diligence.

In order to enter into our *ministry*, (1.) It should enter into our experience; (2.) It should enter into our private counsel.

Usher says we may attain assurance by some means—either *à priori*, by listening to the divine calls; or by other arguments, *à posteriori*, which come from the fruits of faith. These are more evident, but not so sure.

The Rev. J. Pratt—

The Wesleyan Methodists' views are these:—They in general make the forgiveness of sin, and the knowledge of their forgiveness, one and the same thing.

We should distinguish between an assurance of *feeling* and an assurance of *inference*. The Holy Spirit enables the Christian to *infer* from what God has wrought.

This doctrine should enter into our ministry in the way of exciting us to watchfulness and diligence. For, *cæteris paribus*, confidence will be proportioned to diligence. We are to *give diligence* in order to make *our calling and election sure* to ourselves. We are to *hold fast the confidence and the rejoicing of hope firm unto the end* (Heb. iii. 6). *We are made partakers of Christ if we hold the beginning of our confidence steadfast unto the end* (Heb. iii. 14).

We must not preach the duty of assurance as a duty *per se*. But the duty of living in that state with which assurance is connected. And then the duty of entire confidence in the divine assurance and Christ's work, provided conscience justifies us, in full acquiescence with God's will.

There is great danger in preaching assurance in any other manner. It is dangerous to say, as some do, " What have you to do with your misfortunes and your sins? Christ has undertaken all." This is true; but, so stated, is liable to abuse.

Want of assurance generally arises from consciousness of distance and alienation, and want of entire cordiality with God.

The mercy of God has connected assurance with vigilance. Doubts keep many close to Christ who would live carelessly if they had none. I mean doubts of personal interest, not of the truth of God. Toward the close of life, the soul is brought to look off the fruit to the Saviour.

The want of knowledge of Christ shakes assurance. See Watts' second sermon, *Faith founded on Knowledge.*

Remarks of other Members—

Assurance is spoken of in Scripture under other terms. Thus faith is called a *substance,* Heb. xi. 1; an *evidence,* Heb. xi. 1. *Boldness,* Eph. iii. 12, implies assurance. These may be steps towards the *full assurance* spoken of by St Paul, Col. ii. 2; Heb. vi. 11.

Objective assurance, is the assurance of faith. Subjective assurance, the assurance of hope.

Faith respects the truth of God's promises; hope respects our interest in these promises.

Assurance of faith respects our full belief of the divine doctrines and promises. Assurance of hope respects our inference of an interest in them.

Hope has to do with future good. Distinguish faith into objective and subjective. In this view, the assurance of faith will respect the truth of God as an objective act. But it will respect our interest in Christ as a subjective act. The one may be called the assurance of faith, and the other the assurance of sense.

Assurance is often wanting from confounding the covenant of works with the covenant of grace; the work of justification with that of sanctification.

The overwhelming importance of the subject sometimes may withhold assurance.

FEBRUARY 3, 1812.

HOW CAN WE BEST IMPROVE THE APPROACHING FAST?

We have now been nearly twenty years at war. It is evident that God's judgments are abroad in the earth.

Yet such encouragements have arisen in these last twenty years, as have not been seen perhaps since the day of Pentecost.

Some extracts from the Cambridge Annual Bible Society proceedings will shew this.

There is a growing union of Christians of different denominations. An increased regard to the interests of the heathen world. The London Missionary Society, the Society for Missions to Africa and the East [now called the Church Missionary Society], the Baptist Missionary Society, the British and Foreign Bible Society, the Jew's Society, the Edinburgh Missionary Society—have all sprung up of late, and are wishing each other God-speed.

There is a diffusion of religious feeling and activity through the country by the Bible Society : especially at Cambridge, at Bedford, at Hertford, and other places. A flood of infidelity has been likely to overwhelm us.

There is increased attention to the education of the poor. National and Lancasterian schools are doing a good work.

There is a greater regard to the temporal and spiritual wants of the poor.

In the navy and army, there is more leaven of piety. It is the intention of Government to furnish them with the Scriptures. The issuing of such a general order as the Commander-in-Chief has issued, respecting the education of soldiers' children, is most encouraging.

There is a union of even foreign enemies in the grand design of diffusing the Gospel. The Emperor of Russia, King of Prussia, the late and present King of Sweden.

Our discouragements are, that our public sins still continue ; there is a system of traffic by perjury and fraud ; lotteries, gin-drinking, are still crying evils. Our Colonial Legislatures are bad.

The continuance of the King's illness is a great calamity. The state of Ireland is a cause of great anxiety.

Our duty is plain. Urge a praying spirit. Let there be more intercessory prayer. Urge a watchful regard to the footsteps of God.

The uncertainty of future events has a great tendency to awaken this spirit.

Urge a spirit of sympathy with the miseries and sufferings of mankind. One hundred thousand perished in civil war in New Spain. Five times that number have perished in the Peninsular war.

Recollect the distressed state of our manufactories at home.

The grand objects which we should propose to ourselves, as ministers, on every fast day, and we should distinctly tell the people so, are—

1. To bring if but ONE soul to God !

2. To quicken Christians in the exercise of suitable graces.

Our sermons should have a national, not a political cast.

Touch chiefly on sins which the people are guilty of, and by the grace of God may overcome.

FEBRUARY 17, 1812.

HOW SHALL WE DISTINGUISH BETWEEN THOSE EVENTS WHICH ARE THE LEADINGS OF PROVIDENCE, AND THOSE WHICH ARE SENT AS TRIALS OF OUR CHARACTER ?—Proposed by the Rev. H. Godfrey.

Mr Godfrey—

Whatever arises in an apparent way of Providence, if it meet our own inclination, and serve our carnal and worldly policy, we have reason to think a trial and temptation, and not a token of God's favour.

On the next subject we have no notes.

MARCH 16, 1812.

WHEREIN DOES A TRULY RELIGIOUS TENDERNESS OF CONSCIENCE CONSIST, AND HOW IS IT TO BE DISTINGUISHED FROM SCRUPULOSITY OF CONSCIENCE ?—Proposed by the Rev. H. G. Watkins.

The Rev. J. Pratt—

Tenderness of conscience regards God's rule ; as, for example, David breathing after God's word. Scrupulosity frequently regards rules of its own ; as, for instance, the Scribes and Pharisees making the commandments of God of none effect by their traditions.

Tenderness of conscience takes the obvious bearing of God's rule. St Paul would urge the spirit of a rule. Scrupulosity generally rests itself on far-fetched inferences from the rule. Like the Judaising teachers and others wresting the word.

Tenderness of conscience is desirous of light. St Paul—*Lord, what wouldst thou have me to do?* Scrupulosity is frequently obstinate and unwilling to admit light. Saul persecuting the Church.

Tenderness of conscience deals chiefly with the weightier matters of the law ; it attends to the inside of the cup and platter. Scrupulosity is principally conversant with trifles ; the outside.

Tenderness of conscience has a tendency to promote the spiritual interests of the individual ; to deal with what bears on the besetting sin. Scrupulosity frequently has little or nothing to do with those interests.

Tenderness of conscience is candid and liberal toward others. St Paul, how severe was he toward himself ! how liberal toward others ! Scrupulosity is generally uncharitable in its judgment of others. It makes men offenders for a word.

Tenderness of conscience is anxious to promote the spiritual good of others. St Paul, with the utmost tenderness of conscience, devotes himself for his brethren. Scrupulosity is generally indifferent to such interests. It is zealous to win to a party.

Tenderness of conscience is associated with a suitable and entire affiance of Christ. St Paul—*Yea, doubtless, and I count all things but loss for the excellency of the knowledge of Christ Jesus my Lord.* Scrupulosity is self-righteous. See the Judaising teachers.

Scrupulosity is frequently an evidence of a good state toward God, where it arises from the structure of the mind, or the physical constitution of the man.

Tenderness of conscience has a universal regard to the commands of God.

Scrupulosity will sometimes take liberties beyond God's commands.

A person will deny card-playing, but will indulge a censorious worldly spirit.

Ministers should frequently direct and exhort to the cultivation of tenderness of conscience.

Satan will try to direct tenderness into scrupulosity. He will weary and disgust, if not overwhelm, by sin.

Exhort your people to seek light, to keep the mind open to conviction, to pray for humility, to maintain watchfulness.

Remarks of other Members—

We are more in danger of saying to the Divine Spirit, " Go thy way till I have a more convenient season," than of saying, " Dwell in me and walk in me."

Pascal is a striking instance of scrupulosity of conscience.

Scrupulosity frequently arises from a delicate structure of mind.

The man cannot make up his mind.   He is unable to bring himself to a conclusion.

Tenderness of conscience and scrupulosity may exist, at different times, in the same person.   Scrupulosity wants light ; when that light comes, tenderness of conscience succeeds.

Tenderness of conscience respects the glory of God.   Joseph would not listen to his mistress.   Ezra would not ask for a band of soldiers. Scrupulosity respects principally the honour that cometh of man. Herod would not violate his oath.

Tenderness of conscience is joined with humility and tenderness. Scrupulosity, in the unconverted, with bigotry and pride.

Tenderness of conscience is attended with pity of the scruples of others.   Scrupulosity will anathematise.

A tender conscience is sprinkled with the blood of atonement.

A tender conscience will be careful not to go to the borders of Christian liberty.

A tender conscience will lead to self-denial on grounds of usefulness to others.

Saurin remarks that a healthy conscience has a similar relation to the soul that the senses have to the body.   If it were necessary to reason on the quality of food before we eat, we should die of hunger.

It is thus with the conscience.   If we were obliged to investigate every minute matter before we act, we should never act.   But a healthy conscience acts as it were by instinct.

A good conscience will proportion its zeal to the nature of the cause. A scrupulous conscience will manifest disproportionateness.

A good conscience is seasonable in its calls to duty.   A scrupulous conscience is unseasonable.

A good conscience is permanent in its operations.   A scrupulous conscience is uncertain.

There is danger of damping scrupulousness, lest it degenerate into hardness.   There is also a danger of scrupulousness damping tenderness of conscience.

There is great variety in the actings of conscience : sometimes they arise from a change of physical state ; frequently from the activity or decay of grace.

Conscience is a man's judgment of himself in reference to the will of God.   A good conscience is enlightened in its decisions, sprinkled by the blood of Christ, guided by the Divine Spirit, universal in its actings, and permanent in its operations.

On the next topic, THE HARMONY OF THE GENERAL OFFERS OF MERCY CONTAINED IN THE GOSPEL WITH THE DOCTRINE OF PERSONAL ELECTION, we have no notes.

APRIL 13, 1812.

WHAT ARE THE PROMINENT DIFFICULTIES ATTENDING THE ARMINIAN SYSTEM ?—Proposed by the Rev. B. Woodd.

Mr Woodd—

Arminians hold that—

1. God, from eternity, predestinated to everlasting life those whom he foresaw would believe in Christ and persevere to the end.

2. Christ, by his sufferings and death, made atonement for all the sins of all mankind, and of every individual ; but none but believers can be partakers of the divine benefit.

3. True faith cannot proceed from the exercise of natural faculties nor free-will, since man is incapable of thinking or doing any good thing ; therefore, in order to his salvation, it is necessary that he be regenerated and renewed by the Holy Spirit, which is the gift of God through Christ ; but sufficient grace is given to all.

4. This divine energy begins and perfects all that can be called good. It is offered to all, but may be resisted and rendered ineffectual by the perverse will of man.

5. God gives the regenerate the means of preserving themselves in this state ; but they may lose justifying faith, forfeit their state of grace, and die in their sins.

The difficulties of this system are—

1. It makes the will of man the arbiter and ordainer of events.

2. It involves the whole plan of redemption in uncertainty as to its event.

3. The object of the great scheme of mercy might have been rendered fruitless.

4. It detracts from the glory of divine grace, and gives man whereof to glory in himself.

5. It makes the eternal God derive his motives of action from his creatures.

6. It seems confuted by the partial illumination of the world.

7. It seems confuted by instances of individual conversion which are continually taking place.

8. It seems confuted by those constant trains of events which indicate plan and pre-determination.

Objections to both Calvinism and Arminianism—

1. Both systems of Calvin and Arminius infer too much. Calvinism associates too closely with necessity. Arminianism exalts free-will almost above God ; and its consequences seem to involve the denial of particular providence.

2. Calvinists chiefly insist on pre-determination. Arminians chiefly on pre-science. Now, the pre-science of the Arminian seems to involve the pre-determination of the Calvinist.

The following are self-evident axioms :—

1. God is infinitely holy, wise, and good.

2. Man is a moral agent, accountable and rewardable.

3. The redemption of Christ is sufficient for the sins of the world.

R

4. Mercy is universally offered.

5. The rejection of mercy is to be attributed wholly to the wilful obstinacy and sin of man. *This is the condemnation, that light is come into the world, but men love darkness rather than light. Ye will not come that ye might have life.*

6. The acceptance of mercy is wholly to be attributed to the grace of God. *By the grace of God I am what I am. Ye have not chosen me, but I have chosen you.*

7. Man must wait in faith and patience for further information in a better world.

The Rev. W. Goode—

Arminianism undeifies the Deity, and deifies the creature. It leaves every man where Calvinism leaves only the reprobate. It represents God as wishing what is not effected. It denies the total depravity of human nature. It makes salvation depend on the will of a creature, whom the Scriptures represent as totally depraved.

The Rev. J. Pratt—

The different degrees of reward is not a doctrine of Arminianism. It need not be preached, though true. *An abundant entrance* must be the aim.

We may be content to preach in such manner as to be accounted at one time Arminian and at another Calvinistic.

The class of BIBLE-CHRISTIANS increases. Some of them seem to verge toward Calvinism. Others toward Arminianism in some of its points. But all real Christians on both sides, decidedly incline, in experience and in preaching, to honour Divine grace, and to lower man.

Arminianism lowers the doctrine of union with Christ and kindred doctrines.

Neither Calvinists nor Arminians, when truly pious, are consistent with the strictness of their own tenets ; and both preach scripturally.

One advantage of Arminianism, which the pious Calvinist borrows from him, is close and awful appeals to conscience on account of man's accountableness.

A difficulty of Arminianism is the mechanical form which it gives to religious experience.

Say what you will of Arminian difficulties, no difficulty can be greater than that of reconciling the sovereignty of God with the responsibility of man.

The Rev. D. Wilson—

Arminianism has difficulties—

1. As to matters of DOCTRINE.

It lowers the doctrine of the Fall ; it obscures the grace of God ; it denies justification by faith through the imputed righteousness of Christ ; a kind of running account is kept. It obscures the work and influence of the Holy Spirit. It obscures the glory of God.

2. As to the SALVATION OF SINNERS.

If Calvinism is to consist of abstract propositions without reference to the motives and objects for which they are stated in the Scriptures, then Arminianism has a greater effect on the salvation of man.   But there is no abstract proposition in the Bible.   All is for use and energy.

Practical Calvinism is far superior to Arminianism—in respect of the sinfulness of sin, as to the attraction of the Cross, in increasing the difference between godly and ungodly men, in respect to encouragement to turn to God.

3. In respect of EXPERIENCE.

There is danger of Calvinism letting the flesh get the upper hand, and growing careless and presumptuous.   But there is danger of Arminianism puffing up the creature.

Other Members—

On predestination certainly following on prescience, Twisse principally rests in defending Calvinism : and this view made Dr South a Calvinist.

Prescience implies a necessity of immutability, but not a necessity of co-action or force.

It was the revealed will of God that Judas should not betray his master, that the Jews should not shed innocent blood, that Pilate and Herod should not unjustly condemn the righteous.   Yet it is declared that they all acted according to the determinate counsel and foreknowledge of God !   O the depths!

We have no notes on the next topic.

MAY 1, 18112.

HOW SHALL WE CONVINCE AMIABLE CHARACTERS OF THEIR NATURAL DEPRAVITY ?—Proposed by the Rev. B. Woodd.

The Rev. J. Pratt—

Inquire into their opinion of themselves.   You will find self-congratulation ; little allowance for others ; they will be resting on something different from God's foundation.   Shew them the contrariety of this to the word of God.

Inquire into their view of the Law.   Inquire into their view of God and heaven.   The Socratic way of disputation is useful.   Lead them to condemn themselves.   Treat them as our Lord did the Scribe, seize their concessions.   *Thou art not far from the kingdom of God.* Mark xii. 34.

Recommend Watts' *Hopeful Youth falling short of Heaven.*   By the way, your sermon will suggest many grounds of reasoning with amiable persons.

Rather talk *for* than *at* such persons.   Display the elevated character of Christian piety.

A practical reliance is wanted on the Divine spirit in dealing with such persons.

Law's *Serious Call* is of great use in the conviction of such persons.

Remarks of other Members—

Thou shalt love the Lord thy God with all thy heart, and with all thy mind, and with all thy strength—is a clenching argument with amiable persons.

Find out the darling sin. Bring before them active and public characters: such as Swartz. Insist on Christian principles — the depravity of nature.

Shew them their opposition to pious characters. Palliate the evil of other characters. But fall on pious men without mercy. Warn them against trusting to the opinions of others.

Remind them of wandering thoughts. Detect their peculiar prejudices. There was a lady who would submit that her husband should be sent abroad by the King through her spirit of passive obedience, and even that she herself be ordered into his seraglio ; but who resented and resisted his command to enter a Presbyterian meeting.

Shew them the workings of envy. The young lady at the dress or dancing of a rival.

Point to First-Table duties. Amiable persons are apt to take God's name in vain.

Discover the criminality of unbelief.

In Frank's *Best Way of Preaching*, and the 2d chapter of Doddridge's *Rise and Progress*, are excellent suggestions for dealing with such persons.

The sufferings and death of young children are calculated to convince such persons of natural depravity.

The ninth chapter of Daniel gives a striking form of confession of sin.

MAY 25, 1812.

WHAT ARE THE CHARACTERISTICS OF A PUBLIC SPIRIT, AND THE JUST LIMITS OF ITS OPERATION ?—Proposed by the Rev. J. Clayton.

Mr Clayton—

Christianity inspires public spirit; not for the good of any particular nation, but for the good of mankind.

The CHARACTERISTICS of a public spirit are these—

1. It is the part of a whole. There must be personal and family religion before we can pay proper attention to public matters.

2. It is charitable and tolerant, not bitter and censorious ; but sometimes it operates as a licence to disparage others.

3. It is humble and not ostentatious.

The LIMITS within which it is to operate.

(1.) It must not be carried so far as to destroy health.

(2.) It is not to trench on private duties.

(3.) It is not to hinder, in ministers, public preaching.

Much of the present public spirit springs from animal fervour caught in meetings: it is a spirit of restlessness : men are stilted up, who would get no notice in any other way.

God may use these men as the scaffold for the building he is erecting.

When public spirit is refined, its bulk will be diminished.

Remarks of other Members—

A public spirit makes us willing to make sacrifices.

We are better pleased to have good done by others than by ourselves, when a genuine public spirit influences us.

Lord Cornwallis exhibited a fine public spirit in going the second time to India, when he probably foresaw that it would be his grave, because he was persuaded that his character would conciliate the natives.

Public spirit must be limited by the feelings of the man. If irascible, he must not let his spirit carry him so far as to draw him into temptation in his temper.

We may be at home and yet be very frivolous there !

Disinterestedness is a mark of a public spirit.

Self-devotedness, too. *Unum pro multis dabitur caput.*

Consistency. Not for and against reform, merely because the man is in indifferent circumstances. Not to be active and inactive according to the man who supports you.

Purity of principle is a mark of a true public spirit.

Public occupation makes us value the Sabbath as a day, not of argument, but of communion with God. A view of the Cross arrests and collects the spirit.

A true public spirit must originate in a renewed nature. Jehu marred his public spirit by saying, *Come, see my zeal for the Lord.*

Public spirit will often seek retirement. *I beheld the transgressors, and was grieved.* In retirement, it will pray and intercede. Thus did Moses and Samuel.

It will discover itself in domestic cultivation. By neglect of children and servants many do more to injure the public than any efforts abroad can counteract.

It aims to fill up the proper sphere. It co-operates, according to our measure of time and ability, in public and grand efforts for good.

It is distinguishing; it is active; it shews itself in an earnest desire to lay ourselves out for the good of others.

Prudence marks it ; discharging first the immediate duties of our station. Moses lifted his hands ; Aaron and Hur sustained them when sinking ; and Joshua conquered Amelek : each, in his station, did his part.

The Rev. J. Pratt—

A deep sense of redeeming mercy; a single eye to the glory of God ; an endeavour to give all we can—are the springs of a genuine public spirit. Two mites cast into the treasury are the characteristics of a public spirit. So the breaking the box of ointment. The poor man's prayers for his country and the world, the weekly penny, the half guinea, the hundred pounds, are all actings of the public spirit, when the motive is good. The time of the active man devoted to good, and the ardent wishes of the retired, flow from the same.

A willingness to forward real good with any class of men ; a due proportioning of time, and money, and influence to objects as to their nature—these are the actings of a public spirit.

Public spirit will prefer the self-denying service, if more useful, to the gratifying service, if less so.

The divine estimate of public spirit will probably prove to be vastly different from ourselves. God may see more public spirit in the prayer of the retired, than in the *act* of the public man.

It is certain that there is an extraordinary dash of self-gratulation in many admirable men who come forward much in public.

It is a question, what proportion of activity springs from the spirit of self-gratulation, and what from genuine regard to Christ ?

Distinguish between a busy spirit and a public spirit. Much is done in public to promote worldly interests.

God will have his instruments, but will secure to himself the glory.

We must not limit the operation of a public spirit by what is pleasant to ourselves.

Public spirit should put much limit on attendance at public dinners. It should limit itself, not by the entreaties of others but in conscience before God.

June 8, 1812.

WHAT ARE THE CHARACTERISTIC EVILS IN THE SPIRIT OF THE TIMES ? AND IN WHAT MANNER MAY THEY BE BEST COUNTERACTED ?—Proposed by the Rev. J. Pratt.

Mr Pratt—

Much evil is prevalent which is not particularly characteristic. Misjudging of public men is a great evil.

CHARACTERISTIC EVILS are—

(1.) Disdain of authority. This has arisen from the French Revolution. It is very different from the old Whig spirit.

(2.) An eager, even vindictive, attachment to party.

(3.) Ferocity.

(4.) An over-estimate of civil liberty.

(5.) A boldness in profligacy and infidelity. This is seen in debating societies; among what are called "Free-thinking Christians." Meetings have been held to establish "serving on Sundays."

(6.) Religious profession. This is a wide evil, often deep, but generally shallow.

(7.) Ostentation. There is a universal treading of one class on the heels of the classes above.

(8.) Perjury. The state of trade shews this.

The devil rages in opposition to the work of God.

In counteraction of these evils, we must remember that ministers are watchmen of the times. They are peculiarly called to mark and warn : in their personal and social character, we must be ever bearing testimony.

Remarks of other Members—

Men are more deeply selfish and avaricious than ever in political life.

There is a desperate spirit of speculation in the commercial world.

The income-tax has weakened the moral principle.

An extravagant style of living has sprung up. This is the stimulus to commercial speculation.

Frivolity of mind and pursuits mark the times. Periodical works promote this spirit. Circulating libraries feed it. Loose extempore preaching promotes it.

Systematic opposition to Government is a black omen : and the combination of workmen against their masters.

This evil spirit will not go out but by prayer—in the closet, the family, in public.

Dispersion of tracts is a means of counteracting these evils.

Selfishness and insubordination are let loose.

Sunday newspapers are an engine of prodigious mischief. They are mostly democratic, and infect the lower classes. Government is too lenient, as to allowing the promulgation of unsocial opinions.

Nominal and excessive credit is a great evil. " Children pass, not through the fire to Moloch, but through filth to mammon," says Dr Whittaker.

The character of these times is awful, legible, written in letters of blood !

An equalising spirit is another sign. The malicious and revengeful spirit of the times springs much from this equalising spirit.

The influx of foreigners has done harm. This is the history of all falling states. See Juvenal's account of Rome.

Little booksellers, with small tracts, with coarse and impure pictures, infuse poison into the people. Contempt of order is the consequence. This seems to be a dispensation of God in these latter times. God tries men. He shews what man would be if restraint were taken from him.

But let us not despair. Let every one be at his post, watchful and vigorous, and determined. Infidelity crumbles to nothing when opposed aright. The Bible Society is a grand instrument.

The nobles are preaching the Gospel ! The late Duke of Grafton told Mr ——, " I have been cured of Socinianism by the evil characters of Socinians. There is no piety nor charity among them ! Socinianism will not do for old age. I feel I want a Mediator."

June 22, 1812.

What is the Scripture View of Growth in Grace ?—Proposed by the Rev. C. R. Pritchett.

Mr Pritchett—

1. It is entirely of God. *Holding the head, from which all the body, by*

joints and bands, having nourishment ministered, and knit together, increaseth with the increase of God (Col. ii. 19).

2. It arises from an intimate and vital union with Christ. (*Ditto.*)

3. It is produced and carried on by the constant and immediate agency of the Holy Spirit. *I will pour water upon him that is thirsty*, &c. (Isa. xliv. 3).

1. In what point may growing in grace be considered as originating? Marshall endeavours to prove that the very foundation of all growing in grace is an actual persuasion of our reconciliation with God.

2. What are the general marks of growth in grace? The chief are humility and simplicity.

The Rev. J. Pratt—

Submission to grace, desire of grace, conformity to grace, are marks of growth (Eph. iv. 12–16).

Progress in grace is shewn when we are growing in a sense of need of it; have an increasing estimation of its value; shew more decided preference of the things of grace; are advancing in the diligent use of means; have clearer views of sin and Christ; when the spiritual senses are improved; when we have deeper contrition and self-renunciation; increasing charity towards the brethren, more ardent love to Christ's kingdom, and greater maturity.

Remarks of other Members—

Increasing fruitfulness is a sign. *Every branch in me that beareth fruit, he purgeth that it may bring forth more fruit.*

Growing submission to the Divine will; thankfulness for affliction —*It is good for me that I have been afflicted*—are signs of growth.

Growth in grace is important for solid comfort.

It must be gradual, like the insensible motion of the hand on the dial. Like dew: *I will be as the dew unto Israel* (Hos. xiv. 5).

Distinguish between growth in gifts and growth in grace.

The passions, on bereavement, may be set afloat—we may weep, yet not grow in grace.

Growth in grace may be evidenced by the prevailing temper of the heart, humility, absolute dependence on God, submission to God, reverential fear of God, love of God, the affections sanctified, and the mind made spiritual.

Growth in grace is evidenced by growing in evangelical views in our worship and services; depending more on Christ, and living on his fulness; not being satisfied without comfortable frames, but not depending on them.

Growth in grace must be universal, entering into all the parts of the character.

The means of growth are—the milk of the word, and the bread of life.

Grace is a principle of action, arising in a rectified understanding, a sanctified will, divinely-directed affections, and issuing in holy conduct.

Doubts are permitted to set us on investigation. Baxter says, no man really believes a doctrine of which he has had no doubts.

JULY 6, 1812.

WHAT IS THE BEST METHOD OF CONDUCTING PRIVATE PRAYER?—
Proposed by the Rev. H. Budd.

Mr Budd—

The best method is that which detaches the heart most from the
world, and raises it to God. Prayer is the language of the affections
towards God.

The spirit of prayer is promoted by meditation on the divine attributes, reading the Scriptures, remembering the promises, considering
prayer as a privilege, not merely as a duty.

The subject of prayer is ample. As ministers, we should bring
foward the peculiar difficulties and objects of the ministry. We should
have stated periods of going over the flock—the unconverted, the
uncertain, the impressed, backsliders, believers, the mass of unknown.
We should pray for the bishops, and divide the clergy under certain
heads—good men in the Church, those in whom God has put some
good thing, the proud, prejudiced, haughty, bigoted, trifling, gay, and
ignorant.

We should have our time and season for private prayer.

The place to which our prayers should be directed. Heaven is not
so much a place as a nature. Wheresoever God is, there is heaven.
But, as creatures, we must get all aids. Association with particular
places will assist.

The posture. This should be such as to excite attention. Vocal or
mental prayer may be used as most helpful.

Remarks of other Members—

Some of Baxter's prayers at the end of *Poor Man's Family Book* are
a great help. So Patrick's *Help to Prayer.*

The best method is that which suits us best at the time.

Abraham had his altar everywhere. Jacob wrestled with God in
the open field. We should live in the spirit of looking upwards at all
times. *Tota vita Christiani est sanctum desiderium.*

We may use freedom as to manner and posture. Walking, kneeling,
sitting.

It is not so much to be done by rules. Nor need stated seasons for
stated subjects be too closely adhered to.

The SCRIPTURE is the ground of prayer. Read, meditate, and then
pray.

As to place. A church or a chapel is good for private prayer; the
expanse of the place assists.

Bishop Andrews' book is a great help to intercession. So is the
Liturgy.

One evening a-week we should give for intercession. *Making mention
of you in my prayers.* (Eph. i. 16.) The Apostle makes much of the
prayers of others.

We shall gain little by aiming at too much. We are creatures of
the body and sense.

The *habit* of prayer marks the man more than adherence to settled rules. Settled rules, if too minute and precise, will subject to bondage, and lead to self-righteousness.

Our houses are a hindrance from their structure. They do not afford sufficient retirement for pouring out the voice. See Ps. lxxvii. 1.

The spirit of prayer is kept up more by seizing occasions than by dwelling on stated subjects.

The spirit of prayer is portrayed in that passage, *Because ye are sons, God hath sent forth the Spirit of his Son into your hearts, crying, Abba! Father!* (Gal. iv. 6.)

Living in nearness to God in everyday life, as Nehemiah, is the spirit. *A people near unto him.* (Ps. cxlviii. 14.) *Through him we have access by one Spirit unto the Father.* (Eph. ii. 18.) We should consider ourselves to be *of the household of God;* as a *habitation of God through the Spirit.* See also Eph. iii. 12–17; vi. 18. Col. i. 3–9; iv. 2. Rom. xii. 12. 1 Thess. v. 17.

Importunity in prayer is urged by our Lord: Luke xi. 1–13—the friend rising through importunity. Luke xviii. 1–8—the unjust judge.

The characteristics of true prayer are a sense of need, desire of relief, faith in the divine provisions and promises, patient waiting, longing expectation.

Cultivating a thankful spirit is a great aid in prayer. This is frequently urged by the Apostle. An exulting spirit also in God and his children.

The true spirit of prayer is HANGING ON GOD. Enlargement in prayer arises often from natural causes; while a *bound-up* spirit is often a broken one. And, *The sacrifice of God is a broken spirit: a broken and a contrite heart, O God, thou wilt not despise!*

JULY 20, 1812.

WHAT ARE THE MOST LIKELY MEANS OF RECOVERING A BACKSLIDER? —Proposed by the Rev. H. Budd.

See the latter part of Owen on the *Glory of Christ:* also Fuller's *Backslider.*

The Rev. J. Pratt—

An open backslider is to be reclaimed by tenderness, and patience, and unwearied perseverance. Remind such that their case is *natural* to a certain extent. Save them from desperation and presumption. Advise them to fill their head and hands with better things. Guard them against the incentives which lead them astray; and urge a diligent and determined use of means. Recommend the use of Ps. li.

The backslider in heart is to be reclaimed by warning and caution. There are multitudes of such in our congregations. See the epistles to the seven churches.

Remarks of other Members—

Advise them to force themselves out of the way of temptation, even without *a heart* for it, that the *heart may come.* Employ friends to help you who have your confidence. Don't put them on an austere and rigorous course. Be ever willing to receive and kindly discourse with them.

Recommend retirement and reflection: *Remember from whence thou art fallen, and repent!* Urge the ingratitude of a backsliding state. See the latter part of Howe's *Delighting in God.*

Urge the discredit brought on a Christian profession by backsliding. Read chapters ii. and iii. of Jeremiah.

The meetings were adjourned till October. On the first occasion there was only a conversation on the Catholic Question. The subject the next time was, The Ground and Extent of the Gospel Call. We have no notes.

November 9, 1812.

What are the Symptoms and Causes of a Decline in Grace?— Proposed by the Rev. C. R. Pritchett.

What is it to be in grace?

A gracious state is indicated by gracious habits. There is a growing in such habits and a declining in such habits.

The symptoms of decline are—

When the perception of spiritual things is rather from past experience than from present feelings.

A want of feeling, which is probably soon followed by inattention and wandering in prayer. A distaste of Scripture.

Attaching too great importance to worldly circumstances as exciting to grace. Self-righteousness.

A want of retirement. Want of caution in our walk. Indulgence in things lawful though not expedient. Conversing incautiously on religious subjects.

Neglect of the suggestions of conscience. Relaxation in what we purposed for the glory of God.

Habits, rather than acts, are to be looked at as symptoms. Some mistake imaginary decays for real decays. And there are real decays of which men are not duly sensible.

Sluggishness in spiritual things ; the relish for spiritual things gone ; the conscience having lost its tenderness ; opposition to sin not so resolute as formerly; neglect of self-examination—these are symptoms.

Spiritual decays blunt the powers of the soul. Satan labours to produce peace in a state of decline.

Growth in grace is indicated by grief for sin, a savour of divine things, simple reliance on Christ, an endeavour after holiness.

An impaired apprehension of the evil of sin, remaining infirmities not deplored, inattention to the frame of mind in the discharge of duty—these are symptoms of decline in grace.

NOVEMBER 23, 1812.

IN WHAT RESPECT IS JESUS CHRIST TO BE CONSIDERED AS A LAWGIVER ?
—Proposed by the Rev. Mr Simons.

The Rev. J. Pratt—

Christ is a Lawgiver as the Head of the gospel dispensation.

There were never but TWO distinct LAWS—the Law of Innocence,
and the Law of the Fallen.

GOD, in his relation of Creator, is the Lawgiver of the Law of
Innocence. The MEDIATOR, in his mediatorial relation, is the Lawgiver
of Fallen man.

The Adamic, Noahic, Abrahamic, and Sinai covenants were all
gradations of the covenant of grace. They were all imperfect. The
Sinai covenant was also national and peculiar.

The Epistle to the Hebrews is a full comment on Christ's character
and superiority as a Lawgiver.

Moses, the servant of God, in administering the Sinai covenant,
was inferior to HIM, who, *as a son over his own house*, administers the
gospel dispensation. We are *under the law to Christ.* See Ps. cx.

Christ, therefore, was the Lawgiver of the whole dispensation of
grace, in all its gradations. Though we do not find Him called a
Lawgiver expressly, yet the whole Scripture teems with declarations of
His authority and acts as Head of the dispensation of grace.

Remarks of other Members—

Christ is a King : and his kingdom is not of this world. The laws
of the kingdom are HIS laws. The worship of the kingdom is his
worship. He divests the law of its curse, and says, *If ye love me, keep
my commandments.*

Christ vindicated the law from the false glosses of the Jewish
teachers.

Out of Zion shall go forth the law, &c., that is, the Gospel.

Law is a decree, an edict, a statute publicly established. Such is
the Gospel—by miracles, by prophets, by the testimony of the Holy
Ghost.

The Gospel is a law as placing man under a test, as a trial of his
state.

The Gospel is a law as a rule of action : *The grace of God . . . hath
appeared to all men, teaching us, that, denying ungodliness and worldly
lusts, we should live soberly, righteously, and godly, in this present world.*
(Titus ii. 11, 12.)

By the dispensation of pardon, and the grant of the Holy Spirit,
our Lord Jesus Christ establishes the law in all the saved. He
reconciles us, by pardon, to the divine government. He conforms the
heart, by sanctification, to the will of God.

Watt's *Harmony of the Divine Dispensations* furnishes abundant
matter on this subject.

The moral law, as the term of salvation, Christ never gave. But
the moral law, as the rule of life, he gave from the beginning.

Faith and love were enjoined before Christ came, though Christ enforced them by new motives.

See Hooker's conclusion of the first chapter of his *Polity*.

The subject on the next occasion was, WHAT ARE THOSE PARTS OF OUR LORD'S CHARACTER WHICH HAVE MOST STRUCK US IN READING? Mr Pratt was not present, being engaged at the first meeting for the formation of the North-East London Bible Society. He had been one of the principal promoters of that noble institution, the British and Foreign Bible Society, from the commencement in 1804; and was now actively engaged in assisting to organise Auxiliary and Branch Societies and Bible Associations for the City of London and its precincts.

On the next occasion the topic was, WHAT IS THE REAL INTENT OF BAPTISM, AND CAN THE UNBAPTISED ADULT BE DEEMED A MEMBER OF THE BODY OF CHRIST? We have no notes.

At the first meeting in the new year, country members and visitors were chosen as usual. In the list appears the name of the REV. JOHN VENN for the last time. The last occasion on which we have any remarks by him is May 29, 1809. Declining health appears to have interfered with his regular attendance subsequent to that date; and the members accordingly lost the benefit of his calm, thoughtful, wise, and original observations on the various topics which came before them. The subject which stands first in our volume was proposed by him, p. 3. It was Mr Venn who proposed for discussion the question which led to the formation of the CHURCH MISSIONARY SOCIETY, and opened up the subject at large, p. 95. He presided at the public meeting on the 12th April 1799, when that Society was instituted, p. 98; and is justly considered one of its Chief Founders, p. 100. The strain of his remarks, with so many of which this volume is enriched, will amply bear out much that is recorded of him in the following notice which was drawn up for a Tablet to his memory in the Parish Church of Clapham, of which he was Rector for twenty years.

He was endowed by Providence with a sound and powerful under-standing; and he added to an ample fund of classical knowledge, a familiar acquaintance with all the more useful parts of philosophy and science. His taste was simple. His disposition was humble and benevolent. His manners were mild and conciliating. As a divine, he was comprehensive and elevated in his views, and deeply conversant with theological subjects; but he derived his chief knowledge from the Scriptures themselves, which he diligently studied and faithfully inter-preted, anxious to impress on others those evangelical truths which he himself so deeply felt. By his family, among whom he was singu-larly beloved, his memory will be cherished with peculiar tenderness.

Having been sustained, during a long and trying illness, by a stedfast faith in that Saviour whom, in all his preaching, he laboured to exalt, he died, leaving to surviving friends an encouraging example of the blessedness of those who embrace, with their whole hearts, the religion of Jesus Christ. He died 1st July 1813, aged 54 years.

JANUARY 18, 1813.

WHAT ARE THE CHARACTERISTICS AND CONSEQUENCES OF AN INEFFI-CIENT MINISTRY?—Proposed by the Rev. J. Goode.

Mr Goode—

It may be doubtful whether it is proper to mention this subject generally; it should be done cautiously and sparingly.

Every minister is not qualified for every place. Some qualifications may be requisite for particular places.

All blessing is from God. Yet there may be want of success, without anything culpable on the part of the minister.

1. When a minister is low in character, he is likely to be inefficient. If a fribble.

2. If he have peculiarities.

Friends may value him ; but the people in general will not. Friends may feel, " We are thankful for our minister's impediments, or he would have removed to another station."

3. Want of attention and due preparation for the pulpit is a cause of inefficiency.

4. Too much attention to composition and delivery is so too. Such as labour to approve themselves to the taste of their hearers, rather than to their grace, will fail in effect. A blunt iron, when red hot, will pierce deeper into a piece of wood than one that is sharper, but cold.

5. Neglecting to honour the Holy Spirit. This can be done in the study, as well as in the pulpit.

6. Want of affection for the souls of the people—this also is a cause.

Some things on the part of the hearers may be the cause of a minister's want of success.

1. Want of love toward the minister. 2. Want of attention to what is delivered. 3. Wandering from place to place. 4. Neglect of prayer.

Remarks of other Members—

Inefficiency may arise from—

1. Want of lively personal religion in the minister.

2. Want of appropriate talents. Great abilities may not be appropriate to the place. He may be an able divine, but not a lucid preacher.

3. Want of a strong tone of evangelical sentiment in his public addresses. They may not be contrary to the Gospel, yet so blended with what is doubtful or obscure, that it is difficult to prove that the Gospel is preached.

4. Want of prudence in proposing the best end, and fixing on the fittest means.

5. Want of energy in the discharge of the pastoral office.

The Rev. J. Clayton—

We are not to judge of efficiency by the numbers who attend. For efficiency is of two kinds—unholy and holy.

No ministry is efficient but that which BREAKS WHOLE HEARTS, and HEALS BROKEN HEARTS.

1. A ministry is inefficient which does not make Christ the Alpha and Omega.

2. A ministry is inefficient where there is a manifest defect in the spirit. Yet, though God generally employs the animated organ, we must not be discouraged because our frame of mind and character is not so bright as we could wish.

3. A ministry is inefficient where glaring defects accompany the minister, where the temper is bad, where there is a love for good talk, and the people say, "Oh, we know what all his talk of devotion means!"

4. A ministry is inefficient which is indolent. Our Divine Lord was indefatigable. None are likely to be honoured who are not *about their Father's business*.

5. A ministry is inefficient if the minister be not a man of prayer. See Baxter in his *Reformed Pastor*.

Inefficiency may arise from the wickedness of the people; also from their withholding their prayers.

The Rev. J. Pratt—

Deficiency in the pastoral character is a cause of inefficiency. We preach to the people by knowing them. We prepare them by conciliation.

A cold and argumentative way of preaching is a cause of inefficiency. A vague and general mode of preaching is so too; also want of application. Mal. ii. 6 gives a fine description of an efficient and true minister.

A minister may not be inefficient when he is faithfully labouring in order to some further end. *Others laboured, and ye are entered into their labours.*

A ministry may be inefficient comparatively by divine appointment—to shew God's sovereignty, and to humble man.

Deficiency in duties will render a minister inefficient.

Disproportionate statements of doctrine; want of experience; want of sympathy with the people; disproportionate time in the study; acting out of our province; want of accessibleness—all these endanger inefficiency.

The CONSEQUENCES of inefficiency are—1. Few or no communicants. 2. Want of love. 3. A disputatious spirit. 4. Antinomian principles. 5. Conformity to the world.

If a man have had no proper call, the ministry is generally inefficient.

The CONSEQUENCES of inefficiency are, that it (1) lessens respect for the office ; (2) disheartens young beginners ; (3) renders the personal account peculiarly awful ; (4) involves the loss and ruin of the souls of men.

See a paper by T. S., in the *Christian Guardian* for December 1811.

A want of distinctiveness in stating the marks of conversion ; also a neglect of bringing forward Scripture proofs ; a want of philosophy to deal with man, such as man is ; not feeling the great responsibility of the ministry ; neglect of attention to the youth of the flock—these are causes of inefficiency.

The recorder of these notes was absent on the next two occasions, on account of the North-East London Auxiliary Bible Society. The questions were, THE DUTY, LIMIT, AND ADVANTAGE OF FREE INQUIRY ? and, HOW SHALL WE BEST IMPROVE THE APPROACHING FAST ?

MARCH 1, 1813.

IN WHAT RESPECTS IS THE LORD JESUS CHRIST MADE UNTO US SANCTIFICATION ?—Proposed by the Rev. Mr Clayton.

Mr Clayton—

Christ is made our sanctification in various ways—

1. Christ meritoriously purchased the sanctifying influences of the Holy Spirit.

2. Christ dispenses the Spirit.

3. Christ, by his continual intercession, preserves the principle of life communicated.

4. Christ progressively carries on the work, and will, in grace, finish that work.

Sanctification is a fruit of justification. It never exists without justification ; it is never to be conferred without it.

Remarks of other Members—

Christ is called our sanctification, as he is the pattern of sanctification. *Be ye holy, for I am holy.*

As we put on the image of Christ, he is made our sanctification : *Predestinated to be conformed to the image of his Son.*

It may be considered in a sacrificial sense, as He is the sin-offering whereby we are set apart ; as the priests, for example, were set apart by a sin-offering.—Heb. xiii. 12 ; John xvii. 9.

Christ is our sanctification, not by mere influence, but by indwelling in Christians by a believing union.

On the next topic, WHAT ARE THE HINDRANCES WHICH PREVENT RELIGIOUS PERSONS FROM ENJOYING THE COMFORTS OF RELIGION ? we have no notes.

On the next occasion also, March 29, 1813, Mr Pratt was absent, being engaged at a most important India meeting at the City of London Tavern. The East India Company's Charter of 1793 was about to expire, and the friends of Missions were now exerting themselves to the utmost to gain some advantages for the spread of Christian truth in the East. Meetings for deliberation on the best measures to be taken were held by the Church Missionary Society, and also by other bodies; and on the 29th of March a general meeting of all denominations was held at the City of London Tavern, Lord Gambier being in the chair, to petition Parliament. Meetings of the several bodies, and in various parts of the kingdom, rapidly followed. In all, between eight and nine hundred petitions were presented to Parliament at this time on this all-absorbing subject. Mr Pratt took an active part in this great movement. The result of the struggle was, that India was thrown open, without restriction, to missionary enterprise, and the Indian Episcopate was established.*

APRIL 12, 1813.

WHAT IS THE NATURE OF EXPERIENCE IN MATTERS OF RELIGION? AND HOW IS GENUINE TO BE DISTINGUISHED FROM COUNTERFEIT?— Proposed by the Rev. J. Pratt.

Mr Pratt—

The NATURE of EXPERIENCE in matters of religion.

In the widest sense, it is the influence of doctrines on the mind— the influence of our creed on our affections.

For it respects the influence of error as well as of truth; and the wrong influence of truth as well as the right.

But the question respects the right influence of truth, as distinguished from the influence of error or the wrong influence of truth.

" What influence have doctrines on my mind?" This is the first inquiry as to my experience. "What influence has my creed on my affections?" This is the second inquiry. The Scriptures are full of the details of experience: and they abound in exhortations grounded hereon. *Examine yourselves. Prove your own selves. Let a man examine himself. By reason of use* believers *have their senses exercised to discern both good and evil. . . . We glory in tribulations also, knowing that tribulation worketh patience; and patience, experience. . . . .* See the Saviour's example, Heb. v. 7–9. See also 1 Pet. i. 6–8; also the Corinthians—*What carefulness it wrought in you,* &c. 2 Cor. vii. 11. We may mark the effects of experience in others, as well as in ourselves. See 2 Thess. i. 11, 12; 1 Tim. vi.; 2 Tim. ii. 17–23; iii. 13, 16, 17.

The DISCRIMINATION of genuine experience.

1. What are NOT certain signs of genuine experience.

* See Memoir of the Rev. Josiah Pratt, B.D., chap. v.

(1.) Firm persuasion of the mind, or strong religious feelings. For the mind may be firmly persuaded of error. We read of some having *strong delusion, that they should believe a lie.* (2 Thess. ii. 11.) See also John ix. 40. And the affections may be wrought up to a high pitch without any gracious influence.

(2.) Apparent leadings of Providence.

(3.) Delight in religious knowledge and exercises. See Ezek. xxxiii. 31, 32.

(4.) Great knowledge of Scripture and reading.

2. Signs of genuine experience.

Genuine experiences come from the Divine Spirit in the use of appointed means; and are known from their tending—(1.) To humble the sinner; (2.) To exalt the Saviour; (3.) To sanctify the soul.

Remarks of other Members—

The Spirit of God works by the word. If any man professes to experience anything beyond that word, this is enthusiasm.

True experience receives the whole truth of God. It conforms to the precept, as it trusts the promise. True experience knows the value of the promises as a banker does of a bank-note. True experience writes *probatum est* at the foot of the promises.

The Rev. J. Goode—

Experience refers to all the knowledge which the Christian derives from truth and his trials, and to those feelings which are awakened by the operation of truth, &c., on his heart.

Faith and repentance mutually prove each other. If faith put an end to repentance, it proves it to be presumption.

Defective views in our people often proceed from the minister. Dwelling disproportionately on the majesty of God, for instance, begets dread and legal bondage. Dwelling disproportionately on the free mercy of God begets levity and presumption.

Corrupt mixtures attend genuine experience—I mean, of natural and corrupt with what is divine. We may never entirely distinguish genuine from false experience, yet it is our duty to labour after it. The beam of divine light as it comes from God is pure; as it is reflected from us, it is mixed with earthly alloy. There is often a partial influence of some corrupt principle, even while grace is in exercise. Thus our love to the brethren is love to *our* brethren. So the spirit of James and John calling for fire from heaven.

Remarks of other Members—

Our aim and perseverance prove the truth of experience. True experience is the acting of the new nature.

Right sentiments, sound experience, and consistent conduct, constitute a Bible Christian.

Sound experience is a kind of middle link which connects truth with holiness. It gives to the Scripture views of sin and of mercy a sanctifying influence.

" Frost in the pulpit," says some one, " generates ice in the pew."

Truth in harmony is the steady support of the soul: as the symmetry of the arch bears it up against the stream and the storm.

An artificial flower is scarcely to. be distinguished from a genuine one; but expose them to a drenching shower, and the difference is immediately discerned.

Knowledge felt is experience.

APRIL 26, 1813.

WHAT ARE THE NATURE AND EFFECTS OF FAITH AS THE PRINCIPLE OF THE CHRISTIAN LIFE ?—Proposed by the Rev. D. Wilson.

DEFINITION.—Faith, as the principle of the Christian life, is distinct from faith generally, which is credit given to God in his word. It is also distinct from faith in Christ, which is credit given to God's testimony to Jesus Christ, followed by affiance in Christ.

Faith, as the principle of the Christian life, is credit given to the testimony of God as to duties, wherein the Christian's life consists.

Its OPERATIONS.—The Christian walks by faith, stands by faith ; it purifies the heart ; it regards the Son of God ; it works by love ; it overcomes the world.

Our DANGER regarding it.—Ignorance of Scripture ; spoiling it through philosophy ; presumption; pride.   Consider it as it applies to the minister, in choosing texts, in making sermons, in taking up the Cross; as to success, as to not preaching self.

MAY 10, 1813.

WHAT IS THE PROVINCE OF REASON IN MATTERS OF RELIGION ?— Proposed by the Rev. D. Wilson.

Mr Wilson—

Reason apprehends and judges of things brought before it; or it is the power by which one proposition is deduced from another, or consequences from premises.

Reason is given us to improve the notions given by faith, but not to discover new facts.

Reason may be viewed as in a PERFECT creature; its actings are then complete.   Or in a FALLEN creature ; then passions and vice distort the reason.   Or in a RENEWED creature ; the mind is then under the divine influence ; so far as grace prevails, the mind is brought back to its original state.

Reason judges of the evidences of revelation, internal and external ; and is disposed, according to its state, to receive them or not.

Reason judges of the meaning of the terms in which divine revelation is conveyed.

Reason is to distinguish the natural language of history, poetry, prophecy, devotion, proverb, precept, &c., in the various passages of Holy Scripture.

Reason judges of doctrines so far as to deduce them from Scripture. Reason is able to discern more and more the excellence of divine revelation.

Reason is to judge of the effects and power of truth on the hearers.

DANGERS to which we are exposed in the exercise of reason are these.

Reason is beset with danger in the breast of an humble Christian. There is danger that, while we are endeavouring to strengthen reason, we ascribe too much to it. The most dangerous heresies arose from the dangers of leaning too much to reason.

The schoolmen, too, carried reason to foolish and mischievous extremes.

Tuckney says, " Reason is not capable of understanding, nor of legislating respecting, nor of judging in, matters of religion."

The Rev. J. Pratt—

Reason has chiefly to do with the evidence of the record and the meaning of the terms of Scripture.

How whall we best employ the faculty in our hearers ?   By making a continued appeal, not by perfect syllogisms, but by *enthymeme*.*   See Rom. i. 17–20 ; ii. 14, 15.

MAY 24, 1813.

WHAT MEANS MAY BE SUGGESTED FOR AWAKENING THE MINDS OF MINISTERS IN GENERAL TO A CONCERN FOR THEIR OWN SALVATION ?— Proposed by the Rev. B. Woodd.

Cultivate acquaintance with such as are disposed to be on terms. Let us act up to our own character, in a consistent discharge of our own duties.

A series of tracts on Scripture, on Christian doctrines and duties, some entirely selected from the writings of our bishops, would be useful.   So lives of the Scripture saints.   Each of these tracts to be sent to every clergyman in the kingdom, under a cover, from persons unknown, free of expense.

This is important, for whoever wins a minister wins thousands.

Avoid all peculiarities and eccentricities.   Be particularly attentive to discipline.   Enter as much as possible into the case and circumstances of these men.

Burnett's *Pastoral Care*, and Bean's *Zeal without Innovation*, are useful.

Study courtesy towards them.   *Put on, as the elect of God, bowels of mercy and kindness.*

Avoid all trimming, otherwise your effort will fail of its effect ; you will be despised by the men whom it is your intention to conciliate. Forget not fervent prayer for them.

We should be careful of shutting ourselves up in an *esprit du corps*.

---

* *Enthymeme*.—An argument consisting only of an antecedent and consequential proposition ; a syllogism where the major proposition is suppressed, and only the minor and consequence produced in words.

Let us distinguish between vindicating ourselves and our principles in the conviction of our brethren.

Uphold, as far as possible, the dignity of our brethren's office. Exercise self-denial in making the attempt. Deal with openness and candour.

The Bible Society is the means of removing from many clergymen's minds much prejudice.

JUNE 7, 1813.

WHAT ARE THE DISADVANTAGES WHICH ATTEND SUNDAY SCHOOLS, AND THE BEST METHOD OF COUNTERACTING THEM?—Proposed by the Rev. J. Clayton.

The danger is of making young persons too forward. This may be counteracted by the vigilant superintendence of the minister.

Teaching in Sunday schools removes many teachers from ministerial instruction. They lose a sight of their own real character by addressing children. This may be counteracted by their being thus employed only one part of the day.

Married men are removed from their families to the neglect of relative duties.

The sexes are not kept sufficiently separate. This may be counteracted by teachers being separate, or coming on separate times of the day.

There is a desecration of the Sabbath in teaching writing and arithmetic. This may be counteracted by week-day evening schools.

It is injurious to the private devotion of the teachers. It exhausts the animal spirits of the teacher before public worship begins.

Contests arise sometimes among teachers, gossiping, *proselytising*; all this may be counteracted by activity.

A disadvantage often is, that Sunday-schools are entirely managed by young people.

The next topic was, THE NATURE AND NECESSITY OF SEPARATION FROM THE WORLD. We have no notes.

On the next occasion Mr Pratt was absent on account of business at the Church Missionary House. The meetings were adjourned to October. At the first, on the members re-assembling, a general conversation took place. From the next four meetings Mr Pratt was absent for the reason above. The topics were, HOW ARE WE TO UNDERSTAND THOSE DIVINES WHO SPEAK OF COMMON GIFTS AND COMMON GRACE?—ARE ANY INCONVENIENCES LIKELY TO ATTEND THE EXTENSION OF BIBLE ASSOCIATIONS AMONG THE LABOURING CLASSES? AND IF SO, HOW MAY THEY BE BEST OBVIATED?—IS THERE ANY SCRIPTURAL GROUND FOR THE BELIEF OF AN ETERNAL COVENANT BETWEEN THE THREE PERSONS IN THE GOD-

HEAD, AS TO THE REDEMPTION OF MAN?—WHAT EFFORTS OUGHT
EVANGELICAL MINISTERS TO USE, IN ORDER TO OPPOSE THE EXTRA-
ORDINARY EFFORTS NOW MAKING BY THE SOCINIANS TO PROPAGATE
THEIR PERNICIOUS TENETS?

DECEMBER 20, 1813.

THE NATURE, OFFICE, AND RIGHTS OF CONSCIENCE?—Proposed by the
Rev. D. Wilson.

We must consider a good conscience, an evil, an erroneous, a dubious, a scrupulous, a sleepy, a purified, an enlightened, a liberal, a
tender, a faithful conscience.

1. We should listen to the whispers of conscience, lest we should hear
its thunders.

2. We must never entangle conscience by rash and unnecessary
resolutions.

On the 3d of January 1814, the subject was, How TO IMPROVE
THE APPROACHING THANKSGIVING DAY? The long and dreadful
war by which the Scourge of Europe had desolated the continent,
and had drained our own happy island of so much of its life-
blood and its treasure, had been brought to a termination—a termination, as we know, which was the year after suspended only
for a moment, that the usurper, once more at large, might receive
at the hands of the greatest Captain of the age his last and most
signal overthrow. The Fast-Days which had been annually kept
for humiliation and supplication were now turned into praise
and rejoicing. The preliminaries of peace were signed at Paris in
April, and the treaty itself at the Congress of Vienna in July;
and the 7th of that month was set apart as the day of Public
Thanksgiving for the Restoration of Peace.

JANUARY 17, 1814.

THE IMPORTANCE OF MINISTERS INSISTING ON THE MINOR POINTS OF
MORALS.—Proposed by the Rev. D. Wilson.

Mr Wilson—

In the Scriptures are many passages to this effect.

EXAMPLES in which we transgress these points :—

1. Going out of our place and station. When we are ready to do
a duty *out* of our station, rather than in it.

2. When a thing is right, but we disregard the manner of doing it.

3. When we consider the end to warrant, in some measure, a deviation from means strictly right.

4. When we promote worldly interests by the pretexts of religion.

5. When we are lax as to the government of the tongue. *If any
man among you seemeth to be religious, and bridleth not his tongue, that man's
religion is vain.*

6. So in the government of the temper.

7. Inattention to propriety of dress.

8. When we indulge in the flattery of others.

9. When we are not strict in keeping our engagements.

10. When we are busy in recommending persons for stations.

11. Professing ourselves to be qualified for stations when we are not.

12. Smuggling. 13. Simulated papers. 14. Falsehoods in trade.

15. False return of property to tax-gatherers.

It is our DUTY to point out these things—

1. Because there are many who have not time to study their duty.

2. It is necessary for the detection of hypocrites.

3. It is necessary for the discovering of declining Christians to themselves.

4. The detection of such things is the ordinary way by which God works sanctification in the soul : *The very God of peace sanctify you* WHOLLY, &c.

5. It is the way in which excellence in every art and science is obtained.

6. Little evils when left unreformed make room for greater.

7. People are imperfect after all our endeavours.

8. The present times of the diffusion of religion render this of unusual importance.

9. Great divines are great because they enter into detail.

The MANNER in which it should be done.

1. We must not neglect or undervalue the great doctrines of the Gospel.

2. We need not frequently preach sermons on the minor duties ; but throw in occasional hints, put in season, and well pointed.

3. It should be done with sweetness, simplicity, and spirituality.

4. We must be cautious not to overload the understanding and consciences of young Christians. *They* take these things for a covenant of works, &c.

Remarks of other Members—

Saurin's sermon on the *Minor Duties of Religion* may be consulted. *Whatsoever ye would that men should do unto you, even so do ye unto them* —would settle many of these points.

Neglecting the duties of frugality. " He who neglects little things shall fall by little and little."

Saurin's reasons are—

1. They contribute to maintain tenderness of conscience.

2. They offer sources of recovery after great falls.

3. They make up by their frequency what is wanting in importance.

4. Sometimes these things are as indicative of real love as greater duties.

In married life there are no little things, because those little things are just what the temper of either party may make of them. The lover should live in the husband. The bloom should be maintained on the plum.

In parental relation, the child will find delicate regard to his parent happiest. " Waters of consolation flow within the banks of obedience."

"A letter put into the post-office without a direction will reach no one."

See Mrs More's *Practical Piety*, the last chapter in the first volume.

Many of the things mentioned are little, only when little in degree. By little things the character is declared and betrayed. On great points there is a guard.

Jeremy Taylor says, "Men are careless, then presumptuous, then hardened, then damned."

Indulging in habits of expense above our station leads to the utmost evil. Newgate would disclose the magnitude of this evil.

Want of respect to station, want of gratitude, restlessness—are all apparently small evils, but great in their consequences.

See Evans on the *Christian Temper*.

As to manner. Ministers are unpopular oftener from manner than from any objection to the subject. There are occasional touches in the Scriptures which deserve to be well studied. Expounding the Epistles will lead to these minor points.

Many would never hear of their failings, in minor details, but from the pulpit.

By urging minor defects, conviction of sin is more easily fixed on the consciences of amiable persons.

We have now completed our task, having exhausted the materials of the NOTE-BOOK we are so fortunate as to possess. The records during the later years have been more scanty than in the earlier part of the period in which these discussions took place. We have, nevertheless, thought it well to give the whole, as no part is deficient in useful and instructive remarks.

After the year 1814, Mr Pratt ceased to be a member of the Eclectic Society. The cause of his resigning will be found in the following letter, which he addressed to his companions upon the occasion. It sufficiently accounts, also, for the circumstance, that the notes of the discussions were not made latterly with the same fulness as before :—

CHURCH MISSIONARY HOUSE, *Jan.* 2, 1815.

MY DEAR FRIENDS,—I have long struggled with myself before I could bring my mind to request that you would permit me to pass off, for the present at least, as a *miles emeritus*. But when I look at the book, and find that I was present but twice last year, and see no immediate prospect of being able to resume that seat which I have reason to thank God from my heart that I ever held, I cannot continue to occupy a post the duties of which I am disqualified from discharging.

Many of you know well that my occupation at this House is so incessant, that I have neither time nor spirits for anything beyond its walls, except what is of necessity laid upon me. An average engagement for the last two years, perhaps, in the Society's concerns, of from eight to twelve hours a-day, beside frequent journeyings, have made me almost a perfect stranger to my own study ; and have obliged me to look for, what I gratefully acknowledge I have found, the special support and blessing of God. But I assure you, my dear friends, I need, and shall need, this support ; for my spirits and health sometimes give symptoms of failing. But I am persuaded you remember your brethren before that throne round which we shall all, I trust, meet, when prayer shall have yielded to eternal praise.

I remain, in the best of all bonds, your ever affectionate brother and friend, JOSIAH PRATT.

We close the volume with a List of the Members and Visitors, whose names appear as speakers during this period of the Society's history—viz., from 1798 to 1814. The first column will shew, at a glance, the relative length of time that they were severally connected with the Society. Some appear but once or twice, as is seen in the last column, pointing out the pages where their names occur. These were but casual visits upon the introduction of a member. There are but seven who were members through the whole period of these Notes.

PERIODS OF ATTENDANCE.	NAMES OF MEMBERS AND VISITORS.	PAGE
1798 1809	Rev. J. Venn, Rector of Clapham...............	3–459
1798 1814	,, J. Goode, Independent Minister..........	4–522
1798 1811	,, H. Foster, Rector of Clerkenwell.........	4–483
1798 1808	,, R. Cecil, St John's Chapel, Bedford Row	4–423
1798 1814	,, B. Woodd, Bentinck Chapel, Pentonville	5–524
1798 . . . .∴ 1807	,, T. Scott, Chaplain of Lock Hospital.....	5–402
1798 1814	,, J. Clayton, Independent Minister	6–525
1798 1804	,, J. Newton, Rec. of St Mary Woolnoth..	6–330
1798 1814	,, J. Pratt, Assist. Minister St John's Chapel, Bedford Row....................	7–524
1798 1814	,, W. Goode, Rect. St Ann's, Blackfriars	11–506
1798–9	John Bacon, Esq., R.A.............................	12–130
1798 1814	Rev. J. Davies..	41–437
1798	,, Professor Farish, Cambridge...............	41
1798 1814	,, W.J. Abdy, R. St John's, Horselydown	52–492
1798 . 1800	,, G. Pattrick, Lect. St Bride's..............	54–183
1798 1805	,, — Gambier, Rec. St Mary le Strand, 57, 344, 360	
1798	,, T. Dykes, Hull..............................	64
1798	,, J. Stillingfleet, Hotham......................	74
1798 1809	,, J. Storry, Colchester.................... 78, 381, 462	
1798 1811	,, C. Simeon, Cambridge........................	88–490
1799	Charles Grant, Esq.................................	98
1799 1804	Rev. J. Gilbert.................................103, 299, 332	
1799 . 1801	,, H. Jowett, Little Durham...........107, 168, 224	
1800 1814	,, R. Lloyd, Rector of St Dunstan's.........	164–449
1800 . . 3	,, Dr Gilbee..	168, 300
1800	,, E. Edwards, Lynn............................	177
1800 . 2	,, — Vansittart.................................	186, 242
1800 1814	,, — Simons, Paul's Cray....................	198–516
1801 1814	,, S. Crowther, Christ Church, Newgate	218–496
1801	,, — Johnson, Chap. N. S. Wales...........	241
1802	,, — Ring	244
1802 1810	,, T. Robinson, R. St Mary's, Leicester ...	255–476
1802 . 4	,, — Mayor, Collingham........................	269–343
1803 . 5	,, M. Atkinson, Leeds	292, 359
1803 1810	,, W. Fry...	296–480
1804 1814	,, H. G. Watkins, Rector St Swithin's....	315–502

PERIODS OF ATTENDANCE.		NAMES OF MEMBERS AND VISITORS.	PAGE
1804	Rev.	Dr Gilby..	342
1804 1814	,,	D. Wilson, St John's, Bedford Row.....	315–526
1805	,,	Henry Martyn.................................	363
1806	,,	H. Stewart, Percy Chapel..................	374
1806–7	,,	— Shaw..	385, 403
1807 ... 1814	,,	H. Budd, Bridewell Hospital..............	399–514
1807 ... 1814	,,	— Sheppard, Clerkenwell	414–462
1808	,,	S. Marsden, Chap. N. S. Wales...........	423, 7
1808–9	,,	Dr Fearon, Vicar of Ore	463, 463
1810 .. 14	,,	H. Godfrey, aft. Pres. of Queen's, Cam.	474–502
1812 . 14	,,	C. R. Pritchett..................	511, 515

Of this list of FORTY-SEVEN names, ONE only survives to the present day—a Father and Chief Pastor in the Church of Christ; whose memory will be revered for generations yet to come, in both Christian and heathen lands; and whose "joy and crown of rejoicing" in the last day will be the souls whom the Spirit has awakened and edified through his means, by the faithful and powerful preaching of the gospel of the grace of God for more than fifty years.

When his name is numbered with the honoured dead, may a double portion of his spirit rest on us! May there never be wanting in our Church men like Newton, and Cecil, and Venn, and Scott, and Simeon, and Pratt, and this last surviving member of their company, always determining to know nothing as the remedy for a lost and perishing world but JESUS CHRIST AND HIM CRUCIFIED, set forth in all the freeness, fulness, and richness of his saving mercy and redeeming grace.

INDEX.

FINIS.